Philosophy

and the

Turn to Religion

# Philosophy and the Turn to Religion

*Hent de Vries*

The Johns Hopkins University Press
Baltimore and London

© 1999 The Johns Hopkins University Press
All rights reserved. Published 1999
Printed in the United States of America on acid-free paper
9 8 7 6 5 4 3 2

The Johns Hopkins University Press
2715 North Charles Street
Baltimore, Maryland 21218-4363
www.press.jhu.edu

Publication was made possible in part by the support of the Netherlands
Organization for Scientific Research (NWO).

Library of Congress Cataloging-in-Publication Data will be found
at the end of this book.
A catalog record for this book is available from the British Library.

ISBN 0-8018-5994-8
ISBN 0-8018-5995-6 (pbk.)

... und das unbestrittenste Recht hätte *Gott*, dass mit ihm der Anfang gemacht werde . . . / . . . and *God* would have the absolutely undisputed right that the beginning be made with him . . .

G. F. W. Hegel, *Wissenschaft der Logik*
(trans. A. V. Miller, modified)


Dieu déjà se contredit. / God contradicts himself already.

Jacques Derrida, *L'Écriture et la différence*
(trans. Alan Bass)

# Contents

# Preface

AS ITS TITLE PROCLAIMS, this book examines a "turn" to religion in modern philosophy. Although I take my lead in it from the later writings of Jacques Derrida, especially from the recurrence of certain religious and theological motifs in his work, I nonetheless pursue a more general systematic problem: the present-day form and implications of the uneasy relationship between the universal claims of philosophy and the supposed particularisms of religion. This relationship has always been complex, unstable, and full of contradictions.

While sometimes aligned to the point of assimilation, philosophy and religion have often been defined in terms of their analogical relation, based in turn on the doctrine of the analogy of being (*analogia entis*) that was said to exist between the divine and the created realm, as well as on the assumption that the natural light of reason only needed to be supplemented by the supranatural gift of revelation. Martin Heidegger and others have insisted on the ontotheological nature of the history of Western metaphysics from the early Greeks on. Conversely, there are those (most famously Blaise Pascal, in distinguishing between the "god of the philosophers and of learned scholars" and the "God of Abraham, Isaac, and Jacob") who stress the difference from the very outset between the philosophical and the theological. In "Dieu et la philosophie" ("God and Philosophy"), Emmanuel Levinas has suggested, however, that these apparently opposite positions may have more in common than appears at first glance.

Retracing Derrida's engagement with the religious and theological makes it possible to view the uneasy relationship between philosophy and religion in a radically different way, one that is not anticipated or exhausted by any of the better-known classical or modern interpretations of their entanglement or antithesis. In many of the chapters that follow, I attempt to provide arguments for a philosophical reassessment of his work in light of its ever more prominent citation and rearticulation of religious and theological idioms. Derrida's writings exhibit the paradox of a nontheological, and, it would seem, even nonreligious, concern with religion, a type of philosophical reflection that does not simply coincide with itself but lets itself be "doubled," as he would put it, by religion. Only as religion's double can such philosophical reflection be said in turn to "haunt" all (positive or historical) religion. This exposure of the philosophical to the religious and, more indirectly, to the theological may provide us with the best, as well as both the most responsible and the most risky, access to the questions of ethics and politics in the current historical constellation — and, who knows, perhaps beyond.

My book circles around the persistent conceptual and analytical necessity for discourse to situate itself at once close to and at the farthest remove from the resources and current manifestations of the religious and the theological, their traditional and dominant figures, their cultural practices, and the basic tenets of their ethics and politics. This paradox is captured in the familiar French expression *adieu,* which Levinas made into a philosopheme.[1] The *adieu* conveys the departure from all known, all-too-human — positive, metaphysical, ontotheological — names of the divine, and of everything that has come to take its place. Yet if this expression signals a leave-taking, a departure from the postulation of an irreducible realm or being called divine — epitomized by the unity of some unknown, perhaps unpronounceable, name — one might also interpret it as a hint, a gesture toward the absolute (in the etymological sense of the Latin *absolvere,* to set free or untie) that eludes all context and every reference, but that nonetheless marks, enables, and challenges every utterance — and not just prayer or ritual — from within and without. As we shall see, examples of this are legion.

---

1. *Adieu* was a working title of this project for some time; see also my "Adieu, à dieu, a-dieu," in *Ethics as First Philosophy: The Significance of Emmanuel Levinas for Philosophy, Literature and Religion,* ed. Adriaan T. Peperzak (London: Routledge, 1995), 211–20, and the heading of the final paragraph of my "Antibabel: The 'Mystical Postulate' in Benjamin, de Certeau and Derrida," *Modern Language Notes* 107 (1992): 476. The word used in this sense originated with and received its original impetus from Levinas and was later taken up by Derrida. With explicit reference to Levinas, it figures prominently in Derrida's "Donner la mort," in *L'Éthique du don: Jacques Derrida et la pensée du don,* ed. Jean-Michel Rabaté and Michael Wetzel (Paris: Métailié-Transition, 1992), 11–108, trans. David Wills as *The Gift of Death* (Stanford: Stanford University Press, 1995), hereafter cited parenthetically in the text as GD, followed by the English and French page numbers. Derrida subsequently also used it in the titles of his funeral oration for Levinas, published in *Critical Inquiry* 23 (Autumn 1996): 1–10, and of *Adieu à Emmanuel Levinas* (Paris: Galilée, 1997). Jean-Christoph Bailly's *Adieu: Essai sur la mort des dieux* (La Tour d'Aigues: Éditions de l'Aube, 1989) came to my attention only after I had completed the manuscript of this book.

Despite the prominence of Derrida in these pages, as well as in the sequel to this book, entitled *Horror Religiosus*,[2] I address other authors and examples in them as well: Emmanuel Levinas and Eric Weil, Maurice Blanchot and Jean Wahl, Michel de Certeau and Michael Foucault, Paul Ricoeur and Mikel Dufrenne, Edmund Jabès and Jean-François Lyotard, Jean-Luc Nancy and Philippe Lacoue-Labarthe, Jean Greisch and Jean-Luc Marion, Jean-François Courtine and Françoise Dastur, Jean-Louis Chrétien and Marlène Zarader, among others. The work of these interlocutors provides the interpretive context for my own interrogation of the central motifs and argumentative structures that have played a crucial role in Derrida's engagement with the religious and the theological since his earliest writings, and with increasing intensity: they focus in particular on the "Old" and "New" Testaments; the *Confessions* of St. Augustine and the treatises of Pseudo-Dionysius; the sermons of Meister Eckhart and the epigrams of Angelus Silesius; the *Meditations* of Descartes and the critical works of Kant; the early theological writings of Hegel and the dialectical lyric of Kierkegaard; the poems of Hölderlin and the poetics of Celan; the work of Rosenzweig, Kafka, and Benjamin; all approached with a type of questioning that would be impossible without the indefatigable and ultimately polemical reassessment of the work of Husserl and Heidegger that characterizes Derrida's thinking.

I attempt here to comprehend the theoretical significance of religious and theological citations in writings whose roots lie in the phenomenological tradition, although by historical accident they came in the United States to be associated first with the "structuralist controversy" and then with poststructuralism and its purported godfathers, Nietzsche, Marx, and Freud. Attention to the significance of religious and theological motifs in this genealogy rectifies its hasty association with a "hermeneutics of suspicion" (Paul Ricoeur's phrase in *Le Conflit des interprétations* [*The Conflict of Interpretations*]), to say nothing of unhelpful charges of nihilism, skepticism, or relativism.

The turn to religion discussed here must not be understood as a turn to theology in the conventional or confessional sense of the word. Rather, I attempt to rethink the concepts of ethics and politics, their structural and aporetic linkage with practices and institutions. Taken thus, the turn to religion counterbalances a common misunderstanding voiced by Dominique Janicaud's *Le Tournant theologique de la phénoménologie*

2. Forthcoming from the Johns Hopkins University Press.

*française* (*The Theological Turn of French Phemenology*) and echoed by
neohumanist critics of the newest French philosophy. Indicative of the
turn in contemporary philosophy, or so their argument goes, is its invocation of the religious and the theological, as opposed to the sober use of the
language of philosophy and the principles of secular humanism. This view
badly needs correction. In fact, by renegotiating the limits and aporias of
the ethical and the political in light of the religious and the theological,
we can rearticulate the terms and oppositions in which the most pressing
and practical present-day cultural debates are phrased. Thus, here and in
*Horror Religiosus,* I explore how Derrida's texts address the question of
responsibility in its relation to democracy, globalization, and the "politics
of hospitality." More particularly, I explore his views on the nation-state
in its engagement with censorship and religious tolerance, on identity and
its relation to violence, on the politics of the academy in its confrontation with cultural diversity, on the politics of memory and of mourning,
and also on the multimedia and their ambiguous role in the trend toward
globalization and the "virtualization" of reality.

In discussions of these issues, the theoretical and pragmatic obsoles-
cence of certain alternative interpretations—of secularism, modernity,
autonomy, self-determination, progressivism, and humanism—seems to
me more evident than ever. The semantic, symbolic, or intellectual horizon within which these notions have been put to work restricts their
capacity to serve as critical tools in addressing the most pressing questions of our time. The turn to religion provides a genealogical and strategic reformulation or renaming of these notions, one that reveals—and
raises—the stakes involved in their recurrent deployment. It helps to illuminate why there can be no such thing as the ultimate neutrality of a
public sphere in which philosophical, cultural, and political conflicts are
debated. More important, it makes us understand why this insight by
no means implies that the formal and critical task of reason has become
obsolete.

Speaking about religious and theological tropes or figures of speech
and thought, examining the rhetorical features of their occurrences and
reinscriptions, while stressing their fundamental undecidability or un-
readability—all this would certainly have been impossible without the
"Newer Criticism," to employ Rodolphe Gasché's term for the first phase
of the reception of deconstruction, which seemed to make it part of a
canon of "poststructuralism." I sympathize with the more philosophically
focused rereadings of the second phase of Derrida's reception, exempli-

fied by Gasché, which was concerned to demonstrate what should have been clear all along—namely, that Derrida's oeuvre is steeped in the tradition of Western thought, that it should be examined against the background of his philosophical engagement with the concept of reflection and the transcendental, from Hegel, through Husserlian phenomenology, to Heidegger and beyond.[3] My book also presupposes a third and a fourth strain of Derrida's reception, however, which shift toward the ethical and the pragmatic respectively.[4]

Is there still room, then, to attach a "fifth wheel," in Kant's metaphor, to this wagon? To some, it seems already to be traveling at full speed; others see it as sidetracked from the outset and likely soon to come to a halt. In choosing to highlight the religious and theological motifs in Derrida's writing, and in claiming that they bring aspects of it discussed by previous scholarship into "their own," I am, of course, aware that deconstruction and theology have been intensely discussed from the very beginning, at each of the four stages of reception I have indicated. However, rather than attempting to determine the relevance of Derrida's writings for a rethinking of the task and scope of systematic theology,[5] I reverse the perspective, asking: Why is religion a relevant philosophical or theoretical topic at all?

THIS STUDY DATES BACK to 1989, when I did research in Paris after having completed a comparative study of the work of Theodor W. Adorno and Levinas entitled *Theologie im pianissimo.*[6] I embarked on the present

3. Rodolphe Gasché, *The Tain of the Mirror: Derrida and the Philosophy of Reflection* (Cambridge, Mass.: Harvard University Press, 1986).

4. See, for an overview and critical evaluation, Geoffrey Bennington, "Deconstruction and the Philosophers (the Very Idea)," *Oxford Literary Review* 10 (1987): 73–130; id., *Legislations: The Politics of Deconstruction* (London: Verso, 1994), 11–60; and Richard Beardsworth, *Derrida and the Political* (London: Routledge, 1996).

5. For the most radical attempt to sketch a "postmodern a/theology" or a "hermeneutic of the death of God," see Mark C. Taylor, *Erring: A Postmodern A/theology* (Chicago: University of Chicago Press, 1984). See also, for a different approach, Kevin Hart's *The Trespass of the Sign: Deconstruction, Theology and Philosophy* (Cambridge: Cambridge University Press, 1989). Both of these studies appeared before the publication of Derrida's recent interventions with respect to the question of religion, its purported return, and so forth. This is not the case with John D. Caputo's *The Prayers and Tears of Jacques Derrida: Religion Without Religion* (Bloomington: Indiana University Press, 1997). This book covers much the same field that interests me here, but it appeared in print after most of the present study as well as its sequel had already been completed.

6. *Theologie im pianissimo: Zur Aktualität der Denkfiguren Adornos und Levinas* (Kampen, Neth.: J. H. Kok, 1989); forthcoming in translation from the Johns Hopkins University Press.

project with the intention of exploring a different type of questioning and another set of topics, but it soon dawned on me that I was in fact continuing the line of research that had led to the first book. The present work can therefore be seen as a sequel to the former one, even though it is the first book of mine to be written in English, and despite its greater distance from the discipline of theology. As will be clear from *Horror Religiosus* (which was composed at the same time as this book, although both can be read independently), this departure indicates no lessening of interest in the increasing relevance of the religious and the theological to philosophical discourse and cultural analysis.

THE CENTRAL ARGUMENT of this book was tested in seminars held in the German Department of the Johns Hopkins University, in the Philosophy Department of Loyola University, Chicago, and at the University of Amsterdam. Earlier versions of most of the chapters were first presented as papers in the Program of Comparative Literature of the State University of New York at Buffalo, the University of California at Berkeley, the Institute for the Advanced Study of Religion at the Divinity School of the University of Chicago, and the "Graduiertenkolleg Phänomenologie und Hermeneutik" led by Bernhard Waldenfels and Klaus Held in Bochum and Wuppertal. In the final stages of the project, I was exposed to the incisive questions of my students in the Department of Philosophy of the University of Amsterdam, as well as to numerous discussions of a more interdisciplinary nature with my colleagues at the recently founded Amsterdam School for Cultural Analysis, Theory, and Interpretation. However, I was only able to complete the fine-tuning of the text thanks to the hospitality provided during the academic year 1997–98 by the Center for the Study of World Religions and the Minda de Gunzburg Center for European Studies, both at Harvard University.

On these and other occasions, I have greatly benefited from many discussions, first of all with Beatrice Hanssen, whose critical comments helped me to better understand and clarify the general direction in which my research was or should be moving, but also — in an alphabetical order — with Rodolphe Gasché, Jean Greisch, and Werner Hamacher, each of whom in his own way served as my philosophical conscience by constantly reminding me of the virtues of scholarly and argumentative rigor and the necessity of applying it in the boldest, most imaginative fashion; with Martin Jay, Harry Kunneman, and Burcht Pranger, who enriched my historical awareness of the complex landscape of intellectual history in

which certain questions come to fruition, and whose genuinely human-
istic scholarship kept my feet firmly on the ground; with Karin de Boer,
Peter Dreyer, Paola Marrati, Beate Roessler, Jenny Slatman, Martin Stokhof, Helen Tartar, and Saul Tobias, all of whom reminded me of the need
to attend to clarity of expression and to bring out my own voice as much
as possible; and with Samuel Weber, from whom I have learned and continue to learn during our joint inquiries into violence, identity, and self-
determination, on the one hand, and religion and media, on the other,
both of which form part and parcel of the problematics of this book and
have informed it in major ways. Finally, I would also like to thank Jacques
Derrida for numerous attentive and patient responses to my endeavors to
formulate the logic and the implications of the *adieu*. Thanks to all these
interlocutors, the following text has certainly been greatly improved. For
the final result and all its remaining flaws, I remain solely responsible.

# Abbreviations

A    Jacques Derrida, *Aporias* (Stanford: Stanford University Press, 1995); translation by Thomas Dutoit of *Apories* (Paris: Galilée, 1993).

BT   Martin Heidegger, *Being and Time* (San Francisco: Harper, 1962; Oxford: Blackwell, 1993); translation by John Macquarrie and Edward Robinson of *Sein und Zeit* (Tübingen: Niemeyer, 1977).

FK   Jacques Derrida, "Foi et savoir: Les Deux Sources de la 'religion' aux limites de la simple raison," in *La Religion,* ed. id. and Gianni Vattimo (Paris: Éditions du Seuil, 1996), 9–86; translated by Samuel Weber under the title "Faith and Knowledge: The Two Sources of 'Religion' at the Limits of Reason Alone," in *Religion,* ed. Derrida and Vattimo (Stanford: Stanford University Press, 1998), 1–78.

GD   Jacques Derrida, "Donner la mort," in *L'Éthique du don: Jacques Derrida et la pensée du don,* ed. Jean-Michel Rabaté and Michael Wetzel (Paris: Métailié, Transition, 1992), 11–108; trans. David Wills as *The Gift of Death* (Stanford: Stanford University Press, 1995).

GWB  Jean-Luc Marion, *God Without Being: Hors-Texte* (Chicago: University of Chicago Press, 1991); translation by Thomas A. Carlson of *Dieu sans l'être: Hors-texte* (Paris: Quadrige, 1991).

HAS  Jacques Derrida, "How to Avoid Speaking: Denials," in *Languages of the Unsayable: The Play of Negativity in Literature and Literary Theory,* ed. Sanford Budick and Wolfgang Iser (New York: Columbia University Press, 1989), 3–70; translation by Ken Frieden of "Comment ne pas parler: Dénégations," in *Psyché: Inventions de l'autre* (Paris: Galilée, 1987), 535–95.

LH   Martin Heidegger, "Letter on Humanism." In *Basic Writings: From "Being and Time" (1927) to "The Task of Thinking" (1964),* ed. David Farrell Krell (New York: Harper Collins, 1993), 213–65.

MP     Jean-Luc Marion, "Metaphysics and Phenomenology: A Relief for Theology," translated by Thomas A. Carlson, *Critical Inquiry* 20, no. 4 (Summer 1994): 572–91.

NAA     Jacques Derrida, "On a Newly Arisen Apocalyptic Tone in Philosophy," in *Raising the Tone of Philosophy: Late Essays by Emmanuel Kant, Transformative Critique by Jacques Derrida,* ed. Peter Fenves (Baltimore: Johns Hopkins University Press, 1993), 117–71; translation by J. P. Leavy Jr. of *D'un ton apocalyptique adopté naguère en philosophie* (Paris: Galilée, 1981).

NAS     Immanuel Kant, "On A Newly Arisen Superior Tone in Philosophy," in *Raising the Tone of Philosophy: Late Essays by Emmanuel Kant, Transformative Critique by Jacques Derrida,* ed. Peter Fenves (Baltimore: Johns Hopkins University Press, 1993), 51–72; translation by Peter Fenves of "Von einem neuerdings erhobenen vornehmen Ton in der Philosophie," in *Werke in zehn Bänden,* ed. Wilhelm Weischedel (Darmstadt: Wissenschaftliche Buchgesellschaft, 1983), 5: 377–97.

PhRL     Martin Heidegger, *Phänomenologie des religiösen Lebens,* vol. 60 of *Gesamtausgabe,* vol. 60 (Frankfurt a./M.: Vittorio Klostermann, 1995).

SN     Jacques Derrida, *On the Name,* ed. Thomas Dutoit (Stanford: Stanford University Press, 1995); translation of *Sauf le nom* (Paris, Galilée, 1993).

Philosophy
and the
Turn to Religion

# Introduction

THAT RELIGION CAN NO LONGER be regarded as a phenomenon belonging to a distant past, and that it is not a transhistorical and transcultural phenomenon either, is no longer disputed in modern scholarship. Historians, philologists, and cultural critics alike have studied religion's multifaceted manifestations, emphasizing its social, anthropological, and intertextual overdeterminations, the discursive formation of its empirical and symbolic power, and the transformation or displacement of its private and public functions. Philosophers, in contrast, have sought to demonstrate or challenge the very coherence of its leading concepts, often by distinguishing universal natural religion from particular supranatural revelations, and then reducing religion's truth claims more and more to natural causes, category mistakes, or linguistic confusion. Thus, the rationality of its propositions, arguments, and leaps of faith (whether they took the form of a *credo ut intelligam* or of an outright *credo quia absurdum*) was questioned and then dismissed.

What remained after this relentless historicization and conceptual reduction seemed but an empty shell, no more than a name (*sauf le nom*, to cite one of Derrida's titles), whose supposed original content and referent had been destroyed once and for all. In a sense, the conscientious and methodical study of religion seemed to have undermined the very object of its inquiry. No longer identifiable as a clearly demarcated field of research, religion seemed to have become what it probably had been all along: an anthropological and social construct that could serve diverse, even contradictory, purposes. Evidently, the very attempt to give one overarching, general definition of the term *religion* had from the outset been doomed to fail.[1]

Yet quite a few recent books draw on the tradition and the language of religion and theological thinking to address the most pressing questions

---

1. For a discussion, see Jonathan Z. Smith, "A Matter of Class: Taxonomies of Religion," *Harvard Theological Review* 89, no. 4 (1996): 387–403.

at the intersection of contemporary philosophy and cultural analysis.[2] John Milbank's *Theology and Social Theory*, Moshe Halbertal's and Avishai Margalit's *Idolatry*, and Talal Asad's *Genealogies of Religion*, to name three exemplary studies,[3] have begun to outline a mode of inquiry with momentous implications. Each reevaluates the predominant interpretations of the boundaries believed to demarcate the secular from the religious, the profane from the sacred, reason from revelation, representation from alterity, finitude from infinity, and philosophy from theology.

The turn to religion exemplified by these studies does not signal a return to theology or religion per se. The use they make of the concepts of religion and theology, of their histories and systematic resources, is not straightforwardly theological, let alone religious, in itself. These relatively new types of investigation do not present themselves *as* theological or *as* religious. Nor do they turn to religion as to something that had so far remained implicit, waiting only to be brought to light. On the contrary, for these authors, as for those I discuss in this study, religion is never conceived of as the hidden meaning of a secular historical or anthropological truth. The turn to religion they propose is more than an emphasis on turns of phrase that substitute for, exemplify, embellish, or supplement a more original argumentative form and semantic content, which could as easily be expressed without them. They show that citations from religious traditions are more fundamental to the structure of language and experience than the genealogies, critiques, and transcendental reflections of the modern discourse that has deemed such citations obsolete and tended to reduce them to what they are not (or, at least, to what they are not primarily or exclusively): "truth in the garments of a lie" (Schopenhauer), "anthropology disguised as theology" (Feuerbach), "ideology and false consciousness" (Marx), "infantile neurosis" (Freud), "the nonsensical expression of feeling, diffused by metaphysicians without poetic or musical

2. Needless to say, there exists an enormous and admirable body of writings on the philosophy, the sociology, the anthropology, and the psychology or psychoanalysis of religion. To this list we could add the critical theory of religion that takes its lead from the work of Max Weber and Freud. But in the area of cultural analysis and, in particular, cultural studies, the type of inquiry that interests me here seem conspicuously absent. To give just one indication, in his *Keywords: A Vocabulary of Culture and Society* (rev. ed., New York: Oxford University Press, 1983), one of the founding texts of British cultural studies, Raymond Williams does not include an essay on religion.

3. John Milbank, *Theology and Social Theory: Beyond Secular Reason* (Oxford: Blackwell, 1990); Moshe Halbertal and Avishai Margalit, *Idolatry*, trans. Naomi Goldblum (Cambridge, Mass.: Harvard University Press, 1992); Talal Asad, *Genealogies of Religion: Discipline and Reasons of Power in Christianity and Islam* (Baltimore: Johns Hopkins University Press, 1993).

talent" (Carnap), a "category mistake" (Ryle), a "form of life" (Wittgenstein), and so on. Whatever the merits of each of these dismissals, they have proven unable to settle the debate and to silence the religious once and for all.

This is not to argue that the religious is a category sui generis, that it is independent of all contextual and conceptual determination, and, therefore, as it were, irreducible, whether empirically, ontologically, or axiologically, or that it is more resistant to reduction than anything else. Nor is it to suggest that our relation to the religious can be seen as a religious a priori, whether in a neo-Kantian or a fundamentally ontological, Heideggerian sense of the term. Instead, stripped of ever more of its substance, of its logical as well as its ontological claims and foundations, religion not only survives the "death of a thousand qualifications," [4] but can be shown to be itself the abstracting and formalizing movement that brings this virtual death about. The endless, if also inevitably limited, refutations of religion's truth-claims are so many reaffirmations of its ever-provisional survival, ad infinitum. In religion's perpetual agony lies its philosophical and theoretical relevance. As it dies an ever more secure and serial death, it is increasingly certain to come back to life, in its present guise or in another.

NO CONTEMPORARY PHILOSOPHER has provided us with more compelling arguments for this hypothesis than Jacques Derrida. His most direct and powerful account of the "return of" and "turn to" the religious is "Foi et savoir: Les Deux Sources de la 'religion' aux limites de la simple raison" ("Faith and Knowledge: The Two Sources of 'Religion' at the Limits of Mere Reason"), in which he draws on the etymology of the term *religion* to elucidate the paradox that the subject of religion evaporates as it is approached from ever more methodological angles. This paradoxical outcome was surely preceded and facilitated in advance by an even more elementary ambiguity or obscurity on the level of the word, the very concept or idea, of "religion" itself. It is not only the seemingly precise and concise formulations dating back to Cicero's *De natura deorum* (*The Nature of the Gods*), to Augustine and to Aquinas, who take *religio* to stem etymologically from *relegere*, from the renewed *legere*, the "gathering" or "harvesting" that characterizes the observance of cultic obligations vis-à-vis the

---

4. See Anthony Flew, "Theology and Falsification," in *The Philosophy of Religion*, ed. Basil Mitchell, 13–15 (Oxford: Oxford University Press, 1971).

gods; but the meaning of the word *religion* has also been ascribed to *re-eligere*, the restoration of an individual relationship to God after the Fall; and Lactantius and Tertullian trace it to *religare,* from *ligare,* "to tie," in the sense of binding back.[5] Yet even these early pagan and Judeo-Christian determinations of the term *religion* fall short in covering all of this phenomenon's constitutive features. They reduce its original and supposed proper meaning to what Derrida sees as roughly "two possible etymological sources," whose waters flow in the same direction. By pointing to this homogenizing genealogy, Derrida attributes to the Western understanding of "religion" something he deeply suspects in Heidegger's thought of Being—namely, its ultimate horizon of a gathering, a *Versammlung,* that defines the very essence of logos but is never questioned as such: "In both cases (*re-legere* or *re-ligare*), what is at issue is indeed a persistent bond that bonds itself first and foremost to itself. What is at issue is indeed a re-union [*rassemblement*], a re-assembling, a re-collecting. A resistance or a reaction to disjunction. To ab-solute alterity" (FK 37 / 51).

Derrida, by contrast, insists that an "interruptive unraveling" constitutes the very possibility of any "bond" (for example, the social) and thus in a sense forms the "respiration of all 'community' " (FK 64 / 84); he also stresses the "quasi-transcendental privilege" of the at once conceptual, analytical, and testimonial differentiation between

> *on the one hand,* the experience of belief (trust, trustworthiness, confidence, faith, the credit accorded the *good faith of the utterly other* in the experience of witnessing) and, *on the other,* the experience of sacredness, even of holiness, of the unscathed that is safe and sound (*heilig,* holy). These comprise two distinct sources or foci. "Religion" figures their ellipse because it both comprehends the two foci but also sometimes shrouds their irreducible duality in silence, in a manner precisely that is secret and reticent. (FK 36 / 49)

Religion, like the radical evil to which it responds and reacts, but with which it may always enter into an uncanny alliance, is thus divided at its source. Like radical evil, Derrida suggests, it is "not one, nor given

5. On the etymologies of the Latin *religio,* see FK 34, 36–37 / 47–48, 51. Apart from these early pagan and Judeo-Christian determinations of the term *religion,* Derrida mentions W. Otto, J.-B. Hofmann, and Émile Benveniste, in the Ciceronian tradition, and Maximilian Kobbert, the Ernout-Meillet *Dictionnaire étymologique de la langue latine,* and the Pauly-Wissowa *Real-Encyclopädie der klassischen Altertumswissenschaft,* in the patristic tradition. See also Émile Benveniste, *Le Vocabulaire des institutions indo-européennes,* vol. 2: *Pouvoir, droit, religion* (Paris: Éditions de Minuit, 1969), 179–279.

once and for all, as though it were capable only of inaugurating figures or tropes of itself" (FK 9/18). None of the classical and modern etymologies, definitions and reductions, therefore, do justice to the duality—the division and, indeed, divisiveness—at the very origin of "religion."

Even the more radical proposal made by Emmanuel Levinas, in *Totalité et infini* (*Totality and Infinity*), to define *religion* in a meta-ethical manner—at once formally and concretely—as the relation to the other that does not close itself off in any totality (of history, of the political, or of Being), seems at first sight equally blind to some of religion's central characteristics, to wit: its exclusionist and destructive potential, and especially its intrinsic relationship to violence.[6] What remains of religion in Levinas's formula is just another word for a fundamentally ethical relationship to the other (*autrui*). While Levinas leaves no doubt that it is "God" who leaves a trace in this interhuman intrigue (and nowhere else), he insists that the word, the concept, or the name "God" must not even appear if this relation is to be responsible or possible—indeed *religious*—at all. Only thus, Derrida reminds us, is there a clear alternative between a "sacredness without belief," attributed by Levinas to Heidegger, and "faith in a holiness without sacredness, in a desacralizing truth, even making of a certain disenchantment the condition of authentic holiness" (FK 64/84), as advocated by Levinas himself, nowhere more clearly than in his second volume of talmudic readings, *Du sacré au saint* (*From the Sacred to the Holy*).

Although no comprehensive definition or stable concept of religion is available, not least because of its uncertain historical and cultural demarcations, many figures of thought can readily be recognized as religious. Whether acclaimed or loathed, they are perceived as citations from the tradition called "the religious." Resurfacing in the most unexpected of contexts, these motifs do not always signal a belief in certain articles of faith, let alone obedience to some ecclesial or scriptural authority. On the contrary, more often than not, the most reflective and exemplary of these citations serve a decidedly critical—a nondogmatic and even heterodox—purpose. That purpose is to illuminate the unthought, unsaid, or unseen of a philosophical logos that, not only in the guise of modern reason, but from its earliest deployment, tends to forget, repress, or sublate

---

6. See my "Violence and Testimony: On Sacrificing Sacrifice," in *Violence, Identity, and Self-Determination*, ed. Hent de Vries and Samuel Weber (Stanford: Stanford University Press, 1997), 14–43.

the very *religio* (*relegere, religare,* or relation without relation, as Levinas and, following him, Derrida would have it) to which these motifs testify. In so doing—and in utter disregard of its professed enlightenment and its supposedly unbiased attention to its own presuppositions—philosophical discourse also risks a fatal obscurity.

To be sure, this unthought, unsaid, or unseen eludes the reach of formal argument, of both constative propositions and normative rules, because it is marked by a certain performativity that borders on the absolute, what is absolved or set free. It dislodges itself from any context, subtracts itself from any determinable reference, taking on an irreducible and ultimately intractable prescriptivity—one marked by a certain secret, a mystery, that both fascinates and makes one tremble. This may be why the apparent negativity of the unthought (and unsaid or unseen) seeks refuge in the idiom and practices of the positive religions, especially in the most heterodox of their offshoots, those epitomized by negative or apophatic theology, mysticism, messianism, and apocalyptics—in short, all the historical, conceptual, and figural formations from which the self-declared secularism and universalism of modern discourse pretends to be able to set itself apart.

All this is not to deny that the explicit return of the religious to the agenda of philosophy and cultural criticism is prompted less by the definitional or conceptual instability of the term *religion* than by the resurfacing of religion as a highly ambiguous force on the contemporary geopolitical stage. It would be unwise to identify this resurgence or revival with the worldwide "fundamentalisms" often regarded as endangering the modern and modernist projects in whose shadow they fall. Often these "religious nationalisms" are not so much at odds with the institutional arrangements of modern states, by the rules of which they often play—in their resort to violence no less than in their use of its means of communication—as they are with the alleged secularism of those states' ideological self-interpretation.[7]

Not only are these phenomena less anachronistic than is often assumed, they also testify to the uncanny interfacing of what Derrida discusses as a certain performativity discernible in the new media, as well

7. See Peter van der Veer, *Religious Nationalism: Hindus and Muslims in India* (Berkeley and Los Angeles: University of California Press, 1994), and, from a more general perspective, José Casanova, *Public Religions in the Modern World* (Chicago: University of Chicago Press, 1994).

as in contemporary structures of the testimonial and the confessional.[8] Examples include not only the phenomenon of televangelism, the televised stagings of the pope's journeys, and the media portrayal and self-presentation of Islam, but also the fetishization and elevation to virtually absolute status of the televisual and the multimedial as such. One is tempted, Derrida suggests, to muse about the "transcendence of tele-technology" under such headings as "religion and *mechanē*," "religion and cyberspace," "religion and the numeric," "religion and digitality," and "religion and virtual space-time" (FK 2 / 10). For this quasi-religiosity can take many forms — not least, simple wonder at things that seem to reverse the Enlightenment's undoing of myth and fetishization:[9] "One increasingly *uses* artifacts and prostheses of which one is totally ignorant . . . the space of such technical experience tends to become more and more animistic, magical, mystical. The spectral experience persists and then tends to become . . . increasingly *primitive and archaic*" (FK 56 / 74).

It would seem, against this backdrop, that the homology between the hyperessentiality aimed at by certain religious traditions (philosophy is no exception) and the newly explored possible worlds of hypertext is neither accidental nor trivial but based on a certain necessity. Yet while this inner link can, to certain point, be analyzed in terms stemming from the tradition called "religious," it is, strictly speaking, neither religious nor mediated. The religious has always intrinsically been linked to the pragmatic and technological modes of its transmission. These modes have varied, depending on the need for secrecy, censorship, and tolerance, and given religion's changing relationship to the political and public sphere. But the nature of religious communication — of testimony and confession — has undergone several fundamental transformations: quantitatively (and exponentially) with respect to its scale and pace, and also in the infrastructure of its language, its imagery, its mode of presentation.[10] These transformations have affected not only the carriers of the message

8. See also FK 24 and 70–71 n. 17 / 35 and 35–36 n. 13. For a sustained analysis of the philosophical underpinnings and implications of the emerging new media, see Samuel Weber, *Mass Mediauras: Form, Technics, Media* (Stanford: Stanford University Press, 1996). See also Jacques Derrida and Bernard Stiegler, *Échographies de la télévision: Entretiens filmés* (Paris: Galilée / Institut national de l'audiovisuel, 1996).

9. Max Horkheimer and Theodor W. Adorno speak of this with much fervor in *Dialektik der Aufklärung: Philosophische Fragmente* (Frankfurt a./M.: Fischer, 1979), trans. John Cumming as *Dialectic of Enlightenment* (New York: Continuum Books, 1993).

10. See, e.g., Manuel Castells, *The Information Age: Economy, Society and Culture*, vol. 1: *The Rise of the Network Society* (Oxford: Blackwell, 1996).

but also the message itself. "In and for itself," to employ the Hegelian formula that epitomizes the specularity of self-knowledge and self-presence, the message has been changed, to such an extent that it has become difficult to use the phrases "return of religion" or "return to religion" at all. The naive use of these phrases might very well create the illusion that the term *religion* refers to a historical presence, to a delimitable body of writings, or to an intellectual or emotional category that at some time or other may have had the potential of somehow and somewhere remaining itself or intact, regardless of its apparent metamorphoses. It suggests that there is still something to return to, or to be returned to, that has survived the disseminative effects of history, the onslaught of critical thought, of the Enlightenment, of emancipation and "disenchantment." Derrida writes:

> The said "return of the religious," which is to say the spread of a complex and overdetermined phenomenon, is not a simple *return,* for its globality and its figures (tele-techno-media-scientific, capitalistic and politico-economic) remain original and unprecedented. And it is not a *simple* return *of the religious,* for it comports, as one of its two tendencies, a radical destruction of the religious (*stricto sensu,* the Roman and the Statist, like everything that incarnates the European political and juridical against which all non-Christian "fundamentalisms" and "integrisms" are waging war, to be sure, but also certain forms of Protestant or even Catholic orthodoxy). (FK 42 / 57)[11]

Should one nonetheless want to continue speaking of a resurfacing of religion, of a return of or to religion, its cultural remnants, relics, and ruins, one ought to begin by stressing that any such affirmation might be treated as what Kant, in his *Kritik der reinen Vernunft* (*Critique of Pure Reason*), calls a transcendental illusion, and Gilbert Ryle, in *The Concept of Mind,* identifies as a "category mistake." Any rephrasing of a return of or to religion conjures up a spiritual and sociopolitical edifice that may never have existed in the first place, or that never existed as such, in and for itself, identically with itself—in other words, intact. Religion, in the sense that interests us here, is therefore not an anthropological, psycho-

---

11. The ambiguity of the phenomenon in question goes even further, for as Derrida notes somewhat earlier in the text: "I would never have proposed to treat religion *itself,* in general or in its essence, but only a troubled question, a common concern: 'What is going on today with it, with what is designated thus? What is going on there? What is happening and so badly? What is happening under this old name? What in the world suddenly emerges or reemerges under this appellation?'" Yet Derrida immediately adds: "Of course, this form of question cannot be separated from the more fundamental one (on the essence, the concept and the history of religion *itself,* and of what is called 'religion')" (FK 38 / 53; trans. modified).

logical, or sociological invariant. Derrida says as much: "There has not always been . . . nor is there always and everywhere, nor will there always and everywhere ('with humans' or elsewhere) be *something*, a thing that is *one and identifiable*, identical with itself, which, whether religious or irreligious, all agree to call 'religion'" (FK 36 / 49–50).

The ephemeral nature of the religious emerges in one's most intimate thoughts, as well as in philosophical discourse and public debate. It explains the uncanny, indeed, haunting, character of the religious. It manifests itself even without showing its face. Neither verifiable nor falsifiable, reducible, in principle, to nothing other than itself, it surrounds, invades, and sets the tone for everything that it is not. It returns as the repressed, even though the suppression was never of anything in particular. Religion, in this light, resembles the experience of trauma: its modality is the impossible mourning of an immemorial loss.[12] In the writings discussed here, the response to this loss is twofold. It consists, first, in the affirmation of the mere fact of this original bereavement or emptying of language and experience, for which the words *religion* and *God* remain (or have become) the most appropriate names (or simply the best we have come up with so far). Second, this response manifests itself in the affirmation of the impossible yet necessary rearticulation of this troubling fact— a *Faktum der Vernunft* in its own right—in ever-changing idiomatic and institutional contexts.

Instead of concentrating on etymologies, genealogies, and historico-semantic lines of filiation, each of which can be pursued with a legitimate if limited purpose, Derrida stresses therefore that a different questioning should perhaps prevail here and now. One should, he writes, "privilege the signs of what in the world, *today*, singularizes the use of the word 'religion' as well as experience of 'religion' associated with the word, there

12. It is no accident that the concept of trauma makes its most prominent appearance in Freud's *Moses and Monotheism;* see Cathy Caruth, *Unclaimed Experience: Trauma, Narrative, and History* (Baltimore: Johns Hopkins University Press, 1996), chs. 1 and 3. Jakob Taubes finds in Freud's book on Moses, not so much a quasi-historical account of the origin of monotheism, as an insight into the fact that the mode of its transmission is not that of the conscious and active labor of tradition but of a passive collective memory, whose unconscious traces are, moreover, marked by a certain repetitive force (*Zwangscharakter*). See the editors' afterword to Jakob Taubes, *Die politische Theologie des Paulus* (Munich: Wilhelm Fin, 1993), 172–73, and Taubes's own course description: "Under the mask of a psychopathography of the man Moses, Freud develops a theory of recollection and of tradition. His analysis of religious-historical processes of the return of the repressed constitutes an extremely multilayered concept of historical truth" (ibid., 173; my trans.). Taubes suggests that Freud does not so much identify himself with Moses as with Paul (ibid., esp. 122–31).

where no memory and no history could suffice to announce or gather it, not at least at first sight" (FK 35 / 48).

This does not prevent Derrida from risking a "pre-definition" of the meaning of *religion,* one that is sufficiently general and formal—or, perhaps, formally indicative, in Heidegger's sense—so as to capture "religion" both as a historical phenomenon and as a contemporary force to be reckoned with in the most unexpected of contexts, as well as in the very destitution of all context, a meaning that may very well be regulative of all others:

> however little may be known of religion *in the singular,* we do know that it is always a response and responsibility that is prescribed, not chosen freely in an act of pure and abstractly autonomous will. There is no doubt that it implies freedom, will and responsibility, but let us try to think this: will and freedom *without autonomy.* Whether it is a question of sacredness, sacrificiality or of faith, the other makes the law, the law is other: to give oneself back, and up, to the other. To every other and to the utterly other ["autre est la loi, et se rendre à l'autre. A tout autre et au tout autre"]. (FK 34 / 47)

This theme of a responsibility that does not start with autonomy, a responsibility, moreover, that does not limit itself to determinable tasks and duties but is excessive and extends itself, in principle, to everything and everyone—including oneself—as the totally other, is a leitmotif throughout this book. My central concern, however, is not to reconsider the relationship between deconstruction and, say, ethics or politics,[13] but to raise the question of what "religion" has to do with it; and, what is more, to do so in a nontheological fashion, if possible. But to raise this question may already bring into play what is at issue here. Indeed, any inquiry of this kind might very well turn out to rest on a *petitio principii* that, in a sense, is never questioned as such. According to Derrida, even before a distinction between, say, the epistemological and the theological could be made, the questioning of—or into—religion would already have blurred the classical and modern demarcations between faith and knowledge. Any such questioning would, indeed, situate itself "at the limits" of reason, and not of reason alone.

Neither faith nor knowledge nor both at once, the question of religion, Derrida writes, "is first of all the question of the question. Of the

13. See Simon Critchley, *The Ethics of Deconstruction* (Oxford: Blackwell, 1992), and Beardsworth, *Derrida and the Political.*

origins and the borders of the question — and of the response. 'The thing' tends thus to drop out of sight as soon as one believes oneself to be able to master it under the title of a discipline, a knowledge or a philosophy" (FK 39/54). This insufficiency is not merely empirical or linguistic;[14] the well-known issue of the ineffability of the sayable and the unsayable is not the problem here. Religion is to be conceived of as the problem of performative utterance "as such," but of an utterance that does not — not yet or no longer — attain the determinability *qua* content and structure that remains presupposed (without further justification, metaphysically, and in the guise of some "presentism") by the modern theories of the performative (Austin) and of the speech act (Searle). By contrast, the possible success of the religious performative — the very performativity of *religion*, the word no less than its effects, but also the religiosity of every performative — is never guaranteed by preestablished or simply given contextual requirements. Any such "success" is its failure, its lack of respect. The sole successful performative, Derrida remarks somewhere in *La Carte postale* (*The Postcard*), is a "*perverformative.*" Any religious utterance, act, or gesture, stands in the shadow of — more or less, but never totally avoidable — perversion, parody, and kitsch, of blasphemy and idolatry. Again, this holds true for "faith" no less than for "knowledge." As Derrida recalls: "Religion and reason develop in tandem [*ensemble*], drawing from this common resource: the testimonial pledge [*gage*] of every performative" (FK 28/41).

Both as a sociopolitical force and as a theoretical problem, then, the "return of religion" remains inexplicable as long as one continues naively to oppose religion, not only to critique, autonomy, and self-determination, to the profane and the finite, to the technological and the mechanical, to the modern and the postmodern, but also to their concrete manifestations in the secular nation-state and republicanism, the nature of international law, and the future of transnational forms of identity (individual and collective):

> Why is this phenomenon, so hastily called the "return of religions," so difficult to think? Why is it so surprising? Why does it particularly astonish those

14. A little further in the same paragraph, Derrida continues: "[A] serious treatise on religion would demand the construction of new Bibliothèques de France and of the universe, even if, not *believing that one was thinking* anything new, one were to content oneself with remembering, archiving, classifying, and making a memorandum of what one *believed* one already *knew*" (FK 39-40/54; trans. modified).

who believed naively that an alternative opposed Religion, on the one side, and on the other, Reason, Enlightenment, Science, Criticism (Marxist Criticism, Nietzschean Genealogy, Freudian Psychoanalysis, and their heritage), as though one could not but put an end to the other? On the contrary, it is an entirely different schema that would have to be taken as one's point of departure in order to try to think the "return of the religious." Can the latter be reduced to what the *doxa* confusedly calls "fundamentalism," "fanaticism" or in French, "integrism"? (FK 5 / 13)

It does not suffice therefore to think of the intellectual "turn to religion" in terms of a relapse into former stages of thought, as if we were dealing with a reversal of the conceptual onto- and phylogenesis that Auguste Comte projected onto the history of consciousness: from religion through metaphysics all the way up (or down) to the science of the positively given. Neither fideism nor secularism, let alone the religion of positivism that, for Comte, would come to replace them, contains the key to the task that concerns us here: to think or theorize the "religious" and the "theological," their seemingly incessant recurrence, the conceptual tools and chances they offer, but also their ethico-political perils and dangers. We shall have to take more than one step back in order to be able to put this complex set of issues in perspective, to examine its vicissitudes, and to weigh the relative merit of the responses it solicits in the texts under consideration.

Derrida's very title "Faith *and* Knowledge" conveys that one cannot relegate the question of religion to a single discipline — or set of disciplines — that would fall *either* under the rubric of faith (expressed by speculative, systematic, or biblical theology and church dogmatics, but also mystical enlightenment, spiritual exercises, etc.) *or* under that of knowledge (the historical and scientific study of religion or, say, its naturalist reduction to a mere epiphenomenon of other — biological, social, psychological, or linguistic — systems of meaning). Moreover, the title of Derrida's most direct and powerful account of the return or turn to religion implies the need for a certain analytical and critical distance, especially where the very concepts of "analysis" and "critique" can no longer be taken for granted as such, or at least in their common interpretation. Derrida's subtitle, "The Two Sources of 'Religion' at the Limits of Reason Alone," conjures up at least three pertinent philosophies of religion, each of which serves as a foil against which Derrida's own observations take on their distinctive profile: Kant's *Die Religion innerhalb der Grenzen der blossen Vernunft*

(*Religion Within the Boundaries of Mere Reason*), Hegel's *Glauben und Wissen* (*Faith and Knowledge*), and Henri Bergson's *Les Deux Sources de la morale et de la religion* (*The Two Sources of Morality and Religion*). And while the significance of the last two texts is not obvious at first glance, Derrida explicitly raises the question of what, in today's world, a book like *Religion Within the Limits of Mere Reason* would amount to. "Faith and Knowledge" could well be read as the preface to such a rearticulation of Kant's project or, more precisely, of what Derrida calls "the "Kantian gesture." This gesture is complex, Derrida stresses, and includes at least a

> preference for what, in politics, is called republican democracy as a universalizable model, binding philosophy to the public "cause," the *res publica*, to "public-ness" . . . , once again to the "lights" of the Enlightenment [*aux Lumières*], once again to the enlightened virtue of public space, emancipating it from all external power (non-lay, non-secular), for example from religious dogmatism, orthodoxy or authority (that is, from a certain rule of *doxa* or of belief, which, however, does not mean from all faith). (FK 8 / 16)

Although "Faith and Knowledge" recalls those earlier titles of Kant, Hegel, and Bergson, "entering," as Derrida puts it, into "a contract with them," the analyses of his essay are "committed to deforming them, dragging them elsewhere while developing, if not their negative or their unconscious, at least the logic of what they might have let speak about religion independently of the meanings they wanted to say" (FK 40 / 55). This "hijacked translation" (*traduction détournée*) or "rather free formalization" (FK 41 / 56) is explained by the second characteristic of "the Kantian gesture" Derrida mentions: his considerations "attempt to transpose, here and now, the circumspect and suspensive attitude, a certain *epochē* that consists — rightly or wrongly, for the issue is serious — in thinking religion or making it appear 'within the limits of reason alone' " (FK 8 / 16). The two characteristics, however, belong together in ways that are still difficult to divine. The *epochē* in question, Derrida continues, in turn gives a "chance" to the "political event" and is therefore not a mere theoretical operation to be performed by simply abstracting from every empirical and institutional context: "It even belongs to the history of democracy, notably when theological discourse was obliged to assume the forms of the *via negativa*, and even there, where it seems to have prescribed reclusive communities, initiatic teachings, hierarchy, esoteric insularity or the desert" (FK 8 / 17).

According to "Faith and Knowledge," the interpretation of the Western world, especially of its intellectual and political Enlightenment, in terms of modern secularism, rationalism, autonomy, and self-determination has become more and more problematic, if not obsolete.[15] Enlightenment and its philosophical concept of critique can no longer be defined as being merely opposed to, rather than being traversed or haunted by, a faith and a trustworthiness that borders upon heteronomy and therefore inevitably runs the risk of giving way to fideism and, indeed, obscurantism. This possibility, it seems, is inscribed in the very fact of reason. Derrida writes:

> the "lights" and Enlightenments of tele-technoscientific critique and reason can only suppose trustworthiness. They are obliged to put into play an irreducible "faith," that of a "social bond" or of a "sworn faith," of a testimony . . . , that is, of a performative of promising at work right down to lying or perjury and without which no address to the other would be possible. Without the performative experience of this act of elementary faith, there would be neither "social bond" nor address of the other, nor any performativity in general: neither convention, nor institution, nor Constitution, nor sovereign State, nor law, nor above all, here, that structural performativity of the productive performance that binds from its very conception the knowledge of the scientific community to doing, and science to technics. . . . [W]herever this tele-technoscientific critique develops, it brings into play and confirms the fiduciary credit of an elementary faith which is, at least in its essence or calling, religious (the elementary condition, the milieu of the religious, if not religion itself). (FK 44–45 / 59–60)

That the phenomenon of "religion" and everything it stands for — sacrifice, prayer, their respective idioms and idiosyncrasies, but also, in a more general sense, "the chain of analogous motif in the sacro-sanctifying attitude or intentionality," which, Derrida says, "bears several names of the same family" (FK 49 / 66), such as scruple, shame, discretion, restraint, inhibition, modesty: in Kant's vocabulary, *Achtung*, or respect; in Heidegger's vocabulary, *Gelassenheit*, *Scheu*, and *Verhaltenheit*, that is to say, relinquishment, modesty, and "holding-back" (ibid.) — that all this has such a broader relevance could, in sum, be explained by pointing to the unfolding of a singular process. Derrida terms it the process of *mondialatinisation* (FK 11 / 20), which means the becoming ever more

15. Cf. *Violence, Identity, and Self-Determination,* ed. de Vries and Weber.

"Latin" — that is, pagan, Christian, indeed, religious — of the "world" and, inversely (or perversely), the becoming "wordly" of the religious. This neologism, *mondialatinisation*, aptly translated by Samuel Weber as "globalatinization," is introduced, it seems, first of all to avoid the language of modernization and secularization or, at least, globalization without further qualification, none of which would be able to grasp the "credit" or "trust" — the "elementary act of faith" — that, Derrida notes, lies at the very heart of capital in the age, not only of mechanical reproduction, but first and foremost of so-called information technology:

> No calculation, no assurance will ever be able to reduce its ultimate necessity, that of the testimonial signature (whose theory is not necessarily a theory of the subject, of the person or of the ego, conscious or unconscious). To take note of this is to give oneself the means of understanding why, in principle, today, there is no incompatibility in the said "return of the religious," between the "fundamentalisms," the "integrisms" or their "politics" and, on the other hand, rationality, which is to say, the telo-techno-capitalistico-scientific fiduciarity, in all of its mediatic and globalizing dimensions. The rationality of the said "fundamentalisms" can also be hypercritical and not even recoil before what can sometimes resemble a deconstructive radicalization of the critical gesture. (FK 45 / 60)

The theme of *mondialatinisation* is already announced in Derrida's *Spectres de Marx* (*Specters of Marx*) (Marx being an author whose work seems in the nature of a parergon, or ancillary task, in Kantian systematics, rather than the other way around), where it designates the ideological uses and abuses — in short, the one-sided interpretation — of the Hegelian-Kojèvian topos of the "end of history," the "universalization of Western liberal democracy as the final point of human government."[16] But this neologism also mimics and parodies the later Heidegger's preoccupation with the "world" (*Welt*), with the "worlding of world" (*Welten von Welt*). By the same token, it draws on the historical and ontological significance of the Latin and, especially, the Roman that is stressed, notably in Heidegger's *Beiträge zur Philosophie* (*Contributions to Philosophy*). But then again, there is a significant difference as well. Derrida leaves no doubt that the "globalatinization," in its very "Christianicity" (to use Franz Overbeck's term), seems at once pervasive, even virtually omnipresent, and

---

16. Francis Fukuyama quoted from Jacques Derrida, *Spectres de Marx* (Paris: Galilée, 1993), trans. Peggy Kamuf as *Specters of Marx* (London: Routledge, 1994), 72.

marked by an invisible — or should we say virtual? — limit intrinsic to its proper unfolding. More clearly than Heidegger, Derrida insists on this ambiguity. The word *globalatinization,* he writes, "names a unique event to which a meta-language seems incapable of acceding, although such a language remains, all the same, of the greatest necessity. For at the same time that we no longer perceive its limits, we know that such globalization is finite and only projected" (FK 30 / 42).

In its very inflation, it also, Derrida adds, "runs out of breath" (*essouf-flée;* FK 30 / 42); and this "running out of breath" (*essoufflement;* FK 30 / 43) is what is almost impossible to comprehend in its scope, its perils, its changes, its future, and so forth.

"FAITH AND KNOWLEDGE," his most explicit discussion of the theme of religion to date, allows Derrida to bring together different threads that run through his numerous earlier writings. (We shall study them at length in the chapters that follow.) But this essay addresses recent and unforeseen developments as well. First, "Faith and Knowledge" submits that the very concept and growing geopolitical role of what would seem — if only for the purposes of ideological justification — to be religious wars might well offer a key to understanding present-day reality in the Balkans, in the Middle East, and elsewhere.

Second, Derrida emphasizes that religion is not only linked to traditions such as the monotheistic heritage of the Abrahamic religions of the Book, but is also "on line" with the new media. Religion somehow participates in and contributes to the uprooting force of a "radical abstraction" that is not exclusively an attribute of the desertification of contemporary thought, but also marks the "tele-technological transcendence" of a *mēchanē* that creates a virtual, cyber space-time — that reinscribes religion into the realm of the televisual and the digital. This analysis, Derrida suggests, could well be taken as the present-day form of the motif that Bergson evokes in the concluding remark of the final chapter of *The Two Sources of Morality and Religion,* devoted to "Mechanics and Mysticism," when he reminds humankind of the "essential function" of the universe, which consists in its being a "machine for making gods" (FK 41, 51 / 59, 69),[17] rather than the mere perpetuation of life. Indeed, the reference to

17. See Henri Bergson, *Les Deux Sources de la morale et de la religion* (Paris: Presses universitaires de France, 1932, 1951), 338, trans. R. Ashley Audra and Cloudesley Brereton, with the assistance of W. Horsfall Carter, under the title *The Two Sources of Morality and Religion* (Notre Dame, Ind.: University of Notre Dame Press, 1986), 317.

"this machine-like return of religion" (FK 14, cf. 19 / 23, cf. 29), to a turn that is quasi-mechanical, -automatic, and -spontaneous, in short, characterized by and inscribed in a certain technicity — and in that sense, also of an artificial and prosthetic nature — seems one of the most persistent in Derrida's essay. It is interesting that this series of motifs is mentioned in the same breath as that of secrecy and even of mysticism: "Mechanical would have to be understood here in a meaning that is rather 'mystical.' Mystical or secret because contradictory" (FK 41 / 56).

The reason for this seems clear, since in response to the tele-techno-science carried by the new media, religion not only adopts a "reactive" and "antagonistic" stance but, in fact, albeit in less obvious ways, may just as well function as this mechanics' most subtle and most decisive affirmation, its excessive overdrive — that is to say, its transcendence no less than its hyperbolic effect:

> Religion today allies itself with tele-technoscience, to which it reacts with all its forces. It is, *on the one hand,* globalization; it produces, weds, exploits the capital and knowledges of tele-mediatization: neither the voyages and the global spectacularization of the Pope, nor the interstate dimensions of the "Rushdie affair," nor planetary terrorism would otherwise be possible, at this rhythm, — and we could multiply such indications *ad infinitum.* But, *on the other hand,* it reacts immediately, *simultaneously,* declaring war against that which gives it this new power only at the cost of dislodging it from all its proper places, *in truth from place itself,* from the *taking place* of its truth. It conducts a terrible war against that which protects it only by threatening it. (FK 46 / 62).

This at the same time explains why the "strange alliance" between religion and the new media can be at once "hegemonic and finite, ultra-powerful *and* in the process of exhausting itself" (FK 13 / 21–22; emphasis added). The "icons of our time" (FK 70 n. 17 / 35 n. 13) work both for and against religion, for and against a turn — or return — to religion, which they at once signal, epitomize, welcome, diffuse, *and* render increasingly implausible, even counterintuitive. As things stand, there seems to be no way out of this paradoxical or rather contradictory — and, philosophically speaking, aporetic — state of affairs:

> No faith . . . , nor future without everything technical, automatic, machine-like supposed by iterability. In this sense, the technical is the possibility of faith, indeed its very chance. A chance that entails the greatest risk, even the

menace of radical evil. . . . Instead of opposing them, as is almost always done, they ought to be thought *together,* as *one and the same possibility:* the machine-like and faith, and the same holds for the machine-like and all the values entailed in the sacro-sanct (*heilig,* holy, safe and sound, unscathed, intact, immune . . . ). (FK 47–48 / 63)

The world seems marked by an increasingly sophisticated — digitalized and cybernated — culture, which is at once mobilized and exploited by the belligerent protagonists of the so-called new religious wars *and* identified as their major enemy target. In fact, for the present-day advocates of religion, the tele-technico-scientific machine is, Derrida writes, "to be manipulated as much as it is to be exorcised"; in their seemingly "archaic" and "primitive" responses to the machine's expropriating and eradicating force, the religionists must inevitably resort to using its own mechanics to enroot their communities anew in what they conceive to be the proper places, in nonhybrid ethnic identities, and in nations that remain defined as much by the mythology of blood and soil as by collective memories. Hence, the ambiguity, paradox, or aporia: "[W]ith respect to all . . . forces of abstraction and dissociation (deracination, delocalization, disincarnation, formalization, universalizing schematization, objectification, telecommunication, etc.), 'religion' is *at the same time* involved in reactive antagonism and reaffirmatively outbidding itself" (FK 2 / 10).

In other words, what is at issue in the return of religion is a structural or irreducible "interconnectedness" of "religious belief" and the "sacro-sanct," on the one hand, and "knowledge," "technoscience," and "calculation" (FK 54/72), on the other. The task, then, is to comprehend this intertwinement between "faith" and "knowledge," but to do so "otherwise" (ibid.) than, say, Kant, Hegel, and Bergson. But the complexity of the phenomenon in question goes even further. For while there is a mutual implication and exclusion of religion and so-called tele-transcendence (the one engendering and at the same time destroying the other), there is also — paradoxically, aporetically — an inherent tendency toward the beyond of this polarity, one in which the ellipsis is, as it were, eclipsed, albeit never totally or once and for all. "The same movement that renders indissociable religion and tele-technoscientific reason in its most critical aspect reacts inevitably to itself," Derrida writes. "It secretes its own antidote but also its own power of auto-immunity" (FK 44/58).

The term *religion* evokes not only an orientation toward a forever distant and indeterminate future — or *à venir* — but also an obsession with old and new forms of violence, with empirical forms of violence such as censorship and interethnic terror, and with the symbolic violence that marks the privileging of certain conceptual or axiological hierarchies. Indeed, the primacy of specific theologemes and of their logical and ontological order might be said to parallel and enable the manifestation of ethico-political strife and repression.[18] Ultimately, Derrida holds, religion conjures up a specter that Kant saw at the heart of human nature: "radical evil" (*das radikal Böse*), and from his earliest writings on, Derrida has referred to this as *la pire violence* ("the worst violence"). Rewriting Kant's *Religion Within the Boundaries of Mere Reason*) allows him to raise the question of the mutual implication of religion, reason, and radical evil and to ask: "[D]oes radical evil destroy or institute the possibility of religion?" (FK 41 / 55). In a similar way, Bergson's book helps us to rethink the modes of religion's "interminable and ineluctable return" (ibid.), and that means in its always possible relationship to evil and the worst violence. *The Two Sources of Morality and Religion*, Derrida reminds us, was written between the two world wars and "on the eve of events of which one knows that one does not yet know how to think them, and to which no religion, no religious institution in the world remained foreign or survived *unscathed, immune, safe and sound*" (FK 41 / 55).

"Faith and Knowledge" makes clear that *indemne*, the French word so often used to translate Heidegger's use of *heilig* connotes "the pure, the non-contaminated, the untouched, the sacred or the sound [*sain*] before all profanation" (FK 69 n. 16 / 34 n. 12; trans. modified), among other things. *Indemnisation*, then, designates "the process of compensation and restitution, sometimes sacrificial, which *re*constitutes the intact purity" (ibid., cf. 72–73 n. 27 / 59 n. 23). But *indemne* also signals the "absolute imperative," the "living," that which deserves categorical respect, and thus not only *Achtung*, in the precise sense of Kant's practical philosophy, but also the "intentional attitude" of *Scheu, Verhaltenhalt*, and *Gelassenheit*, of which Heidegger speaks in his later writings (cf. FK 49 / 66). Here, Derrida's rewriting of Kant's *Religion Within the Boundaries of Mere Reason* would seem to touch, if only in passing, upon an increasingly important rearticulation of some of the central motifs in Heidegger's *Beiträge zur Philosophie*. A strange alliance, as Derrida is quick to point out:

> The poles, themes, causes are not the same (the law, sacredness, holiness, the god to come, and so on), but the movements appear quite analogous

18. See *Violence, Identity, and Self-Determination*, ed. de Vries and Weber, introduction.

in the way they relate to them, *suspending* themselves, and *in truth inter-rupting themselves*. All of them involve or mark a restraint [*halte*]. Perhaps they constitute a sort of universal: not "religion" as such [*la Religion*], but a universal structure of religiosity. For if they are not in themselves properly religious, they always open the possibility of the religious without ever being able to limit or restrain it. This possibility remains divided. On the one hand, to be sure, it is respectful or inhibited abstention before what remains sacred mystery, and what ought to remain intact or inaccessible, like the mystical immunity of a secret. But in thus holding back, the same halting also opens an access without mediation or representation, hence not without an intuitive violence, to that which remains unscathed. That is another dimension of the mystical. Such a universal allows or promises perhaps the global translation of *religio*. . . . Such a universal, such an "existential" universality, could have provided at least the mediation of a *scheme* to the globalatinization of *religio*. Or in any case, of its possibility. (FK 49–50 / 66–67)

The worst violence: this formula could well be the signature of the "age of extremes," to adopt Eric Hobsbawm's characterization of the major trends of the twentieth century. For Derrida, however, *la pire violence* first of all means abstraction ad absurdum, looking away from every singu-larity that is other or belongs to the other, and, by the same token, the abstraction from the general, and a fortiori from universality, called for by the "democracy to come." The latter is not limited to the forms of rep-resentation or to the ideal of self-determination that have come to define the identity of the West, from the heyday of its imperialisms to the recent call for a "new world order."

Needless to say, the anxiety that feeds the reactive violence — a vio-lence that reacts to the worldwide process of abstraction by abstracting from its formalism and potential universalism, while continuing to use its means of cultural reproduction — shows up in the body politic's obses-sion with a limited conception of the body. In other words: with a sexual politics that exerts its violence to no small degree as a violation, as muti-lation, or at least as the denial of (possible) sexual identities. And this, Derrida suggests in "Faith and Knowledge," is not without relation to an ignorance, forgetfulness, or devaluation of some of the most penetrat-ing insights of psychoanalysis, notably in the Old World, insights, how-ever, that are also ignored if they remain "culturally dissociated" and not "integrated into the most powerful discourses today on right, morality, politics, but also science, philosophy, theology, etc." (FK 54 / 71). Indeed,

Derrida continues: "How can one invoke a new Enlightenment in order to account for this 'return of the religious' without bringing into play at least some sort of logic of the unconscious? Without bringing it to bear on the question of radical evil and working out the reaction to radical evil that is at the center of Freudian thought?" (FK 54/72).

Moreover, Derrida notes in this same context, it would be difficult to aim for a rearticulation of religion and everything it stands for without addressing the death wish, the repetition compulsion, and, last but not least, the relationship between the theoretical gesture, if not the theorems, of psychoanalysis and the "interminable *Jewish question*" or the structure of a certain "messianicity": "It is true that psychoanalytic knowledge can in turn uproot *and* reawaken faith by opening itself to a new space of testimoniality, to a new instance of attestation, to a new experience of the symptom and of truth" (FK 54/72).

This is one of the issues discussed at great length in Derrida's *Mal d'archive* ("Archive Fever"), which tackles the question that interests us here from a slightly different angle.[19] Speaking of Freud's relationship to Judaism, and starting out from a reading of Y. H. Yerushalmi's study of this subject,[20] Derrida here suggests that the legacy of the archive of psychoanalysis — or of any other archive — brings with it the affirmation of an original and originary "impression" that is haunted and made possible by what in the terms proposed by his *Specters of Marx* can be called a "spectral messianicity," distinct from all concrete, positive, messianisms. The archive is at once open toward the future *and* marked — more precisely "circumcised" — by a singular trait, here that of a certain Judaic tradition that cannot be disregarded as merely other or extrinsic to the archive, and that, moreover, cannot be erased without violence. The obligation not to forget, Derrida notes, is based on the ever-recurrent possibility of this violent erasure, the imposition or the realization of "the One."

Continuing this line of thinking, "Faith and Knowledge" gives a provocative analysis of how the concept and the politics of self-determination and the collective and subjective identities it presupposes and produces are fissured and fractured at their very origin. The "double source" of these notions and their cultural representations, Derrida claims, lies not only

19. Jacques Derrida, *Mal d'archive: Une Impression freudienne* (Paris: Galilée, 1995), trans. Eric Prenowitz under the title "Archive Fever: A Freudian Impression," *Diacritics* 25, no. 2 (Summer 1995): 9–63.

20. Y. H. Yerushalmi, *Freud's Moses: Judaism Terminable and Interminable* (New Haven: Yale University Press, 1991).

in autonomy, enlightenment, and the institution of liberal or communitarian political forms, but also in a potentially self-destructive violence. This inherent, endemic, and self-sacrificing violence, which is evident in the very notion of religion and in its sociopolitical practices, is characteristic of all supposedly self-oriented and self-centered determinations, obsessed with just one (nonhybrid) identity, with an identity that deems itself one and indivisible. Indeed, Derrida writes, the religious imposition or self-realization of "the One" or the "Unique" cannot institute or preserve itself without wounding, without murder, in short without violating the other and thereby ultimately doing violence to itself.

By the same token, however, this violence at the source of the self also reveals the need to affirm an original and originary messianicity. The latter term hints at an openness toward the future, but an openness that is nonetheless opened up by a singular trait. In the case of *Specters of Marx* and "Archive Fever," this trait is that of a certain Judaic tradition, one that cannot be disregarded as merely other or extrinsic to what it makes possible—for example, the critical, emancipatory spirit of Marxism, or the discipline and the archive of psychoanalysis—and that cannot be erased without violence. The obligation and the task not to forget, Derrida suggests, is based on the always recurrent possibility of such erasure. To be sure, the ethico-political translation of this task, a task that can, in turn, be considered neither as one, unique option nor as one option among many others, is difficult to imagine. In its departure and distance from all known and all future "-isms," in its affirmation of a democracy that remains forever "to come," it entails at least an exposure to the other, whatever the nature of its determination.

Against this background, it comes as no surprise that Derrida's more recent expositions revolve around the Kantian and Levinasian notions of "hospitality," as well as around the more limited concept of "tolerance." The openness of hospitality and tolerance is a relationship of respect toward the other, toward the others, toward every other as the totally other, toward the other so often determined by the hegemonic ideology of an identity that is dialectically or structurally opposed to it. Here as well the question of religion is significant for its capacity to open up and contextualize or problematize the relationship of the self to the other well beyond its formal juridical implications.

IT IS THE REARTICULATION, then, of these and other texts, as well as the experiences to which they bear witness, that will help us to distinguish Derrida's "unwritten" ethics and politics from the textualism, the transcendental lingualism, not to mention the textual "free play," with which his thought was so unfortunately—and surreptitiously—associated in the earliest phases of its reception. Coming in the wake of the more philosophically oriented attempts to uncover and reformulate the basic assumptions and the analytical force of Derrida's work, the recent endeavors to reassess the ethics and politics of deconstruction should have made that clear enough. Yet it is only by persistently referring to the religious that the reelaboration of these ethico-political traits avoids becoming moralistic, complacent, predictable, and opportunistic—that is to say, naive, prudent, pragmatist, or just another instance of *Realpolitik*. It is, in effect, the exposure to the *horror religiosus,* to the secret, its monstrosity, its madness, and its untimeliness—indeed, as *Specters of Marx* following *Hamlet,* reiterates, to a being "out of joint"—that makes Derrida's "turn to religion" resistant to hasty adaptations and applications.

Speaking of religion in the context of the work of Derrida means addressing myriad themes and strains of thought at once. If one speaks of "theology" one must also speak of different "negative theologies," of an *a*-theology that is nevertheless irreducible to Georges Bataille's *Somme athéologique* (Atheological Summa). But speaking of religion also involves a certain—if not ironic or perverse then at least highly qualified—reassessment of what distinguishes affirmative theologies from negative theologies, as well as of what, precisely, it "is," if anything, that allows affirmative theologies to come into being after (or despite) the passage through the negative. One of the most significant aspects of the body of writings I discuss is that they refuse to take the form of refutations, and therefore do not foreclose these different or even mutually exclusive options, but rather show how each of them can be justified to a certain extent.

To present these analyses under major headings, and thus to center them around crucial religious figures or theologemes—such as confession and prayer, apocalyptics and enlightenment, idolatry and kenosis, revelation and messianicity, sacrifice and divine wrath, demons and specters, mysticism and Babel, shibboleth and circumcision, the sacred space and the desert—is not to imply a logical, ontological, or even chronological order of their appearance or prevalence throughout the writings under the discussion. And yet it would be equally misleading to suggest that these headings are mutually synonymous or merely substitutable. They are not arbitrary topoi meant to illustrate, to embellish, or to trouble a more fundamental theoretical or practical issue that could just as well be articulated without them or independently of their interference.

This brings me back to the central argument that runs as a guiding thread through the chapters to follow. I seek to show that all the figures and texts discussed somehow revolve around the — originally Levinasian — figure of the *adieu*. Derrida discusses and reinterprets the many implications of this notion on several occasions, most explicitly in "Donner la mort" ("Giving Death"; translated by David Wills as *The Gift of Death*). *The Gift of Death* sets the tone for a remarkable recasting of our understanding of the ethical and the political by exposing these concepts, in their ancient and modern overdetermination, to that of the religious tradition, as understood against the historical background of the religions of the Book, especially Judaism and Christianity. The procedure of this turn to religion forces these concepts into a relation of simultaneous proximity with and distance from a phenomenon that they are thus said to both generalize (or universalize) *and* to trivialize, if only by stripping it of its ontological and axiological privilege and substance. *To turn around religion also means here: to turn religion around.* All this is implied from the outset in the phrase *à Dieu* or *adieu*, in all its ambiguity of a movement toward God, toward the word or the name of God, and a no less dramatic farewell to almost all the canonical, dogmatic, or onto-theological interpretations of this very same "God." As if nothing save His name were untouched and left intact. As if the sacred name were not so much lacking (as Heidegger, misreading Hölderlin, believed) but to be found solely in the integrity — or absoluteness, safe and sound — of a host of idiomatic, singular, yet infinitely substitutable names of His name. For good and for ill.

This turn to or around religion should not be confused with the many attempts, old and new, to reduce the problem of morality to that of extrapolating a distinct (concrete, empirical or ontic) conception of the good or the good life — of *Sittlichkeit,* that is — whether from Aristotle through Hegel, all the way up to Alasdair McIntyre and Charles Taylor. Nor should we identify it with the endeavors to mobilize a "political theology," from the various historical messianisms, up to the writings of Carl Schmitt, Walter Benjamin, Jakob Taubes, and the liberation — or so-called "genitive" — theologies of recent decades. Derrida argues that the relation of the ethical and the political to the religious is far more indirect and "immediate" (as Jean-Luc Nancy puts it in his *L'Expérience de la liberté* [*The Experience of Freedom*]), carried as it is by a complex logic of testimony whose instances punctuate its respective histories with an incalculable rhythm. The complexity of this movement of perpetual conversion (*retournement*) is captured by the figure of the *adieu*, borrowed from Levinas, which is given a twist reminiscent of the turn that resonates through the writings of St. Paul and St. Augustine, as read by the early Heidegger. This motif allows Derrida to bring out a simultaneous allegiance and radical distantiation, contrary gestures that are inevitable, it seems, when dealing with the ethical and the political in this way. For to question these notions by reinscribing into the religious tradition is to affirm this tradition all over again—to say the same thing completely otherwise—in a proximity that is almost that of a tautology, yet, as we shall see, also implies the betrayal of a no less radical heterology. True, these mutually exclusive—yet simultaneous—movements are what is already implied in the *terminus technicus* that Derrida introduces and justifies in "Signature, Event, Context" and elaborates in *Limited Inc.,* when he speaks of the concept and practice of "reiteration". And yet, nowhere are these contradictory—yet apparently co-originary—movements expressed more poignantly than in the figure of the *adieu.* The intrinsic ambiguity of this phrase makes in Derrida's recent writings all the difference in the world even though it expresses—repeats and displaces—what seems the very same function of the earlier more formal term (i.e., "iterability"). Why, then, is this reference to religion and to God necessary or useful in the first place? Why is the analysis of the formal and supposedly universal structure of repetition qua change now presented as being contingent upon a particular tradition, here that of the religions of the Book, even though the latter are said to have been made possible by this structure in the first place? What are we to make of this circular relation, which seems to undercut what Derrida elsewhere calls a "logic of presupposition" (i.e., of foundationalism and reductionism, but also of any assumption of possibilization that forms the focus of all quasi-, simili-, ultra-transcendental discourses that seek to escape the predicament of historicism, psychologism, and the like)?

Derrida construes a parallel relationship between religion or faith, on the one hand, and radical evil and ontotheology, on the other. Forcing together Kant's *Religion Within the Boundaries of Mere Reason* and Heidegger's famous essay "Die ontotheologische Verfassung der Metaphysik" ("The Ontotheological Constitution of Metaphysics"), published in *Identität und Differenz (Identity and Difference),* and reiterating the final pages of his own *Apories (Aporias),* Derrida observes: "The possibility of radical evil both destroys and institutes the religious. Ontotheology does

the same when it suspends sacrifice and prayer. . . . Ontotheology en-
crypts faith and destines it to the condition of a sort of Spanish Marrano
who would have lost—in truth: dispersed, multiplied—everything up to
and including the memory of his unique secret. Emblem of a still life [*une
nature morte*] . . ." (FK 65–66 / 86).

   *Necessarily* idolatrous, the *adieu* signals not only that all religious and
a fortiori all theological speech—in short, all "Godtalk"—is irrevocably
tainted by what Kant, in *Der Streit der Fakultäten* (*The Conflict of the
Faculties*), calls an "admixture of paganism": a slippage into the empirical or into anthropomorphism. Conversely, the formula *adieu* accentuates the fact that every discourse, even the most secular, profane, negative, or nihilistic of utterances, directs and redirects itself unintentionally
and unwittingly toward the alterity for which—historically, systematically, conceptually, and figuratively speaking—"God" is, perhaps and so
far, the most proper name. This orientation of all discourse toward the
religious and everything that comes to take its place, is by definition in-
flected, contorted, or even false. It is in this respect that the following
account differs from those that led Michel de Certeau, Jean-Luc Marion,
and others (among them Walter Benjamin and, in middle stage of his
development, Emmanuel Levinas ) to opt for a purely theological, or
rather *heterological,* discourse that is deemed to be capable of escaping,
not only the primary idolatry of the imagery called anthropomorphism,
but also a secondary idolatry, which is far more dangerous, because invisible: what Marion calls the idolatry of the concept, of the intangible
and nonempirical "screen" (*écran*) of Being on which the being of God is
*projected.* Hence the urgency of addressing the central problem of ontotheology, the problem of the dimension of revealability (*Offenbarkeit*)
or of messianicity in its relation to any purported historical or positive
revelation (*Offenbarung*) and concrete messianisms. This aporetic relationship is anticipated in Kant no less than in Heidegger (who explicitly
draws on a comparable notion taken from Franz Overbeck, namely, that
of Christianicity [*Christlichkeit*], which, as in Kant's philosophy of religion, is played out against Christianity's historical and actual forms or
formations).

   With the help of the *adieu,* in all the ambiguity, polysemy, and, ultimately, dissemination of its different connotations or associations, we
find another way, not of redefining the religious, but of indicating its
paradoxical or, rather, aporetic, structure and of redescribing its central
features. To my knowledge, no classical or modern, philosophical, socio-

logical, or anthropological description of religion has so far been able to provide us with an adequate interpretative tool that does justice to historical and sociocultural facts while simultaneously retaining some general philosophical or analytical relevance.[21] Whatever their adequacy at isolated points, all current definitions and interpretations seem to remain somehow beside the point (but is there a point, just one, one and indivisible?), if only because they fail to explain the reemergence of the most enduring appearance — indeed, specter — of religion at the heart and in the very guise of its most fervent denials.

By contrast, the figure of the *adieu* might well succeed in helping us further in this regard and do so without, in its turn, reducing religion to what is taken to define human nature. The structure of the *adieu* is irreducible to the *desiderium naturale,* to a religious a priori, to the physiology or the psychopathology of the mechanism of projection, to the fetishism produced or permitted and fostered by socioeconomic forms of interaction, commodification, or reification, to the fideism presumably internal to certain language games and forms of life, and so on. This list could easily be extended.

Needless to say, the above is merely the formal scheme of an argument that will have to be expounded in detail in order to acquire sufficient plausibility. This book aims at nothing but that. To demonstrate that the apparent entanglement of Derrida's writing in the *via negativa* is a being *on the way* (an *unterwegs* of sorts), not to language (*Sprache*), not to the essence of language, and not to writing, let alone to a science of writing, but, rather, to "God" (*à dieu*) or to what comes to substitute for this name for the totally other yet another totally other (an incommensurable, totally other "totally other"); to argue, moreover, that this entanglement is the culmination and the most powerful illustration of an itinerary that for more than thirty years now has consisted in a radical rethinking, rewriting, undoing, and unwriting of the tradition of metaphysics or ontotheology; all this requires a meticulous reconstruction of the argument of what are often Derrida's least accessible texts in light of what is in principle an infinite series of "finite" — that is, nonsynonymous — placeholders for the "infinite."

Substituting for the "infinite" and ultimately the Infinite, nothing less is at issue in the formula of the *à dieu.* Thanks to this logic of infinite

21. Cf. Asad, *Genealogies of Religion,* ch. 1; Robert Towler, *Homo Religiosus: Sociological Problems in the Study of Religion* (London: Constable, 1974).

substitution, the very idea or concept of "God" already contradicts itself. In his early essay on Edmond Jabès in *L'Écriture et la différence* (*Writing and Difference*), Derrida says as much: "God contradicts himself already" ("Dieu déjà se contredit").[22] Wherever and whenever "God" is named and conceptualized, or even invoked or addressed, the gesture of this speech act is immediately broken. It is folded to the point of collapsing in on itself and reverting into its "opposite." No *coincidentia oppositorum* could hold this notion together. This is what the *adieu* enables us to articulate in its complexity. The expression combines all the ambiguity and coherent incoherence of evoking at once a gesturing *toward* "God" (*à dieu*), a *leave-taking from* "God" (*adieu*), and a "non-God," a being haunted by the other of "God" (of this one God, or of this God as one and the One): *a-dieu* signals the other of the Other as the fracturing and the dissemination of the One. It is not only the historical hegemony of a particular understanding of "God" and the "divine" that can thus be shown to be culturally unstable, philosophically vulnerable, ethically unreliable, or politically volatile. The violence with which the very notion "God" imposes itself remains also necessarily exposed to the violence with which it undermines itself. In Derrida's words: "[T]he One does violence to itself" ("L'Un se fait violence").[23] In fact, this paradox or aporia is its analytical and ethico-political "chance."[24]

Derrida has often suggested that this aporetic structure is reiterated in every genuine piece of testimony. Every attestation worthy of this name is intentionally directed toward an absolute witness, who sees, understands, and knows what happens. Its claim to truth and veracity, indeed, its very

22. Jacques Derrida, *L'Écriture et la différence* (Paris: Éditions du Seuil, 1967), 107, trans. Alan Bass as *Writing and Difference* (Chicago: University of Chicago Press, 1978), 70.

23. Derrida, "Archive Fever," 51/125.

24. It may seem that I use the terms *paradox* and *aporia* too loosely. However, as Derrida observes, there is no aporia "as such," and if the aporia can never be "experienced as such," then there are in fact only *apparent* aporias—that is to say, paradoxes. Moreover, the term *aporia* has various connotations in contemporary thought. In *Temps et récit* (Paris: Éditions du Seuil, 1983–85), trans. Kathleen McLaughlin and David Pellauer as *Time and Narrative* [Chicago: University of Chicago Press, 1984–88]), Paul Ricoeur speaks, for example, of "faire travailler l'aporie" with reference to the perplexities of temporality, a tension that cannot be resolved conceptually but has to be worked through—that is to say, resolved poetically in the medium of narration. This differs from what Derrida means when he alludes, in "Force of Law," to the simultaneous experience of opposed or contradictory validity claims implicit in our most common concepts as the "trial [*épreuve*] of the aporia." See Jacques Derrida, "Force of Law: The 'Mystical Foundation of Authority,'" trans. Mary Quaintance, *Cardozo Law Review* 2, nos. 5–6 (July–August 1990): 965. I cite this bilingual version below. A separate French edition appeared under the title *Force de loi: Le "Fondement mystique de l'authorité"* (Paris: Galilée, 1994).

rationality, requires this. This is just what is implied by saying that something is said in good faith, as Derrida writes in his *Mémoires pour Paul de
Man* (*Memoires: For Paul de Man*), it is "the meaning of a given word."

On the other hand, Derrida insists, if there were any such thing as an
absolute witness — here and now, fully present or even omnipresent, attentive or omniscient — there would, strictly speaking, be no reason why
one would attest to this absolute witness at all. St. Augustine is Derrida's
witness here — not just any witness, since he is presented as the father of
the classical, most pervasive and transgressive model for all testimony,
notably in the form of confession, which has come to dominate the Western theological and literary canon. It is no accident that Derrida returns to
Augustine time and again — in *Limited Inc.*, *Donner le temps* (*Given Time*),
*Mémoires d'aveugle* (*Memories of the Blind*), *Circonfession* ("Circumfession"), and *Politiques de l'amitié* (*Politics of Friendship*), to name only
the most remarkable instances of this spiritual, perhaps, more than spiritual, filiation. Far from being anachronistic in the pejorative sense of the
word, the Augustinian paradigm of confession comes to confirm the current interest in concepts and practices of testimony or attestation. In the
same vein, contemporary authors have provided compelling arguments
in favor of an understanding of testimony that stretches its significance
far beyond the mere communication or expression of some content, the
description of a state of affairs, or statements in a juridical process. What
I am interested in in what follows is the relationship between this philosophical and psychoanalytic rethinking of the testimonial, on the one
hand, and what might be called the surviving instance — the *survivance* —
of the testamentary and especially the confessional, on the other.[25]

In concluding, Derrida might be said to explore the paradoxical circumstance of *being at once close to and at the farthest remove from the
tradition called religious*. How can one think of oneself, Derrida asks in
"Circumfession," as the testamentary executor of religion, of theology, of
its rites, its institutions, its figures of speech, the tropes of its scriptures, of

25. This is not the place to discuss two of the most interesting contemporary interroga-
tions of the testimonial that either go beyond the parameters set by Heidegger's analyses of
*Bezeugung* and *Gewissen* in *Sein und Zeit* or operate independently with respect to them: Paul
Ricoeur's *Soi-même comme un autre* (Paris: Éditions du Seuil, 1990, trans. Kathleen Blamey as
*Oneself as Another* [Chicago: University of Chicago Press, 1992]), and Shoshana Felman's and
Dori Laub's *Testimony: Crises of Witnessing in Literature, Psychoanalysis, and History* (London:
Routledge, 1992). On the former, see my "Attestation du temps et de l'autre: De *Temps et récit*
à *Soi-même comme un autre*," in *Paul Ricoeur: L'Herméneutique à l'école de la phénoménologie*,
ed. Jean Greisch (Paris: Beauchesne, 1995), 21–42.

everything for which it claims to stand, as well as of everything for which
it turns out to stand in fact? What does it entail when Derrida calls himself
the "last of the Jews"? What, moreover, could it mean to identify oneself
as the "last of the eschatologists"?

Clearly, these sobriquets, which are discussed in chapter 1, but whose
implications reverberate throughout this book, play on "the last" in all
the ambiguity of the "latest," the "final," the most advanced and insight-
ful, on the one hand, and the "least" and the "worst," on the other. It is
hard, if not impossible, to reconcile these possible chronological, epistemological, and axiological connotations of "the last." Can one nonetheless think and live them together, be it simultaneously or at least in the
rhythm of a certain alternation or oscillation that goes beyond the logic
of the either/or, of affirmation or negation, continuation or interruption,
fidelity or antinomism, reverence for icons or iconoclasm? Surely this logic
of opposition is not just any convention. Based as it is on one of the first
fundamental laws of thought—the well-known axiom of the excluded
middle, beyond the possibility of either $p$ or non-$p$ (*tertium non datur*)—
it is supposed to safeguard thought against the peril and stagnation that
seems to result from logical contradiction or aporia. What good is it, then,
to expose thought, and thereby experience, life, action, decision, responsibility, testimony, and so on, to their—presumably structural, inherent,
and thus inevitable—contradiction: for example, the aporia of their being
pushed to the very extreme of having to orient themselves at once *nearest to* and *at the furthest remove from* their cultural inheritance? What
does such an exposure accomplish, if not an attestation as opposed to the
establishment of some truth, be it the Truth of all truth?

In *Aporias,* Derrida describes the structure of this "belonging without
belonging"—that is, of "belonging" to two extremes at once—in a sense
that eludes the harmonizing presuppositions made not only by the hermeneutic understanding of our historicity, traditionality, or canonicity
(understood in terms of an *Überlieferung,* an epochal *Seinsgeschick,* or a
*Wirkungsgeschichte*), but also by the dialectical or genealogical conceptions of historical movements, forces, and epistemes. What the attestation
of the religious reveals with respect to the question of continuity and
discontinuity is something entirely different. The movement that characterizes the attestation must rather be thought through with the help of
topological figures that—like the walking on two feet or the choreography
discussed below—do not merely ironize the archaic associations made by
Heidegger's topology of Being (*Topologie des Seins*), in its preoccupation

with the pastoral and the geopolitical, as well as with the earth, the land-scape, the rivers, and the soil. They also target the progressivist ideals of the long revolutionary march, the "great leap forward," as well as of piece-meal social engineering—the step-by-step march through institutions.

My interest in these spatial images is motivated in particular by the fact that they recall the topologies of negative theology that prefigure the features of that radically universalist and utopian democracy that remains forever to come and that cannot appear on any horizon of expectation or anticipation, but rather eludes every concept, every image, and, indeed, every figure. While much attention has been paid in recent years to the "ethics of deconstruction," as well as to the "new sense of the political" prepared (according to some) or impaired (according to others) by it, I venture to claim that the key to the understanding of both the ethical and the political lies in the numerous intersections between Derrida's ana-lyses and the theologico-political displacements of our day, and, perhaps, of all times. Furthermore, it is only against this background that one can hope to highlight the fundamental differences between Derrida's interest in messianicity and the political theologies explored respectively by Wal-ter Benjamin and Carl Schmitt. These differences have become particu-larly clear since the publication of Derrida's *Force de loi: Le "Fondement mystique de l'autorité"* ("Force of Law: The 'Mystical Foundation of Au-thority'") and *Politics of Friendship*, the analyses of which can be read as a critical examination of the "violence" of the "divine." These writings raise the question of whether divine violence, as it figures in the texts of Benjamin and others, should be seen as the inescapable horizon of the de-limitations of the political in its relation to the order of law and of justice, the social and the economic, the mythical as well as the secular and the sacred.

EACH CHAPTER OF THIS BOOK traces the general thrust of the argument I have made here by way of a specific text or religious figure, its contextu-alization and, so to speak, its *refiguration*. The structure of my narrative thus resembles the very thesis it seeks to convey: *retracing* the religious means also—and, perhaps, first of all—*tracing it otherwise*, not allowing it to take on one particular—that is, one universal—meaning once and for all.

Chapter 1, "Revealing Revelations," introduces the terms of a detailed engagement with the idiom, the arguments, and the rhetorical procedures of what Derrida, following a long and predominantly Greek tradition, chooses to call apophatic (i.e., negative, as opposed to cataphatic, affirmative) discourse. I begin by examining in what sense his work—even apart from its explicit engagement with the religious—is irrevocably linked to the formal structure of religion, as well as of theology, notably of negative theology, from its Platonic and Neoplatonic sources through the writings of Pseudo-Dionysius, Meister Eckhart, and Angelus Silesius all the way up to Heidegger, Marion, and—at a greater distance from this heritage— Levinas. I argue that Derrida's contribution is neither a simple extension of this tradition nor its outright refutation. Nor does his indefatigable reassessment of the *via negativa* justify the suspicion that it leaves his writing fundamentally indifferent. In light of this assessment, at least two common misunderstandings, represented here by Mikel Dufrenne and Jean-Luc Marion, lose much of their initial appeal.

In chapter 2, "Hypertheology," I explore some of the central implications of the turn to religion—of its turns of phrase as well as of the turning of thought that it provokes—a turn that has become increasingly dominant or visible in Derrida's most recent writings. Although retrospectively it is apparent that these motifs were a central concern from the very outset, they are emphasized and analyzed in more explicit and detailed terms in his writings of the 1980s and 1990s. In all their startling complexity, these texts have not yet found the systematic and thematic discussion they deserve.

Chapter 3 is entitled "Formal Indications" and discusses the relationship between phenomenology and religion as it is thematized in Martin Heidegger's 1920–21 lecture courses on SS. Paul and Augustine, as well as in the famous 1927 lecture "Phänomenologie und Theologie" ("Phenomenology and Theology"). Further excursions are made into Heidegger's *Sein und Zeit* (*Being and Time*) and "Brief über den Humanismus" ("Letter on Humanism"). This chapter raises two related questions. First, why is it that the question of religion, and in particular the self-explication of the factical life-experience of originary New Testament Christianity (*Urchristentum*), is, for Heidegger, the shortest detour to an adequate understanding of the problem of the "historical"? Second, to what extent and on what grounds can Derrida's own account of the religious be seen along the lines laid down by Heidegger or, for that matter, shed light on Heidegger's most vulnerable presuppositions? To discuss this matter will involve an analysis of Heidegger's crucial yet enigmatic notion of so-called formal indication (*formale Anzeige*) and also of Derrida's early understanding of the Husserlian notion of transcendental historicity. For it is in these notions that we find the key to the understanding of the intricate yet deeply problematic — and, indeed, aporetic — relationship between phenomenology and religion, philosophy and theology, but also, in Overbeck's and Heidegger's terms, of Christianicity (*Christlichkeit*) and Christendom, and, in Derrida's idiom, of messianicity and messianisms.

Chapters 4 and 5 elaborate further on certain motifs that had remained largely implicit in the previous discussion. Chapter 4 contains a detailed analysis of Heidegger's interpretation of our being-toward-death against the background of our reading of the apophatics. Chapter 5 expands on this analysis by including a reconsideration of Derrida's notes on Angelus Silesius, which are brought to bear upon one of his most enigmatic texts to date, "Circumfession."

I then turn to what, by contrast, could be claimed to be religion's and philosophy's "last word," its eschatology, its apocalyptics, indeed, its *ultima ratio*. Chapter 6 retraces the intriguing interrogation of the religious evocation of the "last things," *ta eschata*, the "last days," "the end," and "the end of times," as it appears in Derrida's rereading of Kant against the background of the Revelation of John, in *D'un ton apocalyptique adopté naguère en philosophie* ("On a Newly Arisen Apocalyptic Tone in Philosophy"). Here, the focus is on the "apocalyptic tone" and the "angelic" structure of a critical discourse on "vigilance" that displaces its traditional, ontotheological predecessors and reduces them to the doubly elliptical figure of a "lucid vigil." This wakefulness is read as the ineffaceable remainder, not only of the deconstruction of the Kantian project of Enlightenment, but also of the irrationalistic and obscurantist counterparts that must necessarily continue to cross its path. Like the "yes" that cannot but be affirmed, this vigilant remainder explains why, as Derrida notes, we can never simply "forgo" the quintessential meaning and force of the "good old *Aufklärung*."

The heritage of the vigil and the wake that receives its contours against the background of the New Testament is reminiscent of the Platonic wake (the *meletè tou thanatou*, of which Derrida speaks in *The Gift of Death*). The latter also provides the formal scheme for the keeping-vigil-for-death and ultimately prefigures the Heideggerian understanding, not only of the existential he calls "care" (*Sorge*), but, even more important, of Dasein's "being-toward-death" (*Sein-zum-Tode*), which I discuss in chapter 4.

Surely it is no accident that it is precisely the relationship between "the end," "the last," and Enlightenment — in all of its multifaceted historical forms — that helps introduce the problem of ethics and politics, of their difference and their mutual dependence, of the risks of taking them apart, and of considering them together. As Norman Cohn reminds us in *The Pursuit of the Millennium,* the originally precise and narrow meaning of Jewish and Christian eschatology and apocalyptics that marked the Hellenistic era soon gave way to a host of beliefs and popular movements whose common denominator, millenarianism, became a "label for a particular type of salvationism."[26] What is more, in its desire to force matters by bringing the imminent end—that is, redemption through destruction—even closer, this salvationism may be seen as the precursor of the messianic revolutionary movements that radically threatened the political and cultural hierarchies of later centuries.

There was a time when it seemed that the most powerful and latest successor of these movements had taken on the form of Western, supposedly internationalist Marxism. Has this tradition also left its imprint on what would come to be known as the work of deconstruction? Already in *Positions,* Derrida insists that no deconstructive reading practice can ignore certain premises and protocols of Marxist critique. More than twenty years later, with the publication of *Specters of Marx,* the ontology on which Marx's social *Aufklärung* is said to be based undergoes a rearticulation and displacement similar to Derrida's treatment of its Kantian predecessor. What Derrida's "hauntology" (*hantologie*) retains is "nothing but" the messianicity of Marx's critical spirit, whose specter hovers mournfully over the ashes of its failed embodiments and in our day as in Marx's time—indeed, in Marx's very own thinking—continues to fend off its annihilation through ontologization, its historization, its petrification and reification. The example of Marxism simply confirms the aporia of messianicity as such.

What ethics, then, could the "spirit of critique" or the specter of Enlightenment offer to a reading practice that relentlessly interrogates the metaphysical and ontotheological premises of the classical conceptions of reason, that patiently yet irresistibly ventures beyond the confines of modern formal rationality, without thereby ever becoming irrational? Does not the respect for the appeal of the vigil or wake that solicits reason entrap it in the paralyzing dilemma of a forceless, irresponsible silence and an equally irresponsible betrayal? Moreover, which political model, if

---

26. Norman Cohn, *The Pursuit of the Millennium: Revolutionary Millenarians and Mystical Anarchists of the Middle Ages* (1957; reprint, London: Pimlico, 1970), 13 and 281ff. See also his *Cosmos, Chaos and the World to Come: The Ancient Roots of Apocalyptic Faith* (New Haven: Yale University Press, 1994).

any, could ever hope to respect this irresolvable tension, correspond to its performativity, exemplify it, or, rather, endorse and "sign" it? Could this aporetic structure — for that is what it is — ever be concretized, if not descriptively, dialectically, or phenomenologically, then at least through a certain revolutionary, revisionary, or reformist institutional practice?

The relationship between the emphatic ellipsis of Enlightenment and the demands of institutional practice based on the concept of reason takes the form in Derrida of a polarity that, like an ellipse with two foci, precludes any possibility of discourse closing itself off in a "unifocal," and therefore univocal, dialectical or hermeneutical circle. The quasi-theological overtones that mark the specter of Enlightenment are presupposed by each of Derrida's texts examined in this book. This leitmotif is in the final analysis distinct from the ethics, formulated by Jürgen Habermas, Karl-Otto Apel, and Albrecht Wellmer, among others, that goes by the name of "discourse ethics" (*Diskursethik*), even though it implies an "ethics of discussion" in its own right.

This brings us back to our original question: what is the best — and most responsible — philosophical response to the purported return to religion in an era of globalization, virtualization of reality, and the "deterritorialization" brought about by new media and information technologies? Here, as so often, the question is also that of the appropriate political response to these changes, whose consequences are, perhaps, no longer measurable with the help of terms such as *secularism, postmodernism, multiculturalism, transnationalism,* and so on. This alone might be sufficient reason to reinvoke the semantic, hermeneutic, and critical resources of the historical phenomenon called religion, in both the most traditional and the most heterodox senses of the word. They all constitute an immense archive of concepts and figures, practices and dispositions, whose analytical yet highly ambiguous potential for the present age we have not yet begun to fathom. In this study, I attempt to formalize and concretize just a few of the most promising philosophical answers and strategies that help prepare us for the task of mobilizing the best of religion against the worst of its manifestations. These manifestations may adopt a host of different and mutually excluding forms, whether sacrosanct, profane, or secular. Yet in their very contingency, these forms remain contingent upon a certain formal scheme of sorts that they both betray and allow to be "seen," "intuited," or "named." And the reverse holds true as well. It is in terms of a transcendental historicity that we contrast the idea of revealability (*Offenbarkeit*) with historical revelation (*Offenbarung*), Christianicity (*Christlichkeit*) with positive ecclesial forms, and, indeed, messianicity with the messianisms of all ages. It is in their relationship that the aporia resides that will interest us throughout, which Derrida formulates as follows:

> [I]s revealability (*Offenbarkeit*) more originary than revelation (*Offenbar-ung*), and hence independent of all religion? Independent in the structures of its experience and in the analytics relating to them? Is this not the place in which "reflecting faith" at least originates, if not this faith itself? Or rather, in-versely, would the event of revelation have consisted in revealing revealability itself, and the origin of light, the originary light, the very invisibility of visi-bility? This is perhaps what the believer or the theologian might say here, in particular the Christian of originary Christendom, of that *Urchristentum* in the Lutheran tradition which Heidegger acknowledges owing so much. (FK 16 / 26)

An alternative to, say, the ontological and theological positions in this quest for a logic of presupposition would be simply to suggest that his-torical revelations reveal the general structure of revealability (at least?) as much as the other way around. This is perhaps Derrida's most challenging insight.

In addition to demonstrating the general thrust of my argument in the context of philosophical and theological themes and texts, explor-ing notions and experiences that underlie them and that unsettle their most common (and, perhaps, every possible) interpretation, my project demands an extensive discussion of recent contributions to the abstract questioning indicated by the term *ontotheology*. Yet my aim is not merely to deconstruct the so-called metaphysical coinage of the religious and the theological. Rather, I seek to highlight the overdetermination of philoso-phy that has inspired, enabled, and destabilized the questioning of the religious and the theological that has taken up so much energy in philo-sophical debate from Kant to Heidegger and beyond.

Yet, as will already be clear, the guiding thread of these analyses is the conviction that the topoi introduced to no small degree also signal institutional interventions. One is tempted to speak of the increasingly important place of the political in Derrida's recent writings, as is obvious from his interrogation of the institution of the university, of democracy, of hospitality, of what has emerged from the decline of a species of com-munism and the triumph of a species of liberalism, of the revolution in information technology and the future of the archive, and, last but not least, the role of religion in the contemporary world. This book is oriented at least as much toward these concrete issues as toward abstract philosophical concerns. But then again, as Theodor W. Adorno already knew—I cite the preface to his *Negative Dialektik* (*Negative Dialectics*), which in turn cites Benjamin—the laborious detour through the desert into which the most abstract of discourses lead us more often than not turns out to be the shortest route to what is the most concrete. It is only by starting from and returning to religion, the most singular and in many respects the most dated of idioms, that philosophy may realize its genuine universalist aspirations. This is not to advance a relentless secularization of the religious or the theological in the philosophical concept, as some of Adorno's progressivist dialectical formulations would have it. Nor is it to rehabilitate the "wooden iron" (*hölzernes Eisern*) that Heidegger detects in all religious philosophies and in most philosophies of religion. The logic of the *adieu* that will interest us throughout keeps its distance from these alternatives and puts their respective insights in a different perspective, at the service of a fundamentally different type of inquiry. For neither an overcoming of metaphysics nor a transformation of the foundational aspirations of philosophy is what is aimed at in these pages. What is at issue is a subtle repetition in an almost Kierkegaardian sense of this word: *the same otherwise,* time and again.

Nothing is certain where this relationship between the same and the other is concerned. At least since Plato, the very inquiry into the nature of *to heauton* and *to heteron* has defined the task, as well as the pitfalls, of philosophical thinking, and this book, too, may be understood as yet another attempt to confirm both the opportunities and the dead end—quite literally, the aporia—of this indefatigable *philosophia perennis*: of metaphysics and difference, ontology and theology, tautology and heterology. Although this tradition is more moribund than ever—not unlike the religion from which it draws its energy, on which it reflects, and from which it, regardless of this singular symbiosis, also seeks to set itself apart—it seems less and less likely to die or to end as it dies. Unable to end, in the ambiguous senses of that word, it lingers on in an endless *clôture* that is neither its termination nor its inner telos, as has been noted most clearly in the theoretical matrix that forms the first part of Derrida's *De la grammatologie* (*Of Grammatology*) and its corollary, the interviews in *Positions*. Yet, if the spreading news of its death seems highly exaggerated, this is only because—like religion—it was never truly alive and well. Indeed, if the beyond of metaphysics ever announced itself at all, it was solely in the cracks, the shadows, and, indeed, the twilight of its most cherished conceptual idols. Paradoxically, the very indeterminacy of this modality of difference, of otherness in the very heart of the same—of a difference and otherness *as* religion or in an undeniable relation *with* religion—formed the main source of its continuing lure or appeal. The condition of the possibility of metaphysics (but also of difference, sameness, ontotheology, and heterology) was nothing but its very impossibility.

As pertinent as this familiar argument of the philosophy of difference is to my general purpose, my main interest in this book lies elsewhere. What I examine is the more unsettling, yet mostly ignored, circumstance that the innovations, theoretical and institutional, that go by the name of the philosophy of difference are intimately linked to the "turn to religion." This is nowhere clearer than in the later writings of Derrida. The reasons for this are again partly formal. The relative indeterminacy of their "object" and "objective" makes the writings called deconstructive, on the one hand, and the traditions of negative theology, on the other, silent companions in the attempt to establish new discursive forms and practices of philosophical and cultural analysis, of ethical deliberation and political engagement. For these "inventions of the other" (to borrow the subtitle of Derrida's *Psyché: Inventions de l'autre*), the premises and the rules are not given in advance or once and for all, but instead need to be reinvented along the way, where no invention can claim to come first or last. This alliance between the thought of difference and these often heterodox theological traditions is crucial to my overall strategy, because my agenda is to demonstrate the philosophical relevance of the religious without resorting to the axioms or the types of argumentation of either *metaphysica specialis* (that is, ontotheology) or its mirror image, the empirical study of religion as an ontic or positive (cultural, anthropological, social, psychological, linguistic) phenomenon.

In addition, I trust that my account will not only steer clear of the assumptions that underlie dogmatic theologies—namely, a given faith that, according to a long tradition from Anselm to Karl Barth, seeks understanding (*fides quaerens intellectum*)—but will avoid supposing the ultimate validity or prevalence (ontologically, theologically, axiologically, or even aesthetically speaking) of any particular historical revelation or series of revelations within the context of the so-called historical or positive religions, for example, of the religions of the West, of the Book, and so on.[27] I am aware of their normative orientation and theological archive, but my question is first of all meta-ethical and meta-theoretical; I am interested less in their dogmatic content than in their semantic potential or, rather, disseminative effect; less in their theological message than in the structural inflection of what is commonly held to be possible and what not. Within certain limits, such questioning is at once transcendental—indeed, quasi-transcendental—and pragmatic, provided, of course, that one clarifies the meaning of these terms.

27. The positive religions are often said to presuppose belief in an ultimate and undivided, unveiled Divine Truth, a belief at odds with the relentless rethinking of the strange, yet somehow familiar, expression A dieu. But is this the only possible or even most plausible interpretation of this central premise? For all the legitimate reservations with respect to the truth-claims of historical religion, should one not make an exception, if not for the acknowledgment of the "existence" of this or that "God," let alone for the philosophical necessity of an ens realissimum, then at least for the undiminished (or increasing?) significance and virtual omnipresence of the notion, idea, concept, figure, or name of a "God"? While I focus on a number of different religious or theological tropes and their philosophical translation and transformation, the word and the cultural presence of "God"—and whatever comes to takes "its" place—are the most economical denominator and indicator of the central issue discussed in this book.

# Chapter One
# Revealing Revelations

Much attention has been devoted to the analogies, resonances, and elective affinities that are claimed to exist between the practices of deconstruction, on the one hand, and the argumentative and rhetorical procedures of the tradition of negative theology, on the other. I am thinking here of the writings of Mark Taylor, Kevin Hardt, Rodolphe Gasché, and John Caputo, among others. But no one would claim that the riddle of their apparent mutual implication or elucidation has been solved. The question therefore remains: *why* and *how* does the citation and use of certain theologemes by Derrida reiterate, and in so doing displace, the central concern—if there is one, just one—commonly ascribed to the religious tradition—notably, to the singular legacy that is all too easily defined in terms of negative theology? In particular, if Derrida's analysis and reinscription of these seemingly pre-, extra-, or post-philosophical notions and figures do not simply amount to the modern discursive strategies of "critique" and "parody," what, exactly, are the modes or the status of this reception of the theological and the religious? What would it entail to speak of this rearticulation and redeployment in terms of testimony, of attestation, of affirmation, and, perhaps, even of confession and of prayer?

In "Comment ne pas parler: Dénégations" ("How To Avoid Speaking: Denials"), Derrida provides a reading of some of the most influential stages of the tradition of negative theology, notably in the writings of Pseudo-Dionysius and of Meister Eckhart. This tradition, he proposes, is marked by reference to the Platonic figures of the negative, the hyperbolic, or the superlative. Most significant is the discussion in Plato's *Republic* of the Idea of the Good that illuminates and sustains, or even generates, all other ideas, and that in its very transcendence is said to "be" beyond being or, more precisely, beyond beingness or essence: *epekeina tēs ousias.*[1]

---

1. See Plato's *Republic* 509b–c. It should be noted from the outset that this tradition must not be confused with the one exception that throughout Derrida's most recent writings seems

"How To Avoid Speaking" is not a mere argumentative reconstruction of such historical trajectories. For the treatises and sermons of these authors are presented not only in their structural and thematic complexity—if one can still speak of structures and themes where it is a matter of reference to the unnameable or to that which is out of conceptual reach. What is primarily at issue here is the exemplary aporetics of these trajectories: exemplary because it is precisely this unavoidable or even fatal aporetics that, as Derrida puts it in a different context, can be said to "infinitely distribute itself."[2] This aporetics distributes itself well beyond the realm of negative theology in its ancient Greek and medieval manifestations, as well as beyond its supposedly secular modern successors. In so doing, it is illustrative of the structure of experience in general. The revelations of which negative theology speaks without speaking reveal the most significant modalities of language, meaning, and reference, "as such." Yet, in showing this, negative theology forms only the most revealing example, the example par excellence. For the apparent analogy between the religious and the experiential has reverberations well beyond the supposedly fixed historical delimitation of so-called apophatics. Derrida questions, in fact, whether the apophatic genre has any determinable historical and systematic contours at all. The apophatics gives itself to be seen everywhere and nowhere, or at least shows itself nowhere as such, as itself, in its full integrity. And in this it could, again, serve as a prime example of the structure of experience at large.

In addition to discussing some of the classical stages in the history of negative theology, Derrida's "How to Avoid Speaking" interrogates some of the most challenging contemporary philosophical projects at the limits of the French phenomenological tradition, which center around the elusive notion of a God beyond Being, uncontaminated by Being, of a God, that is, without Being or otherwise than Being, its internal *dunamis*, movement, or *essance*. This is a God whose aporetic modes of giving without giving Himself as such loom large in the work of Jean-Luc Marion and Emmanuel Levinas, to mention only these two most radical representatives of the deontologization of the theological, the religious, the ethical, the liturgical, and, indeed, the political. It need not further concern us here that their rethinking of the meaning of "God"—in the case of

---

to be made for yet another figure of the negative—more precisely of a negative-beyond-or-before-all-negativity—namely, that of *chōra* discussed in Plato's *Timaeus*.

2. Derrida, "Force of Law," 959.

Levinas, of an alterity, *l'Autre, Autrui,* that surprises even before "God" is mentioned—revolves around a reassessment, not only of the boundaries, but also of the possibilities of metaphysics or of first philosophy. What matters is the hypertheological and heterological gesture of their work, to which Derrida seems at once close and at certain remove.

Moreover, Derrida's text concludes with a—in my view lethal—demonstration of the fact that the line of demarcation that Heidegger (both the earlier and the later) claimed to be able to draw between the positive, regional, or ontic science of theology, on the one hand, and phenomenology and the "thought of Being," on the other, is from the outset also divided and indeed erased. This observation, although based here only on some occasional remarks by the later Heidegger, is justified in light of a more fully developed argument that Derrida provides elsewhere, in *De l'esprit: Heidegger et la question (Of Spirit)* and notably in *Aporias.* Heidegger, so Derrida's argument goes in all of these texts, stands at the extreme end of a trajectory that can just as well be characterized—both historically and systematically—as one more *via negativa,* since it is the latter's relentless overcoming; Heidegger's thought can be seen as a reprisal of the Christian cultures of death (of originary guilt, conscience, etc.) just as much as it is their restless formalization. In this, however, Heidegger's work resembles the most salient features of the problematic, the turn to religion, the problematic that interests us here. It exemplifies that one can—or, perhaps, cannot but be—on both sides of the line at once, that is to say, that this line dividing the philosophical and the theological was never given (certain or theoretically justifiable) in the first place.

Heidegger has thus come to typify a mode of thinking—indeed the thinking of *modality* (and, in particular, of the understanding *possible*) as such—from which a more rigorously deconstructive reassessment of the religious must seek to distance itself. But can deconstruction do what it must do? And what, precisely, is the nature or the urgency of this "must"? How are we to avoid Heidegger and everything for which he stands here?

## Two Misreadings

"How To Avoid Speaking" contains Derrida's first explicit and most elaborate discussion of the relationship between "what one calls, sometimes erroneously, 'negative theology'" (HAS 3 / 535), on the one hand, and the thought of the trace, on the other. In this address, first presented as a lecture in Jerusalem, Derrida acknowledges that the isolated remarks on this subject scattered throughout his writings up to the 1980s—notably in *Writing and Difference, Marges de la philosophie* (*Margins of Philosophy*), and *Positions*—had perhaps been too "elliptical and dilatory" (HAS 7/539) in responding to the observation—or more often, insinuation and accusation—of an at least structural resemblance between his own thinking and that which goes by the generic name of negative theology. Derrida recalls his own confident assertion in *Positions* that deconstruction "blocks every relationship to the theological."[3] But he also reminds us of an earlier statement, in "La Différance," that his style of writing might well appear to have a certain similarity to the rhetorical procedures of the *via negativa,* "occasionally to the point of being indistinguishable" from them.[4]

Recent publications by Derrida, however—in addition to "How To Avoid Speaking," notably *Sauf le nom* (*On the Name*), "Circumfession," *The Gift of Death, Specters of Marx,* and "Faith and Knowledge"—have made it possible and indeed imperative to expose and correct at least two widespread misunderstandings that a first or superficial reading of these and other lapidary statements in Derrida's early work might seem to allow. Two of them have recently been effectively criticized by Rodolphe Gasché in his essay "God, for Example."[5] This lucid analysis supplements Gasché's earlier work *The Tain of the Mirror,* which argued that any serious reading of Derrida should begin by paying attention to the philosophical underpinnings of his thinking, in particular to the fact that it is deeply steeped in the tradition of transcendental philosophy, the basic tenets of which it nonetheless subverts. But while *The Tain of the Mirror* sought to state its argument by abstracting, not only from Derrida's more playful texts, but from the countless explicit and oblique references to ethico-theologico-political motifs—an abstraction for which the book has been sharply criticized[6]—most of the essays collected in Gasché's vol-

---

3. Jacques Derrida, *Positions* (Paris: Éditions de Minuit, 1972), trans. Alan Bass (Chicago: University of Chicago Press, 1981), 40/54-55; trans. modified.

4. Jacques Derrida, *Marges de la philosophie* (Paris: Éditions de Minuit, 1972), trans. Alan Bass as *Margins of Philosophy* (Chicago: University of Chicago Press, 1982), 6.

5. Rodolphe Gasché, "God, for Example," in *Phenomenology and the Numinous* (Pittsburgh: Simon Silverman Phenomenology Center, 1988), reprinted in *Inventions of Difference* (Cambridge, Mass.: Harvard University Press, 1994), the sequel and companion volume to *The Tain of the Mirror.*

6. For criticism of Gasché's *The Tain of the Mirror,* see Mark C. Taylor's review in *Diacritics* (Spring 1988), reprinted as "Failing Reflection," in *Tears* (Albany: State University of New York Press, 1990), 87-103, and Richard Rorty in the chapter "From Ironist Theory to Private Allusions: Derrida," in *Contingency, Irony, and Solidarity* (New York: Cambridge University Press, 1989), 122-37, and "Two Meanings of Logocentrism: A Reply to Norris" and "Is Derrida a

ume *Inventions of Difference* (of which "God, for Example" forms a central chapter) seem to make up for these "omissions" without thereby betraying the central claim set out in the first book.

Let me briefly rehearse some central points in Gasché's argument by drawing on "God, for Example," which, I believe, is the best starting point for a serious discussion of these matters and should be read in conjunction with a closely related study entitled "The Eclipse of Difference," included in the same book. I shall also discuss some elements in these misreadings that Gasché passes over in silence, but that shed an important light on the path taken by Derrida in his later writings and thus on the general thrust of the argument to be explored in the following chapters.

## Mikel Dufrenne's Plea for a Nontheological Philosophy

The first misreading that Gasché takes to task is the identification of Derrida's thought with just some new or belated form of negative theology coming after the demise or becoming-obsolete of all prior theology and, perhaps, of theology properly speaking. This identification of deconstruction with negative theology, which here takes the form of an accusation — since we would be dealing with an avoidable pitfall or an *unnecessary relapse* — has been made by the phenomenological philosopher Mikel Dufrenne in the manifesto with which he prefaced the republication of his book-length study *Le Poétique* (Poetics). Under the telling title "Pour une philosophie non-théologique" ("In Defense of a Nontheological Philosophy"), Dufrenne has argued that Derrida's oeuvre, along with the writings of Maurice Blanchot, Gilles Deleuze, and others, should be understood, not so much as representing modern, critical, secular thought, but rather as reviving negative theology in the guise of a philosophy of absence and of difference — a rearticulation that is more often than not oblique, and therefore, Dufrenne suggests, somewhat disingenuous.[7]

What worries Dufrenne is that Derrida, Blanchot, and other authors

Transcendental Philosopher?" both in *Philosophical Papers*, vol. 2: *Essays on Heidegger and Others* (Cambridge: Cambridge University Press, 1991), 107–18 and 119–28 respectively. Gasché responds to these criticisms at some length in the introduction to *Inventions of Difference*. Derrida's reponse to Rorty can be found in his "Remarks on Deconstruction and Pragmatism," in *Deconstruction and Pragmatism*, ed. Chantal Mouffe (London: Routledge, 1996), 77–88. To the same dossier we should add Rorty's essay "Derrida and the Philosophical Tradition," in *Philosophical Papers*, vol. 3: *Truth and Progress* (Cambridge: Cambridge University Press, 1998), 327–50.

7. Mikel Dufrenne, "Pour une philosophie non-théologique," in *Le Poétique*, 2d ed. (Paris: Presses universitaires de France, 1973), 7–57.

obfuscate a possible nondiscursive experience of presence and immediacy, the occurrence of which can be elucidated and prepared for by
a genuine phenomenology of perception and vision alone. Not surprisingly, the author whom Dufrenne quotes most approvingly in this particular context is Maurice Merleau-Ponty, who in his later work, in particular in *L'Oeil et l'esprit* ("Eye and Mind"),[8] explores the ontological
potential of the art of painting and the access it gives to *l'être brut* (or, in
Dufrenne's own terminology, "Nature").

Negative theology, by contrast, is, according to Dufrenne, no less
the agenda of the philosophies of difference than it is the hidden truth-
content of theology. For the latter, if it remains true to its concept, must
hold that neither linguistic attribution nor predication can serve to utter
the name of God or to determine the existence and the essence of His
divine Being. For a theology to be coherent, it must be based on the
premise that all conceptual determination both contains and demands a
negation, privation, or differentiation (in keeping with the well-known
tag "Omnis determinatio est negatio"), and thus forces the theologian
into a movement of infinite regress. God, it is argued, is neither this nor
that, nor that which is excluded by—or lies beyond—each of these two
mutually exclusive alternatives. As a consequence, only an endless retreat
of the referent from any possible semantic reference, only persistent exception to any logic of differential or diacritical opposition, can succeed
in respecting and reaching out to the divine object or addressee, the highest Being, the Highest that no longer even needs to "be," but "is" what
Pseudo-Dionysus calls ὑπερούσιος (*hyperousios*). Only the *via negativa*
or *negationis*—and not merely the *via eminentiae* of praise and hymns,
which are specific forms of affirmation, and thus of a certain nonempirical positivity—is capable of maintaining the proper distance with respect
to God, safeguarding His integrity by endlessly deferring idolatry and
anthropomorphism, blasphemy and parody, not only in the concept or
in predication—that is to say, in propositions and discourse—but also in
any metaphor, figure or image, sound or song.

Now in the thought of difference, more particularly in that of *différance*, Dufrenne asserts, a strikingly similar line of argumentation may
be discerned. Like negative theology, it affirms and traces the effects of a

---

8. Maurice Merleau-Ponty, *L'Oeil et l'esprit* (Paris: Gallimard, 1964), trans. Michael B.
Smith as "Eye and Mind," in *The Merleau-Ponty Aesthetics Reader: Philosophy and Painting,* ed.
Galen A. Johnson (Evanston, Ill.: Northwestern University Press, 1993), 121–49. See also Mikel
Dufrenne's observations on "Eye and Mind" reproduced in ibid., 256–61.

nonpresence that is not simply the absence—or, for that matter, the announcement—of a presence. This nonprivative nonpresence should not
be thought of as a positive, highest Being that can be said to exist somewhere or somehow, and neither are its purported effects—according to
the well-known formula from Derrida's "La Différance," effects without
a cause and thereby hardly effects properly speaking—the visible or invisible result of a creation out of nothing, a *creatio ex nihilo*. Instead, Dufrenne writes, the thought of *différance* seems to revolve around a "*nihil
that creates,*" a *nihil* akin to the *Nichts* of which Heidegger maintains in
"Was ist Metaphysik?" ("What Is Metaphysics?") that it does nothing but
*nichten*, and therefore takes on the form of an "indeterminate determining." We are dealing here, then, with a "pre-god" of sorts, with a "god"
that is hardly the simple negation of God's existence that one expects from
atheism, but, if anything, the "negative of a God" (*un Dieu en négatif* ).[9]
The latter has a virtual presence in the contours of which one recognizes
the unmistakable traits of an ultimately metaphysical, ontotheological
tradition that the work of Derrida and others was supposedly premised
on overcoming, destroying, or deconstructing. In the very notion of *différance*, Dufrenne claims, we thus encounter the features of a God who
does not render His Presence in the present or—phenomenologically
speaking—in our presence, as an intentional object, but who makes Himself felt as a productive absence of sorts:

> To affirm "the absence of a simple origin," is that to turn away from every
> origin? Perhaps this is the point where theology comes into question. For it is
> against the backdrop of the thought of *différance* that theology takes shape as
> a negative theology, since it is the nonpresence that becomes productive. To be
> sure, like Heidegger, Derrida frees himself easily from God conceived as posi-
> tivity: the supreme being, full speech, or absolute *logos* that is at once the judge
> of our actions and a guarantee for our judgments. That God is dead all right in
> the discourse of philosophy. . . . *Différance* is the unconceptualizable concept
> in the name of which every positivity is put under erasure [*sous rature*] . . . the
> origin is nonorigin, the trace dissimulates itself, the *archē* effaces itself. But to
> efface and to dissimulate oneself, these are pronominal verbs that express at
> once an activity and the relation to self; if the trace effaces itself to the extent
> that it is not—and to the extent that it eludes all definition—this means that
> it is; not in the way of a being, but in the manner of a negative that works. . . .
> Derrida always refers, albeit under erasure, to the originary and constitutive

9. Dufrenne, "Pour une philosophie non-théologique," 20; my trans.

character of *différance*. Not a creation *ex nihilo*, but a creating *nihil*, an indeterminate determining. . . . But the question "What is it?" has nonetheless a
use and meaning: but when, and from which point of view? When does writing [*l'écriture*] become language, the trace a sign, presence absence? If one
ascends to an ultratranscendental, one must say how it functions as a condition of possibility. In other words, if presence is not primary, one must say
how it comes about. Derrida may well turn away from the question "What is
it [*la différance*]?" But can he do this with the question "How [does *différance*
work]?" This question can be dealt with in a philosophy of presence, precisely
because it does call the given [*le donné*] into question and has no need of a
giving instance [*donateur*] or even of an origin, unless [this origin is taken, defined, seen] as Nature [*sinon comme Nature*]. But a philosophy of absence cannot do this; if it wants to take stock of presence, it must in a way bring it into
being; such a philosophy borders upon theology: here, a negative theology.[10]

Derrida and the other philosophers of absence and difference are in
this respect no different from the many exponents of "contemporary culturalism," Dufrenne says.[11] While relying on their enigmatic notion of a
productive absence—an enigma that by its very elusiveness "sacralizes"
and gives rise to "religious fabulation"[12]—they are preoccupied with the
way in which actual experience is caught up and permanently displaced
in the differential system, or, rather, open structure of signs and processes
of resignification, and this to the point of being never truly "itself," of
always already absenting itself from "itself."

But, Dufrenne asserts, invoking a central phenomenological doctrine
concerning the very concept of absenting, "when it is absence of [*absence
de*], it is always absence on the basis of presence, as Sartre has shown. We
do not pretend that presence is full, we say that it comes first, that at each
instant it keeps the secret—which is only a secret for knowledge—of the
origin."[13]

This stance can be explained if we pay attention to the notion of presence or, as Dufrenne puts it, of nature. For these concepts have precisely
the function of what Husserl calls a "material a priori." This structure,
Levinas explains, in a review of Dufrenne's *La Notion de l'apriori* (*The
Notion of the A Priori*), which at first glance would seem to draw on a certain psychological Gestaltism, is not that of a formal and general, abstract
idea. It does not stem from the subjective conditions for the possibility of

10. Ibid., 19–20.                              11. Ibid., 42.
12. Ibid., 35 and 48 respectively.             13. Ibid., 45–46.

all experience, let alone from some arbitrary perspectivism or stipulative definition (on the order of "that is simply what we call 'nature' "). For the generality of the material a priori that is at issue in Dufrenne's concept of nature "manifests itself here in the 'correspondances' in the Baudelairean sense."[14] For Dufrenne, the material a priori is read or, rather, *seen* in the very experience of Being and shows itself "as value, as affective quality, as mythical signification."[15] Neither subjective nor objective, its constitutive function is that which in Being allows one to see (*laisse voir*).[16] It is that which gives Being its intelligibility and enables the object to be expressed simultaneously in its singularity—tied as it remains to the "contingencies and necessities of History"—and to pass beyond that very singularity to the extent that "its revelation is its universalization."[17] Yet, as Levinas does not fail to point out, the *unity* of the "existential a priori"—an incarnated, embodied, indeed material essence of sorts—on the one hand, and the order of the empirical, the social, the historical, and the world, on the other, is thought of here in an almost Bergsonian way: for the latter (empirical, wordly) half of the equation is at once the "obstacle" and the "residue" of the former.[18] What is more, the essential unity of the a priori and the empirical—the unity Dufrenne calls Nature—is hardly given in a poetic sentiment that is incapable of becoming a theme for philosophical thought and that steers free of all ontological pretensions. And it is here that the ways of Dufrenne and Levinas inevitably part, in spite of a certain common interest in carrying phenomenology, in particular, the phenomenology of seeing and the gaze, to its limits.

While Levinas, in his essay "A priori et subjectivité: A propos de la 'Notion de l'apriori' de M. Mikel Dufrenne"—written a year after the publication of *Totalité et infini*—welcomes the emphasis it puts on the notion of "expression," he underscores that the *Gestalt* (or whatever phenomenological concept takes its place), in Dufrenne's account, is ultimately founded in a relation marked by difference and, indeed, by separation: namely, in the relation to the *visage* of the other. Levinas writes:

14. Emmanuel Levinas, "A priori et subjectivité: A propos de la 'Notion de l'apriori' de M. Mikel Dufrenne," in *En découvrant l'existence avec Husserl et Heidegger* (Paris: Vrin, 1988), 179–86, 181.

15. Mikel Dufrenne, *La Notion d'apriori* (Paris: Presses universitaires de France, 1959), 55, quoted from Levinas, *En découvrant l'existence*, 180.

16. Levinas, *En découvrant l'existence*, 180.

17. Ibid.

18. Ibid., 183.

From where does the energy of the transcendental movement against the insertion [*l'enlisement*] come, when the world that we inhabit surrounds and
penetrates us and cultures, the "products of our hands," dominate us? The
position of the "transcendental subject" — or what remains of it "in the situation" — would not be conceivable, if man's relations with being were not
immediate ["si l'homme n'entretenait pas avec l'être une relation de face à
face"]. Idealism was certainly wrong in searching for it in the representation
of the world; it was right to postulate it.[19]

To be sure, Dufrenne is aware of an indelible distance between human
beings and the world. And, as Levinas formulates it a little earlier:

It is in discovering the intentionality of consciousness, posited otherwise in
the most classical fashion as consciousness of . . . , but complicated since
by all the other prepositions — consciousness in . . . , consciousness by . . . ,
consciousness for . . . , consciousness with . . . , consciousness toward . . . ,
conscience together with . . . , etc., — that phenomenology pretends to place
itself before the Cartesian distinction of soul and body, before the idealist
distinction between subject and object. From now on, the object is already
explored, . . . , labored, possessed, traversed, or englobed by History — world,
and not nature; from now on, the subject is naturalized, incarnated, social-
ized, historicized — man, and not the unity of the "I think," a pure logical
function. M. Dufrenne has gone all the way to the end: even certain formulations adopted by Merleau-Ponty and Sartre are not radical enough for him.
And yet he shows that man remains a transcendental subject and that the
world remains radically distinct from man.[20]

Paradoxically, for Dufrenne, this distance seems only conceivable against
the background of a preceding unity and immediacy (presence, nature)
that is no longer given to thought, but to aesthetic sentiment alone.
For Levinas, by contrast, *distance presupposes even more distance, or yet
another distance still:* the distance of natural objects (of the stars even)
is founded in the distance that opens up in the very proximity and the
face-to-face relationship between self and other: "All the examples of the
a priori that M. Dufrenne gives, when he opposes himself to general ideas,
are only thinkable in a human order — that is to say, in the order that

19. Ibid., 186.
20. Ibid., 185.

traces itself when the Other [*Autrui*] is revealed to me; this holds true for childhood, Ravel and Franck, and even for the nobility of the horse."[21]

Levinas's ethical reservations about Dufrenne's invocation of presence — of immediacy and nature, in the guise of a material a priori that is to be given or seen in an aesthetic mode alone — are not the first things that come to mind when one asks whether "Pour une philosophie non-théologique" is justified in its portrayal of the authors it takes to task, and, in particular, in its characterization of the writings of Derrida. In fact, one did not need to wait for the publication of the most recent writings on religion as an explicit theme in order to realize that Derrida's deconstruction of the notion of presence — or of nature (for example, in the second part of *Of Grammatology*) — was hardly inspired either by the philosophy of absence or, for that matter, by its shadow, empiricism, whether in the form of "contemporary culturalism" (as Dufrenne has it) or not. Nor can Derrida's resistance to the notion of immediacy, whether of nature or some other presence, be adequately characterized by comparing it with a "contemporary culturalism," albeit in the form of a "transcendental lingualism" that posits the existence and primacy of a differential system or structure, an infinitely expanded web of signifyingness that catches the real in signs of language alone. The latter, were it possible at all, still remains caught in one of the many logocentric presuppositions it pretends to subvert, the assumption, namely, that language is the *primum intelligibele*. We are dealing here with the mere double of one of the central dogmas of empiricism: that we have a direct access to the given as a correcting or corroborating instance of all our concepts and conjectures. Indeed, to insist on the primacy of language is no less problematic than to believe in the duality of words and objects or things.

Nor, to be sure, does the thought of *différance* indulge in what Dufrenne condemns as mere "religious fabulation." Derrida's approach is marked by a different reception and reassessment of the phenomenological understanding of the "material a priori." The latter is rethought in light of a heterodox reading of the Husserlian motif of "transcendental historicity," along lines that, it would seem, neither Dufrenne nor Levinas deems possible or desirable. A completely different logic is at work here.

What remains problematic about Dufrenne's reading is consequently also his suggestion of an apparent *simple resemblance* in form, if not always in content, between the argumentative and rhetorical thrust of apophatics

21. Ibid.

and the strategies of deconstruction. As we have seen, Dufrenne finds deconstruction to be *merely* repeating or mimicking the procedures of classical theology, which, he notes, was in its very essence or in truth—that
is to say, ontologically and conceptually speaking—negative, and this regardless of its dogmatic or its institutionalized form.[22]

Yet Derrida's lecture on *différance* had explicitly cautioned against
precisely such an interpretation:

> *Différance* is not. It is not a present being, however excellent, unique, princi-
> pal, or transcendent. It governs nothing, reigns over nothing, and nowhere
> exercises any authority. It is not announced by any capital letter. Not only
> is there no kingdom of *différance,* but *différance* instigates the subversion of
> every kingdom. Which makes it obviously threatening and infallibly dreaded
> by everything in us that desires a kingdom, the past or future presence of a
> kingdom.[23]

And a little further in the text;

> "Older" than Being itself, such a *différance* has no name in our language.
> But . . . if it is unnameable, it is not provisionally so, not because our language
> has not yet found or received this *name,* or because we would have to seek it
> in another language, outside the finite system of our own. It is rather because
> there is no *name* for it at all, not even the name of essence or of Being, not
> even that of ' "*différance,*" which is not a name, which is not a pure nominal
> unity, and unceasingly dislocates itself in a chain of differing and deferring
> substitutions. . . . This unnameable is not an ineffable Being which no name
> could approach: God, for example. This unnameable is the play which makes
> possible nominal effects, the relatively unitary and atomic structures that are

22. Not unlike Dufrenne, Richard Rorty identifies Paul de Man's deconstructionism with
the project of negative theology: "Reading or writing 'literary language' or 'poetic language'—
the sort of language that makes *evident* that 'language' as such functions differently from the
'phenomenal world,' the realm of 'natural objects' whose 'meaning is equal to the totality of
[their] sensory appearances' [Paul de Man, *Blindness and Insight* (Minneapolis: University of
Minnesota Press, 1989), p. 24]—is, for de Man and his followers, a way of mourning a *Deus
absconditus,* of participating in a divine absence," Rorty writes. "The positive theologians are
the people who think literature is a 'reliable source of information about something other than
its own language.' The initiates, the negative theologians, the worshippers of the Dark God
whose Voice is the literariness of language, are those who no longer believe that 'language
functions according to principles which are those, or which are *like* those, of the phenomenal world' " (Rorty, *Philosophical Papers,* vol. 2: *Essays on Heidegger and Others,* 114–15; cf. 116
n. 18). According to Rorty, Derrida—more precisely, the later "comic" Derrida—would be less
torn and haunted than de Man in this regard (ibid., 117).

23. Derrida, *Margins of Philosophy,* 21–22 / 22.

called names, the chains of substitutions of names in which, for example, the nominal effect *différance* is itself *enmeshed,* carried off, reinscribed, just as a false entry or a false exit is still part of the game, a function of the system.[24]

Yet, if there is any doubling of apophatic thought here—which, as I argue throughout, in agreement with Dufrenne, is hard to deny—this repetition must be analyzed in completely other terms. We are dealing with a reiteration that takes the form of a haunting, spectralization, or even virtualization, Indeed, we find in Derrida's work a movement of *deontologization*—reminiscent of yet far more radical than the *via negativa*—but one that is at the same time affirmative, superlative, and hyperbolical, expressing itself in a way that entails a no less remarkable *reontologization* as well. At once infinitely close to and at an infinite remove from the theological tradition, even or especially in the most heterodox of its manifestations, Derrida's position is therefore more complicated than Dufrenne would want to make us believe. Derrida's invocation of what is traditionally called negative theology relies at least as much on the persistent force of the *via eminentiae* and its rhetorical exaggerations as it does on the *via negationis* and, more generally, the thought of the negative (whether understood in a logical, dialectical, or apophatic way, or in terms of, say, the Heideggerian *Nichten*). This explains the significance and recurrence of Derrida's constant rethinking of the singular performativity of the address and the apostrophe, of prayer and testimony, of the promise and of confession. No clearer example of this double affirmation of the negative in its relation to some—however minimal—affirmation can be found than in Derrida's use of the Levinasian figure of the *adieu* and *à dieu* that rearticulates the two moments that Pseudo-Dionysius invokes in his *Peri mustikēs theologias* (*On Mystical Theology*), namely, the apophatic speaking *away from* speech and its cataphatic counterpart that indicates the movement *toward* speech.

In both types of discourse, the negative and the superlative, the "God" in question seems *either* in transit, *de passage*—always already passed, a "past that has never been present," "un profond jadis, jadis jamais assez," to quote a definition coined by Valéry and often quoted by Levinas—*or,* conversely, forever to come (*à venir*). In fact, however, this "God"—given only in a simultaneous *adieu* and *à dieu*—measures up against both of these possibilities at once (if that is what they are, possibilities or modalities, something that is far from certain). At times it seems that the "God"

24. Ibid., 26–27 / 28.

intended here matches neither of them. For the essential difference that marks His absolute incommensurability in the final analysis resembles nothing but a sublime *in-difference:* something, some Thing (*das Ding, La Chose,* to quote Heidegger and Lacan, whose usage is often adopted by Derrida) that subtracts "itself" from any ascription, from every *hic et nunc,* from all elucidation, that is to say, not only from all conceptual illumination, but also — and first of all — from the Heideggerian understanding of elucidation as an *Erörterung,* which, for all the subtlety of its (no longer) laying bare of grounds, of its step back (*Schritt zurück*), and its patient gathering (*Versammlung*) of the words and sendings of Being, is in its very presuppositions and most outspoken aims not significantly different from the most pernicious of all foundationalisms. (And from this suspicion it only escapes if one reads Heidegger against the grain, in spite of Heidegger, as I attempt to do below).

In Derrida's own writing, by contrast, the adoption of the nonnegative figure of the *without* — notably in its Blanchotian form of the *sans,* which, in turn, radicalizes the Heideggerian procedure of the crossing out (the *kreuzweise Durchstreichung*) — prepares the way for a hyperbolic affirmation that is neither predicative nor simply performative. At first glance, there seems no better example of this logic than the thought of St. Augustine, whose name "haunts certain landscapes of apophatic mysticism," Derrida writes in *On the Name,* observing: "Meister Eckhart cites him often; he often cites the 'without' of Saint Augustine, that quasi-negative predication of the singular without concept, for example, 'God is wise *without* wisdom, good *without* goodness, powerful *without* power'" (SN 40 / 27).

Yet is there indeed a language whose properties or modalities (and use of the "without") allow it to refuse — or to be *in-different* to — the idolatrous act of figural and conceptual appropriation? Is it not the primary concern of Derrida's writings to be suspicious of any such ideal of a purely heterological language and to raise doubts about the very possibility of saying or evoking the other *as such* and, therefore even *as other?*

## Jean-Luc Marion's Heterology of Donation

Jean-Luc Marion's misreading of Derrida's adoption, in "La Différance" and elsewhere, of a style and strategy of writing that borders on the *via negativa* is diametrically opposed to Mikel Dufrenne's. It is put forward in his *L'Idole et la distance* (*Idol and Distance*), reiterated in *Dieu sans l'être* (*God Without Being*), and in a host of articles, as well as, more

implicitly, in his contribution to a recent "symposium" on "God."[25] As
Gasché points out, the claim here is, not that Derrida perpetuates a central theological questioning, but rather that he is indifferent to the very
possibility of such questioning. According to Marion, Derrida only succeeds in deconstructing Heidegger's understanding of ontological difference, an understanding that had sought to overcome the neutralization of
the fundamental distinction between Being and beings, by neutralizing,
in turn, the infinite "distance" that singles out the divine—in Marion's
view, a "Being" without Being—in light of an open but folded dimension
that subjects "God" to yet another generality. This latter generality is not
that of Being, or of the *Ereignis* of Being properly speaking, but that of an
alterity the structure of which is formalizable and coined as *différance* and
the—in principle unlimited—range of what Derrida in "La Différance"
calls "nonsynonymous substitutions." It is precisely this motif of perpetual substitution—"God" and whatever comes to take its place—that,
I would claim, marks the difference between Derrida's rearticulation and
redeployment, indeed reaffirmation, of the tradition called religious and
those of his contemporaries, for example, that of Marion (but, seen from
this perspective, Levinas would often seem to fall into the same category).
But things are complicated here, for, strictly speaking, even the very motif
of substitution and its most privileged names and examples might have
to give way, one day, to something altogether different and be substituted
for, if only momentarily, by something that no longer obeys or allows the
law of substitution. For just as the gift, as we shall see, gives (itself) only
if it gives itself away, so the series of nonsynonymous substitutions must
in principle let itself be substituted for in its turn, and this to the point
where the very structure of substitutability is affected as well. Derrida had
insisted as much when he wrote, in "La Différance," that "the efficacy of
the thematic of *différance* may very well, indeed must, one day be super-
seded, lending itself if not to its own replacement, at least to enmeshing
itself in a chain that in truth it never will have governed. Whereby, once
again, it is not theological."[26]

According to Marion, to "outwit Being [*déjouer l'Être*] would require
more than the revocation of ontological difference in favor of another difference" (GWB 85 / 126).[27] Rather, it means to enter a realm that subtracts

25. Jean-Luc Marion, "Metaphysics and Phenomenology: A Relief for Theology," trans.
Thomas A. Carlson, *Critical Inquiry* 20, no. 4 (Summer 1994), 572–91.

26. Derrida, *Margins of Philosophy*, 7 / 7.

27. Jean-Luc Marion, *Dieu sans l'être: Hors texte* (1982; reprint, Paris: Quadrige, 1991),

itself from what is the last, most persistent and fatal idolatry, namely, that of the "screen of Being," obliterating the sublime interval between God and Being (or beings). This distance, Marion claims, can be revealed by the—nondifferential and thereby nonindifferent—icon alone.

The icon eludes the confusion of God with some visible, tangible, idol —as in the biblical form of anthropomorphism—but also prevents the conflation of "God" with some metaphysical concept, such as the notion of a highest being. The icon is the sole guarantee against the improprieties of blasphemy and iconoclasm alike, because it escapes every horizon, including—or, as Marion seems to suggest, especially—the one that Heidegger never ceased to posit as the condition of possibility of all manifestation or revelation, whether religious or not: the dimension (*Dimension*) and clearing (*Lichtung*) of Being, its truth, and its event, or rather *Ereignis*.

Idolatry, on the contrary, should be attributed to the—for the labor of thought, perhaps, inevitable—ontological presupposition of the anteriority or priority of Being over beings, including the Being called highest, beyond essence even, as in the Platonic idea of the Good, *epekeina tēs ousias,* which, on this reading, is drawn into the realm of *ta eidola,* a term Plato reserves for appearances alone.[28] Yet Marion's charge of idolatry extends well beyond this critique (a "deconstruction" and "destitution," as he puts it) and involves the ontotheological understanding of the *ens perfectissimum* as well. It challenges the primacy of the supreme being that all know or call by the name of God, following the well-known formula at the end of each of the "five ways," that is to say, the ontological and cosmological proofs of the existence of the divine Being proposed by the *Summa theologica* of St. Thomas Aquinas.[29]

---

trans. Thomas A. Carlson as *God Without Being: Hors-Texte* (Chicago: University of Chicago Press, 1991), hereafter cited parenthetically in the text as GWB. "Another difference" here refers to "Levinas and Derrida," as the attached footnote tells us, as well as to the section "L'Autre différant," in *L'Idole et la distance* (Paris: Grasset, 1977), 274–94.

28. See Plato, *Republic,* 520c, and earlier in the text, the allegory of the cave.

29. However, the given examples from Aquinas are highly ambiguous. They point in different directions, as if the very "distance" between iconicity and idolatry is opened up between the divergent formulations of one corpus and, more often than not, in one and the same passage. Marion writes: "Does Christian speculative theology, in its exemplary figures (and I am thinking here first of Saint Thomas Aquinas), belong to metaphysics in the strict sense, or has it responded to the peculiar conceptual demands of the Revelation that prompted it?" (MP 573). On the one hand, it seems, Aquinas "marks a rupture" in the tradition of the divine names, a tradition that dates back to Pseudo-Dionysius, if not to the First Letter of John (4:8) and, even earlier, Exod. 3:14. In keeping with the central premises of the tradition of ontotheology, Aquinas also substitutes the *esse* for the *good,* the *summum bonum.* On the other hand, Marion

Marion agrees with Heidegger that "metaphysics imposes on what it still designates under the disputable title of 'God' a function in the onto-theological constitution of metaphysics: as supreme being, 'God' assures the ground (itself grounded according to the Being of beings in general) of all other derived beings" (GWB xxi). Yet if "God" is the name used and abused to indicate the ground of Being and beings, the principle of which has been the central concern of metaphysics from its earliest beginnings, then it is the death of God that establishes its ultimate failure. This death was not sudden; it came about through the successive onslaughts of "conceptual atheism" called for by the relentless metaphysical search for the ground *itself.* Taken to its logical extreme, metaphysical grounding can therefore only undermine its cause (and, ultimately, its most systematic and historically effective definition of the highest, divine, being as *causa sui*). Yet, in the wake of the "death of a thousand qualifications," to quote Anthony Flew, not only were grounds substituted for other — more remote or more grounding — grounds, but the ground par excellence and, more radically still, the very principle of grounding itself were undermined step by step. First the visible idols, then their (internalized?) conceptual counterparts, and, finally, the "invisible mirror" that metaphysics holds up between experience and phenomena, including the phenomenon (and experience) par excellence, namely, revelation or, more precisely still, donation; for reasons the conceptual necessity of which Marion insists on time and again, they must all give way to — or at least make room for — another seeing, for other names, and for the possibility of an ultimate, mystical, eschatological face-to-face encounter.

Let me briefly unpack the structure of this convoluted argument,

---

hastens to add in the *retractationes* that make up the bulk of the preface to the English translation of *Dieu sans l'être,* "even when he thinks God as *esse,* Saint Thomas nevertheless does not chain God either to Being or to metaphysics. . . . because the divine *esse* immeasurably surpasses (and hardly maintains an *analogia* with) the *ens commune* of creatures. . . . Between metaphysics (with its domain, common Being) and God, the relation, even and especially for Saint Thomas, has to do not with inclusion but with subordination" (GWB xxiii). But also — or, as Derrida demonstrates convincingly, especially — the *via eminentiae* that aims at the hyperbolic excess of all predication and that thus pushes conceptual determination to the point of prayer (as is clear in the function of the hymn or *encomium* in Pseudo-Dionysius and others) belongs to a tradition that it seeks to circumvent while using its very modes of argumentation. The superlative is at once the most radical break and the most subtle perpetuation — the utmost possibility — of the metaphysical tradition that is thus called into question (or that thus calls *itself* into question). Heterology is but the flipside of ontology. Or, put otherwise, all ontology — including or especially all ontotheology — is already more heterological than it pretends (and, for good reasons, must pretend).

which will allow the concept of idolatry to serve as a relay connecting mythologemes, theologemes, and philosophemes with one another and each of them individually with the social construction of political and cultural identities.[30] To the extent that they are rigorous and, indeed, compelling (philosophically, psychologically, or sociologically speaking), Marion claims, conceptual atheisms, are by definition merely "regional."[31] For obvious reasons, they succeed only by targeting a determinate—and therefore necessarily limited or provisional—aspect or concept of "God." But any falsification of a distinctive predicate of God (of his existence, essence, attributes, and works) leaves open—and, indeed, in the case of the *ens realissimum*, Marion writes, necessarily implies—an indefinite or rather infinite possibility of other concepts and properties. It can never forget its perspectivism or claim on rational grounds that its view of the phenomenon in question is panoptic. By imposing its refutation as if it were total, ignoring that its conceptual rigor stems precisely from the fact that every concept—or every chain of concepts—is by definition delim-ited, finite, and therefore structurally incomplete, it becomes at once dog-matic and totalitarian; it must compensate and compromise its principle of "auto-limitation"[32] by relying on violence, whether physical, symbolic, or ideological. Indeed, even the sum of all atheisms—based on all known concepts of the existence and attributes of God—would still be regional, a finite totality, as it were, that leaves the possibility of an infinite number of other concepts untouched.

As it happens, this critique of atheism—a critique *from within*, as it

30. Before being characterized as an intellectual and moral error, and being internalized mentally and socially, "the war against idolatry in the Bible is a war against forms of ritual worship imported from foreign nations," observe Halbertal and Margalit (*Idolatry*, 108). In the historical process of internalization, the first transitions of which can be found already in the Bible, the "focus of the concept of idolatry" is "transferred from the performance of alien rituals to the harboring of alien beliefs" (ibid., 109). Of course, this transference can work in more than one direction alone. At the end of this process, there stand the attempts to rethink ideology in terms of idolatry, in other words, as the reification and fetishization of things and ideas in their very appearance (compare the fact that we speak of cultural icons and idols simultaneously). From here it is but a step to the inversion of the meaning of idolatry by identifying it first of all with the allergy of the modern metaphysical self (in its idealist, egological, or fundamental-ontological interpretation) vis-à-vis the other (or the alien) as such, and from there to materi-alist protectionism, exclusionist policies, hegemony, and internal policing of national states. The ethico-political relevance of this transcription is also signaled by Wendy Doniger in her review of *Idolatry*, entitled "Unspeakable Sins," *New York Review of Books*, April 21, 1994, 55–58.

31. Jean-Luc Marion, "De la 'mort de Dieu' aux noms divins: L'Itinéraire théologique de la métaphysique," in *L'Être et Dieu*, ed. D. Bourg et al. (Paris: Éditions du Cerf, 1986), 103–30, 106.

32. Ibid., 107.

were, one that judges conceptual (rather than dogmatic) atheism by its words—is at once at odds and consistent with the classical denunciation of idolatry of, say, Maimonides, and also of others.[33] What is important to Marion, however, is the fact that any conceptual atheism that deserves the name allows another possibility to reveal itself beyond its own regional—ontico-ontological—confines, if not so much negatively—that is to say, through abstract negation, by pointing to the other of reason that would be a privation of that same reason—then at least *in obliquo:* with an "im-mediacy" (to use a term of Jean-Luc Nancy's) that is believed to escape all dialectics, and much more than that: for example, empirical causation, logical implication, transcendental and phenomenological deduction, but also rhetorical persuasion, poetic evocation, and so on.

In Marion's view, then, it is precisely the historically and systematically adequate definition of metaphysics as the double-edged science of being in general (*metaphysica generalis* or *ontologia*) and of being par excellence (*metaphysica specialis* or *theologia naturalis*) that "renders intelligible the relief that goes beyond metaphysics and takes it up again in a higher figure" (MP 576). This "relief" is enabled by the internal linking of ontology and theology (or "theiology"), each of which is premised on the thought of ultimate grounding. More exactly still, these two poles of Western metaphysics are caught in a circular structure of mutual grounding, one that sooner or later gives way to its own eclipse (or ellipse): "Common being grounds beings, even the beings par excellence; in return, the being par excellence, in the mode of causality, grounds common Being" (MP 576).

This structure does not simply dissolve when the ground itself is rethought in a nonfoundationalist mode (for example, in terms of the Heideggerian interpretation of an *Ur-sprung* or *Satz*, that is to say, as a leaping away from the ground); or when it undercuts itself by raising the paradoxical question of what it is that "grounds," if one can still say so, the ground, the "figure" of the ground. And was it ever more than that: a figure of thought, a figure of figuration, but also of disfiguration, that is to say, a figure that prefigures, precedes, and exceeds whatever figure? Nonetheless, only the "figure" of the ground guarantees an answer to a problem that is as old as Aristotle's *Metaphysics*, which Marion recapitu-

---

33. Compare Halbertal and Margalit, *Idolatry,* 109–12, and Max Scheler, "Die Idole der Selbsterkenntnis," in *Vom Umsturz der Werte,* vol. 3 of *Gesammelte Werke* (Bern: Francke, 1955), 215–92, trans. David R. Lachterman as "The Idols of Self-Knowledge," in *Selected Philosophical Essays* (Evanston, Ill.: Northwestern University Press, 1973), 3–97.

lates by asking: "How can one and the same [*una et eadem*] science treat at the same time [*simul*] of common being (and therefore of no one being in particular) and of the being par excellence (and therefore of a supremely particular being)?" (MP 575).[34] This is only possible if the two poles of this double science presuppose or condition each other mutually; or when they are both subject to a common rule (that is to say, if they rest on a shared principle). And wherever this principle is uprooted — and thus becomes anarchic or unruly — the ontotheological constitution of metaphysics comes to its end. This is nowhere clearer than in the dissolution of the highest being that throughout the history of metaphysics has served the function of an ultimate ground: Nietzsche diagnoses this seemingly irrevocable event as the death of the metaphysical and the moral God. In the twilight of idols — conceptual and other — that ensues, the Platonism of Western philosophy is inverted. Yet, paradoxically, Marion argues, the " 'death of God' immediately implies the death of the 'death of God' " (GWB xxi).[35] The "death of God" paves the way for God's becoming absolved and exempt from all metaphysical concepts, principles, axioms, propositions, predicates, categories, attributes, and horizons (or dimensions). For, again, if metaphysics is defined as the thought of the ground, then to question — or to "ground" — the ground undermines the ontotheological determination of God as *ultima ratio,* or, more precisely still, *causa sui,* that is to say, the modern philosophical name for God.

Heidegger, in his pivotal essay "The Ontotheological Constitution of Metaphysics," which makes up the second half of *Identity and Difference,* suggests as much. Yet Marion pushes the Heideggerian "step back" (*Schritt zurück*) even one step further: "[T]o release God from the constraints of onto-theology can still signify that Being, thought as such, without its metaphysical figure, in the way Heidegger attempted, is still imposed on him. This second idolatry — 'God according to Being'

34. Marion quotes two definitions, one by Thomas Aquinas and one by Francisco Suárez, to solidify the historical basis of this argument. According to Aquinas's commentary on Aristotle: "*Metaphysica* simul determinat de ente in communi et de ente primo, quod est a materia separatum" ("Metaphysics simultaneously determines [how things stand] concerning being in general and concerning the first being which is separated from matter") (quoted from MP 574). According to Suárez's *Disputationes Metaphysicae:* "Abstrahit enim haec scientia a sensibilibus, seu materiabilus rebus . . . , et res divinas et materia separatas, et communes rationes entis, quae absque materia existere possunt, contemplatur" ("This science abstracts from sensible and material things . . . , and it contemplates, on the one hand, the things that are divine and separated from matter and, on the other hand, the common reason of being, which [both] can exist without matter)" (MP 574).

35. See also Jean-Luc Marion, "The End of the End of Metaphysics," in *Epoché,* 1996: 1–22.

—only appears once one has unmasked the first—'God' according to onto-theology" (GWB xxi). The relationship of the later, post- or preontological thought of Heidegger, the thought of the *Ereignis* of Being— that is to say, of the thinking-of Being, of the *Andenken des Seins*—to the "second" idolatry of which Marion speaks here is deeply ambivalent at best. Marion asserts that Heidegger's "other thought" remains in the end characterized, not so much by a genuine desire to repeat and properly appropriate the theological, as by the indecisive ambivalence (*Zweideutigkeit*) that *Being and Time* describes as one of the modes of the inauthentic being of the *Man* or *Man-Selbst*. In its own way, therefore, it lacks *droiture,* immediacy and uprighteousness.

Both forms of idolatry, then, the sensible as well as the intelligible (transcendental, ontological) fall short of the veneration of the icon and the gift of love—of *agapē,* that is—from which Marion's own radical phenomenology and, indeed, theology take their lead.

Unlike Dufrenne, therefore, Marion is not so much interested in philosophy's freedom with respect to the theological—even though he, along with many others (Heidegger among them), insists that the two should not be confused—but first of all in the freedom of God from all metaphysical, ontological, and empirical determinations. Marion illustrates this freedom—God's freedom, that is, from (His own) Being—by referring to the Old and New Testaments and the Fathers of the Church, as well as to Schelling and Shakespeare ("with respect to Being does God have to behave like Hamlet?" [GWB xx]). What is at stake here, however, is an asymmetrical freedom in which God in the very donation of His presence retains the initiative at every single moment:

> At issue here is not the possibility of God's attaining Being, but, quite the opposite, the possibility of Being's attaining to God. . . . Does Being define the first and the highest of the divine names? When God offers himself to be contemplated and gives himself to be prayed to, is he concerned primarily with Being? . . . No doubt, God can and must in the end also be; but does his relation to Being determine him as radically as the relation to his Being defines all other beings? (GWB xix–xx; trans. modified)

These rhetorical questions are not only inspired by strictly phenomenological considerations. They are motivated by exegetical possibilities and theological decisions as well. In fact, Marion writes, it is notably in the problematic of the divine names that one finds an anticipation of the

ambiguity that determines — and destabilizes — the ontotheological constitution of metaphysics from within:

> Biblical revelation seems . . . to give a confirmation of this, or at least an in-
> dication, when it mentions, in the same name, what one *can* (but not must)
> comprehend as *Sum qui sum,* hence God as Being, and what one *must,* at the
> same time, understand as a denegation of all identity — "I am the one that I
> want to be." Being says nothing about God that God cannot immediately re-
> ject. Being, even and especially in Exod. 3:14, says nothing about God, or says
> nothing determining about him.[36]

Many questions might, of course, be raised here. And Marion is the
first to acknowledge their validity for any thought that remains faithful to the central concern of philosophy, of reason, and, perhaps, any
thinking as such. Can the gift transgress, circumvent, or "outwit" Being,
and do so once and for all? In other words, can the gift find ways to
avoid appearing or revealing itself as one of the multiple "ways" by which
Being — or, for that matter, any particular being, for example, the highest
Being — manifests itself, according to Aristotle's τὸ ὂν πολλαχῶς λέγεται
(*to on pollakhōs legetai*),[37] which Heidegger translates as "das Seiende

---

36. GWB 45/71. A little later in the text, Marion seems to nuance this position somewhat:
"[T]he Hebrew verb *hayah* does not suffice to introduce a concept of 'Being'; historically, the
transition from the biblical register to conceptual debate between philosophers and theologians depends on the translation of the Septuagint [i.e., of the *ehyeh asher ehyeh* as]: *egō eimi ho
ōn.* This translation substitutes a participle, *ho ōn,* for a conjugated form, a present persistence
for something unaccomplished; in short, an action can become an attribute, even a name. This
modification remains in the background of the Latin formula *Sum qui sum*" (GWB 73/110).
And should one allow this association of God with (His) being after all, Marion continues, "one
would still have to define whether the name indirectly implied by Exodus 3:14 inevitably precedes other names, like the one that 1 John 4:8 insinuates, *ho theos agapē estin,* 'God is love' . . .
No exegesis, no philological fact, no objective inquiry could accomplish or justify this step;
only a theological decision could do so and retrospectively rely on literary arguments" (GWB
74/111). In sum, however, the divergences between these different statements are less important
than their common attempt to contradict the basic tenets of the appropriation of the phrase
from Exod. 3:14 (or, for that matter, John 8:18) throughout the history of metaphysics, which
has consisted in a tendency to ontologize the range of possible meaning of the biblical verse,
from the Septuangint on. This tendency seems to culminate in the reduction of the biblical formula to a mere formal tautology: "I = I" or "A = A" (Jean-Luc Marion, "Réponses à quelques
questions," *Revue de Métaphysique et de Morale* 96, no. 1 [1991]: 76). Compare also Hendrik
Birus, " 'Ich bin, der ich bin': Über die Echo eines Namens," in *Juden in der deutschen Literatur:
Ein deutsch-israelisches Symposium,* ed. Stéphane Moses and Albrecht Schöne (Frankfurt a./M.:
Suhrkamp, 1986), 25–53; and Frank Moore Cross, *Canaanite Myth and Hebrew Epic: Essays in
the History of the Religion of Israel* (Cambridge, Mass.: Harvard University Press, 1973), 68.

37. Aristotle, *Metaphysics* 4.2.1003a33.

wird vielfach gesagt" (PhRL 56): "Being is expressed in manifold ways"? In Marion's words: "[C]an the conceptual thought of God (conceptual, or rational, and not intuitive or 'mystical' in the vulgar sense) be developed outside of the doctrine of Being (in the metaphysical sense, or even in the nonmetaphysical sense)? Does God give himself to be known according to the horizon of Being or according to a more radical horizon?" (GWB xxiv).

Is there a horizon, we might also ask, that escapes the most general (and most singular) horizon of Being — its situation or dimension, as Heidegger would have it — or that in its radicality explodes the concept of the horizon? In other words, is the gift, as Marion suggests, the "phenomenon" that "saturates" the very horizon of its appearance? Can this gift "manifest itself without passing through Being" (GWB 83/123), without leaving its trace "in" or "on" Being? Can it *not* be, or avoid being? And, lest we assume that the gift, in giving and in giving itself away, determines Being as one of its own multiple "ways," can this gift nevertheless still mark or signal its distance from Being and from "the interplay of beings as such"? (GWB 82–83/123).

Marion stresses that the gift (*le don*) must also be thought of as an abandonment (*abandon*): a gift that does not keep (anything) to itself but rather gives itself totally. For if God is "experienced" as the donation par excellence, then, Marion writes, this "excellence indicates neither sufficiency, nor efficiency, nor principality, but the fact that he gives himself and allows himself to be given more than any other being-given" (MP 588).

What does that mean? First of all, it is clear that Marion, like Dufrenne, opts not for an absence, pure and simple — but no one ever did, least of all the so-called philosophies of absence, difference, or *différance* — but for a certain "dazzling evidence," a "presence without limits (without horizon)" that no object can ever attain: evidence that "voids the saturated horizons of any definable visible thing" and in which God, in a sense to be further explained, "shines by his absence" (MP 589).

Secondly, it must be noted that while Marion here invokes a modality of "excellence" different from those that Levinas and, in his wake, Derrida ascribe to the figure-without-figure of the trace, he remains also at a distance from the Heideggerian understanding of the clearance (*Lichtung*) of Being and its Truth. Marion's analysis relies on a different — genuinely phenomenological — motif, for which, perhaps surprisingly, some confirmation can be found in the modern history of the visual arts, and of modern music no less than of modern metaphysics:

> That he is given par excellence implies that "God" is given without restriction, without reserve, without restraint. "God" is given not at all partially, following this or that outline, like a constituted object that nevertheless offers to the intentional gaze only a specific side of its sensible visibility, leaving to appresentation the duty of giving further that which does not give itself, but absolutely, . . . with every side open, in the manner of the objects whose dimensions cubist painting caused to explode, in order that all aspects might be juxtaposed, despite the constraints of perspective. . . . His evidence displays itself in the atonal tonality of bedazzlement. It follows that God diffuses — what he diffuses remains himself: the Good diffuses itself and therefore what it diffuses still remains itself, perhaps in the way that the modes in which the Spinozist *substantia* expresses itself still remain that *substantia* itself. The donation par excellence implies an ecstasy outside of self where the ecstatic self remains all the more itself.[38]

38. MP 588–89. The reference to the visual arts is less surprising if placed against the background of the intellectual history that informs the present debate on icons, idols, and ideologies, in which Marion's subtle analyses are, by the way, conspicuously absent. See W. J. T. Mitchell, *Iconology: Image, Text, Ideology* (Chicago: University of Chicago Press, 1986), and to a lesser extent his *Picture Theory: Essays on Verbal and Visual Representation* (Chicago: University of Chicago Press, 1994). The first chapter of Mitchell's *Iconology* hints at the theological origins of these concepts, as does Martin Jay's *Downcast Eyes: The Denigration of Vision in Twentieth-Century Thought* (Berkeley and Los Angeles: University of California Press, 1993), ch. 1. Mitchell does not differentiate between the conceptual implications of the icon, on the one hand, and the image (picture, likeness, etc.), on the other. Iconology is taken to refer to "a long tradition of theoretical and historical reflection on the notion of imagery, a tradition which in its narrow sense probably begins with Renaissance handbooks of symbolic imagery . . . and culminates in Erwin Panofsky's renowned 'studies' in iconology" (*Iconology*, 2). Yet, as Mitchell defines iconology more generally in terms of a "rhetoric of images," a certain indelible religious overdetermination of the image, the icon, and their relation to ideology emerges: "In a broader sense, the critical study of the icon begins with the idea that human beings are created 'in the image and likeness' of their creator and culminates, rather less grandly, in the modern science of 'image-making' in advertising and propaganda" (ibid.). And, a little further: "As it happens, the notion of ideology is rooted in the concept of imagery, and reenacts the ancient struggles of iconoclasm, idolatry, and fetishism" (ibid., 4).

As in the case of the new multimedia, one may assume that a systematic, rather than merely historical, thematic, or anecdotal "turn to religion," and, in particular, the necessary yet impossible distinction between the icon and the idol, sheds new light on the status of the image in the visual arts. Particularly revealing in this respect is the subtle interpretation Marion offers in *God Without Being* of Dürer's *Melancholia* (which is reproduced prominently on the cover of the first French edition of the book). And then there is Marion's *La Croisée du visible* (Paris: Éditions de la Différence, 1991). In this book, Marion explores the notion of the icon —

The reference to Spinoza may surprise in this context, but it is only consistent with what Marion proposes here and elsewhere. For even—or especially?—the most relentless version of the philosophy of immanence, testifies to the modality of donation sketched above.[39]

GASCHÉ FORMULATES the difficulty in Marion's position in terms that are reminiscent of Heidegger's "Phenomenology and Theology," a lecture that dates from the same year as *Being and Time* and, like Heidegger's magnum opus, reduces the meaning of "theology" to that of a "positive" science concerning a supposed revelation (*Offenbarung*), which as an ultimately ontic phenomenon is deemed possible only on the basis of a primary manifestation or revealability (*Offenbarkeit*) of Being as such.[40]

---

and, in particular, the figure of Christ as the icon of God, who is "invisible par excellence" (ibid., 102; see Col. 1:15)—in terms of a "kenosis of the image" that follows in the wake of the kenosis of the Word but that translates itself into "aesthetic principles" as well (ibid., 111). This turn to a theologically oriented aesthetic sketches the outlines of a critique of the image that is far from iconoclastic but raises the question of how the "modern (televisual) model of the image" can be countered with a radically different one. This different image of the image would draw on contemporary—nonfigurative, conceptual, or minimalist—art forms no less than on the orthodox position adopted in Nicéa (ibid., 107ff.).

Other examples of a turn to religion in the reading of the visual arts abound. One thinks especially of Derrida's *Mémoires d'aveugle: L'Auto-portrait et autres ruines* (Paris: Éditions de la Réunion des musées nationaux, 1990), trans. Pascale-Anne Brault and Michael Naas as *Memories of the Blind: The Self-Portrait and Other Ruins* (Chicago: University of Chicago Press, 1993), and of Jean-François Lyotard's readings, not so much of Duchamp, as of Barnett Newman, in *L'Inhumain: Causeries sur le temps* (Paris: Galilée, 1988), trans. Geoffrey Bennington and Rachel Bowlby as *The Inhuman: Reflections on Time* (Stanford: Stanford University Press, 1991). See also Marie-José Mondzain, *Image, icône, économie: Les Sources byzantines de l'imaginaire contemporain* (Paris: Editions du Seuil, 1996).

39. See also Jean-Luc Marion, *Étant donné: Essai d'une phénoménologie de la donation* (Paris: Presses universitaires de France, 1997), 192 n. 2, and also 95–96, 167, 294.

40. See Martin Heidegger, "Phänomenologie und Theologie," in *Wegmarken* (Frankfurt a./M.: Klostermann, 1978), 45–78, trans. James G. Hart and John C. Maraldo as "Phenomenology and Theology," in *Pathmarks*, ed. William McNeill (Cambridge: Cambridge University Press, 1998), 39–62. In *Being and Time*, rather than signifying the manifestation or the dimension of Being within which things and events appear or come to pass, the terms *offenbar* and *Offenbarkeit* indicate the realm of a public manifestation and even of publicity: "Everydayness is a way *to be*—to which, of course, that which is publicly manifest belongs" ("Alltäglichkeit ist eine Weise *zu sein*, der allerdings die öffentliche Offenbarkeit zugehört"). See Heidegger, *Sein und Zeit* (Tübingen: Niemeyer, 1977), trans. John Macquarrie and Edward Robinson as *Being and Time* (San Francisco: Harper, 1962), 422 / 371. Hereafter cited as BT, followed by the English and German page numbers.

That the question of religion cannot be addressed without incessant reference to the categories and the realm of the public—or without a consideration of the idea and practice of publicity, of censorship and tolerance, of secrecy, and of media and mediatization—is shown

Could there be an exception to this logic of possibilization, which Derrida calls a "logic of presupposition"? Is not Heidegger himself pointing the way to an alternative model when he speaks of a relationship that is not so much analogous to that between "fundamental theology" and "theological systematics," but rather resembles the relation without relation evoked by the *via negativa?*[41]

Other examples can be found, and some of them are cited and interpreted by Derrida and Marion. But they do not remove the latter's suspicion about the consequences of Heidegger's thought, which Gasché counters thus: "Does such freeing of the notion of God from what Marion sees as the last metaphysical subjection of God to the meaning of Being truly achieve an adequate encounter with God as absolutely Other?"[42] Gasché cites Jean-Luc Nancy's suggestion that to propose to speak *of* and *to* God in terms of "love" or "Father," rather than in terms of a supreme Being that can be believed or even proven to exist—that is possible and necessary, not so much because something exists, as the cosmological proof would have it, but because in its supremacy it alone can be said to exist eminently, emphatically, properly speaking, and par excellence, following a long tradition that states that only God exists in accordance with His essence—risks an even more fatal idolatry than the one feared by the critics of natural and philosophical theology. Gasché argues with Nancy that by invoking such notions or figures as "love," the "Father," and so on, Marion runs the risk of lapsing into the idolatry of representation that precedes conceptual idolatry. In other words, we seem to end up with the very anthropomorphism and blasphemy that, by Marion's own account, postmythical ontology sought to overcome, from Aristotle's *theiology* and the Scholastic *theologia naturalis* all the way up to Heidegger's correction of the ontic remnants of theology proper. And the same could in

---

by Kant in the central argument of *Religion Within the Limits of Reason Alone* and in the first part of *The Conflict of the Faculties.* This argument works in both directions: even in the modern, secular era, the notion of the public, of publicity, of media, and mediatization, becomes intelligible only with recourse to the concept and the institution of religion. This analysis would force us to reconsider some of the premises of the current debates of the concept of the public sphere, of multiculturalism, etc., in the work of authors such as Jürgen Habermas, Charles Taylor, and others. See my *Horror Religiosus* (forthcoming), ch. 1.

41. Martin Heidegger, "Protokoll zu einem Seminar über 'Zeit und Sein,'" in *Zur Sache des Denkens* (Tübingen: Max Niemeyer, 1969), 27–58, 34, 51, trans. Joan Stambaugh under the title "Summary of a Seminar on the Lecture 'Time and Being,'" in Heidegger, *On Time and Being* (New York: Harper Torchbooks, 1972), 25–54, 32, 47.

42. Gasché, *Inventions of Difference*, 153.

principle be said of his destruction of ontotheology in the postmetaphysical thought of Being, regardless of its simultaneous preparation in the
*Beiträge zur Philosophie* for the coming of an indeterminate "last God," or
at least of a God before whom, as *Identity and Difference* has it, one can
once again dance, sing, pray, and sacrifice.

Although Marion seems to succumb to the first idolatry, Nancy and
Gasché maintain, this nevertheless does not mean that his idea of a God
without Being, given in an act of love—of *agapē* and donation—alone,
singles itself out by a greater specificity than, say, the abstract and merely
conceptual God of the philosophers. Far from it, for the latter do not indulge in the fantasy of a pure heterology and at least help us thematize
the chances and perils of the (mutual?) dependency of whatever notion
or revelation of God on the concept (the truth, dimension, event or revealability) of Being: "Proposing a notion of God based on the concept of
charity (*agapē*), and of man's relation to God as one that is to be thought
in terms of *distance*, risks sacrificing the specificity of God. All that one
says about God can immediately be said about anything else, 'about
"event," about "love," about "poetry" and so on and so forth' [quoting
Jean-Luc Nancy]." This is a difficulty to which we shall return repeatedly
throughout this book. God, Gasché asserts, cannot be God—a specific
God and not just any other or otherness as such—"if He does *altogether*
escape the truth of Being."[43]

Marion does not fully deny this. For there to be distance between God
and Being or beings, for "God" to retreat from the mirroring interplay
(the *Spiel* or *Spiegel-Spiel*) between Being and beings (between heaven
and earth, mortals and gods, the elements of the Heideggerian *Geviert*,
or "fourfold"), the nonspatial and nontemporal distance must somehow
or somewhere be marked off in its relation-without-relation to Being,
beings, and their *Spiel*. It must be signaled, if not by these elements, then
at least in or on beings in their very being. It should be gestured, if not
by Being as such or itself, then at least in, on, or even as this very Being.
The last mode of revelation or donation would certainly be the most difficult to grasp: that which gives—or gives itself as—Being would not itself,
in turn, be, or be this Being, its truth, its event, or even its dimension.
For while this donation of Being, if it were possible, would somehow
occupy the same space as the gift of Being, the "*es gibt das Sein, es gibt die
Zeit*"—the very motif by which the later Heidegger overcomes his earlier

43. Ibid., 154 (emphasis added).

allegiance to fundamental ontology and, indeed, to ontology and phenomenology as such—it should nonetheless never be confused with it. *Indistinguishable, it would nevertheless not be the same, but, in a way, the totally other.* But can one think of the totally other in a nonheterological way? Does Marion come close here to what, ironically, both Heidegger, following Hölderlin, and Nancy, in his "theo-topography," attempt to comprehend as the *Winke*—the sign or hint—of the divine or of whatever comes to take its place?[44] Let us leave aside that question for the present and simply recall how Marion describes this modality of the gift:

> [I]f "God is charity, *agapē*" (1 John 4:8), can *agapē* transgress Being? In other words, can it no longer appear as one of the "ways" [*guises*] of being (even if this being has the name of *Dasein*)? Can it manifest itself without passing through Being, and, if it cannot determine Being as one of its—own— "ways," can it at least mark its distance from Being? For in order to free God from Being it does not suffice to invoke, by means of a highly suspect and insufficient return to . . . [*retour à*], another divine name, for example, goodness [*la bonté*]. One still must show concretely how the God who gives himself as *agapē* thus marks his divergence [*écart*] from Being, hence first from the interplay of beings as such. (GWB 82–83 / 123)

It is not difficult to imagine what this might entail for the possibility of any ontology, indeed for any thought of Being, and perhaps for any thought in general. For, if *agapē* marks its distance *from*—as well as *on, in, through,* and even *as*—Being, then the latter can no longer be conceived of as one yet multiple, that is to say, as the one Being that expresses itself in many ways. If Being becomes itself an icon of the gift—again, a being-given in a more radical sense than Heidegger's understanding of the *es gibt* allows—then it is also other than (and beyond or distant from) itself: "Being" beyond Being. A rigorous phenomenological analysis, Marion rightly concludes, would have to show that this holds true, not exclusively for Being as such, or for the being deemed highest, but for any being whatsoever. The divine name of "God" would thus evoke the very structure of experience, language, and thought, in general:

> One would have to extend to every being-given that status of a beyond being-ness [*epekeina tēs ousias*], which Plato reserved solely for the *idea tou agathou.*

---

44. See my "Theotopographies: Nancy, Hölderlin, Heidegger," *Modern Language Notes* 109 (1994): 445–77, and "Winke," in *The Solid Letter,* ed. Aris Fioretos (Stanford University Press, forthcoming).

General metaphysics, as *ontologia,* thus would have to yield to a general phenomenology of the donation of all being-given, of which the *Seinsfrage* [the
question of Being] could eventually constitute but a simple region or a particular case. (MP 583)

Again, ironically, Marion would seem to come close to what Derrida,
in *The Gift of Death* and elsewhere, expresses by the quasi-tautological
dictum "Tout autre est autre" ("Every other is [totally, or every bit]
other"). Yet Marion is reluctant to draw a conclusion that Derrida acknowledges from the outset, and that Gasché summarizes by observing
that if the Heideggerian affiliation and contamination of the gift (or
being-given) with Being constitutes the essence of the last and most effective blasphemy, as Marion suggests, and if, moreover, no thought can escape the horizon of Being *fully* or *for good,* so that no radical heterology is
easily conceivable, a deeply troubling conclusion seems inevitable: "Perhaps God is a necessarily idolatrous notion."[45]

Seen from this perspective, the idea of God is then no longer a coherently conceptual or purely intelligible idea (of transcendence or Spinozistic immanence), since its recurrent appearances, its "chances," are
intimately linked to a (transcendental) history and, rather than being
mere epochal "sendings," impose on it a condition of "being dated" or
even "out of date" that it can never fully escape, purify, or cover over:
God, the very idea of God, would thus be a "false entry" in the game of
praising God, and a "false exit" out of that of our finitude. But, as Derrida argues in "La Différance," there only false entries and exits, and they
form part of the game. There is no straight—methodological—access to
the phenomenon proper or as such. As such, there is no such thing as an
experience (phenomenological or other) as such.

Whenever and wherever the idea of "God" comes to mind (or, as Levinas formulates it, "vient à l'idée"), it is already—unavoidably—tainted
by an inherent and thus irrevocable aporia. This is precisely what Derrida seems to deduce from Edmond Jabès's *Livre des questions* (*The Book
of Questions*) when he writes: "Dieu déjà se contredit" ("God contradicts himself already").[46] Gasché's reconstruction of the debate between
Marion, on the one hand, and Heidegger and Derrida, on the other, pro-

45. Gasché, *Inventions of Difference,* 154.
46. Edmond Jabès, *Le Livre des questions* (Paris: Gallimard, 1963–65), quoted in Derrida,
*Writing and Difference,* 70 / 107.

vides the necessary elements for an explanation of this unavoidability of idolatry.

> If God, for Heidegger, is the destinal figure in which the transcendent pure and simple, Being in other words, retreats, a retreat through which the history of Being begins, God, for Derrida, is the result of an always possible . . . effacement of a quasi-transcendental structure that, as a structure of "thought," is older than the thinking of Being. . . . God's name is the exemplary presentation, and hence oblivion, of a transcendental difference that allows for no name, the name of Being included. . . . The trace or differance must not be understood as a cause that would produce or engender what is traditionally called an effect. The trace does not create. All these activities are . . . ontic relations: that is, relations pure and simple. . . . no relation enters the difference between God and the trace. Now, to determine what happens between a quasi-transcendental structure such as the trace and what it is the structure of is undoubtedly one of the most difficult problems that Derrida's thought poses for us. It stems not only from the fact that the trace . . . is not technically a condition of possibility, though without it no God would come into existence, but also from the fact that, as the retained trace of the *relation* of Other in God, it is a condition of impossibility for a God who can only be the one who He is if He disregards the possibilizing structure of the trace.[47]

The seventeenth-century German mystic Angelus Silesius (Johann Scheffler), whose *Cherubinischer Wandersmann* (*Cherubinic Wanderer*) Derrida discusses at some length in *On the Name*, might be cited as a witness in this context. "*GOtt opffert sich jhm selbst*" ("God sacrifices Himself to Himself"), Silesius says, in an epigram strikingly reminiscent of Derrida's "Dieu déjà se contredit." Both statements evoke a God whose relation to Himself—whose self-relation or auto-affection—is caught up in an irresolvable paradox, or, rather, a performative contradiction. This aporia is as mind-boggling as God's quasi-tautological declaration to Moses: "I AM THAT I AM" (Exodus 3:14).

In all these examples, the very pronunciation of God's word and name is thought as a speech "act" that betrays or rather belies itself in its inner intentional structure and at the very heart of its apostrophe. From here on, any *à dieu*, any toward-God, seems also—and at the same moment—

---

47. Gasché, *Inventions of Difference*, 163–64.

an *adieu,* a bidding farewell to and taking leave of the God it had *seemed* to address or addressed in vain.

Even if God is light and love, even if His first and final word is "Yes" (as Michel de Certeau recalls, the mystics stress the biblical assurance that in God there is only a "yes"), this does not save this God from being doubled, being other than Himself, being Himself as (His) other, but also accompanied, or haunted by a shadow, a darkness, in which the worst of possibilities — an evil more radical than any absence of God — may always insinuate itself. This contradiction of the originary "yes" does not exclude the "yes" for which the divine name stands here (and which Derrida, following Pascal and Montaigne, calls the "mystical postulate") from being infinitely reiterated and undone or annulled by yet another "yes." This is what is implied and formalized by "Tout autre est tout autre," the infinite — yet always finite, that is not to say, nonsynonymous — substitution of the infinite.

All this is, of course, not without consequence for any discourse that seeks to capture or to honor God's names, His existence, and — what in God's case amounts to the same thing — His essence. While relying on an ultimately different phenomenological theologics or heterology, Marion seems to acknowledge as much when, in the preface to the English edition of *God Without Being,* he insists on the intimate link between theology and hypocrisy:

> Theology renders its author hypocritical in at least two ways. Hypocritical, in the common sense: in pretending to speak of holy things — "holy things to the holy" — he cannot but find himself, to the point of vertigo, unworthy, impure — in a word, vile. This experience, however, is so necessary that its beneficiary knows better than anyone both his own unworthiness and the meaning of that weakness (the light that unveils it); he deceives himself less than anyone; in fact, here there is no hypocrisy at all: the author knows more than any accuser. He remains hypocritical in another, more paradoxical sense: if authenticity (remembered with horror) consists in speaking of oneself, and in saying only that for which one can answer, no one, in a theological discourse, can, *or should,* pretend to it. For theology consists precisely in saying that for which only another can answer. . . . Indeed, theological discourse offers its strange jubilation only to the strict extent that it permits and, dangerously, demands of its workman that he speak beyond his means, precisely because he does not speak of himself. Hence the danger of speech that, in a sense,

speaks against the one who lends himself to it. One must obtain forgiveness for every essay in theology.[48]

In a similar vein, Marion explains that this is the case at least until the end of all things, until history comes to a close and we shall be able to see things clearly (that is to say, in Marion's idiom, until the second coming of Christ): "[N]o theology will ever be able to attain the first Parousia by an adequate extension of the text to the referent; for that, nothing less than a second Parousia of the Word would be necessary" (GWB 157 / 220). This is what underlies the inevitable risk of all "theological chatter" and "liturgical bricolage" (GWB 157 / 220). Marion stresses that "forgiveness" for this lack or "delay" of theological interpretation can only be granted, or, rather, given. It is given with and as the love of charity. Not that this gift could be conceived of as possible. Rather, as a pure gift, Marion argues, it is ontologically impossible, even though it can attain a certain intelligibility and "rigor," phenomenologically speaking, that is to say, "within the framework of a phenomenology which is pushed to its utmost possibilities" (GWB xxii).

Marion makes this clear by appealing to a paradoxical figure that, once more, resembles the structure of ethical transcendence and metaphysical desire in Levinas: agapē "appears only as a pure given, with neither deduction nor legitimation. But in this way the given appears all the more as given"; and a little earlier, "God gives Himself to be known insofar as He gives Himself—according to the horizon of the gift itself. The gift constitutes at once the mode and the body of His revelation" (GWB xxiv).

The two "emblematic figures" of this gift of love, of its "mode," as well as of its "body," are, first, the "confession of faith"—that is to say, the for-

---

48. GWB 1–2 / 9–10. Levinas similarly links hypocrisy and the deepening of ethical desire; see his Totalité et infini: Essai sur l'extériorité (1961; The Hague: Martinus Nijhoff, 1961), trans. Alphonso Lingis as Totality and Infinity: An Essay on Exteriority (Pittsburgh: Duquesne University Press, 1969), preface, xii, 24. This explains why in his later writings, Levinas does not always insist on maintaining the word ethics. Ethics is a terminus technicus of Greek origin that, even when it takes the place of first philosophy, of metaphysics, of privileging of theoria, remains indebted to a tradition that juxtaposes ethics with logic and physics, all of which are taken to be secondary with respect to the thought of Being. In and before as well as after ethics, there comes the saintliness and the madness of a responsibility without measure. From here it is just one step to the deconstructive questioning, not of bad faith, but of good conscience, of the act that deems itself to operate in conformity with or even out of pure duty. Any ethics that is not aware—or that does not run the risk—of its exposure to the an- or un-ethical disqualifies itself and is, in that sense, hypocritical.

ever inadequate response to the gift, which, rather than giving in return, increases the gift the more it answers to it — and, second, the Eucharist. The latter, even more paradoxically, is emblematic of *agapē* in that it enacts, rather than representing or symbolizing, the mode and the body of this giving to the point where its distance becomes an "abandonment," a giving by which the divine gives itself away to the world. Here, the "Word" becomes a "body" according to an analysis that seems not only to counter Merleau-Ponty's famous figure of *la chair du monde* (Marion writes *corps,* body, rather than *chair,* flesh, thus again contrasting Christian doctrine — here the dogma of incarnation — with ontology), but also reiterates the Husserlian interpretation of the phenomenon in terms of an originary intuition or donation of its bodily, or *leibhaft,* actuality. Again, this phenomenological motif offers an interpretive possibility of which historical revelation is not so much an instantiation or actualization as, in Marion's terminology, "saturation" par excellence.

The transition from the phenomenological order to the emblematic, the modality of which is what interests us here at least as much as its thematic (or figural) reminiscences, is evoked by the subtitle to Marion's book *God Without Being: Hors-Texte* ("Outside the Text"). The latter is less a reference to the title of the first section of Derrida's *La Dissémination* (*Dissemination*) than an invocation of another *pas d'écriture,* another "step of writing" and at the same time the abandonment of a limited or generalized concept of writing — mere writing or *Écriture* or *texte* — alone:

> *Outside the text* indicates less an addition than a deliverance, or rather a final *corps-à-corps,* where love makes the body (rather than the reverse). The Eucharistic gift consists in the fact that in it love forms one body with our body. And if the Word is also made body, surely we, in our body, can speak the Word. The extreme rigor of charity restores us to speech that is finally not silent. (GWB 3–4/12)

Again, this restoration of speech is not grounded in a revelation or fulfillment "yet to come." Marion's text, in the final analysis, appeals to the New Testament as the place where all is "accomplished at the origin." It is only the affirmation of this completion or fulfillment that renders all (further) speech possible according to the logic of the "again of the already" that Heidegger hints at in his early lectures on the phenomenology of religion. But this is not to say that the completion and fulfillment make this speech necessary, inevitable, or that they make it into that which goes without saying. Certain perils of repetition are unavoidable if the gift is not to lose its character as a pure — irreducible, free, undeserved, and unreturned — gift:

> Once all is given, it remains to say it, in the expectation that the Said itself [the Word, i.e., Christ] should come again to say it. Thus understood, *theo*logical progress would indicate less an undetermined, ambiguous, and sterile groping, than the absolutely infinite unfolding of possibilities already realized in the Word but not yet in us and our words. . . . We are infinitely free in theology: we find all already given, gained, available. It only remains to understand, to say, and to celebrate. (GWB 158 / 221–22)

In Marion's view there could thus never be — and, historically speaking, there never was — a negative theology without an affirmative theology.[49] The latter, like the former, is always more a *theo*logy than a theo*logy*, a prayer followed up and modulated by an encomium or hymn. These, in turn, Marion claims, would have been unthinkable outside the fundamentally ahistorical — symbolic — body of the Church, of its hierarchy and its sacraments, again, particularly the confession of faith and the Eucharist. And it is here that, far from merging with any sensible or conceptual forms of idolatry, Marion believes, they touch upon Being, pierce the veil of its vanity as well as the melancholy and the boredom it inspires. They transfigure it into charity, into an icon of *agapē*.

A certain logic of transfiguration of the realm of Being — that is to say, of the "subordination" of Being to God, rather than of the "inclusion" of God in Being — is thus juxtaposed with an even more radical logic of abandonment. Marion evokes this abandonment by observing that "as soon as Being itself acts as an idol, it becomes thinkable to release oneself from it — to suspend it" (GWB 3 / 11). But this statement, in its turn, is based on the belief, or *credo*, evoked by the title of Marion's book: *God Without Being. Dieu sans l'être*, Marion says, does not imply that "God is not," or, as has been suggested by Derrida and Gasché, that "God is not truly God"; rather it meditates on Schelling's decisive insight that there is an absolute "freedom of God with regard to his own existence" (GWB 2 / 10). This hypothesis or axioma and sine qua non of Marion's phenome-

---

49. The relationship between negative and affirmative theology is analyzed in detail and with speculative force throughout the many phases of so-called apophatic thought, and nowhere more convincingly than in the writings of Pseudo-Dionysius and in *De docta ignorantia* of Nicolaus Cusanus. But other examples abound.

nology and theology undermines the dogmatic assumption of metaphysicians, of neo-Thomists, and of all natural theologians, that "God, before
all else, has to be" (GWB 2/11).

But, we may ask, is this assumption less warranted—philosophically,
phenomenologically, and even theologically speaking—than the heterological alternative that Marion seems to propose? Marion argues thus:
God does not even have to "be." And if God "is," then this, Marion insists, is first of all due to a gift and an abandonment that neither Being nor
beings—whether transfigured or not—can ever hope to contain. If God
"is," it is order to give more, to give everything—that is to say, Himself,
Being and beings:

> If . . . "God is love," then God loves before being. He only is as He embodies
> himself—in order to love more closely that which and those who, themselves,
> have first to be. The radical reversal of the relations between Being and loving,
> between the name revealed by the Old Testament (Exodus 3:14) and the name
> revealed, more profoundly though not inconsistently, by the New Testament
> (First Letter of John 4:8), presupposes taking a stand that is at once theologi-
> cal and philosophical. (GWB xx)

Yet, as in Levinas, the relation-without-relation of beings in an ethical sense, and thus the relation of beings to God, presupposes that these
beings first constitute (contract or hypostatize) themselves as beings, as
naturally atheistic egos. Like Levinas, Marion departs from all natural theology, from the postulated desire for God based in human nature as such.
Between the movement of abandonment and the movement of transfiguration and subordination, there is neither symmetry nor analogy. But one
cannot "be" without the other. And since one movement relies on the
other, or since one releases the other, what we are dealing with here *resembles* what Derrida calls a "logic of presupposition." Those instances
where, as Marion writes with oblique reference to Heidegger, "an opening to God is destined"—in vanity and its counterpart charity—stand as
nondialectical moments in a relationship in which the one somehow conditions or solicits and calls forth the other. And yet, in a way, the poles
of this elliptical movement also cancel each other out. What makes each
of them possible is, as so often, that which makes them impossible as
well: "As love . . . remains essentially inaccessible to us, the suspension
that delivers God from Being becomes feasible for us only in its negative
aspect—the vanity that melancholy pours over the world of beings. . . .

In short, melancholy opens (to) distance" (GWB 3/11). These formulations rearrange the terms of the relationship that Heidegger examines in
"What Is Metaphysics?" even when they adopt and privilege a different
idiom. But it is easy to see how vanity, melancholy, Being, and God have
taken the place of the play of anxiety, the play of the nothing (the *Nichts*)
and, again, of Being. This becomes even clearer if one considers Marion's
analysis of the "interspace" — that is to say, of "an attitude characterized
neither by the idolatrous gaze nor by the iconic face," or if one highlights
once more the place he assigns to a structure reminiscent of the Heideggerian deployment of Hölderlin's *Winke*, or divine nods and hints (GWB
110/160 and 137–38/195 respectively).[50]

IN ALL THESE CONTEXTS, then, Marion continues to insist on the radical
heterogeneity between what Heidegger's "Letter on Humanism" permits
us to think of as the "call of Being" (*Anspruch des Seins*) and the "call of the
Father in Christ" (*Anspruch des Vaters in Christus*).[51] In so doing, he also
anticipates Derrida's renewed attention, in "How to Avoid Speaking" and
elsewhere, to the distinction between the manifestation or revealability

50. The reference to Hölderlin is important, for he serves as a witness on more than one
occasion. In *L'Idole et la distance*, for example, Marion speaks of the need to "think an unthinkable paradox: the intimacy of man with the divine *grows* with the distance that distinguishes
him from it, far from making it smaller. The retreat of the divine would perhaps constitute
its ultimate figure of revelation. Which we tend to single out under the name distance. Two
poems . . . might, as privileged guides, lead us to the evidence of that paradox . . . 'In Lovely
Blue . . .' and 'Patmos'" (114). See my "*Winke*," in *Solid Letter*, ed. Fioretos (forthcoming).
    Furthermore, it is crucial to note that Marion reads Hölderlin along lines that situate
him squarely in the tradition of apophatics. The unsayable, the name lacking in Hölderlin is,
he stresses, not that of a supreme being, but "the unsayable of distance": "It is no longer the
question of saying an object, even transcendent, even supremely 'personal.' It is a question of
signifying the distance where the divine retreat becomes the supreme insistance" (ibid., 181).
But how, then, does one signify this distance that is the very modality of the divine instance,
or, as Marion puts is, of its "insistance"? Marion's answer is that in order to "honor" Hölderlin,
we must begin by "meditating" on Pseudo-Dionysius's *Divine Names* and *Mystical Theology*,
notably on Pseudo-Dionysius's "nonpredicative theory of discourse," which is far from negative in any privative, logical, dialectical, or psychoanalytic sense of the word, but, Marion
stresses, the sole guarantee of a "discourse on the modality of praise [*louange*]" (ibid., 182).
Therefore, we may argue that the "unsayable" must be said and, what is more, must be said
"in two ways [*doublement*]": "as a supreme non-being, as a hyperbolical separation [*écart*]"
(ibid.). The question here, Marion continues, is not so much which discourse faces up to this
double task as "which mode of discourse works already in the Hölderlinean text and assures
its pertinence" (ibid.). This, Marion concludes, is the tradition of the divine names whose lack
provokes the song of praise.
    51. Heidegger, "Brief über den Humanismus," in *Pathmarks*, ed. McNeill, 244, 317.

of Being (Heidegger's *Offenbarkeit*), on the one hand, and the revelation of God (*Offenbarung*), on the other: a distinction that, in Heidegger, is simultaneously—and therefore aporetically—maintained and effaced.

Marion recalls many of the relevant passages where Heidegger seems to insist on the radical distinction, in point of departure and perspective, of metaphysics and philosophy, on the one hand, and faith and theology, on the other. The former is caught up in the essential, constitutive, ambiguity of ontotheology, forced to pursue the question of Being both in its generality and in its excellence, in its supremacy and perfection. As a "theiology" this thought is centered, not around God, without quotation marks, or properly speaking, but around the divine, *to theion*. Whenever it seeks to name "God," it provides us in fact, and of necessity, with a metaphysical concept, and thus fixates the referent and the horizon of the divine name. This is the case, as Marion reminds us in his many studies in the history of modern metaphysics, wherever the meaning of God is determined as the "ultimate ground," as is the case in Leibniz, as *causa sui*, as in Descartes and Spinoza, or, finally, as a "moral God," in Kant, Fichte, and Nietzsche. But the list does not, of course, end here and could be easily extended, both beyond Nietzsche, and, taking many steps back, well before the beginning of so-called modern metaphysics. In a sense, this conceptual idolatry dates from before the emergence of the *theologia naturalis* as one of three branches of the *metaphysica specialis* and as distinguished from the *metaphysica generalis* or *ontologia,* on the one hand, and—much more fundamentally—from so-called revealed or positive theology, or *sacra doctrina,* on the other.

Yet Heidegger's attempt to separate metaphysics (philosophy, phenomenology) from theology proper is not sufficient, Marion insists, in the undertaking to finally "liberate" "God" from the last idolatry, that is to say from His projection onto the "screen" (*écran*) of Being. Heidegger, he writes, "in full accord with his intention, does not elaborate the modalities of an authentically theological discourse, since it remains to him, by hypothesis, foreign" (GWB 63 / 95). For if it is true that Heidegger insists on strict demarcation between the philosophical and the theological—that is to say, between theological science, on the one hand, and the ontic science of the fact of faith,[52] on the other—then this demarcation is also governed by a logic of subordination. Marion argues this as follows:

---

52. This fact (*Faktum*), Heidegger claims, is a positive phenomenon (*Positum, Positivität*), of "Christianicity" (*Christlichkeit*), a term introduced by Franz Overbeck. In the preface to

To liberate theology from the word *Being* now assumes a precise meaning: it is not in any way a question of unbinding [*délier*] theology from *Dasein* but, on the contrary, of according theology a proper domain — faith [*la foi*] — only on condition of submitting it to an ontological "correction." . . . To be sure, it must not employ the word *Being* but by default, not by excess: theology refers to something greater than itself, to the existential analytic of *Dasein,* and later, to the thought of *Seyn.* The theology of faith must avoid [*éviter*] saying the word *Being* because Being expresses itself more essentially than theology can ever glimpse; and for this reason every theology remains subject to the question of Being, as every ontic variant of *Dasein* refers back to bare *Dasein.* (GWB 68 / 103)

And, in a note, Marion formulates a hypothesis that I explore at length in this book: "This ambiguity could explain how Christian theology had been able, biographically, to serve as a path toward that which remains the most foreign to it" (GWB 214 n. 43 / 103 n. 42).

In Heidegger, Marion continues, the question of God undergoes a "double relativization" (GWB 68 / 103): first, by its inscription into theology, or ontotheology — that is to say, metaphysics, specifically, a *metaphysica specialis* or *theologia naturalis* that remains premised upon the presuppositions of the *metaphysica generalis* or *ontologia;* and, second, because although relegated to a separate ontic domain — to theology, properly speaking, a positive science, not of God or of "God," but of faith and "Christianicity" (*Christlichkeit*) — it remains for ever *surbordinated* to and to be *corrected* by the fundamentally ontological analysis of Dasein proper. That this correction means "nothing but" insistence on the double origin and double constitution of the theological concepts in question, which — de facto — stem from two sources (an ontic revelation and the ontological preunderstanding that makes it possible, but that it in turn also supersedes) — does not seem to mitigate Marion's unease with regard to Heidegger's ambiguity:

We see here the independence most certainly of faith and of its theology, but ontic independence, which implies an irreducible ontological dependence. Hence the theology of faith falls within [*relève de*] the domain of *Dasein,* and,

---

his essay "Phänomenologie und Theologie" (in *Pathmarks,* ed. McNeill, 39–62), Heidegger invokes Overbeck's *Über die Christlichkeit unserer heutigen Kultur* (On the Christianicity of Our Present Theology) (1873; Darmstadt: Wissenschaftliche Buchgesellschaft, 1981), a book that also forms a subtext to the lecture notes collected in part 1 of *Phänomenologie des religiösen Lebens* (Frankfurt a./M.: Klostermann, 1995), vol. 60 of the *Gesamtausgabe.*

directly through it, of Being, as the "God" of metaphysics falls within [*relève de*] onto-theo-logy and hence indirectly through it of Being. It seems that the question of "God" never suffered as radical a reduction to the first question of Being as in the phenomenological enterprise of Heidegger. (GWB 69/104)

The question, at this point, is whether this logic of subordination or of "presupposition," to quote Derrida, is phenomenologically sustainable— that is to say, sustainable without relying on presuppositions of its own and unwarranted by whatever it is that is *given* to us to be *seen*. In other words, is Heidegger's logic of subordination not, in turn, "subordinated" to a more complicated logic, which he at times seems to hint at under the heading "formal indication" (*formale Anzeige*), and that Husserl and after him Derrida articulate in terms of a transcendental historicity? Marion broaches this very problematics when he asks:

> How is it that the gap [*l'écart*] between manifestation (*Offenbarkeit*) and revelation (*Offenbarung*), explicitly repeated and traversed, is found to be forgotten and erased [*gommé*], so as to conclude that what determines the one—manifestedness of beings according to the Openness of Being—must necessarily determine revelation as well? In the end, is it self-evident that biblical revelation transgresses neither beings in what they reveal nor Being in the manner [*guise*] of its revelation? Who then decides that the mode of revelation, of which the Bible emphasizes that it speaks *polumerōs kai polutropōs*, "in many refrains, in many different ways" (Heb. 1:1), should have to sacrifice, as a retainer fee, Being? (GWB 70–71/106; trans. modified)

Marion notes, however, that Heidegger's own texts show disparate traces of a "third way," which, if it were chosen methodically and with sufficient rigor, would radically liberate God, not from the first blasphemy (which Heidegger wisely avoids), but from the second—more pernicious, conceptual and ontophenomenological—idolatry and thereby from the very question of Being and its point of departure, the existential analysis of Dasein.

A salient example of this is Heidegger's invocation in the "Letter on Humanism" of the supposed difference between the call of Being and the call of the Father in Christ. That the latter was modeled on the former can be explained, Marion suggests, as the outcome of a long tradition of biblical translation and theological commentary that has left a decisive mark on the central texts of Western metaphysics, from St. Augustine through

Pseudo-Dionysius, St. Thomas Aquinas, Suárez, and Descartes. In these texts what Marion calls a *théologie blanche* can be retraced.

This "white theology," explored in Marion's *Sur la théologie blanche de Descartes* (On the White Theology of Descartes), and taken up without explicit reference to Derrida's earlier interpretation of *la mythologie blanche* (white mythology), stands for a forgetfulness and fundamental indecision at the root of the—decidedly modern—metaphysical project. Unlike the ancient legacy of Christian thought, which relied on the concept of analogy no less than on the tradition of the so-called divine names, modern metaphysics, Marion claims, set out on a relentless search for foundations. Yet it was precisely in this quest for certainty that it could not but point beyond itself. In contradistinction to the position he takes in *Idol and Distance,* Marion acknowledges in his more recent *God Without Being* that in his thinking of the gift, he is at times "close to Derrida" (GWB xxi).[53] Conversely, Derrida says that in some regards Marion's thinking seems "both very close and extremely distant" (HAS 65 n. 9 / 553–34 n. 1). This characterization is significant in that it has a much wider relevance and not only underscores Derrida's increasing or, at least, more and more explicit engagement with the religious tradition and its most significant theologemes, but also captures the exact modality of that interest, namely, as a *being at once extremely close to and, as it were, at an infinite remove from* this heritage. This modality never attains the peaceful stability of a modus vivendi, but takes the form of an incessant and restless oscillation and, indeed, negotiation, the aporetics of which is made into an explicit concern.

On closer scrutiny, the distinction between the two thinkers would seem to lie in their different uses of the term *deconstruction,* the meaning of which Marion, unlike Derrida, defines in a purely heterological— and therefore, I would claim, unhistorical or even ahistorical—manner. Their disagreement here can be explained in terms of their respective receptions of Husserl's analysis of originary donation, which Marion, in *Réduction et donation* (*Reduction and Givenness*) and *Étant donné*

---

53. See Jean-Luc Marion, *Sur la théologie blanche de Descartes: Analogie, création des vérités éternelles et fondement* (Paris: Presses universitaires de France, 1981; Quadrige, 1991), notably p. 450. This "white theology," Marion stresses, goes hand in hand with what he calls a "gray ontology" (ibid., 447). See also Jean-Luc Marion, *Sur l'ontologie grise de Descartes: Savoir aristotélicien et science cartésienne dans les Regulae* (Paris: Vrin, 1975, 1981), and id., *Étant donné,* 108 ff.

(Being Given) takes as his simple point of departure and the *primum intelligibile* of all phenomenological experience, whereas Derrida places it back in the complex genesis of the very ideality of meaning that had troubled Husserl so much in the appendices to *Die Krisis der europäischen Wissenschaften und die transzendentale Phänomenologie* (*The Crisis of European Sciences and Transcendental Phenomenology*). This complexity informs Derrida's introduction to Husserl's *Der Ursprung der Geometrie* (*The Origin of Geometry*), as well his so-called *thèse*, entitled *Le Problème de la genèse dans la philosophie de Husserl* (*The Problem of Genesis in Husserl's Philosophy*).

In Marion's work, moreover, the notion of the gift is not introduced by way of a discussion of Marcel Mauss's *Essai sur le don* (*The Gift*) and Heidegger's dictum "Es gibt das Sein," or "Es gibt die Zeit," which seems, on the contrary, conspicuously absent.[54] Other sources than Heidegger therefore seem more relevant to Marion's insistence on exploring the implications of the being-given of experience that for him constitutes the heart of the phenomenological project: those found in the writings of Hans Urs von Balthasar, Maurice Merleau-Ponty, Levinas, Jean-Louis Chrétien, and, up to a certain point, Derrida himself, to name only a few of the contemporary authors on whose work Marion draws.[55] True, Hei-

54. As Jean Greisch has observed in his essay "L'Herméneutique dans la 'phénoménologie comme telle': Trois questions à propos de *Réduction et donation*," *Revue de Métaphysique et de Morale* 96, no. 1 (1991): 56–57, 62–63, Marion virtually ignores the motif of the *es gibt* in his most detailed analyses of Heidegger to date. This motif, Greisch recalls, plays a central role in Heidegger's thinking from his earliest lectures on, but it is not taken into account in what, in *Réduction et donation*, remains an essentially Husserlian extrapolation of the originary givenness of the phenomenon. And yet, Greisch argues, this motif makes its appearance in Heidegger's development as early as 1919. Another, more relevant example in this context, is the fact that the *es gibt* plays a crucial role in the important 1927 lecture course *Grundprobleme der Phänomenologie*, which further pursues the project of *Being and Time* and for the first time introduces the expression, if not the idea, of the ontological difference (Heidegger, *Grundprobleme der Phänomenologie* [Frankfurt a./M.: Klostermann, 1975], *Gesamtausgabe*, 24: 27). Significantly, the motif of the *es gibt* is understood here against the background of a certain interpretation of the Platonic *epekeina tēs ousias* (ibid., 393–405). The debate between Heidegger and Marion, Greisch suggests, could thus be reconstructed in terms of their radically divergent appropriations of the same Platonic idea that has fueled the tradition of apophatic discourse, from Pseudo-Dionysius all the way up to Levinas and Derrida. See Marion, *Réduction et donation: Recherches sur Husserl, Heidegger et la phénoménologie* (Paris: Presses universitaires de France, 1989), trans. Thomas A. Carlson as *Reduction and Givenness: Investigations of Husserl, Heidegger, and Phenomenology* (Evanston, Ill.: Northwestern University Press, 1998).

55. Marion, "Réponses à quelques questions," 69 and 69–70 n. 1. On Hans Urs von Balthasar, see Marion, *L'Idole et la distance*, ch. 3.4. And see also Maurice Merleau-Ponty, *Phénoménologie de la perception* (1945; reprint, Paris: Gallimard, 1976), 413; Emmanuel Levinas,

degger's thought of the *Ereignis*, after the so-called turn (*Kehre*), is given particular consideration, but it must, Marion insists, be read *against the grain*. Unlike Husserl and the authors mentioned above, all of whom seem to Marion less suspicious in this regard, Heidegger seems also here *at once close to and at the farthest remove from* a genuine thought of the gift. Was a different position even available to us? Marion seems to think so:

> [T]he philosophy that identifies itself absolutely with metaphysics shares the death of the latter. After this, the meditation of the question of being can be pursued, but for the sake of that which Heidegger calls "thought" and for which, by definition, he could not formulate a definition according to logic (that is to say, again, according to metaphysics). Such a "thought" is, moreover, no longer preoccupied with being, which has been taken definitively into the empire of things, but with an event that we name with Heidegger *Ereignis;*

---

*Autrement qu'être ou au-delà de l'essence* (The Hague: Martinus Nijhoff, 1974), 64, trans. Alphonso Lingis as *Otherwise than Being, or Beyond Essence* (The Hague: Martinus Nijhoff, 1981); Jean-Louis Chrétien, *La Voix nue: Phénoménologie de la promesse* (Paris: Éditions de Minuit, 1990), chs. 6, 7, and 12; Michel Henry, *Phénoménologie matérielle* (Paris: Presses universitaires de France, 1990), ch. 1; Jacques Derrida, *Glas* (Paris: Galilée, 1974), trans. John P. Leavey, Jr., and Richard Rand (Lincoln: University of Nebraska Press, 1986); id., *Psyché: Inventions de l'autre* (Paris: Galilée, 1987); and id., *Donner le temps: La Fausse Monnaie* (Paris: Galilée, 1991), trans. Peggy Kamuf as *Given Time: I. Counterfeit Money* (Chicago: University of Chicago Press, 1994). Marion quotes Derrida's assertion in "Comment ne pas parler: Dénégations" (in *Psyché*, 535–95, trans. Ken Frieden as "How to Avoid Speaking: Denials," in *Languages of the Unsayable: The Play of Negativity in Literature and Literary Theory*, ed. Sanford Budick and Wolfgang Iser [New York: Columbia University Press, 1989]) that in comprehending Heidegger's famous dictum, in *Zeit und Sein*, "Es gibt das Sein, es gibt die Zeit," it is crucial to see that there can be "no question of reversing the priority or a logical order and saying that the gift precedes Being. But the thinking of the gift opens up the space in which Being and time give themselves and give themselves to be thought" (HAS 69 n. 27 / 587 n. 1). It is here that one of the differences in intellectual orientation between the two authors comes into view. For, while Derrida questions the logic of presupposition to which such a reversal would remain subject, Marion, in contrast, insists that he is precisely most concerned with the decision concerning the priority of the gift over Being and time. Not to decide here would run counter to the very phenomenological exigency to return to the thing itself. The donation of "ultimate phenomenality" no longer lets itself be projected on the screen of Being, let alone of beings, and thus pierces the veil of "double idolatry" (in other words, of historicism, psychologism, and sociologism, on the one hand, and of metaphysics, ontology, and the thinking of Being, on the other). It can do so, because the donation is characterized by an "original simplicity" and since it is the one "focal point" that "unites" the "instituting act" (Marion, "Réponses à quelques questions," 69 n. 1) of the phenomenological reduction whose essential presupposition it is. And if Derrida's writings — by his own account, "all" of his texts, published "since approximately 1972" — are indeed oriented toward an analysis of the gift, then this might very well mean, Marion suggests, that the anteriority of *différance* over ontological difference must give way to "the still older difference of the gift" (ibid., 70 n. 1). As we shall see below, this interpretation is far from being adequate.

the *Ereignis* attempts to conceive the fact that *there is, es gibt*. Heidegger en-
visions this *es gibt* as a donation, but he objects in advance to our identifying
it properly, since in this way the primacy of beings—*es*, something, or even
some*one!*—would be reestablished. The question of donation consequently
finds itself brilliantly placed at the center of "thought," and closed off in advance. This is because Heidegger decides . . . that donation must be "thought"
from the *Ereignis* and thus, finally, again from, or out of, being.[56]

But does Heidegger not, by Marion's own account, state that the *Ereignis*
gives Being, or that it (*Es*) "is" the very giving of Being and beings? Does
not Marion's concept of charity occupy the same structural—or should
we say, quasi-transcendental—place as Heidegger's *Ereignis* (as well as,
for that matter, of Derrida's *différance*)? Is it just another name for what
the *Ereignis* (or *différance*) gives us to think about? Here is what Marion
writes:

> Donation must not be thought starting from being, but rather from donation;
> this means that the gift unfolds a rigor that is both prior and independent, ac-
> cording to the exigencies of charity. The order of charity surpasses infinitely
> that of being, and governs being—as it does all beings—as one gift among
> others. To receive being as a gift is certainly not learned from the *Ereignis*, but
> from charity. . . .: over and above the ontological difference that metaphysics
> leaves unthought, we must stigmatize its forgetting, even its refusal, to think
> charity and love as such. . . . The ruin of philo*sophy* sets forth . . , the enigma
> within itself of *philo*sophy. . . . Why does philosophy—up to and included in
> the "thought" that Heidegger substitutes for it at the end of metaphysics—
> pass so obstinately in silence over the *philein* that nevertheless inaugurates
> philosophy?[57]

The gift, then, is introduced by Marion as that which remains after
the demise of metaphysics, of ontotheology, the "death of God," and the
"death of the death of God" it implies. It is nothing but the articulation of the originary donation of the phenomenon after the thought of
the ground—including the definition of God as *causa sui*—has exhausted
itself. The latter proves itself to be groundless as soon as it turns its
very own central principle—the principle of reason—against itself. Seen
against this backdrop, the task of phenomenology, that most promising
of all postmetaphysical discourses, is to think the gift or, more precisely,

56. Marion, "End of the End of Metaphysics," 17–18.
57. Ibid., 18–19.

charity, the most theological and most divine of all names: "[A]ccording to an essential anachronism: charity belongs neither to pre-, nor to post-, nor to modernity, but rather, at once abandoned to and removed from historical destiny, it dominates any situation of thought. The thematic of destitution, which strikes all being and all Being with vanity, develops an ahistorical 'deconstruction' of the history of metaphysics."[58]

Derrida's analysis of the gift, by contrast, retains a certain relationship, however complex (as in Levinas, we are dealing here with a "relation without relation") to the historical, and thereby to the metaphysical and to the theological — affirmative and negative — as well as to the very positivity of religion, and especially to the monotheisms of the West. The formal structure of the argument on which this analysis is based can already be found in his early reading of the Husserlian understanding of the transcendental historicity of meaning, of its idealizations, its repetition, and its incarnation.

As things stand, Marion's analysis relies on the distinction between absolute and relative dissymmetries or disproportions in the relation between God and Being, between Being and God, between God and beings, between beings and God, between Being and beings, and, finally, among finite beings as such. These relations presuppose an order or hierarchy that is effectively destabilized by Derrida's enigmatic formula "Tout autre est tout autre," every other is totally other. How, then, can this dictum be reconciled with the transcendental historicity that Derrida pursues in his reading of Husserl? And what is the difference between Derrida's radicalization of this Husserlian motif and Marion's insistence on the a posteriori nature of all a priori's — that is to say, on the radical empiricism of the phenomenological understanding of originary donation, of the being-given, not only of sensuous intuition (as Kant would have it) or of essences and categorial intuition (as Husserl claims), but of all givens in general and in particular of the gift par excellence?

This said, there is yet another type of argumentation that can be found in both Marion's and Derrida's reassessments of the history of Western philosophy. I mean the argument that the deconstruction of the tradition of ontotheology is based on a double — as it were, both internal and external — disturbance that affects the metaphysical edifice simultaneously from within and without. Mutually exclusive, these two operations are also reciprocally constitutive to the extent that one cannot come to pass or

58. Ibid., xxii.

be thought or experienced without the other. And yet, in Marion's analysis, it would seem as if one prepares the ground for the other:

> [T]he definition of *metaphysics* that is most pertinent, both historically and conceptually, also allows one to challenge it. The thought of the ground . . . can also be denied as ground. For if the ground imposes itself metaphysically through its universal capacity to respond to the question, Why a being rather than nothing? it exposes itself to the nihilistic refutation that asks, Why a reason rather than nothing? The ground ensures the legitimacy of metaphysics, but not of itself. Now, the self-evidence of the question Why? can—and undoubtedly must—always become blurred when faced with the violence of the question that asks, Why ask why? And if metaphysics is indeed defined as the thought of universal foundation, it cannot not founder when the self-evidence of the obligation of a foundation of being is called into question. This limitation of "metaphysics" is all the stronger, first, insofar as it results directly from its definition, which is maintained but turned back against itself, and, next, insofar as a mere suspicion (why ask why?) and not even a demonstration is enough for metaphysics to be invalidated in point of fact. The "end of metaphysics" is thus in no way an optional opinion; it is a fact of reason.[59]

It is in this silence or void produced by the immanent critique of metaphysics that the gift as the beyond of metaphysics and the without Being—but also in the original phenomenological sense of the donation of Being—may or may not "insinuate" or "reveal," rather than, say, "manifest" (Heidegger) or "show" (Wittgenstein), itself. Strangely enough, Marion thus upholds a radical distinction between the phenomenological analysis of the structure of all donation and the being-given of the saturated phenomenon (of revelation) itself or as such. Both fit the definition and requirements of radical empiricism, a formulation that Marion takes up, following Levinas's statement, in *Le Temps et l'autre* (*Time and the Other*), that phenomenology is "only a radical mode of experience."[60] Yet the two remain separated, distant from each other:

> Of itself, phenomenology can identify the saturated phenomenon of the being-given par excellence only as a possibility—not only a possibility as

59. MP 577–88. Cf. id., "End of the End of Metaphysics."
60. See Emmanuel Levinas, *Le Temps et l'autre* (Montpellier: Fata Morgana, 1979; reprint, Paris, 1983), 34, trans. Richard A. Cohen as *Time and the Other, and Additional Essays* (Pittsburgh: Duquesne University Press, 1987), quoted from MP 582 n. 17. See also the remarks with which Derrida concludes his "Violence and Metaphysics," in *Writing and Difference*, 79–153 / 117–228, where mention is made of an "absolute" and utimately nonphilosophical empiricism in Levinas's early writing up to *Totalité et infini*.

opposed to actuality but above all a possibility of donation itself. The characteristics of the being-given imply that it gives itself without prevision, without measure, without analogy, without repetition; in short, it remains unavailable. Its phenomenological analysis therefore bears only on its re-presentation, its "essence," and not directly on its being-given. The intuitive realization of that being-given requires, more than phenomenological analysis, the real experience of its donation, which falls to revealed theology. Between phenomenology and theology, the border passes between revelation as possibility and revelation as historicity. There could be no danger of confusion between these two domains. (MP 590)

Derrida takes a different view. According to him, the confusion between the two orders cannot be avoided. On the contrary, it is as inevitable as it is unjustifiable. Yet what thus takes place of necessity—the fatal entanglement of the philosophical and the religious, or, rather, theological, for which the term *metaphysics* in its originary ontotheological determination stands here—cannot simply be replaced by a heterology that would circumvent the pitfalls of confusion, of contamination, of parody, and, indeed, idolatry and blasphemy: "Dieu déjà se contredit." This aporia cannot be escaped and is a *chance* for theology (if not, as Marion would have it, its "relief") as much as it is a stumbling block.

If the confusion is to be avoided at all costs, this would entail limiting revelation in the possible modes of its occurrence. In Marion's terminology, revelation could not be a "saturated" phenomenon at all—one that gives itself without reserve—but would have to define itself a priori and negatively in relation to a horizon. Phenomenology contaminates revealed theology and vice versa; they are inevitably confused. This is not to deny Marion's claim that phenomenology shows philosophy a "new path," without returning to the *metaphysica specialis* or *theologia naturalis*. Nor is it to dispute the fact that "on that path, the rational thought of God, which philosophy cannot forget without losing its own dignity, or even its possibility, finds at least a certain coherence" (MP 591). But then again, coherence can take many different forms, the least promising (plausible or effective) of which is, perhaps, the one favored by radical heterology, with its confessed allergy to contamination, negotiation, and thereby, indeed, "confusion." [61]

61. On more than one occasion, Marion seems to imply as much. While stressing the continuity in his writings from *Dieu sans l'être* (1982) through *Sur le prisme métaphysique de Descartes* (Paris: Presses universitaires de France, 1986) up to *Réduction et donation* (1989), he

## The Example Par Excellence

In "How To Avoid Speaking," Derrida's concern is not merely or even primarily "how not to speak of God," or "how to avoid speaking of God in terms of Being or beings," so much as to avoid speaking of Him (or to Him) in an *onto*-theo-*logical* manner, which is to commit idolatry or blasphemy (in short, an adultery of words or concepts, figures or images). Of more importance than his discussion of an apophatic moment—of the unsaying that follows, accompanies, or corrects the first, cataphatic moment, restoring its relation-without-relation to the beyond of (and the otherwise than) beings and Being, to what "is" *epekeina tēs ousias* or hyperousios—seems Derrida's insistence on the question that corresponds to (and is implied in) "How to Avoid Speaking," to wit, "How to avoid speaking—of Being?" (HAS 64 n. 3 / 540 n. 1).[62] The task outlined

---

acknowledges their respective points of departure in the tradition of the divine names, in the historical emergence of the modern metaphysics of the subject as it is played out between the positions of Descartes and Pascal, and in the basic concepts operative in the phenomenological project from Husserl to Heidegger. Another case in point would be his *Sur la théologie blanche de Descartes*, 455–56. This, however, is not to deny that these studies presuppose each other. The last-mentioned book, for example, deploys a "negative phenomenology" in the wake (*à la suite*) of the negative theology of the first. And even though it is true that *Réduction et donation* situates itself solidly in the phenomenological style of reasoning and must therefore leave a certain "emptiness" (*vide*), this should not lead us to forget, Marion hastens to point out, that this very "emptiness" already carries the trace of what provokes it: "Le 'vide' porte déjà la trace de ce qui le provoque" (Marion, "Réponses à quelques questions," 68). In other words, from the phenomenological description—or experience—of the being-given, the notion of "charity" is not totally absent. The former is, in a sense, "stigmatized" (ibid.) by the latter. Yet has not the risk of "confusion"—of mistaking one for the other—in fact been assumed as soon as one realm or order, to quote Pascal, carries a trace or stigma of the other?

    62. The very ambiguity of asking "How to avoid speaking of . . . ?" corresponds to the double edge of Derrida's inquiry in this essay. First, the question allows one to observe the circumstance that, given the elusiveness of the subject matter (God without Being or essence), it seems impossible to speak of it "henceforth" (HAS 12 / 545) or "in general" (ibid., 15 / 548). Yet, like Marion and in contrast to the early Wittgenstein, Derrida denies—negates or dene-gates—that this silence is possible at all or can be consistently kept. A priori, in the very "origin" or "essence" of its affirmation, the promise that marks all language (and this well before its differentiation into speech or writing, into discourse, encomium, or prayer) is forced it to compromise itself while engaging language or by taking the first step (*pas*) on the way to language. Thus, Derrida can ask, " 'How to avoid speaking' since I have . . . always already started to promise to speak?" (ibid., 16 / 549). Second, and more important (although Derrida seems mostly concerned in this context with the first interpretation of the question), there is the supplementary issue of how to avoid speaking "if one speaks of it" (ibid., 12 / 545), that is, once it has become apparent that one cannot *completely* avoid speaking of it but has already begun speaking, inadvertently, prematurely, and without justification. The question how, in speaking—in not being able not to speak—it is nonetheless necessary or imperative not to

here is to explain how the transgression of the finiteness of Being and beings in the light of (or in view of) the Infinite — as a hyper-being beyond being, the beyond of and otherwise than being — entails in its structure *also,* that is to say, ipso facto, a simultaneous or subsequent turning and returning to these very same beings in their being and thus, albeit indirectly, to the question of Being as such. Paradoxically, therefore, the very radicality of the interrogation of the ultimacy of Being and of beings in their very being does not so much exclude or bracket, let alone eradicate, as, on the contrary, already imply a *reaffirmation,* however cautious, reluctant, and vigilant, of their being, of their being-there, of their historicity or histori(c)ality. And this, we might say, regardless of whether we take these terms in their empirical or ontic, transcendental or ontological sense. The process of what has often been depicted as a movement of transcendence or ascension is, wherever it occurs, accompanied (followed and, in fact, already preceded) by an equally constitutive turn (back) into immanence, that is to say, by a moment of descendence. Together, these movements make up the complex phenomenon of apophatics, of the inner linkage between negative and affirmative theology, but also of kenosis, ascesis, and, indeed, conversion, or, in the Levinasian vocabulary that we have taken as our lead, of the *adieu* and its double, the *à dieu.*

Two linked steps in Derrida's reading of Pseudo-Dionysius may clarify this: first, his acknowledgment of a certain, seemingly formal, parallelism between apophatics and what has come to be known as deconstruction; second, his interpretation of the specific movement of the *hyper* of Dionysius's *hypertheology.* These two join hands, as it were, in Derrida's interpretation of the concept of prayer. In fact, the discussion of prayer — more precisely, of so-called pure prayer in its relation to the hymn or the encomium — reveals the relationship between the apophatic and the cataphatic as simultaneously one of abstraction, formalization, and emptiness

---

speak, this second reading of the "same" question asks what measures should be taken in order to prevent specific inappropriate — anthropomorphic, vulgar, idolatrous, and blasphemous — assertions or figures of speech, rather than predication or rhetoric *as such.* Thus, Derrida concludes, one passes from the problem "How to be silent?" to the question of "which speech to avoid, in order to be speak *well*" (ibid., 15 / 548). In short, one moves from the more general philosophical question "How is it possible not to speak at all?" to the more pragmatic (and, as we shall see, programmatological) problem "How is it necessary [and perhaps even responsible] to speak?" (ibid.). But, of course, the seemingly more interesting second understanding of the question conjures up the first as well: for what measures can be taken where one cannot measure the distance between words and a "referent," where the latter has no common measure with the former, but is incommensurable with all definite, finite, regional, and ontological meaning? And of what else can words speak if they speak at all or speak well?

and an acknowledgment of a certain presence, albeit a presence beyond being, a being otherwise than being, but also—following the very logic of the *hyper*—a being otherwise. To be sure, as in Dionysius, the apophatic moment has for Derrida a certain prevalence, and this leaves its mark on the notion of affirmation adopted here. But the cataphatic is by no means absent.

It is by clarifying this double movement, which never takes place without violence, in both directions and with the risk of coming face to face with the other of the other, with radical evil, the worst, the *a-dieu*—that one is able to explain why Derrida's incessant yet increasingly manifest preoccupation with the religious is neither the appropriation of its truth content or argumentative style, as Dufrenne suggests, nor their neutralization, as feared by Marion. The arguments of Dufrenne and Marion are far more subtle that I have been able to demonstrate here, and each often approaches Derrida's position. Nonetheless, they formulate as alternatives what should be thought and lived as one and the same aporetic experience.

Yet to move beyond these two powerful misreadings cannot mean to interpret the philosophical turn to religion as a mere—logical or theoretical—possibility of Derrida's writing. The turn to religion is also the "condition" or "incondition" of all possibility—of the conditions of possibility, whether they take the form of categories, of transcendentals, or of universals, that structure and orient our access to language, experience, and, indeed, the world.

But the conditioning for which the turn to religion is responsible does not take the form of a transcendental foundation, an existential opening, to say nothing here of the ontic relation of causation, let alone of formal relations of deduction and logical implication. Instead, the structure of the relation in question resembles, if anything, that of the quasi-performative of the promise: of a *quasi*-performative because, on the basis of a logic that Derrida formalizes in "Avances" (Advances), the promise entails and is contaminated by a threat of the worst as well. And this, Derrida points out, implies a break with some of the central presuppositions of the theories of the speech act and their determination of the essential features of the performative (here, of the promise).[63]

All this becomes particularly clear when one ponders the actual refer-

---

63. Derrida, *Adieu à Emmanuel Levinas*, 158.

ence, so to speak, of the apophatic discourse as read by Derrida. At first glance, it does not seem to imply a positive infinity of some superior entity (the highest Being, *ens realissimum, causa sui*), but rather evokes the latter's virtual opposite, without thereby positing something that could be conceived as simply finite, merely empirical, or purely ontic, and, in that limited sense, positive. Neither negative nor positive, the "object" under consideration here is not the referent of theology, which according Heidegger must be defined in its proper or original meaning as a positive science, just as much as, say, chemistry. It is far from certain, however, as will be demonstrated below, whether Heidegger's actual description of the premises and the structure of the science of faith and of Christianicity (*Christlichkeit*) does not unwittingly follow in the footsteps of the tradition of Christian apophatics that it ignores, just as much as it ignores the heritage of Jewish thought, both of rabbinical commentary and of its most severe antipode, Spinoza, whose writings, in their very advocacy of metaphysical immanentism, paradoxically testify to the same concern (as has been observed by Marion).

Derrida's reading of the apophatic also follows the apophatic object or referent in the opposite direction. The deconstructible presuppositions of virtually all negative theologies are relentlessly pointed out, but they are shown to be inevitable. If a "religion without religion" is what is aimed at here, this is likewise the affirmation of a full or fuller presence of sorts; in other words, of a relation to the religious object, albeit one that is not entertained religiously and lacks the deference and the distance—the relation without relation—that according to Levinas defines religion at its best (and, we should add, at its worst).

Here, as so often, one extreme calls forth the other. These different conceptions of the religious and the theological—as virtual almost-absence and as virtual fullest presence—presuppose each other, point to each other, call each other forth, and, finally, collapse into each other, to the point of becoming virtually indistinguishable from each other. And it is against this backdrop that, rather than laying the ground for a new, alternative—postmodern or deconstructive—theology (an *a*theology that, as Mark Taylor has suggested could serve as the present-day form of a hermeneutics of the death of God), Derrida's writings can be taken to reaffirm, if not justify, both the traditional ontotheological notion of God and whatever has come to take its place, or the place of God's name, including its most radical negations and denegations. It is only on this basis that one can understand Derrida's assertion that "the theological is a determined moment in the total movement of the trace." [64]

Yet, if the theological thus presents itself as a constitutive or essential instance or instantiation of *différance* (that is to say, of "the total movement of the trace"), rather than as a merely temporary or provisional one, what exactly is its "determined" function? Clearly, the theological is not the sum total—the alpha and omega—of "the movement of the trace," since it is only the latter's "determinate *moment.*" But does this exclude the hypothesis that the theological is much more than just a "moment"—even a "determinate moment"—among others? My main contention throughout this study is that this is not the case, and that we are dealing here, not with examples—religion, the apophatic, the apocalyptic, the mystic, the messianic, and the list is far from complete—but with the structure of exemplarity per se, which is first of all attributed to (or at least illustrated by) certain examples in particular.

Derrida's incessant reference to religious figures—to God, "for example"—should not (or not exclusively or even primarily) be seen as just one more telling "nonsynonymous substitution" for the notion of the trace or, for that matter, of the gift, of the promise, and so on and so forth. True, like the neologism *différance,* the theological paleonym is caught in and haunted by a "chain" of reiteration and displacement, by which it "lends itself to a certain number of nonsynonymous substitutions, *according to the necessity of the context*" (emphasis added).[65] But, in so doing, does the reference—the citation or re-citation—remain closer to the tradition of philosophical reflection than to that of theology (including negative theology), as Gasché insists? Such a view is based on an interpretation of the religious and theological examples that underestimates their strategic—and more than simply strategic—function; in other words, their economic and testimonial or even testamentary significance or signifyingness. The widespread use and abuse of religious tropes in Derrida's writings, "the theological"—God, "for example"—functions as a privileged example, indeed, as the example par excellence. We touch here on the example of a certain excellence, a performativity at its extreme, which lets itself be simultaneously inspired and haunted by "the

64. Jacques Derrida, *De la grammatologie* (Paris: Éditions de Minuit, 1967), 69, trans. Gayatri Chakravorty Spivak as *Of Grammatology* (Baltimore: Johns Hopkins University Press, 1976), 47, quoted in Gasché, *Inventions of Difference.*

65. Derrida, *Margins of Philosophy,* 12/13.

best" and "the worst," and is therefore not without relation to an emphatic, excessive, paradoxical, or even aporetic notion of "justice."

All this is not to say that these theologico-religious turns—revolving around the letter *a* of the *à dieu* at least as much as around the *a* of *différance*—announced an ethico-theology that had not yet come into its own, found its own voice, or that thus far had simply remained unwritten. One is reminded of the well-known accusation leveled at Heidegger and cited in his "Letter on Humanism," but the parallel holds only in part, since in the case of Derrida, the call for an ethics of sorts seems far more off the mark than it ever was with respect to the project of fundamental ontology or the thought of the Being that followed in its wake. True, the thought signaled by the *a* in *différance*, Derrida writes, is "not the primary prescription or the prophetic annunciation of an imminent and as yet unheard-of-nomination. There is nothing kerygmatic about this 'word.' " [66]

Mutatis mutandis, the same holds true for the *à dieu* and *adieu* that Derrida adopts from Levinas. And, while the reader may be surprised by the fact that Derrida thus insists on demarcating the word *différance* here from what is originally one of the New Testament's guiding concepts— and one, moreover, that is at the very heart of the first (or is it the second?) attempt to use Heidegger's early interpretation of the phenomenological method for the sake of theology: Rudolf Bultmann's hermeneutics of the biblical kerygma—we should not forget that the major aim of this passage is not by any means to discredit the ethical (or the political, the religious, etc.). The latter is not so much "secondarized" as put into a relation of mutual conditioning and possibilization, a relation-without-relation, strictly speaking, and one that undermines and displaces our very understanding of any "condition of possibility" that forms the central presupposition of transcendental philosophy in its classical, modern, and contemporary—transformative—forms.

The ways in which the religious and theological turns are put to work, not in the form of salvific proclamation, but worked through, or, more precisely, submitted to, a process of *désoeuvrement* or *inopération* (to use a formula introduced by Blanchot and rearticulated by Nancy), could be summarized and formalized as follows: they are as many "examples" of a writing and *un*writing that is no longer writing, pure and simple, like

66. Ibid., 27/29.

words brought to paper, but, Derrida says, a *pas d'écriture*. *Pas d'écriture,* in all the ambiguity of the French *pas*: a decisive *step* of writing, of *not* writing, of a *step away from* writing and, in particular, the problematic of *écriture* as such, of a graphical undoing of the written, of a grammatology that from now on, or more explicitly than even before, borders upon the "programmatological," thus putting words or the analysis of words into deeds, or rather exposing those deeds to their "passion," the passion, that is, from which they stem and to which they lead—all these meanings illuminate the complex figure that interests us here. In fact, the *adieu*—naming a movement to and away from "God," and to and away from every other that comes to take "His" place (a movement, lest we forget, that is ultimately *à Dieu* in yet another sense: "up to" "God," and thus up to the other)—cannot only be read as a further "nonsynonymous substitution," to which each of the equivocal characteristics of the *pas d'écriture* is attached, but may also allow us to interpret the aporias of this *pas d'écriture*—and thus of the very "principle" of "nonsynonymous substitution"—in the most economic, strategic, and responsible manner.

Why this is so has more to do with the "necessity of the context" of which Derrida speaks in "La Différance" than with empirical data bespeaking a "return of religion" (whether in the form of newly revived fundamentalisms and nationalisms or in the guise of an unprecedented global virtualization of reality). Rather, it is a consequence of the fact that a singular—and infinitely *finite*—instance may at one point arrive at a certain prominence, if not necessarily hegemony, in what ultimately remains an in principle *infinite* series of nonsynonymous substitutions. Moreover, the said prevalence of the religious, signaled in all its ambiguity by the *adieu,* has everything to do with the persisting relevance—and, indeed, rediscovery—of the "archive" of the religions of the Book, which continues to underpin Western concepts of responsibility (of ethics, politics, Enlightenment, democracy, the human, the animal, etc.). This "archive," it is fair to say, seems the most extensive and most inventive resource for ideas, practices, and beliefs, for good and for ill. And to describe it merely in empirical (historical, philological, archaeological) terms, would certainly be to underestimate the ways in which it has shaped and has been shaped by the central categories, transcendentals, and universals of Western thought. To determine the nature of this mutual influence, we would need a genealogy like the one sketched out by Husserl's *The Crisis of European Sciences and Transcendental Phenomenology,* formalized and forcefully deployed with ever more consequence by Derrida, notably in his

early inquiry into the concept of transcendental historicity in his introduction to Husserl's *The Origin of Geometry*.[67]

As a *pas d'écriture*, the *à dieu* can also be seen as a *pas de Dieu*: a step of
God, toward God, given by God, but also off in another direction, walking with and without God, walking on two feet, as it were, stepping in
the footprints of God and of whatever it is that comes in His wake, without being preoccupied with His existence, essential properties, or proper
names. For the figure, the desire, and promise of "God," while the best
exemplary instance of the structure of the trace (of *différance* and each of
its supplementary substitutions), seems to introduce, first of all, if not an
*indifference,* then at least a certain distance or freedom with respect to the
question of Being, its categories and modalities, its dimension and truth.
In a sense, the *adieu* or *à dieu* "is" always already "there," but, paradoxically, never localizable—that is to say, determinable or decidable. Being
there, it could just as well not have been there at all. It is only there *as
though it were not.* Or, conversely, not quite there, it makes itself all the
more felt and becomes ever more effective in reorienting our gaze, in in-
flecting and, as Levinas used to say, "curving a given social space."

This explains why Derrida can write, for example in *On the Name,* that
the double genitive of the phrase "the desire *of* God" (*genitivus subjectivus*
and *objectivus*) is equivocal, to say the least. Indeed, its origin, direction,
and even addressee are uncertain. What is certain, however, is that, in
an almost clandestine manner, it slips into every history of thought and
representation, whether theological, ontotheological, or neither. Derrida
writes:

> [D]oes it come from God in us, from God for us, from us for God? And as we
> do not determine *ourselves before* this desire, as no relation to self can be sure
> of preceding it, to wit, of preceding a relation to the other, . . . all reflection is
> caught in the genealogy of this genitive. I understand by that a reflection on
> self, on autobiographical reflection, for example, as well as a reflection on the
> idea or on the name of God. (SN 37 / 20)

That said, taking "God" as the example par excellence does not entail
ascribing a supreme mode of existence to His being or to everything for

---

67. Edmund Husserl, *Die Krisis der europäischen Wissenschaften und die transzendentale
Phänomenologie,* ed. Walter Biemel (The Hague: Martinus Nijhoff, 1962), trans. David Carr as
*The Crisis of European Sciences and Transcendental Phenomenology* (Evanston, Ill.: Northwest-
ern University Press, 1970).

which the notion "God" stands. It merely means that "God" is, in a way, the *most substitutable* notion, that is to say, substitutes for most, and substitutes for the most. "God" is the best word for the trace, for its always possible and necessary erasure, not only for every other as the totally other—as Derrida's "Tout autre est tout autre" suggests—but just as much for the other or others of each of these singular others, ad infinitum.

BEFORE DISCUSSING these matters in sufficient detail, it should be noted, in concluding, that aside from being a text on originary affirmation rather than on negativity, denegation, and its functional equivalents, "How To Avoid Speaking" is just as much a treatise on *place*—that is to say, on the trope, the topos, topology—as an inquiry into the specifically linguistic problem of ineffability, of the unsayable in its relation to what can and cannot be said, or to what it is possible and impossible to say, state, and write: "Even if one speaks and says nothing, even if an apophatic discourse deprives itself of meaning or of an object, it *takes place* [emphasis added here]. That which committed or rendered it possible *has taken place*" (HAS 27–28 / 559).

In Pseudo-Dionysius, as in Plato, Eckhart, Angelus Silesius, Heidegger, and Derrida, this privilege of the place determines apophatics in many decisive ways. The apophatic approach to place, as distinguished from the Platonic motif of the *chōra* and its reception, is typified by the claim found in mystical texts, in Pseudo-Dionysius's *On Mystical Theology* as well as in Eckhart's sermons, that one cannot see God face-to-face but can only find access to the divine place where He resides. However, this motif goes hand in hand with an "atopics" of God, for if God gives himself to be contemplated in a place, this place—the divine place—is not itself God.

By the same token, the thought of the gift and the *es gibt* of Being and time—a thought, Derrida writes, that "progressively and profoundly displace[s] the question of Being and its transcendental horizon, time, in *Sein und Zeit*"—must be seen as the "opening up" of space. This relationship between the gift and Being does not primarily consist in the reversal of their logical, ontological, or axiological order. For indeed, the very question of "order" remains internal to a conceptual realm whose givenness is precisely what must be thought. Rather, Derrida concludes, "the thinking of the gift opens up the space in which Being and time give themselves and themselves to thought." The *ultima ratio*, then, of all these discursive strategies and their historical practices—from Plato, through Pseudo-Dionysius, down to Eckhart, Heidegger, and Marion—is, as Derrida, in his incessant references to *le lieu,* to the "place" at the heart or, rather, at threshold of any language of the ineffable, shows, a topology, a "theotopography," or, more precisely, a "theotopolitology."[68]

68. See my "Theotopographies" and "*Winke.*"

# Chapter Two

# Hypertheology

IN THE MODERN PERIOD, Derrida notes, the term *negative theology* no longer exclusively refers to a historically articulated doctrine, but has more and more "come to designate a certain typical attitude toward language, and within it, in the act of definition or attribution, an attitude toward semantic or conceptual determination" (HAS 4/536). It is by a process of increasing formalization of the *via negativa*—a progressive "kenosis" of discourse that tends to abstract from dogmatic content, as well as from its so-called secular reinscriptions—that the range of a diacritical deployment of this figure (and thereby of its possible practical effects) has also been vastly expanded. For the best and for the worst, since the figure in question provides the key to the problem of evil—to *radical evil*, as Derrida puts it, following Kant—no less than to that of justice, not to distributive justice, to be sure, but to justice in the emphatic and excessive, Benjaminian or, rather, Levinasian sense of the word.

But then again, was there ever a substance that allowed us—in retrospect—to measure the distance between the mystic injunction as a pure performative, on the one hand, and a dogmatic content or context from which it sets itself apart? Derrida doesn't say so, but suggests that this presupposition may always have been the illusion—a transcendental illusion of sorts—without which no kenotic attitude toward language can come into its own. Yet stripped of this canonical or heterodox substance, the supposedly negative operation of apophatics was stretched to its limit, and this to the point of becoming virtually indistinguishable from any other purely formal discursive strategy. The *via negativa* thus seemed to have become the privileged "nonsynonymous substitution" for all negative operations, whether philosophical, aesthetic, literary, psychoanalytic, ethico-political, or even existential. God, the notion "God," it would seem, delivered the key to the understanding of the nothing (the *Nichts*) and the particular negative operation (the *Nichten*) of which Heidegger speaks with so much fervor.

Against this backdrop, Derrida proposes a thought experiment based on a possible analogy or family resemblance between an extremely for-malized, one might say consistent, negative theology and any responsible thought of the trace or of *différance:*

> Suppose, by a provisional hypothesis, that negative theology consists of con-sidering that every predicative language is inadequate to the essence, in truth to the hyperessentiality (the being beyond Being) of God; consequently only a negative ("apophatic") attribution can claim to approach God, and to prepare us for a silent intuition of God. By *a more or less tenable analogy,* one would thus recognize some traits, the *family resemblance* of negative theology, in every discourse that seems to return in a regular and insistent manner to this rhetoric of negative determination, endlessly multiplying the defenses and the apophatic warnings: this, which is called X (for example, text, writing, the trace, *différance,* the hymen, the supplement, the pharmakon, the parergon, etc.) "is" neither this nor that, neither sensible nor intelligible, neither posi-tive nor negative, neither inside nor outside, neither superior nor inferior, neither active nor passive, neither present nor absent, not even neutral, not even subject to a dialectic with a third moment, without any possible sub-lation ("Aufhebung"). Despite appearances, then, this X is neither a concept nor even a name; it does lend itself to a series of names, but calls for another syntax, and exceeds even the order and the structure of predicative discourse. It "is" not and does not say what "is." It is written completely otherwise. (HAS 4/536; emphasis added)

The seemingly metaphysical concept of analogy and the more Wittgen-steinian notion of the family resemblance serve as technical terms, chosen here to illuminate a mode of comparison, of interleaving, of intersec-tion, and of resonance that goes well beyond that of a merely accidental, contingent, or purely empirical, some would say ontic, association. An in-delible interplay and co-implication of *chance* and *necessity* (of *tuchē* and *anankē*) is at work here, one that draws on an even older archive, which seems now out of reach; and this, I would venture to say, not only for the strategic or provisional use of such concepts as "analogy" or "family re-semblance" (marked as they are by Aristotelian, scholastic, and pragmatic overtones respectively), but also, in the final analysis, for the very idea of transcendental historicity, which comes closest to being the key to the problem at hand.

But the invocation of *la Chance* and *la Nécessité* does not dispel the obvious difficulty of determining whether the given examples of the non-synonymous substitutions mentioned above should be seen either as so many radical transformative reversals of an ancient paradigm, stripped of its overtly theological connotations, or as that paradigm's secret prolongation. This uncertainty functions as the silent axiom and central theme, if there is one (or just one), of Derrida's "How To Avoid Speaking" and sheds light on its dealing with the question of language, the tropes of space and place, and the oblique discussion of apophatic anthropology. "For essential reasons one is never certain of being able to attribute to anyone a project of negative theology as such," Derrida observes (HAS 3–4 / 535–36).

The least one can say is that in recent forms of critical and post-structuralist theory—for example, deconstruction—the persistence of the negative mode of predication—of denials and denegations, evasions and ellipses—seems as inevitable as its always possible confusion with religious apophatics. In Derrida's own words:

> From the moment a proposition takes a negative form, the negativity that manifests itself need only to be pushed to the limit, and it at least resembles an apophatic theology. Every time I say: X is neither this nor that, neither the simple neutralization of this nor of that with which is *has nothing in common,* being absolutely heterogeneous to or incommensurable with them, I would start to speak of God, under this name or another. God's name would then be the hyperbolic effect of that negativity or of all negativity that is consistent in its discourse. (HAS 6 / 538)

All negative predication would somehow "produce divinity" (HAS 6 / 538), infinitely substituting the name (rather than the concept) of God or of whatever comes to take His place. All genuine or radical negativity could be said to be "haunted" by the ghost of "God" and thus to be responsive to a spectral figure—that of the *à dieu*—that is neither identifiable with a full presence nor reducible to the latter's mere abstract negation. Every thought deserving of the name would be faithful to this promise, to the putting forth of this figure (saying *adieu* and speaking *à dieu,* apophatically and cataphatically) and, in so doing, to putting *itself* before this very figure as well. What is more, it would have to promise to do so, not conditionally, but regardless of the future to come, in *any* future to come.

Conversely, divinity is not only "produced" but "productive"—or promising—in its turn. Put otherwise, "God," under this name or another, is not just the ineffable *telos* of every old and new *via negativa,* but also its very origin, its *archē*, or rather *an-archē*, and, in that sense, its first and last word:

> "God" would name *that without which* one would not know how to account for any negativity: grammatical or logical negation, illness, evil, and finally neurosis, which, far from permitting psychoanalysis to reduce religion to a symptom, would obligate it to recognize in the symptom the negative manifestation of God. Without saying that there must be at least as much "reality" in the cause as in the effect [the classic premise of the so-called cosmological argument for the existence of God—HdV], and that the "existence" of God has need of any proof other than the religious symptomatics, one would see on the contrary—in the negation or suspension of the predicate, even of the thesis of "existence"—the first mark of respect for a divine cause which does not even need to "be."[1]

If deconstruction is seen as the most consistent apophatic discourse, Derrida continues, one could indeed always choose to consider it simply "a symptom of modern or postmodern nihilism," or, on the contrary, "recognize in it the last testimony—not to say the martyrdom—of faith in the present *fin de siècle*. This reading will always be possible" (HAS 7/ 539).

However, to say this is not to deny that the purported analogy between deconstruction and negative theology remains, in a way, also arbitrary, provisional, problematic, hypothetical, and even questionable: a begging of the very question of each of these two radically distinct discursive models, which are different in terms of their historical resources and aspirations. Or so it seems. For it should be clear from what we have found so far that the confessed analogy or family resemblance is by no means a simple retraction of Derrida's earlier statements that the thought of *différance* and the *via negativa* of apophatic theology differ in many crucial respects. If anything, these statements are now qualified or nuanced: *insofar* as negative theology still presupposes a trajectory that is propositional

---

1. HAS 7/538–39. Up to certain point, "God" would occupy the same place as the Nothing, the *Nichts*, that gives itself in the grounding experience (*Grunderfahrung*) of anxiety, or *Angst*, and of which Heidegger speaks compellingly in "Was ist Metaphysik?" (in *Wegmarken*, 103–21, 110, trans. as "What Is Metaphysics?" in *Pathmarks*, ed. McNeill, 82–96, 87). By contrast (although there is no real opposition here), the experience of "God" would resemble "our joy in the presence of the Dasein—and not simply the person—of a human being whom we love" ("die Freude an der Gegenwart des Daseins—nicht der blossen Person—eines geliebten Menschen"), of which Heidegger speaks here.

"and privileges not only the indestructible unity of the word but also the authority of the name" (HAS 7/539); *insofar,* moreover, as negative theology "seems to reserve beyond all positive predication, beyond all negation, even beyond Being, some hyperessentiality, a being beyond Being" (HAS 7–8/540); and *insofar,* finally, as negative theology stands and falls with the assumption (or the promise) of an ultimate intuition, a *visio* and *unio mystica* — *insofar,* then, as each of these deconstructible assumptions or postulates still seem to apply to what is called "negative theology," the latter remains to be sharply distinguished from what has come to be known as deconstruction. The latter, it seems, is analogous only to the most heterodox or the most orthodox — in any case, the most rigorous — apophatic theologies, not to those that go only halfway, leaving many presuppositions intact. However, to the extent that these presuppositions are unavoidable — that is to say, cannot be prevented from returning, but continue to be legible, visible, audible, or otherwise perceptible and intuitable under the marks of their erasure (and, in the era of metaphysics and its simple reversals that happens at every moment, everywhere), the confusion and, indeed, conflation of deconstruction with negative theology will persist, just as much as their radical distinction also remains necessary. Therefore, as Heidegger makes clear, both the ontotheological and the radically heterodox heritages of the *via negativa* cast their shadows indiscriminately well beyond modern attempts to illuminate their premises and implications.[2]

This said, it is clear that Derrida's attempts to reassess the question of "How to avoid speaking" — viewed here according to its form, regardless of whether it speaks of God or of Being — cannot and do not pretend to do justice to either apophatics or deconstruction, or cannot do so without testifying to their seeming confusion, that is to say, to their apparent substitutability. Nor is it clear how speaking of apophatics, how speaking apophatically — but also how speaking of deconstruction or speaking deconstructively — could simply be avoided in this day and age and at least for some time to come.

As a consequence, the question of how to avoid speaking of "God," of Being, and of whatever comes to take their place or adopts their name

2. It is no accident that, from the introduction to *Being and Time* on, Heidegger uses a notion of *Aufklärung* and, more generally, the metaphor of light and darkness in order to point the path from preontological to ontological understanding of the phenomena at hand. This should not be confused with mere repetition or continuation of the so-called project of modern Enlightenment but is not quite separable from it either.

can no longer be assigned a proper place, whether in the discourse of apophatics or in the practice of deconstruction. Nor can one hope to approach this question meta-theoretically, empirically, or historically without immediately being drawn into the equation. Speaking of one, we may well be speaking — in the place or in the name — of the other, or vice versa. It is impossible to tell the difference.

Clarification of the relationship between deconstruction and apophatics is in the end nothing but an unfulfillable promise, and one that threatens to blur all the necessary distinctions at that. In other words, the result of any attempt to disentangle all the relevant threads and overlaps, intersections and overtones, remains for ever pending, not for lack of rigor, but because this is the precise answer we must expect. What is intelligible is only that there is a certain unintelligibility here. "One can never decide whether deferring, as such, brings about precisely that which it defers and alters [*diffère*]," Derrida says. "It is not certain that I am keeping my promise today; nor is it certain that in further delaying I have not, nevertheless, already kept it" (HAS 13 / 546).

As so often, Derrida's analysis performs here what it seeks to circumscribe, speaking of negative theology, not just in terms of a promise or with reference to the promise, but also, paradoxically, "*within the promise*" (HAS 14 / 547; emphasis added). It is only consequent that he indicates a little later in a similar vein: "I thus decided *not to speak* of negativity or of apophatic movements in, for example, the Jewish or Islamic traditions. To leave this immense place empty, . . . to remain thus on the threshold — was this not the most consistent possible apophasis?"[3]

It is precisely this moment of suspense — an *epochē* of sorts — that accounts for the fact that Derrida's reading of negative theology in its traditional and most unexpected modern guises not only mimics or mirrors the structure and privileged figures of the apophatic way but runs the risk of becoming its parody and, indeed, its most severe betrayal. The analysis of apophatics proposed here — which appears as an apophatics of deconstruction no less than as a deconstruction of apophatics, or as both at once — could therefore just as well be a form of ultimate respect as a sign

---

3. HAS 53 / 584. "How to speak suitably of negative theology?" Derrida asks. "Is there a negative theology? A single one? A regulative model for the others? Can one adopt a discourse to it? Is there some discourse that measures up to it? Is one not compelled to speak of negative theology according to the modes of negative theology, in a way that is at once impotent, exhausting, and inexhaustible? Is there ever anything other than a 'negative theology' of 'negative theology'?" (HAS 13 / 546)

of its opposite, that is to say, of blasphemy and idolatry. Again, the difference between these two extremes would be virtually impossible to tell. It
gives itself to be seen only to those who are willing and are able to see and
to testify to it; and this means, paradoxically, only to those who are willing and able to pass through the trial of this uncertainty. If anywhere, it is
here that we would touch upon the heart of the apophatic anthropology
that accompanies the tradition of negative theology and leaves its mark
on Derrida's writing as well.

As long as complete silence is impossible—and even silence speaks
(or can be telling enough) where it turns away from a particular "saying" or "said" or even "contradicts" the virtual totality of all that is said
or can be said—apophatic discourse will always simultaneously say too
little and too much. Again, the difference between these two seemingly
opposite possibilities or extremes is almost impossible to discern. Each
of them is inappropriate and therefore blasphemous, idolatrous, with the
respect to the referent (whether God, a hyperessence, the trace, or some
"nonsynonymous substitute"). In extremis, they converge to the point of
becoming at least formally interchangeable. Saying too much or too little,
as one cannot but do when one speaks—and one cannot but speak—the
difference matters little. The only way out of this impasse, therefore, seems
to be the one Jean-Luc Marion takes from Pascal's *Pensées:* only "God can
well speak of God."[4] Everything else, every attempt to speak well—one
way or another—is vanity, hypocrisy, idolatry.

Yet can we allow God this very possibility, as Pascal and Marion think
we should and indeed must? Does God not already contradict Himself,
as Derrida claims, following Jabès? Is God, the name or the concept, but
also the "positive reality" and "presence" of God, in its very existence or
essence, in and for itself, any more stable than anything else? Can God,
for Himself, address Himself, without missing the point, without speaking already, as it were, off the mark?

True, the very notion of God implies and demands a full presence
of Himself to Himself, an adequate self-reference, self-representation, or
auto-affection, in addition to all divine names, epithets, and predicates,

---

4. Blaise Pascal, *Pensées,* ed. Brunschvicq, no. 799, trans. A. J. Krailsheimer (New York:
Penguin Books, 1966), 123. The Pascal of the *Pensées* is a thinker "in whom one could at times
discern the genius or the machine of apophatic dialectics," Derrida observes in *Sauf le nom
(Post-Scriptum)* (Paris: Galilée, 1993), 88, trans. John P. Leavey, Jr., in *On the Name,* ed. Thomas
Dutoit (Stanford: Stanford University Press, 1995), 72 (hereafter cited parenthetically in the
text as SN, followed by the English and French page numbers).

which the tradition of philosophical theology has investigated with indefatigable inventiveness, to the point where there is almost nothing to
say that has not already been said. Even a superficial reading of Pseudo-
Dionysius's *The Divine Names* and *The Mystical Theology*, to which I turn
below, reveals that almost all thinkable categories and adjectives are carefully recited and reassessed, only to be found wanting to a greater or lesser
degree. Nonetheless, they are never discarded, but remain in place as necessary stepping-stones on the way that leads upward and then downward,
upward by leading downward, and vice versa. Dionysius's usage of these
so-called divine names is — anachronistically speaking — marked by a certain performativity, and thereby repetition, that is far more pertinent
than any search for the one appropriate and holy name. This is hardly
an accident, but obeys a certain historical logic of traditionality, indeed,
of transcendental historicity. A similar motif can be found in Heidegger's insistence, in his early courses on the phenomenology of religion, on
the New Testament — indeed, Pauline — temporality of the *again of the already*, to which I turn in the next chapter. This structure captures the very
dynamics and rhythm of Heidegger's formally indicative method, which,
in turn, forms the heart of the procedure of ontological correction.

## The Unavoidable

Aspiring to rehearse the apophatic gesture and keep its distance at
the same time, Derrida's "How to Avoid Speaking" can, in the end, only
present us with a "fabulous narration" (*narration fabuleuse*) (HAS 30 /
562; see also 60 / 592). In Derrida's vocabulary, informed as it is by both
Francis Ponge's "Fable" (compare the opening pages of Derrida's *Psyché*)[5]
and Michel de Certeau's *La Fable mystique*, the word *fable* does not so
much stand for the fictive or the literary (let alone for a merely aesthetic
mode of presentation), as for the "condition of possibility" of these respective genres: a certain "fictionality" or "literacity" that both fiction
and literature (as well as the aesthetic) share in principle with the philosophical, the ontological, and the theological. This fabulosity is precisely
what qualifies the central meaning, often noted, of what Derrida calls the
quasi-transcendental.

Much more is at stake here, however, than a "condition of possibility,"

5. Francis Ponge, "Fable," in *Proêmes*, 1: *Natare piscem doces* (Paris: Gallimard, 1948) and
*Tome premier* (Paris: Gallimard, 1965). See also Derrida, *Psyché*, 18–19, and *Signéponge/Sign-
sponge*, trans. Richard Rand, bilingual edition (New York: Columbia University Press, 1984),
102–3.

or a redefinition of the concept of the transcendental. Derrida's more re-cent writings — and, again, this is most notable in his interrogations of the religious and the theological — are increasingly concerned with a singular structure of singularity that seems to absolve itself from the logic of the possible as such, from the thinking of "possibilization," and this at least as much as it outwits the conditions that are commonly defined as ontico-ontological, empirical, semantic, pragmatic or symbolic. It seems as if the law of the possible is increasingly suspected of being indebted to a meta-physical tradition that Derrida describes as a "logic of presupposition." Of the latter no clearer example can be found than in Heidegger's fun-damental ontology and existential analytic, which for all its modification and radicalization continues to be a foundationalism, a possibilism, and even a humanism in disguise. In the two following chapters, I shall pro-vide some of the most important reasons that enable Derrida to make this far-reaching claim.

In the writings that interest us here, Derrida's attention is focused on the testimonial, the confessional, and the secret, all of which relate to the question of autobiography. What is more, they each in their singular way redraw the lines of the debate that has come to dominate the reception of J. L. Austin's *How to Do Things With Words,* in speech-act theory as well as in contemporary cultural analysis: the distinction between the consta-tive and the performative, the place of the first person singular and plural, the structure of the promise, the nature of repetition, or rather reitera-tion (or, as Derrida's *Limited Inc.* has it, of iterability), and so on. But the often implicit revisiting of these terms leaves none of them untouched or intact. And this relegation of these basic terms to the metaphysics of pres-ence (in the case of the constative and the prominence of the first person singular), as well as its exposure to or reinscription into the language of religion or apophatics (in the case of the performative and the promise), makes room for — and, indeed, gestures toward — a quite different experi-ence of words and things, one that escapes, not only the parameters of speech-act theory originally or commonly defined, but also the premises of its redeployments in current cultural theory.

Once again, this redescription leaves nothing intact. And the perfor-mativity around which Derrida's analyses of the apophatic and religion "at large" revolve is therefore at once that of a performative called abso-lute (or ab-solute) and one that undercuts the very concept and theory of performatives. It is no accident that in *The Postcard,* in the section entitled

"Envois," Derrida speaks, if only in passing, of the "perverformative."[6] Yet it is precisely in this intrinsic instability or aporetics that the performativity of which we speak here can be said to border upon the most salient features of the *via negativa* and, indeed, of mystic speech. There is no better example of the meaning of the "perverformative" than the dictum that guides this entire discussion: "God already contradicts himself." It both captures the singular structure of performativity that interest us here—a performative contradiction or performative aporetics of sorts— and reminds us that this structure cannot adequately be described *in abstracto*, but should, perhaps, best be seen in terms of a certain historico-theological overdetermination for which "God" is still the best and the most economical name. Hegel was right, then, albeit for other reasons than those the *Wissenschaft der Logik* provides: "und das unbestrittenste Recht hätte *Gott*, dass mit ihm der Anfang gemacht werde" ("and *God* would have the absolutely undisputed right that the beginning be made with him").[7]

The study of Jewish and Arab esoteric thought, a paradigm in our cultural heritage that approaches the apophatic—and thus, by analogy, deconstruction—even more closely than the Greco-Christian tradition, might enable us to grasp this better, Derrida suggests in "How to Avoid Speaking," but this path is not taken there. Discussions of Plato, Pseudo-Dionysius, Eckhart, Marion, Levinas, and Wittgenstein have a prominent place, but references to Jewish and Arabic mystics are absent or remain implicit. Derrida speaks of them—perhaps from within them, away from them, and toward them, apophatically and cataphatically, as it were—but without speaking *about* them, at least not directly.

Instead, he turns to yet another apophatics, one that is neither simply Greek and Christian nor Jewish or Arab, but that may nonetheless very well "resemble the most questioning legacy, both the most audacious and most liberated repetition" (HAS 53 / 584) of Greco-Christian apophatics, to wit, Heidegger's questioning of Western metaphysics. Having questioned the Greek and Christian paradigms, he extends his analysis to

---

6. Jacques Derrida, *La Carte postale: De Socrate à Freud et au-delà* (Paris: Flammarion, 1980), 148, trans. Alan Bass as *The Postcard: From Socrates to Freud and Beyond* (Chicago: University of Chicago Press, 1987), 136.

7. G. W. F. Hegel, *Wissenschaft der Logik* (Frankfurt a./M.: Suhrkamp: 1986), 1: 79, trans. A. V. Miller as *Hegel's Science of Logic* (Atlantic Highlands, N.J.: Humanities Press International, 1969), 78; trans. modified.

the inquiry into "a few landmarks" (HAS 53/584) on Heidegger's path
of thinking. These landmarks help to measure the degree to which the
thought of Being, in its destruction of ontotheology, can itself, in turn,
be shown to touch upon the theological, and to do so, moreover, in ways
that Heidegger is generally at great pains to *avoid*. As is perhaps nowhere
clearer than in Heidegger's texts, the apophatic lets itself neither be bracketed (phenomenologically or otherwise) nor be crossed out. Citing one of
Heidegger's "landmarks," Derrida writes:

> [Heidegger says:] "Faith has no need for the thinking of Being." As he often
> recalls, Christians ought to allow themselves to be inspired by Luther's lu-
> cidity on this subject. Indeed, even if Being is "neither the foundation nor
> the essence of God [*Grund und Wesen von Gott*]," the experience of God (*die
> Erfahrung Gottes*) — that is, the experience of revelation — "occurs in the di-
> mension of Being [*in der Dimension des Seins sich ereignet*]." This revelation
> is not that (*Offenbarung*) of which the religions speak, but the possibility of
> this revelation, the opening for this manifestation . . . [the] *Offenbarkeit* . . . in
> which an *Offenbarung* can take place and man can encounter God. Although
> God is not and need not be thought from Being as His essence or foundation,
> the *dimension of Being* opens up access to the advent, the experience, the en-
> counter with this God who nevertheless is not. The word *dimension* — which is
> also difference — here gives a measure while giving place. One could sketch a
> singular chiasmus. The anguished experience of the Nothing discloses Being.
> Here, the dimension of Being discloses the experience of God, who is not or
> whose Being is neither the essence nor the foundation.
>
> How not to think of this? This dimension of disclosure, this place that gives
> place without being either essence or foundation — would not this step or pas-
> sage, this threshold that gives access to God, yet be the "parvis" (*vorbürge*) of
> which Meister Eckhart spoke? "When we apprehend God in Being, we appre-
> hend Him in His outer sanctuary [*parvis*], for Being is the *parvis* in which He
> resides." Is this a theological, an onto-theological, tradition? A theological
> tradition? Would Heidegger adopt it? Would he disown it? Would he deny it?
> (HAS 58–59/591–92)

Derrida does not answer these questions in any direct or decisive way.
And for good reason. For not only do we touch here upon an undecidable debate, the one that goes on and on, indefinitely, between Heidegger
and the Christian theologians (as is suggested in an almost comical way
by the closing argument and the last few pages of *Of Spirit*); these questions reflect on the status of Derrida's own position as well. In both cases,

they testify to the difficulty one will always have in establishing a proper domain for the question of Being or the philosophical as such, in contradistinction to that of the theological, the apophatic, and the religion of which (on the basis or in view of which) they speak, irresistibly, unavoidably, yet always in vain.[8]

8. In *La Dette impensée: Heidegger et l'héritage hébraïque* (Paris: Éditions du Seuil, 1990), her sequel to *Heidegger et les paroles de l'origine* (Paris: Vrin, 1986), a book prefaced and inspired by Levinas, Marlène Zarader finds in Derrida's *De l'esprit: Heidegger et la question* (Paris: Galilée, 1987), trans. Geoffrey Bennington and Rachel Bowlby as *Of Spirit: Heidegger and the Question* (Chicago: Chicago University Press, 1989), a partial confirmation of her own reading of Heidegger's evasion and reinscription of the religious tradition, notably the one that precedes the Greek and Roman features of Christianity in its determination of *pneuma* and *spiritus* and that is epitomized by the Hebrew notion of *ruah*. She also suggests that Heidegger avoids or denegates the structural resemblance between his ultimate interpretation of *Geist* (spirit) as *Flamme* (flame) in *Unterwegs zur Sprache* (Pfullingen: Neske, 1990), trans. Peter D. Hertz as *On the Way to Language* (New York: Harper, 1971). But she disagrees with Derrida's conclusion that we do in fact find ourselves here in an implicit, virtual debate whose main characteristic is that Heidegger and "the theologians" attempt to outbid each other in their quest for the originary. Following a line of interpretation that we encountered earlier in the work of Gasché, but that must result, perhaps, from any *philosophically* oriented reading of Derrida's writing, Zarader claims that *Of Spirit* seems finally to side with Heidegger. In maintaining that the meaning of *Geist* as flame must, indeed, be thought of as more originary than the meaning of either *ruah, pneuma,* or *spiritus* that it makes possible, Derrida would thus endorse what *Aporias* calls Heidegger's "logic of presupposition" and this regardless of his obvious displacement of the existential analytic (or fundamental ontology) in the direction of the quasi-transcendental thinking of *différance*.

But the gesture that turns Derrida's undertaking, here and elsewhere, into much more than the retrieval of the unthought Hebrew heritage—of the forgotten, avoided, negated, and denegated notions of *yet another spirit in flames,* of *ruah*—is precisely the fact that in his reading, this tradition is *just as much* originated by *Geist* (as *Flamme,* in Heidegger's sense) as the other way around. Each reveals and conceals the other; each is, in a sense, the "unthought debt" of the other. As a consequence, Derrida goes further than stating, as Zarader does, that Heidegger's thought ought to be situated in what it claims to make possible and that it even fails to mention as one of its most significant historical instances. For Derrida seems to insists on a certain co-originarity of the structural (formal or even quasi-ontological), on the one hand, and the concretely historical or traditional, on the other. What is more, the very distinction between the two, philosophically necessary as it may be, is in the end impossible to determine rigorously or once and for all. In Derrida's reading, a certain logic of the undecidable must therefore displace a certain logic of presupposition and its corresponding demarcation of the primary and the derivative, the a priori and the a posteriori, the proper and the impure.

Indeed, Heidegger forgets or avoids speaking of the Hebrew heritage and its understanding of *ruah* and the role the latter may or may not have played in the historical emergence of *pneuma,* of *spiritus,* and, who knows, of *Geist.* Yet the exact reason for Zarader's disagreement with Derrida can be found in the fact that she construes an alternative or dilemma where for Derrida there is none: "In the final analysis, there are only two coherent gestures: either one ignores, as Heidegger does, the Hebraic dimension (and thus chases from history that which exceeds the Greek dawn), or one takes it into account, as Derrida does, one restores it in history—something that necessarily leads to showing, not only the limits of the Heideggerian

## Yet Another "Non-Theo-Anthropological Otherness"

These analyses prepare the ground for an answer to the seemingly simple, yet startling question: Why, notwithstanding the expectations raised by so many of his titles (e.g., "How to Avoid Speaking" and *Sauf le nom*), is Derrida's inquiry into the argumentative and rhetorical protocols of negative theology and mysticism centered, not so much on the problem of the sayable and the unsayable but rather on the question of *le lieu,* the locus, the place, the situation, in which or from which or through which words may be spoken or sent? How, moreover, are we to relate these notions to concepts and tropes such as dimension, horizon, the desert, the island, the gorge, Mount Moriah, and Jerusalem, but also the utopian (*le non-lieu*), not to mention the "space" that has in our day become prefixed by that most transgressive of all apophatic terms, the adverb *hyper?*

In recent years, much attention has been paid to the alliance between deconstruction and certain developments in contemporary architecture, a debate to which Derrida himself has contributed in multiple ways. Par-

---

conception of historicality [*historialité*], but, by the same token [*du même coup*], *the already historical character of what Heidegger presented as pre-originary*" (*Dette impensée,* 197, trans. HdV). Immediately following this statement, Zarader recapitulates the general rule that seems to govern Heidegger's avoidance of the Hebrew tradition, and this not only in the few places, highlighted by Derrida, where he speaks of spirit. It is in this second, more general, assessment of Heidegger's itinerary that Zarader comes closest to Derrida's reading of the religious heritage in Heidegger's work and that of others, including his own: "Instead of privileging one gesture rather than another . . . , ought one not attempt to grasp them *together* [*ensemble*], like to the two faces of one and the same act? And of grasping them together, not only with regard to a particular question (that of spirit), but as characteristics of the Heideggerian questioning as such? . . . How can one think the singular articulation that reveals itself there: the thinker who has, more deeply [*plus amplement*] than any other, *restored* to Western thought the central determinations of the Hebraic universe is precisely the one who has never said anything about the Hebraic as such, who has—more massively than any other—effaced it from thought and, more extensively, from the West?" (ibid., trans. HdV).

   Mutatis mutandis, this quotation anticipates the central thesis I defend throughout this book: *the task—and, indeed, conceptual necessity—of being at once at the furthest remove from and as close as possible to the tradition called religious.* This being said, Zarader assumes on the whole a far greater fidelity with respect to Heidegger's thinking on Derrida's part than, I think, is warranted by even the last three pages of *De l'esprit,* on which she bases her critical discussion, let alone by the many other relevant writings I am attempting to read in a different light in this study. As I have suggested already, Derrida's reservations vis-à-vis Heidegger are perhaps nowhere clearer than in his rereading of the latter's avoidance of the conflation or even intersection of philosophy or thought, on the one hand, and theology or religion, on the other. For Derrida's interpretation of Heidegger's assessment of spirituality and Christianity, as well as the former's reservations with regard to the overhasty attempt to "theologize" fundamental ontology and the thought of Being, see *Of Spirit,* 107 ff. / 176 ff.

allel to this concrete engagement, however, runs another, more theoretical interrogation of the concept of space, based to no small degree on the reading of Plato's *Timaeus,* notably in Derrida's essay "*Khōra*" (i.e., χώρα — space, room, place — which Anglo-American usage would transliterate as *chōra*), but in effect dating back to the very first characterization of *différance* in terms of spacing or *espacement.*[9] In relation to these two explorations of the conceptual and practical underpinnings of "space" and "place," what could be the significance of rethinking the *divine* place, as well as the religious and theological sentiments used and abused to claim geopolitical space? How, moreover, should we interpret the puzzling fact that, in more than one context, Derrida's more recent publications tend to substitute "s'il y a lieu" for the more familiar "s'il faut," "si l'on a l'obligation," or "si l'on a le droit"? These formulations seem to recall Heidegger's reduction, in the "Letter on Humanism" and elsewhere, of the question of ethics to the original Greek understanding of *ethos* in terms of a dwelling. But this analogy can easily mask the more decisive differences between these two authors, differences in perspective, in tone, in steps taken, and so on and so forth.

For all the stress on the notion of space and place vis-à-vis the ineffable, Derrida's repeated reference to the Platonic *chōra* evokes and keeps open a "possibility" — less or more than a possibility, in the philosophical, metaphysical sense of this word — that escapes the possibility, indeed the possibilizing function of Meister Eckhart's threshold (*Vorbürge,* or *parvis*) and the Heideggerian dimension of Being whose revealability (*Offenbarkeit*) precedes and enables all revelation (*Offenbarung*). The repeated invocation of the motif of *chōra* points beyond the "possibility" for which Derrida, most prominently in *Specters of Marx,* reserves the name of messianicity.

*Chōra,* Derrida says in "Faith and Knowledge" seems a nothingness irreducible to the *Nichts* that according to Heidegger's "What Is Metaphysics?" opens up Dasein to the very question of Being as such. Conversely, Derrida continues, *chōra*

> does not even announce itself as "beyond being," in accordance with a path of negation, a *via negativa.* As a result, *chōra* remains absolutely impassable and heterogeneous to all the processes of historical revelation or of anthropotheo-

---

9. On *chōra,* see Jacques Derrida, *La Dissémination* (Paris: Éditions du Seuil, 1972), 184–85, trans. Barbara Johnson as *Dissemination* (Chicago: University of Chicago Press, 1981), 159–60, and *Khôra* (Paris: Galilée, 1993), trans. Ian McLeod, in SN 89–127.

logical experience, which at the very least suppose its abstraction. It will never have entered religion and will never permit itself to be sacralized, sanctified, humanized, theologized, cultivated, historialized. Radically heterogeneous to the safe and the sound, to the holy and the sacred, it never admits of any *indemnification.* . . . It is neither Being, nor the Good, nor God, nor Man, nor History. . . . an utterly faceless other. (FK 20–21/31)

*Chōra,* then, is the Greek name for that which has remained irrecoverable even for the Greek—read Platonic—heritage itself: "[I]t says the immemoriality of a desert in the desert of which it is neither a threshold [*seuil*] nor a mourning [*deuil*]" (FK 21/31).

Derrida leaves no doubt that Plato's *Timaeus* also has the character of a canonized archive that threatens to vanish behind the countless glosses superimposed on it. In "Avances," he observes that, for more than one reason, one might see this text even as "a sort of Bible *avant la lettre.*" In both cases, Derrida continues, we would seem to be dealing with an interpretation of the "origin of the world," with "that which comes *before anything else* [*avant tout*]," with the "absolute *antecedent*"; what is more, we touch here upon a troubling and fundamentally aporetic insight, namely, that of a "more than one [or no longer one: *plus d'un*] at the origin of the world." He raises the interesting question in this context of whether or to what extent the *Timaeus* should be read "*before* every Christian revelation and especially what this 'before' can mean." The question is significant in an author who interrogates the legitimacy or the limits of the "logics of presupposition," which implies, precisely, a certain coming "before," if not de facto (empirically, ontically), then certainly de jure, that is so say, in the order of reasons (as modern philosophy would have it), or, far more often and more perniciously, ontologically, theologically, axiologically, and so on. For Derrida, the very presupposition of the coming- or being-before (*l'être-avant*) is therefore not merely theoretical but linked in an intimate yet complex way to the questions of ethics, politics, and religion. It somehow implies or entails or inadvertently institutes and prescribes a debt (*un être-devant,* as in the being-before-the-law of which Derrida speaks with reference to Kafka, but not Kafka alone) with respect to what is thought of as coming first (again, if not chronologically, then at least logically).[10]

There is the invocation of another "non-theo-anthropological otherness," then, the respect of which would still—by hypothesis or on the basis

10. All citations from Jacques Derrida, "Avances," in Serge Margel, *Le Tombeau du dieu artisan: Sur Platon* (Paris: Éditions de Minuit, 1995), 11–43.

of a minimal (formal and, perhaps, formally indicative) definition — be *religio.* Derrida says as much when he speaks, in "Faith and Knowledge,"

> of a *third place* that could well have been *more than* archi-originary, the most anarchic and anarchivable place possible, not the island [Capri, Patmos, perhaps the Kantian archipelago — HdV] nor the Promised Land [the telos of messianism — HdV], but a certain desert, that which makes possible, opens, hollows or infinitizes the other. Ecstasy or existence of the most extreme abstraction. That which would orient here "in" this desert without pathway and without interior, would still be the possibility of a *religio* and of a *relegere*, to be sure, but *before* the "link" of *religare*, problematic etymology and doubtless reconstructed, *before* the link between men as such or between man and the divinity of the god. It would also be like the condition of the "link" reduced to its minimal semantic determination: the holding-back [*halte*] of scruple (*religio*), the restraint of shame, a certain *Verhaltenheit* as well, of which Heidegger speaks in the *Beiträge zur Philosophie*, the respect, the responsibility of repetition in the wager [*gage*] of decision or of affirmation (*re-legere*) which links up with itself in order to link up with the other. Even if it is called the social nexus, link to the other in general, this fiduciary "link" would precede all determinate community, all positive religion, every onto-anthropo-theological horizon. It would link pure singularities prior to any social or political determination, prior to all intersubjectivity, prior even to the opposition between the sacred (or the holy) and the profane. This can therefore resemble a desertification, the risk of which remains undeniable, but it can — on the contrary — also *render possible* precisely what it appears to threaten. (FK 16–17 / 26–27)

The thought of this desert — of a desert in the desert, which is given or which gives only in the absolute and most abstract desertification of thought — could help to prepare another thought, may help prepare another space, no longer restricted to a fixed ground, matrix, or receptacle. Only the experience and the trial or "ordeal" (FK 20 / 31) of such openness, before or beyond any horizon of expectation, may eventually inspire the welcoming of what Derrida chooses to call the *arrivant absolu,* and thereby "a new 'tolerance' " (FK 21 / 32), or, better, a new *hospitality.* In this new hospitality — which entails a new vigilance and indeed Enlightenment as well — any actual politics of hospitality would be premised at least as much as on the economical, juridical, and cultural limitations of migration, immigration, and international refuge.

As a consequence, one would have to rethink the concept of hospitality, which is not without severe repercussions for our understanding of tolerance, of its idea, and, indeed, its very practice. Derrida explicitly notes that he puts

> quotation-marks around this word [*tolerance*] in order to abstract and extract it from its origins. And thereby to announce, through it, through the density of its history, a possibility that would not be solely Christian. . . .
>
> Another "tolerance" would be in accord with the experience of the "desert in the desert," it would respect the distance of infinite alterity as singularity. And this respect would still be *religio, religio* as scruple or reticence, distance, dissociation, disjunction, coming from the threshold of all religion in the *link of repetition to itself,* the threshold of every social or communitarian link.
>
> Before and after the *logos* which was in the beginning, before and after the Holy Sacrament, before and after the Holy Scriptures.[11]

Derrida aims at thinking of this desertification *across* or *via* the two other sources of religion to which he refers "provisionally" and, he adds, "for pedagogical and rhetorical reasons," to wit, "the *messianic,* or messianicity without messianism" (FK 17 / 27), and the *chōra.*

At times, *chōra* seems to come even "closer," if one can still say so, to the experience of desertification toward which Derrida gestures. *Chōra* becomes here, as it were, itself a name for the "desert in the desert." As such, it seems to point even further beyond itself and its past and present interpretations than the motif of the messianic and messianicity without messianism, both of which retain many—indeed, the most decisive— traits of the historical revelations that they, paradoxically, make possible in the first place (and by which they are thus affected, as it were, retroactively, after the fact). Nothing of the kind, it would seem, can be said of

11. FK 21–22 / 32–33. In the same section, Derrida notes that "the concept of tolerance, *stricto sensu,* belongs first of all to a sort of Christian domesticity. . . . It was printed, emitted, transmitted and circulated in the name of the Christian faith and would hardly be without relation to the rise, it too Christian, of what Kant calls 'reflecting faith'—and of *pure morality* as that which is distinctively Christian. The lesson of tolerance was first of all an *exemplary* lesson that the Christian deemed himself alone capable of giving to the world, even if he often had to learn it himself. In this respect, the French Enlightenment, *les Lumières,* was no less essentially Christian than the *Aufklärung*" (FK 22 / 32). Quoting the lemma "Tolerance" from Voltaire's *Dictionnaire philosophique* to the effect that, of all the religions, "Christianity is without doubt that which ought to inspire the greatest tolerance, even if until now Christians have been the most intolerant of men," Derrida suggests that "by their vehement anti-Christianity, by their opposition above all to the Roman Church, as much as by their declared preference, sometimes nostalgic, for primitive Christianity, Voltaire and Heidegger belong to the same tradition: proto-Catholic" (FK 69 n. 13 / 33 n. 9).

the singular name and the concept of *chōra*, which outwits its historical overdetermination far more easily than its messianic counterpart. Indeed, even Plato uses the term *chōra* in his *Timaeus*, Derrida writes, "without being able to reappropriate it in a consistent self-interpretation":

> From the open interior of a corpus, of a system, of a language or a culture, *chōra* would situate the abstract spacing, *place itself,* the place of absolute exteriority, but also the place of a bifurcation between two approaches to the desert. Bifurcation between a tradition of the "via negativa" which, in spite of or within its Christian act of birth, accords its possibility to a Greek— Platonic or Plotinean—tradition that persists until Heidegger and beyond: the thought of that which is beyond being (*epekeina tēs ousias*). This Greco-Abrahamic hybridization remains anthropo-theological. In the figures of it known to us, in its culture and in its history, its "idiom" is not universalizable. It speaks solely at the borders or in view of the Middle-Eastern desert, at the source of monotheistic revelations and of Greece. It is there that we can try to determine the place where . . . "we" persist and insist. If we insist, and we must for some time still, upon the names that are given us as our heritage, it is because in respect to this borderline place a new war of religions is redeploying as never before to this day, in an event that is *at the same time both interior and exterior.* It inscribes its seismic turbulence directly upon the fiduciary globality of the technoscientific, of the economic, of the political and of the juridical. (FK 19–20 / 29–30)

The so-called return of religion or of the religious—not merely as philosophical or more broadly scholarly theme, but as geopolitical concern or risk (and chance?)—can, Derrrida claims, never be understood if we do not take these two movements and sources into serious account. But then again, also here, speaking of the "desert in the desert," a certain essential scruple seems imperative. This reticence has everything to do with Derrida's deconstruction of the "logic of presupposition" that he sees as a continuation of the tradition of the *prima philosophia* and its modern reversals. For the response to this one-dimensional or -directional logic consists in a double attempt to give new meaning simultaneously to the phenomenological (Husserlian rather than Heideggerian) principle of *Voraussetzungslosigkeit* and to the original—or should we say *originary* and *pre-originary*—meaning of *religio.* These two poles of Derrida's exposition are not simply collapsed into each other. They revolve around each other in an elliptical relationship that at times seems asymmetrical, since one pole, while never without the other, seems somehow to weigh more heavily than the other: the apparent and inarticulable indecision between these two — philosophical and religious — motivations being precisely what Derrida calls "religion." But then again, is this not simply what *gives* itself to be *seen,* without further presupposition? Phenomenology might well be at the heart of "religion," and vice versa. The answer to this question, Derrida suggests, must be left open:

> The question remains open, and with it that of knowing whether this desert can be thought and left to announce itself "before" the desert that we know (that of the revelations and the retreats, of the lives and deaths of God, of all the figures of kenosis or of transcendence, of *religio* or of historical "religions"); or whether, "on the contrary," it is "from" this last desert that we can glimpse that which precedes the first [*l'avant-première*], what I call the desert in the desert. The indecisive oscillation, that reticence (*epochē* or *Verhaltenheit*) . . . (between *revelation* and *revealability, Offenbarung* and *Offenbarkeit,* between event and possibility or virtuality of the event), must it not be respected for itself? Respect for this singular indecision or for this hyperbolic outbidding between two originarities, the order of the "revealed" and the order of the "revealable," is this not at once the chance of every responsible decision and of another "reflecting faith," of a new "tolerance"? (FK 21 / 31–32)

These observations help us comprehend that, as Derrida notes, the apophatic leaves everything or almost everything "intact." And yet something has taken place. This something, some Thing (see FK 48 / 64), *la Chose,* as Lacan writes in *L'Éthique de la psychanalyse* (*The Ethics of Psychoanalysis*), or *das Ding,* as Heidegger writes in "Das Ding" (The Thing) in *Vorträge und Aufsätze* (Lectures and Essays), marks the radical difference between this most difficult — and, indeed, most generous — of Derrida's observations and Wittgenstein's well-known dictum that philosophy leaves everything as it is. But then again, Wittgenstein too continued to allow for the exception and exceptionality of the mystical (*das Mystische*) that can neither be said to *be* nor claim to be intelligible, but that *gives* ("Es gibt allerdings Unaussprechliches") or merely *shows* itself.

Regardless of this difference or similarity, which need not concern us here, the "taking place" of which Derrida (unlike Wittgenstein) speaks "is" as difficult to grasp, as transitory, and even as "virtual" as the multimedial "reality" produced by the other (more profane?) modes of quasi-mechanical abstraction, mechanization, and formalization that have come to be known under the general denominator of hypertext. In fact, if, as Derrida notes in "Faith and Knowledge," religion shares at least the same condition of possibility as the tele-techno-scientific world of the new media, it is produced by them as much as it in turn produces them. This is not to deny that religion must, in a sense, also deny this very "mechanics" that *seems* to deny it its proper cause, its *sui generis* and its *causa sui,* that is to say, its exclusivity and irreducibility, as well as its originator, its God.

## Thearchy and Beyond

If, for Derrida, any discourse can be said to touch upon the theological, then this apophatic feature is, in turn, possible, sayable-unsayable, or thinkable, only insofar as it is "opened, dominated, and invaded by the word '*Being*'" (HAS 60 / 592). It has to be at least troubled or, as Derrida would say, haunted by the word, the concept, and the verbal or transitive character of Being, the very spell of which is cast upon every attempt to dispel its transcendental violence, its neutrality and indifference, its idolatry and injustice. The logic and rhetoric of the *via negativa* make this very clear.

The "beyond" or "without being" necessarily *abandon* themselves to Being if they give themselves—as their "concept" or "idea" demands— without reservation, totally, without holding anything back. "God," in the very mode and substance of His revelation, "is" nothing but this gift: the absolute gift of the absolute, which absolves itself from Being no less than from being "itself" and thus from being, precisely, this "beyond" or "without Being." Paradoxically, aporetically, the pure gift must also give itself, give itself up as gift, that is, if it is to give (itself) at all. Without or beyond Being, without or beyond being itself, it collapses into Being, becomes indistinguishable from Being, substitutable by Being, *as if nothing had happened.* The gift takes place, as if nothing had taken place at all; it is, if it is possible at all ("s'il y a le don," as Derrida cautions time and again), invisible, and thus retains all the elements of the secret (its *Geheimnis,* its being *unheimlich,* etc.). One lives the secret as if there were none.

The ontotheological mistake, its fatal idolatry and blasphemy, is therefore by no means either accidental or avoidable. It is the inevitable result or accomplice of any movement that absolves itself absolutely, totally, and does in so relation to everything, including itself. There is no better figure for this paradox or aporia than the New Testament notion of the kenosis,[12]

---

12. The word *kenosis* is taken from Phil. 2:7, where St. Paul says that Christ "made himself nothing" or "emptied himself." See Hans Urs von Balthasar, "Kénose," in the *Dictionnaire de spiritualité ascétique et mystique* (Paris: Beauchesne, 1974), 8: 1705-12.

reclaimed, like the *adieu*, first by Levinas and then by Derrida: a movement of passage, of emptying out, of making oneself (and one's words and thoughts) nothing, leaving everything behind and gaining everything in its place. This, nothing else, is the paradox of faith, its reversal, inversion, conversion.

Hence also the speculative force that Marion for his part attributes to the Eucharist, to the liturgical commemoration of the becoming-body of the Word. According to this central doctrine and its accompanying sacrament, God touches upon the finitude of the being that we humans are thereby reenacting, in fact or symbolically, the *being-one of essence*, expressed by the Nicean term ὁμοούσιος (*homoousios*), signifying that in the incarnated Christ there exist a divinity and humanity that are both complete yet *neither discrete nor combined*. This incarnation of the infinite in the finite — an abandonment of the beyond-being that is an abandonment, precisely, to Being — is nevertheless coherent, albeit in a way that is neither logically deducible, the outcome of a dialectical sublation, nor, for that matter, the inherent teleology of an unfolding process, but aporetically and, much more than paradoxically, *coherently incoherent*.[13]

Hyperbolically, then, at its utmost extreme, the hyperessential gift calls forth — solicits rather than causes, implies, or possibilizes — its other, that is to say, Being. As a matter of fact, this movement can be retraced at the earliest beginnings of the historical formation that we now know as the *via negativa* and that stretches from Plato's idea of the good "beyond being or beingness," the *epekeina tēs ousias*, to the modern and contemporary examples that interest us here.[14]

13. See J. N. D. Kelly, *Early Christian Creeds* (Longman: New York, 1972), 242ff. The theology of *God Without Being* is at odds here, not only with the philosophical theology of Hegel's *Vorlesungen über die Philosophie der Religion*, but also with the paradox of faith according to Kierkegaard, with the radical Protestantism of Karl Barth (from the *Römerbrief, Fides Quaerens Intellectum* up to the *Kirchliche Dogmatik*), and with the so-called process theology that emerged in the wake of A. N. Whitehead's *Process and Reality* (1929). With the possible exception of the last example, which is based throughout on an ontology of the "event," all of these projects can be described in terms of their struggle with either the "realization of Being" or "the return to Being." None of them, however, takes its lead from a thought or phenomenology of the gift such as the one sketched out in Marion's *Étant donné*. True, analysis of the gift plays an important role in the discussion of Hegel's early theological writings and philosophy of right in Derrida's *Glas*, but there Hegel is read "against the grain." The gift is hardly Hegel's avowed concern.

14. See, for a useful overview, Deirdre Carabine, *The Unknown God: Negative Theology in the Platonic Tradition, Plato to Eriugena* (Louvain: Peeters Press, W. B. Eerdmans, 1995), and Alois M. Haas, *Mystik als Aussage: Erfahrungs-, Denk- und Redeformen christlicher Mystik* (Frankfurt a./M.: Suhrkamp, 1996), as well as, of course, Marion's *L'Idole et la distance*. Of par-

## The Movement Upward

*Hyperbolē*, Derrida reminds us in *On the Name*, is the name for the very "movement of transcendence" that, as Plato claims in the *Republic*, "carries or transports *epekeina tēs ousias*." Yet the movement "upward" or "beyond" in all of the linguistic, literal, conceptual, or interpretative translations it has subsequently received and still receives (for example, in Derrida's writings) seems tainted from the outset by an ambiguity or rather undecidability that transforms every philosophical and theological transgression that follows in its wake into an inescapable aporia. Every attempt at thinking and saying "X 'is' beyond what 'is,'" indeed every formalization or re-instantiation of the movement *hyper, ultra, über, au-delà,* or *en-deçà* that which is said to "be" is somehow tied—and called—back to this very same "being." As with Icarus, transcendence beyond being, in the direction of the light—and in the texts under consideration the Good is almost always symbolized by the sun, by a light that may well be a dark and blinding radiance, "the vision of a dark light," a "more than luminous [*hyperphoton*] darkness"—burns up the wings that carry it.

It is because of this circumstance that a puzzling question arises. Derrida formulates it as follows: "In regard to Being or the word 'Being,' does it always have the mode that we have recognized for it in the apophatic theologies? For Heidegger, would these be examples of aberration or of the 'squared circle'—namely Christian philosophies or unacknowledged ontotheologies?" (HAS 55 / 587). Derrida notes that Heidegger, too, in a surprising repetition of the apophatic, analyzes the transcendence of Dasein by drawing on the Platonic *epekeina tēs ousias.* Yet it is no less remarkable that he merely takes its movement to stretch beyond the totality of what is (i.e., the sum total of beings, and notably of the realm of beings ready at hand), and therefore does not allow this transcendence to aim at whatever it "is" that lies beyond the "beyond" of this totality itself. Being as such, and to begin with Dasein's proper being—its ownmost being that reveals itself in its very finitude, that is to say, in its being toward death (*Sein zum Tode*)—is never really called into question or transcended in a manner that is similar or measures up to the radicality of the apophatic way. And yet, Derrida proposes, the "hyperbolic" movement of the latter,

---

ticular importance is Michel de Certeau's *The Mystic Fable,* which I discuss in my "Anti-Babel: The 'Mystical Postulate' in Benjamin, de Certeau and Derrida," *Modern Language Notes* 107 (April 1992), 441–77.

epitomized by a certain "Platonic, Plotinian, or Neoplatonic style" (SN 65/73–74) of thinking and writing, nonetheless casts a revealing light on the contextual horizon that enables—and indeed delimits—Heidegger's questioning from the very outset. It seems clear that if it were not for this background, the question of the meaning of Being (*Frage nach dem Sinn des Seins*) would have gone unnoticed; it would have been impossible, imperceptible, and therefore, in a sense, also unsurpassable, beyond correction.

We might be tempted here to invoke and, perhaps, reverse the perspective proposed by Heidegger's "Phenomenology and Theology." For it is in the first place the indelible historical and indeed ontic overdetermination of phenomenological science (of fundamental ontology or existential analysis) as well as of the positive science called theology that allows for a certain process of *correction* (in the double sense of Heidegger's use of the word *Korrektion*), which is both that of a corrective critique and, more important, of a "co-direction" or *Mitleitung,* and thereby invokes, once more, two sources of religion or at least of theological discourse on religion.[15] The traditional imprints left by the *via negativa* are not only *co-originary* with—and *equally directive of*—the ontological questioning that they enable in its very possibility, they also mark or even stigmatize the latter's conceptual, imaginative, and ethico-political limitation.

In this, the radicality of the "hyperbolic movements" can hardly be overestimated. They do not only interrogate the pertinence of existing predicates of God—including the predicate of existence or substance as such (God's being, God's being the supreme being)—they even "precipitate," Derrida writes, beyond the understanding of God, "as name, as naming, named, or nameable, insofar as reference is made there to some thing" (SN 65/74). In doing so, they seem to question the very *integrity* of the concept of "God," of His identity—His "Self" or being "selfsame" — and, as a consequence, also of the unity and indivisibility of His "divinity"; in short of all those properties or qualities that would allow one to elaborate a "positive" theology, or, more fundamentally, a "discourse on the divinity (*theion*) of the divine," that is to say, a "theiology" (SN 65/74). Not unlike Heidegger, the apophatic reaches beyond this ontico-onto-theological program by taking its discourse *one step further*—or, what comes to the same thing, *one step further back*—in the direction of its most proper "possibility," which it can never attain as such but somehow

---

15. See Heidegger, "Phenomenology and Theology," in *Pathmarks,* 52/64.

presupposes or rather affirms at each step along the way. This "possible" is at odds with the classical and modern definition of the possible in terms of a *dunamis, potentia, Möglichkeit,* or a *possible world.* It merely stands for an indeterminable "referent" toward which apophatic discourse gestures in multiple ways, *via negativa et eminentiae.*

## Angelus Silesius's *über*

What exactly, then, is the radicality of the apophatic way, and in what, precisely, does its aporetics consist? In *On the Name,* Derrida underpins his analysis of the negative way begun in "How to Avoid Speaking" by recalling that in several aphorisms in his *Cherubinic Wanderer,* the seventeenth-century mystic Angelus Silesius speaks of the necessity of going *beyond God* in view of the beyond of God, the Beyond-Godhead, or the *Over-Divinity:*

> Die über-GOttheit.
> Was man von GOtt gesagt, das genügt mir noch nicht:
> Die über-GOttheit ist mein Leben und mein Liecht.

> *The beyond divinity.*
> What was said of God, not yet suffices me:
> The beyond divinity is my life and my light.[16]

The term *über-GOttheit* and the earlier apodictic statement that one must surpass God — "Man muß noch über GOtt" — betray all the ambiguities I have hinted at. For there is nothing that guarantees that the beyond of God cannot be read, after all or once more, as the Beyond-God in the sense of God's Beyond, God's being beyond, God's Being insofar as it is beyond the common being, that is to say, beyond the being of common beings. As *über-GOttheit,* God would *be* all the more, that is to say, exist more, more emphatically, in a more godly fashion, hyperbolically, hypertheologically. Seen in this light, the transcending movement can no longer be said to transgress Being at all or once and for all. Put otherwise, it is in the very transgression of Being that Being seems affirmed once again and, perhaps, more radically than ever before. The step toward infinity, toward God and the beyond divinity, is infinitely small and, as it

16. SN 65/74–75, quoting Johann Scheffler, *Des Angelus Silesius Cherubinischer Wandersmann,* ed. Louise Gnädinger (Stuttgart: Reclam, 1984), 29, trans. Maria Shrady as *The Cherubinic Wanderer* (New York: Paulist Press, 1986). This translation offers only a selection from the original, but contains a very informative introduction.

were, never taken at all: indeed, it might always be taken as being no step at all. Paradoxically, the step beyond ontology would be more ontological than any ontology that denies the very possibility of this (step) beyond or simply advises against it. Here, once more, the apophatics would be the very truth of the theology: ontotheology carried to its very extreme. By giving itself up, it comes into its own.

### Pseudo-Dionysius's *hyper*

Derrida anticipates and gives further evidence of this at once hyperbolic and aporetic logic of the apophatic way when, in "How to Avoid Speaking," he supplements his reading of Plato with a close reading of some fragments of Pseudo-Dionysius's *The Divine Names* and *The Mystical Theology*. These works stand here first of all as *pars pro toto* for a fascination and "uneasiness" that has to do first of all with the way in which they continue to promise a vision of intuitive plenitude in spite of (or thanks to?) their emptying of all categories and all modalities of being, including the being called highest: "The promise of such a presence often accompanies the apophatic voyage. It is doubtless the vision of a dark light, no doubt an intuition of "more than luminous [*hyperphoton*] darkness," but still it is the immediacy of a presence. Leading up to union with God" (HAS 9 / 542–43, trans. modified).[17]

As the opening chapters of *The Mystical Theology* and *The Divine Names* teach us, this union with God is a singular — and, one is tempted to add, nonphenomenologizable — experience, which situates itself well beyond any intellectual or sensory synthesis or impression. It is for this reason that the second chapter of *The Mystical Theology* speaks of a mystical darkness, that is to say, an ignorance with respect to the divine that is, paradoxically, also the most elevated and sublime form of knowledge of Him. In the third chapter of *The Mystical Theology*, this entering into

17. See Pseudo-Dionysius, *The Complete Works*, trans. Colm Luibheid in collaboration with Paul Rorem (New York: Paulist Press, 1987). For the Greek text, see the version edited by B. Corderius in *Patrologia Graeca*, ed. J. P. Migne, vol. 3 (Paris, 1857). For a discussion of past and present interpretations, see Carabine, *Unknown God*, 279–300; John N. Jones, "Sculpting God: The Logic of Dionysian Negative Theology," *Harvard Theological Review* 89, no. 4 (1996): 355–71; and Haas, *Mystik als Aussage*, 58–61. Pseudo-Dionysius's *Divine Names* makes clear that the divine light is that of an "intangible and invisible darkness," which, moreover, is "unapproachable" precisely because "it so far exceeds the visible light" (Pseudo-Dionysius, *Complete Works*, 107). Less and more than light at once, the divine radiance can be indicated only aporetically, according to the logics of the *hyper*, that is to say, of the *hyperphoton*.

the mystical darkness is circumscribed as the absence of language and thought.

When for Pseudo-Dionysius this beyond exceeds the logical antithesis of affirmation and negation, when it, moreover, escapes the very alternative of the positive, of all positing, on the one hand, and of all privation, on the other, if it can for that reason be neither predicated as either this or that nor be understood as either lacking or negating or denying this or that, then it must be, precisely, the *in-between-of-all-things-present-or-absent* that singles out its very "being." This hyperbolic being is both *other* and *more* — a being-otherwise as much as an otherwise than being; it can not only be said to break away from our historical or common understanding of the concept of being, but must also be seen as the attempt to *stretch, inflate*, or, perhaps, *revisit* and *reinvest* this concept's semantic potential, or, in yet another register, the range of its differential possibilities. Derrida puts this as follows:

> As for the *beyond* (*hyper*) of that which is beyond Being (*hyperousios*), it has the double and ambiguous meaning of what is above in a hierarchy, thus both beyond and more. God (is) beyond Being but as such is more (being) than Being: *no more being* and *being more than Being:* being more. The French expression *plus d'être* (more being, no more being) formulates this equivocation in a fairly economical manner.[18]

At first glance, only a notion of *an-archy*, in the sense Levinas has given to this term, or of a *hierarchy*, as Marion understands it — two notions that are both stripped of all ontic, including all political, determinations —

---

18. HAS 20/552. In *Sauf le nom*, a text to which I shall return at some length below, Derrida stresses this double — contradictory — logic of the apophatic gesture that consists in simultaneously disavowing and reaffirming tradition, thus being at once at an infinite remove and infinitely close to the legacy of ontotheology. The apophatics is therefore neither strictly heterodox nor orthodox or, rather, both at once:

> On the one hand . . . placing the thesis in parentheses or in quotation marks ruins each ontological or theological proposition, in truth, each philosopheme as such. In this sense, the principle of negative theology, in a movement of internal rebellion, radically contests the tradition from which it seems to come. . . . This contract rupture programs a whole series of analogous and recurrent movements, a whole outbidding of the *nec plus ultra* that calls to witness the *epekeina tēs ousias*, and at times without presenting itself as negative theology (Plotinus, Heidegger, Levinas).

> But *on the other hand*, and in that very way, nothing is more faithful than this hyperbole to the originary ontotheological injunction. The *postscriptum* remains a *countersignature*, even if it denies it. (SN 67–68/78–79)

would seem to be able to situate the being-other or the being-more *other-wise*. Upon closer scrutiny, however, Derrida remarks that the notions of anarchy and hierarchy only *seem* to escape the more common, classical and modern, interpretations of the other (of otherness and of the otherwise). The difference in question is—and, indeed, must be—one of *appearance* alone and therefore (almost) impossible to tell. And yet, it is precisely this indecision—an undecidability and in-difference, of sorts—that makes all the difference in the world.

## Emmanuel Levinas's *autrement*

In the same vein, Emmanuel Levinas's evocation of an *overdetermination of ontology* that transforms ontological terms into ethical ones ends up by showing that ethics—or, for that matter, saintliness—is, in an emphatic sense to be determined, *more ontological than ontology*, following the very same logic of the *plus d'être* discussed in connection with Pseudo-Dionysius and Angelus Silesius. Ethical discourse would be *more*—and, as a matter of fact, also *less*—than ontological: the condition of its very possibility but also that of its limitation and, thereby, of its impossibility. Preceding ontology, as we know it, pervading the order of knowledge and the knowable, ethical discourse—yet another faith of sorts—would hint at that which "is" no longer or not yet, or that "is" otherwise-than-being, in any case, ontological *autrement* (otherwise). Derrida rightly notes that this ambiguity both obstructs and enables the distinction of the speech of (on or vis-à-vis) the Other from ontology and ontics (as summed up in Levinas's terms in *Totality and Infinity*, the finite totality of all that is, or, as rephrased by Levinas in *Autrement qu'être ou au-delà de l'essence* [*Otherwise than Being, or Beyond Essence*], the *conatus* or *essance* that is Being's – and any being's – intrinsic drive to persevere in its own being). Like any negative theology or any meta-ontology, Levinas's invocation of an ethical transcendence or an-archy remains accompanied or even haunted by what it seeks to overcome. Conversely—but there is no real opposition here—every affirmative, positive theology, and, indeed, each hymn receives its distinctive features or qualities only against the backdrop of an indeterminacy that no dogmatic decision can ever dispel: a void or nothingness of sorts, a negativity, but one that precedes or exceeds or traverses any preestablished concept of dialectical, logical, or psychoanalytic negation, denegation, or denial.

Derrida explores the Levinasian logic further in a thoughtful reflection on the uncommon title of Levinas's *Otherwise Than Being, or Beyond Essence*. In this second major reading of Levinas's work, devoted to the writings published after *Totality and Infinity*, Derrida observes first of all that we are dealing here with a discourse offered in the mode of a *quasi-phenomenological gesture of attestation*. The very title of Derrida's essay, "En ce moment même dans cet ouvrage me voici" ("At This Very Moment in This Work Here I Am"), underscores this testimonial structure, one that speaks from (and to) a singular constellation, which seems to be reduced to the almost silent gesturing of the "Here I am," the *me voici* (a structure echoed and, paradoxically, testified to by the very response and responsibility it provokes in the reader, or rather the addressee). Indeed, Derrida stresses that we find here an almost idiosyncratic argumentative and rhetorical pattern that does not lend itself to any descriptive or constative rendering, but can only be *affirmed*—indeed, *assumed*—by a singular or indeed absolute performative, one that "is," if one can still say so, *otherwise than being*. The reasons for this are clear, for this "performative" does not fulfill the contextual requirements of the performative considered as speech act. Nor does it originate in a sender or interlocutor who in the first person indicative says "I." And for structural reasons, such an absolute performative should even be seen not only as *otherwise than being* but also as *otherwise than the "otherwise than being"* to which it thus testifies. It is therefore a "perverformative" of sorts:

> In a singular comparative locution that does not constitute a phrase, an adverb (*otherwise*) immeasurably wins out over a verb (and what a verb: to be) to say something "other" that cannot make nor even modify a noun or a verb, nor this noun-verb which always amounts/returns to *being*, in order to say something else, some "other" thing that is neither verb nor noun, and especially not the simple alter*ity* that would still submit the *otherwise* (that modality without substance) to the authority of a category, an essence or being again. The beyond of verbalization (constitution into a verb) or nominalization, the beyond of the *symplokē* binding the nouns and the verbs by playing the game of essence, that beyond leaves a chain of traces, an other *symplokē* already "within" the title, *beyond essence*, yet without allowing itself to be included, rather deforming the curvature of its natural edges.[19]

19. Jacques Derrida, "En ce moment même dans cet ouvrage me voici," in *Psyché: Inventions de l'autre* (Paris: Galilée, 1987), 167–68, trans. Ruben Berezdivin as "At This Very Moment in This Work Here I Am," in *Rereading Levinas*, ed. Robert Bernasconi and Simon Critchley (Bloomington: Indiana University Press, 1991), 18.

Two seemingly conflicting consequences could be drawn from this formalization of what Derrida chooses to call the *sériature,* or "seriasure," of the Levinasian text, consequences that have had a lasting influence on his writing. Indeed, they determine the—at bottom aporetic—structure of any plausible and truly innovative argument, of any rhetoric or poetics of the other, of temporality, of the ethical, the political, and, last but not least, of the religious.

The first consequence is that the apophatic is necessarily at war (in a *différend*) with the language of propositions, of concepts, in short of any implicit or explicit deployment of the verb "to be" in the first person indicative and all the genres of thought, of writing and speaking, that are dependent on it: that is to say, all genres, and, first of all, with the very concept of genre as such.

The second consequence is that, conversely, this apophatic has no other refuge than to inscribe itself somehow—enigmatically—in the language that tends to exclude it a priori. It is here, Derrida argues, that a certain logic of citation should be invoked, a logic that no one has mobilized more inventively than Levinas by demonstrating that the philosophy of the Same (*le Même*) in the major texts of its chief proponents nonetheless ventriloquizes the Other (*l'Autre, Autrui*), and by showing, therefore, that the central task of philosophy is not to say something else, but to say the Same *otherwise* (*autrement*) or at least *to the Other* and thus, ever indirectly, *à Dieu.*

## Jean-Luc Marion's Analogy of Hierarchy

Seen in this light, the very title of Jean-Luc Marion's book *God Without Being* seems, in its polysemy, marked by an ontological complicity that it cannot outwit. Insofar as it implicitly espouses a predicative structure—God is without Being, without even having to be (albeit the being called highest)—it tacitly affirms the precedence of the very being it seeks to call into question. In addition, it leaves a certain unity and integrity of the word and name *God* intact. Although there are remarkable similarities between Marion's phenomenology of donation and abandonment, on the one hand, and that of Levinas and Derrida, on the other, the motif of the *adieu,* in all its ambiguity as a farewell, an address (*à dieu*), and an exposure to the other of the Other (*a-dieu*), bears witness to Levinas's and Derrida's very different sensibility, namely, that of the dictum "Dieu déjà se contredit," which for Marion would seem to be, if not downright idolatrous, then at least at odds with the so-called saturated phenomenon. For all its insistence on the unthinkable, Marion's theology seems intent on escaping the full consequences of the aporetics that interests us here.

A more solid foundation for this suspicion is provided by examining the forms of the inevitable link between the "beyond Being" and the ethico-political orientation of the existing socio-institutional realm. The difficulty here, as Derrida has convincingly shown, becomes particularly clear when one considers the concept of hierarchy (introduced by Pseudo-Dionysius, notably in the third chapter of his *The Celestial Hierarchy*) and how it entangles itself in the confusion of two hierarchies, one empirical, historical, and sociopolitical, and the other metaphysical, or, as Marion would have it, theological or ecclesial. For Pseudo-Dionysius, of course, the question is not so much one of linking the sociopolitical order and the sacred order of hierarchy as of the correspondence—the distance and analogy—between the celestial and ecclesial hierarchies. But, regardless of this important difference, the difficulty of translating a categorially distinct realm into terms of another remains. For one thing, it implies that one traverse the distance of an infinite space, the space that opens up the possibility of the Infinite revealing itself in the first place—and, as it were, *ex nihilo*—even though this same revelation, paradoxically, in turn calls this very same space into being. Derrida formulates this difficulty as follows: "How is it possible that 'distance'—in the sense Marion gives to this word and which also makes up the distance between the two hierarchies—can let itself be overstepped or 'traversed' and *give place to the analogical translation of one hierarchy into another?* . . . What would be the good political translation of the hierarchy as a 'sacred ordinance'?" (HAS 65 n. 9 / 553–54 n. 1).

In a sense, this critical question concerns every theoretical and institutional intervention called deconstructive as well. What is problematic about it cannot be the fact that there *is* translation or "overstepping" at all here. In Marion's own work, this transposition from one realm to the other—from the "beyond Being" to the world of beings—is somehow called for and not simply postponed ad infinitum. We are not dealing with a surreptitious lapse here, but with an essential or constitutive moment of one and the same figure. Yet everything hinges on discerning the radical difference that opens up between the idolization or aesthetization of the body politic, on the one hand, and the institutional symbolization of an iconic and spiritual, if not necessarily invisible, body, or *corpus Christi,* on the other. For Marion, the latter can be found in the Church, the apostolic tradition, its ritual calendar, its sacraments, and its hierarchy, rather than in, say, the antinomian and iconoclastic messianisms of the past. But this does not mean, of course, that his phenomenology of the gift would not allow for an understanding of a sensible politics for the contemporary world.

For Derrida, too, this problem of negotiation and reinscription lurks at every corner, after every *epochē*, every suspension, every erasure. Yet it is no less clear that for him this return to the empirical takes on a different pragmatic form than it does for Marion, in whose theological work at least this iconic embodiment is guided by a (different) norm. For the measure of a good translation between Marion's conception of the sacred order of hierarchy, on the one hand, and the sociopolitical order, on the other, could be said to be analogical with and oriented toward an original accomplishment that, according to Marion is saturated in itself and only needs to be unfolded, comprehended, and celebrated in its infinite possibilities. Despite all the "freedom" that thereby comes to rest on our shoulders, for Marion, no present or future political theology resulting from the sacred canon — and, indeed, no democracy to come — could ever in good faith supplement that canon's theological structure, vary its contents, or stretch its frame of reference, let alone disseminate its meaning, in the nontrivial, that is to say, nonpolysemic, sense that Derrida has given to this term. One might even wonder to what extent Marion's writing is in the tradition of apophatic theology, if it is indeed true, as Derrida claims, that the characteristic feature of the *via negativa* is precisely its "passing to the limit, then crossing a frontier, including that of a community, thus of a socio-political, institutional, ecclesial reason or raison d'être" (SN 36 / 18).

But then again, on Derrida's own reading, the question of belonging to the apophatic tradition would always be one of belonging *while* not belonging, a belonging *without* belonging, a belonging *by* not belonging. And the very same structure would apply to all those forms of political and institutional critique that resist or ignore all theological motivation. They, too, would correspond at least formally, in their very structure, to this aporetics of negation and affirmation, transgression and repetition.

The significance of Derrida's engagement with the question of negative theology, then, can be seen, in part, in the demonstration that it is precisely in the movement of this most rigorous of all abstractions (from thought, the world, and the very attributes, essence, or existence of God) that the criteria for determining the "virtual or actual" (SN 41 / 27) participation of a given discourse in the apophatic tradition become uncertain. The reason for this seems clear: for there is no single philosophical, literary, or even theo*logical* "genre" from which these criteria could be derived or that would guide their application. But this observation is only a partial justification, and one that explains merely the singularity of the *via negativa* and everything that follows in its wake, to the point of becoming almost indistinguishable from it. More important is the fact that this "belonging while not belonging" ("belonging without belonging," "belonging by not belonging") is hardly contingent or historically arbitrary and has consequences that are neither simply empirical nor purely normative. Nor is the "effect" of this "belonging in not belonging" that of the trace alone — that is to say, an effect without cause, which is therefore no effect at all in the traditional, metaphysical, or common sense (so the well-known argument in "La Différance"). Rather, the effect in question seems to find its chance, some would say, the condition of its possibility, in an intricate relationship that apophatics maintains between even its most radical ruptures with the language of tradition, with the concepts and argumentative structure of ontotheology: ruptures that are punctuated — paradoxically, aporetically — by as many reaffirmations, repetitions, renegotiations, and reinscriptions of this very same heritage, and this to the point where it can be said to *say the same all over again* or to *say the same, but completely otherwise;* in other words, *as if nothing had been said at all,* and, again, *as if this saying seemingly nothing at all could very well make all the difference in the world.* To say this confirms a seemingly simple but, as we shall see, far-reaching insight that Alois Haas expresses in the following theses:

1. Mysticism ratifies that which is.
2. Mysticism gives proof of the double determination of man, namely that as a Christian he
2.1 is not of this world,
2.2 but is nonetheless in this world (cf. John 17, 11, 14, 16)[20]

   If the forgoing analysis is at all plausible, two questions impose themselves with renewed urgency. First, can attempts to break away from metaphysical or common syntax and semantics hope to succeed, whether phenomenologically, dialectically, theologically, or mystically? One cannot exclude the possibility that any such discourse might succeed (by failing) *after all,* that is to say, by speaking or writing *anyway,* translating the untranslatable, measuring up against what exceeds it by means of

---

20. Haas, *Mystik als Aussage,* 69.

exaggeration, emphasis, and rhetorical ecstasis, hyperbolically and in the best tradition of the *via eminentiae.*

Second, where does this leave the question of so-called aphophatic anthropology broached earlier? The subject as subject, the modern *subjectum,* that underlies and initiates or in freedom assumes its duty or responsibility, dissolves here into the mere addressee — indeed the "passion" — of an appeal that it can neither anticipate nor evaluate, neither match nor counter in any appropriate way. The apophatic subject situates itself well beyond — or should we say before? — the conceptual distinction between autonomy and heteronomy that marks modern Enlightenment thought and most of its contemporary analytic, hermeneutic, and pragmatic transformations. The details need not interest us here. Let me only note that to the motif of the "God without Being," there necessarily corresponds the idea of an " 'I' outside Being" ( *Je hors d'être*) or a " 'There' outside Being" (*Là hors d'être*). This intrinsic link, which is also that of a further phenomenological corroboration, is signaled, as Jean-Luc Marion has observed, in his own itinerary from *God Without Being* up to *Reduction and Givenness* and *Étant donné.* A similar amplification takes place in Derrida's writings, in particular in those contexts that discuss the notion of the *subjectile* (notably, " 'Il faut bien manger' ou le calcul du sujet" [" 'Eating Well,' or the Calculation of the Subject"] and the analysis that Derrida published as an introduction to Antonin Artaud's sketches, entitled "Forcener le subjectile" ["To Unsense the Subjectile"]). There is a direct correspondence, therefore, between the movement away from anthropomorphism in the direction of, say, "anthropophatism" — the belief in, or mystic postulation of, a transpersonal rather than impersonal God, the One-beyond-being — on the one hand, and the affirmation of an anthropology or subjectivity that is apophatic, indeed uncircumscribable, in almost equal degree, on the other.[21] Pseudo-Dionysius suggest as much

21. See Marion, *Reduction and Givenness,* esp. 161, 198 / 240, 297; Jacques Derrida, " 'Il faut bien manger' ou le calcul du sujet," *Cahiers Confrontation* 20 (1989): 91–114, trans. as " 'Eating Well,' or the Calculation of the Subject: An Interview with Jacques Derrida," in *Who Comes After the Subject,"* ed. Eduardo Cadava, Peter Connor, and Jean-Luc Nancy (London: Routledge, 1991), 96–119; Jacques Derrida, "Forcener le subjectile," in id. and Paule Thévenin, *Antonin Artaud: Dessins et portraits* (Paris: Gallimard, 1986), 55–108, trans. Mary Ann Caws as "To Unsense the Subjectile," in Derrida and Paule, *The Secret Art of Antonin Artaud* (Cambridge, Mass.: MIT Press, 1998), 61–157. Anthropophatism: see Henry Duméry, *Le Problème de Dieu en philosophie de la religion* (Paris: Desclée de Brouwer, 1957), trans. Charles Courtney as *The Problem of God in Philosophy of Religion* (Evanston, Ill.: Northwestern University Press, 1964), 120 n. 32.

when he says of ecstasy: "We should be taken wholly out of ourselves and become wholly of God, since it is better to belong to God rather than to ourselves."[22] This should not surprise us for yet another reason: apophatic theologies operate in a genuine phenomenological way: their kenosis of discourse, their "mystic speech," to use Michel de Certeau's formulation, reflects on the subject that speaks — or that is addressed — as well. The subject in question becomes as other — and as other to itself — as the God or the Beyond-God toward which it directs itself in prayer as to its Cause and telos.

Thus, for all the insistence on finitude — "la différance infinie est finie" — and for all the emphasis on ends of man far more radical than, say, Kant and Heidegger, Kojève and Sartre, would have dreamed, we are nonetheless dealing here, in Derrida's texts, with a certain quasi-mystic *deification;* not, to be sure, because of some *unio mystica,* pure and simple, but because the self becomes as other as the totally other for which "God" is still the most exemplary — in a sense, the most substitutable — name.

Indeed, few thinkers have gone as far as Derrida in probing and challenging the limits of the modern discourse on religion, of its metaphysical presuppositions, as well as its recent transformations in the much-debated linguistic, structuralist, narrativist, pragmatic, and culturalist turns. No writer, I would add, has been more consistent in foregrounding the unexpected and often uncanny alliances that thus emerge between the most radical interrogations of the history of Western thought and a certain religious inheritance. We have seen that there are certain formal analogies between deconstruction's textual practices and the argumentative and rhetorical procedures of the traditions known as negative theology, apophatics, or mysticism. Yet much more is at stake in these structural similarities and occasional thematic intersections between discourses that, at first glance, would seem to draw their inspiration and intellectual force from very different cultural sources, that address themselves to a different audience, and that orient themselves toward a different "other," or at the very least toward a fundamentally different understanding of the "other," of "God," for example. For the fact that deconstruction and apophatics situate themselves simultaneously extremely close to *and* at an infinite remove from each other — often resembling each other *to the point of confusion* — has important ethical, political, and even institutional implications as well.

22. Pseudo-Dionysius, *Complete Works,* 106.

Not the least important consequence of this analysis would be that it shows how in any decision, in any act, we are exposed to the risk of the worst, to the ultimate confusion, to the confusion of ultimates. Why is this so?

The Levinasian argument would seem to be the following. By being nonteleological, nondialectical, nonintentional, and nondialogical, the *à dieu* indicates a structure of giving to the other, of giving oneself up— abandoning oneself, one's own self, or of being just one self—*to the point of* being invaded, hollowed out, and dispersed by a surplus of non-sense over sense (a risk to be run, since it alone makes sense—as a genuine signal of and to the other—possible in the first place).

The in-direct, im-mediate, ab-solute relation to the Ab-solute would thus seem to imply a relation to the other of the Other, to the oblique and nether side of God, to what Levinas calls the haunting of the *il y a* in the trace—the echo or the shadow—of the *illéité*. And while it would be true that one cannot describe the relation to God (*à Dieu*) without speaking of the relation to the neighbor, the other man (*autrui*), it should also be said—by implication or otherwise—that this relation finds a condition of its possibility in what always threatens to make it impossible, that is to say, in the other of the Other, the other other, the other than other, the otherwise than other, the otherwise than otherwise than being or, rather, the otherwise than being yet otherwise still.

## The Affirmative First

The central motif of the preceding paragraphs may be seen as the affirmation of an original and originally constitutive "first word," the alpha and omega of all discourse and of every practice. This affirming alpha (in Hebrew, *aleph*) introduces us to the *yes* that precedes any literal spoken or written "yes"—a *yes* that is already reiterated, doubly affirmed, Derrida says: a *oui, oui*. "Gott spricht immer nur ja" ("God only ever says yes"), Angelus Silesius says, echoing the New Testament's assertion that in God there is only a "yes," a dictum parodied and varied by Nietzsche and James Joyce, and analyzed in Michel de Certeau's historical studies in *La Fable mystique* (*The Mystic Fable*).[23] What are the most apparent differences between Derrida's writing and what might be seen as these successors of Dionysian apophatics?

23. Michel de Certeau, *La Fable mystique: XVI^e–XVII^e siècle* (Paris: Gallimard, 1982), trans. Michael B. Smith as *The Mystic Fable* (Chicago: University of Chicago Press, 1992). See further my "Antibabel."

Aside from being irreconcilable with a postulated hyperessentiality and the intuited telos of a *visio* or *unio mystica*, the discourse of the other revolving around a nonnegative "negativity"—or "affirmation"—is, Derrida claims, irreducible to the philosophemes of a speculative and negative—that is to say, Platonic, Hegelian, or Adornian—dialectics, to the theorems of Freudian or Lacanian psychoanalysis, or to the professed silence of Wittgenstein's logical atomism. These three classical and modern types of discourse remain as problematic as the ancient and medieval forms of the apophatic way to the very extent that they also rest in part on deconstructible presuppositions, and this perhaps—as in the case of theological apophatics—inevitably so. Let me briefly pause at the reasons why this is so. Derrida discusses them in roughly chronological order, according to their subsequent emergence in the history of thought.

First of all, and regardless of the striking similarities that appear to exist between apophatics and dialectics, the thinking of the former—and whatever comes in its wake—remains "essentially alien" to the latter. This holds true, Derrida continues "even if Christian negative theologies owe much to Platonic or Neoplatonic dialectic; and even if it is difficult to read Hegel without taking account of an apophatic tradition that was not foreign to him (at least by the mediation of Bruno, hence of Nicholas of Cusa and of Meister Eckhart, etc.)" (HAS 30 / 562). As is clear from Derrida's discussion, in *Glas,* of Hegel's philosophy of religion and the family, his speculative dialectics finds its ultimate referent in an absolute knowledge that it in its exposition both invokes and disavows. As a result, Hegel's mode of proceeding is at once infinitely close to *and* at an infinite remove from the central argument propounded by so-called deconstruction.

Likewise, there is a certain disjunction between apophatics and psychoanalysis, notwithstanding that both orthodox and heterodox psychoanalytic schools rely on the same deconstructible premises that Derrida detects in the dominant self-understanding of the Greco-Christian apophatic and mystic discourses and their modern substitutes. For even though the name of God seems only sayable, as Derrida is the first to acknowledge, "in the modality of . . . secret denial"—the modality of saying, "Above all, I do not want to say that" (HAS 26 / 557)—this kind of a saying without saying (that is, without wanting to say) is ultimately at odds with the Freudian interpretation of the denial (*Verneinung*), repression, slips of the tongue, and so forth. The secrecy involved in the *via negativa*—more precisely, in what remains of it after the deconstructibility of its premises has been brought to light, from within and without, that is

to say, with inner consequence and by turning it against itself—is mis-
construed by psychoanalytic discourse insofar as the latter is sustained by
a theorem of the unconscious. Indeed, as Derrida has stressed all along,
from "La Différance," *Of Grammatology,* and *Positions* on, it is difficult to
conceive of a psychoanalytic theory or practice that does not rely on this
fundamentally metaphysical and thereby ontotheological presupposition
of an originary lack that functions as an absent (and thereby all the more
effective) center of gravity or, inversely, as a centrifugal, and thus decentering, force.[24] Derrida would seem to agree here with Mikel Dufrenne's
concern that the very notion of the "enigma"—in this case, the riddle of
the unconscious—allows for a certain sacralization that is never either
fully convincing or without many risks. In his "In Defense of a Nontheological Philosophy," Dufrenne writes:

> Perhaps some philosophies of desacralization—of suspicion, as P. Ricoeur
> says—still give in to the prestige of the enigma. I am thinking here of a cer-
> tain usage of psychoanalysis: to tear the subject loose from the roots that it
> plunges into the individuality of the living, to take literally the topological
> imagery that divides and fragments it, to conceive of desire as an earthquake
> without epicenter, as a storm that blows from nowhere, all this can be a man-
> ner of ontologizing the lack [*le manque*], of theologizing the absence: from
> there, it is not far to making oneself a priest of a new religion, not farther than
> this distance that separates the School from the *Séminaire.*[25]

Finally, and on similar grounds, the analysis of apophatic discourse
and its sequels proposed here parts ways with the "current interpretation"
(HAS 11 / 544) of the final propositions of Wittgenstein's *Tractatus Logico-
Philosophicus.* Not unlike the theorem of the unconscious, the claim that
the mystical (*das Mystische,* the mere fact that the world is) can only
somehow *show* itself, still implies too much. This was already noted by
one of the first and most perceptive of Wittgenstein's readers, Otto Neurath, who in 1931 made the following observation concerning the implied
"something" that the final thesis of the *Tractatus* seems to incorporate into
the system of its deductions: "The conclusion of the *Tractatus*—'What
we cannot speak about, we must pass over in silence'—is confusing, at
least linguistically; it sounds as though there were a 'something' of which
one cannot speak. We would say: if one really wants to completely avoid

24. To give just one example among many, see Derrida's remarks in *Of Grammatology,* 69,
88, 159, 160 / 102, 132ff., 228, 230.
25. Dufrenne, "Pour une philosophie non-théologique," 35 n. 2; my trans.

the metaphysical mood, then 'be silent,' but not about 'something.'[26] Of course, for Neurath it makes sense to say that one *can* and *must*, in fact, avoid metaphysical moods if one is to speak meaningfully at all. Derrida, by contrast, would seem to doubt the very possibility of such an avoidance and the promise of a meaningful language.

The question remains, of course, whether we might not reinterpret these dialectical, psychoanalytic, or analytical modes of argumentation in a way that would to a large extent immunize them against Derrida's claim that their respective presuppositions — irrespective of the radicality of these projects — remain vulnerable and indeed deconstructible. Elsewhere I have claimed that such a case could indeed be made for Theodor Adorno's conception of a negative dialectics. Could a similar case be made for psychoanalysis? And is this not precisely an agenda that Derrida has himself relentlessly pursued in his readings of Freud (in "Freud and the Scene of Writing," and "To Speculate — on 'Freud,'" in *The Postcard*), of Lacan (in "The Purveyor of Truth" and "Pour l'amour de Lacan"), as well as of Nicholas Abraham (notably in "Fors") and Yerushalmi (in "Archive Fever")? Finally, should not something similar be expected of those strands in modern analytic and postanalytic philosophy that not only take their lead from the *Tractatus* but seek to come to terms with the Wittgenstein of the *Philosophical Investigations,* the *Lectures on Religious Belief,* the aphorisms of the *Vermischte Bemerkungen* (published in English as *Culture and Value*), and *On Certainty?* If the "current interpretation" of Wittgenstein's most famous proposition is problematic, as Derrida seems to suggest, what, then, would be the premises for a reading of Wittgenstein's work that could clarify or accommodate the analysis of apophatics given so far?[27]

26. Otto Neurath, "Soziologie im Physikalismus," *Erkenntnis* 2 (1931): 393–431, 396: "Der Schluss des 'Tractatus': 'Wovon man nicht sprechen kann, darüber muss man schweigen' — ist wenigstens sprachlich irreführend; es klingt so, als ob es ein 'Etwas' gäbe, von dem man nicht sprechen könne. Wir würden sagen: Falls man sich wirklich ganz metaphysischer Stimmung enthalten will, so 'schweige man', aber nicht über 'etwas.'" In his *A Companion to Wittgenstein's "Tractatus"* (Ithaca, N.Y.: Cornell University Press, 1964), 378, Max Black quotes two distiches by Angelus Silesius (Johann Scheffler) apropos of Wittgenstein's concluding proposition: "Schweig, Allerliebster, schweig: kannst du nur gänzlich schweigen, / So wird dir Gott mehr Gut's, als du begehrst, erzeigen" and "Mensch, so du willst das Sein der Ewigkeit aussprechen, / So musst du dich zuvor des Redens ganz entbrechen."

27. On the subject of Wittgenstein and religion, we should perhaps distinguish between interpretations of the final propositions of the *Tractatus logico-philosophicus* (London: K. Paul, Trench, Trubner; New York, Harcourt Brace, 1922) about the mystical, on the one hand, and the later *Lectures and Conversations on Aesthetics, Psychology, and Religious Belief* (Berke-

Marion quotes Wittgenstein's famous dictum at the conclusion of the *Tractatus-logico-philosophicus* as a parallel to Heidegger's confession in *Identity and Difference* that whoever knows theology from within would do well to be silent with respect (out of respect) to God (*von Gott zu schweigen*). Yet, Marion writes:

> the highest difficulty does not consist in managing to reach, with Wittgenstein and Heidegger, a guarded [*réservé*] silence with regard to God. The greatest difficulty doubtless consists more essentially in deciding what silence *says:* contempt, renunciation, the avowal of impotence, or else the highest honor rendered, the only one neither unworthy nor "dangerous." But already we pay so much attention to securing the place where only silence is suitable that we do not yet try to determine the stakes and the nature of this silence. The silence concerning silence thus conceals from us that, finally, nothing demands more of interpretation than the nothingness of speech — or even that, to have done with silence, keeping silent does not suffice. Silence, precisely because it does not explain itself, exposes itself to an infinite equivocation of meaning. In order to keep silent with regard to God, one must, if not hold a discourse on God, at least hold a discourse worthy of God on our silence itself. (GWB 54 / 82–83; trans. modified)

Two observations are necessary here. First, Marion sees silence as the central characteristic of the idol, just as Levinas attributes silence to the mask, the portrait, indeed, to the whole make-believe of art, whether it is representational or figurative or not: "To remain silent does not suffice in order to escape idolatry, since, preeminently, the characteristic of the idol is to remain silent, and hence to let men remain silent when they no longer have anything to say — not even blasphemies" (GWB 107 / 154). Second, it is clear that Marion does not simply advocate an ideal of pure heterological speech that would be appropriate to its referent. He does not indulge in a respectful silence before the ineffable. The question for him, too, is

ley and Los Angeles: University of California Press, 1966, 1972) and *Vermischte Bemerkungen,* trans. Peter Winch as *Culture and Value* (bilingual ed., Chicago: University of Chicago Press, 1984), on the other. See, for an interpretation, Hilary Putnam, "Wittgenstein on Religious Belief," in *Renewing Philosophy* (Cambridge, Mass.: Harvard University Press, 1992), 134ff., who stresses the importance of Kierkegaard's *Concluding Unscientific Postscript* for Wittgenstein's later views.

See also Philip R. Shields *Logic and Sin in the Writings of Ludwig Wittgenstein* (Chicago: University of Chicago Press, 1993). I have greatly profited from discussing these matters with Martin Stokhof during a seminar we conducted together in the spring of 1997 at the University of Amsterdam on the subject of "Wittgenstein and Heidegger."

how to speak well, if speaking is unavoidable, if one can apparently not keep silent, and if, moreover, an improper silence may very well turn out to be irresponsible, unfaithful, indeed, idolatry: "The surprising thing is not our difficulty in speaking of God but indeed our difficulty in keeping silent. For in fact, with regard to God, overwhelmingly [*massivement*], one speaks. In a sense we speak only about that, and much too much, with neither modesty nor precaution" (GWB 55 / 83; trans. modified). Apostasy and, perhaps, even aphasia are part and parcel — and not merely a risk or possibility — of theological language. This, and nothing else, can be the consequence of the dictum "Tout autre est tout autre," which Marion would, no doubt, consider yet another example of "idolatry of substitution" (GWB 56 / 86). For Marion, the latter can take two forms: "On the one hand, one presupposes a concept as exhausting the name of God, in order to reject the one by the other; on the other hand, one presupposes that a God guarantees that which another concept signifies more, in order to qualify [*qualifier*] the one through the other. There is here a double impotence to keep silent about God, which silences him all the more" (GWB 56 / 86; trans. modified). The only sincere respect paid to God, then, would be to "free "God" from "his quotation marks" (GWB 60 / 91), that is to say, from idolatry, from metaphysics, from the thought of Being. But, then again, "can one think outside of Being?" (ibid.). Does this not erase the possibility of thought, based as it is, not so much on nomination, on the integrity of the name, for example, of "God," as on conceptual determination, as well as on the self-effacement of the gift that gives itself away?

## The Diacritical Moment of Prayer

How is the gift of thought returned, if not by thought, then at the very least thoughtfully? In principle, only a discourse prior to any concrete or articulated discourse would seem capable of respecting and conveying the truth of the totally other (*tout autre*) that is ipso facto betrayed by the metaphysical and, in the final analysis, ontotheological grammar of language and thought. Is there such a discourse, one that would be neither dialectical, psychoanalytical, analytical, empirical, formal, and merely tautological nor, for that matter, a simple language of silence and gestures, one insensible to sensible idols, and inaccessible to conceptual schemes? Or is any such discourse forever caught in an aporetics that betrays the other?

At times, it seems that Derrida allows for the possibility of such another discourse on (and of) the other (or Other). At times, he seems to associate this possibility with that of a structure that, once again, resembles the paradoxical features of the promise, namely, that of a pre-predicative prayer. Yet on closer scrutiny it becomes clear that the peculiar discourse of prayer also misses the mark when it directs itself to the absolute referent. Strictly speaking, every prayer—including the prayer that precedes the act of predication—is with respect to its addressee inappropriate, not to say blasphemous.

This is not to argue that prayer should—or could—be avoided. From the moment that one speaks a language, from the first instance that one enters into a symbolical order of sorts—in a manner that will always be singular, one way, my way, that is to say, marked by a mineness (*Jemeinigkeit*), as Heidegger knew all too well—one has already begun to pray, one has already become guilty.[28] Derrida for his part cites the inevitable evocation of the name of God in a way that announces a more extensive discussion of so-called originary affirmation, the acquiescence vis-à-vis just about any singular engagement of (and with) language "as such":

> This is what God's name always names, before and beyond other names: the trace of the singular event that will have rendered speech possible even before it turns back toward—in order to respond to—this first or last reference. This is why apophatic discourse must also open with a prayer that recognizes, assigns, or ensures its destination: the Other as Referent of a *legein* which is none other than its Cause. (HAS 29 / 560)

And yet, this unavoidable address nonetheless always risks the worst. The very practice and sincerity of prayer always remains vulnerable to parody and mechanical repetition; not because of some false content (it has or should have none), but for reasons that are intrinsic to the very structure of its address (utterance, apostrophe).

What makes one version of the apophatic address or recall (*rappel*) different from another seems first of all the prayer—the pre-confessional credo—that accompanies and corrects, inspires and interrupts it. In tune with his analysis of the aporetic structure of "perverformative," Derrida insists on the necessity *and* ultimate impossibility of the distinction between two different traits of prayer: a pre-predicative—and thus non-theological—gesture of invocation or supplication and what he chooses to call, with reference to Pseudo-Dionysius, a celebration or encomium (a

28. And in that sense, Heidegger is indeed right, albeit it for reasons other than he intended, when he insists, in *Being and Time,* that thrownness (*Geworfenheit*) and guilt (*Schuld*) are co-originary.

*hymnein* in Greek, *louange* in French).[29] Although both modes of prayer resemble performatives — not constatives, but utterances that, as Aristotle knew, are neither true nor false — only the first moment of prayer, Derrida writes, "implies nothing other than the supplicating address to the other . . . to give the promise of His presence as other" (HAS 42/574). This first moment, then, is that of *pure* prayer, and as such never given as such. In its very invocation of the "promise" of a "Presence," it still has the status of a promise, and one that cannot be kept as such. Whoever insists on retaining it as a merely analytical, diacritical, yet unsurpassable, moment should also acknowledge that this first moment of prayer is from the outset and forever divided in and against itself and therefore, strictly speaking, neither analytical nor diacritical at all.

> An experience must yet guide the apophatics toward excellence, not allow it to say just anything, and prevent it from manipulating its negations like empty and purely mechanical phrases. This experience is that of prayer. Here prayer is not a preamble, an accessory mode of access. It constitutes an essential moment, it adjusts discursive asceticism, the passage through the desert of discourse, the apparent referential vacuity which will only avoid empty

29. That prayer is like a chain leading man up to God is argued by Pseudo-Dionysius in *Divine Names*, ch. 3. A central question remains: where in Derrida's analysis of the different modalities of prayer can we situate the prayer that cries out, in other words, the lamentation, the elegy, the *in memoriam*, indeed, the *adieu*? Could one not conceive of an originary negativity (in precisely this sense) just as easily — and with, perhaps, even more reason — as of an originary affirmation? And, is that not what is hinted at in the leitmotifs of passion and, as we shall see, of kenosis? Of course, there is no strict opposition or antinomy here, as Derrida points out. For the affirmation does away with all *fermeté* and all *fermeture*. But why, then, favor one term over the other? The answer to the question can be found in part in Derrida's efforts to keep a certain distance with regard to the metaphysical underpinnings of dialectics, on the one hand, and the ethico-political reverberations of the problem of nihilism or, for that matter, of negative ontology, on the other.

What, finally, can be said of the shadow that another regime, if not of semantics and reference, then at least of the ontological casts over the proper structure and direction of prayer? In *Being and Time*, Heidegger leaves no doubt that there is as much continuity as there is discontinuity between the manifestation of truth and the gesturing of prayer. Like apophatic discourse (*Rede*), prayer reveals, but in another way:

> In discourse (ἀπόφανσις), so far as it is genuine, *what* is said [was *geredet ist*] is drawn *from* what the talk is about, so that discursive communication [*die redende Mitteilung*], in what it says [*in ihrem Gesagten*], makes manifest [*offenbar*] what it is talking about, and thus makes this accessible to the other party [*dem anderen*]. This is the structure of the λόγος as ἀπόφανσις. This mode of making manifest [*Modus des Offenbarmachens*] in the sense of letting something be seen by pointing it out, does not go with all kinds of "discourse" [*Rede*]. Requesting [*Bitten*] (εὐχή), for instance, also makes manifest [*offenbar*], but in a different way. (BT 56/32)

deliria and prattling, by addressing itself from the start to the other, to you. (HAS 41/571-72)

Prayer, then, speaks in a first gesture *to* rather than *of* the Other and gives itself to this Other, *à dieu:* "In every prayer there must be an address to the other as other, *for example . . . God [Dieu par exemple]*" (HAS 41/572). In so doing, this invocation or supplication does not ask for anything in particular: "The pure prayer demands only that the other hear it, receive it, be present to it, be the other as such, a gift, call, and even cause of prayer" (HAS 41/572). This first moment of prayer should be radically distinguished from the Dionysian encomium or hymn, which inaugurates a second movement beyond (or in?) the first "pure" address by supplementing it with a certain determination, if not dogmatic content. It is here that both the apophatic and the cataphatic attributions are situated, both of which come after—or are accompanied by the very performative gesture of—the pure invocation of the other as other. This second moment, Derrida claims, does not simply annul the first—fleeting and all too momentary—one. For the latter remains unsurpassable, even though, in full rigor, it can never claim a proper place or existence as such: "Even if this address is immediately determined by the discourse of encomium and if the prayer addresses itself to God [*à Dieu*] by speaking (to Him) of Him, the apostrophe of prayer and the determination of the encomium form . . . two different structures" (HAS 42/574).

Despite this difference between a pre-discursive, gestural saying and an articulate said—a differentiation that recalls not only the Levinasian distinction between *le Dire* and *le Dit* but that between Heideggerian revealability (*Offenbarkeit*) and revelation (*Offenbarung*), and between Kantian rational religion and its many historically revealed instantiations—the silent praying that precedes, inaugurates, or accompanies the apophatic movement at each of its steps (or *pas*) runs the risk—inevitably, and like any apostrophe or address—of being immediately stripped of its purported purity. But then again, this risk of being reified in citation and recitation, mechanical repetition and parody—a risk that is not so much an empirical fact as an ever-present, looming possibility, a necessity, or *anankē,* that is also a chance—is inscribed on the face of every mark, not only of language but in all experience. Indeed—"fortunately," Derrida writes—this circumstance is "also a piece of luck" (HAS 5/537). For without this always possible derailment of each single meaning, of all "signifyingness," to quote Levinas, no prayer, no gesture, no address, would be possible in the first place.[30]

Prayer, then, is never *pure* properly speaking. Only as an *analytically unsurpassable* moment, only as a momentary gesture, as a breath, as it were, does it come to pass at all. From the very moment of its inception, it exposes itself to contamination. There is no prayer without idolatry. Or, if we take idolatry to refer to images and, more indirectly, to ideas and concepts, we are dealing in every prayer with blasphemy, with an inappropriate use of words and phrases, whether silent or spoken and chanted. And yet prayer is never entirely reducible to either blasphemy or idolatry alone. Neither blasphemy nor idolatry can ever be pure or coincide with itself. To say that everything said or gestured is either blasphemy or idolatry or both would be just as false as to insist on the purity and the presence-to-self of an addresser and addressee in prayer. Just as the hypothesis of a generalized fetishism or of the omnipresence of simulacra is only the reverse of the metaphysics of presence, the assumption that everything religious is merely based on a blasphemous or idolatrous anthropomorphism or projection remains parasitic on the very theology, or ontotheology, it seeks to overcome.

But if we grant this, we may still ask how negative theology—or any other apophatics—can ever hope to circumvent a mode of speech that contains an element of contamination, of predication, or even of nomination. What difference is there between a prayer that by its very reiteration runs the risk of being perverted and a prayer that (like that of Pseudo-Dionysius) links its performance to a language of predicates and constatives and holds "that the passage to the encomium is the passage to prayer itself or that between these two the passage is immediate, necessary, and in some ways analytic" (HAS 66 n. 16 / 572–73 n. 1)? Would prayer—

30. Seen in this light, Jean-Luc Nancy's suggestion in *Des Lieux divins* (Mauvezin: Trans-Europ-Repress, 1987), 15, trans. Michael Holland as "Of Divine Places," in Jean Luc Nancy, *The Inoperative Community*, ed. Peter Connor (Minneapolis: University of Minnesota Press, 1991), 121, that, for example, recitation, as "a litany laid bare," "merely sustains the reality of a lack of prayer," or "prays for want of praying," seems questionable. It pays tribute to a notion of immediacy that, if not analyzed carefully—that is, in terms of neither mediate nor simply immediate "*im-mediacy*"—falls prey to the reservations sketched above. Freud ties the emergence of prayer to that of doubt, which in turn is a sign of the repression that marks the transition from the magical and animistic worldview to that of faith (and prayer) based on piety. See *Totem and Taboo: Some Points of Agreements Between the Mental Lives of Savages and Neurotics*, trans. James Strachey (New York: Norton, 1989), 105–6, esp. 106 n. 16.

even pure prayer—not be impossible, unsayable, unthinkable without this transition, or rather slippage, into the language of predication? Derrida seems to acknowledge as much.

Conversely, no prayer could undo itself from its petrified forms were it not capable of distancing itself from these determining predications—that is to say, if it were not also pure aspiration: an absolute beginning and a rupture at once. Only this interval of "pure" prayer makes different or many prayers possible in the first place. Pseudo-Dionysius was right then to state, in his *Divine Names,* that "before all things, and particularly before theology, one must begin by prayer." [31] But, as Marion reminds us, for Dionysius this prayer is not analytically distinguished from the encomium (the *hymnein*) as such. As a gesture of praising the good, of celebration and jubilation, it guards over all predication and denomination: it opens them up and exposes their "impropriety." To ignore this distinction between the performance of prayer, as pure address, on the one hand, and the encomium or celebration that, although it is not simply attributive language, "nevertheless preserves an irreducible relationship to the attribution" (HAS 42 / 572), on the other, a distinction that, Derrida notes, is "inadmissible for Dionysius and perhaps for a Christian in general," comes down to denying "the essential quality of prayer to every invocation that is not Christian" (HAS 42 / 574). To respect the possibility of other, non-Christian prayers would thus seem to demand that one affirm an essential, structural indeterminacy of the address (of its addresser and of its addressee) and thereby on the necessity of a passing—and however structurally unstable or, indeed, aporetic—moment of pure prayer. But then again, the latter has no existence, no relevance or no effect, outside of the concrete prayers (or apophatic discourses) that it inaugurates, inspires, interrupts. It does not fall from heaven but remains, in a sense, parasitic upon or orientated toward the historical and positive determinations that it makes possible in the first place. More precisely still: it is made possible by what it makes possible. That is its aporia.

On Derrida's reading, then, we would seem to be dealing here with a relation (without relation) between two analytically distinguishable poles—pure prayer and its predication, the encomium—that imply and exclude each other somehow, secretly, incomprehensibly, yet with the same necessity. The enigma of this aporetic, reciprocal reference—that is to say, of each one calling forth *and* annulling the other—can hardly be

31. Pseudo-Dionysius, *Divine Names* 3.1, quoted in GWB 157.

underestimated. For much more (or much else) seems at stake here than in the classical and modern conception of a semi-foundational relationship in which categories, transcendentals, or existentials lie at the source, the bottom, of what they make possible, or condition and determine in its very essence. Traditional first philosophy, metaphysics no less than its most radical transformations, does not think of this conditioning or possibilization as being *reversible,* working two ways at once. Yet where the conditioned conditions the condition (or where what is made possible in turn makes possible what made it possible), the very concept of conditioning (or of possibilization) becomes problematic, to say the least.

That this troubling insight may have very old credentials indeed, is, as Derrida points out, already clear from the fact that it resembles the call for a "double language," "double inscription," "double tradition," and "double mode of transmission" that Pseudo-Dionysius assigns to the so-called mystical theology—that is to say, to the apophatic, negative way in its internal or intrinsic connection to the cataphatic, affirmative way:

> on the one hand unspeakable, secret, prohibited, reserved, inaccessible (*aporreton*) or mystical (*mystiken*), "symbolic and intitiatory"; on the other hand, philosophic, demonstrative (*apodeiktiken*), capable of being shown. The critical question evidently becomes: How do these two modes relate to each other? What is the law of their reciprocal translation or of their hierarchy? What would be its institutional or political figure? Dionysius recognizes that these two modes "intersect." The "inexpressible" (*arreton*) is woven together or intersects (*sympeplektai*) "the expressible" (*tō retō*). (HAS 24/556–57; trans. modified)

Taken together, they form an elliptical figure of thought, language, and experience, whose very center is split—doubled—and withdraws itself from sight and from predication. And the same, Derrida concludes, must hold true of discourse—for example, his own—directed toward it. Moreover, such discourse will "keep to the place, which cannot be an indivisible point, where the two modes cross—such that, properly speaking, the crossing itself . . . belongs to neither of the two modes and doubtless even precedes their distribution" (HAS 24–25/557). We are touching here upon a "crossing point" of "two languages, each of which *bears* the silence of the other" (HAS 25/557).

The analysis of the structure of prayer—of the necessity, the task, and the impossibility of prayer, of pure prayer, that is, *strictly* or *properly* speaking—could well serve here as an introduction to the analogous

model or mode of speech and writing, thinking and testimony, responsibility and practice that has come to be known under the name of deconstruction. Derrida seems less preoccupied with the negations or denials
that inevitably accompany the *via negativa*—let alone with the negation
of those negations, which would seem the main characteristic of positive,
thetic, or dogmatic theologies and their secular (for example, atheist) de-
tractors—as with pursuit of a certain indelible, indeed unavoidable, *affirmation*. More specifically, Derrida's analysis could be said to circle around
the notion (again, neither a name nor a concept) of an originary affirmation, of the "yes," or rather, of the reiterated, doubly affirmed, "yes,
yes," that precedes and enables any subsequent discourse on negativity
and allows it to have a secondary, derived place at best. Neither negative
nor positive, this originary affirmation would seem to serve as a condition of possibility of any apophatics, of the *via negativa* as well as the *via
eminentiae*, were it not for the difficulties we have begun to discover in
each of these concepts (condition and possibility) and their functioning
in the tradition of classical and modern transcendental philosophy.

What, then, does Derrida's notion of originary affirmation mean and
entail? First and foremost, Derrida's treatise is an inquiry into what appears as a simple—and almost rhetorical—question, "Is an obligation
before the first word possible?" (HAS 3 / 535). It is around this *prévenance*,
and indeed this prevalence, that "How to Avoid Speaking" seems to revolve, at least as much as *On the Name* and *Of Spirit*. Indeed, part of the
answer to the question can be found in the much discussed long footnote to *Of Spirit* where Derrida elaborates a topic to which "How to Avoid
Speaking" alludes only in passing when it makes mention of "that which
a question . . . must *already* contain in itself and which no longer belongs to the questioning" (HAS 66 n. 12 / 561–62 n. 2), in other words, that
which turns it into a secondary, belated response to or denial of a prior
provocation. *Of Spirit* speaks of it in terms of an originary acquiescence,
or *Zusage*, that precedes and exceeds, enables and disables apophatic discourse as much as the prayer that opens it, inspires it, and guides it toward
its ultimate destination.

Given the primacy of this originary affirmation, every possible address, every question, is already a response. This "recall," Derrida notes,
will always have taken place *prior* to "every proposition and even before
all discourse in general—whether a promise, prayer, praise, celebration"
(HAS 28 / 560). The "most negative discourse, even beyond all nihilisms
and negative dialectics" (HAS 28 / 560) would, were it were possible at all,

already betray the trace of an other who calls this discourse into being in the first place and thus remains its ultimate addressee. Even when nothing is said, even if everything is said in vain and misses the mark, this structure remains in place: "To speak for *nothing* is not: not to speak. Above all, it is not to speak to no one" (HAS 6 / 538).

"How to Avoid Speaking" takes this point further: "From the moment I open my mouth, I have already promised; or, rather, and sooner, the promise has seized the *I* which promises" (HAS 14 / 547), that is to say, even *before* it has intended to speak, to speak well, or to speak no longer.

This circumstance explains why the immemorial, involuntary, pre-reflexive promise of the "yes" or the *Zusage* will never be classifiable in a theory concerning itself first of all with acts of speech, with its constative or performative quality, with its felicity or failure, enabling contexts, and so forth. To state that the promise is "older than I" contradicts the very premise of this theory, which, from J. L. Austin to John Searle and beyond, stipulates that just like any other "genuine" performative, "a promise must be made in the present, in the first person (in the singular or in the plural)," or, more precisely still: "It must be made by one who is capable of saying *I* or *we*, here and now . . . and where I can be held responsible for this speech act" (HAS 14 / 547). In the case of the promise in question (and, indeed, in every question we may want to raise about it), this requirement is neither fulfilled nor fulfillable, nor, for that matter, appropriate or meaningful. On the contrary, the promise escapes this "demand of presence," in part because it is itself that which "renders possible every present discourse on presence" (HAS 15 / 547).

Again, such an analysis would require that one not stop here, speaking merely of a quasi-transcendental condition of the possibility of all that is — or of all that is possible in the present and as a presence, but that itself neither belongs to that order of presence nor falls under the law of some possible. True enough, to a certain extent, the motif of originary affirmation resembles the formal structure of all transcendental reflections, from, say, Kant through Husserl and Heidegger, all the way up to Saussure, formal pragmatics, even speech-act theory, and beyond.[32] An important

32. Let us not forget that this singular structure of quasi-transcendental "conditioning" appears in many ways in the most diverse of contexts. Wittgenstein reminds us of this in his *Philosophical Investigations:* "There is one thing of which one can say neither that it is one meter long nor that it is not one meter long, and that is the standard meter in Paris. But this is, of course, not to ascribe any extraordinary property to it, but only to mark its peculiar role in the language game of measuring with a meter rule" (Ludwig Wittgenstein, *Philosophical Investigations* [1953], ed. and trans. G. E. M. Anscombe and R. Rhees [Oxford: Blackwell, 1963;

difference, however, exists in the fact that the former does not ignore the singularity—the performativity or rather "perverformativity"—of its philosophical stance and does not mistake it for a meta-theoretical statement of sorts:

> The experience of negative theology perhaps holds *to* a p omise, that of the other, which I must keep because it commits me to speak where negativity ought to absolutely rarefy discourse. . . . .Why can't I avoid speaking, unless it is because a promise has committed me even before I begin the briefest speech? If I therefore speak of the promise, I will not be able to keep any metalinguistic distance in regard to it. Discourse on the promise is already a promise: in the promise. (HAS 14 / 547)

Even though the negative way adopts a strategy of rigorous abstraction, it will nonetheless have been preceded by an affirmation that antedates even the most critical turn to the origins of anything whatsoever and that turns it from an all-out questioning into a belated response. And,

---

2d bilingual ed., 1997], 25). What is interesting in this statement is the quasi-transcendental structure it implies—the condition of possibility of determining any meter is not itself, in turn, a meter, properly speaking. This is not to ignore that it can be misleading, as Saul Kripke shows in *Naming and Necessity* (Cambridge, Mass.: Harvard University Press, 1972; reprint, 1980), 54.

A similarly loose formulation of the transcendental can be found on the opening page of J. R. Searle's *Speech Acts*. After having raised the central question of the philosophy of language: "How do words stand for things? What is the difference between a meaningful string of words and a meaningless one? What is it for something to be true? or false?" Searle notes:

> [W]e do know that people communicate, that they do say things and sometimes mean what they say, that they are, on occasion at least, understood, that they ask questions, issue orders, make promises, and give apologies, that people's utterances do relate to the world in ways we can describe by characterizing the utterances as being true or false or meaningless, stupid, exaggerated or what-not. And if these things do happen it follows that they are possible for them to happen, and if it is possible for them to happen it ought to be possible to pose and answer the questions which examine this possibility. (John R. Searle, *Speech Acts: An Essay in the Philosophy of Language* [Cambridge: Cambridge University Press, 1977], 3)

Searle further explains:

The philosophy of language is the attempt to give philosophically illuminating descriptions of certain general features of language, such as reference, truth, meaning, and necessity; and it is concerned only incidentally with particular elements in a particular language; though its method of investigation, where empirical and rational rather than *a priori* and speculative will naturally force it to pay strict attention to the facts of actual natural languages. . . . The "data" of the philosophy of language usually come from natural human languages, but many of the conclusions about e.g. what is it to be true or to be a statement or a promise, if valid, should hold for any possible language capable of producing truths or statements or promises. (ibid., 4)

Derrida insists once more, "it is always possible . . . to call this assumed origin of speech by the name of God":

> Translated into the *Christian* apophatics of Dionysius (although other trans-
> lations of the same necessity are possible), this signifies that the power of
> speaking and of speaking *well of* God already proceeds from God. This is the
> case even if to do this it is necessary to avoid speaking in one manner or
> another, or even if, in order to speak *rightly* or *truly,* it is necessary to avoid
> speaking entirely. This power is a gift and an effect of God. (HAS 28 / 560)

All responsibility *must* thus respond to God, *à Dieu,* to this "gift of the gift" (HAS 28 / 560), a *promise, order,* and *threat,* at once, and one that in-scribes and immediately effaces itself in the content and structure of every speech, of every language, of all experience.

More radical here than Heidegger, in his famous analysis of Dasein's "thrownness" (*Geworfenheit*), Derrida thus departs from — or returns to — what is irreducible to any *déjà-vu* and indeed to any determinable point of departure, that is to say, from the "the 'already-there' [*déjà-là*] of a phrase."

> A trace has taken place. Even if the idiomatic quality must necessarily lose
> itself or allow itself to be contaminated by the repetition which confers on it a
> code and an intelligibility, even if it *occurs only to efface itself,* if it arises only
> in effacing itself, the effacement will have taken place, even if its place is only
> in the ashes. *Il y a là cendre.* (HAS 29 / 560-61)

Again, in this always-already-there, a "must" and an "ought" — a "ne-cessity" and an "injunction" — are somehow intertwined. They "force" and "oblige" us asymmetrically, before we can possibly assume and con-sent to this call, even before we can say, "Here I am!" Yet this provocation, preceding every deliberation as well as any free engagement, "in no way mitigates my responsibility" (HAS 30 / 561). On the contrary, Derrida writes, it is only in this unconditionality and indeed impossibility that obligation can become an issue at all:

> There would be no responsibility without this *prior coming* (*prévenance*) of
> the trace, or if autonomy were first or absolute. Autonomy itself would not
> be possible, nor would respect for the law (sole "cause" of this respect) in the
> strictly Kantian meaning of these words. In order to elude this responsibility,
> to deny it and try to efface it through an absolute regression, it is still or al-

ready necessary for me to endorse or countersign it. When Jeremiah curses
the day he was born, he must yet — or already — *affirm*. (HAS 30 / 561–62)

In reaffirming this inescapable moment of affirmation, Derrida does
not relapse into a pre-Kantian — heteronomical, dogmatic, or, for that
matter, obscurantist or mystagogic — conception of moral and religious
obligation. A further analysis of the origin or referent of the imperative
in question — an imperative *before, in,* and *beyond* every question — may
make this clear.

Derrida demonstrates that every attempt to define the precedence of
trace — the fact that language has "started without us, in us and before
us" — in terms of its infinity or divinity, as theology would seem to in
good conscience ("This is what theology calls God" [HAS 29 / 561]), remains in the end — philosophically and phenomenologically speaking —
arbitrary. Paradoxically, the tracing of traces is "finite, insofar as it is infinite" (HAS 29 / 561). It does not exempt any supposedly transcendental
signified from the chain, the flux, the stricture, or the *sériature* of marks
(linguistic and other).

This consideration gives rise to a final twist in Derrida's argument. For
it is here that the very distinction between the finiteness of all singular experience and the "infinity" of what caused it becomes blurred and, in a
sense, secondary (HAS 29 / 561):

> What *différance*, the *trace*, and so on, "mean" . . . is "before" the concept, the
> name, the word, "something" that would be nothing, that no longer arises
> from Being, from presence or from the presence of the present, nor even from
> absence, and even less from some hyperessentiality. Yet the onto-theological
> reappropriation always remains possible — and doubtless *inevitable* insofar as
> one speaks, precisely, in the element of logic and of onto-theological gram-
> mar. One can always say: hyperessentiality is precisely that, a supreme Being
> who remains incommensurate to the being of all that is, which *is* nothing,
> neither present nor absent, and so on. If the movement of this reappropria-
> tion appears in fact irrepressible, its ultimate failure is no less necessary. But I
> concede that this question remains at the heart of a thinking of *différance*. . . .
> It remains a question. (HAS 9 / 542)

In fact, it remains more than a merely theoretical or rhetorical question,
something — some "thing," *la Chose* — evading yet pervading all questioning. For as the "element" of traditional "logic" and ontotheological "grammar," the originary affirmation is reaffirmed time and again,

from the moment one opens one's mouth, starts to write, or entertains a thought.

## Analytical Confirmations

This analysis of the apophatic (of mystical theology and, more in particular, of a mystic speech or mystic postulate, as in Derrida's "Force of Law"), does not start out with what would seem like an ontic example only to lead us to an ontological or quasi-transcendental structure that somehow matters more. The ontic example is not simply stripped of its concrete historical determinations, in a process that, as Heidegger insisted, is neither that of abstraction nor that of formalization, but one of so-called *formal indication*.

Rather, what is at stake in Derrida's turn to "religion" is a movement in the opposite direction, and thereby one of *reverse implication*. In the texts discussed, the seemingly transcendental and ontological structure is *folded back into*—once again implicated in—the history of the tropes, topoi, and even commonplaces that it had been thought merely to open up, so as to provide it with a dimension, a horizon, and the condition of its possibility. Yet this reversal of the philosophical perspective that runs counter to—and, indeed, counterbalances—the movement of transcendental and phenomenological reduction, no less than that of formal indication, is anything but an empirical reductionism. Its procedure of *deformalization* does not favor concrete history (fictions, fables) over the transcendental. Instead, Derrida's most recent turn is a rearticulation of his earliest engagement with Husserl's motif of *transcendental historicity*. The latter consists in the fact—a fact of reason of sorts—that history, as Husserl writes, is "from the start nothing other than the vital movement of the coexistence and the interweaving of original formations and sedimentations of meaning."[33] It is in the analysis of this concept that Derrida's discussion of Husserl's phenomenology touches upon the theological, the apophatic, the mystical, and, as we shall see, the spectral. For while transcendental historicity indicates first of all the inner structure of the meaning in question, its originary foundation (*Urstiftung*) does not only

---

33. Edmund Husserl, *The Crisis of European Sciences and Transcendental Phenomenology: An Introduction to Phenomenological Philosophy*, trans. David Carr (Evanston, Ill.: Northwestern University Press, 1997), 371–80. For an excellent discussion of the so-called genesis of the transcendental, see Paola Marrati-Guénoun, *La Genèse et la trace: Derrida lecteur de Husserl et Heidegger* (Dordrecht and Boston: Kluwer Academic Publishers, 1998).

demand its reiteration (in refoundation, or *Nachstiftung*) but also implies
the very postulation and realization of a certain telos (or *Endstiftung*).

As early as his introduction to Husserl's *The Origin of Geometry*, Derrida had already pointed out that the phenomenological principle of all principles, and in particular the originary foundation, or *Urstiftung*, that Husserl analyzes throughout *The Crisis of European Sciences and Transcendental Phenomenology* touches upon a certain notion of God, albeit hardly the God of transcendental theology, which for Kant, as I shall show in chapter 6, is embedded in the very idea of reason, as its most fundamental and ultimate regulative idea. In Husserl's *Ideen zu einer reinen Phänomenologie und phänomenologischen Philosophie* (*Ideas Pertaining to a Pure Phenomenology and to a Phenomenological Philosophy*), to name yet another significant context, it is stressed that while the transcendence of God must be bracketed by and falls under phenomenological reduction, this transcendence can nonetheless be described, first, as a "transcendence" that is totally different from the transcendence of the world, and, next, as an "absolute" that is absolute in a radically other way than the absolute of transcendental conscience ("*Es wäre also ein 'Absolutes' in einem total anderen Sinne als das Absolute des Bewusstseins,* wie es andererseits ein *Transzendentes in ein total anderem Sinne* wäre gegenüber dem Transzendenten im Sinne der Welt").

As Husserl formulates it, the transcendence of God is the "polar opposite" of the transcendence of the world. Like the world, however, and unlike the absoluteness of the I, the transcendence of God with respect to the world, and with respect to the I, is not immediately given in consciousness — or with consciousness — after the phenomenological reduction has been performed. The phenomenological analysis necessarily leads to the point where a "ground" of the world comes into view. However, the relationship between this ground and that which it grounds is not that of a causal relationship between things. It obeys a structure of its own and one that cannot enter the explication of phenomenology as Husserl understands it, that is to say, as a rigorous science. As will be the case for Heidegger, it goes without saying that for Husserl the task of understanding of these theological motifs — here of the "absolute" and "transcendent" that are absolute and transcendent with reference to the absoluteness of consciousness and the transcendence of the world — is not that of philosophy. To the extent that it understands itself properly and limits its explication to that of the intentionality of consciousness proper — or in its purity, that is to say, *qua* transcendental ego — it must reduce and bracket the other absolute and the other transcendence that it, as Husserl leaves no doubt, also somehow presupposes.[34]

At this point, the reader might be tempted to regard this concept of God as nothing but an idée fixe on the part of continental European phenomenology, an idea, moreover, that could just as easily be dispensed with as soon as one adopts a more analytic style of reasoning (and along with it a more rigorous theory concerning semantics, the nature of reference, the meaning of meaning, conceptual schemes, and so on). Before we draw this conclusion, it might be useful to note that (albeit in a very different register) the American philosopher Saul Kripke would seem to endorse several of the central claims I have been making.

For Kripke, too, "God" can be understood as a singular term, a name or proper name, as it is called in so-called natural language, that — precisely in its role of example par excellence — reveals something of the structure of signification and attribution in general. "God," whether viewed aporetically (in the very ambiguity of the *à dieu, adieu, a-adieu,* and even *Ahhhh . . . dieu*) or metaphysically (as the *ens perfectissimum* and *summum bonum*) is a "singular term" in the very sense that Kripke gives that phrase in his book *Naming and Necessity.* Accordingly, "God" is interpreted as a "non-descriptive," unique denominator, or "rigid designator," to use a vocabulary derived from Kripke's work on modal logic and possible world semantics in the early 1960s, but one, he insists, that in fact also corroborates a "natural" or "direct intuition" about names in "ordinary language," although at odds with the "conventional description theory" of proper names, meaning, and reference, developed at the beginning of the century by Gottlob Frege and modified by Bertrand Russell.[35] But then again, "God" is mentioned by Kripke — indeed, named, and this, I am inclined to conclude, out of a certain necessity — only in passing. For Kripke, this example is an example par excellence, but one that is disavowed at the very moment it is invoked. Or so it seems. "In the case of

---

34. "Auf dieses 'Absolute' und 'Transzendente' erstrecken wir natürlich die phänomenologische Reduktion. Es soll aus dem neu zu schaffenden Forschungsgebiete ausgeschaltet bleiben, sofern dieses ein Feld des reinen Bewusstseins selbst sein soll" (Edmund Husserl, *Ideen zu einer reinen Phänomenologie und Phänomenologischen Philosophie* [Halle a.d. S.: M. Niemeyer, 1928], vol. 1, par. 58). Cf. Derrida's introduction to Husserl, *L'Origine de la géométrie,* trans. id. (Paris: Presses universitaires de France, 1962, 1974), 3–171, 21 n. See also Paul Ricoeur, "Husserl et le sens de l'histoire," in id., *À l'école de la phénoménologie* (Paris: Vrin, 1986), 21–57, and id., "L'Originaire et la question-en-retour dans la *Krisis* de Husserl," in ibid., 285–95; and Nathalie Depraz, *Transcendance et incarnation: Le Statut de l'intersubjectivité comme altérité à soi chez Husserl* (Paris: Vrin, 1995).

35. Kripke, *Naming and Necessity,* 5, 14.

some terms, people might have doubts whether they are names or descriptions; like 'God' — does it describe God as the unique divine being or
is it a name of God? But such cases needn't necessarily bother us," Kripke
writes.[36]

Both descriptions and proper names are "designators," but only the
latter can be called "rigid." Descriptions may be definite, referring to only
one object that satisfies all the conditions of the designation. But they
are not "rigid" in the way names are. Names find their origin and referring capacity in a situation that Kripke calls "initial baptism." This "initial
baptism" — and the need for an example of this decidedly religious motif
is hardly fortuitous — need not be an event that is "identifiable"[37] with
the help of simple temporal and spatial coordinates alone. It is important
to note this, for while the so-called causal theory of names is certainly
a dominant and influential element of Kripke's account, his work allows
different appropriations as well, including the ones that interest us here.

This view contrasts with that put forward by Frege and Russell, which
held that the proper name, "properly used, simply was a definite description abbreviated or disguised."[38] In *Naming and Necessity*, Kripke maintains that this interpretation is clearly false:

> [A]ccording to Frege, there is some sort of looseness or weakness in our lan-
> guage. Some people may give one sense to the name "Aristotle," others may
> give another. But of course it is not only that; even a single speaker when
> asked "What description are you willing to substitute for the name?" may be
> quite at a loss. In fact, he may know many things about him; but any particu-
> lar thing that he knows he may feel clearly expresses a contingent property of
> the object.[39]

A common solution to this problem, Kripke notes, is the one suggested by the later Wittgenstein, by Peter Strawson, and by John Searle,
among others, all of whom seem to hold that the name is associated, not
with a single description, but with a range or "cluster" of descriptions that
show a certain "family resemblance."[40] This theory, Kripke points out,

36. Ibid., 26–27.                    37. Ibid., 162.
38. Ibid., 27.                       39. Ibid., 30.
40. See Wittgenstein, *Philosophical Investigations;* P. F. Strawson, *Individuals: An Essay in
Descriptive Metaphysics* (London: Methuen, 1959); and Searle, "Proper Names," in *Speech Acts,*
162–74. See also Ernst Tugendhat and Ursula Wolf, *Logisch-semantische Propädeutik* (Stuttgart: Reclam, 1993), 146 ff, and *Eigennamen: Dokumentation einer Kontroverse,* ed. Ursula Wolf
(Frankfurt a./M.: Suhrkamp, 1985).

has the obvious advantage that the name "Moses," say, does not need to have "a fixed and unequivocal use for me in all possible cases," but it has some weaknesses of its own. Kripke's reference here is to Wittgenstein's *Philosophische Untersuchungen* (para. 79), from which this quotation is taken. On this view, Kripke continues: "Whatever in some sense satisfies enough or most of the family is the referent of the name."[41] Others, by contrast—and, at this point, Kripke cites Paul Ziff[42]—hold that even though the cluster descriptions may determine referents of names, in the final analysis, names "don't have meaning at all, they are not a part of language in some sense."[43] It is between these two extreme positions that Kripke locates his own.

How, then, are we to understand a name, a proper name, a singular term, for example "God"? Against the backdrop of this discussion, how should we understand Derrida's explicit warning: "Never treat as an accident the force of the name in what happens, occurs or is said *in the name of religion*" (FK 6/14)? In other words, what light does Kripke's *Naming and Necessity* shed on the analysis Derrida propounds in "Faith and Knowledge," when the latter lists the many

> questions of the name or noun "religion," of the names of God, of whether the proper name belongs to the system of language or not, hence, of its untranslatability but also of its iterability (which is to say, of that which makes it a site of repeatability, of idealization and therefore, already, of *technè*, of technoscience, of tele-technoscience in calling at a distance), of its link to the performativity of calling in prayer (which as Aristotle says, is neither true nor false), of its bond to that which, in all performativity, as in all address and attestation, appeals to the faith of the other and deploys itself therefore in a pledge of faith. (FK 6/14)

For one thing it would seem that we have to take the name *God* (or, for that matter, the noun *religion*, functioning here as a name) as a "rigid designator." A "designator" is "rigid" as opposed to a "nonrigid" or "accidental," Kripke claims, "if in every possible world it designates the same object."[44] Or, more cautiously: "When we think of a property as essential to an object we usually mean that it is true of that object in any case where

41. Kripke, *Naming and Necessity*, 31.
42. Paul Ziff, *Philosophical Turnings* (Ithaca, N.Y.: Cornell University Press; London: Oxford University Press, 1966), 94–96.
43. Kripke, *Naming and Necessity*, 32.
44. Ibid., 48.

it would have existed. A rigid designator of a necessary existent can be called *strongly rigid*."[45] The central "intuitive" thesis of *Naming and Necessity* is thus that names—names properly speaking, proper rather than common names, names of persons, things, cities, and so on—are rigid, if not necessarily strongly rigid, designators in precisely this sense. This implies saying that the particulars singled out by names are

> nothing but a "bundle of qualities," whatever that may mean. If a quality is an abstract object, a bundle of qualities is an object of an even higher degree of abstraction, not a particular. Philosophers have come to the opposite view through a false dilemma: they have asked, are these objects *behind* the bundle of qualities, or is the object *nothing but* the bundle? Neither is the case; this table is wooden, brown, in the room, etc. It has all these properties and is not a thing without properties, behind them; but it should not therefore be identified with the set, or "bundle," of its properties, nor with the subset of essential properties.[46]

A little earlier in the text, Kripke makes clear that the problem of naming, to say nothing here of identification across possible worlds (so-called "transworld identification"), remains for all its rigidity tied up with a irreducible "vagueness" that is all too often ignored by logicians. "Vagueness" in designation does not exclude "rigidity," or, for that matter, imply mere "accidentality."[47] The name stands for an "object" but has no meaning that would be captured by a description made up of a finite number of verifiable propositions. And while the "object" can thus be indeterminate (empirically and logically speaking), the name can still be said

45. Ibid.
46. Ibid., 52.
47. Engaging the possibility of a "non-actualized" situation, Kripke writes, and

> given certain counterfactual vicissitudes in the history of molecules of a table T, one may ask whether T would exist, in that situation, or whether a certain bunch of molecules, which in that situation would constitute a table, constitute the very same table T. In each case, we seek criteria of identity across possible worlds for certain particulars in terms of those for other, more "basic," particulars. If statements about nations (or tribes) are not *reducible* to those about more "basic" constitutents, if there is some "open texture" in the relationship between them, we can hardly expect to give hard and fast identity criteria; nevertheless, in concrete cases we may be able to answer whether a certain bunch of molecules would still constitute T, though in some cases the answer may be indeterminate. I think similar remarks apply to the problem of identity over time; here too we are usually concerned with determinacy, the identity of a "complex" particular in terms of more "basic" ones. (For example, if various parts of a table are replaced, is it still the same object?) (ibid., 50–51)

to designate it rigidly. Conversely, it should also be noted that while the attribution of identity—the "identity relation"—is "vague," it also "may seem intransitive; a chain of apparent identities may yield to an apparent non-identity."[48] This, Kripke suggests, is a risk that cannot be excluded: "It seems . . . utopian to suppose that we will ever reach a level of ultimate, basic particulars for which identity relations are never vague and the danger of intransitivity is eliminated."[49] It should have come as no surprise, then, that Kripke's analysis could be taken to imply the advocacy of "universal substitutivity of proper names"[50] or at least a demonstration of the inevitability of such interchangeability (albeit one depicted by him as a "danger" rather than as a chance).

If *God* is a name, then what is designated by this name can only be found by backtracking through the innumerable steps of its causal or historical effects—passed on to us "by tradition from link to link"[51]—yet these effects are also "effects" after the fact, after-effects of an original yet immemorial "baptism," an "initial baptism" not to be confused with an accurate descriptive rendering, but that is at once invention and intervention, interpretation and affirmation. The so-called causal and historical chain of communication does not therefore lead back from the name— the rigid designator—to some simple origin that would be describable at wish in mere empirical or, say, naturalist terms and propositions. Initial baptism would hardly be the *primum intelligibile* that starts off the series of namings. As the putative origin of the causal chain, it is itself a missing link, a transcendental illusion of sorts: the "first" of its nonsynonymous substitutions. The very identity of the name—its rigid designation of sorts—is thus a trace of the other.

Although Kripke does not say so, we would, in a sense, be dealing here with an absolute, if not absolutely arbitrary—or "accidental"—performative, since it does not rely on contextual conditions whose descriptive features are relevant to the act of naming. Only its effects could form the guarantees and vehicles of its subsequent reidentification, repetition, reiteration, citation, recitation, parody, and invocation. And along the way, confusion cannot be excluded. For the rigidity thesis does not mean that each name must have only one bearer. Names do not necessarily have unique references. Names may be homonymous. *Naming the same, they may very well name the other.*[52]

48. Ibid., 51 n. 18.                    49. Ibid.
50. Ibid., 20.                          51. Ibid., 106.
52. That Kripke's theory is relevant to the interpretation of other cultural or political sig-

IT IS WORTH NOTING that the problematic of the proper name—in particular the secret proper name—haunts both the writing of Walter Benjamin, as is clear from the signature at the end of "Critique of Violence," to which Derrida has drawn attention, and that of Derrida himself, and this nowhere more explicit than in "Circumfession," whose central preoccupation it seems to be. And it is precisely this problematic of the name that gives us access to the question of the belonging and allegiance to tradition. It is in *Schibboleth pour Paul Celan* ("Shibboleth: For Paul Celan") that Derrida speaks most directly of an affirmation of Judaism that obeys a formal scheme similar to the one discovered in the temporality of the date, notably, the so-called poetic date. This affirmation indicates an en-

---

nifiers as well, has been noted by several authors such as Slavoj Zišek, in *The Sublime Object of Ideology* (London: Verso, 1989), 87–102, and, with some critical reservations, by Judith Butler, in *Bodies That Matter: On the Discursive Limits of "Sex"* (London: Routledge, 1993), 153–54, 208ff., 280 n. 18. Both discuss the apparent similarities between the rigid designation of the singular term or name in Kripke and the "ideological" or "identity-conferring function" of names, especially in relation to the writings of Jacques Lacan. Butler writes:

> Zizek argues that what the philosopher Saul Kripke understands as the proper name's status as a rigid designator is parallel to this identity-conferring function of the name in Lacan. . . . Like Lacan, Kripke understands the proper name to secure the identity of the object over time; the proper name is referential, and the identity to which it refers cannot be substituted for by any set of descriptions.
>
> Significantly, both Kripke and Lacan agree to hypostatize a *pact,* a social agreement that invests the name with its power to confer durability and recognizability on that what it names. And in both cases, it is always a social pact based on the Law of the Father, a patrilineal organization that implies that it is *patronymic* names that endure over time, as nominal zones of phallic control. . . . Moreover, the proper name can be conceived as referential and *not* descriptive only to the extent that the social pact which confers legitimacy on the name remains uninterrogated for its masculinism and heterosexual privilege. Once the proper name is elaborated as a patronym, then it can be read as an abbreviation for a social pact or symbolic order that structures the subjects named through their position in a patrilineal social structure. The durability of the subject named is not, then, a function of the proper name, but a function of a patronym, the abbreviated instance of a hierarchical kinship regime.
>
> The name as patronym does not only bear the law, but institutes the law. Insofar as the name secures and structures the subject named, it appears to wield the power of subjectivation: producing a subject on the basis of a prohibition, a set of laws that differentiates subjects through the compulsory legislation of sexed social positionalities. (ibid., 153–54)

Needless to say, these considerations would have to be brought to bear upon the question of religion, of its return, and of the political theologies it may yet again come to inspire. As we shall see in chapter 6, the question of sex and gender pertains to the very heart of one of Kant's most telling expositions of the tasks of a moral philosophy that deems itself pure and formal. And the same holds true of the question of sexual difference as it is raised and erased in the writings of Heidegger and Levinas.

gagement that is neither the awareness or acceptance of a matter of fact (let alone a fact of life) nor, conversely, a purely arbitrary decision taken outside of any specific and historically determined context. On the contrary, to affirm means here to assume a singular responsibility, and one that has always already preceded the "I" who says "yes" (or the one who repeats the supposed original "yes" by reiterating "yes, yes"). Strictly speaking, the nature of being Jewish, discussed in a commentary on Paul Celan's short prose piece "Conversation on the Mountain" ("Gespräch im Gebirg"), is precisely to have *no* nature or essence, that is to say, to have no describable identity.[53] No one is more consistent than Celan in "inscribing Babel in the body of each poem,"[54] which does not exclude but implies the singularity of so-called rigid designation, a designation whose structure is neither that of *deixis* nor that of empirical reference, which is not to say that it is simply differential. What is comprehensible about it lies in its incomprehensibility alone. Like the shibboleth of which Derrida speaks in his study of Celan, the proper name of the Jew, in Celan's prose piece, is unpronounceable—that is to say, translatable into another idiom (of, say, constatives or evaluatives) only at a high price.[55] This, and nothing else, constitutes its fundamental—and fundamentally aporetic—performativity, its "perverformativity."

Finally, as Derrida reiterates in "Faith and Knowledge," it is "rational analysis" that brings to the fore that, paradoxically,

> the foundation of the law—law of the law, institution of the institution, origin of the constitution—is a "performative" event that cannot belong to the set that it founds, inaugurates or justifies. Such an event is unjustifiable within the logic of what it will have opened. It is the decision of the other in the undecidable. Henceforth reason ought to recognize what Montaigne and Pascal call an undeniable "mystical foundation of authority." The *mystical* thus understood allies belief or credit, the fiduciary or the trustworthy, the secret (which here signifies "mystical") to foundation, to knowledge, . . . to science

---

53. On Benjamin's understanding of the affirmation (the *Bejahung*) of the Jewish identity, see the letter of October 1912, published in *Gesammelte Schriften,* ed. Rolf Tiedemann and Hermann Schweppenhäuser, vol. 2.3 (Frankfurt a./M.: Suhrkamp, 1980), 839.

54. Jacques Derrida, *Le Monolinguisme de l'autre* (Paris: Galilée, 1996), 130, trans. Patrick Mensah as *Monolingualism of the Other; or, The Prosthesis of Origin* (Stanford: Stanford University Press, 1998), 69.

55. Derrida, *Postcard,* 197 / 212, speaks of a difficult—and, in a sense, deadly—thematics of allegiance and nonallegiance to Jewish tradition in the cases of both of Benjamin and Celan with the help of an uncanny figure, namely that "rojudeo-suicide."

as "doing," as theory, practice and theoretical practice—which is to say, to a faith, to a performativity and to technoscientific or tele-technological performance. Wherever this foundation founds in foundering, wherever it steals away under the ground of what it founds, at the very instant when, losing itself thus in the desert, it loses the very trace of itself and the memory of a secret, "religion" can only begin and begin again: quasi-automatically, mechanically, machine-like, *spontaneously*. *Spontaneously*, which is to say, as the word indicates, both as the origin of what flows from the source, *sponte sua*, and with the automaticity of the machine. For the best and the worst, without the slightest assurance or anthropo-theological horizon. (FK 19 / 28–29)

"Religion," then, is the insinuation of a story where there is none, in the forgetfulness of the secret (namely, that there is none). It is the concrete form of something posited—a *positive* religion of sorts—that covers over a missing ground. Yet "religion" is, by Derrida's own account, also the old-new "tolerance" with regard to "the distance of infinite alterity as singularity," and singularity is all that is at issue in justice, regardless or rather precisely because of its universalist intent. And this tolerance or "respect"

> would still be *religio, religio* as scruple or re-ticence, distance, dissociation, disjunction, coming from the threshold of all religion in the link *of repetition to itself,* the threshold of every social or communitarian link.
>
> Before and after the *logos* which was in the beginning, before and after the Holy Sacrament, before and after the Holy Scriptures. (FK 22 / 33–34)

Religion or the mystic becomes thus almost a *terminus technicus* for an analysis of the very foundation of ethics, politics, and the law that is strictly speaking "neither foundationalist nor anti-foundationalist."[56] Herein lies the continued relevance of discussing political theology and theocracy,[57] as no one saw more clearly than Benjamin, whose so-called "Theologico-Political Fragment" speaks of nothing else.[58]

---

56. Derrida, "Force of Law," 931.

57. Derrida seems to acknowledge as much too:

It would be too easy to show that, measured by the failure to establish liberal democracy, the gap between fact and ideal essence does not show up only in . . . so-called primitive forms of government, theocracy and military dictatorship (supposing even, *concesso non dato*, that all theocracy is foreign to the ideal State of liberal democracy, or heterogeneous to its very concept). But this failure and this gap also characterize, *a priori* and by definition, *all* democracies, including the oldest and most stable of so-called Western democracies. At stake here is the very concept of democracy as concept of a promise that can only arise in such a *diastema* (failure, inadequation, disjunction, disadjustment, being "out of joint"). That is why we always propose to speak of a democracy *to come*, not of a *future* democracy in the future present, not even of a regulating idea, in the Kantian sense, or of a utopia — at least to the extent that their inaccessibility would still retain the temporal form of a *future present*, of a future modality of the *living present*. (*Specters of Marx*, 64–65 / 110)

See also Horst Turk, "Politische Theologie? Zur 'Intention auf die Sprache' bei Benjamin und Celan," in *Juden in der deutschen Literatur: Ein deutsch-israelisches Symposium*, ed. Stéphane Mosès and Albrecht Schöne (Frankfurt a./M.: Suhrkamp, 1986), 330–49.

58. Walter Benjamin, "Theologisch-politisches Fragment," in *Gesammelte Schriften*, vol 2.1, ed. Rolf Tiedemann and Hermann Schweppenhäuser (Frankfurt a./M.: Suhrkamp, 1980), 203–4. For an excellent discussion of Benjamin's conception of history, see Beatrice Hanssen, *Walter Benjamin's Other History: Of Stones, Animals, Human Beings, and Angels* (Berkeley and Los Angeles: University of California Press, 1998).

# Chapter Three
# Formal Indications

In *The Gift of Death,* more clearly than anywhere else, Derrida re-considers the concept of ethical responsibility by inscribing it in the history of religions, notably of the monotheistic and Abrahamic religions of the Book (Judaism, Christianity, Islam). He does so with repeated reference to the Czech phenomenologist Jan Patočka's *Heretical Essays on the Philosophy of History,*[1] asking in what measure the history of ethical responsibility is intimately linked with the history of religion, notably its *mysterium tremendum.* One of the most telling examples of the latter, Derrida writes, is "the dread, fear and trembling of the Christian in the experience of the sacrificial gift." It is in the analysis of this figure, moreover, that we stumble upon the "secrets of European responsibility" (the title of Derrida's first chapter), which he finds lie in responsibility's intrinsic linkage to the metamorphoses of mythical, religious, and secular paradigms, from the Platonic to the Christian and beyond. These paradigms, Patočka contends, constitute the different and often contradictory layers of "our" history, but, as Derrida's reading stresses, we also encounter here the structural or inherent (and, it would seem, nonempirical) aporias of the very concept of responsibility. In effect, this turn to religion consists precisely in establishing a relationship between these two constitutive elements of what has to be thought of and lived as one and the same experience, as one and the same antinomy. And it does so by transcribing the religious drama into the language of philosophy and vice versa. More specifically, it does so without resorting to the dialectical mediation and speculative sublation of phenomenality and ideality. If there is an alternative to this Hegelian trap, it must be sought in a very different type of

An earlier version of this chapter appeared in *Modern Language Notes* 113 (1998): 635–88.

1. Jan Patočka, *Heretical Essays in the Philosophy of History,* trans. Erazim Kohák, ed. James Dodd (Chicago: Open Court, 1996); originally published as *Essais hérétiques sur la philosophie de l'histoire* (Lagrasse: Verdier, 1981). For an English translation of Roman Jakobson's afterword to the French edition, "Le Curriculum Vitae d'un philosophe tchèque," see *The New Republic,* May 7, 1977.

renegotiation, reelaboration, reenactment, or "redeployment," which, it should be added, is not merely "strategic." For while it is true that the language of religion is too important, too pervasive, indeed too dangerous, to leave it in the hands of those whose relationship to this idiom is one of blind submission, thoughtless adoration, or calculated interest, it cannot and must not be merely parodied or instrumentalized for critical purposes either. Religion must first of all be affirmed in a sense that is not to be confused with fideism. Religion is related to the ethical and the political — to history even — by a complex and contradictory inheritance. At one point in his discussion of Patočka, Derrida cites a series of concepts that reveal part of this other genealogy of responsibility, steeped as they nonetheless are in a discourse (Christian, dialectical, psychoanalytical, etc.) that is deconstructible: "conversion," "sacrifice," "reversal," "sublation" "incorporation," "interiorization," "repression," and so on. Each of these terms, however, may count as a partial redescription of this aporetic "relation without relation," for which the term *religion*, the relation to God, and notably the *à Dieu adieu*, is the most concise and indeed most precise formula. For, as *The Gift of Death* demonstrates, the "relation without relation" can best be formalized with the help of the analytical potential of this phrase, which evokes a turn at once *toward* and *away from* God, *toward* and *away from* the totally other (every totally other, in all the ambiguity of the *tout autre*) and, indeed, as a face-to-face encounter with the other of *this* other, that is to say, with the "Same," but also with monstrosity, the demonic, the diabolical, radical evil, the worst (or, in New Testament idiom, the Antichrist).

DERRIDA CONTRASTS Heidegger and Jan Patočka in *The Gift of Death* as the protagonists of two opposite phenomenological readings of the relationship of the philosophical to the religious. The opposition here is not so much between a fundamental ontological analysis and a fundamentally ontic genealogy of the religious, or between the supposed bracketing and the apparent (i.e., heretical) affirmation of a certain Christian heritage, as between two types of ontologization, neither of which is acceptable to Derrida, at least not in its entirety. Derrida writes:

> Heideggerian thought was not simply a constant attempt to separate itself from Christianity (a gesture that always needs to be related — however complex this relation — to the incredible unleashing of anti-Christian violence represented by Nazism's most official and explicit ideology, something one tends to forget these days). The same Heideggerian thinking often consists,

notably in *Sein und Zeit,* in repeating on an ontological level Christian themes and texts that have been "de-Christianized." Such themes and texts are then presented as ontic, anthropological, or contrived attempts that come to a sudden halt on the way to an ontological recovery of their own originary possibility. . . . Patočka makes an inverse yet symmetrical gesture, which therefore amounts to the same thing. He reontologizes the historic themes of Christianity and attributes to revelation . . . the ontological content that Heidegger attempts to remove from it. (GD, 22–23 / 29–30)

Aside from the idea of infinity or infinite love, which has a central function in Patočka as the foil against which so-called originary guilt can be understood (an almost Cartesian and Levinasian motif), but as a theme is virtually absent in Heidegger (although taken up by Hannah Arendt in her dissertation on St. Augustine), there are at least two thematic differences between these two authors that would in principle merit a much longer discussion. Derrida notes them only in passing. For whatever their divergence, these views far from contradict or outweigh the striking parallels in formal structure and basic orientation between these phenomenologists: their *step back* and return toward an at once simple and convoluted — some would say manifold or at least double — origin of Western thought, of religion, and, as Patočka has it, of "European responsibility," as well as their respective (and seemingly opposed) tendencies toward an ontologization of that origin.[2] This ontologization either treats Being — that is to say, its meaning, openness, situation, horizon, dimension, event, and truth — as the condition of the possibility of the ontic phenomenon of religion and its purported revelations, in the case of Heidegger, or insists, inversely, on the fact that the revelations in question are in essence the basis of the ontological, in the case of Patočka. But what, in spite of the latter's adoption of a similar strategy of supposition, are their alternative thematic preocccupations, and what exactly do these methodological affinities entail for the specific content of their respective philosophies? Derrida writes:

2. Cf. also Jan Patočka, "Questions et réponses: Sur *Réponses et questions* de Heidegger," in id., *Liberté et sacrifice: Écrits politiques* (Grenoble: Éditions Jérôme Millon, 1990), 333–65; and Françoise Dastur, "Patočka et Heidegger: La Phénoménologie et la question de l'homme," *Cahiers de Philosophie* 11–12 (Winter 1990–91), special issue, *Jan Patočka: Le Soin de l'âme,* 83–92. Patočka had been one of Husserl's last and most promising students. For an excellent account of his philosophical development, see "Entretien avec Jan Patočka," in *Jan Patočka: Philosophie, phénoménologie, politique,* ed. Etienne Tassin and Marc Richir (Grenoble: Éditions Jérome Millon, 1992), 7–36, where he mentions that he participated in one of Heidegger's seminars on Hegel, in 1932–33.

The theme of authenticity, the links among care, being toward-death, free-dom, and responsibility, the very idea of a genesis or a history of egological subjectivity, all such ideas certainly have a Heideggerian flavor to them. But this genealogy is hardly Heideggerian *in style* when it takes into account an incorporation of an earlier mystery that blurs the limits of every epoch. With-out wanting to assign Patočka a particular heritage at all costs, one might say that certain of his genealogical tendencies seem at times more Nietzschean than Husserlian or Heideggerian. (GD 19 / 26; emphasis added)

Patočka's *Heretical Essays* are genealogical to the extent that they re-trace the ongoing process of a transvaluation, incorporation, and spiritu-alization of values in ways that would seem to echo the central argument of Nietzsche's *Zur Genealogie der Moral* (*Genealogy of Morals*). And, along these lines, the essays under consideration also prefigure what Derrida, in "Faith and Knowledge," terms the "mondialatinisation" (translated by Samuel Weber as "globalatinization"), indeed, the becoming Christian of the modern world (or, for that matter, the becoming worldly and, in a sense, abstract, of Christianity). This process, Derrida notes, reiterating the argument of his *L'Autre Cap* (*The Other Heading*), is linked to the faith (and fate) of a certain Europe.

Somewhat later in the text, Derrida points to yet another difference, this time between Patočka, on the one hand, and Heidegger *and* Levinas, on the other. Indeed, the work of Levinas plays a central and, as it were, mediating role in the constellation that interests Derrida in *The Gift of Death*, since from a certain perspective Levinas's most important insights seem at once close to and at an equally far remove from *both* Patočka and Heidegger:

> It is not only Patočka's Christianity that separates him from these two think-ers (for argument's sake let us follow the hypothesis that in what they say in general Heidegger and Levinas are not Christian, something that is far from being clear). Along with Christianity there is a certain idea of Europe, its his-tory and future, that also distinguishes him from them.[3]

3. GD 48 / 51–52. To be sure, this theme — Europe — in itself constitutes an eminently phe-nomenological preoccupation, from Husserl's *The Crisis of European Sciences and Transcen-dental Phenomenology* (1962) to Derrida's *L'Autre Cap* (Paris: Éditions de Minuit, 1997; trans. Pascale-Anne Brault and Michael B. Naas as *The Other Heading: Reflections on Today's Europe* [Bloomington: Indiana University Press, 1992]). See also Klaus Held, "Husserls These von der Europäisierung der Menschheit," in *Phänomenologie im Widerstreit: Zum 50. Todestag Edmund Husserls*, ed. Christoph Jamme and Otto Pöggeler (Frankfurt a./M.: Suhrkamp, 1989), 13–39, and Nathalie Depraz's introduction to and commentary on the French translation of the 1935

For Heidegger, the sense of guilt—of *das ursprüngliche Schuldigsein*—is hardly contrasted to an idea of perfection, that is to say, to an idea of the infinite that inspires a whole tradition, from Plato through Augustine, Descartes, and Pascal down to Levinas and Patočka. Derrida leaves no doubt that it is here that one should locate the difference in point of departure, content, and referent, if not necessarily in argumentative structure, between the respective phenomenologies of Patočka and Heidegger. Patočka's assertion that "individuality has been related to infinite love and man is an individual because he is guilty, *always* guilty with respect to that love," Derrida comments, is the basis for his analysis of the difference in context and style between the phenomenological writings of these authors, a difference that, again, leaves room for striking structural parallels:

> Patočka emphasizes "always": like Heidegger he defines there an originary guilt that doesn't wait for one to commit any particular fault, crime, or sin, an apriori guilt that is included in the conception of responsibility in the originary *Schuldigsein*, which one translates as "responsibility" as well as "guilt." But Heidegger has no need to make reference, no explicit reference at least,

Vienna lecture that formed a sort of manifesto and the nucleus of the *Crisis* (268ff., 314ff.), published as *La Crise de l'humanité européenne et la philosophie* (Paris: Hatier, 1992), 3–49.

What is remarkable about Derrida's dealings with the topic of "Europe" in this context is that, in the wake of Patočka, he deals with it not so much from the perspective of the history of modernization and secularization, which have helped to establish and guarantee a certain neutrality of the public sphere, as from that of the history of religious intolerance, which has all the appearance of having revived in recent years as the return of the repressed. "Difficult to say 'Europe' without connoting: Athens-Jerusalem-Rome-Byzantium, wars of Religion, open war over the appropriation of Jerusalem and of Mount Moriah, of the 'here I am' of Abraham or Ibrahim before the extreme 'sacrifice' demanded of him, the absolute offering of the beloved son, the demanded putting-to-death or death given to the unique descendent, repetition suspended on the eve of all Passion," Derrida observes (FK 4–5 / 13).

Derrida's "Faith and Knowledge" continues and radicalizes the necessary analysis of the *mysterium tremendum* and the demonic in its intrinsic relation to the mechanical and the technological, a theme that Patočka and *The Gift of Death* only announce: "Contrary to what is normally thought, technological modernity doesn't neutralize anything; it causes a certain form of the demonic to re-emerge. . . . There is an affinity, or at least a symmetry, between a culture of boredom and an orgiastic one. The domination of technology encourages demonic irresponsibility" (GD 35–36 / 40).

Neither Levinas nor Marion would agree. According to Marion, the experience of boredom or vanity and melancholy does not bring us back to the wonder of the idols—and what else would the orgiastic be?—but instead opens up the possibility of the "without Being." According to Levinas, this appreciation of the technological is deeply mistaken. For it is precisely the deracination of human beings by technology that by decontextualizing it makes true responsibility possible in the first place.

to this disproportion with respect to an infinite love in order to analyze the originary *Schuldigsein*. (GD 52/55)

Nonetheless, Heidegger's existential analytic or fundamental ontology and Patočka's *Heretical Essays in the Philosophy of History*, amount to the same thing, because they both assume that *either* ontology *or* religion — here Christianity — must be *first* or *primary* or *decisive* in conditioning or founding the other in its very possibility. Both authors let themselves be guided by what Derrida, in *Aporias*, would come to term a "logic of presupposition." This logic is both subtle and complex, and it should be radically distinguished from other metaphysical, empiricist, historicist, or otherwise reductionist attempts to determine or derive the exact relationship between philosophemes and theologemes, or phenomenological intuitions and their formal indications, on the one hand, and the purported revelations of the positive religions, on the other. Nevertheless, the "presupposition" of this logic is far from invulnerable, and, in a sense, it is full of presuppositions of its own. Not only does it entangle and undercut itself in what — at least from a formal perspective-has much about it of an infinite regress: in the case of Patočka, this is clear from the assumption, never justified as such, that the genealogy of the Western concept of responsibility, "supposes a double rupture: both with orgiastic mystery *and* with Platonism," an assumption that in fact enables him to interpret this — essentially European — responsibility in predominantly Christian terms as a perpetually repeated process of *conversion* and, more particularly, "*as* culpability, sin, salvation, repentance, and sacrifice" (GD 50/54 and 56/58 respectively).

According to Patočka, Western, or, rather, European, responsibility has to be rethought against the backdrop of the "irresponsibility" or "nonresponsibility" that characterizes the demonic, the orgiastic mystery, the mythical — in other words, that which precedes the subject's being able to say "I" and to relate itself to an absolute Other — by means of yet another structure of secrecy, namely, that of the *mysterium tremendum* (GD 3/12). This disciplining of the orgiastic by putting it into relation with the realm of responsibility, sincerity, and truth is, Patočka insists, the very germ of religion, properly speaking. Religion can be found wherever sacrality is held in check.[4] Paradoxically, however, this is only possible

4. Patočka writes: "Human comportment aimed at the development of openness and its realm, perhaps its tradition, is not . . . contained solely in language, in propositions and their

where responsibility understands itself, in turn, as exposed to an unintelligible and terrifying mystery of faith. In this sequence, then, of "supersession,"[5] the history of European responsibility is marked by "a chain reaction of ruptures and repressions that assures the very tradition they punctuate with their interruptions" (GD 7 / 16).

In Heidegger, by contrast, the logic of presupposition relies on a limited or restrictive interpretation of the transcendental mode of philosophical questioning. I shall argue throughout that it is precisely the metaphysical or ontological privilege of this motif, as well as its inherent tendencies — not toward foundationalism, but toward a no less problematic *possibilism* — that Derrida's most recent writings have come to interrogate and displace with far more consequences than his continued use of the figure of the *quasi*-transcendental would suggest.

The analogies between Heidegger's destruction of the tradition of Western ontotheology and Patočka's attempt at rethinking the concept of responsibility "as European" — that is to say, "through the decoding [*décryptage*] of a certain history of mysteries, of their incorporation and their repression" (GD 48 / 52) — are more revealing than the differences. Patočka's essays are heretical with respect to the Husserlian and Heideg-

---

formations. There are modes of development and transmission of openness in religion, myth, and sacrifice. . . . Each of these activities, each such comportment, contains a special mode of unconcealment of what there is or perhaps of being" (*Heretical Essays*, 9). Later, he asks: "[I]s there not a history of religion in a rich differentation of religious experience long before the emergence of the Greek *polis* and the Ionian *historia?* . . . Is there not a whole range of evidence that precisely in the sphere of religion it is *conversion,* something like death and rebirth, that is, finding a fundamentally new meaning, that is the focus of all experience? History may be at its core a history *of the world* in the sense of an antecedent complex of our human possibilities, but then it will be primordially a history of religion" (ibid., 139–40). But what, then, is religion? For Patočka, the name should be reserved for a particular transition or, indeed, conversion. In *Heretical Essays,* he defines it only once: "Religion is not the sacred, nor does it arise directly from the experience of sacral orgies and rites; rather, it is where the sacred qua demonic is being explicitly overcome. Sacral experiences pass over into the religious as soon as there is an attempt to introduce responsibility into the sacred or regulate the sacred thereby" (ibid., 101; trans. modified).

     5. I borrow the word *supersession* neither from Derrida nor from Patočka but from Charles Taylor, who, in his *Sources of the Self: The Making of the Modern Identity* (Cambridge, Mass.: Harvard University Press, 1989), 65, speaks of a structurally and perpetually "conflictual" nature of cultural identities: "Platonism in one way, and the Judaeo-Christian religious revelations in another, both have been defined as historical supersessions — of the Homeric-inspired honour ethic and of various forms of idolatry, respectively — and both remain as sources of radical criticism of existing practices and beliefs.

     An ethical outlook organized around a hypergood in this way is thus inherently conflictual and in tension."

gerian concept of history and historicity, and this even more so, as Paul
Ricoeur observes in his preface to the French edition of *Heretical Essays*,
than in their obvious repudiation of the orthodox interpretation of Marxist historical materialism (Patočka was one of the of the 243 writers, art-
ists, and intellectuals who signed Charta 77, a call for basic human rights
that became a focus of opposition to the communist regime in Czecho-
slovakia, and the text of *Heretical Essays* first circulated as a samizdat
publication in 1975).[6] As Ricoeur goes on to point out, Patočka's version
of the Husserlian "regressive, questioning method" does not "recover" a
natural world that is described in terms of a pre-scientific "lifeworld,"[7] as
in Husserl's *The Crisis of European Sciences and Transcendental Phenomenology*, but a prehistoric age that lies at the origin of Western European
history and politics, philosophy and religion. This prehistoric origin has
been lost sight of, but it continues to cast its light (and, in Patočka's account, a grim light at that) on the contemporary political domain. In
Patočka's "strange, frankly shocking passages about the dominance of
war, of darkness and the demonic at the very heart of the most rational
projects of the promotion of peace,"[8] Ricoeur observes, we find a tonality
very different from that of Hannah Arendt (on whose work Patočka draws
in part) or even of Heidegger. For while Patočka sides with Heidegger in
his break with Husserlian idealism, or "philosophical subjectivism,"[9] and,
like Heidegger, no longer takes the transcendental ego or the transcendental and eidetic reductions as his point of departure—that is to say, as
the *via regia* to the natural world and the origin—he nonetheless doubts

6. Paul Ricoeur, "Preface to the French Edition of Jan Patočka's Heretical Essays," in Patočka, *Heretical Essays*, vii–xvi, ix. Ricoeur's preface to the French edition is revealing in more
than one respect. He does not only mention the analogy and difference between Patočka's
undertaking and that of Husserl's *Krisis*, he also compares the *Heretical Essays* to the work
of Merleau-Ponty: "[I]n the works of the successors of Husserl and Heidegger, the *Heretical
Essays* occupies the same place as *The Visible and the Invisible*; namely, by showing a path that
stays faithful to as well as diverges from the two standard versions of phenomenology. Beyond
that, these essays, like the posthumously published writings of Merleau-Ponty, have that dense
beauty of certain figures of Rembrandt, emerging out of the vibrant obscurity of the background. Readers are unable to pull themselves away from the sense of grandeur even when
their progression is retarded by a certain impenetrability and the nonlinear character of the
presentation" (ibid., vii–viii).
7. Ricoeur, "Preface," x. *The Natural World as a Philosophical Problem* had been the title
of Patočka's *Habilitationsschrift*, written in 1936 and published in French translation in 1976
as vol. 68 of the Phaenomenologica series under the title *Le Monde naturel comme problème
philosophique*, trans. Jaromír Daněk and Henri Declève (The Hague: Martinus Nijhoff, 1976).
8. Ricoeur, "Preface," viii.
9. This is Patočka's own term; see *Heretical Essays*, 150.

whether Heidegger's insistence on the concealment and simultaneous unconcealment of Being and its epochs adequately portrays the "problematic condition characteristic of the age of history."[10]

Nonetheless, Patočka's *Heretical Essays* adheres to a logic of "presupposition" that is fully in tune with Husserl's and Heidegger's phenomenology in that it construes the history of responsibility in terms of
a complex, multilayered, and often obscure lineage, and thereby, once
again, in terms of the very conditions of history's (and responsibility's)
innermost possibility. What, then, are these conditions and in what sense
do they make responsibility — the history of that responsibility described
as distinctively *European* — possible?

In Patočka's view, a pervasive historical force of conversion and re-
translation runs from the Platonic *anabasis* through the Christian *meta-
noia* all the way up to the modern philosophies of history, to the theories of secularization, modernization, and the technological age. In all of
these, the Judeo-Christian-Islamic concept of sacrifice is of a decidedly
philosophical rather than merely religious importance. For both Heidegger and Patočka, as well as for Levinas and Freud, among others, Derrida
observes, the construction of the history of responsibility consists chiefly
in reinterpretation of the *theme* and *modality* of the sacrifice: "[T]he arguments intersect in spite of their differences. They ground responsibility,
as experience of singularity, in [an] apprehensive approach to death. The
sense of responsibility is in all cases defined as a mode of 'giving oneself
death'" (GD 43 / 47).

Derrida's own recounting of this history, of Christian religion, of the
question of Being, and of their intimate yet ultimately problematic —
unresolvable — relationship, sets itself apart from the ontologizations for
which the names Heidegger and Patočka stand here, if only by rearrang-
ing the elements and the referents of their respective discourses. Central to
this reading is the emphasis on the motif of sacrifice — on the humiliation
and self-humiliation of discourse that Derrida elsewhere calls "kenosis."
Other words, nonsynonymous substitutions in their own right, come to
mind: ascesis, abstraction, desertification. But none of these figures — if
that is what they are, these figures of all figuration and of defiguration as
well — has the force and uncanny resonance of the term that dominates
and organizes the text of *The Gift of Death*, namely, *sacrifice*. For Derrida,

10. Ricoeur, "Preface," xi. For Patočka's own account of his departure from Husserl's and
Heidegger's respective conceptions of history, see, in particular, *Heretical Essays*, 44ff.

as for Patočka and Heidegger, it is first and foremost the understanding of sacrifice, and, in Derrida's case, particularly the sacrifice of Isaac, as related in Genesis 22 and reiterated in every passion, that should govern the analysis of responsibility in its complex and ultimately aporetic relation to the political foundations of modern Europe and the perennial return of the religious, of messianisms, and of so-called fundamentalisms. All of these phenomena are premised upon a crisis whose very structure seems to be prefigured, anticipated, and announced by the sacrifice. It is the notion of sacrifice that is gradually given prominence over all the other key concepts that structure and punctuate Derrida's reading, in *The Gift of Death*, of Patočka, Heidegger, Kierkegaard, and others: *incorporation, interiorization, internalization, sublation, work, discipline, repression.*

The figure, the motif, and the modus of sacrifice—of a sacrifice, lest we forget, that also sacrifices itself—are privileged in many other contexts as well, including Kierkegaard's *Fear and Trembling*, although Patočka mentions Kierkegaard in his *Heretical Essays* only once.[11] Derrida's confrontation of the transcendental and indeed phenomenological "logic of presupposition" with what might tentatively be called a logic of the sacrifice or sacrificial logic finds its inspiration—or rather instigation—in different sources, not the least important of which are the many discourses on the gift, on the "all-burning" (*brûle-tout*), circumcision, the shibboleth, and so on.

As in Patočka's and Heidegger's discourses, a similar question is at issue. Derrida describes it as the question, not only of "what links historicity to responsibility," but also of what, in turn, links responsibility (at least European responsibility) to historicity, to the historical, and, more particularly, to the "history of religion" (GD 5/14). And the latter, unavoidably, conjures up the religions of the Book, the so-called positive or historically revealed religions, negative theologies, mysticisms, their rhetorical strategies, their prayers, hymns, and so on and so forth.

The two different aspects of this double and seemingly circular or quasi-tautological binding of historicity to responsibility and vice versa—linking this responsibility to the historical, in the ontic no less than the ontological sense—are extremely difficult to comprehend or assess in their inner structure, in their apparent symmetry, and with regard to the actual range of their systematic and practical implications (both philosophical and theological, but also existential, ethical, and political). It

11. Patočka, *Heretical Essays*, 112.

comes as no surprise, therefore, that Derrida claims here that the relation of these concepts to one another has *something of a secret.*

What is at issue in *The Gift of Death* is nothing less than the secret of history and responsibility and the secrecy of their intimate relationship, as well as, conversely, the history of and responsibility toward (and, as Derrida often puts it, "before") that secret. *Donner la mort*, "Giving Death," is the name, the content, and the modus, if not strictly speaking the modality, of the secret par excellence, and, specifically, of the secret of European responsibility and its history, its relation to history, to politics, to democracy, to hospitality, and so on.

Derrida here reiterates the argument of "Préjugés-devant la loi" (translated under the title "Before the Law"), which consists of a subtle reading of Kafka's short story "Vor dem Gesetz." In this reading, Derrida makes reference to the narrative of Freud's *Totem and Taboo* and recalls how responsibility, in the most classical and modern of its definitions, is also thought ultimately here to *resist* or *subtract* itself *from* all historical determinations. In other words, *in order to deserve its name, responsibility must be neither conditioned nor conditional. Nor, in turn, should responsibility be conditioning:* "Even if there is undeniably a history of freedom or responsibility, such a historicity, it is thought, must remain *extrinsic.* It must not touch the essence of an experience that consists precisely in tearing oneself away from one's historical conditions. What would responsibility be if it were motivated, conditioned, made possible by a history?" (GD 5/14). And a little further Derrida continues:

> [T]he classic concept of decision and responsibility seems to exclude from the essence, heart, or proper moment of responsible *decision* all historical connections (whether they be genealogical or not, whether their causality be mechanical or dialectical, or even if they derive from other types of motivation or programming such as those that relate to a psychoanalytic history). It is therefore difficult to *acknowledge* [*avouer*] such a historicity and, to the extent that a whole ethics of responsibility often claims to separate itself, as ethics, from religious revelation, it is even more difficult to tie it closely to a history of religion. (GD 5/14; trans. modified)

Conversely, Derrida maintains, history in its turn "can be neither a decidable object nor a totality capable of being mastered, precisely because it is tied to *responsibility,* to *faith,* and to the *gift*" (GD 5/14). Put otherwise, there is no history, no concept or conceptualization of the historical, without the evocation or without the provocation of some testimony, of a structure of heritage that escapes—exceeds, precedes, or supersedes—not only teleologies and genealogies, in short, all the philosophies of history and their subsequent destructions (from, say, Hegel through Nietzsche and Foucault), but also the hermeneutic understanding of effective history (or, as Gadamer says, of *Wirkungsgeschichte*), the posthermeneutic evocation of metaphysical epochs, seen by the later Heidegger as so many "sendings" of Being, its event, and its truth.

But then again, the attestation in question calls the historical into being. It constitutes it from within, and in so doing, it just as much resists the pattern (so often celebrated) of discontinuity, of contingencies, of the revolution of and breaks with paradigms and epistemes. A completely different logic is at work here. The "logic of sacrifice" is neither the continuation nor the reverse of the "logic of presupposition." It inhabits the same "space" that was once taken by the conditions of possibilities (of categories, transcendentals, existentials, universals) so often invoked by the foundationalist philosophies of all ages and their more cautious modern transformations. But it organizes and structures, formalizes and deformalizes this "space"—now perceived or refigured as a "desert" or a "desert in the desert"—in a very different, if not radically new or "original," way, and does so with diverging consequences.

Derrida suggests as much when he notes with reference to Patočka: "If the orgiastic remains enveloped, if the demonic persists, incorporated and dominated, in a new experience of responsible freedom, then the latter never becomes what it is. It will never become pure and authentic, or absolutely new" (GD 19–20 / 26–27). This, Derrida concludes, constitutes Patočka's essential heresy: the fact that he inscribes the history of responsibility, notably of Western, Christian, and European responsibility, into a history of the transfiguration and metamorphoses of the *mysterium tremendum,* of the secret in its relation to the *demonic*—that is to say, of the substitution of one secret by the other—that most would much rather want to forget about altogether, if only they could. What is more, Derrida claims, this constitution of responsibility is rethought in terms of a *gift of death,* of a *giving oneself*—or *others,* or even the *Other*—*death,* according to a logic, no longer of presupposition, at odds with some of (at least modern) philosophy's most cherished assumptions:

This history of secrecy that humans, in particular Christians, have difficulty thematizing, even more so acknowledging, is punctuated by many reversals [*renversements*] or rather conversions. Patočka uses the word "conversion" as one often does to render the ascending movement of *anabasis* by which Plato refers to the turning of one's gaze towards the Good and the intelligible sun, out of the cavern. . . . The word "conversion" is regularly rendered by words such as "turning back" . . . or "about turn". . . . The history of secrecy has the spiral form of those turns [*tours*], intricacies [*tournures*], versions, turnings back, bends [*virages*], and conversions. One could compare it to a history of revolutions, even to history as revolution. (GD 7–8 / 16–17)

In this, Patočka's genealogy seems to have all the structural features of the Levinasian and Derridean use of the *à dieu,* the toward-God that is at once a turning-away-from-God — an *adieu,* a taking leave of an earlier interpretation or form of the secret — as well as a gesture by which one exposes oneself to the *mysterium tremendum,* to the demonic, the *a-dieu,* as it were, the *horror religiosus* that Derrida reads with and against Kierkegaard, Levinas, Patočka, and Heidegger.

For in the final analysis, the genealogy of responsibility, reread as a history of giving oneself death, or appropriating the meaning of death, is a critical engagement of the work of Heidegger, and most notably of his existential analytic of the being toward death (*Sein zum Tode*). All the paradoxes, aporias, scandals, and conversions — in short, all the historical narratives and formalizations of *a responsibility that does not come into its own but remains tied to a history of irresponsibility,* and this to the point where the good, the best, and the worst have all the appearance of resembling one another in their "origin" and their structure, and start haunting one another *to the point of substitution* — all this, then, sheds a bleak light on the task and the limits of philosophy, of thought, of all action, of every decision that deserves its name: "Paradox, scandal, and aporia are themselves nothing other than sacrifice, the revelation of conceptual thinking at its limit, at its death and finitude" (GD 68 / 68).

The discourse under consideration shares, if not the intention or the explicit aim, then at least a mode of proceeding with the trajectory followed by negative theology as it manifests itself in the tradition of apophatics and in certain mysticisms. In both cases, we are dealing with discourses marked by a process of abstraction, desertification, and formalization, each of which strips religion of all or almost all of its dogmatic content, of its purported substance, indeed, of all remaining deconstructible presuppositions; and this means, in all rigor, that religion is here as it were liberated from the very concept, method, and practice of presupposition as such.

If we look at other texts by Derrida, such as *On the Name,* we find a similar approach to these very same issues, this time, however, not so much in the language of responsibility and sacrifice as in that of phenomenology, repetition, and kenosis.

Before we turn to the details of these texts and their vocabularies, let me first take a few steps back and analyze some key motifs and central arguments in Heidegger's lectures on the phenomenology of religion in the early 1920s, as well as in his subsequent dismantling of onto-theology, notably in the "Letter on Humanism." I shall focus here exclusively on those issues that are directly relevant to my general purpose throughout this book, namely, to explain in what *systematically compelling* and *semantically innovative* sense philosophy—more particularly, modern philosophy from Kant through Heidegger up to Patočka, Marion, and Derrida—can be seen as undertaking a turn to religion.[12]

## Heidegger and Insubordination

I do not contest that we are in fact in this world, but it is a world where we are altered. Vulnerability is the power [*pouvoir*] to say farewell [*adieu*] to this world. One says farewell [*adieu*] to it by aging. Time passes in the guise of this leave-taking [*adieu*] and of the to-God [*l'à-Dieu*].

—EMMANUEL LEVINAS, *De Dieu qui vient à l'idée*[13]

Early on in his *The Genesis of Heidegger's "Being and Time,"* Theodore Kisiel observes: "Heidegger's breakthrough to his lifelong philosophical topic is inherently tied to a personally felt religious topic, in ways we have yet to 'divine.'"[14] Many penetrating studies have been devoted to the riddle of the relation of life and work, in particular where religion is concerned, but it may never be solved. The reasons for this are far from obvious. They seem to lie in the structural inscrutability or incomprehensibility that—from the final pages of Kant's *Grundlegung zur Metaphysik der Sitten* (*Groundwork of the Metaphysic of Morals*), through the writings of Freud and Heidegger, down to Levinas and Derrida—has come

---

12. See also my "Violence and Testimony," in *Violence, Identity, and Self-Determination,* ed. de Vries and Weber, and its more expanded version in my *Horror Religiosus* (forthcoming). I shall leave aside here and reserve for later a discussion of the relevant passages in *Identity and Difference,* the lecture courses on Hölderlin, and the *Beiträge zur Philosophie.*

13. Emmanuel Levinas, *De Dieu qui vient à l'idée* (Paris: Vrin, 1982), 208, cf. 134.

14. Theodore Kisiel, *The Genesis of Heidegger's "Being and Time"* (Berkeley and Los Angeles: University of California Press, 1993), 19.

to be analyzed with increasing subtlety under the heading of the secret, the *Geheimnis,* the enigma, the ellipsis, and so on. These notions are not identical, but they can be read as a chain or series of "nonsynonymous substitutions" (to quote Derrida's "La Différance") formalizing a complex historical phenomenon and, perhaps, the phenomenon of historicity as such, that is to say, of historicity as we know it, but also of a historicity that Derrida in his earliest studies in phenomenology, following Husserl rather than Heidegger, calls "transcendental."

More than one compelling reason why religion remains a "topic," perhaps even a "lifelong topic," for Heidegger — and this "in ways we have yet to 'divine' " — can be found in several of Derrida's later readings of Heidegger, notably in *The Gift of Death, Aporias,* and *On the Name* (in particular, the essay "Sauf le nom"), which stand out by reason of their explicit discussion of the concept of religion, of the theological, of apophatics and mysticism, often with explicit reference to Heidegger, and differ in this respect from the earlier discussions of Heidegger's work in *Of Grammatology, Positions, Margins of Philosophy, The Postcard,* and the interviews collected in *Points de suspension (Points . . . ).* Yet the more recent texts also take up and further elaborate — or formalize — an argument that had been roughly sketched out in the final pages of "How to Avoid Speaking," in *Psyché,* and, more extensively, in the imaginary dialogue between Heidegger and the Christian theologians that concludes *Of Spirit.* All these expositions — some of them systematic, while other are more episodic, parodic, or elliptical — are provisionally summed up in one of the last sections of Derrida's "Faith and Knowledge: The Two Sources of 'Religion' Within the Limits of Mere Reason." This text, introduced and discussed at some length in the opening chapter of this book, will guide my interpretation, since it effectively bundles some of the guiding threads that have run through Derrida's reading of Heidegger from its earliest beginnings.

Regardless of all the confessed importance of the "personally felt religious topic," it was Heidegger himself who stated time and again that philosophical, phenomenological, or fundamental ontological analysis should be kept at an equally far remove from both empirical (anthropological, psychological, biological) *and* theological preconceptions of Being and human existence. In its very mode of proceeding — and in its very essence, to the extent that it is a phenomenological and philosophical undertaking — the existential analytic, Heidegger maintained, *comes before* and is *superordinate* to that of the so-called ontic and positive (read,

empirical and formal) disciplines. For instance, in discussing the demarcation (*Abgrenzung*) between the existential analysis of death—of Dasein's being toward death, that is to say, its most distinctive or most proper
possibility—and other possible interpretations of death and dying, Heidegger insisted:

> Methodologically, the existential analysis is superordinate to the questions of
> a biology, psychology, theodicy, or theology of death. Taken ontically, the re-
> sults of the analysis show the peculiar *formality* [*Formalität*] and emptiness
> [*Leere*] of any ontological characterization, However, that must not blind us
> to the rich and complicated structure of the phenomenon.[15]

It is precisely with regard to these attempts to ascertain the princi-
pal difference between the task of thinking proper—that is to say, of the
phenomenological or ontological *Urwissenschaft* called philosophy—and
the whole spectrum of scholarly or scientific disciplines indebted to ontic
presuppositions and oriented toward some empirical content (in the case
of mathematics and logics, to abstract, indeed formal, principles),[16] that a
serious suspicion might nonetheless arise. This suspicion seems to affect
virtually all of Heidegger's conceptual delimitations. In *Aporias,* Derrida
formulates this difficulty as follows:

> [S]ince it thus precedes all content of knowledge, such an analysis may seem
> to be formal and empty, at least from the viewpoint of ontical content. . . .
> Heidegger recognizes this, but he sees here only an appearance, which should
> not blind us to the differentiated richness of the phenomenological structures
> described by such an analysis. . . . we [must however] raise the question of
> whether, in order to sustain this existential analysis, the so-called ontologi-
> cal content does not surreptitiously reintroduce, in the mode of ontological
> repetition, theorems and theologeme pertaining to disciplines that are said
> to be founded and dependent—among others, Judeo-Christian theology, but
> also all the anthropologies that are rooted there. (A 54–55 / 101–2)

Is this is just another way of saying, then, what Heidegger himself
states at the outset of *Being and Time,* namely, that in the final analysis the existential analytic is, indeed, *rooted* in a concrete existential (i.e.,

---

15. BT 292 / 248.

16. That is to say, to the extent that these disciplines operate as, say, normal sciences and
do not enter into a crisis. For wherever so-called regional sciences or disciplines touch upon—
that is to say, revolt against—their conceptual and presuppositional limits, they become *philosophical,* at least de facto. See, e.g., BT 29–30, 71 / 9–10, 45.

factual and ontic) "possibility"?[17] Yet in what sense, exactly, can or must
the ontological remain ontically *grounded*? Or must we think of the relationship between religion—here the Christian religion—and fundamental ontology in yet another way? Should we assume, for instance, that one
is an inevitable transcription or echo—a belated effect of sorts—of the
other? And what, then, is it that explains this inevitability? History? Tradition? A heritage that one cannot but affirm and attest to? Or do all of
these come down to the same "necessity," that is to say, to the same "possibility," in Heidegger's formal sense of this word? And what, finally, does
"formal" mean here? Of what, exactly, is it an indication, methodologically, ontologically, and, perhaps, even theologically speaking?

Surely, if a similarity between the ontological and the ontic can be discerned or assumed at all—if not in substance or content then at least in
formal structure—it will not have fallen from heaven. The singular, that is
to say, nonidealist, factical aprioricity that we shall be dealing with here,
and that forms part and parcel of Heidegger's formally indicative hermeneutics, can hardly be understood in terms of an atemporal, unhistorical
essence. What is more, it cannot be determined and articulated—or, as
Heidegger says, explicated—without invoking the historical dimension
and constitutive, structural elements that it is somehow able to retrieve
and set free. Arguably, this was already the case in Husserl, on whose work
Heidegger was to draw heavily, if not without reservations or severe criticism, in his introduction and first development of the procedure of formal
indication. In *Being and Time*, Heidegger speaks of the said aprioricity—
which could well serve here as first determination of formal indication—
in no uncertain terms:

> But to disclose the *a priori* is not to make an "*a-prioristic*" construction.
> Edmund Husserl has not only enabled us to understand once more the mean-
> ing of any genuine philosophical empiricism; he has also given us the neces-
> sary tools. "*A-priorism*" is the method of every scientific philosophy which
> understands itself. There is nothing constructivistic about it. But for this very
> reason *a priori* research requires that the phenomenal basis be properly pre-
> pared. (BT 490 n. x / 50 n. 1)

In the context of his own first major work, Heidegger goes on to explain, this means the following: "The horizon which is closest to us, and

17. "But the roots of the existential analytic, on its part, are ultimately [*sic*] *existentiell*, that
is, *ontical*" ("Die existenziale Analytik ihrerseits aber ist letzlich [*sic*] *existenziell*, d.h. *ontisch*
verwurzelt") (BT 34 / 13).

which must be made ready for the analytic of Dasein, lies in its average everydayness" (ibid.). For all the abstraction of its alleged *formalism*, the path taken by fundamental ontology—and by the later thought of Being and its *Ereignis*—never therefore succeeds in fully escaping—in preceding and possibilizing, strictly speaking—the realm of the empirical and the ontic that it is said to open up, but from which it must nonetheless also keep itself apart, if a proper understanding is to be attained at all. Paradoxically, aporetically, *it is made possible by what it makes possible.*

In the rest of this chapter, I give a few examples of the relevance of this Heideggerian problematics to the general issue that interests us throughout: the peculiar form of modern philosophy's invocation of—and turn to—religion. These examples are not the ones given by Derrida, but they may very well further illustrate and corroborate what is at stake in the readings he pursues in different contexts, especially in his discussion of the necessary, yet impossible, demarcations of fundamental ontology and existential analysis, of the persistence and recurrence—in spite of or thanks to these demarcations—of some of the most remarkable theologemes, taken from but transported beyond the tradition of Christian dogmatics and biblical exegesis, and of Heidegger's interpretation of a being toward death that distinguishes itself from the seemingly alternative approaches to death of, say, Freud or Levinas, whose central insights it also, however, seems to confirm or anticipate.

My first example stems from the notes on Heidegger's early lecture course on the phenomenology of religion, published in 1995; the second comes from the well-known "Letter on Humanism." As will become clear in due course, my analysis comes down to raising a seemingly simple question, whose implications and consequences may very well reach beyond the task of interpreting Heidegger, his itinerary, his "lifelong topic," and his engagement with "religion." At issue is a more general systematic question concerning the specificity of philosophy—here phenomenology—in relation to other disciplines, and, as Heidegger would have it, to the very experience of factical life.

## Shortcuts

One should not be surprised by the fact that already in his early lectures, Heidegger portrays the historical (*das Historische*) as the phenomenon that opens the way to a proper understanding of philosophy's tasks, origin, goal, and limitations ("The historical is the phenomenon that ought to provide us with access to the self-understanding of philoso-

phy" [PhRL 34]). Indeed, as early as the winter semester of 1920/21, his
thought seems already to have come into its own, and this well before
his actual reception—and, if one can say so, actualization—of Aristotle,
a reception that has often been seen as the very inception of Heidegger's
turn to a decidedly ontological inquiry into factical life experience, facticity, existence, their temporality, and their historicity. This claim would
seem to rest on the highly questionable presupposition that Heidegger's
turn to and decisive insight into Aristotle, the turn to his "lifelong topic,"
needs no further elucidation, but contains, as it were, the condition of its
very possibility—indeed, its own *Ursprung*—in itself. Nothing, however,
is further from the truth. For what is it that makes Aristotle *fragwürdig*, in
both senses of the word, in the first place? And what is it that continues
to filter through—casting its peculiar light and shadow, its *clair-obscur*,
another *Lichtung* of sorts—the cracks that mark Heidegger's eventual attempt to deconstruct the history of Western metaphysics in toto?

For a clearer understanding of these questions and in order to prepare
a plausible answer to them, it may be worthwhile to carefully examine the
argument that Heidegger propounds in his 1920/21 lecture course "Einleitung in die Phänomenologie der Religion ("Introduction to the Phenomenology of Religion").[18] As Kisiel notes, it is in the early lectures—
which, in addition to the "Einleitung," also include his "Augustinus und
der Neoplatonismus" ("Augustine and Neoplatonism")—that we find

> the in-depth development of 1) the *Bekümmerung* of life, first introduced at
> the end of SS [*Sommersemester*] 1920 and now traced back to its patristic
> and biblical roots; and of 2) the dimension of history which, as Schleier-
> macher and Dilthey had already taught Heidegger, was absolutely central to
> the religious life. The distinction between object-historical and actualization-
> historical, first introduced in this year, will prove to be an indispensable
> "formal indication" for the latter problematic of "Being *and* Time."[19]

Yet one can only be struck by the circumstance that in these early
lecture courses, which precede, and, perhaps, solicit or provoke, the question of the meaning of Being and its multiple senses, Heidegger's other
"lifelong philosophical topic," it is in effect first of all a particular understanding of religion—or, more precisely, of religion *qua* religion, and,
provided this distinction can be made in all rigor, of the phenomenology

18. In Heidegger's *Phänomenologie des religiösen Lebens*, cited parenthetically in the text
as PhRL. All translations from PhRL are my own.
19. Kisiel, *Genesis of Heidegger's "Being and Time,"* 149.

of religion—that opens up the central phenomenon of the "historical." For this astonishing assumption—namely, that "religion" provides access, indeed, the shortest detour, to the "historical"—no explanation is ever given. We are dealing with what seems an outspoken presupposition on the part of Heidegger, brought up as a possible question only in the concluding paragraph of the transcript of the first introductory lecture course (PhRL 124), to which I shall return later. It is simply stated—apodictically affirmed and reiterated with lapidary formulations—that Christian factical life experience lives temporality, or, more precisely, that "Christian experience lives time as such" ("Die christliche Erfahrung lebt die Zeit selbst") (PhRL 82).

In sharp contrast, then, with Heidegger's repeated insistence on a variety of phenomenological principles and procedures, there is no genuine folding of religion out of (or into) the phenomenon—the core phenomenon (*Kernphänomen*)—called historical or *the* historical. Now and then, religion and the historical seem merely to *co-exist*, albeit it not altogether peacefully, as co-originary possibilities caught in a perpetual flight both *away from* and, oddly enough, also *toward* each other. It is as if Heidegger were suggesting that whenever either religion or the historical stabilizes itself, in a concept, a category, an objectifiable domain, or a doctrine, it has somehow forgotten its origin, ground, and limitation, to which only the other can call it back. Just as often, however, it seems that the two resemble each other *to the point of being virtually interchangeable;* in Heidegger's reading, they seem to become, if not identical, then at least *substitutable.* Even the most undisputed conceptual and disciplinary boundaries such as the ones indicated above thus threaten to break down, or are at least robbed of their ultimate justification. Why is this so? And is this an accidental unclarity or, rather, a structural—or formal—necessity of Heidegger's thought (and, perhaps, not of Heidegger's thought alone)?

The answer to this question cannot be found, I believe, in the many—and often contradictory—anecdotal *faits divers* of Heidegger's biography, autobiography, isolated citations, and retrospective self-stylization.[20] Nor, for that matter, can the apparent confusion be ascribed to the much decried "formalism" in Heidegger's use of the terms *historical* and *religion.* Are these synonyms for, say, the flux of factical life as such, in its purity, before and beyond its inevitable petrification into the innumerable and

20. For a helpful documentation of Heidegger's itinerary and the history of its reception, see Pero Brkic, *Martin Heidegger und die Theologie: Ein Thema in dreifacher Fragestellung* (Mainz: Matthias Grünewald, 1994).

relatively stable ontic, positive, and empirical *forms* of this very "life"? No single detail provides us with an unambiguous answer to this question or enables us to resolve the riddle in any rigorous way, let alone at a stroke.

How, then, are we to understand the explication of the phenomenon of religion—and thereby (but how precisely?) of the historical—that Heidegger pretends to undertake here in a *formally indicative* way? To what extent, moreover, is this mode of proceeding—the *formale Anzeige*—representative of the works to follow and, perhaps, "in ways we have yet to 'divine,'" also of enduring significance for all those who are no longer at ease with Heidegger's "lifelong topic," with its point of departure or its putative results?[21]

I shall return to this question below, but must raise a preliminary issue first: why exactly is it that the shortest route to the explication of the phenomenon of the historical is found in the phenomenology of religion? Are we dealing here with a shortcut, a cul de sac, or an aporia?

A possible answer to this question is offered by Karl Lehmann, who notes that it was only the primal Christian experience of factical life that in Heidegger's eyes constituted "the other" in contrast to the ontology of the Greeks, and thereby a vantage point from which the latter could be seen in its limitations and in toto.[22] Conversely, Lehmann goes on to suggest, it was, of course, only Heidegger's intimate relationship with the Greek authors that enabled this originary Christianity to appear as

---

21. See Kisiel, *Genesis of Heidegger's "Being and Time,"* 152: "No less important than the discovery of the kairological character of lived time, in the second part glossing the Pauline letters, is this development of the formal indication in the methodological first part of the course. (Kairology and formal indication will together constitute the *most* essential, but largely unspoken, core [of BT])." On the concept of καιρός, see Henry George Liddell and Robert Scott, *A Greek-English Lexicon* (rev. ed., Oxford: Clarendon Press, 1977), and Gerhard Kittel et al., eds., *Theologisches Wörterbuch zum Neuen Testament* (Stuttgart: W. Kohlhammer, 1933–73), trans. and abridged in one vol. by Geoffrey W. Bromley (Grand Rapids, Mich.: William B. Eerdmans, 1985). In these lexica, καιρός is defined as a decisive point in time (or, more rarely, in situation and place). Significant for the temporal meaning is the fact that the καιρός is viewed as divinely ordained. Within these parameters, the καιρός can either pass as a general index of time or as the *terminus technicus* for the Last Judgment (as in Rev. 1:3: "for the time is near). In the plural, the term can indicate the times or state of affairs; in the singular, a stretch of time, but also a critical moment of opportunity—often of good fortune—whose chance needs to be seized. The *Theologisches Wörterbuch* notes that the "connection with ethics" of the καιρός, stressing the "responsibility of meeting the demands of the *kairós*," can also be found in Stoicism, for example.

22. Karl Lehmann, "Christliche Geschichtserfahrung und ontologische Frage beim jungen Heidegger," in *Heidegger: Perspektiven zur Deutung seines Werkes,* ed. Otto Pöggeler (Königstein: Athenäum, 1984), 140–68. For an excellent discussion, see Zarader, *Dette impensée,* 165ff.

"other" in the first place. In other words, Lehmann claims, only if one assumes that the early Christian experience of time—of the eschatology of
the καιρός (kairos), or fitting season and occasion, and the coming of the
παρουσία (parousia)—had in effect (and for whatever reasons) for Heidegger this pivotal function, can one comprehend that he was indeed able
to take a "step back" (Schritt zurück) and portray the Western tradition as
an apparent—forgetful yet also deconstructible—homogeneous whole.
But how and why exactly is this step taken at all? Lehmann's explanation
would almost seem to point in the direction, not of some perspectivist
contrast, but of a dialectical relationship of opposition or polarity that
would only let itself be resolved in the overcoming (or rather Verwindung)
of metaphysics, in the epochē of all epochs, that is to say, of all reifying
coinages of Being in terms of this or that being or beingness. But this all-
too-Hegelian reading (engaged in by Heidegger himself in Identity and
Difference) fatally oversimplifies matters.[23]

To be sure, Heidegger notes that a certain generality has so far been
considered to be philosophy's privileged object. At least since Aristotle,
philosophy has aimed at an understanding and categorization of the
"totality of beings" (Gesamtheit des Seienden). Aristotle's Metaphysics,
and notably the famous dictum τὸ ὂν πολλαχῶς λέγεται, testifies to
this theoretical preoccupation with the general structures and regions of
Being. Yet Heidegger hastens to add that Aristotle's text harbors other
possibilities as well, which have been insufficiently realized and may very
well still be ahead of us:

> For Aristotle rather means still something different from what one has seen so
> far. In him, not only do we find ontological considerations, but a totally other
> consideration reverberates unnoticed ["es schwebt eine ganz andere Betrach-
> tung unabgehoben mit"]. The Aristotelian metaphysics has perhaps already
> gone further than we ourselves are nowadays in philosophy. (PhRL 56)

Yet to argue that Heidegger was already able to find his lever in Greek
ontology itself in Aristotle's understanding of the multiple senses of
Being, and especially in the attention Aristotle himself pays to the notion
of the kairos[24]—should not lead us astray or allow us to ignore the fact

---

23. For a discussion of the influence of Hegel on Heidegger, see Karin de Boer's lucid study
Denken in het licht van de tijd: Heideggers tweestrijd met Hegel (Assen: Van Gorcum, 1997); English translation in preparation.

24. See, e.g., Dieter Thomä, Die Zeit des Selbst und die Zeit danach: Zur Kritik der Textgeschichte Martin Heideggers, 1910–1976 (Frankfurt a./M.: Suhrkamp 1990), 145–46, 156. Thomä

that primal Christianity nonetheless figures as a *privileged model* for the
explication of factical life experience and the problem of the historical,
and, perhaps, also for access to Aristotle's text. But then again, to insist
on the experienced radical otherness of originary Christianity vis-à-vis, if
not the totality, then at least the hegemony of a specific Western system
of thought, is not to deny that this otherness is also contested, which is
simply to say that in its role of the other, it was never *alone,* nor, perhaps,
even *first.* What I would suggest, following Lehmann's interpretation, is
that it is solely in the experience of an otherness that contrasts with what
is common, known, or established (empirically, ontologically, axiologically, aesthetically, theologically), that the world of phenomena—here:
the phenomenon of the historical or of temporality—can appear (and indeed appear as *fragwürdig*) at all.

At yet another point in his lecture course, Heidegger describes the
function of this *distanciation* in terms of a strategy of delaying (*Retardier-
ung*) (PhRL 120). In choosing this word, he indicates that the distantness,
which, in a way, forms the condition of the possibility of all experience, is grounded in—or, perhaps, even identical with—a structure of
temporality; this structure, which enables all experience as well as all
theoretization, cannot be theoretically deduced or be experienced in any
empirical sense of the word. It can only be existentially assumed and reaffirmed, that is to say, reenacted, and this, Heidegger insists, only in a
*Vollzugszusammenhang mit Gott.* This figure of temporality—*Retardier-*

---

sharply critizes the common hypothesis, defended by Lehmann, Sheehan, and Pöggeler, among
others, according to which Heidegger's conception of temporality somehow found its "grounding" in the original Christian experience, which he allegedly discovered after he turned away
from Catholicism and supposedly drew closer to Protestantism. Nonetheless, Thomä also
speaks of a "philosophical metamorphosis" (*Verwandlung*) (ibid., 147) of theological transcendence, a transition (*Übergang*) from religion to philosophy in which this religion does not fully
disappear but remains obliquely intended (ibid., 148). But this, he continues, is neither "modernization [*Modernizierung*] of Pauline theology nor an abolishing of religious premises; there
is rather . . . a systematic connection between a 'life' that asserts itself against the 'values' and a
'grounding experience' with which the '*system* of Catholicism,' of a dogmatically petrified religiosity that depends on God, is given up" (ibid., 149). In short, Thomä thinks that reference
to the originary Christian motif is insufficient for a plausible account of Heidegger's later interpretation of futurity and the *Augenblick* (ibid., 160–61), and that a more important source
can be found in Aristotle. "The *Grundprobleme der Phänomenologie,* from 1927, attribute the
discovery of the *kairos* to the sixth book of the *Nichomachean Ethics,* yet this discovery would
have been covered over in favor of a determinate ontological option. . . . The contested end
of the ninth book of the *Metaphysics* thinks Being and truth in the way that Heidegger looks
for," Otto Pöggeler writes in a similar vein in his afterword to *Der Denkweg Martin Heideggers*
(Neske: Pfullingen, 1983), 331.

*ung*—forms, it would seem, the counterpart of the spatial figure of the "step back" (*Schritt zurück*) that Heidegger was to adopt much later (for example, in *Identity and Difference*): it allows one to see the world, one's own world, in its very *genesthai*, becoming, or thrownness, as the result, not of fate or mere contingency, but of an act of creation and of grace. That which would have seemed to come before, the already-there, is seen—or repeated—in this early lecture course as that which comes, if not in fact, then at least in its very essence, "later," or as that which is not yet, but remains still and, perhaps forever, to come.

## Reading St. Paul Methodically

The second part of Heidegger's course is devoted to a "Phenomenological Explication of Concrete Religious Phenomena Drawing on Pauline Letters" ("Phänomenologische Explikation konkreter religiöser Phänomene im Anschluss an Paulinische Briefe"). What does this mean? How does this second part of the lecture course relate to the interrupted—and allegedly too abstract (too formalist?)—exposition of the central problem of phenomenology, to wit, the historical and its most direct approach by way of the procedure of formal indication and the revealing example provided by the phenomenology of religion? Heidegger is quoted as stating his aim in seemingly clear terms. It is his—as we shall soon verify, unsuccessful—attempt to establish clear-cut conceptual distinctions and disciplinary demarcations that is of most interest here:

> In what follows, we do not aim to give a dogmatic or theological-exegetical interpretation, nor a historical consideration or a religious meditation, but merely an occasion [*eine Anleitung*] for phenomenological understanding. What is proper to the understanding of the phenomenology of religion is to gain a preunderstanding [*Vorverständnis*] for an original way of access. To that end, the method of the history of religion must be incorporated, and this in such a way that one tests it oneself in a critical manner. The theological method lies beyond the scope of our considerations. It is only through phenomenological understanding that a new avenue for theology is opened. The formal indication refrains from having a final understanding, which can only be given in genuine religious experiencing [*Erleben*]. It aims only at opening the access toward the New Testament. (PhRL 67)

From the very outset, Heidegger gives his insights into the key words, phrases, and verses of the biblical text a very peculiar status. They are not so much statements (*Sätze*) concerning matters of fact that might in principle be proven or corroborated or justified (empirically, historically, exegetically, dogmatically). Instead, he argues, we start out with preconceptions that figure merely as provisional, if not arbitrary, means, and that do not so much get hold of as gain access to the phenomenon in question. Yet, if the latter (religion, the historical) is ultimately given, it is solely in a genuine and singularizing religious experience, in an act of divine grace, which remains irreducible even to the authenticity of existence proper, as well as to the enactment of phenomenological understanding as such.

Formal indications have the character of stepping-stones that enable thought to explicate and thus eventually to understand the phenomenon under consideration; here, the experience of factical, historical life, for which original and originary Christianity—or, as Heidegger, following Franz Overbeck, would eventually say, Christianicity, *Christlichkeit*—seems to be the example par excellence. Yet Heidegger is quick to point out that formal indications are in fact stumbling blocks as well. This intrinsic ambiguity—a dual status that is an aporia in its own right—is, precisely, what marks the very nature and function of formally indicating concepts, and, perhaps, of philosophical concepts in general. The peculiar phenomenological problematic of formal indication that Heidegger introduces in the early lecture course—notably its central concern with the experience called religious and, through it, with the historical—thus seems to have a much wider relevance, which extends not only far beyond the domain of the existential analytic, of the fundamental ontology, espoused in *Being in Time,* but ultimately also well beyond the ulterior thought of Being, its *Ereignis,* and its Truth.

The formally indicative concepts are first of all hypothetical, underlying and preceding any possible thesis, in that they target or touch upon the phenomenon—lived experience—yet do not lead us to the very heart of this phenomenon itself. In a sense, they lead up to a way that still remains to be followed *all the way* and first of all *in a genuine way.* The very act of the determination characteristic of formally indicative concepts is therefore, in a sense, *pre-* or *proto-*, and thereby *methodo-methodological* (rather than, say, *meta-methodological*) alone. It is, it seems, only when they disclose the access to the fundamental meaning of the phenomenon that they allow certain methodological principles and procedures to be deduced in the first place: "These founding determinations are first of all hypothetical. When the fundamental meaning of Christian belief [*Religiosität*] has been hit upon [*getroffen*] with them, we ask, what follows from this methodologically?" (PhRL 80).

Religion, faith, and theology are thus presented in a formal schema that, as Heidegger reiterates, ultimately does not capture the proper meaning of the phenomenon in question. It would almost seem that the formal indication becomes, as it were, obsolete in the enactment (or reenactment) — *Vollzug* — of phenomenological understanding as such, even though it is itself paradoxically what gives access to the phenomenon in the first place. But the latter finds its proper measure — a measure beyond measure — only in a synthetic and, we might add, *synergetic* enactment and reenactment with God.

However, Heidegger's emphasis on this singular and singularizing structure of the *Vollzugszusammenhang mit Gott* does not prevent him from making what seems a vast and contradictory general claim; for with reference to the basic presupposition of all hermeneutics, ancient and modern, he notes: "Without a preunderstanding of the whole context, one cannot grasp one single trait" (PhRL 95). It is difficult, indeed impossible — and this is the heart of the aporia that characterizes this text, like so many others, among them *Being and Time* — to reconcile this assertion with the fact that it is solely in the specific modality of the Pauline experience of the *kairos* and the *parousia* that Heidegger views the *locus classicus* of the upsurging of theology, defined as the explication and self-articulation of faith. There is an irresolvable tension here that expands itself beyond Heidegger's actual (or actualizing) reading of St. Paul into his overall concern with the phenomenology of religion, and thereby — via a shortcut that is simply posited as the shortest possible detour — with the core phenomenon of philosophy, that is to say, the historical itself. This tension can be ascribed neither to the idiosyncrasies of Heidegger's thought nor to the conceptual limitations of phenomenological methodology. Rather, it is revelatory of a general philosophical problem and, perhaps, even of the proper — and this means the necessary, yet ultimately impossible — specificity of philosophy (as a discipline and a way of life) itself. The central concerns of these elliptical notes on phenomenology, history, and religion are philosophical idealization and the ways in which any conceptualization is triggered, carried forward, and interrupted by the experience of factical life, according to a logic that is not so much one of "presupposition" (as Derrida suggests in *Aporias* with reference to *Being and Time*) as of "transcendental historicity" (a concept that structures Derrida's earliest studies of Husserl).

Heidegger argues that early Christianity, and thereby factical life *tout court* — but what, exactly, justifies this analogy, extrapolation, or implication, if not, in turn, an act, indeed a leap, of faith?—is marked by an irreducible uncertainty or restlessness. It is in part this Augustinian motif of the *cor inquietum* that, as Kisiel rightly notes, "inaugurates the gradual emergence of 'care' as more 'strenuous' characterization of the *dunamis* of intentionality."[25] For this view more than one confirmation can be found, not only in the early lecture course, but also in a footnote to *Being and Time,* where Heidegger observes:

> Even as early as the Stoics, μέριμνα was a firmly established term, and it re-curs in the New Testament, becoming "*sollicitudo*" in the Vulgate. The way in which 'care' is viewed in the foregoing existential analytic of Dasein, is one which has grown upon the author in connection with his attempts to inter-pret the Augustinean (i.e., Helleno-Christian) anthropology with regard to the foundational principles reached in the ontology of Aristotle. (BT 492 n. vii / 199 n. 1)

For the clarification of this motif of restlessness, then, other testi-monies—testimonies both much older and much more recent than St. Paul's letters—are therefore relevant. They all resonate throughout Hei-degger's text. Yet it is impossible to decide which comes first or which has left the most decisive traces. Uncertainty, it seems, belongs to the very genealogy and definition of the concept or the motif of restlessness itself. But why, then, is a certain privilege accorded—at least verbally, rhetori-cally, and, perhaps, strategically—to the experience of early, or so-called primal and originary, Christianity?

Heidegger turns to Galatians and subsequently to Thessalonians 1 and 2, because it is in them, and in the situatedness from which these letters speak to us here and now—and, precisely, out of *their* here and now—rather than in the more retrospectively oriented narrative recon-structions of, say, the Acts of the Apostles and the four Gospels that he expects to gain access to the original Christian experience of facti-cal life. As the editors of this very first part of the *Phänomenologie des religiösen Lebens* observe: "Starting out from the phenomenon of the Pauline gospel [*Verkündigung*], he works out . . . the determining features [*Grundbestimmungen*] of originary Christian belief [*Religiosität*], in light of which [*an denen*] the enactment character [*Vollzugscharakter*] of facti-cal life as such becomes noticeable [*erkennbar*]" (PhRL 342).

25. Kisiel, *Genesis of Heidegger's "Being and Time,"* 114.

Yet this seemingly simple observation hides a puzzling obscurity. For how exactly, and according to which criteria—or, for that matter, any other, more fundamental, *krinein*—can this transition (leap or *Ur-sprung*) from the testimony of originary Christianity to the structural enactment of factical life ever be accomplished, let alone justified? In what sense does the phenomenological explication—to begin with the procedure of formal indication on which it relies—differ from what might just as well be an unwarranted extrapolation, generalization, abstraction, idealization, or formalization? What guarantees that the *formale Anzeige* indicates or touches upon the phenomenon at all, if only provisionally, and like the proverbial ladder that must be pushed away after having completed its function?

## Eschatology, the καιρός, and the παρουσία

According to Heidegger, eschatology, specifically the experience of the καιρός and the παρουσία (apparently seen as synonyms), lay at the center (*Zentrum*, PhRL 104) of early Christian life, even though this was forgotten and repressed (*verdeckt*, ibid.) from at least the first century of the Christian era on (and other fundamental Christian concepts would soon suffer the same fate). Heidegger is quoted as stating:

> The meaning of this temporality is . . . foundational for factical life experience, also for problems such as that of the eternity of God. Already in the Middle Ages these problems were no longer understood in a fundamental [*ursprünglich*] way as a consequence of the penetration of Platonic-Aristotelian philosophy into Christianity, and our contemporary speculation, which speaks about God, increases the chaos. The culmination of the confusion has been reached in these days with the projection of the concept of value into God. (PhRL 104)

Complicating matters even more, Heidegger stresses that the heart of the original Christian life was in its very originality and primacy, that is to say, in its grounding motif, *far from original and far from being first*. In passing, he notes that the distinctive nature of the "eschatological problem" was of a much older origin, which early Christianity forgot, albeit it in a less fatal manner than the forgetfulness attributed to the Middle Ages and the age of modernity. For whereas the Platonic-Aristotelian and Neoplatonic systematization and canonization of Christian faith and the history of modern ontotheology, of the *metaphysica specialis,* and natural theology, were based on an expanding forgetfulness, the Pauline concept of temporality remained an authentic modification (or *Umbildung,* PhRL 105) of the primary—pre-Christian—impulse.

It is not fully correct, therefore, to suggest, as Marlène Zarader does, that for Heidegger the impetus of so-called *Urchristentum* is simply marked by an "absolute beginning."[26] In a truly Kierkegaardian sense, the novelty of the New Testament and in particular of the Pauline letters— and, within that corpus, notably Galatians and 1 and 2 Thessalonians— is already a repetition or imitation, a *Wiederholung.* And, even while Heidegger does indeed not cite, say, Ecclesiastes 9:12, he nonetheless does not deny that the concept of *kairos* remains "unintelligible outside the Hebraic conception of time."[27] He could just as well as have said this; but, of course, does not, or at least not in so many words.

The reference to pre-Christian eschatology, though, does not contradict the circumstance that St. Paul's teaching is, in its essence and proper movement, also *unprecedented.* The conversion of which Paul—and Heidegger with him—speaks with so much fervor was and is to be discovered and reenacted by each single individual, which must happen each time anew. Heidegger sums it up in the following way:

> The eschatological [*das Eschatologische*] in Christianity was already obscured by the end of the first century. Later, all the original Christian concepts are misconstrued. In contemporary philosophy, too, the Christian conceptualizations are still hidden behind the Greek attitude [*Einstellung*]. One should draw here on the Gospels—the great eschatological discourses of Jesus in Matthew and Mark—from which the fundamental positing of the problem arises. The fundamental eschatological orientation is already late Judaic; Christian consciousness is a peculiar modification [*Umbildung*] of it. (PhRL 104–5).

In saying that the eschatological orientation is "already late Judaic," Heidegger refers to the so-called apocryphal Apocalypse of Ezra, the fourth book of Ezra, written at the end of the first century. No reference is made to earlier—Old Testament—apocalyptics; nor does Heidegger choose to inscribe the Pauline eschatology into the history of a—political—messianism that on the reading of interpreters such as Gershom Scholem and Jakob Taubes, stretches from biblical times, through modern chiliastic

26. Zarader, *Dette impensée,* 172ff.
27. Ibid., 178 and 177 respectively.

"antinomism," all the way up to writings of Marx and Freud, Benjamin and, to a certain extent, Levinas.[28] Of this canon of the messianic — at least

28. Shortly before his death, Jabob Taubes gave a few lectures on St. Paul's Letter to the Romans, which were published as *Die Politische Theologie des Paulus*, ed. Aleida Assmann and Jan Assmann (Munich: Wilhelm Fink, 1993). The meaning of St. Paul's theology had formed the subject of Taubes's last seminars at the Free University of Berlin, where he held a chair in philosophy and, more particularly, in hermeneutics. And, indeed, on first glance, it seems that the relevance of St. Paul's letters — the founding documents of early Christianity — for a broader nontheological audience, notably, students in philosophy, occupied Taubes most in these courses, which focused mostly on the Letter to the Corinthians. What we find in *Die politische Theologie des Paulus*, however, is not only a tour de force interpretation of St. Paul's single most influential text, the Letter to the Romans, but also nothing less than an intellectual testament, presented without notes and compiled on the basis of tapes and recollections of the participants. Taubes insisted on the publication of what he considered to be a final articulation of his life's work and, indeed, that of a whole generation.

*Die Politische Theologie des Paulus* offers a highly original reading of St. Paul that not only reinscribes him in the Jewish tradition (by now almost a commonplace in New Testament scholarship thanks to authors such as E. P. Sanders), but first of all seeks to give new meaning to the very idea of a political theology. Political theology, as understood here by Taubes, should be radically distinguished, in its inspiration, scope, and implications, from the so-called liberation theologies of the 1960s, which were often characterized by the attempt to bring the concepts and methods of theoretical Marxism (Western and non-Western) to bear on biblical texts. In Taubes's presentation references to anticolonial struggles and anticapitalism are completely absent. If anything, his frame of reference is the intellectual and political climate of the interbellum, of the spiritual climate of the Weimar Republic, with its discussions of a demythologized understanding of the New Testament, dialectical theology, critical theory, psychoanalysis, existential analysis, and the revival of the Jewish philosophy of religion (notably in the works of Cohen, Rosenzweig, and Buber). Nor should Taubes's project of a political theology be confused with the ambiance of the works of Carl Schmitt, the infamous legal theorist, with whose conception of a *Politische Theologie* Taubes's position has certainly much in common, even though he does not share Schmitt's reactionary political tenets. Taubes edited several volumes devoted to Schmitt's work, and the book under consideration contains a revealing account of his personal exchange with Schmitt. Yet something different is at issue in these lectures. If Schmitt's work is characterized by an apocalyptics according to a top-down model, Taubes's universe, by contrast, is marked by a sense of history as catastrophe, that is to say, by an apocalyptics that is not contained by political schemata, but disrupts the categories of immanence from the bottom up.

Taubes situates his reading in the history of Jewish interpretation of St. Paul, from Leo Baeck and Martin Buber on, seeking to emphasize a liturgical, rather than, say, theologico-dogmatic, reading of the texts under consideration. Taubes distances himself from the earlier Buberian attempts to radically differentiate between a primary, natural, Jewish faith, or *emuna*, that expresses itself in a collective belonging, on the one hand, and the supposedly Greek conviction of faith as a merely individual and singularizing conversion, that is to say, of a *pistis* that reduces itself to the *belief in* certain propositions or matters of "fact." The irony, he writes, is that *pistis* forms the heart of a messianic logic with the help of which St. Paul situates himself squarely in the tradition of Jewish prophecy and apocalyptics.

It is important to note, however, that this is not yet another attempt to revive the so-called Jewish-Christian "dialogue" (an idea for which Taubes has nothing but contempt). Taubes's key witnesses point in another direction. They are Gershom Scholem ("meinen Lehrer") and, more indirectly, Walter Benjamin, as well as — with many more reservations and qualifications — the aforementioned Carl Schmitt. In their writings, Taubes finds the paradoxical logic of messianism (of apocalyptics and eschatology), which forms the organizing principle of St. Paul's gospel, no less than of so-called antinomian movements such as Cabalism and Hasidism, and, as a matter of fact, of any unprecedented *act* founding a people or state. What all such movements and events have in common is a certain paradox, something that runs counter to the evidence of common sense, of what can be known or predicted.

In their afterword, the editors of *Die Politische Theologie des Paulus* rightfully characterize Taubes's lectures as "a deconstruction of the effective history [*Wirkungsgeschichte*] of the Letter to the Romans that at least since Luther had been obsessed with the formula 'faith instead of works'" (ibid., 144). Taubes's reading, they propose, takes issue with the most influential classical and modern interpretations of the Letter to the Romans, notably those of St. Augustine, Luther, Karl Barth, and Rudolf Bultmann, all of whom he accuses of having in the end reduced St. Paul's theology to an existentialist-ontological dogma. Heidegger is also taken to task for having wanted to "neutralize" the Christian in Kierkegaard and the genuinely theological element in the New Testament. And, Taubes writes, to the extent that Heidegger seemed to suggest otherwise, for example, in his engagement with the circle around Bultmann in Marburg, he simply "played along" and this for merely strategic and tactical reasons (ibid., 91). Again, what Taubes stresses instead in his reinterpretation is the functioning and systematic force of what he calls here a "messianic logic." This formulation is reminiscent of similar interests pursued by Benjamin, Scholem, Levinas, and, most recently, Derrida, among others, some of whom Taubes discusses in passing. Taubes's own version of messianic logic, however, is marked by insights that, I would claim, are less central to these authors, but that nonetheless deserve careful attention in any further discussion of messianism (of eschatology and of the apocalyptic), as, say, a historical category, a theologeme, and, let us not forget, a philosopheme.

Messianic logic has everything to do with the question of memory, with the present force of the past. For this a model can be found in the psychoanalytic understanding of trauma. Taubes sees in Freud's book on Moses not so much a quasi-historical account of the origin of monotheism as an insight into the fact that the mode of its transmission is not that of the conscious and active labor of tradition but of a passive collective memory, whose unconscious traces are marked by a certain repetitive force (*Zwangscharakter*). This is clear from Taubes's own course description: "Under the mask of a psychopathography of the man Moses, Freud develops a theory of recollection and of tradition. His analysis of religious-historical processes of the return of the repressed constitutes an extremely multilayered concept of historical truth" (ibid., 173). In addition, Taubes claims that Freud does not so much identify himself with Moses as with St. Paul (ibid. and esp. 122–31). Freud is described as following in the trace of Paul: "ein direkter Nachfahre des Paulus" (ibid., 123).

Mixing the genres of biblical exegesis, history of ideas, and philosophical commentary, Taubes presents his views in a discourse that is deeply personal and at times autobiographical. Moreover, Taubes makes it very clear that the separation of questions commonly relegated to the faculty of theology from questions designated as philosophical is in the end detrimental to both disciplines (he notes, albeit it in passing, that a chair in Old and New Testament studies as well as one in Church history should perhaps be part of every philosophical faculty). In other words, theological issues form the ABC of any instruction in philosophy. That this is not recognized is made clear by the general *"Bibel-Ignoranz,"* which, he notes polemically, is owing to the dominant *interpretatio graeca* of European history, more precisely, to the interpretation of culture as "Humanismus-Humboldt-Kultur." Nothing less than a historically well informed and systematically challenging attack on the silent premises of this limited interpretation of culture, its meaning and transformation, is at stake here.

of its inherent messianicity—Derrida's *Specters of Marx* would seem to be the latest, the most telling, and also the most hesitant or reluctant example. Be that as it may, in the chapter following the one containing the reference to late Judaic eschatology, Heidegger goes on to note what seems also a fundamental difference, and one due to the fact that Christian eschatology, in its Pauline form, seems more consequent than its precursor and model. What is the difference?

> For the Christian, only the τό νῦν [now, at present] of the enacting synthesis, in which he properly locates himself, can be decisive, not the expectation of a separate event at some time in the future. In late Judaism, the expectation of the Messiah is primarily [*primär*] oriented toward such a future event, toward the appearing of the Messiah, at which other human beings will be present. Esra 4 already shows a familiarity with the Christian prevalence of the enactment over as opposed to the expected congeries of the event [*Ereigniszusammenhang*]. Something like temporality springs only from enacting such a synthesis with God [*Vollzugszusammenhang mit Gott*]. (PhRL 114)

At the end of this exposition, Heidegger further amplifies this putative difference through a discussion of the concept of *parousia;* in spite of the subsequent changes of its meaning throughout the ages, this concept, he suggests, conjures up a radically "different [*andersartige*] Christian life-experience" (PhRL 102). In the wake of others, above all Kierkegaard and Overbeck, Heidegger identifies this experience with that of a specific modality of temporality, as well as with the unique—yet infinitely repeated—disposition it requires. This disposition is hardly that of the grounded expectation (*Erwartung*) of an upcoming event, but rather the experience of a restless vigilance (*Wachsamsein*) vis-à-vis the imminence of a futurity, a to-come or *à venir* that—in our lives and deaths—remains forever uncertain or highly ambiguous, and toward which no theoretical attitude will ever be appropriate; this *eschaton* is given solely in the *re-* and *co-* enactment with God, the *Vollzugszusammenhang mit Gott*.[29] In Heidegger's own words:

> In classical Greek, παρουσία means "arrival" [*Ankunft*] (presence [*Anwesenheit*]), in the Old Testament (and the Septuagint, respectively): "the arrival

29. See Françoise Dastur, "Heidegger et la théologie," *Revue Philosophique de Louvain*, nos. 2–3 (May-August 1994): 226–45, 230–31.

of the Lord at the Day of Judgment"; in late Judaism, "the arrival of the
Messiah as placeholder [*Stellvertreter*] of God." For the Christian, however,
παρουσία means: "the appearing again of the already appeared Messiah" [*das
Wiedererscheinen des schon erschienenen Messias*], which in the first place is
*not* literally expressed by the term. The whole structure of the concept is,
however, concurrently altered by this.

One might think at first: the fundamental disposition toward the παρουσία
is an expectation and the Christian hope . . . a special case of it. But that is
completely wrong! We shall never get from mere analysis of the consciousness of a future event to the relational meaning [*Bezugssinn*] of παρουσία.
The structure of Christian hope, which is in truth the meaning of the relation
[*Bezugssinn*] to the παρουσία [*Parusie*], is radically different from all expectation.[30]

What is striking is, first, that there seems to be no common measure
between the παρουσία and the (past, future, or present) presence that
underlies the horizon of expectation of classical Greek philosophy no less
than of Old Testament and, again, of late Jewish thought, all of which
seem, in Heidegger's reading, at best ambiguous. Sometimes they get it,
sometimes they don't. Moreover, the παρουσία is not a specific case that
differentiates, exemplifies, or — in more than one sense of the word — betrays a general structure. Nor, finally, does this temporality let itself be
deduced from the intentionality of consciousness as such. On the contrary — but then again, there can be no real opposition here, where a certain incommensurability holds sway over all conceptual delimitations —
the παρουσία is nothing more or less than the *instance* and *instantiation*

30. PhRL 102. For the different meanings of παρουσία, see Liddell and Scott, *Greek-English
Lexicon*, and esp. Kittel et al., *Theologisches Wörterbuch*, which define the παρουσία as a presence, a coming or arrival and (in New Testament use) an advent. In the Greek translation of the
Old Testament, we find the term referring to the coming of God in self-revelation and in the
cultus, or to the coming of the messiah. In the New Testament, Kittel reminds us, παρουσία is
not used of the first coming of Christ; thus, there is "not a twofold *parousía.*" Moreover, where
St. Paul employs παρουσία, the Gospels speak of the coming in glory as the "day of Lord," and
the pastoral letters use ἐπιφάνεια (*epipháneia*), appearance, manifestation. Revelation, which,
as we have seen, virtually opens with the invocation of the καιρός, lacks the term παρουσία.
On the whole, Kittel goes on to suggest, St. Paul's letters are premised on the belief that the
"turning point has already come," and that, as a consequence, the παρουσία is seen as "a defini-
tive manifestation when God's eternal rule supersedes history." "In Plato the word [παρουσία]
is still a secular [*sic*] one, and it is not prominent in Stoicism, but it acquires a cultic sense
in Hermes mysticism and Neoplatonism," Kittel comments. "Typical uses are for the invisible
presence of the gods at sacrifices and for the appearance of divine fire."

of a radically singular alterity, of the totally other (*das ganz Andere,* as Rudolf Otto puts it, or the *tout autre,* as Derrida writes).

The structural change in the concept of παρουσία rather than the range of its actual meaning throughout history is what interests Heidegger most here. The anticipation of the second coming of Christ is at odds with any idea of some future presence: its structure is a different one, namely, the coming of what, in a way, is *already there.* And it is only the formulation of this structure that can serve as a formal indication that may help us gain access to the radically other structure of the phenomenon of Christian hope. The latter, Heidegger remarks, should not be taken either as an expectation, well-grounded or not, or as a waiting for an event that will come to pass in some future time. The structure in question does not let itself be reduced to any intentional correlation between a *noesis* and a *noema.* Instead, we are dealing here with an eschatology that is at once consequent and could be interpreted as an "absolute teleology," and, perhaps, as Benjamin would have it, as a teleology *ohne Endzweck.* It signals a different approach to the question of time, to the here and the now. This and nothing else explains the introduction at this very point of Heidegger's exposition of the privileged — Kierkegaardian — moment of the *Augenblick:*

> "Time and Moment" [*Augenblick*] (1 Thess. 5:1: Περὶ δὲ τῶν χρόνων καὶ τῶν καιρῶν, always spoken in one breath) pose a particular problem for the explication. The "when" is no longer grasped originally, to the extent that it is grasped in the sense of a suspended and fixated [*einstellungsmäßigen*] "objective" time. Neither is the time of "factical life" in its falling, unaccentuated, non-Christian sense meant. Paul doesn't say "when," because that word is inadequate for what has to be expressed, because it does not suffice.
>
> The whole question is for Paul not a matter of knowledge. . . . He does not say "then and then does the Lord come again"; nor does he say, "I don't know when he will come again," — rather, he says: "You know very well. . . ." This knowledge must be a very peculiar one, for Paul refers the Thessalonians back to themselves and to the knowledge that they have as those who have become what they are [*als Gewordene*]. From this mode of answering, it follows that the decision of the "question" depends on their own lives. (PhRL 102–3)

As in the interpretation of Galatians, where the dogmatic or thetic differences between faith (or grace) and the works of the law are reduced to the single difference in orientation in factical life for which they supposedly stand, so the reading of 1 Thessalonians is also seen in light of the radical distinction between the *how* of two contrasting forms of communication (or *Mitteilungen*). The alternative here is that between the message of those who feel themselves inclined to say *anything at all* regarding the "what" and "when," and who are thus, Heidegger stresses, primarily interested in "peace and security" (PhRL 103; cf. 1 Thessalonians 5:3) and those who remain faithful to the truly eschatological and kairological temperament of the apostle:

> Those who find rest and security in this world are those who cling to this world, since it prepares them peace and security. . . . Sudden decay [*Verderben*] befalls them . . . They are surprised by it, they do not expect it. Or rather, they are exactly in the suspended and fixated mode of expectation [*in der einstellungsmäßigen Erwartung*]; their expectation absorbs itself in that which life brings them. Since they live in this expectation, the peril [*das Verderben*] hits them in such a way that they cannot escape. They cannot save themselves, because they do not have themselves, because they have forgotten the proper self, because they do not have themselves in the lucidity of proper knowledge. (PhRL 103)

Is this the final word? Not quite. For Heidegger leaves no doubt that, according to 1 Thessalonians 5, the uncertain arrival of the παρουσία does not only come as a thief in the night for those who are asleep or drunk. Should this be the case, one could—on a somewhat perverse reading— argue that, paradoxically, only the improper, fallen, existence of the sons of darkness and the night may entertain a relation with the time of the decisive moment of the καιρός (albeit indirectly, or, rather, *in obliquo*— that is to say, in the very mode of forgetfulness). And, indeed, at times, Heidegger seems to suggest as much—for example, when he is quoted as saying: "For *those,* who have no hope and then trouble [*Trübsal*], but who have a fake joyfulness and security, it comes as 'sudden' and inescapable; *unexpected,* not prepared for it; no means for overcoming and taking a position, they are *handed over* to it [*ausgeliefert*]" (PhRL 150–51). Only the nonbelievers, it would thus seem, relate to the παρουσία in its very unpredictability. Yet the distinction at issue here is, of course, that between those paralyzed by an inauthentic fright (*falschen Schrecken*) and those whose response ought to be understood in a completely different register, reminiscent of the phrase from Philippians 2:12 taken up by Kierkegaard, namely, that of "religious fear and trembling!!" (*religiöser Furcht und Zittern!!* PhRL 154). Over and against the first mode of exis-

tence, in the hectic or fixed curiosity of its fallenness, Heidegger pits the
tranquil lucidity and restless wakefulness of the sons of light and of the
day, whose attitude toward the παρουσία and the καιρός is described in
a way that would seem to contradict the most obvious (and Heidegger's
own) interpretation of 1 Thessalonians 5:3: "For those who are wise the
day does not come (like a thief in the night)" — not "with suddenness and
inescapability," Heidegger elaborates (PhRL 151). Nonetheless, this circumstance does not take away from, but, on the contrary, increases this
second coming's essential uncertainty, an uncertainty that seems to spill
over into Heidegger's own attempt to give a reenacting interpretation of
the Pauline text. But what, exactly, is this uncertainty?

On the one hand, it seems, the faithful are called upon to stay awake
lest the day of the Lord — the παρουσία — surprise them as a thief in the
night. On the other hand, they are assured that they *already* are sons of
light and of the day — that they *already* know — and that they are in that
sense far from being unprepared for that which allows for no determinable anticipation, and thus, strictly speaking, for no preparation whatsoever. The οἴδατε, you "know" — a prefiguration of the "understanding"
(*Verstehen*) that *Being and Time* stresses — has here, fundamentally, the
status of an "I know not what," it comforts without providing any advance knowledge that could remove or still the fear and the trembling.

Let me note in passing that it is not insignificant that this comfort-
without-comfort is extended by St. Paul to those who have *already* fallen
asleep with that other sleep called death (biological death rather than the
inauthentic mode of existing that most of the time marks one's being
toward death). Yet this is something Heidegger passes over in silence, for
reasons that are, perhaps, not so different from his ulterior unwillingness
or inability to attribute a primary or constitutive role to the death of the
other in *Being and Time*. This unwillingness or inability — an oversight of
phenomenological seeing of enormous proportions, for which Heidegger
has been taken to task by both Levinas and, in his wake, Derrida — will
occupy us at some length in the next chapter and need not concern us in
the present context.

Now does all this mean, then, that the fundamental uncertainty regarding the παρουσία is exclusively on the part of those who do not
believe and of those who have not believed and are no longer with us?
Not so. There remains a double uncertainty here, one that once more
would seem to prefigure some of the most striking features of Heidegger's
later thought, in *Being and Time* and elsewhere. Heidegger insists that

the Antichrist, the threat of whose coming St. Paul announces with vivid
imagery, in fear and trembling, raises the stakes and presents as it were a
παρουσία that is, on the one hand, *not quite* or *not yet* it—and therefore
not the παρουσία proper—but that, on the other hand, differs in nothing
observable from the real one, that is to say, from the coming again of the
one who had in fact already come before:

> Nobody and especially not those who speculate and chatter can say: " 'the
> day has come" [*ist da*], "now" the "now" is coming about, since "before" all
> this the Antichrist must first appear. (No "history" that still goes on there,
> an "accident," but something essential, albeit something negative, that en-
> counters God and Christians. It does not all come down to a mere before
> and after. "Before" is not some kind of *order* and a disposition [*Einstellung*],
> respectively, but concern [*Bekümmerung*]—something existentially mean-
> ingful.) . . . Thus the when is always uncertain also for the believer; for him,
> when faced with the Antichrist, everything comes down to perseverance [*das
> Durchhalten*]. (PhRL 155)

There seems to be no doubt in Heidegger's mind that the coming of
Christ is not so much a coming *in time*—or, by any human measure, a
coming *on time*—that is merely preceded by a violent prelude. For the
coming of the Antichrist of which Paul speaks at the beginning of 2 Thessalonians 2 is interpreted, not so much as the penultimate phase in the
completion and fulfillment of a supposedly linear biblical time (running
from creation, through revelation and incarnation up to the apocalypse
and the second coming), but as the *modality* of Christ's return.

What does that mean? Well, first of all that the ultimate, pure—and
purely purifying—possibility of human existence comes closest to the
possibility at the other extreme of the spectrum of the existential possibility that makes up factical life experience—namely, of the human
being's deepest fall, of fallenness at its worst. This is yet another falling
without halt, but one, as it were, in the wrong direction, namely, that of
the finite, doomed world, and comes down to an improper loss of self:
"In the last and most decisive and purest concern for oneself lingers the
possibility of the most abyssal [*abgründigsten*] fall and the proper loss of
oneself [*Sichselbstverlierens*]" (PhRL 240–41).

Second, it means that the modus of this second coming—or coming
*again*—is far from being unequivocal; the terrifying uncertainty is inscribed on the very face of it. This becomes clear if we look more closely
at what St. Paul says of the counterfeit miracles and their fatal decep-

tion: "And for this cause God shall send them strong delusion, that they should believe a lie: / That they all might be damned who believed not the truth, but had pleasure in unrighteousness" (2 Thessalonians 2:11–12, King James Version).

Of course, it is clear that for St. Paul there is also this: it is God who first holds the wicked one back and who will eventually also annihilate him. This is another central element in Paul's text that is ignored, as if it were no longer part of the experience that can be explicated — or formally indicated — by the phenomenology whose methodological confines (and chances) seem the chief concern of Heidegger's lecture. In this, the phenomenology of religion is once more in accord with the fundamental ontology of *Being and Time,* as well as with the later works, among them the *Beiträge zur Philosophie* and the "Letter on Humanism," that pretend to overcome the most questionable of this major work's guiding presuppositions. Like the "experience" of death in itself, the experience of the end — of the *eschaton,* of the Apocalypse — defies all description and phenomenological understanding. It is here, then, that the analysis of existence and Heidegger's early self-explication of factical life find their ineluctable and internal limit.

It is not as if one should have to remain silent about time in its worldly, linear, or cyclical sense and speak instead about the one and unique καιρός that annuls this time or puts it in perspective as a created, finite, and finished — yet to be fulfilled — time, as a time also that does not count, if worst comes to worst (and *eschaton* and Apocalypse mean nothing else). Paul refuses to speak about the καιρός as if it were a determinate and determining point in time. In the New Testament, we should not forget, the καιρός is mentioned not in the singular but in the plural; its privileged moment or rather momentum is "one of a kind," to be sure, but this singularity is not or no longer characterized by its being *one* or indivisible. It confirms the analysis just given when Heidegger is quoted as saying: " 'Christian belief [*Religiosität*] lives temporality.' It is a time without an order of its own or fixed places, etc. Starting out from whatever objective concept of time, it is impossible to hit upon this temporality. The when is by no means objectively graspable" (PhRL 104). The *when* is reduced to the *how,* to a *how,* moreover, the proper explication of which subtracts itself from all objective, dogmatic, meditative, or edifying discourse. The *Wann* is a *wie,* not a moment *in time* or *of time,* but precisely the *having* (or not having) of this time, of any time, a certain way of having time when there is — in fact — no one left, but also when there is no time to lose, and where it is always already too late. Paul Celan would seem to provide us with a key to this *Wann* when he associates it with the *Wahn*, the "madness" — the "madness of the day," the *folie du jour,* as Maurice Blanchot would say — the madness also to which, according to St. Paul, all the wisdom of the world is doomed before God.

The very structure of the καιρός thereby confirms nothing less than a transcendental truth — a *veritas transcendentalis* of sorts — which consists in the discovery that a certain undecidability and restlessness form the necessary condition for wakefulness, for conversion, and finally for resoluteness, all of which contribute to the enigma of faith as well as, *by analogy,* to that of factical life experience as such — that is to say, of human existence in its proper meaning. But again, what precisely constitutes this analogy? Are we dealing here with a parallel that is merely *formal?* And in what exactly does this *form* — or is it a *formalism?* — that seems similar in both phenomena consist? Or are we dealing here with what is at bottom one and the same phenomenon, if only because religious faith is fundamentally a modification of factical life, or, conversely, because this life is in the end to be understood in terms of faith, or, perhaps, because both are merely epiphenomena of yet another more originary phenomenon, for example, the core phenomenon called the historical? Or, finally, are all these phenomena co-originary, to use a formulation that plays an important role in *Being and Time?* These are difficult questions indeed.

Two possible interpretations of the said analogy between faith and factical life can be given. If I am not mistaken, they somehow exclude each other, even though each is in a sense fully adequate. This constitutes the very aporia that interests us here. First, it could be maintained that early Christian eschatology prefigures the ontology of Dasein and the analytic of existence proper. Heidegger could thus be said to have redefined early Christian temporality in terms of resoluteness (*Entschlossenheit*), the religious reminiscences of which were subsequently ignored, denied, or played down.

Second, it seems no less plausible to say that the formal indication of existence that finds its extensive elaboration only in *Being and Time,* in a sense, already *informs* — or precisely *forms itself in* — the understanding of early Christianity, of its restlessness, its wakefulness, its knowledge of having to become what one already is, and so forth.

No hermeneutic circle resolves the tension between these two possible yet incommensurable interpretations, each of which seems equally compelling. And perhaps we should not let ourselves be forced to choose here, where a certain indecision—or, as Derrida stresses throughout in "Faith and Knowledge," a certain scruple, restraint, respect, and, thereby, by definition, *religio*—is de rigueur. To know how to judge, the very secret of *krinein,* is precisely to know when (and how) *not* to judge.

Be that as it may, on both readings, the emergence of the existential analytic or fundamental ontology—and thus, as the introduction to *Being and Time* would have us believe, the beginning of phenomenology proper—seems to obey *a Christian logic.* This logic enters into a complex relationship with the "logic of presupposition," which Derrida claims both organizes and destabilizes the basic tenets of the central argument of Heidegger's magnum opus, and this nowhere clearer than in its interpretation of Dasein's being toward death. What, then, is this Christian logic? Does it escape the "logic of presupposition," and, if so, in what sense and to what extent?

The first thing to be noted here is that the Christian logic is premised on a structure broached above, namely, that of the *again* of the *already.* This structure, it would seem, differs from that of the logic of presupposition in an important way, since it does not imply a distinction in principle —or de jure—between the repetition and what it is a repetition of. The latter is not only the condition of the possibility of the former, which, in turn, is not simply its derivation or actualization, since the reverse holds true as well: the repetition is at least as much the condition of what it is a repetition of as the other way around. Needless to say, such a reversibility of two terms undermines the very meaning of "conditioning," of "possibilization," and indeed of the transcendental upon which *Being and Time* is premised. On this reading, the early lectures would for all their fragmentation seem to be well advanced beyond the premises of Heidegger's so-called mature work, in that they allow it to be seen that the latter's logic of presupposition is inscribed in a structure of testimony—or, indeed, *religio*—by which it is grounded in its very possibility at least (or just?) as much as it in turn illuminates and indeed reveals this structure. In a sense, it is unclear which of the two comes first, and, as a consequence, the very principle of transcendentality would appear to be split, doubled, haunting every determination (conceptual and existential) with an uncertainty whose modality is that of a respectful indecision, and thereby, again, of *religio.* Upon close scrutiny, the very destruction of metaphysics and ontotheology announced by *Being and Time,* and undertaken in the writings that followed, would be but the re-citation of the *verbum internum* of Christian faith, and this regardless of its professed atheism, agnosticism, and even paganism. Phenomenology, ontology, existential analytics, the thought of Being and its *Ereignis*—they would all be made possible by a structure of faith that they are said make possible (or understandable) in the first place. And the acknowledgment of this paradox, or aporia, is precisely what could be called religion in more than one sense of the word. In her study on Heidegger and the Jewish tradition, Marlène Zarader comes close to drawing this conclusion:

> It does not suffice . . . to say that Heidegger understands the essential structure of Dasein in a way that an experience such as that of the *kairos* can find there the condition of its possibility. One must add that Heideggerian thought uses [something of] the *kairos* [*use du kairós*] in order to *rethink the essence of time itself,* an essence . . . which is not a simple form, but indeed the full determination of the content.[31]

Yet this mutual dependency of fundamental ontology and ontic rootedness, Zarader confirms, is never acknowledged as such, that is to say, in explicit terms. This may well surprise, she continues, since in so many other contexts Heidegger always insists on taking the analysis of a given phenomenon—and first of all the core phenomenon of the historical, of originary temporality—several steps back toward the originary words (*Urworte*), etymologies, and the singularity of a past (*Herkunft*) that, as he insisted on more than one occasion, remains forever a future to come (*Zukunft*). One could maintain, therefore, that Heidegger's fundamentally ontological concepts—especially his use of notions such as guilt, fallenness, and conscience—inhabit the world of the New Testament idiom (as well as that of St. Augustine, Luther, Pascal, and Kierkegaard) *as though* they were not part of it; they echo it without being implicated in this world, as though they were merely its ontological repetition, and one that leaves everything as it is—intact—while nonetheless also putting everything in a radically new light.

Yet Heidegger pretends that the originary Christian idiom—as noted, the very paradigm, the example par excellence, of the phenomenon of factical life and the historical as such—*invades* the philosophical problematic *without* ever challenging the latter's ontological primacy. Whatever the theological or religious overdeterminations of so many of the so-called existentials, according to Heidegger, they never threaten the professed separation between the ontological and ontic disciplines (especially the

31. Zarader, *Dette impensée*, 171–72.

positive science called theology); nor do they infringe upon the apparent formality of ontology's formally indicative concepts. These concepts as well as the existentials to which they lead, so the argument goes, do not mean what they would seem to mean at first glance (or *zumeist und zunächst*, to quote the phrase whose scansion dictates the rhythm of Heidegger's text). But then, again, is to say this not precisely to reiterate—perhaps unwittingly—the essential strategy of appellation that Heidegger himself attributes to early Christian life? "For the Christian, however, παρουσία means 'the reappearance [*Wiedererscheinen*] of the Messiah who has already appeared,' which at first glance [*zunächst*] does *not* lie in the literal expression" (PhRL 102). To deny the Christian heritage, then, to limit ontological understanding of its idiom to a meaning that goes well beyond its original or current use, all this means still to pay tribute to a logic—that of early Christianity—that is for the rest also portrayed as secondary and derived. In short—and in the absence even of any psychoanalytical necessity—the denial confirms exactly what it seeks to deny.

## "As Though It Were Not"

Heidegger notes that the relation to the παρουσία of the wakeful true believers is marked neither by ignorance nor by lack of concern. Rather, it stands out by reason of a remarkable *indifference*. What does that mean? And how does this indifference relate to the figure of the ὡς μή (*ōs mē*), or "as if not," of which Heidegger speaks somewhat later? Heidegger says that the ὡς μή should not be understood along the lines of the Kantian regulative idea (let alone—but Heidegger does not say so explicitly—in terms of the fictionalism adopted by the neo-Kantian Hans Vaihinger in his *Philosophie des Als-Ob* [Philosophy of the As-If]).[32] Neither negative nor merely imaginative, the ὡς μή has a properly positive or rather affirmative structure, albeit premised upon a certain indifference to the distinction between being and nothingness:

> One is tempted to translate the ὡς μή with "as if" [*als ob*], but that doesn't work. "As if" conveys an objective concatenation and suggests that the Christian should cancel [*ausschalten*] those links to the world. This ὡς positively speaking adds an entirely new meaning. The μή conceals the enacting syn-

32. Hans Vaihinger, *Die Philosophie des Als Ob: System der theoretischen, praktischen und religiösen Fiktionen der Menschheit auf Grund eines idealistischen Positivismus* (Leipzig: Felix Meiner, 1920). For a discussion of the peculiar "indifference to be" of the ὡς μή;, the "as if," or *comme si*, see Jean-Luc Marion's GWB 83ff. and 126ff. / 124ff. and 181ff.

thesis [*Vollzugszummenhang*] of Christian life. At each single moment of the
enactment, all of these links [to the world] undergo a retardation [*Retardier-ung*], so that they emerge from the origin of the Christian synthesis of life
[*Lebenszusammenhang*]. Christian life is not unilinear [*geradlinig*], but bro-
ken: all contextual [*umweltlichen*] links have to go through the enacting synthesis of the having become what one is [*Gewordenseins*], so that this one is
co-present [*mit da*], while the links themselves and that to which they relate
are in no way affected [*angetastet*]. Who can grasp it, should grasp it ["Wer es
fassen kann, der fasse es"]. The isolation of Christian life sounds negative. . . .
Yet there is in Christian life also an unbroken synthesis of life at a level of
spirituality, which has *nothing* to do with the harmony of a life. (PhRL 120)

The repetition alluded to in the expression of the *again* of the *al-*
*ready* is revelatory of the intrinsic structure, the logic or *verbum internum,*
of the peculiar, nonepistemic knowledge for which faith stands here (as
*wissendes Glauben,* as recalled, Heidegger stresses, by St. Paul's appeal
to the οἴδατε: "you know"). It is clear that the ways in which the different threads of meaning (the *Sinnzusammenhänge*) are gathered into the
enacting synthesis with God (the *Vollzugszusammenhang mit Gott*), obtain the features of an ὡς μή;, an "as though it were not," which means
that the undelimitable difference that is made by the παρουσία in relation to the historical chronology of cosmic time — as an *Augenblick* that
escapes, yet troubles, any now, then, or later — finds its counterpart in an
experience, a turning around or new birth, that likewise leaves no observable, let alone objectifiable, marks on the believer and his or her dealings
with the world, with others, and with him- or herself. The difference made
by the παρουσία, the *Augenblick,* the καιρός, on the one hand, and the
imperceptible change of heart it inspires or provokes, on the other, lies in
the fact that they both stand under the regime of the ὡς μή, of the non-
ironic indisposition that leaves everything as it is even though it makes all
the difference in the world. In both cases, in the παρουσία and in *faith,*
the difference is only there for those who are willing, able, and destined —
*predestined* — to see it. It depends on how one sees it, if one sees it. There
is nothing more to say.

Does this mean that those who believe relate to time — in the chronological, vulgar-historical sense of the word — in the same manner as to
the *Umwelt,* the *Mitwelt,* and the *Selbstwelt,* namely, in the modus of
ὡς μή? In other words, is the ὡς μή St. Paul's and, indeed, Heidegger's
answer to the question of the "how?" Is the ὡς μή the decisive charac-

teristic of the *Vollzugszusammenhang mit Gott?* Does the latter take place as though nothing happened at all, as though everything were bracketed, suspended, put under erasure, and crossed out, while remaining what it is, and thus, in a sense, fully intact? Is the most radical change (of heart and in the order of things) invisible, imperceptible, and this to the point of bringing almost no change at all? This is indeed how one might, for example, be inclined to interpret 1 Corinthians 7:29–31:

> I mean, brethren, the appointed time [καιρός] has grown very short; from now on, let those who have wives live as though they had none, and those who mourn as though they were not mourning, and those who rejoice as though they were not rejoicing, and those who buy as though they had no goods, and those who deal with the world as though they had no dealings with it. For the form [σχῆμα] of this world is passing away.[33]

Again, what is at issue here is an intentional attitude or rather *disposition* that in its Pauline form — but also its Augustinian, Lutheran, Kierkegaardian, and Heideggerian guises — remains principally at odds with every possible psychological, anthropological, historical, epistemological, and axiological characterization; one, moreover, that may manifest itself everywhere and nowhere, that is everywhere at home — and therefore nowhere at home — and that, finally, is *in* this world (in all its complexity of the *Selbstwelt, Mitwelt,* and *Umwelt*) but not *of* this world, or, put otherwise, in this world but ὡς μή:

> In the calling [*Berufung*] in which someone is, he should remain. The γενέσθαι is a μένειν. With all the radical transformation something remains. In what sense should we understand the remaining? . . . Schematically: something remains unchanged, and yet it is radically changed. Here we have a pandemonium [*Tümmelplatz*] of speculatively rich [*geistreicher*] paradoxes, but this doesn't help a bit! Smart formulations explicate nothing.
>
> That which is changed is not the relational meaning [*Bezugssinn*] and even less so that which concerns the content [*das Gehaltliche*]. Thus the Christian does not step outside the world. (PhRL 118–19)

33. New Revised Standard Version, 2d ed. (1971), in Nestle-Aland, *Greek-English New Testament* (Stuttgart: Deutsche Bibelgesellschaft, 1992). The King James Version has: "But this I say, brethren, the time *is* short: it remaineth, that both they that have wives be as though they had none; / And they that weep, as though they wept not; and they that rejoice, as though they rejoiced not; and they that buy, as though they possessed not; / And they that use this world, as not abusing *it:* for the fashion of this world passeth away."

This is not to say that the world, its goods, and human relations become thereby a mere ἀδιάφορον (*adiaphoron*), a matter of indifference (PhRL 122). On the contrary, they are not nothing, but that which can here and now be appropriated in an authentic manner, in the *Vollzugszusammenhang mit Gott*. With reference to 1 Corinthians 7:20, Heidegger notes that the calling in which one is and the one whom one is—that is to say, the *Umwelt* and *Selbstwelt*—by no means determine the facticity of the Christian. Yet they are nonetheless there and are appropriated in the Christian life: in fact only the becoming and the thrownness of the latter turns them into what they truly are, namely, mere temporal goods (PhRL 119).

What does that mean? Again, Heidegger bases himself on the interpretation of 1 Corinthians 7:29–32 and suggests that this temporalization is first of all indicative of the Christian's way of relating to the world, to its authorities, to others, and to himself. Paradoxically, it is precisely in their relative in-difference that all these relations attain their proper measure and, indeed, their particular urgency: "Only a short time still remains, the Christian lives persistently in the only still to come [*Nur-Noch*] that enhances his affliction [*Bedrängnis*]. The compressed temporality is constitutive for Christian religiosity: an 'only still to come'; there remains no time for delay" (PhRL 119).

To say much more, Heidegger warns, means to lapse into the pitfalls of enthusiasm, of *Schwärmerei*, but also of the scientific *Einstellung*, that is to say, into the epistemic disposition toward and thereby cessation of the flux of factical life experience, attempting to find some *Halt*, some footing or support, in it or—worse still (but fundamentally there is no difference here)—to find a *Halt* in God. The latter, Heidegger says with an unflattering reference to Karl Jaspers's *Psychologie der Weltanschauungen* (*Psychology of Worldviews*), in particular the section "Der Halt im Unendlichen" ("The Support in the Infinite"),[34] comes down to nothing less than committing "blasphemy":

> The Christian does not find in God his "support" [*Halt*] (cf. Jaspers). That is a blasphemy [*Blasphemie*]! God is never a guarantee [*Halt*]. But to "have a support" is always enacted in view of a certain meaningfulness [*Bedeutsamkeit*], attitude, worldview, insofar as in giving support and gaining it God is the cor-

34. Karl Jaspers, *Psychologie der Weltanschauungen* (Berlin: Springer, 1919; reprint, 1960), ch. 2c. See also Heidegger's "Comments on Karl Jasper's *Psychology of Worldviews*," trans. John van Buren, in *Pathmarks*, ed. McNeill, 1–38/1–44, a text that once more takes up the question of formal indication.

relate of a meaningfulness. Christian worldview [*Weltanschauung*]: properly speaking an absurdity [*Widersinn*]! (PhRL 122; see also 200).

One may well wonder, of course, whether one cannot, in Heidegger's own terms, envision a *Halt* that is experienced in the mode of the ὡς μή. Indeed, how are we to differentiate between finding one's footing in God, on the one hand, and a genuine act of faith, on the other, if the latter's sole characteristic is to have none whatsoever, that is to say, if the true faith is, in the end, indiscriminable, invisible, and thus virtually indistinguishable from every *Halt*, but also from its opposite?

## Formal Indication: The Very Idea

Heidegger does not provide us with an answer but instead resorts to a characterization of the genuine enactment of Christian life that seems as good as any other. He insists that to believe — to adopt faith — means ipso facto to involve oneself in trouble or put oneself in a situation marked by trouble (*Trübsal*):

> The experiencing is an absolute affliction [*Bedrängnis*] . . . , which belongs to the life of the Christian itself. The taking upon oneself [*Annehmen*] . . . is a putting oneself in a situation of need [*Not*]. This affliction is a fundamental characteristic, it is an absolute concern on the horizon of the παρουσία, of the second coming at the end of time [*endzeitlichen Wiederkunft*]. (PhRL 97–98).

But what is an "absolute worry" on the "horizon" of the παρουσία? What does it mean to think of the latter as horizon, or, as Heidegger would eventually say, as a dimension? This question is difficult to answer, not in the least because, for Heidegger, the παρουσία is an absolute singularity every time and for each single human existence. It is singular also in the sense of absolute, according to the etymological meaning of the Latin *absolvere*. Could any such singular envelop, situate, or welcome or anything else? For this question to be answered in a satisfying way, we should begin by clarifying the precise nature of this singularizing worry (concern, or care) and by asking how it springs up as a possibility — the utmost possibility — of so-called factical life.

The transition, transfiguration, new birth, or conversion called faith is, according to Heidegger, a turn to a factical life that is incomprehensible in terms of life *tout court*, let alone in terms of life in its everydayness. Nonetheless, it is a turning away from life *to* life, more precisely, a turn of life itself as it turns itself, in itself, against itself, that is to say, against

its older self. This turnabout is a process vis-à-vis or before an absolute witness—God: "What is at issue is an *absolute turnabout [absolute
Umwendung]*, further a turning *toward [Hinwendung]* God and a turning
away [*Wegwendung*] from the idols [*Götzenbildern*]. . . .The taking upon
oneself consists in putting oneself in the need [*Not*] of life. With this a joy
[*Freude*] is connected that comes from the Holy Ghost and is incomprehensible to life. . . . The taking upon oneself is in itself a transformation
[*ein Wandel*] before God" (PhRL 95).

Heidegger is aware of the fact that this "how" of our relation to life
proper is hard to grasp. Nothing less than a God's-eye view seems demanded here. But then again, this difficulty of testifying to the difference
marked by the turn is at the same time that of every phenomenological
understanding worthy of the name. What is more, it has nothing to do
with an "individuality" that is inaccessible in its infinite complexity. What
Heidegger aims at here is a problem that becomes increasingly paradoxical or aporetic, becomes ever more mysterious, as we approach the phenomenon itself. In a sense, this difficulty is given with the nature of understanding as such, but as one traverses more and more "stages" (*Stufen*)
and "steps" (*Schritte*) of the so-called explicative schema, and as the phenomenon is approached from ever more angles, it becomes increasingly
clear that the task of understanding—in its proper instantiation, which is
a repetition and reenactment of sorts—becomes more and more urgent:

> Understanding has its difficulty in its enactment itself; the difficulty grows
> steadfastly with the approach to the concrete phenomenon. It is the difficulty
> of putting-oneself-into-the-situation [*Sich-hinein-Versetzens*], which cannot
> be replaced by a fantasizing-one's-way-into-it [*Sich-hinein-Phantasieren*], by
> an "approximative understanding" [*Anverstehen*]; what is required is a proper
> enactment. (PhRL 100)

In this respect, phenomenological understanding belongs to the world of
the "self" evoked by Paul, which is characterized by an intrinsic and irrevocable uncertainty, by a weakness, that is, which is in essence its greatest strength, the very locus and modality of its resoluteness. Here one
finds the strange reversal according to which it is in being virtually nothing—close to the Nothing—that one comes closest to God:

> Only when he is weak, when he perseveres in the needs [*die Nöte*] of his
> life, can he enter into an intimate connection with God [*Zusammenhang mit
> Gott*]. This fundamental requirement of having-God [*Gott-Habens*] is the

opposite of all bad mysticism. Not the mystic plunging [*Versenkung*] and the particular effort, but the perseverance of the weakness of life becomes decisive. Life is for Paul not a mere sequence [*Ablauf* ] of events, it *is* only, insofar as he *has* it. (PhRL 100)

This uncertainty also pertains to the texts under consideration, St. Paul's epistles and Heidegger's interpretation of them, which are neither theological treatises (dogmatic prolegomena, biblical exegeses) nor philosophical speculation. On the contrary, to the extent that Heidegger's reading is a singular testimony, just like Paul's—a *writing again* of the epistles, as it were, of the very same gospel, *with and beyond* Paul, in a repetition whose modality is apparently more important than their purported content—it is characterized by a logic connected with the procedure of formal indication ( *formale Anzeige*). Heidegger distinguishes the latter from mere formalization (generalization, abstraction, idealization) that subsumes and dissects the phenomenon in terms of what it is—or *has*—not, thereby violating precisely the specific judgment or *krinein* appropriate to it.

What, then, does the procedure of formal indication entail?[35] Why is it that it alone makes possible what Heidegger identifies as κρίνειν λόγῳ (*krinein logō*), "distinguishing . . . understandingly" between truth and untruth (cf. BT 265 / 222–23). Heidegger addresses the first of these questions most explicitly in the first, methodological, part of the lecture course, which was soon cut short by protests concerning its apparent lack of concreteness, its not living up to its billing, namely to give an introduction into the phenomenology of, precisely, *religion*. He only returned to it at comparable length in his 1927 lecture "Phenomenology and Theology," which defines theology as the positive science of a *Christlichkeit* whose very heart is faith. This lecture, it has been noted, can very well be taken as offering a corollary to the *Grundlagenkrisis* that is mentioned in passing in *Being and Time*,[36] for example in the following:

35. See Georg Imdahl, *Das Leben verstehen: Heideggers formal anzeigende Hermeneutik in den frühen Freiburger Vorlesungen* (Würzburg: Königshausen & Neumann, 1997), 19: "It is inherent in the methodological intention of formal indication that philosophy not only formulates its thought with the help of concepts, but also that, beyond that, philosophy wants to initiate an authentic situation; application is a central theme of the formal indication." Cf. ibid., 23, 142ff.

36. This is suggested by Jean Greisch in his *Ontologie et temporalité: Esquisse d'une interprétation intégrale de "Sein und Zeit"* (Paris: Presses universitaires de France, 1995), 427–54.

*Theology* is seeking a more primordial interpretation of man's Being towards God, prescribed by the meaning of faith itself and remaining within it. It is slowly beginning to understand once more Luther's insight that the "foundation" on which its system of dogma rests has not arisen from an inquiry in which faith is primary, and that conceptually this "foundation" not only is inadequate for the problematic of theology, but conceals and distorts it. (BT 30; cf. 29 / 10; cf. 9)

Instead of clarifying this statement against the foil of the 1927 lecture, let me take another step back and ask again what an appropriate conceptual foundation (*Begrifflichkeit*) would look like. This brings us back to procedure of formal indication, which is first and foremost an indication of the proper—that is to say, the best or least distortive—access to and provisional view of the phenomenon under consideration. In the 1920/21 lecture course, Heidegger explains that the formality intended in the phrase "formally indicative concept" should be understood, in the first place, against the background of an important terminological distinction introduced by Edmund Husserl in his *Logische Untersuchungen* (*Logical Investigations*) as well as in the first volume of *Ideas Pertaining to a Pure Phenomenology and to a Phenomenological Philosophy.* Heidegger is quoted as saying:

The methodical use of a meaning [*Sinnes*], which becomes directive for the phenomenological explication, this is what we call the "formal indication." What the formally indicative meaning carries in itself is that with regard to which the phenomena are reviewed [*abgesehen*]. The methodological consideration should make clear in what sense the formal indication, although it governs the consideration, nonetheless does not carry a preestablished opinion into the problems. One should be clear about the meaning of the formal indication lest one relapse either into a consideration marked by a fixed disposition [*einstellungsmässige Betrachtung*] or into regional limitations [or demarcations: *Einschränkungen*] that one then deems absolute. (PhRL 54)

It is important to note that Heidegger develops this phenomenological procedure of formal indication by lifting it out of the original Husserlian context of the analysis of so-called theoretical acts. Furthermore, Heidegger insists that the methodical use of concepts *qua* formal indication is at odds with their usage in common parlance, or, for that matter, in traditional and modern philosophical vocabulary and discourse. This is nowhere clearer than in the specific use Heidegger has here for the concept that names the core phenomenon (*Kernphänomen*) from which phenomenology, indeed, philosophy in general takes its lead.

What is central to both of these aspects of formal indication is that they view this procedure first of all as a "phenomenon of discrimination" (*Phänomen des Unterscheidens*), and that means of critique, indeed, of *krinein* and thereby, indirectly, of a necessary correction (*Korrektion*). That the use of formally indicative concepts enables us to correct theological categories—in more than one sense of the correction—this and nothing else is final word of "Phenomenology and Theology." No mention is made here that the correction might very well be *reciprocal* and thus work in two ways at once.

A certain tendency toward generalization is typical of philosophy from at least Aristotle through Kant all the way up to Husserl. In Heidegger's view, this generalizing scientific attitude is an *Einstellung*, that is to say, a predisposition, but also fixation or cessation of the flux and the unrest of factical life. Philosophy, according to the tradition that Heidegger takes to task here, is ontology, the categorization of the totality of whatever is (the *Gesamtheit des Seienden*) in regions and disciplinary domains. Of this tendency of Western philosophy to investigate the order of the world of objects in its generality and specificity, Husserl's transcendental phenomenology—in its reduction of every given to its originary constitution in intentional consciousness—is, according to Heidegger, the most rigorous example. The history of Western philosophy can, therefore, be summed up as follows: "In ontological respects, philosophy deals with being [*dem Seienden*]; with respect to consciousness, it deals with the original laws of the constitution of consciousness" (PhRL 57).

Heidegger thinks in particular of Husserl's concept of formal objectivity (*formale Gegenständlichkeit*) in the sixth of the *Logical Investigations*. This concept concerns a categorial intuition that can no longer be understood in terms of a generalization (as the "red" in a red thing, as the color in the "red," as the quality in the color), but must rather be seen as a formal characteristic that is not tied to one specific object domain. Yet the question of how a certain general perspective comes about is never satisfactorily answered in Husserl's philosophy.

In "Introduction to the Phenomenology of Religion," Heidegger takes his lead (he speaks of a *weiterbilden*) from a distinction, made by Husserl in *Ideas* (vol. 1, para. 13). Within the general concept of *Verallgemeinerung*, Husserl differentiates between *Formalisierung* and *Generalisierung*. "Generalization" marks the transition to the larger category, within the confines of a certain object domain—Heidegger speaks of a *Stufenordnung* (PhRL 61)—and therefore implies a hierarchization that is respectful of the continuity between the highest, the first, or the most general, on the one hand, and the lowest, the last, and the most particular, on the other. Generalization, in other words, is a procedure that characterizes the many naturalisms that derive normative principles from empirical abstractions, instead of from, say, categorial intuitions that are genuinely phenomenological.

The procedure of formal indication, by contrast, initiates a *leap* and forces a *rupture* with any given object domain, with respect to which it remains fundamentally "free" (PhRL 58). In one of the first review articles devoted to Heidegger's *Phänomenologie des religiösen Lebens,* Dominic Kaegi rightly observes:

> Contrary to the specification or, in the other direction, contrary to the species-oriented [*gattungmässigen*] generalization [*Verallgemeinerung*] that Heidegger—with Husserl—calls *Generalisierung,* the formalization remains "with respect to its content free" [*sachhaltig frei*]: . . . The "formal predication" [PhRL 58] conveys no contents, but that *as what* [*als was*] given contents are in each single case intended—as object [*Gegenstand*], state of affairs [*Sachverhalt*], as unity or plurality, etc.; formal-ontological categories are "extrapolations [*Ausformung[en]*] of a relation" [PhRL 62], not the indication of a given content.[37]

And yet, the formal indication is neither a construct, nor a hypothesis, nor a heuristic principle. Rather, we touch here upon a philosophical—and ontotheological—motif that has a much longer history and that dates back as far as the ancient and medieval doctrine of the *analogia entis*. In his *The Genesis of Heidegger's "Being and Time,"* Theodore Kisiel counts this motif among Heidegger's oldest interests: "The very idea of 'formal indication' in fact finds its first stirrings in the Scotian version of the Aristotelian-scholastic doctrine of the analogy of being. Regarding the Scotus dissertation as a precursor brings out the elements of a 'hermeneutics of facticity' already operating in filigree in what Scotus might have called his 'speculative formal grammar of thisness.' "[38]

37. Dominic Kaegi, "Die Religion in den Grenzen der blossen Existenz: Heideggers religionsphilosophische Vorlesungen von 1920/21," *Internationale Zeitschrift für Philosophie* 1 (1996): 133–49, 141. And see also PhRL 58–59.
38. Kisiel, *Genesis of Heidegger's "Being and Time,"* 20. Kisiel summarizes Heidegger's position in the following way:

The opposition, then, between generalization and abstraction, on the one hand, and formal indication, on the other, is that between a *synchronic, immanent-structural* fixation of the object, and a *diachronic, transcendent-transitive* and therefore fundamentally *free* approach to the phenomenon as such. In the latter, we no longer presuppose an established relation between fixed or commensurate terms. Instead, we find or invent here what Derrida, following Levinas and Blanchot, calls a relation-without-relation, which he formalizes in his own terms under the heading of "paleonymics" (notably in *Dissemination*) and "hauntology" (especially in *Specters of Marx*).

Formal indication does not merely entail a "reference" (*renvoi*) to the "formal conditions of possibility" of a given phenomenological experience, while leaving its ontic content suspended or in abeyance.[39] Rather, the formal indications with which Heidegger operates in the early work first of all serve a function that is not very different from the procedure he adopts in his latest writings, to wit, the "crosswise erasure" (*kreuzweise Durchstreichung*), the warning signal that indicates that a given phenomenological experience — for instance, the historical — should be evoked, if not so much apophatically, *via negationis*, or emphatically, *via eminentiae,*[40] then at least with as many precautions and

---

How does the historical itself stand to factic Dasein, what sense does it have out of factic Dasein itself? But does not the question itself introduce a particular, and perhaps even disturbing, sense of the historical? Do I not already have a particular sense in mind, in terms of which I decide in what sense the historical happens to factic life experience? But the question cannot be broached and approached in any other way, if I want to discover the historical *itself* in factic life. This difficulty is a recurrent disturbing element in all phenomenological analyses. . . .

We shall call the methodic use of a sense which is conducive to phenomenological explication the "formal indication". Its task is to prefigure the direction of this explication. It points the way and guides the deliberation. The phenomena are viewed on the basis of the bearing of the formally indicated sense. But even though it guides the phenomenological deliberation, contentwise it has nothing to say. Methodological considerations must make clear how the formal indication, even though it guides the deliberation, nevertheless interjects no preconceived opinions into the problems, in no way prejudices the content of the explication. Such a clarity of the sense of the formal indication is necessary to avoid lapsing into attitudinally objective tendencies or into regional domains which are narrow in content and yet conceived as absolute. (ibid., 164)

39. As Zarader suggests in *Dette impensée*, 168.
40. Heidegger circumvents the question of the viability of the apophatic way, for example, at BT 499 n. xiii / 427 n. 1, where he writes: "The fact that the traditional conception of 'eternity' . . . has been drawn from the ordinary way of understanding time and has been defined with an orientation towards the idea of 'constant' presence-at-hand, does not need to be discussed in detail. If God's eternity can be 'construed' philosophically, then it may be understood

corrections as possible. In both cases, in the procedure of formal indication and in that of the crosswise erasure, a certain liberty is bestowed
on the phenomenon, lest its explication be prejudged from the outset,
whether ontically, ontologically, theologically, axiologically, or otherwise.

Mutatis mutandis, the distinction between generalization and formal
indication corresponds to that between "elaboration" or "extrapolation"
(*Fortführung*), on the one hand, and "conversion" (*Umstellung*), on the
other, that Heidegger puts to work in "Phenomenology and Theology."
In "Introduction to the Phenomenology of Religion," "formal indication" indicates the proper movement of philosophy—indeed, of science
and the theoretical as such—as opposed to generalizations of the regional
sciences and the different historicisms. Along similar lines, "Phenomenology and Theology" puts all the emphasis on a turnabout (*Umstellung*)
that is said to typify the proper feature of the *Urwissenschaft* called philosophy in its absolute difference from the positive disciplines of which
theology, as the science of faith and Christianicity (*Christlichkeit*), forms
the chief example here.

In both contexts, therefore, the difference between mere generalization, on the one hand, and genuinely indicative formalization, on the
other, is that the first presupposes a *relative progression*, whereas the latter
inaugurates a *qualitative*—and in that sense, precisely, *absolute*—transition: a categorial and *categorical leap* whose apparent immediacy resembles the Kierkegaardian leap of faith in its structure, if not necessarily
in its content. In the generalization, the phenomena—here the objects
within a given empirical, ontic, or positive domain—are ordered in a
direct way; in the procedure of formalization, they are ordered merely indirectly; the formal indication, finally, *precedes both*. The gesture or the
enactment (*Vollzug*) is all that seems to matter to it, not the formal indicative schema that is said to be its result.

In order to assess the importance, indeed, the methodological and
more than simply methodological primacy of the concept of formal indication, we need only realize that Heidegger takes the very definition
of "phenomenon" and "phenomenology" in a formally indicative sense.
The procedure of formal indication gives access to—or reveals the very
meaning of—phenomenology and of the phenomenon, rather than the
other way around. Heidegger observes: "What is a phenomenon? What is

---

only as a more primordial temporality which is 'infinite.' Whether the way afforded by the *via
negationis et eminentiae* is a possible one remains to be seen."

phenomenology? This can itself only be formally indicated here" (PhRL 63). Strictly speaking, the formal indication does not yet therefore belong to phenomenology and, stretching our interpretation a little bit further, it does not itself form part of the order of phenomenality, to which it is merely the *via regia*. To complicate matters more, the very phrase "formal indication" seems to be used by Heidegger in a consistently formal or even formally indicative, way:

> In the discourse about "formal indication," does the word *formal* have the meaning of the formalized or does it gain a new one? What formalization and generalization have in common is that they stand under the aegis of "general" whereas formal indication has nothing to do with generality. The meaning of *formal* in the "formal indication" is *more originary [ursprünglicher]*. (PhRL 59)

More original than Husserl could have imagined. Or so it seems. Formal indications, Heidegger challenges, have nothing to do with the theoretical propensity that has dominated philosophy—or ontology—from its earliest beginnings in its very desire to order the beings in different regions. However, the phenomenological—read Husserlian—countermovement (*Gegenbetrachtung*, PhRL 60) that stressed the role of consciousness in the experience of the given, which emerged so late in the history of thought, is merely the correlate of this earlier ontological hegemony. Heidegger does not hesitate to claim that the domain of consciousness is still interpreted here as a region, now characterized in terms of its original activity (*Tätigkeit*) and constitution. With one stroke, Husserl is thus inscribed into the onto-theoreticist movement that runs from Aristotle—albeit not the Aristotle who knew otherwise and who remains, paradoxically, still ahead of us—all the way up to the Neo-Kantians. This common theoretical *Einstellung* blocks the way to any genuine appraisal of the religious[41] and, through it—but how exactly? this is our question—of the *Kernphänomen* of the historical, the experience of factical life, its flux, its temporality, and, finally, its thrownness and its understanding (signaled by the Pauline emphasis on the *genesthai* and the *eidenai* respectively).

41. For an impression of the neo-Kantian contribution to the philosophy of religion, see Hans-Ludwig Ollig, "Die Religionsphilosophie der südwestdeutschen Schule," in *Materialien zur Neokantianismus-Diskussion*, ed. id. (Darmstadt: Wissenschaftliche Buchgesellschaft, 1987), 428–57. That Heidegger remains silent on Hermann Cohen's influential writings is surprising (see Kaegi, "Religion in den Grenzen der blossen Existenz," 137), but Cohen's *Religion der Vernunft aus den Quellen des Judentums* (Wiesbaden: Fourier, 1978) was published only posthumously, in 1919.

In distancing himself thus from the ontotheoreticist presuppositions of classical-transcendental phenomenology, Heidegger radically reinterprets the significance of the Husserlian *eidetic reduction,* which in his view never progresses beyond a certain capacity to keep the phenomenon up in the air (*in der Schwebe*). But he also transforms the phenomenological understanding of the *transcendental reduction;* for in Heidegger's view the phenomenological gaze does not halt at the intentional consciousness to the extent that latter is still thought of in terms of a certain region (which, of course, Husserl would categorically deny). Furthermore, it is perhaps not an accident that Heidegger gives the *terminus technicus* of indication—of the formal *Anzeige*—such a strategic function, given the significance that Husserl, in *Logical Investigations,* had attributed to the distinction between the *Anzeichen,* on the one hand, and the *Bezeichnung,* on the other.[42] As is well known, the difficulty Husserl has in upholding a rigorous distinction between these two is the guiding thread of Derrida's seminal *La Voix et le phénomène* (*Speech and Phenomena*).

Nonetheless, Heidegger baptizes the notion of formal indication as the central methodological supplement of any phenomenology worthy of the name. It is the one single motif that marks the radical—indeed absolute—distinction between phenomenology and the primal science of being and beings and the more limited preoccupations of the positive, regional, ontic, and formal sciences:

> The indication should in advance indicate the relation to the phenomenon [or the constellation of phenomena—HdV]—in a negative sense, that is, as it were as a warning! A phenomenon must be given in advance in such a way that the meaning of its link [*Bezugssinn*] is kept pending. One should be cautious about assuming that the meaning of its link is originally the theoretical one. The relation and enactment of the phenomenon is *not* determined in advance; it is kept in abeyance. That is a position in sharpest contrast with that of science. There is no insertion into an objective realm, but on the contrary: the formal indication is a *defense* [*Abwehr*], a preceding *guarantee* [*Sicherung*]. . . .The necessity of this precaution results from the falling tendency of factical life experience, which always threatens to slip into the world

---

42. But then again, Heidegger is very close to Husserl here too. See, e.g., PhRL 129–30, where Heidegger notes that genuine phenomenological understanding does not reduce the experience of factical life and its flux to something "regional," nor, for that matter, to its "opposite." Instead, it seeks to explicate the phenomenon in its own terms ("*in sich selbst zu erweisen und ins explizite phänomenologische Verständnis zu heben*") (ibid., 130).

of objects [*Objektmäßige*], out of which we nonetheless must lift up the phenomena. (PhRL 63–64)

In adopting the strategy of formal indication, one steers free of every preconceived theoretical order and leaves everything pending, or in abeyance ("man lässt gerade Alles dahingestellt," or, Heidegger notes, "in der Schwebe" [PhRL 64]). The function of formally indicative concepts therefore corresponds on a methodological level with that of the ὡς μή at the level of existential conversion: they leave everything as it is and signal merely negatively, in the guise of warning signs, that no single concept—nor, for that matter, the totality of all possible concepts—conveys the true, full, or genuine meaning of the phenomenon and the flux or unrest of factical life. The latter can only be said to be exemplified by—and modeled after?—the phenomenon of religion in its most original manifestation (in Paul's letters, in Augustine, in Luther, and in Jewish eschatology).[43] But what does that mean concretely—that is to say, in the analysis of the elementary structures of factical life, of human existence?

In the formally indicative hermeneutics of facticity, factical life is not merely analyzed in its constitutive elements, or constructed or reconstructed out of disparate empirical givens, let alone speculatively or a priori, without reference to any experience whatsoever. Heidegger's aim is rather to understand the—three—constitutive aspects of the meaning of factical life, of the historical, in their internal structure, unity, and co-originariness:

> However, these three directions of meaning (the meaning of content, relation, and enactment [*Gehalt-, Bezugs-, Vollzugssinn*]) do not simply stand next to one another. "Phenomenon" is a totality of meaning [*Sinnganzheit*] in these three directions, "Phenomenology" is the explication of this totality of mean-

43. Heidegger fails to discuss, not only representatives of the Jewish tradition—the Old Testament prophets, the rabbinic commentators, the Jewish mystics, and Jewish philosophers, from, say, Maimonides up to Hermann Cohen, but (more surprising, given Heidegger's intellectual heritage), Blaise Pascal, whom Hegel, in the concluding words of *Glauben und Wissen*—in a passage invoked by Heidegger in the essay "Nietzsches Wort 'Gott ist tot' "—cites as a witness to the modern feeling: "Gott selbst ist tot," or, in Pascal's words: "[L]a nature est telle qu'elle marque partout un Dieu perdu et dans l'homme et hors de l'homme" (G. W. F. Hegel, *Glauben und Wissen*, ed. Hans Brockard and Hartmut Buchner [Hamburg: Meiner, 1986], 134; trans. Walter Cerf and H. S. Harris as *Faith and Knowledge* [Albany: State University of New York Press, 1977]). See Martin Heidegger, "The Word of Nietzsche 'God is Dead,' " in *The Question Concerning Technology and Other Essays*, trans. William Lovitt (New York: Harper & Row, 1977), 58–59. For a discussion, see Henri Birault, "Philosophie et théologie: Heidegger et Pascal," in *Heidegger*, ed. Michel Haar (Paris: Éditions de l'Herne, 1983), 514–41.

ing, it gives the λόγος of the phenomena, λόγος in the sense of a *"verbum internum"* (not in the sense of a logical abstraction [*Logisierung*]). (PhRL 63)

In this *trias* of co-originary structural moments, we may suspect an early anticipation of several distinctions made throughout Heidegger's later work;[44] the most notable being, perhaps, the way in which, in *Being and Time*, he brings the three co-originary dimensions or *extases* of time together in one single analysis of the structure and the impetus of originary temporality. Of importance, in the context of the early lecture, is the circumstance that Heidegger views this *trias* as an explication—here an *Ausformung* rather than an *Umstellung*—of the one fundamental possibility that, as the Aristotelian dictum τὸ ὂν πολλαχῶς λέγεται (PhRL 56) already suggests, allows all others to come into their own. To understand this in a proper way does not mean to contribute to a general theory of the world of objects, as Husserl had falsely assumed in his formal ontology, but rather to resort to an altogether different phenomenology of the formal (see PhRL 62). Of this phenomenology of the formal, Heidegger says that it by no means prejudges the given, but, on the contrary, presents—or, rather, enables and awakens—the proper task of all genuine philosophical inquiry, to wit, openness to the given and, eventually, to so-called originary donation as such. That this donation, regardless of its anti-theoretical thrust, indicates yet another return and rearticulation of the phenomenological, and, more precisely, Husserlian, project has been argued in many detailed studies, most notably in Jean-Luc Marion's *Reduction and Givenness* and its sequel, *Étant donné*.[45] In addition, Heidegger's view could be seen as a variation on the phenomenological theme of so-called *Voraussetzungslosigkeit,* that is to say, of the avoidance of any

---

44. As Thomas Sheehan notes, it is "in the distinction of content-sense [*Gehaltsinn*], relation-sense [*Bezugssinn*], and enactment [*Vollzugssinn*] [that] we may perhaps begin to see a primitive articulation of the latter distinction between *das Seiende* (the thematic entity), *Seiendheit* (the beingness of that entity = the Greek *ousia*), and *das Sein selbst* (the event of being itself). . . . the *Vollzugssinn* or enactment-sense looks like a first name for *Ereignis*" ("Heidegger's 'Introduction to the Phenomenology of Religion,' 1920–21," in *A Companion to Martin Heidegger's "Being and Time*," ed. J. J. Kockelmans [Washington, D.C.: Center for Advanced Research in Phenomenology and University Press of America, 1986], 51–52). This essay offers an interesting account of the manuscripts of the lecture notes, well before their publication in volume 60 of the *Gesamtausgabe* and preceded only by more general accounts by Pöggeler (*Denkweg Martin Heideggers,* 36–45, 327–31, 334, 337) and Lehmann ("Christliche Geschichtserfahrung und ontologische Frage"). For an outspoken account of the difficulties in interpretating early Christianity, see also Sheehan's *The First Coming: How the Kingdom of God Became Christianity* (New York: Random House, Vintage Books, 1986, 1988).

45. Marion, *Réduction et donation* and *Étant donné.*

presupposition that is not warranted by the phenomena themselves or given in an orginary way:

> To the extent that the formal-ontological determinations are formal they do not prejudge anything. Therefore it is appropriate to reduce philosophy to them [or to lead philosophy back to them: "die Philosophie auf sie zurück-zuführen"]. When we ask whether the formally ontological prejudges something for philosophy, then this question has meaning only when one accepts the thesis that philosophy is *not* a [theoretically fixated and suspending] disposition [*Einstellung*]. For us there stands in the background the thesis that philosophy is not a theoretical science. (PhRL 62)

Nothing is simple in these seemingly unambiguous statements. For when Heidegger says, "*Insofar* as the formally indicative determination are formal," does he thereby imply that concepts are in fact or of necessity never *fully* "formal" or "indicative," in the strict sense of these words? Is this, perhaps, the reason why there can never be more than a formal indication of formal indication, with the consequence that no formal indication ever comes into its own, and that there is thus no formal indication as such, in all purity, or properly speaking? If this is the case, as I believe, then we must conclude that even the most formal — that is to say, the most indicative — of all formal indications ultimately falls short of freeing the phenomenon from illicit preconceptions. In other words, even the most rigorous formal indication would remain *blasphemous, idolatrous,* tainted by an ontic and objectifying prejudgment and fixation on the phenomenon. But if we grant this, then we must also acknowledge that to the extent that Heidegger's concepts are indeed advanced in a truly formal and formally indicative way, they hardly live up to the claim — also made here with even more fervor — that they "prejudge nothing."

The formal indications warn against an overhasty determination of the phenomenon, but also serve as its corrective stipulation, conducive to its explication. All this takes place in view of and by means of a more proper *krinein* — knowing, being able to judge, when to stop judging, when to take things, not for granted, but as given, donated in an act of divine grace, and thus *beyond any criteriology.* This grace allows one not to acquiesce, since it makes one all the more insecure, all the more certain to be tested and tempted, haunted by the specter of betrayal, which is here, in St. Paul's universe, represented by that other coming that is neither the first nor the second but the third, in between the first and the second, which masks itself as Christ, but is, if anything at all, *not quite* and *not yet* Christ — rather, a proxy, a counterfeit Christ, a totally other *Stellvertreter* of God, an Antichrist, albeit one without whose coming the second coming of Christ Himself could not take place.

In Heidegger's reading, it seems that the Antichrist is the figure of a coming whose otherness is as radical and as ineluctable as the radical evil of which Kant speaks in *Religion Within the Boundaries of Mere Reason.* Yet a remarkable difference should be noted as well. For the possibility of which Heidegger speaks here with so much fervor — with fascination, indeed, in fear and trembling — is hardly one that can be called "human." It befalls human existence as a perverted act of grace, of a grace turned sour, as the reverse of the divine, and does so necessarily, albeit with a necessity that is neither that of an analytical truth nor that of empirical causation. "For Christian life there is no security; the persistent insecurity is also the characteristic of the fundamental determinations of factical life. The uncertainty is not accidental, but necessary. This necessity is neither a logical one nor that of a natural order" (PhRL 105). The relation between the divine and its double has to be thought of completely otherwise.

## Fiat Flux

Based as it is on what the editors of volume 60 of Heidegger's *Gesamtausgabe* call the "secondary authentic constitution" ("'sekundär authentischen' Textkonstitution" [PhRL 341]) of these texts, which were compiled from different sets of notes and transcriptions by students, supplemented with a few, sometimes illegible, glosses in Heidegger's own hand,[46] the preceding interpretation may seem all too speculative. However, it is sufficiently confirmed by other writings of Heidegger's, notably "Phenomenology and Theology" and the "Letter on Humanism," but also *Identity and Difference, Beiträge zur Philosophie,* and the Hölderlin lectures, all of which preserve the same formal scheme intact.

This formal schematics, we have found, has the task of protecting the phenomenon against all those historical, philosophical, and metaphysical presuppositions or prejudgments that form part and parcel of the objectifying *Einstellung,* of a predisposition, that is, that — no one knew better than Heidegger — is not warranted by the facts, by the given, by the phe-

---

46. Indeed, the problem with this "secondary authentic text constitution" is, as Kaegi rightly points out, that there is no such thing, properly speaking. The term itself hints at the fundamental aporia that I have sought to bring to the fore here, but, according to Kaegi, it is merely a poor way of expressing a philological peculiarity. See Kaegi, "Religion in den Grenzen der blossen Existenz," 148–49.

nomena, let alone by the phenomenon that Heidegger treats with such special care: the *Kernphänomen,* history, the experience of factical life, in the very conflicting tendencies of its flux. Indeed, *fiat flux* would be an adequate summary of some of the core elements of Heidegger's activist, not to say decisionist, rewriting of the gospel according to St. Paul; and this in spite of his no less explicit denunciation of the appropriateness of oppositions such as static and dynamic, active and passive, each of which falls short of grasping the movement and the restlessness intrinsic to factical life (something, one is tempted to add, that holds true for the distinction between freedom and grace too).

This reading should not lead us to forget, however, that in Heidegger's subsequent lecture course on "Augustine and Neoplatonism" — as well as in the analyses of care and fallenness in *Being and Time* — at least as much emphasis is put on *continentia,* a gathering and holding (on) to oneself that is mobilized against the dissipation (*Zerstreuung, teuflische Zerstreutheit,* or, as St. Augustine has it, *defluxio*) that is an equally dominant tendency inherent in factical life. "By continence we are collected together and brought to the unity from which we disintegrated into multiplicity" ("per continentiam quippe colligimur et redigimur in unum, a quo in multa defluximus"), Augustine observes.[47]

Upon closer scrutiny, there is perhaps no real contradiction here. Or, more precisely, what seems a mere inconsistency is in fact a confirmation and reiteration of the aporetic structure that I am seeking to map out at more than one level of Heidegger's thinking. Thus, in this particular context, the flux of the enactment of existence proper forms the very element (modality, essence, and, perhaps, content) of a becoming oneself — *one* self — over and against the temptation of the many and the manifold, that is to say, of the *Manselbst* of which Heidegger speaks so eloquently in *Being and Time* and with explicit reference to the Augustinean motif of *curiositas,* among others.

Let me once again sketch the principle features of this Heideggerian aporetics. Perhaps the words with which Kaegi's review reminds us of the structural ambiguity — more precisely, the inherent aporia — of factical life experience and the conversion to the faith (indeed, the life, its flux, and *continentia*) that it both allows, enables, and, in a sense, also obstructs, would be a good starting point:

47. St. Augustine, *Confessiones* 10.29, trans. Henry Chadwick (New York: Oxford University Press, 1991), 202; *Confessions,* trans. W. Watts (Cambridge, Mass.: Harvard University Press, 1996), 150.

[A]lthough philosophizing emerges with a leap out of factical life experience, it can only be thought as a "turning around" [*Umwendung*] or "metamorphosis" [*Umwandlung*] of factical life experience—in this lies [its] "principle difference" from science.

"Turning around" of factical life experience, even the captivity [*Befangenheit*] of positive science in the factical life experience are Husserlian subjects, yet unlike Husserl, Heidegger does not understand the turning around that initiates philosophizing as a *change in disposition* [*Einstellungsänderung*]. To describe philosophy in terms of a particular, "counternatural" disposition would mean precisely to extrapolate the orientation with respect to the contents and "things"[*Sachen*] that rule factical life experience into the philosophizing. ... For philosophy not to be simply "a disposition toward the determination of the object" [*einstellungshafte Objektbestimmung*], for the turning around of factical life experience not to be a mere change in disposition, one must be able to indicate a moment in factical life experience itself that points beyond the dispositional determination of the object and thereby motivates philosophizing; beyond the dispositional determination of the object points the *historicity* [*Geschichtlichkeit*] of factical life experience, the "phenomenon of the historical."[48]

What seems to interest Heidegger, then, is formally indicative access to the phenomenon of religion as a shortcut to a fuller explication of the central problem and core phenomenon of the historical. A far-reaching conclusion regarding the relationship between phenomenology and religion, philosophy and theology imposes itself with renewed force, however, in light of the special status of formal indication, which is not a concept among others, but contains Heidegger's seminal insight. For if the conversion, not only of the intentional gaze,[49] but also of the turning around of concepts toward a formally indicative use is not without relation to the phenomenon called religion, *through which it passes,* then a tantalizing uncertainty with regard to the demarcation between phi-

48. Kaegi, "Religion in den Grenzen der blossen Existenz," 139–40. The reference to Husserl is to his *Ideen zu einer reinen Phänomenologie und Phänomenologischen Philosophie* (The Hague: Martinus Nijhoff, 1950), vol. 1 paras. 30–32; trans. as *Ideas Pertaining to a Pure Phenomenology and to a Phenomenological Philosophy* (The Hague: Martinus Nijhoff, 1980–82).

49. "Perhaps it will even become manifest that the total phenomenological attitude and the *epoch* belonging to it are destined in essence to effect, at first, a complete personal transformation [*Umwandlung*], comparable in the beginning to a religious conversion [*Umkehrung*], which then, however, over and above this [*sic*], bears within itself the significance of the greatest existential transformation which is assigned as a task to mankind as such," Husserl observes (*Crisis of European Sciences and Transcendental Phenomenology,* 137, 140).

losophy or phenomenology, on the one hand, and religion and theology, on the other, returns unannounced, like a thief in the night. This uncertainty—and, indeed, undecidability—catches us by surprise, or, if we flatter ourselves that we are awake and wakeful ("knowing," believing already), as an uncertainty that will forever, till the end of time, cast its shadow over all of the endeavors that we take upon ourselves, not in a state of paralysis or terror, or with false hopes, but in *fear and trembling*, with a *horror religiosus* that only a few, Kierkegaard among them, have been able to stand and to communicate.

Heidegger's pious assurance that philosophy and theology, phenomenology and religion proper, have no common measure—which turns their attempted fusion into *hölzernes Eisen*—is therefore somewhat disingenuous and in the end unwarranted. Perhaps this explains why, aside from the many reassurances to the contrary, there are at least as many passages in which a greater continuity or even *substitutability* between these disciplines—or between all disciplines and so-called religion—seems to be suggested, albeit often indirectly. It seems that our uncertainty concerning these demarcations—demarcations that are somehow "known" but always contested, tempted, and therefore in need of reconfirmation— has much in common with the fundamental uncertainty haunting the believers to whom St. Paul addressed his letters.[50]

---

50. For these reasons, I tend to disagree on this issue with Rüdiger Safranski, who, in his excellent biography, *Ein Meister aus Deutschland: Heidegger und seine Zeit* (Munich: Carl Hanser, 1994), insists on a different turn (or return) to religion than the one that interests me here. Safranski says that Heidegger no longer took the position of the 1927 lecture on "Phänomenologie und Theologie" (in *Pathmarks*, ed. McNeill, 39–62). At that time, Safranski continues, "in good Lutheran manner, he had separated thought and faith. Faith would be the uncaculable event [*Ereignis*], through which God breaks into life. Thought could only determine the breakthrough spot [*Einbruchstelle*]. The divine event [*Gottesereignis*] is not itself a matter of thought.

"Yet to precisely this ambitious project, to experience the real presence of the divine [*die reale Gegenwart des Göttlichen*] from thought, Heidegger devoted himself in his *Beiträge*. But since the divine assumes no clear contours in thought, Heidegger resorts to a neat solution: *Proximity to the last god is silence [Die Nähe zum letzten Gott ist die Verschweigung]*" (quoting Martin Heidegger, *Gesamtausgabe*, vol . 65: *Beiträge zur Philosophie (Vom Ereignis)* [Frankfurt a./M.: Klostermann, 1989], 12). What is wrong with this interpretation is the fact that it overlooks two things. First, the line of demarcation between phenomenology and theology is far from clear in the 1927 lecture. As I have argued, there is an undeniable continuity between Heidegger's ambiguous position in the early courses on religion and the one he adopted in "Phenomenology and Theology" that supposedly contains Heidegger's clearest statement on this matter. It is no accident that it is precisely in these two contexts that we find the most detailed expositions of the problem of formal indication. Second, also in the *Beiträge*, the modality of the coming of the (last) God that Heidegger attempts to think in vain here is hardly that of a "real presence," as Safranski suggest, but that of a passage, passing, visitation, and

One could, of course, go one step further and argue that it is precisely this uncertainty that forms the transcendental condition of the possibility of the *turn* (*Umwendung, Wiedergeburt, conversio*) that defines what both philosophy and theology, phenomenology and religion, can do, and perhaps what they are—that is to say, in the structure of their *Vollzug* and perhaps also in the very meaning of their content. If such an interpretation can be risked, this is because we are dealing here with at least two ambiguities, which not only complement but also reinforce each other.

In the first place, there is the ambiguity of the Janus face of factical life experience as such, marked as it is by a tendency toward complacency, petrifaction, and objectivation, but also by the flux that Heidegger sees as the core phenomenon of the historical (that is to say, the phenomenon for which *Being and Time* reserves the term *Geschichtlichkeit,* historicity or historicality).

In the second place, there is the ambiguity of the modality of the core phenomenon, characterized as it is by the troubling circumstance that in it two extreme possibilities—those of the most proper and the most improper—coexist, as it were, simultaneously. There would seem to be a permanent oscillation, then, between the best and the worst, between rebirth and the end, the eschaton and the apocalypse, the second coming of Christ and the haunting of his double, the "Christ"-instead-of-Christ, the "Christ"-against-Christ, the "Christ-who-is-not-Him" but the so-called Antichrist.

The one could not come without the other; one must accompany—foreshadow and, indeed, cast its shadow on—the other. The act and sub-

---

(or as) retreat, alone. Again, it is no accident that Jean-François Courtine sees a thematic and structural resemblance between Heidegger's early consideration of the *kairos*—for example in his reading of St. Paul—and the language of the *Beiträge.* The implication is not only that there is a "continuity" between the latter and the project of "fundamental ontology" (of which "Phenomenology and Theology" forms a central part, no less than an interesting supplement); but that the early lectures left their mark on the "capital document of the famous turning," *Beiträge zur Philosophie.* Courtine also reminds us that the passage of the (last) God is not to be confused with a *parousia.* (See J.-F. Courtine, "Les Traces et le passage du Dieu dans les *Beiträge zur Philosophie* de Martin Heidegger," *Archivio di filosofia* 1, no. 3 [1994]: 525, 533.) Indeed, if one takes the term παρουσία in the way *Being and Time* proposes in its opening pages, namely, as meaning a "presence" or *Anwesenheit* (BT 47 / 25), then the difference between this notion and the trace or *Wink* of the (last) God of which the *Beiträge* speak could not be more striking. Yet, as we have seen, Heidegger reads the word *parousia* in a decidedly New Testament, Pauline sense in the early lectures. The coming again of Christ, announced as it is by its double—the Antichrist—has the same structure therefore as the passage of the (last) God, and this regardless of the latter's unmistakably anti-Christian reverberations (see Courtine, ibid., 528–29).

stance of faith are thus divided against themselves. Which is yet another way of saying that in order to gain oneself, one must lose oneself. To come into its own, the self must risk letting itself be haunted by its other. And what can be said of this core of factical life experience holds true of so-called theology as well. The demarcations between theology and, say, idolatry, blasphemy, and apostasy, on the one hand, and science — the science of origins, philosophy, and the nontheological sciences called positive — on the other, can no longer be taken for granted where theology is no longer seen as church dogmatics or biblical exegesis, but as the self-articulation, exposition, and reenactment of faith, that is to say, of the crucifixion of Christ, a reenactment that brings us face to face, not with God, but with our forgetfulness vis-à-vis God.

Why, then, does Heidegger insist so desperately on the supposedly absolute separation — both in fact and de jure — between philosophy or phenomenology, on the one hand, and religion and theology, on the other? Moreover, why and how is it that these two domains can or even must nonetheless enter into a relationship of mutual dependence and supplementarity, or, as Heidegger puts it, of *correction* (albeit a correction that is in his view hardly mutual)?

In order to answer these questions, we should look into Heidegger's sources. In the foreword to "Phenomenology and Theology," Heidegger reminds us of two texts that form part of the intellectual background against which to understand his resistance to conflating the domains of phenomenology and theology. Not surprisingly, both sources revolve around a reinterpretation of the meaning and the fate of original Christianity. With apparent approval, Heidegger refers in the first place to Franz Overbeck's insistence, in *Über die Christlichkeit unserer heutigen Theologie* (On the Christianicity of Our Present Theology), on "the world-denying expectation of the end as the basic characteristic of what is primordially Christian" ("die weltverneinende Enderwartung als den Grundzug des Urchristentums").[51]

51. Heidegger, *Pathmarks*, 39, 46. See Overbeck, *Über die Christlichkeit unserer heutigen Theologie*. More significant even than this pamphlet of 1873 is Overbeck's book-length study, posthumously published in 1919, entitled *Christentum und Kultur: Gedanken und Anmerkungen zur modernen Theologie*, ed. Albrecht Bernoulli (Darmstadt: Wissenschaftliche Buchgesellschaft, 1973). Notably the the first two chapters are of interest, it seems, since it is here that Overbeck reiterates that Christianity, in the strict sense of the word, begins with St. Paul (ibid., 28, 62); for him, it is Pascal (ibid., 126ff.) who figures as a key witness, as the last Christian in the modern world, not Kierkegaard. Yet this difference with Heidegger should not make us for-

The second text invoked by Heidegger is the *Unzeitgemässe Betracht-ungen* (*Unfashionable Observations*) of Overbeck's friend Nietzsche, who is nonetheless taken to task in the lecture course for having completely misunderstood the nature of faith and its relation (without relation) to the world: "The synthetic relations [*Zusammenhänge*] of Paul should *not* be understood *ethically.* Therefore it is a misapprehension when Nietzsche accuses him of *Ressentiment.* That does not belong in this realm. In this context, *Ressentiment* cannot be at issue at all. If one gets involved with that, it shows that one has not understood a thing." [52]

For all their differences, Overbeck's and Nietzsche's texts both shed light on the task that Heidegger set himself in the 1927 lecture on "Phe-nomenology and Theology," which, he notes, "might perhaps be able to occasion repeated [*wiederholt*] reflection on the extent to which the Christianness of Christianity and its theology merit manifold question-ing [*das vielfältig Frag-Würdige*]; but *also* on the extent to which phi-losophy, in particular that presented here, merits questioning." But, as Heidegger observes here too, the relevance of this task is much wider. It illuminates both his earlier thoughts, in the 1920/21 lecture course, and his later writings on "the glorious Hölderlin," the holy, the coming god, and the relationship between theology and the *theiological.* Here, in the preface to "Phenomenology and Theology," he implies that the two *Frag-Würdigkeiten,* the Christianicity of Christianity and its theology and that of philosophy, are related. But, again, why and how exactly? A tentative

---

get that *Christentum und Kultur* reiterates the antithesis between an eschatological-apocalyptic *Urchristentum,* on the one hand, and its immediate theologico-dogmatic betrayal, on the other. What is more, Overbeck begins this book with an extensive reflection on the notion of tem-porality, duration (*Dauer*), and the nature of historiographical discourse, and concludes with a meditation on death, on the memento mori, and does so in a confessional or highly per-sonal style ("Von mir selbst und vom Tode," ibid., 287 ff.). For a helpful acccount of Overbeck's central ideas and their influence on Karl Barth and early dialectical theology, see Bruce L. McCormack, *Karl Barth's Critically Realistic Dialectical Theology: Its Genesis and Development 1909–1936* (Oxford: Clarendon Press, 1997), 226–35. That by 1922 Heidegger was deeply involved in the reading of Overbeck is noted both by Kisiel (*Genesis of Heidegger's "Being and Time,"* 556–57, no. 15) and by Jeffrey Andrew Barash, *Heidegger et son siècle: Temps de l'être, temps de l'histoire* (Paris: Presses universitaires de France, 1995), 127 n. 2. See also Jacob Taubes, "Ent-zauberung der Theologie: Zu einem Porträt Overbecks," in id., *Vom Kult zur Kultur: Bausteine zu einer Kritik der historischen Vernunft,* ed. Aleida Assmann, Jan Assmann, Wolf-Daniel Hart-wich, and Winfried Menninghaus (Munich: Wilhelm Fink, 1996), 182–97.

52. PhRL 120. Friedrich Nietzsche, *Unzeitgemässe Betrachtungen,* in *Sämtliche Werke,* Kri-tische Studien Ausgabe, ed. Giorgo Colli and Mazzino Montinari, 1: 157–510 (Berlin: Walter de Gruyter, 1988); trans. Richard T. Gray as *Unfashionable Observations* (Stanford: Stanford Uni-versity Press, 1995).

answer to these questions can, perhaps, be derived from the particular status Heidegger ascribes to the texts of Overbeck and Nietzsche, as well as to the ones—including his own—that they have made possible: "To say both writings are unseasonable also in today's changed world means: For the few who think among the countless who reckon, these writings intend and point [*weisend*] toward that which itself perseveres before the inaccessible [*Verharren vor dem Unzugangbaren*] through speaking, questioning, and creating."[53]

Yet this is hardly the final word. The difficulty consists in the fact that Heidegger wants to keep the religious and the theological separate from the phenomenological and the philosophical—and says so explicitly—but then immediately goes on to forge them together again. Perhaps this is nowhere clearer than in the words with which Heidegger concludes the 1920/21 lecture:

> The genuine phenomenology of religion does not originate in preconceived concepts of philosophy and religion. But from a particular belief [*Religiosität*] —for us the Christian—stems the possibility of its philosophical understanding [*Erfassung*]. Why it is in particular the Christian belief [*Religiosität*] that forms the central focus [*Blickpunkt*] of our consideration is a difficult question; it can only be answered by solving the problem of historical connections [or syntheses, *Zusammenhänge*]. The task is to gain a genuine and originary relationship to history that is explicable by our own historical situation and facticity [*aus unserer eigenen geschichtlichen Situation und Faktizität zu explizieren ist*]. It depends on what meaning history can have for us [*was der Sinn der Geschichte für uns bedeuten kann*], for the "objectivity" of the historical "in and for itself [*an sich*]" to dissipate. There is only one history out of a present [*aus einer Gegenwart heraus*]. Only thus can the possibility of a phenomenology of religion be taken up. (PhRL 124–25)

The separation between the phenomenological and the theological is in Heidegger's work thus both required and undercut. For all its implicitness, this blurring of the lines of a demarcation that remains nonetheless essential is—in its ultimate consequence—quite dramatic. Where the distinction between the philosophical and the religious is no longer certain —and, moreover, this uncertainty is increased as understanding comes into its own, precisely by becoming, living, and affirming what, in a way, it already *is*—existence turns into a mystery to itself. Being *in* the world,

---

53. Heidegger, *Pathmarks*, 39 and 40, 45 and 46; emphasis added and trans. modified.

we are no longer *of* this world, but as Levinas knew, altered, aging, made vulnerable by a suspense and suspension, as indicated by the *adieu* that forms the very modality of the *à-Dieu.*

## On Becoming a Mystery to Oneself

Needless to say, my interpretation runs counter to a widespread opinion concerning the development and the content or the phenomenological method of Heidegger's thought. A common strategy is to insist on the distinction between the actual use and the proper meaning of religious terms or theologemes and to emphasize their transformed — formal indicative — use throughout Heidegger's text. Thus, Kaegi, to give just one example, stresses that

> as far as the *use* is concerned, the theological motifs in the lectures on the "phenomenology of religious life" are already no longer theological. From the outset, the incorporation of grace into the conscience by which Dasein extricates itself from fallenness [in *Being and Time*] fundamentally results from an access to the originary Christian life experience that is not so much anti- as "meta-theological." For Heidegger, Christianity counts as an external proof, indeed as a historical paradigm, of a form of existence that revolves around the "world of the self" [*Selbstwelt*] and whose conceptual explication alone is the concern [*Sache*] of philosophy; religion does not advance a determinate understanding of the content of existence, it confirms this understanding, and only to the extent that it does so is it philosophically relevant. Heidegger does not describe existence in theological concepts; he describes religious life in terms — and thereby within the limits — of existence.
>
> *Within* these boundaries, Heidegger's lectures on the philosophy of religion admittedly document a remarkable proximity to Christianity, without the pagan pretensions [*Allüren*] of the later work, but also without recourse to Judaism; . . . Heidegger's phenomenology of the religious is a phenomenology of *Christian* life . . ., in many places clearly with an apologetic impetus, too, after the renunciation of the "system of Catholicism." [54]

On the basis of the interpretation I have attempted above, I would tend to disagree with most of these claims. Let me give a few more arguments that sustain the view I have advocated instead.

Theology and the phenomenology of religion that gives access to the New Testament and provides the shortest detour to the core phenome-

54. Kaegi, "Religion in den Grenzen der blossen Existenz," 137. See also ibid. 134–36.

non of the historical are based on an existential and conceptual turning or conversion that repeats an original and originary possibility of factical life and of temporality or history as such. It is in this turning toward and away from factical experience in one or the other form that it has assumed—in its flux, that is, or in its petrifaction—that Heidegger locates the emergence of concepts, their formation and explication. Theology proper, but, mutatis mutandis, the same also holds true for any other (phenomenological, philosophical) discourse worthy of the name, has its origin, its beginning and upsurging, its *Ur-sprung*, in this singular twist of life as it reorients itself toward its other—and, Heidegger believes, toward its ownmost or most proper—possibilities. It is in and with this turn alone that one may actually become and appropriate or repeat what one already is in fact: "The knowledge concerning one's own having become what one is [*Gewordensein*] is the point of departure and the origin of theology. In the explication of this knowledge and the conceptual form of its expression, one finds the meaning of a theological concept formation."[55]

To shed light on the turn in St. Paul's life—and, mutatis mutandis, in the life of any believer, or even all human existence—Heidegger points to several passages in Galatians (among them 2:19–20 and 5:11) that seem to summarize Paul's dogmatico-theological and mystical position. Their centrality, Heidegger suggests, lies in the fact that they define faith in the final analysis in terms of being crucified with Christ, alone, in one's singular existence, and time and again. The "stumbling-block of the cross" (τὸ σκάνδαλον τοῦ σταυροῦ), Heidegger says, is "the proper foundation [*das eigentliche Grundstück*] of Christianity, in relation to which there is only faith or unbelief" (PhRL 71).

This crucial motif also organizes the lecture "Phenomenology and Theology," which likewise treats it as the heart and central movement of Christian faith. In *The Sickness unto Death,* a text often referred to by Heidegger in the early lectures, Kierkegaard does not hesitate to call it the "offense"—or, more precisely, the "possibility of offense"—that characterizes the essence and paradox of Christianity.[56]

Again, at times it would seem that this characterization brings Hei-

55. PhRL 95. In his notes, Heidegger speaks of an "Ur-sprung der Theologie" (PhRL, 145).
56. For the reference to Kierkegaard's *The Sickness unto Death,* see PhRL 248; for a reference to *The Concept of Anxiety,* see PhRL 257. On the philosophical relationship between Heidegger and the aforementioned writings of Kierkegaard in the context of a discussion of a New Testament "theology of time," the "praying faith" (*Gebetsglaube*) of Jesus, and the "temporality of being a Christian," see Michael Theunissen, *Negative Theologie der Zeit* (Frankfurt a./M.: Suhrkamp, 1991), 321–77.

degger to adopt a genuine — and, I would add, universal — *singularism* in his account of faith in particular and of existence in general. Nothing seems to count in his description of these exemplary phenomena of the historical but their very modality, their *how,* which, stripped of every content, is assessed in terms of its proper logic — its *verbum internum* — alone. To understand means here to reenact and thus, in a sense, to write Paul's letters again, with Paul, but also here and now, and time and again. Heidegger suggests as much:

> Baptism is not the decisive thing, but the gospel [*Verkündigung*] and in particular *how;* not in the discourse of wisdom [*Weisheitsrede*] so as not to empty the cross by all too much chatter, but simply through its appropriate-modest speech [*angemessen-schlichte Rede*]. This is the only thing, and here there is no possibility of babbling, if only one has grasped the how; cross and preaching of the cross. . . .
>
> This preaching is precisely such that with it absoluteness, nonartificiality, can be determined [*an ihr Absolutheit, Nichtgekünsteltheit sich entscheidet*]. It poses one with an either-or and leaves no room for ambiguities [*Halbheiten*] and opinions, — great discourses, which cover over what is proper [*das Eigentliche*].
>
> The impetus [Anstoss] *ought not be caught and diminished by an adaptive disposition* [Aufnahmestellung] *that through discourses and wisdom overlooks it and therefore does not keep itself radically open. And radically prepares the situation of existential concern* [Bekümmerung] *in itself.* (PhRL 144).

The question that remains to be raised is whether Heidegger's explication of Christian life — and thereby (but, again, how exactly?) of the historical of which religion forms the privileged example — does not weaken the impetus (*Anstoss*) of the gospel (*Verkündigung*), by modeling it on the larger contours of a "horizon" or "dimension," as Heidegger would eventually come to call it. There are no clearer examples of this than those pointed out by Jean-Luc Marion in *God Without Being,* in particular with reference to the "Letter on Humanism," to which I briefly return in the next section. But the seeds of idolatry and blasphemy, by Heidegger's own exacting standards — standards against which he himself holds up so many other authors, Scheler and Jaspers among them, with the possible exception of a certain Aristotle, St. Augustine, Luther, and Kierkegaard — had already been sown in the early lectures on the phenomenology of religion. In other words, *idolatry and blasphemy make their appearance at the very heart of the same ontological "correction" that is supposed to rid all theological discourse from its improprieties and, indeed, its hypocrisy.*

And yet Heidegger was engaged on a lifelong basis in the "correction" of the religious, whether in the form of a phenomenology of factical life, of fundamental ontology and existential analysis, of the thought of Being, its truth, and its *Ereignis,* or of the rhetorical "delirium" that some have decried in *Beiträge zur Philosophie.* In each case, he was faced with the necessity of both respecting and violating the distinction that appears to demarcate the religious from the phenomenological, as well as the theological from the philosophical. As a result, one no longer knows exactly on which side of the line one starts out — or ends up — when charting the phenomenon (e.g., the historical) *as such,* that is to say, in its very essence, in its purity, intact.

*On the one hand,* Heidegger is quoted as stating almost categorically, in the lecture course on "Augustine and Neoplatonism," that a distinction should be preserved between the theological and the philosophical, if only because the real question lies elsewhere and precedes, pervades, and exceeds the very process and conceptual fixation of their differentiation or demarcation:

> The borders of the theological and the philosophical should . . . not be confused (no philosophical watering down [*Verwässerung*] of theology, no make-believe religious "deepening" [*religiöstuerische 'Vertiefung'*] of philosophy). Rather, the step back behind both exemplary formations of factical "life" should (1) principally show for once to what extent [something] and what lies "behind" both, [and] (2) how a genuine problematics results from this; and all of this not atemporally [*überzeitlich*] and for the construction of a culture that may or may not arise, but in the manner of a *historical enactment* [*vollzugsgeschichtlich*]. (PhRL 173)

*On the other hand,* Heidegger does not merely provide a "Religion Within the Limits of Existence Alone" here, as is surmised by Kaegi. For just as in the case of Kant's *Religion Within the Boundaries of Mere Reason* — as well as in the case of Paul Natorp's *Religion innerhalb der Grenzen der Humanität* (Religion Within the Boundaries of Humanity), or, for that matter, Derrida's "Faith and Knowledge: The Two Sources of 'Religion' at the Limits of Reason Alone" — it is not so much that there is a mystery *beyond* what can be said about mere existence (*Vernunftreligion,* as Kant has it, or *la simple raison,* as Derrida puts it); the enigma is rather to be found in the very understanding of this existence (or of *Vernunftreligion, la simple raison,* etc.) itself. Everything that is said of the mystery of and ultimate inscrutability and hence uncertainty of faith—but also of the lack thereof, that is to say, of sin, of faith as a *Kampf,* as a being tempted and tested by the worst, especially, as St. Paul seems to think, at the end of time—holds true of existence and its decision as well. *Where it comes into its own, existence becomes a mystery to itself.*

Again, the demarcation that Kaegi wants to maintain here between the existential and the genuinely theological perspective cannot be upheld. With reference to Heidegger's analysis of conscience (*Gewissen*) in *Being and Time,* Kaegi writes: "For Heidegger what is tempting [*versucherisch*] is only the They [*das Man*] to which Dasein in its care for itself 'always already and then again' falls prey [*verfallen*]. The religion beyond the limits of mere existence would begin there where the temptation of God by man is to taken more seriously than the temptation of man by himself."[57]

But when religion is defined as a *Vollzugszusammenhang mit Gott* and temptation is provoked not so much by others as by the ambiguous modality of a coming in which the Antichrist is virtually indistinguishable from Christ Himself, do we know where to draw the line between the existential and the religious, the human and the divine, the profane and the sacred?

Heidegger's somewhat elliptical remarks on Rudolf Otto's *Das Heilige* (*The Idea of the Holy*) perhaps provide the best answer.[58] To understand

57. Kaegi, "Religion in den Grenzen der blossen Existenz," 148.

58. In the preparatory notes for an uncompleted review of Rudolf Otto's *Das Heilige: Über das Irrationale in der Idee des Göttlichen und sein Verhältnis zum Rationalen* (1917; Munich: C. H. Beck, 1997), trans. John W. Harvey as *The Idea of the Holy: An Inquiry into the Non-Rational Factor in the Idea of the Divine and Its Relation to the Rational* (New York: Oxford University Press, 1958), a book appreciated by Husserl and others as one of the first systematic attempts at writing a phenomenology of religion (Kaegi, "Religion in den Grenzen der blossen Existenz," 148), Heidegger distances himself from any endeavor to graft the religious upon the ill-understood concept of the irrational, saying: "Die Aufpropfung des Irrationalen auf das Rationale muss vermieden und bekämpft werden" (PhRL 333). However, it should be noted that Otto himself insisted in retrospect, in his foreword to the first English edition, that before embarking upon the project that would eventually lead him to publication of *Das Heilige,* he had first made careful study of the "*rational* aspect of that supreme Reality we call 'God'" (referring to his earlier books *Naturalistische und religiöse Weltansicht* and *Die Kant-Friesische Religions-Philosophie*); he leaves no doubt therefore that no one "ought to concern himself with the 'Numen ineffabile' who has not already devoted assiduous and serious study to the 'Ratio aeterna.'" Moreover, it is no less remarkable that the final chapter of *Das Heilige* sketches, albeit all too summarily, the interlocking of the two constitutive aspects of the holy that, in the preceding chapters, he had defined as at once an a priori category of the human spirit *and* an

St. Paul, Heidegger had noted, cannot mean: "To interpret [him] on the basis of a historical connection in which Galatians is placed" (PhRL 78). Instead, it means to explicate the proper meaning, or *Sinn*, of Galatians, and in order to understand the latter we need to pursue the "fundamental determination of original Christian belief [*Religiosität*]" (ibid.). Heidegger stresses that none of these notions, let alone the phenomenon for which they stand, can be grasped by introducing a categorial distinction between the rational and the irrational or the numinous: "With these terms nothing is said as long as one does not know the meaning of *rational*" (PhRL 79). The latter, however, has so far been characterized by "notorious indeterminacy" (ibid.).

This said, Heidegger's strategy seems to hinge on two contradictory approaches. On the one hand, he maintains that simply to leave it at that and to view the religious as an otherness opposed to reason makes mere "aesthetic play" of the phenomenology of religion: "Everything that one says of the remainder that reason cannot dissolve, and that should have existence in all religion, is merely an aesthetic game with misunderstood things" (PhRL 79). In his notes on Otto's *Das Heilige*, Heidegger seems to draw a further consequence from the fact that the phenomenological concept of *Sinn*—and thereby the holy—should neither be understood in terms of this phenomenon's cognitive meaningfulness (cf. also PhRL 85, 131, 311), as the correlate or *noema* of a theoretical intentional act, nor as the latter's opposite (*Gegenwurf*) or even limit (*Grenze*, PhRL 333). Rather, he insists here on an "originarity" (*Originarität*) and proper or self-constitution (*Eigenkonstitution*, PhRL 333) of the holy and assumes that one that should radically distinguish between the "pure holy" and the different forms (worlds and objects) it espouses or constitutes—but how exactly?—on its course through the history of religion ("Differentiate: the pure holy and the constituted holy worlds and objects," PhRL 334). Unlike his contemporary Wilhelm Windelband, for instance, Otto would have neglected these methodological precautions.[59] And Heidegger is the first to admit that we lack adequate insight into "the living consciousness and its original worlds, which in a completely originary [*völlig originär*] way

outward appearance. Rather than taking it as an innate or fundamentally aesthetic notion, Otto seems intent on taking the inner and outward aspects of the holy as a single phenomenon that reinstantiates itself throughout—or as?—the history of the positive religions and that should be explicated in its own terms.

59. On Windelband's "Das Heilige," see Ollig, "Religionsphilosophie der südwestdeutschen Schule," 430–37.

nonetheless have a common, albeit multilayered rooting [*Verwurzelung*] in the grounding meaning [*Grundsinn*] of a genuine personal existence" (PhRL 333).

What we do know, however, Heidegger says here, not without paradox, is that for all its principle independence — an incommensurability it retains in particular when measured in terms that are not its own, such as the terms and paradigms (*Gesetzlichkeiten*) of cultural criticism or any other criterion of validation — the holy can nonetheless be seen as the correlate of an act of faith that, in turn, is related to the historical, to a transcendental historicity of sorts:

> The Holy ought not be thematized as a theoretical *noema* — nor to be sure as an irrationally theoretical *noema* — but as correlate of the act character "belief" that itself can only be interpreted out of the fundamentally essential synthetic experience [*grundwesentlichen Erlebniszusammenhang*] of historical consciousness. That does not mean the explanation of the "Holy" as a "category of validation" [*Bewertungskategorie*]. Rather, what is primary and essential about it is the constitution of an originary objectity [*originären Objektität*].[60]

Yet it seems that, according to Heidegger, there is also an appropriate way to leave the holy for what it is — that is to say, in its peculiar inscrutability (which may very well be the inscrutability of its invisible marking

60. PhRL 333. Clearly, Heidegger did not share the reservations of Karl Barth, in his *Kirchliche Dogmatik*, and, much later, of Levinas, in *Difficile liberté: Essais sur le judaïsme* (2d rev. ed., Paris: A. Michel, 1976), trans. Seán Hand as *Difficult Freedom: Essays on Judaism* (Baltimore: Johns Hopkins University Press, 1990; paperback reprint, 1997) — cf. the essay "Une Religion d'adultes" — and *Du sacré au saint*, about the association of the self-revealing "Word of God," as a *dicere*, that is — or, for that matter, as a "holiness" that exhausts itself in ethical responsibility for the other human being — with an understanding of *das Heilige* that takes it in the first place to be the numinous. All three seem to *agree*, however, that the concept of the holy should under no circumstances be defined in terms of the irrational.

On Barth and Otto, see McCormack, *Karl Barth's Critically Realistic Dialectical Theology*, 341, who, in the accompanying footnote (n. 35), quotes the following passage from Barth's *Church Dogmatics* (KD I/1, 140; CD I/1, 135): "Whatever 'the holy' of Rudolf Otto may be, it certainly cannot be understood as the Word of God, for it is the numinous, and the numinous is the irrational, and the irrational can no longer be distinguished from an absolutized natural force. But everything depends upon this difference if we are to understand the concept of the Word of God." More interesting, of course, is the attempt by Levinas to differentiate between the nonempiricalness, or nonnaturalness, that characterizes both of the two forms of the holy that seem to haunt the West: the Judaic (and Christian?) interpretation of the holy as the trace of God, of the Infinite, of the *illéité*, on the one hand, and the, as it were, (neo)pagan invocation of the holy as *das Heilige*, the numinous, and the *il y a*, on the other.

of the same world, but repeated as no longer the same, *as though* no longer itself or primary, but given, created, revealed, manifested as a mystery). This approach to the phenomenon of the holy—but is it, precisely, under the aspect of its "purity" still or already part of the order of phenomenality?—reveals yet another central feature of phenomenology and of formal indication itself:

It is the peculiarity of phenomenological understanding that it can understand in particular the unintelligible [*Nichtverstehbare*], especially insofar as it radically *leaves* it in its unintelligibility [*Unverstehbarkeit*]. But this itself is only comprehensible when one has understood that philosophy has nothing to do with a scientific consideration of object and subject....

The access is fundamentally determined by the fact that the *phenomenon* to be attained (Christian belief [*Religiosität*]–Christian life–Christian religion) *is already at the outset of the explication grasped in the direction of its grounding meaning [Grundsinnrichtung]*. These connections of meaning may at first . . . still be far removed from the proper understanding; it suffices when they are relentlessly kept and if they are not given out of hand for the enactment of the explication, but are ever more radically ascertained. (Thereby is the certainty of the corroboration not determined in the sense of a scientific general validity and necessity of reason, but by originality [originariness, *Ursprünglichkeit*] and approximation with respect to the concern [*Bekümmerung*], as is demanded absolutely.). (PhRL 131)

These are fundamental issues, but—theoretically, that is to say, ontologically and axiologically, hermeneutically and exegetically—any attempt to respond to them in ways other than by a singular repetition or testimony is left pending or rather in abeyance. This is precisely what phenomenology is all about here; in its method of formal indication, it hints at the site of decision to be made time and again. But its hint is also an exemplary instantiation and thereby a—nongeneralizable, nonformalizable, indeed inscrutable—testimony.

Needless to say, this leaves many questions open, not the least important of which is to know how, in the constitution of the holy and its manifestation, not only the *fascinans* and the *tremendum,* but also the "best" and the "worst" relate. We have touched on this question apropos of the function of the Antichrist in Heidegger's reading of St. Paul. In his preparatory notes for reviewing Otto's book, Heidegger writes only this: "The 'numinous': the 'particular element [*Sonderelement*]' in the Holy *minus* the ethical and rational moments. On what grounds the bond of the latter with the former? And does it in a way belong to the originary structure of the numinous?" (PhRL 333)

Perhaps, all this is what is meant by Heidegger when he speaks, in the "Letter on Humanism," of man's need to exist in the dimension of the nameless (*im Namenlosen*). This phrase does not therefore so much hint at a secret dialogue with the tradition of the Cabala, as Derrida muses in "Violence and Metaphysics"—although this formal analogy can never be excluded—as it should be taken as saying that here, at the decisive moment, there is nothing more to say.[61] Indeed, there where the holy is somehow present, words, the holy names, must be lacking. "Holy names are lacking" ("Es fehlen heilige Namen"), Hölderlin writes, demonstrating not so much his indebtedness to the *via negativa,* to the tradition of apophatics—although, again, this parallel can never be simply excluded—as his endorsement of yet another thought of divine presence: this time of a presence that is present in certain hints or *Winke* alone and that therefore *is* but *as if not,* ὡς μὴ, marked by an *im-mediacy* that is neither dialectical nor empirical, in other words, that escapes the grasp of ontotheology and can no longer be based on the *positum* of historical revelations alone.

## "Religion *qua* Religion": Heidegger's Humanism

If the objection is made that this is hardly what Heidegger had "in mind" or what Heidegger is "all about," then I can only insist once more on the radicality, the singularity, the *singularism* of his claims. For Heidegger's insistence on the enactment of interpretation (*vollzugsgeschichtlich* once more) is based, not on a disputable concept of *Einfühlung* informed by a certain hermeneutics, but on each of us writing St. Paul's epistles with Paul all over again, each time anew, in struggle (*Kampf*) and uncertainty, fear and trembling that leaves no room for any objectifiable knowledge as to *where, what,* and *who* we are, and, least of all, as to *when* to expect the end of all things, the second coming (and the coming between the first and the second of the Antichrist and the necessary *Not* for which it stands).

This is at bottom nothing but the prefiguration of the *mineness,* the *Jemeinigkeit,* of which *Being and Time* speaks so incisively, albeit without, perhaps, being willing to draw its full consequences. For we are dealing here, I think, with nothing less than a singular logic of the singular, a singularism that begins by avowing the aporia that feeds it.

61. See LH 223 / 316; Derrida, *Writing and Difference,* 137 / 201.

Yet articulation of the structure of mineness does not prevent Heidegger from immediately forgetting and covering over the abysses that this singular determination of interpretation opens up. This denial and betrayal of his single most decisive philosophical innovation occurs in the lectures on the phenomenology of religion no less than in Heidegger's mature writings.

Again, the most economical way—the shortest detour—toward verifying that hypothesis is by focusing once more on Heidegger's dealings with the *Kernphänomen* of history and factical life experience as exemplified or instantiated (or mimicked) by religion: that is to say, not so much by religion in its positive forms as thematized, objectified, and canonized by the history of religions, by biblical and dogmatic theology, as by the restlessness at the heart of existence, by religion within the limits of mere existence, and this means, for Heidegger, for religion proper, by religion *qua* religion.

Religion *qua* religion: there is another word for that—more than one even—in the "Letter on Humanism." Without wanting to stretch the analogy too far, I would suggest that the function of the phrase "religion *qua* religion" is virtually taken over by that of the truth of Being, the holy (*das Heilige*), the essence of divinity, in short by the "dimension" in which religions and revelations manifest themselves *necessarily*, if, that is, they manifest themselves at all.

This pluralization of religion *qua* religion in terms that will subsequently give way to the mirroring play—the *Spiegel-Spiel*—of the Fourfold, would have been unthinkable without the pagan, read Hölderlinean, turns that Heidegger at this point has already taken; turns, since there is not just one, and they move in more than one direction at once. But while this pluralization may be explained by invoking Hölderlin, the poet of whom it is prophesied that he "does not belong to 'humanism,' precisely because he thought the destiny of man's essence in a more original [*anfänglicher*] way than 'humanism' could" (LH 225/318), Hölderlin thus becomes a witness for similar reasons to St. Paul, St. Augustine, Luther, and Kierkegaard, who likewise led the human back to its nonsubjectivist and nonobjectifiable essence, existence, that is to say, to its thrownness, ecstatic temporality, homelessness, and openness. However, when Heidegger reduces this poet's poetry to so-called *Dichtung*—to a poetizing, moreover, that comes to stand here for the saying of the holy (as had already been noted in the afterword to "What Is Metaphysics?")—he also subjects Hölderlin to a redoubtable procedure of hierarchization. Like the *parousia* and *kairos,* which are at once captured in their singularity and formalized, as it were, beyond recognition, Hölderlin's words, too, are interpreted in terms of an architecture of conditionality and possibilization. Once more, one thing (but not a *thing,* exactly, rather a certain *nothingness*) here forms the horizon in whose dimension alone another may or may not appear.

Now if humanism in its different historical forms is taken to task for not having been able to properly value *humanitas,* in its *Würde,* that is, and in its *height,* then this latter notion of *humanitas* serves a similar function as the religion *qua* religion of which Heidegger speaks with so much insistence. For what else does it mean to speak of a more originary interpretation of humanism, rethinking it in light of the "more essential" *humanitas* of the *homo humanus,* and thereby, I would venture to suggest, in terms of a humanism *qua* humanism? Heidegger states that it is the task of thought to

> think the essence of man more primordially. With regard to this more essential *humanitas* of *homo humanus* there arises the possibility of restoring to the word *humanism* a historical sense that is older than its oldest meaning chronologically [*historisch*] reckoned. The restoration is not to be understood as though the word *humanism* were wholly without meaning and a mere *flatus vocus* [empty sound]. The "*humanum*" in the word points to *humanitas,* the essence of man; the *ism* indicates that the essence of man is meant to be taken essentially. This is the sense that the word *humanism* has as such. To restore a sense to it can only mean to redefine [rather, to determine further, *weiterbestimmen* — HdV] the meaning of the word. (LH 247–48 / 341)

Does this mean that Heidegger from now on uses the term *humanism* or *humanitas* in a formally indicative way? As a stepping-stone and a stumbling block? Or that its classical, modern, and theological connotations are subjected to ontological correction, in the precise sense that the lecture "Phenomenology and Theology" gives to the word *Korrektion?*

No clear answers to these questions are given. The very methodology for which these technical terms — *formal indication* and *ontological correction* — stand seems to give way to the mere poetic evocation of man's being in terms of a *Wächterschaft* whose modality is that of responsiveness pure and simple:

> *Humanism* now means, in case we decide to retain the word, that the essence of man is essential for the truth of Being, specifically in such a way that

what matters is not man simply as such. So we are thinking a curious kind of humanism [*einen Humanismus seltsamer Art*]. The word results in a name that is a *lucus a non lucendo* [literally, a grove where no light penetrates]. (LH 248/342)

If we assume that the word *humanism* is not a mere *flatus vocis*, that it retains a conceptual specificity of sorts, albeit one that needs to be further determined, should we then not also accept that it in its very formal, and, if one can say so, semantic characteristics, forms an exact analogy of the word *religion*, as understood in the early lectures?

At first glance, religion as well seems older than any historical, chronological datability can grasp; it, too, is a *lucus a non lucendo*. And just as Heidegger's uncommon use of the word *humanism* reminds us of the *humanitas* of the *homo humanis*, that is to say, the essence of man, so also the singular use of *religion*—of the word and the concept—leads us back to a religion *before* and *beyond* religion, to a religion *qua* religion that differs in nothing from the structure of factical life experience that Heidegger would come to define in terms of existence, or being there.

Both *religion* and *humanism* are, therefore, used in formally indicative, revealing ways. They reveal Being, man's being, as much as they are, in turn, revealed by Being as such. "[T]he essence of man is essential for the truth of Being, specifically in such a way that what matters is not man simply as such [*lediglich als solchen*]," Heidegger observes (LH 248/ 342), and one may well wonder whether there is any determinable difference between this and the definition of religion—or rather—faith in, say, "Phenomenology and Theology." For there, too, all emphasis is put on a singular *asymmetry*, which can be summarized as follows: no revelation, no grace, no second birth without there being a singular addressee, a sinner, either individually or collectively, as a people. But the latter do not matter as such. They are, if not mediators or vehicles, then at most the sounding boards of a gift for which they prepare but cannot anticipate or initiate as such.

Regardless of this formal analogy, the difference between these two structures of asymmetry (i.e., of religion or faith and of humanism in the uncommon sense) remains decisive, and this precisely insofar as it remains still—always still—to be decided, by each of us, or, rather, Heidegger seems to suggest, by the few of us who are awake, sober, on our guard.

And yet, the difference rests just as much on an ultimate *in-difference* that has nothing to do with nihilism, or even with ethics or politics, since it forms the very condition of their possibility. For while it might be claimed that Heidegger inscribes the question of Being into that of religion and humanism by pursuing their respective meanings back to their source, his discourse is here also characterized by an uncanny lack of interest in what either of them is *about* in terms of historical reference and empirical effect. In the end, it seems, neither religion nor humanism matters *much* or, if you like, *as such.* In both cases, the supposedly essential meaning of these terms is played out against their respective historical idiom, just as the *positum* of faith is distinguished from — and then privileged over — the multifarious positive forms of the so-called positive religions. By the same token, *humanitas,* or the essence of man, is pitted against humanisms deemed too metaphysical, too anthropological, too theological. And on both counts, following the "logic of presupposition," the former is thought as the condition of the possibility of the latter.

While the historical names of religion and *humanitas* are retained, they are thus at the same time formalized, and this to the point where they become virtually or at least structurally *interchangeable* with each other. And not only with each other, but also *with the existence toward which they are said to provide possible access, or even, in the case of religion, the shortest detour.* Paradoxically, they are, in Heidegger's reading, nothing but a word for the experience of Being, and yet at the same time nothing but avenues *toward* that experience of Being, toward an experience that is never given beyond this being-toward, beyond this being toward a Being deemed pure, if not simple.

As so often, Heidegger's thought reaches here for the *as such,* the *als solches.* This idée fixe orients the search, not only for religion *qua* religion, *humanitas* properly understood, but also — and first of all — for Being — and ultimately the *Ereignis* — itself. Note how the "Letter on Humanism" reiterates this most persistent of Heidegger's concerns: "Yet Being — what is Being? It is It itself. ["Doch das Sein — was ist das Sein? Es ist Es selbst"]. . . . "Being" — that is not God and not a cosmic ground. Being is farther than all beings and yet nearer to man than every being, be it a rock, a beast, a work of art, a machine, be it an angel or God" (LH 234/ 328). Being, in other words, is not a deus ex machina that makes its sudden appearance on the stage of thought and experience; it is already there, given in an almost uncanny proximity that is at once a sublime distance. This explains why thought and experience all too often fail to grasp it as such, and instead commit the gravest idolatry and blasphemy; why they always already keep Being (it, *Es,* itself) at what is merely a *false distance,* or, conversely, why they bring it into a *false proximity* by representing it by beings or even as the generality and the ground of beings as such: "Being is the nearest. Yet the near remains farthest from man. Man at first [*zunächst*] clings always and only to beings. But when thinking represents beings as beings, it no doubt relates itself to Being. In truth, however, it always [*sic*] thinks only of beings as such; precisely not, and never, Being as such" (ibid.). From one as such to the other, from the as such that is not quite it (but, say, derivative and improper) to the as such *qua* as such: this is the strange and unsettling movement of Heidegger's thought.

Religion and *humanitas* — humanism in a new, but, in fact, the oldest, or, rather, older than oldest, meaning of the word — become structurally analogous to the transcendence for which existence and being-a-shepherd-of-Being stand, but they are at the same time also enveloped by the latter. Coming first, they are immediately secondarized, allowed to manifest or reveal themselves only in the *dimension* of this Being that they — again, paradoxically — also open up. What *in fact* comes first, or at the same place, comes *de iure* later. Or so it seems. What makes access to Being possible in the first place comes second or later, much later even than any historical time as we know it could possibly capture.

There is no better illustration of this *hierarchization* — and the "logic of presupposition" that it entails — than the well-known passage in the "Letter on Humanism" that speaks of this *one-dimensionality* of the experience of Being and thought in their relation to God, gods, the holy, and mortals:

> Only from the truth of Being can the essence of the holy be thought. Only from the essence of the holy is the essence of divinity to be thought. Only in light of the essence of divinity can it be thought or said what the word "God" is to signify. Or should we not first be able to hear and understand all these words carefully if we are to be permitted as men, that is, as existent creatures, to experience a relation of God to man? How can man at the present stage of world history ask at all seriously and rigorously whether the god nears or withdraws, when he has above all neglected to think into the dimension in which alone that question can be asked? But this is the dimension of the holy, which indeed remains closed as a dimension if the open region [*das Offene*] of Being is not cleared and in its clearing is near man. Perhaps what is distinctive about this world-epoch consists in the closure of the dimension of the hale [*des Heilen*]. Perhaps that is the sole malignancy [*Unheil*].

But with this reference the thinking that points toward the truth of Being as
what is to be thought has in no way decided in favor of theism. It can be theistic as little as atheistic. Not, however, because of an indifferent attitude, but
out of respect for the boundaries that have been set for thinking as such, indeed set by what gives itself to thinking as what is to be thought, by the truth
of Being. (LH 253–54 / 347–48)

In this context, Heidegger leaves no doubt that there is an intrinsic link between the experience or the thought of Being and a certain
struggle, between the most proper and the most uncanny, between the
best and the worst. Again, there is a formal analogy or structural parallel
between the eschatology discussed in the early lectures — notably, in their
apocalyptic invocation of the coming between the first and the second of
the Antichrist — and the invocation of Being in terms of *das Strittige.* Both
ambiguities — of the coming of Christ and the *Ankunft* of Being — raise the
stakes of experience, decision, and thought, underscoring the fundamental ambivalence or ambiguity of Being's manifestation, by showing that
whatever it *is* that makes existence possible is also that which threatens to
make it impossible.

Yet while Heidegger thus claims that the revelation of positive religions is somehow made possible by the revealability or "dimension" of
Being, it can be argued on internal grounds that the reverse thesis holds
true as well. In speaking about religion and in speaking about humanism,
Heidegger speaks about the same subject, about a subject, however — the
question of Being, *as such* — that is never thematized directly and that is
never addressed *as such.* It is hard to determine whether this subject receives a different color, tone, or inflection when it arises in the context of
the phenomenology of religion or in that of humanism, or, for that matter, somewhere else (in, say, the body, the flesh, old and new media).

At times it would seem that the religious overtones gain a certain
prominence in Heidegger's writing that is never attained by the idiom of
humanism. One thinks here of the way in which *Being and Time* retains
and rearticulates some of its most central motifs. In fact, it seems fair to
say that Heidegger's engagement with humanism is circumstantial, accidental, triggered as it is by a specific debate (the publication of Jean-Paul
Sartre's pamphlet *L'Existentialisme est un humanisme* [*Existentialism and
Humanism*], and the question posed by Jean Beaufret to Heidegger after
the war: "Comment redonner un sens au mot 'Humanisme'?" ["How can

meaning be restored to the word *humanism?*"] [LH 219 / 313]) [62] that came
to him relatively late in his career. It was never motivated by an inquiry
into his own *Herkunft*, which, as he insisted on more than one occasion,
is not merely biographical and remains forever one's *Zukunft.*

The implication is, at least, that the essence of religion is more essential than *humanitas,* which is already more essential than humanism in
its historical, positive, forms, and, as we have seen, older than history
itself. Yet, to complicate matters, we should not forget that the more
essential essence of religion—religion *qua* religion—is *less old,* and, in
that sense, less originary, than the essence of humanism, than humanism
*qua* humanism. For religion, at least in the early lecture courses, is given
precisely with—and implied in—the phenomenon of history and the stirrings of factical life as such.

And it is, perhaps, for this reason, that it may remind us more than
anything else—more than humanism in its more than oldest meaning at
least—of a conditionality that is not merely empirical, biographical, or
ontic, but, precisely, historical and at the same time transcendental, this
time in a Husserlian rather than Kantian sense of the word.

What motivates the invocation of religion—of religion *qua* religion,
but of a religion also that, in its very concept, remains tainted, indeed
stigmatized, by the history of religions from which it sets itself apart—
is its unique and uncanny ability to evoke a transcendental historicity of
which it is—for Heidegger—the example par excellence.

What, then, is this wider relevance of the attempt to relate Heidegger's
early understanding of religion *qua* religion to his later insistence on the
"more essential" *humanitas* of *homo humanus,* on humanism *qua* humanism? For one thing, the formal analogy makes us aware that the question
of Being cannot but announce or reinscribe itself in the discourses and the
practices from which it—according to Heidegger and according to its own
internal logic—must also set itself apart. The question of Being, in other
words, never leaves the horizon—indeed the dimension—of the complex syndrome that Jean-François Courtine calls "onto-theo-anthropo-
logy," [63] and that Derrida identifies as "onto-theo-teleo-eschatology."

62. Jean-Paul Sartre, *L'Existentialisme est un humanisme* (Paris: Éditions Nagel, 1946; reprint, 1970), trans. Philip Mairet as *Existentialism and Humanism* (1948; reprint, Brooklyn,
N.Y.: Haskell House, 1977). See also Tom Rockmore, *Heidegger and French Philosophy: Humanism, Antihumanism, and Being* (London: Routledge, 1995), chs. 4, 5, and 6.

63. Jean-François Courtine, *Heidegger et la phénoménologie* (Paris: Vrin, 1990), 55ff.

I do not want to insist on the pertinence of these neologisms, but simply wish to stress, once more, that the so-called ontic and empirical determinations and overdeterminations are conditions of the possibility of the question of Being—of Being as such—*at least as much* and *for the same reason*—as they are in turn made possible by this question—by the notion of Being.

Of course, such a hypothesis has all the appearance of a contradiction, an aporia, a *Holzweg*, and a *circulus vitiosus* at that. And there is no way of telling whether this is how thought begins or, on the contrary, comes to its end, begins by ending or ends by beginning—the point being precisely that there is none, that nothing has been said, that everything remains to be said, indeed, to be determined further, and that what will still be said in fact amounts to nothing at all, that is to say, to nothing that is determinable, whether ontically or ontologically, whether empirically or axiologically, and so on and so forth.

The classical and modern objection to this aporia—the challenge of the very *tertium non datur*—is, of course, that it allows one to say just about anything. That in the course of the repetition of concepts and motifs, each one of them may come to signal something else, and this, it would seem, almost at random. But then again, this is precisely the point: that no single point can claim priority.

One can certainly agree, therefore, with Kaegi who, in his review of Heidegger's *Phänomenologie des religiösen Lebens* and in a criticism of the views of Otto Pöggeler, Christoph Jamme, and others, writes:

> Already the extensive propedeutic regarding the relationship between philosophy, factical life experience and science . . . should correct the widespread view that Heidegger would find "life in its *hic et nunc* facticity . . . forgotten . . . by Western tradition" in "early Christianity" [*Christenheit*]. Factical life experience is not originary Christian life experience, but originary Christian life experience is factical life experience, and especially: the covering over [*Verdeckung*] of factical life experience does not result from a (or the) Western tradition, but from the objectivism of factical life experience itself.[64]

But then again, should one not rather maintain that the originary Christian experience of factical life provides at least just as much a key to the understanding of factical life as the other way around? Is originary Chris-

---

64. Kaegi, "Religion in den Grenzen der blossen Existenz," 142.

tian life experience for Heidegger merely an "example" (*Exempel*),[65] albeit
the most revealing instantiation of a general structure, called facticity? Or
does the reverse of these hold true as well? Of course, to argue that any
*general* structure remains parasitic upon that which it makes possible is
not to imply that the latter takes the function of a *concrete*, that is to say,
ontic or empirico-positive, condition of the possibility of the former. For,
as we have seen, the concreteness of the unrest and the flux of Christian
factical life experience is much less that of mediatizable whole (as would
be the implication of the Latin *concrescere*) as that of an absolute yet re-
peatable *singularity*. As a matter of fact, this singularity would therefore
be at least as elusive—indeed, as abstract or as formal—as the most abstract and most formal of all structures (categories, transcendentals, existentials, universals).

## Transcendental Historicity

I have would not have been able to interpret Heidegger's exegesis of
St. Paul—and, more broadly, to formulate a hypothesis concerning his
relation to religion "in general"—had I not been guided by the writings
of Jacques Derrida, notably *Of Spirit, Aporias, The Gift of Death*, and *On
the Name*.

Conversely, however, I cannot but help ask whether these writings of
Derrida's, where they address Paul, Augustine, or religion "in general," are
not prefigured and premeditated, as it were, in Heidegger's early notes,
compiled and published by others. Surely, this adumbration of Derrida's
exegesis of Heidegger in the exegesis Heidegger gives of Paul (and of Augustine) is not simply thematic and only indirectly a question of method.

As suggested already, both discussions hinge above all on a certain
reception and reassessment of the work of Husserl. In the case of Heidegger, as we have seen, explicit reference is made to Husserl's *Logical
Investigations* and *Ideas* for an understanding of formal indication, the
procedure that governs the central methodic steps in *Being and Time*, but
finds its first and most explicit elaboration in the early lectures on the
phenomenology of religion, as well as in the lecture on "Phenomenology
and Theology."

Mutatis mutandis, a similar operation seems to take place in the writings of Derrida, especially when he speaks of a "transcendental histo-

65. Ibid.

ricity" that makes its appearance in the later writings of Husserl. This crucial motif is discussed most extensively in the introduction to Husserl's *Origin of Geometry*,[66] but also, and more implicitly, on numerous other occasions, especially where religion is a central concern.

Both the Heidegger of the early lectures and Derrida in his most recent writings on so-called negative theology seem to situate themselves in fact *at once extremely close to and at an infinite remove from* the phenomenon called "religious." This fact is hardly ever acknowledged by Heidegger, who continues to secondarize religious revelation in favor of a dimension of revealability that makes the former possible in the first place. In Derrida, by contrast, the uneasy balance between *Offenbarung* and *Offenbarkeit* is preserved most of the time. As result, his analyses situate themselves beyond — or, if you like, on this side of — the divide that is supposed to separate philosophy and theology, phenomenology, thought, and religion, discursiveness and, say, prayer. But then again, as we have seen, the indecisiveness or undecidability with regard to these last and most pernicious of all binary oppositions may very well be the ultimate gesture of the respect — indeed, the *Verhaltenheit*, the *Scheu* — that marks the essence of religion, whatever form it takes.

To my knowledge, no clearer expression of this circumstance can be found than the one given — or should we say confessed to? — in Derrida's "Circumfession," the subliminal text that accompanies one of the more rigorous formalizations of his works to date. In "Circumfession," the so-called logic of presupposition gives way to a logic of substitution — of "the first" becoming "the last," "the least," and vice versa. Yet this second or secondary logic, a logic of supplementarity, already announces itself in Heidegger, albeit obliquely and under cover of his more explicit intentions and formulations. As so often, one must therefore read Heidegger *with* and *against* Heidegger, Heidegger *with* Derrida, Derrida *against* Heidegger.

Interpreting Heidegger in the way I have proposed thus comes down to charging him with — or complimenting him on — two related yet contradictory positions: (1) the transformation of philosophy, the thought of Being, into one gigantic tautology, and (2) introducing a radical — or should we say phenomenal? — heterology, for the repetition of "the same" does not exclude otherness, but implies it, since "the same" is always

---

66. Jacques Derrida, "Introduction," in Husserl, *Origine de la géométrie*, 3–171. See also Jacques Derrida, *Le Problème de la génèse dans la philosophie de Husserl* (Paris: Presses universitaires de France, 1990), 247ff., esp. 272–83.

actually said, thought, and experienced *otherwise*. The formal indication of theologemes, no less than of humanism, results in a generalization no less than a trivialization, in a repetition that inscribes an indelible difference in the repeated. To be sure, this is hardly ever acknowledged as such either by Heidegger or by those who have followed in his footsteps. Wherever this logic of substitution — of an aporetic hetero-tautology — appears, however, it is not only denied primacy but ignored in its very coexistence with the tautology, the repetition of "It," *Es*, Being, itself. It is here that we discern the chance missed by Heideggerian discourse, which is alluded to only obliquely by Heidegger himself and to my knowledge has been grasped and articulated only by Derrida.

Again, to read Heidegger in this way means to read him against the grain — indeed, deconstructively — but also in a way that, I maintain, is first of all Levinasian, if not in its inspiration or in its method, then at least in its argumentative thrust. For it is in Levinas, notably in his *Otherwise than Being, or Beyond Essence,* that we find a logic of substitution that radicalizes and extends the Heideggerian analysis, in particular, as I demonstrate in the next chapter, by rearticulating — and reorienting — the formal structure and, if one can still say so, the substance of Dasein's being toward death. In so doing, Levinas makes it clear that to cite one given concept or motif rather than another — speaking, for instance, of "religion" or "humanism" rather than of anything else — can only be relegated to a singular testimony that, for all its situatedness, keeps its distance from the philosophical and the religious tradition and finds therein its freedom, albeit a freedom that is contradictory and therefore always contested.

# Chapter Four

# The Generous Repetition

IN THIS CHAPTER I consider two remarkable examples that further illustrate the perplexity that emerges whenever we ask how
the structural and thematic turn of the philosophical to the religious
comes to pass, or can responsibly be conceived of.[1] The two chosen examples are hardly fortuitous, since they deal with two *absolute signifiers*—
signifiers of some absolute as much as signifiers that absolve or loosen
themselves from all conceptual and cultural analysis; from the realms of
thought and of experience; from the transcendental as much as from the
empirical. They concern *death*—the being toward death that, Heidegger
says, in its proper modality forms the secret ground of the historicity of
Dasein[2]—in its relation to *God,* the notion of God as it evokes the experience of a certain death, and, therefore, raise the problem of the very
conceptual or figural interchangeability of these extremes. More specifically, I seek to highlight some central aspects of a text that I consider to
be one of the most intriguing and enigmatic of all the studies of the theological that interest me here, Derrida's *Sauf le nom (Post-Scriptum).*[3]

1. On the "répétition généreuse" to which the chapter title alludes, see Jacques Derrida,
"Ousia et grammè," in *Margins of Philosophy,* 48 / 54.
2. "Authentic Being-towards-death—that is to say, the finitude of temporality—is the
hidden basis of Dasein's historicality" ("Das eigentliche Sein zum Tode, das heisst die Endlich-
keit der Zeitlichkeit, ist der verborgene Grund der Geschichtlichkeit des Daseins"), Heidegger
notes (BT 438 / 386).
3. First published in English under the title "Post-Scriptum: Aporias, Ways and Voices," in
*Derrida and Negative Theology,* ed. Harold Coward and Toby Foshay (Albany, N.Y.: State University of New York Press, 1992), this has been reissued in SN in a new translation by John P.
Leavey, Jr., along with two closely related essays by Derrida, *Passions* and *Khōra.* Each of
these, Derrida notes, sheds a certain light on the other two: "Under the mobile syntax of these
titles, one could read *three essays on a name given* or on what can *happen to the name given*
(anonymity, metonymy, paleonymy, cryptonymy, pseudonymity), hence to the name *received,*
indeed, to the name *owed,* on what one perhaps *ought* to give or to sacrifice as well as what one
*owes* to the name, to the name of the name, hence to the sur-name" (SN xvi). On the general
problematics of the name and the relationship between Derrida's three essays, see Jean Greisch,
"Nomination et Révélation," *Archivio di filosofia* n. 1–3 (1994): 577–98.

*Sauf le nom* presents itself as a dialogue in the tradition of *polylogues* adopted by Derrida in *Éperons: Les Styles de Nietzsche* (*Spurs: Nietzsche's Styles*), in "At This Very Moment in This Work Here I Am," in *Parages*, and elsewhere. The subtitle *Post-Scriptum* refers, however, to the genre of autobiography, to the confessional mode, notably in St. Augustine. As in Heidegger's reading of St. Paul, the analysis of the name, in particular the divine name, in the tradition of apophatics, but also, more obliquely, in that of the secret—more precisely, the *passion*—at the very heart of the ethical and the political (in Kant and others), has everything to do with a singularizing reenactment of sorts, a *Vollzugszusammenhang mit Gott.* Derrida suggests as much when he points out that his discussion of the *passion*—of a *passion* that occurs in the plural and that is "at once essential and foreign" to what is commonly named a secret—takes place, among other things, "within the more or less fictive repetition of a 'this is my body' " (SN xiv). I shall return to this matter in the next chapter.

## Save the Name

*Sauf le nom*'s adoption of the rhetorical procedure of the *polylogue* seems justified by its first few phrases, which remind us that the phenomenon of negative theology is not only *one of a kind* but is also based on inherent aporias that force it to speak through more than one voice alone. It is always necessary for more than one (*plus d'une*) voice to speak, especially when the subject is God or death or both. And, Derrida writes, this holds true "[s]till more . . . when one claims to speak about God according to the apophatic [*l'apophase*], in other words, according to the voiceless voice [*la voix blanche*], the way of theology called or so called negative. This voice multiplies itself, dividing within itself: it says one thing and its contrary, God that is without being or God that (is) beyond being" (SN 35/15). This ambiguity or, rather, internal contradiction, of which it is not certain that it is logically and ontologically *possible* at all, can be discerned, Derrida claims, in all the texts traditionally associated with the tradition of apophatics, of which the treatises of Pseudo-Dionysius, the sermons of Meister Eckhart, and the epigrams of Angelus Silesius are the better-known examples. And, mutatis mutandis, what has come to be known under the name of deconstruction would seem to fall into the same category. The reasons for this possible resemblance have occupied us earlier. Here, in *Sauf le nom,* Derrida adds yet another consideration, one that recalls a particular phrase that occurs almost unexpectedly in

Angelus Silesius's *Cherubinic Wanderer* and assumes a central role in Heidegger's existential analysis, in *Being and Time,* of Dasein's being-toward-death:

> Far from being a methodological technique, a possible or necessary procedure, unrolling the law of a program and applying rules, that is, unfolding possibilities, deconstruction has often been defined as the very experience of the (impossible) possibility of the impossible, of the most impossible, a condition deconstruction shares with the gift, the "yes," the "come," the decision, testimony, the secret, and, perhaps, death. (SN 43 / 31–32)

Perhaps death. Possibly death. Would death be a possible name of one of the elements of this series, then, and if so, in what sense? Is death a possible name for testimony and notably for the impossibility by which it is said to be characterized? Is death possible or, perhaps, impossible? Can this be decided? Or is death itself, in its very phenomenality, undecidable and therefore, so to speak, an ultimate "perhaps"? But then again, what does it mean to speak of death itself and *as such?*

Perhaps death. Possibly death. Everything would depend here on how one thinks the possible for which this apparent possibility named death — the impossibility of being there that is death — stands; on how, moreover, it is possible to demarcate it from the thanatological overdeterminations of given cultures, from anthropologies and ontotheologies of death, from a certain, for example, Judeo-Christian interpretation of the giving of death, from sacrifice, but also from the question of culture as such. For, as Derrida argues, the very circumstance that all culture is ipso facto an engagement with death contributes to the impossibility of addressing death in purely phenomenological terms.

The whole discussion of the relation of God to death in *Sauf le nom* revolves around a single enigmatic assertion by Angelus Silesius: "The most impossible is possible" ("Das überunmöglichste ist möglich"), which allows Derrida to reiterate one of the central arguments expounded earlier in "How to Avoid Speaking" and to stress that the excess implied in the *über* suggests an expansion and transformation, or even interruption, of the realm of Being, of ontology, of the theological, and of the possible. Yet "this beyond, this *hyper (über)* obviously introduces an absolute heterogeneity in the order and in the modality of the possible. The possibility of the impossible, of the 'more impossible' that as such is also possible ('more impossible than the impossible'), marks an absolute interruption in the regime of the possible that nonetheless remains, if this can be said, in place" (SN 43/32–33). How can an "absolute interruption in the regime of the possible" occur, be attempted, or be successful as long as this "regime" remains "in place" or intact? Needless to say, Derrida does not rely here on the formal or dialectical logic according to which a double negation—the "more impossible than the impossible"—equals affirmation, sublation, or even elevation. Rather, Derrida seems to refer here to the singular logic of the hyperbolic "more," *über, plus,* which, in a manner reminiscent of Maurice Blanchot's deployment of the *sans* ("X *sans* X"), enables a movement of emphasis and excess aimed, not unlike the ancient *via eminentiae,* at an ultimate respect for the singularity of "whatever it is" that is named or evoked. Perhaps this logic lets itself be pushed to the very limit of the possible and beyond, indeed, toward the "most impossible" and even the "more impossible than the impossible." For, as Derrida reminds us, the *über* in *überunmöglichste*—like the Greek prefix *hyper* in the apophatics of Pseudo-Dionysius—might "signify just as well 'most' or 'more than': the most impossible or the more than impossible" (SN 44/33). And this would explain why the *via negativa* and the *via eminentiae,* in the very ambiguity of their abstractions and superlatives, enable a writing and thinking to be at once revolutionary and traditional, uprooting and marked by a desire for the originary, for the origin of the origin.

In what follows, I seek to analyze the double meaning of this excessive thought of the *über,* as well as the double gesture of the apophatics that it allows or provokes, so as better to clarify, first, how this double movement is reiterated and enabled, not only by the *via negativa,* but also by the discourse of phenomenology, more precisely, the kenosis of its discourse. This correlation between apophatics and phenomenology finds its best illustration in the rearticulation by Derrida of the mutual implication of revealability (*Offenbarkeit*) and revelation (*Offenbarung*), of Christianicity (*Christlichkeit*) and Christianity (*Christentum*), and of messianicity and messianism. These dual sources of the religious and their relation—that of their respective bipolarities but also that of the series—are at the heart both of the writings of Angelus Silesius and of Heidegger's *Being and Time,* each of which, Derrida suggests, can be read as a commentary on the other.

Stretching his argument a little further, Derrida demonstrates what the impossible thought of the impossible, the more than impossible, in short the *other than possible,* might entail for an uncommon, heterodox reading of Heidegger. For it is in Heidegger's existential analytic of death in *Being and Time* that we may locate a conceptual and figural analogy with some of the most radical traditions of negative theology, notably with Angelus Silesius's formulation "Das überunmöglichste ist möglich." Derrida writes:

> The possibility of the impossible, of the "most impossible," of the more impossible than the most impossible, that recalls, *unless it announces,* what Heidegger says of death: "die Möglichkeit der schlechthinnigen Daseinsunmöglichkeit" ["the possibility of the absolute impossibility of Dasein"]. What is, for *Dasein,* purely and simply impossible is what is possible, and death is its name. I wonder if that is a matter of a purely formal analogy. What if negative theology were speaking at bottom of the mortality of *Dasein?* And of its heritage? Of what is written after it, according to (*d'après*) it? (SN 44/33–34; see BT 293/250)

The reference to this supplement, based on the hypothesis that *Being and Time* might to some extent be seen as a sequel to the work of Angelus Silesius, as a postscript whose relation to what precedes it—to its prescript, as it were—extends well beyond its being a "purely formal analogy," is, of course, to its first chapter of the second division on Dasein and Temporality. The second voice of *Sauf le nom* continues even more boldly by stating that if a parallel and secret correspondence can indeed be said to exist between these two authors, then, conversely, the apophatic texts of the mystics, first and foremost those of Angelus Silesius, might just as well

> be read as powerful discourses on death, on the (impossible) possibility of the proper death of being-there that speaks, and that speaks of what carries away, interrupts, denies, or annihilates its speaking as well as its own *Dasein.* Between the existential analytic of being-to-death, in *Being and Time,* and the remarks of Heidegger on the theological, the theiological, and above all on a theology in which the word "being" would not even appear, the coherence seems to me profound and the continuity rigorous. (SN 44–45/34–35)

How can this be? And what does it teach us about the relation between the philosophical, ontological, and phenomenological, on the one hand, and the empirical, ontic, and theological *positum* (whether positive or negative, neither or both), on the other? And where, on which side of this apparently fixed or undivided line that runs through a good deal of the history of metaphysics at least from its classical modern exposition up to its contemporary linguistic, semiotic, or formal-pragmatic transformation, does religion fit into the equation? On the side of the more or less abstract transcendental (a structure or dimension of possibilization) or rather on the side of the concrete instantiation of any such transcendental? Must religion, perhaps, be located on *both* sides of this apparent alternative? Or rather *between* them, that is to say, as the modality of their relation, a relation that, as we have seen, is precisely a relation-without-relation, and in this regard fits Emmanuel Levinas's definition of *religion* in *Totality and Infinity*?

Angelus Silesius's text, Derrida is quick to point out, cannot simply be treated as "a treatise of philosophy or theology, not even as a sermon or a hymn" (SN 42 / 30). In what sense, then, can it be said to "anticipate" the Heideggerian discourse on death (and this, moreover, in a way that is marked by a "profound coherence" and a "rigorous continuity")? And, in what sense does the latter's discourse, in turn, belong to the tradition called theological?

One way of answering the first question would be to argue that the apophatic way of Angelus Silesius's *Cherubinic Wanderer* resembles Heidegger's analyses in its formal structure; in Heidegger's words, in its formal indication (*formale Anzeige*). Both ways of proceeding, the first practiced by the mystics and the second adopted by Heidegger, are marked by paradox, by aporia, by the desire for a similar preoccupation with an impossible retreat that increases in the measure that it approaches God and death, respectively or simultaneously. But there is thus a thematic resemblance here as well. Both authors direct their expositions toward absolute signifiers that remain tied to and contingent upon the very givens of a history, tradition, or culture that they are said to open up — inspire and orient — in the first place.

JUST AS THE CHRISTIANITY of which Heidegger speaks in his early writings and the messianicity of which Derrida speaks in *Specters of Marx* is made possible by what it makes possible, so being toward death remains tainted, overdetermined, and haunted by what Derrida would come to call the historical and religious "cultures of death." Like the messianisms that pervade and mark history, they also make possible what makes them possible. Yet the apparent circularity of this aporetics — of the conditioned conditioning its condition and vice versa — should be distinguished, not only from a merely formal (and logically formalizable) contradiction, but also from a hermeneutic circle whose vicious nature, Heidegger contends, is a matter of mere appearance alone. It has to be thought in a completely different register, one whose implications we are just beginning to fathom, even though they lead us back to the very origins of ontotheology, of religion, of the thought that makes religion possible, and that, in turn, is made possible by it.

Referring to the work of the self-described "historian of death" Philippe Ariès, notably his *L'Homme devant la mort* (*The Hour of Our Death*), Derrida observes that in discussing the many "arts of dying," Ariès in the end "insists upon the recurrence of ideas that *announce* the Enlightenment before the Enlightenment and that, no matter how 'anachronistic' or 'exceptional' they may seem, are nonetheless recurrent, 'verified and confirmed' by testimonies" (A 49 / 92). *But can something announce what announces it in turn?* Can this other logic, if it is one, ever be comprehended in terms of a logic of conversion, interiorization, and repression, as is suggested by Jan Patočka in his *Heretical Essays?* Moreover, does what Derrida develops in his interpretation of the relationship between the apophatics and fundamental ontology still fit the "logic of presupposition" that Heidegger deploys in *Being and Time?* Do the implications of the foregoing analysis not reach beyond the conceptual delimitations that govern the method of formal indication? And, finally, is not Derrida's insistence on the mutual conditioning of formal structures and their historical announcements or reverberations the most effective strategy to undermine, not only the multifarious reductionisms that go by the name of empiricism, psychologism, and historicism, but also the philosophical foundationalism of some, perhaps all, types of ontology and transcendental philosophy, whether existential analytic or not?

In order to answer these questions, let me retrace the relevant steps of Heidegger's existential analysis of death as developed in *Being and Time.* Heidegger sets out by defining Dasein's ipseity or selfhood (*Selbstheit, Selbständigkeit*) as a "way of existing" (*eine Weise zu existieren*), according to which it may choose, win, and lose itself (see BT 312 / 267). Derrida summarizes this as follows: "*Dasein* is not an entity that is here in front of me or that I can put my hands on, like a substantial object, as *Vorhandenes*. Instead, the essence of *Dasein* as entity is precisely the *possibility*, the being-possible (*das Möglichsein*)."[4]

Dasein, then, is a being, a being-there, that is in the first place (if

---

4. A 63 / 113–14. See also BT 67–68 / 42: "*The essence of Dasein lies in its existence.* Accordingly those characteristics which can be exhibited in this entity are not 'properties' present-at-hand of some entity which 'looks' so and so and is itself present-at-hand; they are in each case possible ways for it to be, and no more than that. . . . And because Dasein is in each case essentially its own possibility, it *can,* in its very Being, 'choose' itself and win itself; it can also lose itself and never win itself; or only 'seem' to do so."

not *zunächst* and *zumeist*) possible. Yet while Dasein is said to be able to choose, win, and lose itself (as a possibility and as possible), it can never lose itself beyond its own ultimate possibility, *toward* which and *as* which it *is*, from the earliest moment of its coming into the world (at its birth) and as long as it remains a "way to exist"—that is to say, as long as it is (its) there (*Da*). Death, however, as the very possibility of its impossibility, of the cessation of its being in the world, is regarded as Dasein's utmost possibility. Yet Derrida reminds us that if the ontological distinction between Dasein and *Vorhandensein* (or *Zuhandensein*) should in the end prove vulnerable—as is argued in the series of studies devoted to Heidegger's "hand" and "ear"[5]—then this discourse on the possible and on death as this possible's most proper possibility risks losing much of its philosophical rigor.

The fact that, according to Heidegger, death is "the most proper possibility" of the possibility that is Dasein explains why the interpretation of death may rightfully claim to be exemplary for the existential analysis of Dasein. For Heidegger, death, more precisely, *my* death, more exactly still, the being toward the *possibility* that is my own death, rather than my relation to the death or the mortality of the other in and outside me (and thus to mourning), constitutes the very event of singularization. It is in the being toward the end (and "as something of the character of Dasein," death is nothing but *my* existential relation to death, the *Sein zum Tode*, Heidegger asserts) that Dasein can be "whole," that is to say, a being-whole (*Ganzsein*) (BT 276–77 / 234).

How does Heidegger determine this singular being-whole, which leaves no room for any retreat into the manifold possibilities, but confronts Dasein with its own utmost possibility, with the possibility of its very impossibility, that is to say, with the possibility of Dasein's no longer being "there" or "in-the-world"? He does so by underscoring the irrefutable appeal (*Anspruch*) of death, which is addressed to or concerns *me* alone and cannot simply leave me indifferent.[6] It is the very certainty or

5. See Jacques Derrida, "La Main de Heidegger (*Geschlecht* II)," in *Psyché*, 415–51, trans. John P. Leavy, Jr., as "*Geschlecht* II: Heidegger's Hand," in *Deconstruction and Philosophy: The Texts of Jacques Derrida*, ed. John Salis (Chicago: University of Chicago Press, 1987), 161–96; Jacques Derrida, "L'Oreille de Heidegger," in *Politiques de l'amitié*, trans. as "Heidegger's Ear: Philopolemology (*Geschlecht* IV)," in *Reading Heidegger: Commemorations*, ed. John Salis (Bloomington: Indiana University Press, 1993), 163–218.

6. See BT 308 / 263: "Death does not just 'belong' to one's own Dasein in an undifferentiated way; death *lays claim* to it as an *individual* Dasein. The non-relational character of death, as understood in anticipation, individualizes Dasein down to itself. This individualizing is a

*Gewisssein* of *my* own death that lies at the bottom of the call of conscience (*Gewissen*), properly speaking. Both are without possible substitution. More precisely, the singularity of the possibility of my being toward death (toward *my* death) provides as it were the measure for the proper understanding of the call of conscience directed to me — and, it should be noted, *by* me — alone. In both cases, the relation of Dasein to its death and to its call is one that is reversible yet not substitutable. Here, Dasein can only substitute itself, call itself, and relate to its own death alone. Even if one dies for another ("für einen in den Tod gehen," is how Heidegger's puts it), one cannot remove death as the other's own utmost possibility, as the possibility that marks the cessation of each of this other's possibilities. Through the very structure of mineness, or *Jemeinigkeit*, I cannot substitute for the other's death. As Derrida formulates it: "I can give the other everything except immortality" (GD 43 / 47).

In *Being and Time*, this truism is the single most important key to an originary understanding of the concept of truth. For the certainty in question is circumscribed by Heidegger as a truth that is "heterogeneous to any other certainty (apodictic, theoretical, or empirical, that is to say, derived or induced — for example from the spectacle of the other's demise)" (A 67 / 120). Whenever and wherever Dasein chooses or circumvents, escapes and forgets the "self-evidence" of this truth — and in Heidegger's analysis of Dasein's everydayness and fallenness, this means almost everywhere and most of the time — this being that "we" are persists in an improper mode of existing that Heidegger identifies with "untruth" (*Unwahrheit*) (BT 264 / 222):

> No one can take the Other's dying away from him. Of course someone can "go to his death for another." But that always means to sacrifice [*sic*] oneself for the other "*in some definite affair.*" Such "dying for" can never signify that the Other has thus had his death taken away in even the slightest degree. Dying is something that every Dasein itself must take upon itself at the time. By its very essence, death is in every case mine, insofar as it "is" at all.[7]

---

way in which the 'there' is disclosed for existence. It makes manifest that all Being-alongside the things with which we concern ourselves, and all Being-with-Others, will fail us when our ownmost potentiality-for-Being [*das eigenste Seinkönnen*] is the issue."

7. See BT 284 / 240: "*No one can take the Other's dying away from him.* Of course someone can 'go to his death for another.' But that always means to sacrifice oneself for the Other '*in some definite affair*' ['*in einer bestimmten Sache*']. Such 'dying for' can never signify that the Other has thus had his death taken away in even the slightest degree. Dying is something that every Dasein must take upon itself at the time. By its very essence, death is in every case mine,

The other, then, cannot replace me in *my* death; nor can I ultimately substitute for the other in his or her death. It is, Derrida reminds us, only this irreplaceability that makes it possible for something like self-sacrifice (a *sich opfern* or a *don de soi*) to take place at all. *Being and Time* stresses a similar point, arguing that the ontological (analysis) plays the role of a necessary yet insufficient condition of possibility of the ontico-ontological possibility of what could be called (but Heidegger does not do so) the ethical and the political. This, then, is the way in which death, in its very ontological determination, is relevant to (or ought to bear on) the "concrete situation" of our daily actions (which does not go without saying, but is a serious question in its own right, for as Heidegger himself asks: "What can death and the 'concrete Situation' of taking action have in common?" [BT 349 / 302]):

> The ownmost, non-relational possibility is *not to be outstripped* [*unüberhol-bar*]. Being towards this possibility enables Dasein to understand that giving itself up impends for it as the uttermost possibility of its existence. Antici-pation, however, unlike inauthentic Being-towards-death, does not evade the fact that death is not to be outstripped; instead, anticipation frees itself *for* ac-cepting this ["*gibt sich frei für* sie"]. When, by anticipation, one becomes free *for* one's own death, one is liberated from one's lostness in those possibilities which may accidentally thrust themselves upon one; and one is liberated in such a way that for the first time one can authentically understand and choose among the factual possibilities lying ahead of that possibility which is not to be outstripped. Anticipation discloses to existence that its uttermost possi-bility lies in giving itself up [*die Selbstaufgabe*], and thus it shatters all one's tenaciousness to whatever existence one has reached. In anticipation, Dasein guards itself against falling back behind itself, or behind the potentiality-for-Being which it has understood. It guards itself against "becoming too old for its victories" (Nietzsche). Free for its ownmost possibilities, which are deter-mined by the *end* and so are understood as *finite,* Dasein dispels the danger that it may, by its own finite understanding of existence, fail to recognize that it is getting outstripped by the existence-possibilities of Others, or rather that it may explain these possibilities wrongly and force them back upon its own, so that it may divest itself of its ownmost factical existence. As the non-relational possibility, death individualizes — but only in such a manner that,

---

in so far as it 'is' at all. And indeed death signifies a peculiar possibility-of-Being in which the very Being of one's own Dasein is an issue."

as the possibility which is not be outstripped, it makes Dasein, as Being-with, have some understanding of the potentiality-for-Being of Others.[8]

Does this mean that death or the being toward death that is Dasein's utmost possibility is an *in-finite* or, if one can say so, *a-finite, trans-finite* and *pre-finite* possibility? Let us leave this question unanswered for the moment and simply note that the phenomenon of Dasein's being free for death (*Freiheit zum Tode*) is simultaneously a being open to permanent threat. This threat is not an external infringement upon Dasein's existential integrity. Heidegger insists that it belongs to the structure of being-there itself that has to be assumed.[9] The indeterminate experience of this permanent threat is *Angst*: Being toward death, Heidegger says, "is essentially anxiety" (BT 310 / 266). It is as if Dasein were its own best and most intimate friend, no less than its own most formidable enemy. But these notions, so the argument goes in *Politics of Friendship* and somewhat more elliptically in *The Gift of Death*, should not be used naively. Solely in this *Angst*, Heidegger writes, does Dasein find itself "before the nothing" of death—that is to say, before the possible impossibility of its existence ("*vor dem Nichts der möglichen Unmöglichkeit seiner Existenz*") (BT 310 / 266). The formulation should give one pause. For what, precisely, does it mean to equate the possible impossibility of Dasein's existence with a nothingness, a *Nichts?* What, moreover, does it imply to state that the *Angst* of being toward death brings Dasein literally *before* or *onto the threshold*—"*vor*"—of this nothing?[10] Heidegger modifies the relentless identification of Dasein's proper being-there with a being fun-

---

8. BT 308–9 / 264: "Frei für die eigensten, von *Ende* her bestimmten, das heisst als *endliche* verstandenen Möglichkeiten, bannt das Dasein die Gefahr, aus seinem endlichen Existenzverständnis her die es überholenden Existenzmöglichkeiten der Anderen zu verkennen oder aber sie missdeutend auf die eigene zurückzuzwingen — um sich so der eigensten faktischen Existenz zu begeben. Als unbezügliche Möglichkeit vereinzelt der Tod aber nur, um als unüberholbare das Dasein als Mitsein verstehend zu machen für das Seinkönnen der Anderen."

9. BT 310 / 265: "In anticipating [*Vorlaufen zum*] the indefinite certainty of death, Dasein opens itself to a constant *threat* [*Bedrohung*] arising out of its own 'there.' In this very threat Being-towards-the-end must maintain itself. So little can it tone this down that it must rather cultivate the indefiniteness [*Unbestimmtheit*] of the certainty."

10. "Was ist Metaphysik?" further formalizes this structure of the *Angst* of the *zum Tode* in terms of a transcendental and transcending for-nothing, a *zum Nichts*, as it were, which is said to ground and open up all relatedness to beings, whether one's being or (that of) other beings, whether to other beings in the original structure of *Mitsein*, or to beings that are not so much dead objects but ready at hand (*zuhanden*). Essential thought would no longer simply calculate (*rechnen*), but would define itself in light of the other-than-being (*aus dem Anderen des Seienden*), that is to say, the other than *Mitsein* and *Vorhandensein*.

damentally (if not *zunächst* and *zumeist*) possible when he writes that the anticipation (the *Vorlaufen*) of death *"reveals to Dasein its lostness in the they-self [Man-selbst]."* What is more, it thus brings Dasein *"before the possibility . . . to be itself."* [11] Neither *into* the possibility nor as the possibility itself, but before, on the threshold of, the possibility, the anticipation (the *Vorlaufen*) keeps a certain distance from the possible. The attestation of the possible impossibility of Dasein's existence is not itself already a possibility or the utmost possibility, the possibility of Dasein's impossibility. Neither possible nor impossible (lest we interpret the impossible as a mere privation of the possible), it fulfills a totally different function. The attestation of Dasein's most proper possibility consists in confronting Dasein with this possibility, bringing Dasein before it, rather than simply stating or communicating it. The structure of this relation to the possible is one of *infinitization,* in which the utmost possibility increasingly takes on the features of a *mere* possibility. According to a strange, paradoxical logic of distanciation through approximation, or vice versa, the possible retreats into an immeasurable remoteness. And it is only thus that it obtains the quality of *a pure and thereby purifying possible.* The analytical and formally indicative process of abstraction goes hand in hand with a peculiar and uncanny intensity whose *cathartic* function seems to be Heidegger's chief concern — something never explicitly stated as such.

Here, more than elsewhere, Heidegger's analysis oversteps the limits that the phenomenological method has set itself. For it is difficult to understand how the articulation and understanding of this possibility could still claim to have some minimal phenomenological concreteness. For the given (or the gift) of the relation to death is hardly a relation to what is concretely or phenomenologically given. It has all the appearance, then, that the descriptions of the *Sein zum Tode* recede at this crucial point from the very ground, or *Boden* (BT 311 / 267) that Heidegger promises to give to it, or that he at some point acknowledges to have to be able to provide so as to free his analysis of its most unwarranted pretensions. As such, the analysis of Dasein's utmost possibility, of its possible impossibility, would have to refrain from prescribing whatever ontic "ideal" could come to concretize the formal threads of this structure. The fundamental ontological description of Dasein does not permit one to "depict" a "concrete" ideal of existence (*ein 'inhaltliches' Existenzideal*) or to impose that on Dasein "from without" (BT 311 / 267). And yet, Heidegger

---

11. BT 311 / 266.

immediately adds, the purely existential being toward death remains "a fantastical exaction" ("Und trotzdem bleibt doch dieses existenzial 'mögliche' Sein zum Tode existentiell eine phantastische Zumutung") (BT 311 / 267). It remains insignificant until it has been shown that there is in fact a corresponding ontic possibility, or, what comes down to the same, that there is at least the testimony (*Bezeugung*) of the appeal (*Forderung*) to exist accordingly. Thus, it should be asked, first of all,

> whether to *any* extent and in any way Dasein *gives testimony* [*Zeugnis gibt*], from its ownmost potentiality-for-Being, as to a possible *authenticity* of its existence, so that it not only makes known that in an existential manner such an authenticity is possible, but *demands* this of itself.
>
> . . . If we succeed in uncovering that attestation phenomenologically, together with what it attests, then the problem will arise anew as to *whether the anticipation of* [zum] *death, which we have hitherto projected only in its **ontological** possibility, has an essential connection with that authentic potentiality-for-Being which has been **attested**.* (BT 311 / 267)

These last words are quite central to Heidegger's concern: testimony in its most proper sense should somehow be shown to correlate to a primary structure of relatedness, not that of a mourning for the other's death or that of the gesture of saying "Dear Lord" in prayer (i.e., praying "*mon dieu*") but, first of all, of the certainty of the singularizing indeterminacy of my individual death alone.

But should it not be inferred from this that *every* or *each single* instance of my Dasein's *zu sein*—and not just my relation to my very own death—is always already the most proper possibility of my Dasein, a call for decision, an occasion for testimony (see BT 307 / 263)? Should we not conclude that if all *zu sein* is in its very *transitivity* marked by an irreducible mineness and thrownness,[12] there is nowhere and never—in nothing that affects or concerns me—substitutability (*Vertretbarkeit*) in any strict sense of the word? Even in Heidegger's own terms, it would seem, death is not the only future we cannot escape. How then, could Dasein ever hope to delegate all the other possibilities—again, except the possibility of its impossibility, of its being toward its own death—in which it has been thrown or toward which it projects itself? How, finally, could there be an unproblematic line of demarcation between the in principle

---

12. BT 68 / 42: "Das Sein," Heidegger writes, "*darum* es diesem Seienden in seinem Sein geht, ist je meines. . . . Es hat sich immer schon irgendwie entschieden, in welcher Weise Dasein je meines ist."

infinite series of *relative possibilities* (see BT 305 / 261) and that apparently absolute — albeit absolutely finite — possibility called death?

Derrida raises this very same issue in somewhat different terms when he remarks in *Aporias* that if death

> names the very irreplaceability of absolute singularity (no one can die in my place or in the place of the other), then all the examples can precisely illustrate this singularity. Everyone's death, the death of all who can say "my death," is irreplaceable. So is "my life." Every other is completely other. ["Tout autre est tout autre"]. Whence comes a first exemplary complication of exemplarity: nothing is more substitutable and yet nothing is less so than the syntagm "my death." It is always a matter of a hapax, of a hapax legomenon, but of what is only said one time each time, indefinitely only one time. (A 22 / 49)

In this singular structure, in this structure of singularity, one can find grounds for the formal analogy — if that is the right word — between the relation to my finitude or "my death" and the relation to infinity as evoked by praying *mon dieu.* There is a structural similarity between my being toward death and my being toward God. We are dealing here with two relations — relating without relation — which seem to collapse into each other in the figureless figure of the *à dieu,* which is at once an *adieu* and an *a-dieu.*

In sum, if the being toward death and the *à dieu* and their intricate relations are exemplary for virtually *all* others — and this up to the point where Derrida's dictum "Tout autre est tout autre" becomes almost inevitable — then this can only be because death, as Heidegger conceives of it, is hardly the only "possibility" we cannot avoid. True, my being toward my death seems the only possibility in which my being in the world as such is at stake, since we are confronted here with an impossibility of existence without further remainder.

But again, if all possibilities thus turn out to be a relation (without relation) to the *tout autre,* how then can we justify the suggestion that the relation to death or, for that matter, to God is a privileged one and one, moreover, that has a certain regulative, paradigmatic, or revelatory status with respect to all others, as both Heidegger and Derrida (and also Levinas) would seem to suggest?[13]

13. For one example, see BT 289–90 / 245.

## The Impossibility of Possibility

And how can we think of death starting from *adieu* rather than the inverse?

—JACQUES DERRIDA, *The Gift of Death*

As Levinas reminds us in *Dieu, la mort et le temps* (God, Death, and Time), being toward the end is fundamentally a relation toward the *not-yet* (*Noch-nicht, pas encore*), which signifies "always another step yet to take"—the meaning of the word *pas* being both "not" and "step"—and one that is *stretched out* to an imminence or menace that cannot be waited or hoped for, and to which only a vigil or vigilance can be truly responsive.[14] As should be clear by now, one of Levinas's most telling titles, "De la conscience à la veille" ("From Consciousness to Wakefulness"), could serve as a summary of Heidegger's "lifelong topic," which was to raise (to repeat and retrieve) the so-called question of Being.[15] By now we have sufficient reason to claim that Heidegger's writing can be viewed neither as a further elaboration of the work of intentional analysis in the domain of religion, the historical, and the existential, say, nor as a phenomenology that remains premised on the idea of philosophy as a "rigorous science" (a model, by the way, that Levinas himself had already begun to question in the concluding pages of his dissertation, *La Théorie de l'intuition dans la phénoménologie de Husserl* (*The Theory of Intuition in Husserl's Phenomenology*), in part with reference to Heidegger). Rather it might be seen as a singular testimony (or *Bezeugung*) that *cuts across* the disciplinary demarcations of the ontological and the empirical, the phenomenological and the religious, the philosophical and the theological, which form the very *doxa* (or, for matter, pragmatic arrangement) of modern life, but rest upon unquestioned presuppositions and hardly do justice to the phenomena themselves.

According to Heidegger, Levinas comments in *Death and Time*, the fact that Dasein has to be, that it is the sole being that in its being is concerned with being, means ipso facto that it also has to die or even that it is *already* dying, in the precise sense Heidegger gives to this word (*Sterben*). Death is not some distant future event that will take even-

---

14. Emmanuel Levinas, *Dieu, la mort et le temps*, ed. Jacques Rolland (Paris: Grasset, 1993), 15–134.

15. Emmanuel Levinas, "De la conscience à la veille: A partir de Husserl," in *De dieu qui vient à l'idée*, 34–61.

tually place at some time. On the contrary, the original and originary modality of temporality is a having to be, that is to say, a having to die.[16] The self-appropriation of Dasein (and Heidegger presupposes without any further justification, as if he were relying here on the silent axiom, indeed, the *veritas transcendentalis,* of all ontological inquiry, that this self-appropriation is Dasein's sole, major, or ownmost concern) manifests itself as a "being before death," as a "being toward death" (in Levinas's words, an *être-pour-la-mort* or *être-à-la-mort*). It is this very "before" and "toward," Levinas goes on to explain, that entails a surprising—indeed maddening—modality: "being to the point of death (in the sense in which one can love to the point of madness, which means to love in a way that implies a going almost out of one's mind" ("*être-à-la-mort* [au sens où l'on aime à la folie, ce qui signifie aimer d'une manière qui implique d'aller jusqu'à la dé-raison"]).[17]

Levinas stresses the *transitivity* marked by this *à* (or *jusqu'à*). This transitivity is at once close to Heidegger's major insight in a verbal and, in that sense, nonsubstantive and undemonstrable meaning (for Heidegger of Being in its difference from beings) *and* at an infinite remove from this (in Levinas's view) particular meaning's neutralizing "sonority."[18] A little later, Levinas alludes to the fact that the relation toward death lies primarily in its certitude (or *Gewissheit,* as Heidegger would have it), and not in confronting the possibility of annihilation (*anéantissement*); the very impossibility of experiencing death—the "truism" on which Heidegger's whole analysis is built—signals itself first of all in "an affection more passive than traumatism" and, Levinas continues, "a passivity beyond shock."[19] And these modalities are first and foremost those of our relation to others, more precisely, to the mortality and death of others.

Since this possibility of Dasein's being toward its end cannot be delegated or taken away, we are dealing here with a singular relationship:

16. Levinas, *Dieu, la mort et le temps,* 52: "Avoir à être, c'est avoir à mourir. La mort n'est pas quelque part dans le temps, mais le temps est originairement *zu sein,* c'est-à-dire *zu sterben.*" On the sequence, *à-être, à-mourir, à-venir,* and *à-Dieu,* see ibid., 66, 132.

17. Ibid., 54. Toward the end of his course, Levinas speaks of a "folie pure," "absurdité," or "pur rapt" (ibid., 134) that caracterize my being toward death far more accurately than the Heideggerian formula of the possibility of the impossibility. An example of the passivity and thereby relation to the Infinite, Levinas concludes, would be the intercession of Abraham for the inhabitants of Sodom while acknowledging that he himself is "but dust and ashes" (Gen. 18:27).

18. Levinas, *Dieu, la mort et le temps,* 33.

19. Ibid., 18–19.

"The relation toward death as a possibility is an exceptional *toward,* an exceptional *before,* one that is privileged."[20] This implies at least two things. First, that death is not "the ending of a duration composed of days and nights, but a *possibility* that is always open."[21] Second, that death is "the most proper possibility, *exclusive of the other,* isolating" and making one stand alone, all by oneself (*esseulante*).[22] The *à* is *prior* to all other *à*'s or *zu*'s or *unto*'s and *toward*'s (such as that of the "being before oneself" [*être-au-devant-de-soi*] or *Ek-sistenz;* the "being already in the world" [*d'ores-et-déjà-au-monde*] or, what comes down to the same, the *Faktizität;* and the "close to or together with things" [*auprès-des-choses*] of *Verfallenheit*). The *à* of the *à-mort* "is," if one can still say so, *prior* and in this respect a priori, not in the sense of a given or elementary structure of transcendental consciousness, but as a condition or rather in-condition of Dasein's being-thrown into the world, or, as the earlier work would have it, into "life." Death, the toward- or unto- or before-death, properly understood, Heidegger writes, is "a way to be, which Dasein takes over as soon as it is. 'As soon as a man comes to life, he is at once old enough to die' ['Sobald ein Mensch zum Leben kommt, sogleich ist er alt genug zu sterben']" (BT 289 / 245).[23]

Now the Levinasian figure of the *à dieu* (or *adieu*), and this my central thesis, could be said to substitute for the—in Heidegger's view unsubstitutable—relation toward death.[24] The invocation of the figure of the *à*

20. "La relation à la mort comme possibilité est un *à* exceptionnel, un *pour* exceptionnel, privilégié" (ibid., 56).

21. "[L]a finition d'une durée faite de jours et de nuits, mais une *possibilité* toujours ouverte" (ibid., 58).

22. Ibid., 62.

23. Heidegger is quoting *Der Ackermann aus Böhmen* by Johannes von Tepl (1350?–1414?), vol. 3, pt. 2 of *Vom Mittelater zur Reformation: Forschungen zur Geschichte der deutschen Bildung,* ed. K. Burdach (Berlin: Weidmann, 1917), p. 46. For an English version, see *Death and the Plowman; or, The Bohemian Plowman: A Disputatious and Consolatory Dialogue About Death from the Year 1400,* trans. Ernest N. Kirrmann (Chapel Hill: University of North Carolina Press, 1958).

24. For a similar suggestion, see Derrida, *Adieu à Emmanuel Levinas,* 150. Derrida also recalls that the formulation "the possibility of the impossible" figures prominently in the central chapter of Levinas's *Autrement qu'être ou au-delà de l'essence* (*Otherwise than Being or Beyond Essence*), entitled "La Substitution" ("Substitution"). Here, Levinas speaks of a "passivité qui n'est pas seulement la possibilité de la mort dans l'être, la possibilité de l'impossibilité; mais impossibilité antérieure à cette possibilité, impossibilité de se dérober" (quoted from Derrida, *Adieu à Emmanuel Levinas,* 150). Derrida comments by stating that this passivity is therefore "[n]otre responsabilité, en somme, avant la mort, devant la mort, devant les morts, au-delà de la mort" (ibid.). On the relationship between Heidegger and Levinas, see also Françoise Dastur,

*dieu* underscores the indeterminate, paradoxical, or, rather, aporetic features of the *distant nearness* of death. What is more, it reinscribes this structure into a highly overdetermined horizon of interpretation, whose ethico-political remainders Heidegger chooses to ignore or efface. Thus, the relation toward death is substituted for by the relation to the infinite, by a relation, that is, that absolves itself from every ontico-ontological relation and therefore takes the form (without form) of an infinitization (or "*infinition,*" to quote Levinas). This strategy of substitution, I would claim, is not absent from Derrida's debate with Heidegger either. With reference to the "indeterminacy of death," Derrida writes:

> Fundamentally, one knows perhaps neither the meaning nor the referent of this word. It is well known that if there is one word that remains absolutely unassignable or unassigning with respect to its concept and to its thingness, it is the word "death." Less than for any noun, *save God* [ *fors celui de Dieu* ] — and for good reason, since their association here is probably not fortuitous — is it possible to attribute to the noun "death," and above all to the expression "my death," a concept or a reality that would constitute the object of an indisputably determining experience. (A 22 / 49; emphasis added)

*God,* like *death,* would thus stand for an aporetic and *substitutable notion of the unsubstitutable.* It is the experience and the trial of this impossible possibility (or possible impossibility) that constitutes the enigma and drama of finitude, that is to say, of the infinite substitution, of the substitution of the infinite, of the *infinite as substitution.* Now, could this "possibility" still be articulated by the thought of finite Being or, conversely, by the thought of the infinite Other for which the names of Heidegger and Levinas stand here? Is this not precisely what both seem to exclude: the epitome of "in-difference" (to *God* and *death*) but of a being in difference that hardly leaves us indifferent and makes all the difference in the world? An in-difference, finally, from which all violence, whether empirical, conceptual, or transcendental, springs?

Jean-Luc Nancy suggests in *Des lieux divins* ("Of Divine Places") that it is in the figure of a certain *à dieu* that we might be tempted to "force together," if only for a moment, the names and the works of Levinas and

---

*La Mort: Essai sur la finitude* (Paris: Hatier, 1994), 43 ff. In the introduction to this book, Dastur insists on the inseparable link between the concept of death and that of the divine. More than any apophatic theology, she notes (ibid., 6), meditation on death is the foil against which the gods (immortality, infinity) can appear or be thought at all.

Heidegger. This is not to deny that there are important differences between their respective descriptions of the structure for which this figure
stands. Nor should the suggestion of a certain intersection of the writings
of these authors on the subject of the *à dieu* make us forget that each of
them privileges a different element of this figure so as to evoke its philosophical and existential or ethical relevance.

Nancy summarizes this difference in the following manner: "[T]he
*à-Dieu* of Levinas is constitutive of 'the passivity more passive than passivity' in which immanence is breached; Heidegger's *being-unto-God* (or
unto-the-god) is merely a possible [*ein mögliches Sein zu Gott*]: opened
up, offered (but equally withheld, withdrawn) in the finite transcendence
of being-unto-death." [25] In other words, while for Levinas the revelation
and the testimony of the "toward God" marks the instance at which Being
and the *conatus essendi* are inverted and point beyond themselves—that
is to say, to the "otherwise than being"—for Heidegger it is the very manifestation of Being's ownmost openness, marked by the vigil over death,
and a structure analogous to the revealability (*Offenbarkeit*) of Being that
is distinguished from any concrete revelation (*Offenbarung*) whose *possibility* it is.

And yet at least a formal resemblance dictates the relation between the
philosophical options for which these proper names—Levinas and Heidegger—stand. Both the Levinasian "one for the other" (*l'un pour l'autre*)
and the Heideggerian being toward death (*Sein zum Tode*) stand under
the sign of the *à-dieu* and secretly communicate with each other, if, indeed, the *donner la mort,* the giving of death, as Derrida suggests, marks
our relation to the other. If the formal structure of sacrifice determines
the interhuman relation to *autrui* no less than my relating to my ownmost
death, then this relation echoes the internal division and divisiveness or
even *polemos* of the *à dieu* in all the ambiguity of this phrase (*adieu, a-
dieu*). Neither Levinas nor Heidegger portrays these relations in terms of
a peace (*paix*) or an accord and harmony (*das Innige*) alone.

In his polemics with Heidegger, Levinas insists that the mystery (*mys-
tère*) of death, as the relation to the unknown, to the absolute otherness, of
its "eternal to-come [*éternel à venir*] [26]—the future also that "gives death
[l'avenir que *donne la mort*]" [27]—does not constitute the subject's temporality at its most fundamental level (as is claimed by *Being and Time*).

25. Nancy, "Of Divine Places," 121/14.
26. Levinas, *Le Temps et l'autre*, 59: "éternel à venir."
27. Ibid., 68; emphasis added.

Strictly speaking, my being toward my own death does not truly capture time at all. Time, Levinas asserts, comes from, or is given by, the other, by another other, other others, the virtual totality of all others, that is to say, by *autrui, le tiers, tous les tiers*. And if the relation to other(s) can thus be said to form the terminus ad quem as well as the terminus a quo of temporality,[28] then it must also be added that in this relation no terminus — no termination, no end-term, no determination, resolution or resoluteness — can ever be found. For Levinas, the other is *at least as* interminably indeterminate as death, in Heidegger's sense. Nonetheless, it can be noted that different passages in Levinas's work give evidence to Nancy's observation that, in the figure of the *à dieu*, a parallel with Heidegger *Sein zum Tode* can be found. The *à dieu* could not only be said to substitute for the "to be" (the *à-être* or *Zu-sein*, the *être à être*, and thereby the Dasein "qui a à être*," since, as Levinas formulates the being-there, the *être-là* is "the manner in which the to-be articulates itself").[29] The *à dieu* also takes the place of the "unto death," of the *à mort* (the *zum Tode*), while transforming — reorienting — the "egological" structure of mineness (*Jemeinigkeit*)[30] of both of these notions into a mode of gesturing toward the other.

In both cases, the *à dieu* displaces Heidegger's definition of the essence (*Wesen*) of the Dasein, which in *Being and Time* is formulated in terms of the possible modes of (its very ownmost) being. It is beyond these possibilities — and, perhaps, beyond the category and the modality of the "possible" as such, beyond the "possible" insofar as it is a modality — that this Levinasian figure situates itself. In so doing, it also mobilizes a Kantian motif against the basic tenets of Heidegger's thought, although Kant, too, pays tribute to a possibilism whose presuppositions or implications are at odds with the thought and the experience, if one can say so, of the *à dieu*. Be that as it may, there is no doubt that for Levinas, Kant's philosophy, notably his *Kritik der praktischen Vernunft* (*Critique of Practical Reason*), plays the role of an important counterexample. Among a few other instances throughout the history of Western philosophy (motifs of transcendence in Plato, Plotinus, Augustine, Descartes, Pascal, and Bergson), Kant's insistence on "hope," on the postulate of the immortality of the soul (albeit in a radically different sense than that of a prolonged duration in time) shows that the "reduction" of meaning to the finitude

28. Ibid., 69: "La situation de face-à-face serait *l'accomplissement du temps*" and "La *condition du temps* est dans le rapport entre humains"; emphases added.
29. Levinas, *Dieu, la mort et le temps*, 65.
30. Emmanuel Levinas, *Entre nous: Essais sur le penser-à-l'autre* (Paris: Grasset, 1991), 179.

of Being need not be the last word; rather, Kant would seem to testify to a "temporality *other* than that of being-toward-death."[31] Challenging Heidegger's interpretation, Levinas asserts:

> The question "*What can I know?*" leads to finitude, but "*What should I do?*" and "*What can I rightfully hope for?*" go much further and in any case in a different direction than in that of finitude. These questions do not reduce themselves to the comprehension of being, but concern the duty and the redemption [*le salut*] of man.
>
> In the second question, if one understands it formally [*formellement*], there is no reference to being. That meaning [*le sens*] can signify without reference to being, without recourse to being, without comprehension of being given [*étre donné*], that is by the way the great contribution [*apport*] of the Transcendental Dialectic of the *Critique of Pure Reason*.[32]

Levinas explains this as follows: for Kant, being is thought of as that which is constituted as a phenomenon by the synthetic activity of the categories of understanding (as well as, of course, by the a priori forms — time and space — of inner and outer perception). Yet the appeal to the whole (or the totality) of the given, which, on Kant's account, is equally constitutive of the task and the progress of all empirical knowledge, is given only as a transcendental ideal, which, Levinas adds, "never receives the *predicate* of existence" and is never given as such: "The transcendental ideal is thought by Kant *in concreto,* but Kant refuses it being, guided as he is by the prototype of being that is the phenomenon. In that sense, Reason has ideas that go beyond being."[33]

The *Critique of Practical Reason* further amplifies this paradoxical limitation of the finitude of being. In Levinas's words: "There is a mode of practical signification that remains, next to [*à côté de*] the theoretical access to being, an access to a meaning that is irrecusable, access to a signification where the after-death [*l'après-mort*] cannot be thought as an extension of time from before death until after death, but where the after-death has its own motivations."[34]

31. Levinas, *Dieu, la mort et le temps,* 73 and 76 respectively. A classic formulation of the importance of this Kantian motif can be found in Levinas's *Autrement qu'être ou au-delà de l'essence,* 166.

32. Levinas, *Dieu, la mort et le temps.* Cf. Heidegger's *Kant und das Problem der Metaphysik* (Bonn: F. Cohen, 1929), trans. Richard Taft as *Kant and the Problem of Metaphysics* (5th ed., Bloomington: Indiana University Press, 1997).

33. Levinas, *Dieu, la mort et le temps,* 71.

34. Ibid., 72.

It is this proper motivation that for Kant is hope. This hope finds neither a theoretical nor an ontological warrant but "comes to pass in time and, in time, goes beyond time."[35] There is a sense here, Levinas notes, of a restlessness (*inquiétude*)[36] that is from now on no longer conceivable as a modality of being, as a "projecting itself in the possible," or, for that matter, a "projecting itself toward the possible."[37] And it is precisely by questioning this central presupposition that everything takes (its) place in Being, in the dimension or horizon of Being, as its modality or as mode of its gesture, its truth, and *Ereignis*, that one begins to "contest the first pages of *Sein und Zeit*."[38] For Levinas, there is a far more fundamental and responsible question (*une question plus questionnante*),[39] which consists in addressing the "things" (*choses*) that produce themselves when being face-to-face with our being—the very persistence in our being—is no longer that which counts: the death of others.[40]

MUTATIS MUTANDIS, all of the above can be said of the rearticulation Derrida offers of the *à dieu* and the possible in *The Gift of Death* and, indirectly, in *Aporias*. Even the Levinasian invocation of Kant finds its parallel in Derrida, most notably in "Passions," but also in "On a Newly Arisen Apocalytic Tone in Philosophy," which contains a reelaboration of the concept of eschatology and wakefulness with oblique reference to Heidegger.

## The Death of the Other

Unlike Derrida, Levinas never convincingly responds to Heidegger by exploring in any detail the possibilities of the latter's understanding of my being toward death (toward the death that is my innermost possibility) as a possible condition of possibility for my being open or even hospitable toward the possibilities of others (that is to say, toward their existence as well as their death, or, rather, their being toward their death). Nor does Levinas ever consider the complex relation between Heidegger's analysis of death and our understanding of the others who are already dead or no longer simply dead, since—while dead or as dead—they continue to be haunting and/or mourned. Granted, this is a topic addressed only elliptically in *Being and Time*, in isolated allusions to "signs of mourning" (*Trauerzeichen*) and "being with the dead" (*Mitsein mit dem Toten*)

35. Ibid.
37. Ibid., 68.
39. Ibid.
36. Ibid., 70.
38. Ibid., 69.
40. Ibid.

(BT 108/77 and 282/238, respectively). For Levinas, it is above all (and, indeed, exclusively) in the immediacy of the *face to face* with the other human being (*autrui*) here and now, that this other is seen as vulnerable, denuded, and ultimately exposed to death. The face of the other is, in a sense, nothing but the sign of his or her mortality—the "visage" is to be thought, Levinas writes, "comme la *mortalité* même de l'autre homme"[41]—our relationship to which is

> at once [*à la fois*] the relation to the absolutely feeble . . . to the one who is alone and may suffer the supreme solitude [*esseulement*] of what is called death; consequently, there is in the Face of the Other always the death of the Other and thereby, in a way, a provocation to murder [*incitation au meurtre*], the temptation to go all the way to the extreme [*jusqu'à bout*], of completely neglecting the other—and at the same time [*en même temps*], and that is the paradox, the Face is also the "Thou shalt not kill" . . . it is the fact [*le fait*] that I cannot let the other die alone.[42]

I discuss this doubling aspect of the relation to the other at more length in a different context and against the background of the *horror religiosus,* to which both Levinas and Derrida, in response to Kierkegaard's *Fear and Trembling,* pay minute attention in seemingly diverging ways.[43] For now, it will suffice simply to note that, for Levinas, it is the responsibility for the *other's*—actual or potential, visible or invisible—death that alone is capable of singularizing the self. Hence, it is solely in the *unsubstitutability of the other's death* that I, in being uniquely responsible, am somehow involved or even included: "I am responsible for the other in the sense that he is mortal. The death of the other is the primary death."[44]

By contrast, Heidegger could be said to ignore an important possibility that is hardly ontic or *existenziell.* His analysis revolves around the possibility of a death that can neither be experienced *as such* in others,[45] nor, for that matter, be given to me directly. I can witness neither my own demise (*Ableben*) nor my own dying (*Sterben*); they cannot become part of an *Erlebnis, hic et nunc.* But could one not maintain that Dasein is

41. Levinas, *Entre nous,* 186.
42. Ibid., 122; my trans.
43. See my "Violence and Testimony," in *Violence, Identity, and Self-Determination,* ed. de Vries and Weber, and *Horror Religiosus* (forthcoming).
44. Levinas, *Dieu, la mort et le temps,* 54.
45. BT 282–83/238–39.

marked first and above all by a being toward the possible rather than the actual death of the other? Would not the relation to the possible rather than the actual end or death of my own Dasein be more fundamental, ontologically speaking, than my being toward the possible impossibility of the other and of (all) others? Should we not insist, then, that the relation to the possible death of the other and of (all) others responds to a different modality of the possible than the one tirelessly varied by Heidegger? If this is the case, the expression *mortalité de l'autre* does not only elude the definition of the possible in terms of a logical, abstract, theoretical or statistical possibility, but also any possible in the ontico-ontological interpretation of the possible that Heidegger puts (or keeps) in place. And *mortalité de l'autre* means vulnerability, fragility, the unmistakable trait of aging, fatigue, in short, phenomena that challenge the delimitation and description of the understanding of the phenomenon, that is to say, all phenomenology.

It is, perhaps, in analyzing these experiences (experiences that also challenge the most common determination of the concept of experience) that Levinas comes close to one of Derrida's central insights: namely, that the structure of mourning (*deuil*) for the other is "more originary" than,[46] and constitutive of, my being toward my own death, indeed, of my very being-there in the first place. Derrida describes this in terms reminiscent of Levinas, but scarcely of Heidegger: "Even before the death of the other, the inscription in me of his [or her, or its?] mortality constitutes me. I am filled with mourning, therefore I am."[47] Is this another way of saying that one must (or ought to) think death on the basis of the *adieu* rather than the other way around, as Levinas seems to claim? Or would the primacy of mourning and its *à dieu / adieu / a-dieu* have to be thought along lines that would make this alternative, if not obsolete, than at least secondary?

Levinas's objection to the premises of Heidegger's existential analytic, for all its paradoxicality, is genuinely phenomenological. What is con-

46. Jacques Derrida, *Points de suspension: Entretiens* (Paris: Galilée, 1992), trans. Peggy Kamuf et al. as *Points . . . : Interviews, 1974–1994* (Stanford: Stanford University Press, 1995), 322 / 332.

47. Ibid., 331: "Avant même la mort de l'autre, l'inscription en moi de sa mortalité me constitue. Je suis endeuillé donc je suis." In the passage in which Heideggger seems to evoke an inscription of the other in the self (in the *Selbstsein* as much as in the *Man-Selbst* of Dasein), speaking of the "voice of the friend that every Dasein carries with itself" (BT 206 / 163), he does not think it necessary to specify whether this friend is alive or dead, mourned, and still haunting (see Jacques Derrida, *Politiques de l'amitié* [Paris: Galilée, 1994], trans. by George Collus as *Politics of Friendship* [London: Verso, 1997], 000 / 345; and cf. also 000 n. 0 / 362 n. 1).

demned is the reduction of the other *à,* that of the *zum Tode des Anderen,*
to an innerworldly occurrence. What is proposed is a radical reversal of
this reduction: it is not the other's death that comes second but rather *my*
death that is, phenomenologically speaking, secondary—that is to say,
the affair of others and not my primary concern. Quite literally, it cannot
concern me, touch me, overcome me, be experienced by me, let alone be
encountered face to face. Yet not being concerned with one's own death is
a "positive" phenomenon and, other than Heidegger chooses to believe,
the very event of my singularization.

Even when I do not desert the other, *my* relation to *his or her* death
(rather than the relation, my relation, to death *in general* or, for that matter, to *my death*) is "already guilty" (*déjà une culpabilité*),[48] if only because
*I survive.* This relation, Levinas suggests, must obtain even before the
question of any guilt or innocence in a moral or moralistic sense can arise.
What is more, this relation is absolutely independent of that other truism that springs from Heidegger's determination of original guilt, which
is nothing but the undeniable fact that for Dasein certain possibilities
will always already have been "lost," "missed," or simply have come and
gone without being realized or actualized. To be hostage, on the contrary,
means, not that *one* in general, but that *I* alone have to respond to the
possibility of the other's death *before* and *beyond* being concerned with
that utmost possibility of impossibility that, in Heidegger's analysis, is my
own death.[49]

Levinas's articulation of the *à dieu* both substitutes it for the *zum Tode*
and retains the phenomenological structure of *Jemeinigkeit* by taking it,
not as the formal indication of my concern with the being-there that I
am, but as the concrete description of the very asymmetry of my responsibility for the other, regardless of the concern that the other may—or
may not—have for me. By contrast the "finitude of time" that *Being and
Time* situates in being toward death remains "imprisoned in the immanence of *Jemeinigkeit*,"[50] or, in other words, in a structure of *Jemeinigkeit*
interpreted as immanence. In spite of his explicit intentions, Heidegger
thus remains a captive of the "philosophy of presence." Responsibility or,
rather, fear (*crainte*) for the other, Levinas asserts, does not enter into
the Heideggerian phenomenology of *Befindlichkeit.* Such responsibility

48. Levinas, *Dieu, la mort et le temps,* 15.
49. Ibid.
50. Levinas, *Entre nous,* 193.

consists precisely in being able to hear and understand (*entendre*) "the meaning of a *future* beyond that which happens to me," and thus beyond my end.[51] In his phenomenology of death, Heidegger does not push his analysis of the relation of the modes of ending to its very extreme (*jusqu'au bout*). And here, Levinas concedes, one encounters the limits of phenomenology, not only of the "noetico-noematic correlation," but also of any understanding of a relation whose terms do not absolve themselves of the relation-without-relation into which they enter. The terms in question do not belong to the same spatio-temporal realm. Their relation is one of diachrony and nonsimultaneity.

The *à dieu* is characterized by another temporality than that of my being toward or for death. It is marked by another time, the time of the other, the in-finity calling the self *in* its very finitude and from beyond its own utmost possibility, that is to say, from beyond its own impossibility—from beyond and *beyond* its own death. This occurs not in view of a life or resurrection after this death, but in response to a call that originates neither in a Dasein that is called back to its proper being nor in a Dasein's being faced with the possibility of its own end. Rather, we are dealing here with an "obligation" from which death (my death and the death of the other) does not absolve us; an "imperative" signification that comes from a future independent of and beyond my own death: "Significance of an authority that signifies *after and in spite of my death* [*après et malgré ma mort*]: signifying to the finite Me [*Moi fini*], to the Me vowed to death [*voué à la mort*], an order that is judged to be significant beyond that death. . . . The original meaning of the future!"[52]

Levinas goes so far as to suggest that we are dealing here with a "rupture of the natural order of being" that might well be called supernatural (*sur-naturel*). This and nothing else would be the "word of God or, more exactly, the coming itself of God to the idea and his insertion in a vocabulary."[53] Instead of a proof of God's existence, this coming to mind of God (or, as Levinas has it, the *tombée de Dieu sous le sens*) would reveal the singular structure and purity—*pur futur*—of temporality itself. As St. Augustine already knew, time as such may be seen as the relation (in Levinas's view, the relation-without-relation) to God, and thereby as the very *à Dieu* of theology: "le temps comme l'à-Dieu de la théologie!"[54]

In Levinas's reading, then, the "adventure" or "intrigue" of the *à dieu*

51. Ibid.                                    52. Ibid., 192.
53. Ibid.                                    54. Ibid., 193.

can "neither be constituted nor better said starting from any category or
'existential.' All the figures and words that try to express it—such as *transcendence* or *beyond*—are already derived from it." And, in the same vein,
Levinas continues: "The *to-God* is neither the thematization of theologies,
nor a finality, which goes to a term . . . nor the eschatology preoccupied
with ultimate ends or with promises rather than with obligations with regards to humans"; "the presuppositions themselves, including the *to* and
the *pro* are already only metaphors of time, and could not serve in its constitution."[55]

The vigilance of the *à dieu*, of the being before and being toward God
(as well as the being before and toward the other, or the other side, of
God) is described by Levinas as an *éveil dans l'éveil*.[56] For if vigilance truly
marks a rupture with the formal structure of intentionality, it no longer
retains the features of a *vigilance à;* the "*éveil* as such [*comme tel*] becomes
a state of affairs [*un état*]—what is needed therefore is *un éveil de cet éveil*.
There is an iteration of the *éveil*. . . . An *éveil* where the unknown, where
the non-sense of death, is the obstruction of every installation in some
sort of virtue of patience."[57]

Levinas describes this condition by accentuating that the impossibility of having oneself replaced in one's responsibility—that is, of one
taking the place of, or substituting for, the other—is a passivity, indeed,
a "patience that must [and ought] to risk itself in the eventuality of non-
sense and even face to face with the discovery of the arbitrary"; for if
its meaning were that of an "inevitable obligation," if there were not the
danger and the threat of "madness," it would become "self-sufficient," an
"institution" with a "statute" and an "enterprise."[58] This necessary possibility of nonsense, then, is not only guaranteed by a deference with respect
to death (*déférence à la mort*), which does not let itself be "situated" and
cannot be "objectified"; it also recalls the "reverse side of a unthinkable
dimension" (*versant d'une dimension impensable*).[59]

The Levinasian figure of the *adieu* or *à dieu* introduces an impossibility, the "impossibility of possibility,"[60] that is neither Dasein's own

55. Ibid., 195. Levinas, *Time and the Other,* 118–19 / 000.
56. Levinas, *Dieu, la mort et le temps,* 25.
57. Ibid. 25–26; emphasis added.
58. Ibid., 23
59. Ibid., 23
60. Emmanuel Levinas, *Sur Maurice Blanchot* (Montpellier: Fata Morgana, 1975), trans.
Michael B. Smith as "On Maurice Blanchot," in *Proper Names* (Stanford: Stanford University
Press, 1996), 132 / 16.

innermost possibility nor the possibility of Dasein's impossibility. The
former is the impossibility of the latter's possibility as much as of its
impossibility. But, as this impossibility, it is not as such, in turn, possible, or *a* possible. Indeed, as the possible impossibility of Dasein's possibilities and its impossibility, it "is," again, some kind of death: the
death of its death. The *à dieu* situates itself well beyond the ontic and
ontico-theological conceptions of the divine as an infinite, omnipresent
or absent, *ens realissimum* (if there is any *ens realissimum*, it is Dasein in
its fallenness); since it cannot assure itself of the (possible) existence or
death of its object or addressee, it resembles in its very structure the spectrality, the being haunted by a ghost or by ghosts (the *à dieu* being multiple and divided in and against itself). What is said of Marx's specters
thus holds true of every singular *à dieu*, of every singular Dasein, of its
most "proper" decisions as well as of the singular possibility of its death.
It is there without being there. It is there without being one, proper, properly speaking. And this doubling of Dasein—beyond its own possibilities,
beyond its own utmost possibility, that is to say, death—which, in an uncanny and yet strangely familiar way, constitutes its very *Unheimlichkeit*.
This spectrality is not, in turn, somehow there, before, behind, aside, or
beyond the Dasein it comes to haunt from its very first breath. The specter
is the impossible un-conditionality of Dasein's possibilities, as well as
of the possibility of its impossibility.[61] Dasein, in its relation to itself, to
its very being, as well as to its death, to its possibility no less than to its
impossibility, is thus in advance—that is, from its very inception, in its
very thrownness or constitution—marked by an indelible *jeandersheit*, an
always-already-and-forever-otherness, a being *je anders*, always other, or,
more elliptically still, simply an *anders*, an *otherwise*, an *autrement*, which
can no longer even be said to be: a singular other, irreducible to the general structure of the *Existenzial*, its modifications and its possibilities.

## The Aporetic as Such

For Heidegger, too, of course, there is a certain retreat of death in its
very imminence. It has not often been observed that this paradoxical aspect of being toward death in its distant nearness, in the distanciation of
its approximation, strongly resembles the retreat or infinitization of the

61. Derrida, *Specters of Marx*, 100/165; cf. 195 n. 38/274 n. 1: "Le spectre dont parlait . . .
Marx était là sans être là. Il n'était pas encore là. Il ne sera jamais là. Il n'y pas de *Dasein*
du spectre mais il n'y a pas de *Dasein* sans l'inquiétante étrangeté, sans l'étrange familiarité
(*Unheimlichkeit*) de quelque spectre."

desired in the description of the structure of desire in Levinas's *Totality and Infinity*. For all its emphasis on relating to death as such, on dying properly speaking, on properly dying, Heidegger leaves no doubt that dying as such is not given by one stroke. Rather than being a determinable event in time and space, it is elusive and abyssal to the point of letting its "as such" sink and die away as such. Heidegger writes:

> [A]s one comes closer understandingly, the possibility of the possible just becomes "greater." *The closest closeness which one may have in Being towards death as a possibility, is as far as possible from anything actual*. . . . Death, as possibility, gives Dasein nothing to be "actualized," nothing which Dasein, as actual, could itself *be*. It is the possibility of the impossibility of every way of comporting oneself toward anything, of every way of existing. In the anticipation of this possibility it becomes "greater and greater"; that is to say, the possibility reveals itself to be such that it knows no measure at all, no more or less, but signifies the possibility of the measureless impossibility of existence. In accordance with its essence, this possibility offers no support for becoming intent on something, "picturing" to oneself the actuality which is possible, and so forgetting its possibility.[62]

The being-whole of being-there, then, goes hand in hand with a "not yet" (*Noch-nicht*) that forms the essence of care, of the *Sorge*, of Dasein's potentiality-for-being, which, Heidegger insists, must not be mistaken for "the anticipation of a completion or accomplishment": "In the 'not yet' that bends us toward death, the expecting and waiting is absolutely incalculable; it is without measure, and out of proportion with the time of what is left for us to live" (A 69 / 123). And while "How to Avoid Speaking" had overhastily concluded by stating that in Heidegger's published texts no prayer ever occurs, this view is modified in *Aporias*. Here, in an intense and rigorous reading that further pursues the line of argument prepared by "Ousia et grammé," *Of Spirit*, and "La Main de Heidegger" ("Heidegger's Hand"), Derrida now makes room for the suggestion that in the indefatigable analysis of being toward death, toward the haunting of its imminence, as described by *Being and Time*, one "necessarily passes from the ontological 'not yet' (*Noch-nicht*), insofar as it says what is, in the indicative, to the 'not-yet' of prayer and of desire, the murmured ex-

62. BT 306–7 / 262. Death is not an event of life for Wittgenstein either: "Der Tod ist kein Ereignis des Lebens. Den Tod erlebt man nicht" (*Tractatus logico-philosophicus* 6.4311). Yet the way in which we relate to this nonevent seems to be thought along very different lines.

clamation, the subjunctivity of the sigh: that death not come, *not yet!*" (A 69/123). Indeed, the very formulation of the most proper possibility, *die eigenste Möglichkeit,* is characterized, Derrida says, by a "slightly liturgical tone" (A 70/124). This tone is fueled by the fact that, like the anxiety through or, rather, *as* which it announces or manifests itself—*Sein zum Tode* is in its very essence *Angst,* even though *Angst* is said to bring Dasein only before the possibility of *Entschlossenheit*—death is a peculiar "presence." For, if death never comes as such, then, conversely, the threat of its imminence cannot be removed either. As we have seen, Heidegger's words at this point reveal an intriguing ambiguity in the interpretation of the possible impossible: "The closest closeness [*die nächste Nähe*] which one may have in Being towards death as a possibility, is as far as possible [*so fern als möglich*] from anything actual [*einem Wirklichen*]." [63] Death, Derrida concludes, is not merely "the paradoxical possibility of a possibility of impossibility: it is possibility *as* impossibility" (A 70/125).

What this means—if the word of meaning (*Bedeutung* or *Sinn*) is still relevant here at all—is discussed in some detail in the final pages of *Aporias.* But the question arises in *Sauf le nom* as well. Both texts seek to demonstrate that the very ambiguity of the possible must be distinguished from any possible in the most common and strict sense of the word. How are we to understand this ambiguity, and in what, precisely, does the impossible possibility—the possible *as* impossible—that it calls forth consist?

On the one hand, the said possibility indicates a mere "logical" possibility of impossibility. On this reading, the possibility of impossibility is that of mere or determined negation, of the negation that organizes Hegelian dialectics, or of the *Verneinung* that Heidegger in *What Is Metaphysics?* relates to *das Nicht* as distinct from *das Nichts.* As an impossible possibility, death, Derrida suggests, is not, is not a way to be, is not (a) possible, in any rigorous or generally accepted meaning of *is,* of the possible, of being, of being possible. If possible, the impossible possibility, must be thought completely otherwise, namely as the "more impossible still than the impossible" (*plus impossible encore que l'impossible*) or, in any case, "more impossible than the impossible if the impossible is the simple negative modality of the possible" (SN 43/32). The apophatic turn thus reveals an affirmative rather than a merely negative operation, in

---

63. BT 306–7/262.

short, a different logic than the "logic of presupposition" adopted by Heidegger in *Being and Time*.

On the other hand, however, Derrida suggests that the possibility in question is also reminiscent of "the manifestation of the possible *as* impossible, the 'as' (*als*) becoming the enigmatic figure of the monstrous coupling [of the possible and the impossible]" (A 70 / 124). On this second reading, the impossibility hints at an abyssal mode of experience in which the experienced can never belong to the order of the actual, or, for that matter, the possible as such.

On both counts, Derrida infers, the most proper possibility of Dasein, namely, its impossibility, turns out to be its "least proper," its *least actual* or, in other words, its least appropriable possibility. As we shall see, it is this very same paradoxical structure that informs Derrida's puzzling statements, made in "Circumfession," according to which he considers himself to be "le dernier des Juifs," "the last and the least of the Jews," as well as "le dernier des eschatologists," "the last and the least of the eschatologists." The ambiguity of these expressions enables him to envision a thought that says at once the same and something completely other than the most orthodox and heterodox traditions. What is more, it is this structure that will allow Derrida to read to apophatic *hyper* or *über* as at once a more of the same and a movement toward the totally other. In all these instances, we encounter a subtle reversal of the most possible and the most proper into the least possible, the impossible, and the least proper, the improper, and vice versa. One collapses into the other. As a consequence, the inherited conceptual and existential delimitations become, if not obsolete, then at least fractured, porous, unstable, tentative, provisional, and thus — in principle — negotiable. Again, this is nowhere clearer than in the reading *Aporias* proposes of Heidegger's magnum opus.

What is closest to Dasein secretly corresponds with what for Dasein, as long as it exists, will forever remain the most distant. Not even its proper death or end gives Dasein this possible impossibility "in hand," not even its being toward-death brings Dasein closer or even before its utmost possibility (at least not in any intelligible, spatio-temporal meaning of *closer* and *before*). And we might well ask, Derrida writes, "how a (most proper) possibility as impossibility can still appear *as such* without immediately disappearing, without the 'as such' already sinking beforehand and without its essential disappearance making *Dasein* lose everything that distinguished it — both from other forms of entities and even from the living animal in general . . . . And without its *properly dying* being originarily contaminated and parasited by the *perishing* and the *demising*."[64]

Dasein's utmost or most proper possibility is its very impossibility, its being no longer there, its being no longer what it is or its being no longer *as* what it is, namely, Dasein. We witness here the "ruin," that is to say, the "end," the "perishing," the "demise," or endless "dying" of "properly-dying" (A 74/129). And it is, perhaps, in part this very *inactuality* and *virtuality*, or, as Derrida writes, this "impracticality" of the existential understanding of death that explains and necessitates its "original pre-scriptivity." For it is only in the face of this and similar aporias that a praxis and a certain decision (or, for that matter, resoluteness) become thinkable or imperative at all. This holds true, not only for decisions of a practical or existential nature, but also for decisions pertaining to the analytical and conceptual demarcations that are supposed to make these notions possible in the first place.

> If death, the most proper possibility of *Dasein*, is the possibility of its im-possibility, death becomes the most improper possibility and the most ex-propriating, the most inauthenticating one. From the most originary inside of its possibility, the proper of *Dasein* becomes from then on contaminated, parasited [*sic*], and divided by the most improper. Heidegger indeed says

---

64. A 71/125–26. See also A 35/68–69: "If the distinction between (properly) *dying* and *perishing* cannot be reduced to a question of terminology, if it is not a linguistic distinction, for Heidegger (extending well beyond *Being and Time*) it nevertheless marks the difference of language, the impassable difference between the speaking being that *Dasein* is and any other living thing. *Dasein* or the mortal is not man, the human subject, but it is that in terms of which the humanity of man must be rethought. And man remains the only example of *Dasein*, as man was for Kant the only example of finite reasonable being or of *intuitus derivativus*. Heidegger never stopped modulating this affirmation according to which the mortal is whoever experiences death *as such*, as death. Since he links this possibility of the 'as such' (as well as the possibility of death as such) to the possibility of speech, he thereby concludes that the animal, the living thing as such, is not properly a mortal: the animal does not relate to death as such. The animal can come to an end, that is, perish (*verenden*). . . . But it can never properly die." Derrida goes on to quote a passage from *Unterwegs zur Sprache*, where Heidegger states: "Mortals are they who can experience death as death [*den Tod als Tod erfahren können*]. Animals cannot do this [*Das Tier vermag dies nicht*]. But animals cannot speak either. The essential relation between death and language flashes up before us, but remains still unthought" (quoted from A 35/69–70; Heidegger, *On the Way to Language*, 107/215). Further confirmation can be found in *Being and Time*. Thus, while Heidegger acknowledges that Dasein can be seen as "pure life," he hastens to add that this perspective is secondary with respect to the purely ontological view (BT 290–91/246). Elsewhere, Heidegger seems even less certain that the biological-physiological inquiry could solve all the riddles (BT 396/346).

that inauthenticity is not an exterior accident, a sin or an evil that comes by surprise to existence in its authentic mode. This is where Heidegger at least claims to dissociate *Verfallen* from the original sin and from any morality as well as from any theology. But he crucially needs the distinction between the authentic and the inauthentic, as well as that among the different forms of *ending: dying properly speaking, perishing* and *demising*. These distinctions are threatened in their very principle and, in truth, they remain impracticable as soon as one admits that an ultimate possibility is nothing other than the possibility of an impossibility and the *Enteignis* always inhabited *Eigentlichkeit* before being named there—indeed, this will happen later. (A 77 / 134–35)

The vanishing of the "as such" is a common characteristic of all sorts and modes of being, but this hardly implies that everything (*tout*) is reduced to a bleak homogeneity. Rather, this difficulty signals the "impossibility of an absolutely pure and rigorously uncrossable limit (in terms of existence or concepts) between an existential analysis of death and a fundamental anthropo-theology and moreover between anthopological cultures of death and animal cultures of death" (A 75 / 132).

The consequences of this analysis are immeasurable. If I quote these passages at some length, it is not least because they form the conceptual matrix and the interpretative key to the relationship that interests me here in the first place, namely, the one between philosophy and religion. What holds true of the deconstructible analytic distinctions of Heidegger's major work applies to the relationship between the most critical thought and the theological as well.

Strictly speaking, Derrida's analysis could be said to be self-defeating. It has the effect of reproducing or, rather, displacing the aporia it seeks to describe or evoke, and thus entails the experience of performative contradiction in its turn. And inevitably this affects the logical, epistemological, and phenomenological status of the very argument *Aporias* attempts to expound. If the aporia pointed out here invalidates the presupposition of a certain hierarchical order of beings and concepts, of ontological modalities, and of possibilities (not every possibility is, according to Heidegger, as possible as others), then, it should also be noted that this aporia does not give *itself* to be thought *as such*, that is to say, in its purity or entirety. Derrida makes this clear in no uncertain terms:

> [I]f one must endure the aporia, if such is the law of all decisions, of all responsibilities, of all duties without duty, and of all the border problems that ever can arise, *the aporia can never simply be endured as such*. The ultimate

aporia is the impossibility of the aporia *as such*. . . . Death, as the possibility of the impossible *as such,* is a figure of the aporia in which "death" and death can replace — and this is a metonymy that carries the name beyond the name and beyond the name of the name — all that is only possible as impossible, if there is such a thing: love, the gift, the other, testimony, hospitality and so forth.[65]

Rather than reaffirming a transcendental or quasi-transcendental foundation, system, or infrastructure of being or beyond being (let alone some given ontico-empirical position), Derrida's dictum "Tout autre est tout autre" calls for a completely different "logic" that does justice to both its tautological and its heterological implications. However, neither the same nor merely the other, this "logic" nonetheless remains vulnerable to the very ontico-ontological *parti pris* and presuppositions for which it seeks to substitute. For ultimately, no logic can fully "protect itself from a hidden bio- or anthropo-thanato-theological contamination" (A 79 / 138).

SITUATING ITSELF beyond the grasp of the existential analysis of fundamental ontology, without therefore becoming a mere ontico-empirical event, betraying itself as a "nonsaid" and a "denied revelation," death only manifests itself, Derrida writes, as a "secret that cannot be kept and that presents itself cryptically"; it thus takes the form of a "shibboleth," whose language resembles that of "a sort of hidden religion of the *awaiting* (oneself as well as each other) with its ceremonies, cults, liturgy, or its Marranolike rituals. A universal Marrano, if one may say, beyond what may nowadays be the finished forms of Marrano culture" (A 74 / 130; "Marrano" alludes to the Christianized Jews of medieval Spain).

There is a secret correspondence between the inherent prescriptivity of Heidegger's text and the many passages Derrida has devoted in recent years to the classical concept and conceptual transformations of testimony, of attestation, and of confession. Heidegger's *Being and Time* is found to be marked by "a certain prevalence of the phenomenological tradition" (A 56 / 103), which is shown to reiterate the biblical figure of the kenosis, a figure also invoked by Levinas, Blanchot, and Derrida. What is more, this "kenosis of discourse" — a humiliation and an annihilation of sorts — can with equal right be attributed to the apophatic tradition of negative theology. The method of the existential analytic or funda-

---

65. A 78–79 / 136–37; trans. modified. Reiterating the position taken in *Sauf le nom,* Derrida adds parenthetically: "and this is a metonymy that carries the name beyond the name and beyond the name of the name."

mental ontology and the *via negativa* of mystics such as Angelus Silesius
thus seem to converge to the point of becoming virtually indistinguishable from each other. The phenomenologically articulated *revealability* of
Being reveals the *revelations* claimed by the positive religions (on whose
resources even the most negative of theologies continue to draw). But, in
so doing, this revealability is at least as much in turn revealed by these
historical revelations (or the accounts thereof). Needless to say, this circularity affects the very structure, purity and privilege of the "logic of presupposition" and therefore has severe consequences for the fundamentally
ontological claims of *Being and Time* and its formally indicative method.
The presupposition of ontological revealability thus presupposes that of
which it is the presupposition. *Stricto sensu,* there is no presupposition,
let alone a "logic of presupposition" at work here at all, but a questioning
of tradition, of ontotheology as well as of the more heterodox tradition
of mysticism, which is just as much its radical affirmation. Heidegger can
thus be seen, Derrida suggests, as at once the least and the most Christian
or, for that matter, apophatic, of all authors.

  This, in a nutshell, is the central argument presented in the final pages
of both "How to Avoid Speaking" and *Of Spirit.* And "Faith and Knowledge" states the same insight in explicit terms, which pull Heidegger's
text in a direction from which it had attempted to steer clear: that of a
certain Latin — and therefore Roman Catholic, rather than Lutheran and
Protestant — culture. Heidegger's work, Derrida notes, from its earliest
formulation of the existential analytic up to the thought of the truth of
Being, "continually reaffirms" what could be called a "certain *testimonial
sacrality,* let's say even a professed faith [*une foi jurée*]." [66] Not only the explicit mention made of the concept of attestation or of originary guilt, but
"*all* the existentials" receive their conceptual determination within the
horizon of an "ontological repetition" that is marked (if not overdetermined) by a Christian tradition.[67] Hence the need to retrace the decisive
features of a Roman tradition: "To think 'religion,' that means to think the
'Roman.'" [68] And, as we have seen, "Faith and Knowledge" goes so far as to
suggest that not only our tradition but our present world as a whole can be
characterized in terms of a "mondialatinisation," or "globalatinization,"
that is simultaneously a movement of dissemination and of abstraction.

  This process or movement of abstraction is taken as a blessing and as a

66. FK 61, 80, trans. modified.
67. Ibid.
68. Ibid., 4, 12.

curse. And in this very ambiguity, Derrida notes at the outset of his meditations in "Faith and Knowledge," it forms the very heart of religion. The
reference here is, of course, to Hegel, to the Hegel of *Glauben und Wissen* (*Faith and Knowledge*), who provides Derrida with the paradox that
pervades the latter's text and that is saved and abstracted from the apparent concreteness of the dialectical mediation. Hegel writes: "Denken?
Abstrakt?—*Sauve qui peut!* Rette sich, wer kann!" And Derrida introduces this quotation with a question for which no a priori—or abstract?—
answer is readily available: "Must one save oneself through abstraction or
save oneself from abstraction? Where is salvation to be found?" ("Où est
le salut?").[69]

## Heidegger's Possibilism

What interests Derrida in *Aporias* is the way in which *Being and Time*
adopts a conceptual strategy in order to uphold a radical distinction between the fundamental ontology or existential analytic of death, on the
one hand, and the regional or ontic approaches to death, on the other.
The latter do not only include the positive sciences or disciplines such as
biology, anthropology, theology, and even metaphysics, but also any concrete and singular existential position (*existenziellen Stellungnahme* [BT
290–92 / 246–48]). With respect to all other discourses, Derrida writes,
Heidegger's analysis claims to be "both anterior and free, first and neutral" (A 51 / 96) on methodological grounds, grounds that have everything to do with the problematics of formal indication discussed before
(but largely implicit in *Being and Time*):

> All the disciplines . . . named, and thereby identified within their regional
> borders, notably "metaphysics" and "biology" . . . necessarily presuppose a
> meaning of death, a preunderstanding of what death is or what the word
> "death" means. The theme of the existential analysis is to explain and make
> explicit this ontological preunderstanding. . . . the delimitation of the fields
> of anthropological, historical, biological, demographic, and even theological
> knowledge, presupposes a nonregional ontophenomenology that not only
> does not let itself be enclosed within the borders of these domains, but
> furthermore does not let itself be enclosed within cultural, linguistic, na-
> tional, or religious borders either, and even within sexual borders, which
> crisscross [*retraversent*] all the others.[70]

69. Ibid., 19.
70. A 27 / 57. See also A 44 / 84: "Forms of anthropological knowledge supposedly treat

What is more, all regional and ontic interpretations of death *cannot but fail to indicate and respect* the essence of Dasein (which is neither that of a substance nor an object or subject, but a pure possibility and, properly speaking, the being-possible [*das Möglichsein*] as such), "because they exclude or do not recognize this strange dimension of the possible, all these problematic closures lock Dasein into an ontological determination that is not its own, that of the *Vorhandensein*. And if they lock it up, that is already in order to give in to a confusion between death and an end leveled by the average, mediocre, and leveling everydayness of Dasein" (A 63 / 114). However, if the notion of the being-possible — which, as Heidegger claims, characterizes Dasein *exclusively* — turns out to be affected (from within or from without) by ontological determinations taken from the realm of *Vorhandensein* and *Zuhandensein* after all; if, moreover, these latter modes of being let themselves, in turn, be redescribed in terms of the possible, in Heidegger's very own use of this word, that is, in view of their being themselves possibilities or possibilizations that condition possibilities, in turn — if this is the case, then the existential analysis risks "losing something of its fundamentality" (A 63 / 114).

The theme and strategy of *Aporias* is to lay bare these paradoxes and contradictions inherent in *Being and Time*. In its formal scheme, Derrida writes, the "order of orders" advocated by Heidegger's work "belongs to the great ontologico-juridico-transcendental tradition, . . . impossible to dismantle, and invulnerable . . . *except* [*sauf* ] perhaps in this particular

---

death according to culture and history; bio-genetic disciplines presumably treat death according to nature. No matter how necessary and enriching they may be, these forms of knowledge must presuppose a concept of death properly speaking — this is, in sum, what Heidegger says. Only an existential analysis can provide such a concept of death to the forms of knowledge." This, Derrida says a little further, is what lies at the very heart of the "logic of presupposition," the presupposition, namely, that in philosophy one should begin by being concerned as to "what, already and from the outset, makes possible every statement, every determination, every theme, every project, and every object. In this context, such a logic of presupposition is also a logic of, or a request for, foundation. Indeed, Heidegger says that the existential interpretation of death precedes, is presupposed by all other discourses on death, but also founds (*fundiert*) them" (A 45 / 86). The logic of presupposition, then — this is what the "in this context" implies — could take many other, say, nonfoundationalist, forms as well. It is for this reason, I believe, that Derrida's deconstruction of the logic of presupposition reaches much further than either the classical or modern critiques of foundationalism and goes to the heart of any *possibilism* in general. In part, this displacement can already be associated with the strategic use of the formulation *quasi-*, or *simili*-transcendental. But I would venture to say that a more consistent strategy can be found in the often largely implicit shift from the "law of the possible" to the more nuanced "modalities" of the *peut-être* and the *vielleicht*.

case called death, which is more than a case and whose uniqueness excludes it from the system of possibilities, and specifically from the order that it, in turn, may condition" (A 45 / 86–87). Derrida does not hesitate to mobilize these aporias against the central premises and implications of the "onto-phenomenological" project Heidegger undertakes here and elsewhere. More precisely, his strategy is that of "approaching the place where such aporias risk paralyzing the ontological, hierarchical, and territorial apparatus to which Heidegger lends credit. These aporias risk interrupting the very possibility of its functioning and leading it to ruin. Death would be the name, one of the names, of this threat, which no doubt takes over from what Heidegger himself very early on called 'ruination.' "[71]

Death is at once "the name" and "one of the names" of the threatening aporia, and this ambiguity is no accident, no imprecision in the formulation on Derrida's part, but central to the insight that "Tout autre est tout autre," even though not every other reveals this otherness as incisively as another, or for all times and each place. If God and death are the examples par excellence of this aporia, this does not mean that others may not one day come and take their place. And when this comes about, it will find its basis, not so much in a causal chain of empirical events that could be described in a definite set of propositions (as certain theories of naming and meaning would have it), but in a singular act — or rather passion — of testimony, in which words and names are renamed and, indeed, rebap-

---

71. A 28 / 57–58. On the central demarcation between death, or properly dying (*Tod, eigentlich sterben*), and ending (*verenden*) as it relates to the living — but not Dasein — as such, Derrida remarks, putting all his cards on the table:

> If, in its very principle, the rigor of this distinction were compromised . . . the entire project of the analysis of *Dasein*, in its essential conceptuality, would be, if not discredited, granted another status than the one generally attributed to it. I am thus increasingly inclined to read ultimately this great inexhaustible book in the following way: as an event that, at least in the final analysis, would no longer simply stem from ontological necessity or demonstration. It would never submit to logic, phenomenology or ontology, which it nonetheless invokes. Nor would it submit to a "rigorous science" (in the sense that Husserl intended it), not even to thought (*Denken*) as that which parallels that path of the poem (*Dichten*), and finally, not even to an incredible poem — which I would be nevertheless inclined to believe, without, however, stopping on this point for obvious reasons. The event of this interrupted book would be irreducible to these categories, indeed to the categories that Heidegger himself never stopped articulating. In order to welcome into thought and into history such a "work," the event has to be thought otherwise. *Being and Time* would belong neither to science, nor to philosophy, nor to poetics. Such is perhaps the case for every work worthy of its name: there, what puts thinking into operation exceeds its own borders or what thinking itself intends to present of these borders. (A 31–32 / 63–64)

tized. Why this must be so follows, again, from Heidegger's own analysis, even though one may question some of its central—and, it seems, un-questioned—presuppositions, namely, what I would call his *possibilism*.

Dasein's utmost or most proper possibility, we have seen, is its very impossibility, its being no longer there, its being no longer what it is, as possible, namely, Dasein. And yet some caution is required here, for this paradox or aporia is not thought of as an impasse that is, say, historically contingent, that could have been avoided or overcome. Nor does it take the form of a Kantian antinomy, which although it is inevitable does not need to paralyze the analysis if the latter lets itself be restricted within certain delimitable confines. Neither empirical nor transcendental, the aporia in question can only be testified or attested to, one way or another:

> Insofar as it is its most proper possibility, and precisely as such, death is also for *Dasein*, Heidegger ultimately says, the possibility of an impossibility. There are several modalized occurrences of this nuclear proposition. It is often cited. However, its gripping paradox is hardly noted, and the impor-tance of all the successive explosions that it holds in reserve, in the under-ground of the existential analysis, is probably not measured. . . . Is it an aporia? Where do we situate it? In the impossibility or in the possibility of an impossibility (which is not necessarily the same thing)? What can the possi-bility of an impossibility be? How can we *think* that? How can we *say* it while respecting logic and meaning? How can we approach that, live, or *exist* it? How does one *testify* to it? (A 68 / 121)

It seems clear that the testimony that is called for is not that of some epistemic quality. Derrida notes that whenever Heidegger reiterates the "nuclear proposition" in question, he does so

> without ever lending the least attention or the least thematic interest to the logical form of the contradiction or to what goes against meaning or common sense. In the persistence of this apparently logical contradiction (the most proper possibility as the possibility of an impossibility), he even seems to see a condition of the truth, the *condition of truth*, its very unveiling, where truth is no longer measured in terms of the logical form of judgment. (A 70 / 123–24)

But this reservation with respect to the logocentric and epistemologi-cal determinations and limitations of the rigor of thought is based on a different set of presuppositions, whose metaphysical connotations and overtones are no less obvious. For if a "certain thinking of the possible

is at the heart of the existential analysis of death," this "possible" should
be understood, not only as the "virtuality" or "imminence," but as the
"chance" of an impending future that at any given moment may come to
claim its due, and that one must therefore expect at all times. The possible
is not just any occurrence or futurity that opens up a possible horizon of
expectation. The *Möglichkeit* on which this discourse hinges also recalls a
certain *Vermögen*, an "ability," "power," or "potentiality." Derrida notes
that these two possible meanings of the possible—as mere logical possibility and as a *dispositional capacity* or *ontological resource* implicit in
being-there as such—"co-exist in *die Möglichkeit*."[72]

Needless to say, deconstructive thinking cannot ignore this ambiguity
in the Heideggerian "logic of presupposition," let alone its silent insertion
of potentiality into the notion and the formal indication of the possible,
unless it is willing to adopt Paul Ricoeur's suggestion, in *Soi-même comme
un autre* (*Oneself as Another*), that we ought to reaffirm a certain ontological notion of Being (including our being) as a being *en acte* (a notion
anticipated by the Aristotelian understanding of *dunamis* no less than by
the Spinozistic thought of the *conatus essendi*). This motif is conspicuously absent from Derrida's writings, which betray a different attitude
toward the modality of the possible, especially where the language of
transcendental philosophy (and thus of conditions of possibility) is not so
much eschewed as rearticulated. Derrida prefers to invoke the logic of *la
Nécessité* and *la Chance*, in which Epicurean, Freudian, and Mallarmean
motifs are closely intertwined.[73]

72. A 62 / 113. As Ernst Tugendhat and Ursula Wolff point out in their *Logisch-semantische Propädeutik*, 244, the ambiguity of the concept of the possible is noted by Aristotle (*Metaphysics* 5.12). Marion is equally sensitive to the fact that the possibilities of existence—and the very in-terpretation of existence in terms of mere possibility—is characterized by a certain "mastery" (*maîtrise*) (GWB 213 n. 38 / 101 n. 37).

73. In *Jenseits des Lustprinzips* (*Beyond the Pleasure Principle*), Freud asserts that what op-poses man's narcissism and forces him to hand some of his omnipotence over to spirit (thereby giving rise to his first theoretical achievement) is *anankē*, and, above all, death (Derrida, *Postcard*). Bergson's critique of the concept of the possible "en tant que possible" is invoked by Derrida in "Ousia et grammè" (*Margins of Philosophy*, 62 n. 36 / 72 n. 24), in a context that draws our attention to the "force," "potentiality," and "dynamique" (ibid., 69) implied in the metaphysical concept of time. Plotinus's language of presence hardly fits into the Heideggerian determination of the Platonic epoch of metaphysics and is shot through with figures of non-presence, that is to say, of the *morphē* that is a trace of the *amorphous*: a "trace" that is, strictly speaking, "ni présence ou absence, ni sur quelque mode que ce soit, un compromis second" (ibid., 77 n. 27). On the Unmoved Mover, see Aristotle's *Physics* 5.256a28–29 and *Metaphysics* 12.1070a. On the "aleatory," "*tukhē*," and "luck," see Derrida, *Given Time*, 123ff. and 133 / 157

and 169. And then there is, of course, Derrida's rethinking of the motif of chance and necessity, of the throwing of the dice, in the context of Stéphane Mallarmé's "Un coup de dés" and
"Igitur," in *Dissemination.*

One should distinguish, then, between the thought of the possible and the thought and
experience of a certain chance. The first remains faithful to an implausible, deconstructable
metaphysics of possibilism, whether in an Aristotelean guise or by using the concept of the
possible in the sense of a mere *formal indication* or in terms of an abstract law of the possible. The latter, the thought and the experience of chance, by contrast, opens an avenue that
is as Epicurian as it is messianic and indebted to a certain messianicity and even messianism,
whose historical contours cannot and ought not be fully erased or forgotten. At times, Derrida
identifies it as the aleatory; at times, he defines it as the future-to-come, as the promise of an
*avenir* or *à venir.* But whereas the thought of the possible seeks to set itself apart — if not in fact,
then at least *de iure* — from the actual, the actualized, or the actualizable, that is to say, from
the ontic, the empirical, the real, reification, mechanization, and the technological media they
presuppose or call into being, the thought and the experience of chance (*la Chance*) is in its
turn nothing without simultaneous affirmation of necessity (*la Necessité, anankē*). Not only do
these two poles of all experience, language, and thought intersect in what Derrida at times calls
the *"line of life"* (*ligne de vie*), "destiny," or "a singular way of not being free" (*Points . . . , 118 /
127*), they can also seem to revert into each other. Thus necessity can be called the dream, the
desire, the phantom, and the promise of the idiomatic, which in its very *apparent* accessibility
is the sole chance for the event, the word, the gesture to come to pass at all, yet which, should
it ever arrive as such, in its unity and full presence, is a fatal threat as well: the annihilation of
difference and therefore a certain death (ibid., 136 / 145–46). What must be promised, must not
arrive. It is on both of these necessities (of thought and experience) that chance must rest, if
there is to be chance at all. This dual or double necessity — indeed, the necessity of two necessities that exclude each other in their very possibility — is the aporetic "condition" of chance.

Necessity, then, is neither based on the epistemological notion of aprioricity, which, as
Kripke notes in *Naming and Necessity,* 34, may still allow for a possible exception, if not for
human or artificial minds, then at least for others, for God or for "the Martians"; nor is it based
on a mere causal empirical sequence that can only be known a posteriori. It belongs to neither
of these two realms, assuming that a fundamental distinction can be maintained between their
concepts, whose supposed difference has dominated much modern critical (Kantian) and neo-
positivist, logical empiricist philosophy, from Hume's so-called fork (the distinction between
"relations of ideas" and "matters of fact") all the way up to Rudolph Carnap's reiteration of the
logical distinction between analytical and synthetic truths. It hardly needs to be recalled that
this supposition has been radically undercut in postwar philosophy, in neodialectical thought,
in neopragmatism, and, perhaps, even more effectively in so-called postanalytical philosophy,
beginning with W. V.O. Quine's famous essay "Two Dogmas of Empiricism" (1951).

Neither (epistemo)logical nor physical necessity is what is meant here, in Derrida's insistence on *la Nécessité,* but, in a sense to be determined — in a sense, Kripke writes, that
is "non-pejorative" (*Naming and Necessity,* 36) — *metaphysical* necessity. Kripke's whole argument revolves around the central claim that the notion of necessity and that of aprioricity are
not simply "interchangeable" or even "coextensive"; which opens up the possibility — no, the
necessity — that "necessary a posteriori truths, and probably contingent a priori truths, both
exist" (ibid., 38).

Two further stipulations, quite literally, should be added here: Kripke makes it a "matter
of stipulation" that "an analytic statement is, in some sense, true by virtue of its meaning and
true in all possible worlds by virtue of its meaning. Then something which is analytically true
will be both necessary and a priori" (ibid., 39; cf. 56 n. 21, 122–23 n. 63). Necessity, therefore,

But then again, we should not forget that Derrida's analysis of the different aspects and implications of the possible is haunted by an ambiguity as well, owing neither to a mere conceptual obscurity nor to the potentialist metaphysics that continues to overshadow Heidegger's attempt to overcome the ontology of the West, but, rather, to a structural, internal necessity and uncertainty. As will be seen, the ambiguity of the possible — of the perhaps and potential — has a counterpart (or should we say "double") in Derrida's exploration of all the multiple aspects and implications of the formulation *plus d'une langue,* which simultaneously means more and no more language (or more and no more of one language).

As I indicated earlier, it is therefore only consequent that the logic of the possible, of the possible even of the impossible, calls forth an equally equivocal movement of the potential and the potentializing movement of the possible in the direction of the *überunmöglichste.* Just as the apophatic *via negativa* can be shown to reveal or engender its other, to wit, the inevitable presence or hyperessence of a Being beyond Being, the existential analytic cannot but supplement itself with what it — properly speaking and in its very quest for the proper — ought to and must exclude.

One example might clarify this. Even if we should grant that Heideg-

---

is neither interchangeable nor necessarily coextensive with analyticity. Secondly, something similar could be said with regard to the relation of "certainty" to aprioricity, analyticity, and necessity. Kripke writes: "Whatever certainty is, it's clearly not obviously the case that everything which is necessary is certain. Certainty is another epistemological notion. Something can be known, or at least rationally believed, *a priori* without being quite certain" (ibid., 39). Certainty, in other words, is a subjective, psychological notion, a state of mind. Kripke's understanding of necessity, moreover, circumvents or even undercuts the distinction between what some would call "essentialism, the belief in modality *de re*" and "mere advocacy of necessity, the belief in modality *de dicto*" (ibid., 39). The first position is untenable, bad metaphysics, whereas the latter one limits the analysis to statements or describable states of affairs, in short, to what can be (clearly) said at all.

The necessity of which Derrida speaks is "metaphysical" in the precise sense that Kripke gives to this term; the necessity in question rests on the intuitive consideration of possible worlds rather than on analyticity, and therefore on a certain phenomenological procedure, donation or, in Derrida's words, fiduciary act. Of course, this notion of a "possible world," introduced into semantic theory in the wake of so-called modal logic, should not be confused with my ironic depiction of the world of the possibilists with a merely possible world, with the reduction of the actual or factual world to a possibility to be measured and appropriated in light and view of the utmost and purest possibility. In *Naming and Necessity,* it is made clear that the concept of the "possible world" can serve a completely different function (ibid., 44).

Finally, for an analysis of physical or natural as well as logical and mathematical necessity in terms of "Hume's regularities, culminating here and there in what passes for an explanatory trait or the promise of it," see W. V. O. Quine, "Necessary Truth," in *The Ways of Paradox and Other Essays,* rev. ed. (Cambridge, Mass,: Harvard University Press, 1976), 68–76, 76.

ger's interpretation of the essence of *Bezeugung* (testimony) in *Being and Time* does not claim to convey the psychological or existential event of Dasein's death directly or immediately, that is to say, in its *hic et nunc;* even if we acknowledge that this testimony only attests to the permanence of the imminence of this death—in its difference from all other imminences and as it announces itself in its retreat—it must be stressed that Heidegger's interpretation of this attestation continues to take its "measure" (A 51 / 97) in a phenomenological understanding of the *Erlebnis* that it had set out to question in the first place. What is more, this measure is itself measured by a prescriptivity whose very nature challenges the common nonprescriptivist interpretation of the attestation (*Bezeugung*) of the voice of conscience, in which Dasein fundamentally calls to itself from a long distance and calls itself away into a distance (*aus der Ferne in die Ferne*), albeit never from *itself,* that is to say, from its own innermost possibility (i.e., the possibility of its impossibility).

Being toward death, then, in particular the *Vorlaufen* in the possibility that is death, is to engage rather than to realize a *pure purifying possibility,* a possibility that is *cathartic* to the extent that it is entertained—Heidegger's word is *ausgehalten*—as a mere possibility.[74] As a *purely* purifying possibility, it is nothing else. It is not so much the modality of taking one's responsibility for oneself, let alone for the other, even though Heidegger leaves no doubt that it is only this most proper of all possibilities that brings Dasein into its own and that thus—indirectly—also allows for a proper being with and for others.

> Being-possible is proper to *Dasein* as entity, and death is the most proper possibility of this possibility. This typical statement distributes itself, modulates itself, and is argued in many ways. . . . This possibility of being is not a simple characteristic to be noted or described. In its essential and constant imminence, it must be *assumed;* one can and one must testify to it; and the testimony is not a mere constative report: the statements of the existential analysis are originally prescriptive or normative. More precisely, they analyze

74. See BT 305 / 261: "[I]f Being-towards-death has to disclose understandingly the possibility which we have characterized, and if it is to disclose it *as a possibility*, then in such Being-towards-death this possibility must not be weakened: it must be understood *as a possibility*, it must be cultivated *as a possibility*, and we must *put up with* it *as a possibility*, in the way we comport ourselves towards it." ("Im Sein zum Tode . . . , wenn anders es die charakterisierte Möglichkeit als *solche* verstehend zu erschliessen hat, muß die Möglichkeit ungeschwächt *als Möglichkeit* verstanden, *als Möglichkeit* ausgebildet und im Verhalten zu ihr *als Möglichkeit ausgehalten* werden.")

an irreducible prescriptivity, which itself stems from being as being-possible, but they do so in the mode of phenomenological attestation . . . : "Death is a possibility-of-being that Dasein itself has to take over [*zu übernehmen*] in every case. With death, Dasein awaits itself [*s'at-tend lui-même, steht sich . . . bevor,* stands before] in its ownmost potentiality-for-Being" [BT 294 / 250: "With death, Dasein stands before itself in its *ownmost* potentiality for being" / "Mit dem Tod steht sich das Dasein selbst in seinem *eigensten* Sein-können bevor"]. (A 64 / 115–16)

In the final analysis, a paradoxical *attestation* comes to determine any analysis that—rightfully or wrongly—claims to describe the conditions of possibility, indeed, the co-originary structures, of all modes of our (or, more precisely, *my*) existence. And the same holds true of the existential interpretations one would want to give of the concrete, historical and contemporary examples of this attestation.

The existential analytic of the relation to death is marked by an "irreducible prescriptivity" that, for Heidegger, Derrida maintains, "itself stems from being as being-possible," even though the latter, in turn, can only be offered "in the mode of phenomenological attestation" (A 64 / 115). In an almost circular mode, then—and this reveals the aporetic—*the attestation is made possible by what it makes possible.* In other words, this prescriptivity manifests itself only in the mode of a *quasi-*, if not *un-* or *anti-*phenomenological gesture of testimony, which does not lend itself to any descriptive or constative rendering, and has for that reason to be *affirmed* and *assumed* by a singular performative. This performative, moreover, is absolute in the etymological sense of the Latin *absolvere:* it loosens itself from every context, from every horizon, from every dimension, even from the situation that Heidegger characterizes as "thrownness." Otherwise than being possible, then, and otherwise than the "otherwise than being" to which it testifies, its resembles the very structure of the *à dieu.*

Could this "irreducible prescriptivity" be thought of, as Heidegger contends, as the result or the effect or even as the testimony of a *being-*possible, of a possibility of *being*, of a *possibility* that can be said to exist? Is it necessary or even possible to retain the very notion of a modality—indeed, of the possible—where precisely a certain categoricity in its very relation to the question of being *as such* seems to lose, if not its perennial pertinence, then at least, its primacy? And is it not here that one might envision escape from a certain transcendental and methodological logic of presupposition, along with the fundamentally metaphysical tradition of possibilism (of *dúnamis* and *possibilitas*) that it implies? For let us not forget: Heidegger does attribute to the possible a doubly qualified (and thereby restricted or modified) power or force, speaking, almost in passing, of "*die stille Kraft des Möglichen*"; of "*die 'Kraft' des Möglichen*"; and of a Dasein that, in its anticipation of death, "lets death become powerful in itself" (*den Tod in sich mächtig werden lässt*).[75] Are there alternatives to the overdetermined modality of the said modality, such as, for example, the "perhaps," the *vielleicht*, that Heidegger so frequently intersperses in his text?[76]

75. BT 446, 447; 436 / 394, 395; 384. For a more general exposition of "The Primacy of the Possible," see Kisiel, *Genesis of Heidegger's "Being and Time,"* 439 ff.

76. Derrida, *Politics of Friendship*, 45–46 n. 5 / 48–49 n. 1; see also 186–87 / 213–14. Here, in the context of a chapter that advocates the need for a "systematic study of the 'category,' if it is one, . . . of the 'perhaps' in all languages and in all the world's cultures," Derrida refers to an essay ("Perhaps—A Modality? On the Way with Heidegger to Language," *Graduate Faculty Philosophy Journal* 16, no 2 [1993]: 467–84), in which Rodolphe Gasché raises the issue of whether the "perhaps" can still be seen as a modality. In the background lie the philosophical reservations (of Hegel and others) with respect to the "perhaps," which is seen as "an empiricist slip back into the approximate formulations of ordinary language. 'Perhaps' would belong to a vocabulary which should remain outside philosophy. That is to say, outside certainty, truth, even outside veracity" (ibid.). "And what if perhaps modalized a discourse which no longer proceeds by statements (declarations, affirmations, assertions) without being for all that less rigorous than the discourse of philosophy?" Derrida quotes Gasché as asking ("Perhaps," 469; cf. Gasché, *Inventions of Difference*, 194, 228). The basic function of modalizing terms such as *perhaps* (and, perhaps, even *c'est-à-dire* and *autrement dit*, formulations used nowhere more intensively than by Levinas, for example, in the final section, the postscript, as it were, of *Autrement qu'être ou au-delà de l'essence*) is to signal a certain moment of *suspension* (and, perhaps, *suspense*) *in* and *of* the assertion and thereby (a) to qualify its logical, onto-, theo-, and deontological status, and (b) to influence, intensify, or mitigate its effect on the hearers and readers. This rhetorical aspect is directly related to the modication of the nature of what it is that is being asserted (without being asserted, i.e., predicated or attributed, in the strict sense of these words). Elsewhere, Derrida pays minute attention to the adjectives *probably* and *perhaps* in the writing of Levinas. Commenting on a central Levinasian statement— "Responsibility which, before the discourse bearing on the said, is probably the essence of language"—Derrida explains that the qualifier "probably" that is used here, as in so many other contexts, "contains nothing empirical or approximative, it removes no rigor from the utterance it determines." And with reference to another observation of Levinas's—"But the language of thematization, which at this moment we are using, has perhaps only been made possible itself by means of that Relation, and is only ancillary"—Derrida clarifies:

> A perhaps ("has perhaps only been made possible") still affects this assertion: yet it nonetheless concerns a condition of possibility, the very thing philosophy subtracts from every "perhaps." This is consonant with the earlier "probably," and the "only" making possible is to be read also, perhaps, in two ways: (1) It has *not* been made *possible* except by that Relation (classical form of a statement on a condition of possibility); (2) It has only been rendered *possible* (probable), a reading that better corresponds with the ordinary syntac-

For Heidegger, notably in his later work, but already quite manifestly in *Being and Time*, Being *itself* is defined as the possible or, as the "Letter on Humanism" has it, the *Mög-liche*. In *Being and Time*, it is clear, Derrida recalls that if "being-possible is the being proper to *Dasein*, then the existential analysis of the death of *Dasein* will have to make of this *possibility* its theme": "the analysis of death is submitted to the ontological law that rules the being of *Dasein*, whose name is 'possibility' " (A 63/114).[77] What does this mean? Perhaps no better elucidation of this leitmotif can be found than the passage in the "Letter on Humanism" that compares the notion of the possible to that of a possibilizing affecting, affection, or even love:

> Thinking comes to an end when it slips out of its element. The element is what enables thinking to be a thinking. The element is what properly enables: it is the enabling [*das Vermögen*]. It embraces thinking and so brings it into its essence. . . . To embrace a "thing" or a "person" in its essence means to love it, to favor it. Thought in a more original way such favoring [*Mögen*] means to bestow essence as a gift. Such favoring is the proper essence of enabling, which not only can achieve this or that but also can let something essentially unfold in its provenance, that is, let it be. It is on the "strength" of such enabling by favoring that something is properly able to be. This enabling is what is properly "possible" [*das "Mögliche"*], whose essence resides in favoring. From this favoring Being enables thinking. The former makes the

tic order, and with the insecurity of a *perhaps*. (Derrida, "At This Very Moment in This Work Here I Am," 23)

77. We should not forget, at this point, that for Kant no less than for Heidegger, there is a certain primacy of the possible. Unlike Heidegger, however, Kant is aware of the fact that the possible is at bottom or ultimately a *theological idea*. In the idea of God, stripped of all—or almost all—of the ontotheological and substantialist determinations that typified it in the *metaphysica specialis*, the possible is retained as the formal determination of all concepts in view of the regulative idea of the full range of the possible: "die Bestimmung aller Begriffe in der Idee eines vollständigen Inbegriffs des Möglichen" (Immanuel Kant, *Prolegomena zu einer jeden künftigen Metaphysik, die als Wissenschaft wird auftreten können* [Riga: J. F. Hartknoch, 1783], trans. Gary Hatfield as *Prolegomena to Any Future Metaphysics That Will be Able to Come Forward as Science* [Cambridge: Cambridge University Press, 1997], par. 43. On the primacy of the possible, see ibid., par. 4). But an at least formal similarity remains: the possible is the horizon of reason and of morality. Hannah Arendt reminds us of a motif that is central to this thought: "an inborn voice says: Thou shalt, and it would be a contradiction to assume that I cannot where my own reason tells me that I should (*ultra posse nemo obligatur*: what exceeds the possible obliges no one)" (Hannah Arendt, *Lectures on Kant's Political Philosophy*, ed. Ronald Beiner [Chicago: University of Chicago Press, 1982], 50).

latter possible. Being is the enabling-favoring, the "may-be" [*das Mög-liche*]. As the element, Being is the "quiet power" of the favoring-enabling, that is, of the possible. Of course, our words *möglich* [possible] and *Möglichkeit* [possibility], under the dominance of "logic" and "metaphysics" are thought solely in contrast to "actuality"; that is, they are thought on the basis of the definite — the metaphysical — interpretation of Being as *actus* and *potentia*, a distinction identified with the one between *existentia* and *essentia*. When I speak of the "quiet power of the possible" I do not mean the *possibile* of a merely represented *possibilitas*, nor *potentia* as the *essentia* of an *actus* of *existentia;* rather, I mean Being itself, which in its favoring presides over thinking and hence over the essence of humanity, and that means over its relation to Being. To enable something here means to preserve it in its essence, to maintain it in its element.[78]

Could a prescription ever stem from a being-possible, then? Can it emerge from a being-impossible that, as Heidegger thinks, is possible and that is intrinsic to Being, to being-there, that is, Dasein? Can it stem from a being impossible that is possible in its being impossible, that is the possibility of an impossibility, thereby of the impossibility of the possibility, rather than from a possible that is possible only *as* impossible and, therefore, not possible as such? Without suggesting that prescription must or should come from the realm of the factual in the sense of reality (*Wirklichkeit*) as opposed to possibility (*Möglichkeit*), should one not rather maintain that *all prescriptivity stems from what has already come to pass,* lies behind us or preceded us, and that is therefore neither possible nor impossible; from that which, far from being *passé,* can neither be anticipated nor projected or invented, but only *mourned,* with a sense of loss that is both irremediable and inappropriable?

Original prescriptivity, on this reading, should be tied to mourning rather than to the being possible that for Heidegger culminates in death. This mourning's proper temporality is not so much that of some futurity, grounded in ecstatic temporality, but of *a spectral return of the prior in the posterior, in the posteriority also that is posterity.* It manifests itself in the affirmation of a heritage that is neither natural nor cultural, and that does not let itself be confined within the common features of historical conscience, the voice of conscience, original guilt, the cultural present, but is truly a *survivance du passé* (to employ a phrase from Bergson's *Essais sur les données immédiates de la conscience* [*Time and Free Will*]).

78. Heidegger, "Letter on Humanism," in *Pathmarks,* 241–42 / 313–14.

At times, it would seem that Heidegger acknowledges this importance of mourning. *Being and Time,* of course, *does* speak, albeit in passing, of signs of mourning and of commemoration, of a "being with the death," that is characterized by a proper structure, and so on. But the *Trauerzeichen* are just one example among others in a list of *Zeichen* in general,[79] and the *Mitsein mit den Toten*[80] remains grounded in the primary ontological structure of Dasein's relation to its own death. In other words, for Heidegger, mourning is not a possibility of primary concern, let alone a possibility that opens or orients or haunts all others. For Derrida, by contrast, mourning does have a central place, albeit not as a possibility, as a possibility properly speaking, as a possibility of the proper, as a possibility that can be appropriated — or, for that matter, appropriate — as such. Indeed, the experience of mourning is, if anything, impossible. It is overtaken by the desire, as *Specters of Marx* puts it, "to ontologize remains, to make them present, in the first place by *identifying* the bodily remains and by *localizing* the dead (all ontologization, all semanticization — philosophical, hermeneutical, or psychoanalytical — finds itself caught up in this work of mourning, but, as such, it does not yet think it . . . )."[81]

To think mourning — or to think mournfully — demands that one question the simple logic of either presupposition or interiorization, of repression, and of introjection in light of a more complex and more paradoxical or aporetic structure. This is precisely what interests Derrida in Patočka's *Heretical Essays,* in which the genealogy of European responsibility is thought of as at least in part a history of "conversion." Of the transition between the Platonic and Christian principles, Derrida writes:

> This all takes place . . . as if conversion amounted to a process of mourning, facing up to a loss, in the sense of keeping within oneself that whose death one must endure. And what one keeps inside at the very moment that there comes into play a new experience of secrecy and a new structure of responsibility . . . is the buried memory or crypt of a more ancient secret. (GD 9 / 18)

History as a process of mourning, or of thinking mourning and of thinking mournfully — the idea is certainly not new. What is new, however, is

79. See BT 108 / 77, which lists *Trauerzeichen* among *Wegmarken* and the *Flursteine;* and BT 108 / 78 on the *Spur, Überrest,* and *Denkmal.*

80. See BT 282 / 238.

81. Derrida, *Specters of Marx,* 9 / 30. On thinking mourning, see Jacques Derrida, *Ulysse gramophone: Deux mots pour Joyce* (Paris: Galilée, 1987), 90, 117, 136–37; "Ja ou le faux bond," in *Points . . .* ; and, of course, *Mémoires: Pour Paul de Man.*

the fact that this history is thought from the perspective of the history of
religion, of responsibility as a kind of religion, or at least as something
whose very idea and genealogy remain unthinkable *without* or *outside*
religion. Religion is the very experience of mourning. Religion, in a sense,
enables mourning to be thought.

Does Heidegger think it? Following the letter and the spirit of Heidegger's text, it could be claimed that the topos of immortality—a topos,
Derrida reminds us, that in its very structure resembles "any form of
survival or return [*revenance*] (and society, culture, memory, spirit, and
spirits are made only of that—only for that)"—is not so much the negation, denial, or overcoming of Dasein's being toward death; for, Derrida
notes, "it does not contradict it, it is not symmetrical with it, because it is
conditioned by being toward death and confirms it at every moment" (A
55–56 / 103). Regardless of the absolute independence, anteriority, neutrality, or even indifference of the being toward death with respect to the
affirmation or negation of the possibility of the afterlife and its respective
religious, mythological, idealist, or materialist interpretations, Heidegger
stresses the fact that his analysis is inscribed in a perspective that is radically *finite* and, consequently, purely this-wordly, "*rein 'diesseitig.'*" It is
almost as if we were dealing here with a methodological atheism or secularism that takes its point of departure on this side—from there where
apparently "we humans" happen to see something at all—without therefore prejudging, it would seem, as to what may lie beyond, or, for that
matter, on this side (*diesseits, en-deça*) of the purely this-wordly:[82]

82. Derrida is clearly skeptical with respect to what he calls Heidegger's "methodologism,"
which, as he goes on to note, "poses as its axiom that one can only *start* from *here, from this
side*: the best point of departure is the point from which we can start and that is always here.
Where does one start from, if not from here? Such is the thrust of a question that may not be
as invisible as it looks" (A 53 / 99). A first precaution is that such an apparent methodological
decision is never simply this, but much more (or much less), if only because it is based on the
preliminary decision that it is good to have or to follow a method in the first place (A 56 / 104).
But then, again, nobody has so consistently insisted that we always begin somewhere—*quelque
part où nous sommes*—than Derrida. Is this "somewhere" not "here," then, or not simply identifiable with the *hic et nunc,* with a "here" that is thought of as one and indivisible? What is
it, if anything, that constitutes and singularizes the "here" whence we—of necessity and with
a chance far more aleatory than any thrownness, facticity, or *Geschick*—shall always already
speak? And can this "here" ever be thought of and experienced without constant reference to
the "over there," without therefore invoking some dialectical truth or metaphysical correspon-
dance (as was the case in the traditional speculative and idealist philosophies of the infinite)?
This difference between Derrida's view and Heidegger's would be in part the following: as is
pointed out in *Aporias,* the methodological "order of orders" is for Heidegger "(1) an order in
the sense of the logic of a whole, an element, or a milieu . . . ; (2) it is also an order as order of

The existential analysis is . . . anterior, neutral, and independent with regard
to all the questions and all the answers pertaining to a metaphysics of death:
the questions and answers that concern survival, immortality, the beyond
(*das Jenseits*), or the other side of this side (*das Diesseits*), that is, what one
should do or think *down here* before death (ethical, juridical, and political
norms). . . . after having excluded from the existential analysis all considerations about the beyond and the here (the "on this side," *das Diesseits,* which
must not be translated by the Platonic or Christian "down here"), arguing
that they are founded, dependent, and derivative with regard to the existential
analysis, Heidegger nevertheless stresses that the existential analysis stands . . .
purely on this side: it is *rein "diesseitig."* It is on this side, on the side of *Dasein*
and of its here, that the oppositions between here and over there, this side
and beyond, can be distinguished. In the same direction, one could say that it
is by always *starting from* the idiomatic hereness of my language, my culture,
and my belongings that I relate to the difference of the *over there.* (A 52 / 98)

Now, while the factual coming about of death would annihilate the
Dasein that is toward-death itself, the becoming possible (and thus betrayal) of mourning would consist in the annihilation of the other (as well
as of the other also that may just as well be the self). Derrida's own emphasis on the to-come (*à venir*) of the future event, of the futures that
mark any event, and the *hospitality* that is the very name for the *awaiting
of the event* remain subjected to this structure of mourning.

There is not much future in Derrida, then, in this analysis of Dasein's
futurity, as well as in the interpretations it may or may not provoke, if
only because the future belongs to what has no future, but is haunted by
the past, by the immemorial, by the *profond jadis,* to quote Levinas quoting Valéry. In short, by that which characterizes the mode and the mood
of mourning. This motif of a past that has never belonged to any "present"
is already cited in "La Différance" as the expression Levinas adopts, in
a way that is radically different from that of psychoanalysis, in order to
evoke the trace of the other. And it is, Derrida notes in this same context,

---

progression, sequence, forward motion, or irreversible procedure, a step, a way of proceeding
or of progressing; (3) it is finally a given order of sequential linkage or consequence: begin here
and *end* there!" (A 45 / 86). This order, *Aporias* goes on to argue, should be contrasted with an
"entirely other 'logic' of the order" (A 47 / 87), and one no longer premised on a questionable
presupposition. In Derrida's words: "[I]f there are legitimate and powerful questions about the
foundation and the 'already' of the condition of possibility, then they are themselves made possible by a relation to death, by a 'life-death' [*la vie–la mort*] that no longer falls under the case
of what it makes possible" (ibid.).

precisely within the confines and on the basis of this, if not formally, then at least structurally indicative character of the trace that the thought of *différance* could be said to imply the Levinasian deconstruction (Derrida writes "critique") of Western metaphysics and modern ontology.

However, is this singular pastness or past without past — and everything it would seem to imply — not at odds with Derrida's equally important insistence on the to-come, the *à venir?* Perhaps. But the to-come is not the coming of something determinate. Rather, it is coming of a certain not (*pas*) that does not even attain the structure of the not-yet (in the Heideggerian understanding of the *Noch nicht*).

Whereas for Heidegger, being toward death is Dasein's utmost possibility of relating to its impossibility, mourning for Derrida is an impossible relation to what is no longer possible, or, for that matter, impossible, if the impossible is taken as a mere privation or the reverse of the possible. Here, there would be nothing to choose, not even the *Nachholen* or the *Wählen einer Wahl* ("making up for not choosing" or explicitly choosing [BT 313 / 268]) that Heidegger defines as the only appropriate response to the call of conscience. But does not Derrida himself, in turn, state that mourning is impossible, that it is the impossible par excellence, and this for reasons quite similar to the ones that lead Heidegger to speak of the impossibility that is Dasein's utmost possibility? Is not also mourning possible, precisely, *as* impossible? If this is the case, then it entails that there can be no mourning *as such,* and that the question and the phenomenon of mourning will always already touch upon structures and events whose concrete manifestations throughout history are far from irrelevant. In effect, to isolate mourning radically from, say, revelation or messianism would require that one reiterate the conceptual demarcations of the existential analytic in one form or another.

If this rearticulation of the structure of being toward death in terms of a being-toward-mourning seems to come close to what in *Being and Time* is analyzed as the *Nachholen einer Wahl* or the *Wählen dieser Wahl,* then this comparison is merely that of a formal analogy that leaves room for substantial differences.[83]

83. In *Being and Time,* this *Nachholen,* or retrieval, comes close to the "generous repetition" of Derrida's "Ousia et grammè," but the "repetition" is also seen as the becoming manifest and explicit of Dasein's "fate":

> The repeating of that which is possible does not bring again [*Wiederbringen*] something that is "past," nor does it bind the "Present" back to that which has already been "outstripped." Arising, as it does, from a resolute projection of oneself, repetition does not let

For in the repetition (haunting, doubling) that constitutes mourning there is finding—and, perhaps, a finding again—that is not so much a finding or refinding of one's true self as of that self *as other*. And if this possibility (if it is one) of finding oneself *as another* is revealed by the attestation of a voice—a voice that for Heidegger is one, unambiguous, and the instantiation of conscience (Heidegger speaks of its "Instanzfunktion für die Existenz des Daseins")—then Derrida's analysis should make us pause again and raise the following questions.

When Heidegger writes: "In terms of its *possibility*, Dasein is already a potentiality-for-Being-its-Self, but it needs to have this potentiality attested" ("Das Dasein bedarf der Bezeugung eines Selbstseinkönnens, das es der *Möglichkeit* nach je schon ist") (BT 313/268), it must be asked: first, whether this ontico-ontological possibility is not itself, in turn, made "possible" or, rather, evoked and provoked by that which precedes or exceeds the logic of presupposition and the potentiality or the power that, regardless of its attempted formalization, continues to determine the regime of the possible from within. One might well doubt, therefore, whether *Selbstseinkönnen* or *Entschlossenheit* are the best names for the response and the responsibility that is called for by the attestation in question.

"The call of conscience has the character of an *appeal* to Dasein by calling it to its ownmost potentiality-for-Being-its-Self; and this is done by way of *summoning* it to its ownmost Being-guilty" ("Der Gewissenruf hat den Charakter des *Anrufs* des Daseins auf sein eigenstes Selbstsein-können und das in der Weise des *Aufrufs* zum eigensten Schuldigsein"), Heidegger writes (BT 314/269). But should this call be taken to come from Dasein to Dasein? Is it not first of all a call *addressed to* this Dasein

---

itself be persuaded of something by what is "past," just in order that this, as something which was formerly actual, may recur. Rather, the repetition makes a *reciprocative rejoinder* to the possibility of that existence which has-been-there. But when such a rejoinder is made to this possibility in a resolution, it is made *in a moment of vision* [*Augenblick*]; *and as such* it is at the same time a *disavowal* of that which in the "today" is working itself out as the "past." Repetition does not abandon itself to that which is past, nor does it aim at progress. In the moment of vision authentic existence is indifferent to both these alternatives. . . .

Resoluteness implies handing oneself down by anticipation to the "there" of the moment of vision; and this handing down we call "fate." This is also the ground for destiny [*Geschick*], by which we understand Dasein's historicizing in Being-with-Others. In repetition, fateful destiny can be disclosed explicitly as bound up with the heritage which has come down to us. By repetition, Dasein first has its own history made manifest [*offenbar*]. (BT 437–38/385–86)

296 Philosophy and the Turn to Religion

and "measured" in terms of the possibilities, more precisely, the never (or not yet) actualized possibilities of this Dasein? And is this not precisely what would follow from Heidegger's own analysis if only one pushed just a step further his insistence that the voice of conscience can neither be described in terms of a psychological state of mind, nor explained biologically, nor interpreted theologically?[84] What are the consequences of stating, as Heidegger repeatedly does, that the distance between the fundamental ontological analysis of conscience is at an equally far remove from the psychological, the biological, and the theological determinations of that phenomenon?

THAT FOR Heidegger dying (*Sterben*) is a process that is "neither natural (biological) nor cultural" (A 42 / 79–80) has far-reaching implications, not the least important of which is the fact his analysis does not allow for a "politics of death" in the same way that, say, Levinas's or Derrida's analyses do. In Derrida's words: "The existential analysis does not claim any competence (and indeed it has none) for dealing with political problems of burial, of the cult of the death, and, above all, of war and of medicine" (A 59 / 108).

Yet the deconstruction of the very distinction between the ontological and the empirical should make it clear that there is no death, no being toward death, without the invocation, however indirect, of a "culture of death" just as "culture" (or, for that matter, politics [see A 61–62 / 112]) will always be premised on a concept of—and relation to—death that is, to a certain extent, formalizable, if not necessarily ontologizable:

> culture itself, culture in general, is essentially, before anything, even a priori, the culture of death. Consequently, then, it is a history of death. There is no

---

84. See BT 313 / 269. For Heidegger, the sense of guilt is not contrasted to the idea of perfection, or, rather, of the infinite, that inspires Plato, St. Augustine, Descartes, Pascal, Levinas, and Patočka, among others. In *The Gift of Death,* Derrida makes it clear in an important parenthetical remark that it is here that one should locate the difference in *content* or in *point of departure* and *referent,* if not in *structure,* between Patočka and Heidegger. "[I]ndividuality has been related to infinite love and man is an individual because he is guilty, *always* guilty with respect to that love," Derrida quotes Patočka as writing, and comments parenthetically: "Patočka emphasizes 'always': like Heidegger he defines there an originary guilt that doesn't wait for one to commit any particular fault, crime, or sin, an a priori guilt that is included in the conception of responsibility in the originary *Schuldigsein,* which one translates as 'responsibility' as well as 'guilt.' But Heidegger has no need [*sic*] to make reference, no explicit reference at least, to this disproportion with respect to an infinite love in order to analyze the originary *Schuldigsein*" (GD 52 / 55).

> culture without a cult of ancestors, a ritualization of mourning and sacrifice, institutional places and modes of burial, even if they are only for the ashes of incineration. . . . The very concept of culture may seem synonymous with the culture of death, as if the expression "culture of death" were ultimately a pleonasm or a tautology. But only such a redundancy can make legible the cultural differences and the grid of borders. Because each culture entails a treatment of death, each of them treats the end according to a different partition. (A 43 / 83–84)

For Derrida, death is much more than what Paul de Man calls a "displaced name for a linguistic predicament";[85] it is a singular and singularizing relation to the other, to all others, including those no longer with us, and to all others as, precisely, totally other. But the Levinasian emphasis on the death of the other and Derrida's stress on the structure of originary mourning also seem to chart death as a concept, referent, or experience that is nonbiological, and noncultural, in short, that cannot be understood in naturalistic terms. What, then, is the difference? Why does one seemingly abstract or formally indicative structure let itself be translated into a politics, here a politics of death, *more easily and more responsibly* than another?

## Virtual Debates

Speaking of death, as *Being and Time* does, as "the possibility of the pure and simple impossibility for Dasein [*die Möglichkeit der schlechthinnigen Daseinsunmöglichkeit*]," is, Derrida would seem to suggest, saying too much and too little. *Too little,* since Heidegger does not fully explore the aporetic that underlies or pervades, but also precedes and follows, his analysis. *Too much,* for whatever the formalism of the existential analytic of death, it is, as Derrida notes, "not certain that Heidegger does not ultimately give us a discourse on *the best,* indeed *the most proper and the most authentic,* relation to dying: hence, *de bene moriendi*" (A 60 / 110). A certain given death, a *mort donnée,* would come to foreclose, that is, to sacrifice, another, which is the death of the other and his spectral return in mourning.

It would seem as if Derrida were arguing that "Il faut bien mourir," that indeed one must die, but that *in dying not everyone dies as well.* Not every death is an instance of ontologico-existential death or of death as

85. Paul de Man, "Autobiography as De-Facement," in id., *The Rhetoric of Romanticism* (New York: Columbia University Press, 1984), 67–81.

such. And where the simple opposition of life and death loses its simplicity or even its pertinence, everything takes the form, if not of survival,
let alone of eternal life, then at least of a living-on (a *survie*); not of an
afterlife but of an *überleben*, an overlife as it were, of *la vie–la mort* and
of a *living through it all over again*. In a sense, this would come down to
an arrest of death, an *arrêt de mort*, to quote Blanchot, so often quoted by
Derrida.[86]

What is central, then, to these considerations is that what Derrida
says here of Heidegger's conceptual and existential-analytic demarcations
concerning being toward death or dying—of *death,* that is, in its very
distinction from *perishing* and *demise,* and in contrast with every other
thinkable form of imminence, as well as with all other modes of relating to
being and beings—holds true a fortiori for the delimitations between the
transcendental, in the sense of the *veritas transcendentalis,* and the theological and the religious, in the sense of the ontic, empirical, and positive
phenomenon that is ascribed to so-called revelations. Here too, the conclusion must be that there can be no "ontologico-existential problematic
that anthropology must presuppose and that concerns the being-until-
death of *Dasein,* beyond any border, and indeed beyond any cultural,
religious, linguistic, ethnological, historical, and sexual determination"
(A 42 / 79). Yet this is precisely what Heidegger pretends. Especially where
the relation of Dasein to death (that is to say, to its own death rather than
any other) is concerned.[87]

*Aporias* shows that the three modes of ending or relating to the end
that Heidegger takes great pains to keep apart are in fact difficult to distinguish.[88] Even more important is Derrida's suggestion that if differentiation
between these modes were possible at all—an assumption that is difficult
to accept after all we have found so far—then it would permit one to uncover a secret correspondence, an unexpected alliance, indeed a chiasmic

---

86. See my essay " 'Lapsus absolu': Remarks on Maurice Blanchot's *L'Instant de ma mort,*"
*Yale French Studies* 93 (1998), 30–59.

87. See BT 293 / 248–49: "The fact that in an existential analysis of death, existentiell possibilities of Being-towards-death are consonant with it, is implied by the essence of all ontological
investigation. All the more explicitly must the existential definition of concepts be unaccom-
panied by any existentiell commitments, especially with relation to death, in which Dasein's
character as possibility lets itself be revealed most precisely. The existential problematic aims
only at setting forth the ontological structure of Dasein's Being-*towards*-the-end."

88. Derrida is referring to the sentences that "formalize the three modes of ending (*enden*):
*perishing, demising,* and *dying*" (A 38): "Dasein never perishes [*verendet nie*]. Dasein, however,
can demise [*ableben*] only as long as it is dying [*solange, als es stirbt*]" (BT 291 / 247).

relation, between the aporias of the existential analytic of death and those other discourses on finitude and mortality whose most significant articulations, Derrida claims, can be found in the writings of Freud and Levinas: "When one keeps in mind the distinction between *verenden* [perishing] and *sterben* [dying], Heidegger's statements are not irreconcilable with the double Freudian postulate according to which there is an irreducible death drive, although neither biological *science*, nor our *belief*, nor our unconscious testifies to our mortality, an essential, necessary, or intrinsic mortality" (A 38 / 74). *Aporias*, like "Speculer — sur 'Freud' " ("To Speculate — on 'Freud' "),[89] seeks to establish a relation — indeed a "virtual debate" (A 79 / 137) — between Heidegger's existential analysis and the "two major concurrent discourses on death in this century, which could be identified by the names or metonymies of Freud and Levinas" (A 38 / 74).

To be sure, all three of these discourses seem to agree that in the analysis of death *sexual difference* does not need to be considered, or as Derrida phrases it: "[S]exual difference does not count in the face of death. Sexual difference would be a being-*up-until*-death" (GD 45 / 49). Their concurrence, Derrida stresses in *Aporias*, is not that of two parallel or opposite articulations of the relation between self and other, God and death. Instead, it is that of the unexpected intersection or even overlapping of radically different forms of analysis, which collapse into each other when pushed to their extreme. Here one might thus be tempted to challenge the very line of demarcation that Heidegger attempts to draw between the existential analytic or fundamental ontology, on the one hand, and psychoanalysis, on the other. Conversely, one would find here an additional confirmation of the central argument of "To Speculate — on 'Freud' " that the differentiation between psychoanalysis and the discipline of philosophy is, perhaps, less secure than Freud's genealogy of his own work suggests. With respect to these two authors, Derrida takes great pains here and elsewhere to show that their texts are, in a secret way, "preoccupied with each other, passing all their time in deciphering each other, in resembling each other."[90] Thus, the introduction of the death drive, of

89. Jacques Derrida, "Spéculer — sur 'Freud,' " trans. Alan Bass as "To Speculate — on 'Freud,' " in *Postcard*, 259–409 / 277–437.

90. Derrida, *Postcard*, 357 / 379. It is not only where the discourse on death is concerned that the central psychoanalytic theorems and the basic tenets of Western transcendental philosophy resemble each other. "Does not everything that Freud ventures on the subject of time in these environs have to be related to the auto-affective structure of time (that which there gives itself to receive is no present-being) such as it is described in Husserl's *Lectures on Internal*

the "immanence of death in life," of its "internal necessity," the ananke,
or constraint, of life, all this, Derrida claims, could easily be translated
into the language of *Being and Time*, of the *Sein zum Tode*. Any skepticism
with respect to the Freudian analysis would therefore leave its reverberations in Heidegger's as well.[91]

> Similarly, it may be enough to distinguish between *demise* [*Ableben*] and
> *dying* [*Sterben*] in order to avoid Levinas's objection to Heidegger regard-
> ing the originary and underivable mineness of dying. When Levinas accuses
> Heidegger of privileging, in the existence of *Dasein*, its proper death, what is
> at stake is *Sterben*. Indeed, it is in dying proper and properly speaking that
> "mineness" is irreplaceable, that no one can die for the other, in the experi-
> ence of the hostage or of the sacrifice, in the sense of "in the place of the
> other," and that no testimony can testify to the contrary. But, conversely,
> when Levinas says and thinks that, against Heidegger, he is saying "the death
> of the other is the first death" and "it is for the death of the other that I am
> responsible, to the point of including myself in death." This may be phrased
> in a more acceptable proposition: "I am responsible for the other insofar as

---

*Time Consciousness* or Heidegger's *Kantbuch?*" Derrida asks (ibid., 359 / 387). Like death, time
is that which *there is*, or *il y a*, with a mode—no longer a modality—whose aporetic features
are analyzed in a work that "Speculer — sur 'Freud' " announces in a note: *Given Time*.

91. Based on Freud's interrogation of the "proper path toward death" in *Beyond the Pleasure Principle*, Derrida formulates some rhetorical questions of relevance to the existential
analytic as well:

> A critical question on the part of the scientist: and if this alleged propriety, more literally,
> this notion of the immanence of death in life, if this familiar domesticity were nothing but
> a consoling belief? And if it were an illusion destined to help us, as the Poet ( ... ) says "to
> bear the burden of existence" ("*um die Schwere des Daseins zu ertragen*")? To make it more
> bearable as *Ananke* than it would be as accident or chance? Let us translate: and if the au-
> thenticity proper to *Dasein* as *Sein zum Tode*: if its *Eigentlichkeit* were but the lure of a prox-
> imity, of a self-presence (*Da*) of the proper, even if in a form which would no longer be that
> of the subject, of consciousness, of the person, of man, of living substance? And if it were
> precisely the *poem*, the poetic itself, this death which is immanent or proper to life? A great
> narrative poem, the only story that one always tells oneself, that one addresses to oneself,
> the poetics of the proper as reconciliation, consolation, serenity? The only "belief" too, or
> rather counter-belief, for this belief is not original? (Derrida, *Postcard*, 363 / 386)

And if Freud suspects here that the structural relation of life to death is based upon a "belief"—which gives the analysis a poetic quality (the poet referred to is Rilke)—then something
similar holds true for Heidegger's existential analysis of being toward death. On Freud's *Beyond
the Pleasure Principle*, see also Samuel Weber, *The Legend of Freud* (Minneapolis: University
of Minnesota Press, 1982), 121ff. On Freud and Derrida, see id., "The Debts of Deconstruction
and Other, Related Assumptions," in *Institution and Interpretation* (Minneapolis: University of
Minnesota Press, 1987), 102–31.

he is mortal,"[92] these statements either designate the experience that I have of the death of the other in demise [*Ableben*] or they presuppose, as Heidegger, does, the co-originarity of *Mitsein* and of *Sein zum Tode*. This co-originarity does not contradict, but, on the contrary, presupposes a mineness of dying [*Sterben*] or of being-toward-death, a mineness not that of an ego or of an egological sameness. (A 38–39 / 74–75)

In addition to these dazzling attempts at fracturing the self-stylized borderlines — lines of demarcation, it should be noted, on which not only Heidegger but also Freud and Levinas themselves insist — Derrida broaches a topic whose centrality is ignored by each of these individual authors (even though it could not have been introduced without them). For at this point, Derrida continues, one should "take into consideration a sort of original mourning, something that . . . neither Heidegger, Freud, nor Levinas does" (A 39 / 75). A little further on in the text, Derrida explains this topicality of mourning and its organizing force within and between the conceptual delimitations that we have discussed so far:

death is ultimately the name of impossible simultaneity and of an impossibility that we know simultaneously, at which we await each other, at the same time, *ama* as one says in Greek: at the same time, simultaneously, we are expecting this anachronism and this contretemps. . . . Taking into consideration the anachronism of the waiting for each other in this contretemps of mourning would certainly change the commonly and hastily assumed premises of the triangular debate that we assigned to Freud, Heidegger, and Levinas: with respect to death, the death of oneself, and the death of the other. (A 65–66 / 117–18)

By way of an addendum to the analysis of mourning provided by *Mémoires: For Paul de Man* and so many other texts, *Aporias* would thus demonstrate that this aporetic experience implies – in fact and in principle — a *secondarization* or even *trivialization* of the question of which comes first: my relation to my own death or my relation to the other's mortality. For if the other — dead, alive, or otherwise, as a guest or a ghost, through analogical apprehension or as a specter — comes to haunt the self *from within,* from the very first moment of its constitution (as an *idem,* as Ricoeur would say) but also in the determination of this self *as other* (as an *ipse*), then the very difference between *jemeinig* and *jeanders* becomes obsolete:

92. The reference is to Levinas's *Dieu, la mort et le temps.*

If *Jemeinigkeit,* that of *Dasein* or that of the ego (in the common sense, the psychoanalytic sense, or Levinas's sense) is constituted in its ipseity in terms of an originary mourning, then this self-relation welcomes or supposes [or, we might add: suffers and supports] the other within its being-itself as different from itself. . . . The relevance of the question of knowing whether it is from one's proper death or from the other's death that the relation to death or the certitude of death is instituted is thus limited from the start. (A 61/111)

In an important interview published in *Points* . . . , Derrida reiterates the conclusion to be drawn from this analysis, namely, that the question of who comes first—my being toward death or the death of the other—is secondary and, in a sense, trivial when measured against the no longer phenomenologizable (impossibly-possible) experience of originary mourning:

Doubtless the death of the other is irreplaceable. I do not die in the place of the other, who does not die in my place. But I can have this experience of "my own death" by relating to myself only in the impossible experience, the experience of the impossible mourning at the death of the other. It is because I "know" that the other is mortal that I try to keep him or her in me, in memory. But from that moment on, he or she is no longer radically other. In the experience of fatal, original, and impossible mourning, I anticipate my own death, I relate to myself as mortal. Even if I am the only one to die, I apprehend this solitude on the basis of this impossible mourning. I do not know if this "logic" is very Heideggerian. It should lead one to say that my being-for-death is always mediated (but that word is not very good: one would have to say immediately mediatizable [*médiatisable*], not only by the spectacle or the perception of the other's death, but in the experience or in the "non-experienceable" structure of impossible mourning. Mourning would be more originary than my being for death.[93]

Derrida's analysis of "originary mourning" could up to a certain point be said to correct and further amplify the phenomenological finding described by Levinas that death, in particular the other's death (*my* death being the other's primary concern), should not be understood in terms of a simple "*end* of the being-in-the-world," as an "annihilation" (*anéantissement*), as seems to be proposed by Heidegger.[94] For Heidegger's interpretation not only inscribes the unknown and the *sans-réponse* of death into

93. Derrida, *Points* . . . , 321–22/332.
94. Levinas, *Dieu, la mort et le temps,* 41.

the question of being and not-being, thus ignoring the extent to which the phenomenon of the end marks "the end of the phenomenon," that is to say, "a movement opposed to phenomenology,"[95] and introducing an enigma. It also fails to explain that and how the certainty of the other's death is more than a case of the *Man stirbt*. Prior to, over and against, our own innermost *Daseinsgewissheit*,[96] the death of the other constitutes or rather provokes the call of conscience (*Ruf des Gewissens*), which is first and foremost that of a *bad conscience,* as Levinas would have it, or a haunting presence of the other in impossible mourning, according to Derrida. In *Being and Time,* by contrast, it is further argued in *Aporias,*

> the existential analysis does not want to know anything about the ghost [*revenant*] or about mourning. Everything that can be said, . . . would certainly stem, in Heidegger's view, from derivative disciplines such as psychology or psychoanalysis, theology or metaphysics. It would concern the figures or the experiences of demise (*Ableben*) rather than death properly speaking. Such would be his fast answer . . . to whoever would be tempted to consider mourning and ghosting [*revenance*], spectrality or living-on, surviving, as non-derivable categories or as non-derivable derivations (non-reducible to the fundamental debate in which . . . Freud, Heidegger, and Levinas make up the three most determinant angles). (A 60–61 / 110–11)

Heidegger's answer to the question of which (or who) comes first, phenomenologically and ontologically speaking, is, Derrida claims, hardly convincing. This does not imply that the existential analytic questioning thereby becomes obsolete. Derrida's claim is far more nuanced and consists of two related observations. It pertains first of all to a different assessment of the peculiar status of Heidegger's—and, perhaps, any philosopher's—work as it transgresses upon the very conceptual and disciplinary boundaries whose very validity it seeks to impose. And while he formulates this conclusion in an almost elliptical manner, its consequences are no less radical: "Whoever tries . . . to draw the necessary consequences (they are incalculably numerous; they are the incalculable itself), would find himself accused of still presupposing the existential analysis of *Dasein* at the very moment when he would, on the contrary, claim to extract its presuppositions or to extract himself from its presupposed axioms. But . . . *the reciprocal axiom would also be necessary"* (A 61 /

95. Ibid., 55.
96. The "Gewiss-sein gegenüber den Tod" is, Heidegger writes, "eine ausgezeichnete *Daseinsgewissheit*" (BT 300–301 / 256).

111–12; emphasis added). It thus becomes clear, secondly, that a simple distinction between the phenomenological and the religious, the ontological
and the theological, the perspective of methodological atheism and that
of faith and testimony, can no longer be upheld. *Aporias* would therefore
seem to corroborate the suspicion, uttered for the first time in "Violence
and Metaphysics," that the two eschatologies discernible in Heidegger
and Levinas are in an unexpected way mutually dependent on each other.
Each of them, Derrida suggests, provides the eschatology of the other.
In Derrida's words, "the question about the Being of the existent [*l'être
de l'étant*] would not only *introduce* — among others — the question about
the existent-God [*l'étant de Dieu*]; it already *would suppose* God as the
very possibility of its question, and as the answer within the question.
God always would be implied in every question about God, and would
precede every 'method.' " [97]

97. Derrida, *Writing and Difference,* 150 / 223; trans. modified. On eschatology in the work
of Heidegger, see also Pöggeler, *Denkweg Martin Heideggers,* 327–31, 334, 337.

# Chapter Five
## The Kenosis of Discourse

𝕏 THE PRECEDING INTERPRETATION of Heidegger's *Being and Time* affects key concepts of the transcendental as that which makes possible, allows, conditions, determines — indeed possibilizes — possibles (whether existential, apophatic, religious, or other). In this chapter I shall try to make this clearer by reexamining Derrida's suggestion, in *Sauf le nom* and elsewhere, that the path of phenomenology parallels the apophatic way — for example, that of the mystic Johann Scheffler, known as Angelus Silesius.

### Angelus Silesius's *Cherubinic Wanderer*

Angelus Silesius's epigrams confront us with a procedure of abstraction that annihilates everything (or almost everything) that would seem to make genuine testimony possible.[1] It is as though the latter were created out of nothing, out of a "possibility" beyond or before all possibility. But the nothing here is not the result of mere negation, privation, absence. If anything, it resembles the rarefaction that we encountered before in St. Paul's phrase ὡς μή. A paradoxical, nondialectical inversion lies at the very root of Silesius's faith, a faith that relates death and God, as in the dictum "Nichts werden ist GOtt werden / Nichts wird was zuvor ist" ("To become Nothing is to become God / Nothing becomes what is before"), which speaks, Derrida notes, not only of a "becoming" that is "birth and change," "formation and transformation," a coming into being ex nihilo, but also of a process that takes place although impossible, that appears possible only *as* impossible, with the consequence that the impossible becomes something more and other than "the simple negative modality of the possible" (SN 43 / 32).[2]

---

1. Scheffler's *Des Angelus Silesius Cherubinischer Wandersmann* thus partakes in the process that Derrida in "Faith and Knowledge" describes in terms of an abstracting delocalization and desertification of thought, but not of thought alone. See the Introduction to this book.

2. See BT 482 / 431, where Heidegger says with reference to Hegel: "Becoming is both arising and passing away" ("Werden ist sowohl Entstehen als Vergehen"). That the nothingness

How can an impossible possibility ever be said to be other — and more — than a merely "negative modality" of the possible or other — and more (or less) — than the very category of "modality," whether in its Kantian critical or Heideggerian fundamental ontological interpretation or, for that matter, in its more recent transformations in modal logic, possible world semantics, and so on and so forth? It can only do so by submitting itself to a double and doubly inclusive reading.

In apophatics, Derrida claims, two forces — "*two powers*" or "*two voices*" (SN 66/76) — are simultaneously at work: in the first place, a "hypercritique" that leaves nothing unquestioned and suspects idolatry and blasphemy in everything (a process of abstraction that affects philosophical, theological, and scientific truth no less than the opinions of common sense); and, in the second place, a hyperbolic affirmation in the form of an imperturbable "monolingualism or soliloquy" that almost "mechanically" reiterates what had been thought and said before — leaving everything as it is in the very movement of its transcendence — and does so in a "tone of dogmatic assurance" (SN 66–67/77). Derrida's *polylogue* stages this double and doubling movement of the apophatic model. On the one hand,

---

of which Angelus Silesius speaks finds its parallel in Heidegger's existential determination of the essence of Dasein becomes clear a little earlier on in BT: "We have conceived death existentially as . . . the possibility of *im*possibility of existence — that is to say, as the utter nullity [*schlechthinnige Nichtigkeit*] of Dasein. Death is not 'added on' to Dasein at its 'end'; but Dasein, as care, is thrown (that is, null [*nichtige*]) basis for its death. The nullity by which Dasein's Being is dominated through and through, is revealed to Dasein itself in authentic Being-towards-death" (BT 354/306). This nothingness (*Nichtigkeit*) should, however, be understood in terms of an originary culpability that, Heidegger claims, differs from its counterpart in Christian theology, and this precisely insofar as the former forms the condition for the latter. But then again, while the two are thus somehow related — one enabling and "correcting" the other — they must also be thought of as completely distinct and, indeed, indifferent to each other. This is the aporia that pervades the very procedure of formal indication, of existential analysis and any ontology that calls itself "fundamental," while continuing to draw on certain indelible features of the ontic:

> The Being-guilty which belongs primordially to Dasein's state of Being must be distinguished from the *status corruptionis* as understood in theology. Theology can find in Being-guilty, as existentially defined, an ontological condition for the factical possibility of such a *status*. The guilt which is included in the idea of this *status*, is a factical indebtedness of an utterly peculiar kind. It has its own attestation [*Bezeugung*], which remains closed off in principle from any philosophical experience. The existential analysis of Being-guilty proves nothing either *for* or *against* the possibility of sin. Taken strictly, it cannot even be said that the ontology of Dasein *of itself* leaves this possibility open; for this ontology, as a philosophical inquiry, "knows" in principle nothing about sin. (BT 496 n. ii/306 n. 1)

... this theology launches or carries negativity as the principle of auto-destruction in the heart of each thesis; in any case the theology suspends every thesis, all belief, all *doxa* ...

— In which its *epokhē* has some affinity with the *skepsis* of scepticism as well as with the phenomenological reduction. . . . transcendental phenomenology, as it passes through the suspension of all *doxa,* of every positing of existence, of every thesis, inhabits the same element as negative theology. One would be a good propaedeutic for the other. (SN 67/77–78)

On the other hand, however, this movement of eradication and conversion through which negative theology signals its leave-taking (or *adieu*) is already a postscript, a reaffirmation, reiteration, or countersignature (or *à dieu*):

nothing is more faithful than this hyperbole to the originary ontotheological injunction. . . . In the most apophatic moment, when one says: "God is not," "God is neither this nor that, neither that nor its contrary" or "being is not," etc.; even then it is still a matter of saying the entity [*étant*] such as it is, in its truth, even were it meta-metaphysical, meta-ontological.[3]

In this sense, the apophatic mode still somehow holds the "promise of saying the truth" of the tradition it comes to subvert. And since the line of demarcation between the tradition and its subversion thus becomes porous, no text could from this moment on be said strictly to belong to *either* negative theology *or* metaphysics or ontotheology. The very unity, indivisibility and self-identity of tradition, of its continuation and discontinuation, as a consequence turns out to be highly questionable. It would be difficult to reduce the text of Angelus Silesius to the tradition of the *via negativa* to which — by definition — no text belongs "pure and simple." And, conversely, Derrida surmises, there will be

no text that is not in some way contaminated with negative theology, and even among those texts that apparently do not have, want, or believe they have any relation with theology in general. Negative theology is everywhere, but it is never by itself. In that way it also belongs, without fulfilling, to the space of the philosophical or onto-theological promise that it seems to break [*renier*]: to record . . . the referential transcendence of language; to say God such as he is, beyond [*par delà*] his images, beyond this idol that being can still be. (SN 69/81)

3. SN 68/80; see also 67–68/78–79.

One way of describing this paradox of a belonging without belonging, strictly speaking, of a repetition in the very moment of rupture (or vice versa), of faithfulness in the hour of infidelity (or vice versa), of integrity in the very act of betrayal (or vice versa) would be to say that this negative theology loosens its relation to a dogmatic content or horizon by which it remains nonetheless highly overdetermined, because the latter continues to accompany it as its inescapable shadow, for good and for ill, as the source of its bad or good conscience. This is not to deny, Derrida goes on to say, that

> in what one *could believe* to be the interior of a history of Christianity . . . the apophatic design is also anxious to render itself independent of revelation, of all the literal language of New Testament eventness [*événementialité*], of the coming of Christ, of the Passion, of the dogma of the Trinity, etc. An immediate but intuitionless mysticism, a sort of abstract *kenōsis,* frees this language from all authority, all narrative, all dogma, all belief—and at the limit of all faith. At the limit, this mysticism remains, after the fact [*après coup*], independent of all history of Christianity, *absolutely* independent, detached even, perhaps absolved, from the idea of sin, freed even, perhaps redeemed, from the idea of redemption. Whence the courage and the dissidence, potential or actual, of these masters (think of Eckhart), whence the persecution they suffered at times, whence their passion, whence this scent of heresy, these trials, this subversive marginality of the apophatic current in the history of theology and of the Church. (SN 71 / 85–86)

And yet, conversely, its heresy—in Derrida's words, yet another "*pharma-kos* to be excluded or to be sacrificed"—could at the same time be read as the ultimate or most consequent keeping of the promise of the confession that it seems to dismantle, or to which it had seemed at best indifferent. Thus, while, on the one hand, the mystic heresy challenges every tradition with an almost antinomian and iconoclastic zeal, it is, on the other hand, also true that—again, in the example of Angelus Silesius—"the dissident uprooting, *responding* thus to the call and to the gift of Christ . . . can claim to fulfill, in its most historic sense, the vocation and the promise of Christianity" (SN 72 / 85–87; trans. modified).

This is the aporia that characterizes the structure of every decision (whether ethico-political or conceptual) and for which apophatics may well serve as the example par excellence. And one might wonder, once again, what it is that makes this analogy possible or plausible in the first place. Even though "everything" remains "intact" after it has passed through the operation of the apophatic kenosis, its abstractions and for-malizations, a minimal — imperceptible, inaudible — difference will have been made. Why this must be so can be understood when it is recalled that the mystic reiteration of central religious motifs and theologemes does not so much announce itself *within* a given or future hermeneutic horizon that would determine its constative or performative truth or fe-licity, but, as Michel de Certeau has shown in his groundbreaking work *The Mystic Fable,* first of all *with* it.

The theological tropes under consideration cannot be reconstructed in terms of the redeployment of a semantic or metaphorical *potential* that had been deemed obsolete. Nor does the citation and re-citation of these religious figures reproduce a new dogmatic content as it puts old meanings into a radically new perspective. Neither a continuation nor a rupture — or, rather, both at once — the *via negativa* and *eminentiae* obey a different logic. Nonetheless, there is something here (again, some thing, *la Chose, das Ding,* to cite Lacan citing Heidegger and cited by Derrida in turn) that is repeated and changed, and that, in the process, invisibly alters the intellectual and sociocultural landscape. The marks left by this process are as many singular instances that from here on *open up the pos-sibility of future events and decisions,* albeit not so much as the *condition* of their *possibility,* but in a way that must be thought — or, rather, at-tested to — completely otherwise. In their very singularity, these markers (or dates, as Derrida has it, following Paul Celan), *trigger* — and *lose them-selves in* — a process of formalization, generalization, and abstraction, that conjures up the transcendental, its very illusion (as Kant knew), but also the necessary idealizations of speech and thought. Tradition, it would seem, is based on this mechanism of a generalized singularism, as a con-sequence of which it can no longer be seen as one, as indivisible, and as identical with itself. This, nothing else, is meant by the "generous repeti-tion" of tradition: in the repetition of the same, it inspires and gives way to the other. Paradoxically, apophatics would be the most telling example of this sameness in the Western tradition's very "self-difference."[4]

It is the non-coincidence of any tradition with itself (whether that tradition be philosophical, theological, apophatic, or other), as well as the circumstance that it thus ipso facto "passes over the other edge of

---

4. See SN 71/85: "[I]t is the idea itself of an identity or a self-interiority of every tradi-tion (*the one* metaphysics, *the one* onto-theology, *the one* phenomenology, *the one* Christian revelation, *the one* history itself, *the one* history of being, *the one* epoch, *the one* tradition, self-identity in general, the one, etc.) that finds itself contested at its root."

itself," that makes singularities and idiosyncrasies "translatable": "What makes philosophy go outside itself calls for a community that overflows its tongue and broaches a process of universalization" (SN 70/84).

Such a rereading of the heritage of religion and of theology, whether negative and mystic or affirmative and dogmatic, might be said to consist of a process of *generalization*, or even virtual *universalization*, of the structure of its address that simultaneously intensifies and trivializes its intent or meaning. And yet, while it is impossible to decide between these apparent alternatives — intensification and trivialization — on the basis of theoretical or philosophical arguments, the very distinction between these two is in the end all that matters ethically, politically, and religiously.

Thus, Derrida suggests, when Angelus Silesius writes that "GOttes Eigenschafft" ("God's characteristic") is "sich ins Geschöpff ergiessen / Allzeit derselbe seyn, nichts haben, wollen, wissen" ("to pour forth in creation, / To be always the same, to have, want, know nothing"), this may well signal that, far from resting on a "creationist dogma," creation is to be understood as "expropriating production," and that, indeed, "wherever there is expropriation there is creation" (SN 73/90; trans. modified). In other words, this formalization and virtual universalization of the concept of "creation," its pertinence *everywhere* where a certain gift and thereby an "expropriating production" come to pass — that is to say, *almost everywhere* — would tell us something about the structure of experience in general and of ethics and politics in particular. Derrida continues:

> What if that were only a redefinition of the current concept of creation? Once more, one should say of no matter what or no matter whom what one says of God or some other thing. The thought of whomever concerning whomever or whatever, *it doesn't matter* ["Pensée du quiconque au sujet de quiconque ou du quelconque, *n'importe*"]. One would respond thus in the same way to the question "Who am I?" "Who are you?" "What is the other?" "What is anybody or anything as other?" "What is the being of beings [*l'être de l'étant*] as completely other?" All the examples are good ones, even if they all show that they are singularly though unequally good. The "no matter" of the "no matter whom" or of the "no matter what" would open the way to a sort of serene impassibility, to a very shrill insensibility . . . capable of being stirred by everything, precisely because of this element of indifference that opens onto no matter what difference. (SN 73/90; trans. modified)

For Derrida, this apparent indifference that makes all the difference in the world, by being the very access to it (to the world and any ontic difference in it), reminds one of the tradition of *Gelâzenheit* (or *Gelassenheit*) that, from Eckhart up to Heidegger evokes a dis-position that "lets go without abandoning" or, more precisely still, "abandons without forgetting or forgets without forgetting" (ibid.). This aporetic experience of a forgetting without forgetting enables the substitution of one concept for another. It explains how it is that one motif (whether philosophical or theological, ontological or ontic) gives way to another and gives itself away to that other. Is this how the ontological and the ontic come to intersect? Is this how the transcendental—far from becoming irrelevant or obsolete—*makes a pass* at the empirical and solicits it by traversing it? Is this the movement that reinscribes its transcendence—its *transcendere* in Heidegger's rather than Kant's sense—in the realm of presence, of the *ens realissimum* (which is for Heidegger the realm of *Vorhandenheit*), but also of the empirical, the historical? Messianicity or revealability, in Derrida's view, neither creates nor generates the empirical or historical instances it calls forth or allows to come into being (without, therefore, *making them possible*). Conversely, the concrete positive revelations or messianisms are not so much instantiations of a pregiven and stable "structure of openness," since the latter has no existence "outside," "before," or "without" them. Perhaps it has a future "beyond" them, which becomes clear if one discerns the similarity in structure, if not content, between messianicity and hospitality, between the messianic (or the Messiah) and the futurity called the *absolut arrivant*, whose privileged examples are the guest, the foreigner, the immigrant, the contemporary successors, as it were, of the biblical figures of the widow, the orphan, the hungry, whom Levinas invokes on so many occasions.

Hospitality might well be the contemporary successor of messianism.[5] But even if modern states are based on the principle of hospitality, as is argued in Kant's *Zum ewigen Frieden* (*Perpetual Peace* [1795]), the specter of the messianic is not so far off and comes to uproot or disturb the purported predictability of the historical process. Derrida suggests as much when he says the following about the "*messianic*, or messianicity without messianism":

> This would be the opening to the future or to the coming of the other *as* the advent of justice, but without horizon of expectation and without prophetic prefiguration. The coming of the other can only emerge as a singular event

5. See Derrida, *Specters of Marx*, 65/111. On the "phrase messianique," see id., *Politics of Friendship*, 37/55ff. and 173/197.

> when no anticipation *sees it coming,* when the other and death—and radical
> evil—can come as a surprise at any moment. Possibilities that both open and
> can always interrupt history, or at least the *ordinary* course of history. (FK 17 /
> 27)

In a sense, Derrida continues, this may well assume the "apparently passive" features of a decision that is ultimately taken by the other. The
messianic is the *"decision of the other"* (ibid.) and thereby, in a sense, the
very structure of any decision. This circumstance, Derrida emphasizes, by
no means lessens but, on the contrary, deepens or intensifies *my* responsibility. And behind the haunting specter of the other there looms yet
another. This other specter of the other, the specter of another other, is
the one that makes us "work for our salvation in *fear and trembling,"* as
St. Paul, Kierkegaard, Heidegger, and Derrida all suggest: "The messianic
exposes itself to the absolute surprise and, even if it always takes the phenomenal form of peace or of justice, it ought, exposing itself so abstractly,
be prepared (waiting without awaiting itself) for the best as for the worst,
the one never coming without opening the possibility of the other" (FK
17–18 / 28). We are dealing here with the "general structure of experience"
(ibid.), whether past, present, or to come. But why would the messianic
or, for the matter, the apophatic, be the best analogy, indeed, the example
par excellence, of this "structure"? Is this a resemblance or exemplarity
that is based on merely formal similarities, on a semantic potential, albeit
emptied almost beyond recognition, on the mere historical weight of certain discourse practices that continue to inform—and form themselves
in—the most abstract of our concepts?

   The search and desire for the appropriate speech with respect to God
is a quest for the proper that consists in "expropriating itself" and in
"having nothing of its own [*en propre*]" (SN 69 / 82).Angelus Silesius's
distich on "GOttes Eigenschafft" urges us to understand this *accidencia-
liter,* that is to say, as saying that God has no *contingent* properties and has
or wants or knows everything that he has or wants or knows essentially,
in its essence, as well as in an essential fashion. But this essential property—a property beyond property properly speaking—remains forever
beyond human grasp. For Angelus Silesius as well as for the many others
whose "heir" and "post-scriptor" he is—Derrida mentions Christoph
Köler, Johannes Tauler, Jan van Ruysbroeck, Jakob Böhme, and "above
all Eckhart"—God remains an unknown, unacknowledged and unrecognized God:

*Der unerkannte GOtt.*
Was GOtt ist weiss man nicht: Er ist nicht
Licht, nicht Geist,
Nicht Wonnigkeit, nicht Eins
Nicht Weissheit, nicht Verstand, nicht Liebe, Wille, Güte:
Kein Ding, kein Unding auch, kein Wesen, kein Gemüthe:
Er ist was ich, und du, und keine Creatur,
Eh wir geworden sind was Er ist, nie erfuhr.

*The Unrecognized God*
What God is one knows not: He is not light, not spirit,
Not delight, not one, not what is called divinity:
Not wisdom, not intellect, not love, will, goodness:
No thing, no no-thing either, no essence, no concern:
He is what I, or you, or any other creature,
Before we became what He is, have never come to know. (SN 52 / 49–50;
    trans. modified)

There is nothing but the name, save the name, *sauf le nom,* as the surviving instance, in Derrida's words, "the survivance of an internal onto-logico-semantic auto-destruction" (SN 55 / 55), an instance saved, but also one that must and ought still be saved, if not for always, then at least for the time being, that is to say in the historical and political constellation in which we happen to find ourselves, and that is marked by a return of religion, by an almost mechanical production and repetition of religion, as is suggested by "Faith and Knowledge."

The word *survivance* hints at a "more than life and more than death," a "living-on" that is the effect, the remainder of an immemorial and perennial erasure of the differential, no less than semantic, signifyingness of language and hence signals its transfiguration into mystic speech. Neither the phenomena as such, nor the phenomenon of the (phenomenological) *as such,* can be saved, as a long essentialist and foundationalist tradition (long before and well into phenomenology) would have it. Nor is what is saved merely their names, as certain nominalist positions would insist. What is saved is *the* name—*le nom*—the named, which again is not named *as such,* but for which "death" and "God" are the best names, *so far* and for some time to come.

Reiterating an insight from "Des tours de Babel," where, in a reading of the biblical story of Genesis, the dissemination of names—and thereby the deconstruction of the imposition of one particular idiom—is attributed first of all to a divine anger,[6] *Sauf le nom* leaves no doubt that " 'God' 'is' the name of this bottomless collapse, of this endless *desertification* of language" (SN 55–56 / 56; emphasis added). Consequently, "God" is a name that no longer names *anyone* or *anything*. "God" is neither a proper (Christian) name, for example, that of a divine person (or three in one, as in Holy Trinity) nor merely a common noun, for instance, the designation of an abstract entity, albeit the most elevated of all beings, the divinity (*to theion, GOttheit*). Rather, Derrida writes, "the singularity of the unknown God overflows the essence and the divinity, thwarts the oppositions of the negative and the positive, of being and nothingness, of thing and nonthing, and thus transcends all the theological attributes" (SN 52 / 49). What is more, it escapes all nontheological attribution too. Yet as the erasable—indeed, always already erased—trace of a "negative operation," this notion—just like the hyper- or virtual or spectral reality for which it stands—"inscribes itself *in* and *on* and *as* the *event* [*l'événement*]" (SN 56 / 56), whether that of a particular language or that of language and of experience in its generality or as such. And since an indelible singularity is inscribed at the heart of the as such, the latter is no longer itself. Paradoxically, the as such is no longer thinkable or experienceable as such.

The very mode of the "negative operation," as it inscribes itself *in* or *on* the face of things, calls for a reconsideration of the concept of place and all of its ramifications, that is to say, of the *topos*, of *topoi*, of the Platonic *chōra* as well as of the Heideggerian interpretation of *Ort* and *Erörterung*, of space-time and architecture, of the desert no less than of cyberspace, of the *oikos*, the home, the tomb or the crypt, but also the redrawing of borderlines in contemporary geopolitics. The oblique reference to the place (*le lieu*)—the *corpus*, the desert—should be distinguished from all attempts to delineate this space in terms of a horizon, a dimension, a receptacle, in short, a matrix. For the mere "there is" (*il y a*) of the inscription or the remainder is intractable to any attempt to determine its exact location with the help of a system of coordinates (a map, a radar, a scanner). Intractable, God's omnipresence is *utopian*. Never really there, God's existence and essence or hyper-essence even—or, rather, first of all—escapes the turning toward the place that characterizes Heidegger's later thought. Both Heidegger and Angelus Silesius would seem to

6. Jacques Derrida, "Des tours de Babel," in *Psyché*, 203–35, trans. in *Difference in Translation*, ed. Joseph F. Graham (Ithaca, N.Y.: Cornell University Press, 1985), 165–248.

be caught in a discourse of the possible, in a certain *possibilism,* even though they evoke or thematize the possible in radically different ways. Elucidating or displacing and dislocating the stakes of thought *that*—or *there,* in this merely possible world, this realm of possibles—is no longer the issue.

After Heidegger, topologizing Being and beings could no longer mean fixing or grounding thought in its conditions of possibility—thereby letting the possibility of conditions or, for that matter, the conditioning of our thought in possibles go unquestioned—but, rather, grafting them onto what exceeds every condition, every possible, and all of their combinations. And here Angelus Silesius may well be one step ahead of Heidegger and venture into new territory, unknown to fundamental ontology and a certain limited interpretation of deconstruction alike:

> There is [*Il y a*] this event, which remains, even if this remnance is not more substantial, more essential than this God, more ontologically determinable than this name of God of whom it is said that he names nothing that is, neither this nor that. It is even said of him that he is not what is *given there* in the sense of the *es gibt:* He is not what gives, his is beyond all gifts (*GOtt über alle Gaben*). (SN 56 / 56–57)

A little later in the text, Derrida notes that a similar motif can also be found in Plotinus: "God 'therefore has no longer anything' and, if he gives, as the Good of Plotinus (*Enneads,* 6, 7–15–16–17), it is also what he does not have, insofar as he is not only beyond being but also beyond his gifts (*kai tou didomenou to didon epekeina ēn*)" (SN 70 / 83–84). For Silesius, God is more and other than whatever gift, more and other than the gift of Being, and yet, somehow, God has to be thought as the one who gives this all, while giving Himself in giving Himself away. By underscoring this remarkable observation, Derrida not only replaces Heidegger's notion of the gift but also, rearticulates the premises of his very own thinking revolving around this notion, as undertaken in *Glas* and all the way up to *Given Time* and *The Gift of Death.*

It is at this point, I would argue, that one must reopen the debate between Derrida's and Jean-Luc Marion's seemingly diverging rereadings and reaffirmations of the apophatic tradition. Not unlike Marion, Derrida seems to discern in the very notion of gift (*le don*) the possibility or even the conceptual necessity of its abandonment (*l'abandon*), that is, of its giving itself up, of its giving itself away. Both Marion and Derrida locate in this movement a transition to a positive infinity, whether as embodiment, incarnation and inscription, or otherwise. In its Christian and Levinasian sense, this theological trope is well described in *The Gift of Death* apropos of Patočka's heretical genealogy of European responsibility:

> On what condition does goodness exist beyond all calculation? On the condition that goodness forgets itself, that the movement be a movement of the gift that renounces itself, hence a movement of infinite love. Only infinite love can renounce itself and, in order to *become finite,* become incarnated in order to love the other, to love the other as a finite other. This gift of infinite love comes from someone and is addressed to someone; responsibility demands irreplaceable singularity. Yet only death or rather the apprehension of death can give this irreplaceability, and it is only on the basis of it that one can speak of a responsible subject. (GD 50–51/54)

And yet, for Derrida, the meaning of abandonment has to remain suspended between this notion of "God's love for the world" and ultimate despair. In other words, the first possibility is, if not counterbalanced, then at least continually haunted by the possibility of its impossibility, that is to say, by *la pire violence:* in Christian terminology, by the crucifixion and death of God's Son, which is not followed up by a resurrection, or by a speculative Good Friday, which does not (as Hegel would have it) turn itself for dialectical reasons into Easter, into the subsequent proliferation of the spirit, and, finally by a second parousia that is known and sublated in absolute knowledge. This latter position is, of course, precisely the one Marion intends to undercut. To be sure, his phenomenological description of the emblematic figure of the reenactment of the crossing out of God is everything but a sample of speculative dialectics. Yet the presupposition of a nonspeculative, given completion remains. It is at this juncture that Derrida, like Levinas, pushes the hollowness of discourse — the biblical kenosis that is taken to resemble or even to anticipate phenomenological reduction — at least one step further. The debate between Derrida and Levinas, on the one hand, and Marion, on the other, thus indistinguishably comes down to a disagreement about the phenomenological theorems and themes of reduction and donation in their relation to the ontological difference. But, it is no less a conflict of interpretation concerning kenosis.[7] This figure finds a parallel in the notion of *Gelassenheit,* which plays an important role in the tradition in which

---

7. For the discussion between Levinas and Marion, see the preface to the second edition of the former's *De l'existence à l'existant* (Paris: J. Vrin, 1978).

Angelus Silesius inscribes himself, and that, Derrida notes, runs from Meister Eckhart to "at least" [sic] Heidegger: "It is necessary to leave all, to leave every 'something' through love of God, and no doubt to leave God himself, to abandon him, that is to say, at once to leave him and . . . let him (be beyond being-some-thing)."

> Das etwas muß man lassen.
> Mensch so du etwas liebt, so liebstu nichts fürwahr:
> GOtt is nicht diß und dass, drumb laß das Etwas gar.
>
> One must leave the something.
> Man, if you love something, then you love nothing truly:
> God is not this and that, leave then forever something. (SN 78–79 / 100–101)

Derrida notes that there remains the question of what gives rise and place to the play, or *Spiel*, that Silesius ascribes to the process of divine creation ("Gott spielt mit dem Geschöpffe"). The enigma lies in the elusiveness of this unlocalizable place, as well as of the aporia that it signals — namely, that one is *not yet there and cannot get there*, where a decision may come to pass; but also that this circumstance is precisely the condition — or, rather, the *in-condition* — on the basis of which responsibility is both possible and impossible (that is to say, never lived up to completely). Not to reach it is to "reach" it, but not to reach it as such, in full rigor, or with good conscience. And it is here alone that, in a sense, the other — the Other, God, but also, on Derrida's reading, the other that I can be for myself — could be said to speak as illustrated by another of Silesius's couplets: "Geh hin, wo du nicht kannst: sih, wo du sihest nicht: / Hör wo nichts schallt und klingt, so bestu wo Gott spricht" ("Go where you cannot: see where you see naught: / Hear where nothing sounds and rings, and be thus where God speaks"). Derrida comments:

> [The] adverb of place [*wo*] says the place (*wo*) of the word [*verbe*] of God, of God as word, and "*Der Ort ist dass Wort*' (1:205) indeed affirms the place as word [*parole*] of God.
> — Is this place created by God? Is it part of the play? Or else is it God himself? Or even what precedes, in order to make them possible, both God and his Play? In other words, it remains to be known if this nonsensible (invisible and inaudible) place is opened by God, by the name of God (which would again be some other thing, perhaps), or if it is "older" than the time of creation, than time itself, than history, narrative, word, etc. It remains to be known (beyond knowing) if the place is opened by appeal (response, the

event that calls for the response, revelation, history, etc.), or if it remains im-
passibly foreign, like *Khōra,* to everything that takes its place and replaces
itself and plays within this place, including what is named God. . . .
    — Do we have any choice? Why choose between the two? Is it possible? But
it is true that these two "places," these two experiences of place, these two
ways are no doubt of an absolute heterogeneity. One excludes the other, one
(sur)passes the other, one does without the other, one is, absolutely, *without*
the other. But what still relates them to each other is this strange preposition,
this strange with-without or without-with, *without* [English in original]. (SN
75–76/93–95)

There is thus, Derrida asserts, a "singular chance in the transfer or the
translation of that of which negative theology would be a sort of *analogon*
or general equivalent, in the translatability uprooting but also returning
this *analogon* to its Greek or Christian economy" (SN 81/104–5). This
singular chance is that of an aleatory singularity that does not belong to
the category of the subjective, but without therefore "losing itself in the
community." This chance of signaling a singular belonging does not let
itself be captured by the concepts of the human and the divine, which
always tend to obey an "anthropotheocentric" order, and from which
even Heidegger's *Geviert* does not escape, since it condemns to oblivion
that mortal (living) being called the animal.

## Save . . . the Name

    After having pointed out that the desert is a recurrent figure in Ange-
lus Silesius's *Cherubinic Wanderer,* after having discussed how this exemplary "paradoxical figure of the *aporia*" signals a discursive strategy of
desertification that brings language into a crisis affecting much more than
its constative or denotative aspects alone, Derrida's *polylogue* goes on to
elucidate what it is, if anything, that can be said to *remain* after all is said
and done:

    — Despite this desert, then, what we call negative theology grows and cul-
    tivates itself as a memory, an institution, a history, a discipline. It is a culture,
    with its archives and its tradition, and accumulates the *acts* of a tongue. . . .
    However much one recalls . . . that negative theology "consists," through its
    claim to depart from all consistency, in a language that does not cease testing
    the very limits of language, and exemplarily those of propositional, theoreti-
    cal, or constative language . . .
    — By that, negative theology would be not only a language and a testing

of language, but above all the most thinking, the most exacting, the most intractable experience of the "essence" of language: a discourse on language, a "monologue" (in the heterological sense that Novalis or Heidegger gives to this word) in which language and tongue speak for themselves and record [*prennent acte de*] that *die Sprache spricht*. Whence this poetic or fictional dimension, at times ironic, always allegorical, about which some would say that it is only a form, an appearance, or a simulacrum . . . It is true that, simultaneously, this arid fictionality tends to denounce images, figures, idols, rhetoric. An iconoclastic fiction must be thought. (SN 54 / 53–54)

In fact, the very opening pages of *Sauf le nom* recall Leibniz's judgment, cited by Heidegger in *Der Satz vom Grund* (*The Principle of Reason*), according to which Angelus Silesius's epigrams are full of "difficult metaphors . . . inclining almost to Godlessness [*beinahe zur Gottlosigkeit hinneigend*]" (SN 36, 49 / 16, 44).[8] Yet, for all its destruction of constative language, of the proposition, of semantics, of the word even, the *via negativa* must in its very excess or surplus also succeed in somehow or somewhere making its point, if any point (or *one* point) there is. In order to make itself known or to make any difference at all, it must somehow and somewhere leave its mark. As Derrida notes, "by testifying it *remains*" (SN 54 / 54).

Everything, then, comes down to understanding what this remaining might mean. Derrida raises this issue by asking, "Is it a modality of 'being'?" (SN 55 / 54), leaving hardly any doubt that the answer to this question must be negative. Is it a *possibility* of Being? Or is it, rather, the mere, that is to say, never fully actualized, virtual, and thus nonactualizable "possibility" of the impossibility, of the impossibility of Being — or of our being — to somehow and somewhere persist in this very being? Does the apophatics or, for that matter, that *of* which and *from* which it speaks — that from which it speaks *away* or *in vain*, in *speaking-without-speaking*, or even downright blasphemously — take place in the realm of Being? Does negative theology and the subject or object around which it revolves and to which it testifies claim or need to be? As a consequence, can negative theology itself be seen as "something (determinable) and not nothing," or as a theology that "wants to be or become something rather than nothing"? (SN 55 / 55).

Derrida gives no clear answers to these questions and the chosen form

8. See Martin Heidegger, *Der Satz vom Grund* (Pfullingen: Neske, 1957), 68; trans. Reginald Lilli as *The Principle of Reason* (Bloomington: Indiana University Press, 1992), 35.

of the dia- or polylogue permits him not take sides here (or to be on both
sides at once). In other words, the aporetics that is studied, practiced,
and perhaps even cultivated here allows and forces him to have it both
ways. On the one hand, this discourse aspires to say nothing, nothing that
is inappropriate with respect to God or the Beyond-Godhead, that is to
say, everything that belongs to the order of the created, of the finite, as
well as of the infinity of (His) Being. On the other hand, this "transascen-
dance" or "transdescendance" of discourse (to quote Jean Wahl's *Traité de
métaphysique* (Treatise on Metaphysics), cited by Levinas at the outset of
*Totality and Infinity* and elsewhere), that is to say, this movement beyond
or on this side of discourse, if one can say so, itself somehow and somewhere signals, attests, and "imprints" itself in the "body" or the "corpus"
of a language:

> —Some trace remains right in this corpus, becomes this corpus as *sur-
> vivance* of apophasis (more than life and more than death), survivance of an
> internal onto-logico-semantic auto-destruction: there will have been abso-
> lute rarefaction, the desert will have taken place, nothing will have taken place
> but this place. Certainly, the "unknowable God" . . . says nothing: of him
> there is nothing said that might hold . . .
> —Save his name [*Sauf son nom;* "Safe, his name"] . . .
> —Save the name that names nothing that might hold, not even a divinity
> (*Gottheit*), nothing whose withdrawal [*dérobement*] does not carry away every
> phrase that tries to measure itself against him. "God" "is" the name of this
> bottomless collapse, of this endless desertification of language. But the trace
> of this negative operation is inscribed *in* and *on* and *as* the *event* (what *comes*,
> what there is and which is always singular, what finds in this kenōsis the most
> decisive condition of its coming or its upsurging). (SN 55–56 / 55–56)

Since one might well wonder as to whether the *askesis* or kenosis of
this discourse makes a halt before the integrity of the name—whether as
a common, proper, or even divine and holy name, for example, the unpronounceable Tetragrammaton—the name that is saved is both less and
more than an empty signifier. The name that is saved collapses into this
one word—*sauf, safe*—that is here not so much ascribed or attributed to
God as paratactically aligned or juxtaposed to "his name," separated from
it by the interval or interspace of an invisible colon or comma, as if Derrida were writing, with an readable-unreadable pause, *Sauf* (pause) *son
nom.* In the end, therefore, the very title *Sauf le nom* would seem to take
on the very meaning of a simple yet breathtaking *Sauf . . . le nom.*

This, then, could be the historical and interpretative background for the fact that this single retained (or saved) name—*sauf*—is one of the important elements of the in principle provisional series that Derrida addresses at greater length in "Faith and Knowledge," and that includes, as we have seen, the tropes of the *indemnis,* the *sacred,* the *holy,* the *intact,* but also the *immunity* and the so-called *auto-immunization,* all of which, Derrida suggests, come closest to the heart of *religio. Sauf* opens or enters or, for the time being, closes, the whole series of names and figures that evoke one of the sources of any religion that would want to manifest itself within the limits of a reason that defines itself in a more or less abstract, formal or perhaps even formal indicative way.

How, then, does this apophatic motif relate to the second source of religion that can be found in the realm of history. In other words, how does the motif of the *sauf* make its way into the realm of the empirical, the political, and ethical life (e.g., *Sittlichkeit*), to be distinguished from the realm of pure morality and, indeed, pure prayer?

THE *via negativa* SIGNALS "perhaps today," Derrida remarks with a double precaution—perhaps and, if so, only today—the transition and the "passage" of all "idiom" into "the most common desert"; as such, its singular structure describes and calls forth "the chance of law [*droit*]," as well as, Derrida writes with reference to Kant, the chance of "another treaty of universal peace (beyond what is today called international law, that thing very positive but still so tributary of the European concept of the State and of law, then so easy to arraign [*arraisonner*] for particular States)" (SN 81/105).

This is not to say that there would be such a thing as a "politics" or a "law" of the *via negativa,* pure and simple. No ethico-political maxims or imperatives can be deduced from this chance of theology, from the chance of this theology, from the theology of this chance. But, Derrida notes, there would be no politics, law, or morals without the seemingly aleatory path of the apophatic, that is to say, "*without* this possibility, the very possibility that obliges us from now on to place these words [*politics, law, morals*] between quotation marks" (SN 81/106).

Here, again, as in Heidegger, the possible seems to take the lead, albeit now in a decisively different way, if only because this possibility, as it is said, "obliges," begins by obliging, and therefore does something more and other than simply forming the opening, the condition, the horizon, or the dimension of every possible decision (and this regardless of whether this decision is taken responsibly, irresponsibly, or not at all). Here, the possible is neither ontologized nor attains the qualities of virtually fixed pre- or pro-reality (be it under the name of "areality," to use a term introduced by Jean-Luc Nancy in "Of Divine Places"). Still we may ask: can a possibility, of whatever modality—or even, if possible, beyond the implications of any ontological possibilism—ever "oblige"? Can a possibility, however defined, ever solicit, enable, or convey an obligation of sorts? Does obligation belong to the order of the possible?

It is striking that in this particular context, Derrida charts the singular possibility by invoking first of all a notion of *democracy* rather than by giving, say, a formal—or formally indicative—analysis of the testimonial structure of the messianic or, for that matter, the eschatological (as was the case in the early Heidegger). The idea of democracy discussed in *Sauf le nom* is not limited to the purely formal-representational features that function as a model in modern liberal states, and Derrida's idea does not regulate itself fully after the Kantian (or, for that matter, formally pragmatic) postulation of an infinite approximation. Instead, the idea of democracy is seen as that which at every instant and in each single instance remains an always yet "to-come" (*à venir*). As that which at every given point in time is always yet another step ahead and can never be anticipated as such, it never reaches a full plenitude or presence (to itself) but attains instead the elusive yet no less urgent quality of infinite, albeit also infinitely finite, future (*avenir*).

Now, it is this paradoxical notion of a never-present, irrepresentable, "democracy as promise," of a democracy, Derrida writes, that is no more defined "than the apophatic defines God," whose "path passes perhaps today in the world through (across) the aporias of negative theology" (SN 83/108–9). Not that we should immediately resort here to a new political theology, whether in its Schmittian or its Benjaminian form, but the theological, apophatic language enables and reinforces a necessary rearticulation of the premises, the axioms or postulates, as well as the figures or topoi of the political, that is, of any future politics worthy of the name. At the same time, this notion is just as much "threatened" as it is "promised" by the apophatics, by the with and without of its redoubling and opening up of traditions, by the interplay of its formalization and universalization, on the one hand, and of singularization and idiomaticity, on the other.

For this the figure of Babel is, according to Derrida, at once the best and the worst or, at least, both relevant and an inadequate example:

—To let passage to the other, to the totally other, is hospitality. A double
hospitality: the one that has the form of Babel (the construction of the Tower,
the appeal to universal translation but also the violent imposition of the
name, of the tongue, and of the idiom) *and* the one (another, the same) of the
*deconstruction* of the Tower of Babel. The two designs are moved by a certain
desire of universal community, beyond the desert of an arid formalization,
that is, beyond economy itself. (SN 80 / 102-3)

Linked to the history of Babel, to all the Babels of history, and to history as an infinitely repeated and diffused event of Babel, the apophatic
way responds to two contradictory—yet mutually dependent—imperatives: the paradoxical desire to construct *and* deconstruct a shared idiom
in the name of some universalism, of genuine universalism, and ultimately of that which lies well beyond the opposition of the particular and
the general upon which the very concept of the universal remains premised.[9] The Babelian and anti-Babelian scene thus accompanies, enables,
and exemplifies the path of deconstruction. In a way, the very concept and
practice of deconstruction are announced by the biblical story that it illuminates—and announces?—in turn. For just as a structural resemblance
between religion and deconstruction imposes itself, the latter's call for a
democracy "to-come" both mimics and prefigures the formal features of
a *religion to come.* This co-implication is a necessity, a fatality, and risk,
but a chance as well.

The desire for a "universal tongue" to undo the dissemination of
names resulting from the divine deconstruction of the aspiration to construe one language, based on the hegemony of a single idiom, moves back
and forth "between formalism, or the poorest, most arid, in effect the
most desertlike techno-scientificity, and a sort of universal hive of invio-
lable secrets, of idioms that are never translated except as untranslatable
seals. In this oscillation, 'negative theology' is caught, comprised and
comprehensive at once" (SN 80 / 103). And again: "What permits localizing negative theology in a historial site and identifying its very own idiom
is also what uproots it from its rooting. What assigns it a proper place is
what expropriates it and *engages* it thus in a movement of universalizing
translation." This movement disseminates it beyond the boundaries that
historically, theoretically, and politically demarcated the Christian West

9. See my "Antibabel."

from the non-Christian remainder, the religious and the theological from
the irreligious and the nontheological, and so on:

> How, today, can one speak . . . on the subject of and in the name of negative
> theology? How can that take place today, today still, so long after the inaugu-
> ral openings of the *via negativa*? Is negative theology a "topic" [English in
> original]? How would what still comes to us under the domestic, European,
> Greek, and Christian term of negative theology, of negative way, of apophatic
> discourse, be the chance of an incomparable translatability in principle with-
> out limit? Not of a universal tongue, of an ecumenism or of some consensus,
> but of a tongue to come that can be shared more than ever? (SN 46–47 / 38–39)

And yet, despite all the precautions these formulations would allow
us to make, the reference to the Babelian "narration" would still be that
to a "(hi)story" and, to that extent, be "Too full of sense" (SN 80 / 104).
In its very rigor, the aporetic under consideration would not so much be
the one that plays between the Babelian "project" and its "deconstruction"
but, rather, the one that marks the "invisible limit" between the

> Babelian place (event, *Ereignis*, history, revelation, eschato-teleology, mes-
> sianism . . . and deconstruction) and "something" without thing, like an
> indeconstructible *Khōra* . . . : the place that gives rise and place to Babel
> would be indeconstructible, not as a construction whose foundations would
> be sure, sheltered from every internal or external deconstruction, but as the
> very spacing of de-construction. There is where that happens and where there
> are those "things" called, for example, negative theology and its analogues,
> deconstruction and its analogues. (SN 80–81 / 104)

By invoking the Platonic *chōra*, Derrida reminds us here of a "possibility" that eludes both Meister Eckhart's *Vorbürge* or *parvis* and Heidegger's *dimension* of *Offenbarkeit*, as well as, it would seem, Derrida's
own insistence on the preliminary and proleptic structure of messianicity.
*Chōra* is the blind spot of all of these postulates, which—in this perspective or taken in isolation—turn out to be deconstructible presuppositions
in their own right. *Chōra* therefore reminds us that with the exploration
of messianicity and Christianicity in their respective relations to the phenomena of so-called positive religion, not everything—and not even the
"essential"—has yet been said.

## Revealing Revelations Once More

The history of religions reveals the perpetual interplay between a general structure of revelation and a series (or *sériature*) of singular instances. *Revealing revelations* — this dictum implies, first, and in contradistinction to Mikel Dufrenne's interpretation of the relationship between deconstruction and the apophatic (see chapter 1), that Derrida distances the general structure of revealability (or *Offenbarkeit*) analytically from the concrete forms it adopts in real life, in the testimonies that mark the history of religious revelation (or *Offenbarung*). Here, the quasi-transcendentality of conditioning differs from what it is said to make possible. This is precisely the reason why *différance*, the trace, and iterability have a certain nontheological character. And yet the formulation "revealing revelations" cannot be reduced to a merely programmatic statement that would urge us to reveal this constitutive structuring and destructuring of purported revelations. For it equally indicates the fact that the general infrastructure "is" "nothing" *outside, before,* or *beyond* — over and above — the singular revelations that it is deemed to make possible. Far from being indifferent, however, as Jean-Luc Marion seems to fear, the general structure is as much called for by singular instances as it, in turn, enables those instances to come into their own. The singular conditions the general as much as it is conditioned by it. One is the "element" and the "effect" of the other.

More complicated still, this mutual conditioning — or possibilization, if that is the right word, where the language of possibilism finds its end or limitation — is at the same time a relation without relation in which revelation and consequently also revealability become *im*possible. Each of them is prevented from coming into its own, whether as intelligible or discernible structure or as historical fact or phenomenon. Revealability and revelation would thus seem to be virtual — neither possible nor impossible — extremes or poles, neither of which can, however, claim existence as such.

In saying this, am I not giving in to the temptation of "conventionalism," to the convenience of an empiricism, that is, whose prime error is that it mistakes itself for a philosophical position (as the concluding pages of Derrida's "Violence and Metaphysics" remind us)? Have I not neglected the fact that Derrida's most explicit statements concerning the religious in its most down-to-earth empirical, historical, and positive formations are guided by a reticence that should make one pause and think twice? Perhaps. But then again, the foregoing analysis should first of all be taken as an attempt to understand Derrida's enigmatic assertion according to which the structure of messianicity (but, again, the same holds true of Christianicity and, indeed, of every formally indicative concept of religion "at the limits of mere reason") is characterized by a certain indeterminacy. In speaking about his turn to religion, Derrida writes, one should "distinguish the specter not only from the icon and idol but also from the image of the image, from the Platonic phantasma, as well as from the simple *simulacrum* of something in general." The specter is affirmed precisely in the hesitation and indecision between life and death that metaphysics since Plato has sought to exorcise.[10]

And as Derrida insists in *Specters of Marx*, the "logic of the specter" (*la logique du fantôme*) implies a "thinking of the event" that goes well beyond the restrictive determinations of "binary or dialectical logic," since it resists the very conceptual or factual distinction between historical products or effects and a supposed ideality.[11]

10. Derrida, *Specters of Marx*, 7 / 27, 147 / 235: "The 'phantasma,' which the *Phaedo* (81d) or the *Timaeus* (71a) do not separate from the *eidola*, are figures of dead souls.... The idol appears or lets itself be determined only against the background of death." On the relation between the specter and the theme of *la vie-la mort*, the *sur-vie*, etc., see ibid., 109 and 186–88 n. 7 / 177 and 177–79 n. 1. Yet the dividing line that demarcates the difference between Platonico-idealist metaphysics, on the one hand, and Derrida's hauntology, on the other, does not prevent *Specters of Marx* from inscribing the specter in the long tradition of interpretation — from Neoplatonism through Heidegger down to Levinas — of the so-called form of the Good beyond essence in which the classical doctrine of ideas as put forward in the *Politeia* culminates and perhaps ruptures the very set of hypotheses on which it had been built (lest we should forget: the highest idea is the *anhypothaton*): "The specter, as its name indicates, is the *frequency* of a certain visibility. But the visibility of the invisible. And visibility, by its essence, is not seen, which is why it remains *epekeina tēs ousias*, beyond the phenomenon or beyond being" (*Specters of Marx*, 100 / 165). This lineage should make one pause even if one takes it as an illustration of the fact that the specter, the phantom, as Derrida puts it a little later in the text, is "not just one figure among others," but the "hidden figure of all figures," the one figure that escapes any attempt at capturing it figuratively, or with the help of some "meta-rhetoric" (ibid., 120 / 194). Nor, for that matter, would the specter let itself be captured by a "psychology of imagination" or a "psychoanalysis of the imaginary," let alone an "ontology" or "me-ontology" (ibid., 148 / 236). And, Derrida writes, if Marx at his best moments succeeds in reinscribing the phantom in a "socio-economical genealogy" or in a "philosophy of work and production," then these reductions continue to presuppose the "possibility of the spectral survivance [*survie*]" (ibid.). Of course, the "possibility" of a *survie*, and a fortiori the survivance that is called spectral, is not a possibility of either being or not being. That it is to say, it not a possibility at all or as such. Here, again, it is the more elusive notion of the virtual that comes to substitute — or to haunt — the metaphysical overdeterminations of the "possible" in terms of a potential or reserve, on the one hand, and a mere ideal or logical option, on the other. What Derrida does is to introduce an emphatic notion of *la Chance* and *la Nécessité*, or *anankē*, that allows for a rethinking of the possible in terms of the "virtual," the spectral, and the phantomatic.

11. Derrida, *Specters of Marx*, 63 / 108: "un pensée de l'événement qui excède nécessaire-

It would almost seem as though we are dealing here with what Heidegger, alluding to Count Paul Yorck von Wartenburg's correspondence with Wilhelm Dilthey, calls the "virtuality" (*Virtualität*) of the essential feature (*Grundcharakter*) of history.[12] Provided, of course, that we do not confuse the "spirit" of history, which, according to Wartenburg, is the ground of this "silent" and "non-specular" virtual history, with the specter as it is understood by Derrida (and, in part, by Marx). All the difficulty lies in distinguishing between these two, between two conceptions of history, of the spirit, and of the virtual. This distinction is not merely empirical. But is it conceptual, formal, analytical, intelligible, or, again, spiritual, spectral, virtual? Perhaps, in following the ghost of history, we are just as much followed by it, "persecuted by the very chase we are leading?"[13]

The formulation "revealing revelations" might thus well summarize Derrida's analyses of the messianic, as well as of the formalism of a messianicity that abstracts from all specific dogmatic, propositional, and axiological content, while retaining its promise and its threat. In *Specters of Marx*, Derrida introduces the notion of messianicity against the backdrop of a reconsideration of Marxism. Like the critical spirit of the Enlightenment, the "spirit" of Marxism testifies, Derrida says, to a structural "messianicity" that no one can simply forgo and forget. The "spirit of Marxism" that one should be reluctant to "renounce," Derrida writes, "is not only the critical idea or the questioning stance (a consistent deconstruction must insist on them even as it also learns that this is not the last or first word). It is even more a certain emancipatory and *messianic* affirmation, a certain experience of the promise that one can try to liberate from any dogmatics and even from any metaphysico-religious determination, from any *messianism*."[14] The spirit of Marxism thus not only plays against the dogmatism that characterizes so many of Marxism's historical doctrines, but at least as much against anti-Marxisms that reintroduce an evangelico-messianic eschatology whose ontotheological premises and

---

ment une logique binaire ou dialectique, celle qui distingue ou oppose *effectivité* (présence, actuelle, empirique, vivante — ou non) et *idéalité* (non-présence régulatrice ou absolue)."

12. BT 453 / 401, referring to Count Paul Yorck von Wartenburg's correspondence with Wilhelm Dilthey: "With history, what makes a spectacle [*Spektakel*] and catches the eye is not the main thing. The nerves are invisible, just as the essentials [*das Wesentliche*] in general are invisible. While it is said that 'if you were quiet [*stille*], you would be strong,' the variant is also true that 'if you are quiet, you will perceive [*vernehmen*] — that is, understand [*verstehen*].' "

13. Derrida, *Specters of Marx*, 10 / 31: "Qu'est-ce que suivre un fantôme? Et si cela revenait [*sic*] à être suivi par lui. . . ."

14. Ibid., 89 / 146–47.

"contents" are far more problematic (or, as Derrida says, "deconstruct-ible")[15] than Marx's thought ever was.

Derrida leaves no doubt that the *epochē* that characterizes the "formal-ism [or formality, *formalité*] of such a structural messianism," of a "mes-sianism without religion," of a "messianism without messianism" will be unacceptable to the adherents of both historical religion and its func-tional equivalents. To the extent that this formalization, while respecting their idiom, sacrifices the very semantic content and horizon of these doctrines—that is to say, almost everything—it comes to stand for noth-ing but a "thinking of the other and of the event to come."[16] In so doing, however, not everything is erased. We should distinguish here, Derrida maintains, between "everything" and "almost everything," between *tout et presque tout,* the *presque* alluding to nothing in particular, to nothing determinate, but welcoming and opening up the chance of the future's to-come as well as of futures to come. And this distinction would be difficult to accept for Marxists and anti-Marxists alike, for radical atheists no less than for adamant believers.

All this is not to forget that the notion of messianicity should be used with great caution. In "Force of Law," Derrida differentiates between an "infinite 'idea of justice' " (beyond right or law), on the one hand, and a "regulative idea (in the Kantian sense)," a "messianic promise" and "other horizons of the same type,"[17] on the other. In this particular context, Der-rida does not distinguish between the "idea of justice" and some concrete example of messianism taken from the history of positive religion but, rather, sets this idea apart from a certain structure of the messianic that retains a common measure with an ideal of approximation within an open space or horizon that canalizes and thus—in a formal sense—anticipates or predicts what is still to come.

*Specters of Marx* will reiterate that the messianisms that retain this structure establish a continuity between their inaccessible—intelligible or utopian—*avenir* and the "temporal form of a *future present,* of a future modality of a *living present.*"[18] This form of most, perhaps all (*presque tous*), messianisms should not be confused with the destructuring struc-ture of messianicity as it is introduced in this more recent work. Here, we

15. Ibid., 90 / 147.
16. Ibid., 59 / 102.
17. Derrida, "Force of Law," 965.
18. Derrida, *Specters of Marx,* 65 / 110; cf. 65–66 / 111–12.

are dealing with an *à venir*, with a temporality *out of joint*, marked, quite literally, by the splitting of *avenir* (future) into *à venir* (to-come).

We should not let ourselves be distracted, then, by the fact that, in "Force of Law," Derrida circumscribes the idea of justice in terms of a sense of absolute urgency, while *Specters of Marx* insists, by contrast, on a messianic "hesitation."[19] For in both cases the emphasis is on the necessary distinction between an end that announces itself (and eventually takes place) within a horizon of possible expectation, on the one hand, and a structure of infinity that stands for and enables an appeal here and now—here and now being without assignable time and space—that cannot wait, on the other.

What is perhaps surprising, though, is that the term *messianicity* is written in the singular, while it is suggested, at the same time, that the messianic gives itself to be thought, not as a multifaceted phenomenon, but as a *nonphenomenologizable multiplicity*. This observation could be reconciled with Derrida's suggestion, in "Force of Law," that "in fact"—de facto, rather than de iure—there is "only one aporia, only one potential aporetic that infinitely distributes itself."[20]

In fact, it might well be asked whether there is indeed only one. What is more: is this one aporetic "potential," a "potential"? Are we not here, as Derrida himself notes, "in a realm where, in the end, there are only singular examples," with as consequence that, strictly speaking, "Nothing is absolutely exemplary,"[21] not even the messianic, let alone messianicity? And, if this is the case, can messianicity, as the formalized theological topos that in *Specters of Marx* receives the status of a quasi- or meta-category and crypto-modality, still be thought as being singular or as a structure? Is what revelations reveal, presuppose, and obfuscate not rather the plurality of innumerable and incommensurable messianicities? What more could messianicity be but an envoi, which, instead of retaining the formal structure—the *Offenbarkeit*—of a *Geschick des Seins*, gives itself only in the plural, that is, as envois? What else could the messianic signal but the interruption, inflection, or fracturing of the social space that is multidimensional, multiple—more than one and, perhaps, no longer one or just *one*, indeed *le plus d'un, n + Un*[22]—and, in that sense precisely,

19. Ibid., 169 / 268–69.
20. Derrida, "Force of Law," 959.
21. Ibid., 977.
22. FK 65 / 85. Cf. Derrida, *Specters of Marx*, 135 / 214: "Number is the specter."

more than a mere sociopolitical, historical, contemporary, or epochal phenomenon? Here, again, it is not to some indistinct futurity that a certain primacy is given, but rather to the distinct pastness of the dead. The structure of openness is related to a being exposed to death, not to the death of oneself (of myself, of *Dasein*, or of just one self), but to the death of innumerable others that must be feared or mourned in every singular death.

In a recent reading of Yosef H. Yerushalmi's study *Freud's Moses: Judaism Terminable and Interminable,* entitled "Archive Fever: A Freudian Impression,"[23] Derrida describes the said structure in terms of a "Jewishness beyond all Judaism," hinting at a being "open toward the future" that would be "Jewish." Such openness could be called messianic and could be formalized with the help of the quasi-transcendental notion or meta-category—and simili-modality—of "messianicity." To adhere to a particular, concrete, historical form, practice or figure of messianism tends, if not to abolish, then at least to obfuscate the structure of messianicity. Merely to describe the to-come in terms of a general structure would be at least as problematic, however, since it annuls messianicity's link with singularity. Not that this singularity occurs in the singular, for whenever and wherever the singular takes place or comes to pass, we are already dealing with what is unique as well as divided in and against itself, or, more carefully, this intrinsic doubling or tripling is always already possible, a necessary no less than impossible possibility, which explains its iterability *and* spectrality, its universality *and* the "virtuality" of its reality. Such as it is, it does not come into being as such.

A supposed revelation (*Offenbarung*), then, reveals as much as it is itself in turn revealed by a structure of revealability (*Offenbarkeit*), which is, properly speaking, nothing determinable outside or before or beyond —over and above—the said (concrete, positive, empirical ontic) revelation or account thereof. Historically speaking—as with the Saussurian *système de la langue* in its relation without relation to the *parole*—the latter could even be said to come first or earlier. But strictly, systematically and philosophically speaking, we would be caught in an unresolvable aporia here:

23. Yerushalmi, *Freud's Moses;* Derrida, "Archive Fever." Cf. also Michel de Certeau, "La Fiction de l'histoire: L'Écriture de *Moïse et le monothéisme*," in id., *L'Écriture de l'histoire* (Paris: Éditions du Seuil, 1975), 312–58, trans. Tom Conley as "The Fiction of History: The Writing of *Moses and Monotheism*," in *The Writing of History* (New York: Columbia University Press, 1988), 308–54.

Since there is no presence before and outside semiological difference, what Saussure has written about language can be extended to the sign in general: "Language is necessary in order for speech to be intelligible and to produce all of its effects; but the latter is necessary in order for language to be established; historically, the fact of speech always comes first."

*Retaining at least the framework, if not the content, of this requirement* formulated by Saussure, we will designate as *différance* the movement according to which language, or any code, any system of referral in general, is constituted "historically," as a weave of differences.[24]

One "conditions" the other, albeit not necessarily in the same way or to the same extent at the same time. Here, as always, everything would depend on contextual parameters that are historically, culturally, and pragmatically overdetermined, and that forbid us to think of this relation in terms of mere abstract anticipation and concrete prefiguration. "Archive Fever" formulates this aporia as follows:

does one base one's thinking of the future on an archived event — with or without substrate, with or without actuality — for example on a divine injunction or on a messianic covenant? Or else, on the contrary, can an *experience,* an *existence,* in general, only receive and record, only archive such an event to the extent that the structure of this existence and of its temporalization makes this archivization possible? In other words, does one need a first archive in order to conceive of originary archivability? Or vice versa? This is the whole question of the relation between the event of the religious revelation (*Offenbarung*) and a revealability (*Offenbarkeit*), a possibility of manifestation, the prior thought of what opens toward the arrival or toward the coming of such an event.[25]

24. Derrida, *Margins of Philosophy*, 12 / 12–13; emphasis added.
25. Derrida, "Archive Fever," 52 / 127. See also FK 16 / 26:

In its most abstract form, then, the aporia within which we are struggling would perhaps be the following: is revealability (*Offenbarkeit*) more originary than revelation (*Offenbarung*), and hence independent of all religion? Independent in the structures of its experience and in the analytics relating to them? Is this not the place in which "reflecting faith" [Derrida uses the term from Kant's *Religion Within the Boundaries of Mere Reason*] at least originates, if not this faith itself? Or rather, inversely, would the event of revelation have consisted in revealing revealability itself, and the origin of light, the originary light, the very invisibility of visibility? This is perhaps what the believer or the theologian might say here, in particular the Christian of originary Christendom, of that *Urchristentum* in the Lutheran tradition to which Heidegger acknowledges owing so much.

Derrida suggests that it is nothing but the logic of repetition of the "after-the-fact," the belatedness or *Nachträglichkeit,* that forces us to think of two moments in another way than as the succession of two moments of *presence,* or, for that matter, two moments that are simultaneously *present.* This brings me to yet another way of thinking (comprehending-without-comprehending) the relationship between the trace—as the folded, multifaceted and infinitely finite destruction, dissemination, and rearticulation of *Offenbarung*—and the religious, the theological, and the ontotheological. Mutatis mutandis, the relation of one to the other might be structurally analogous to the relation-without-relation of *différance* to the ontico-ontological difference as it is developed by Heidegger's "un-circumventable meditation." Just as *différance* is simultaneously internal and external to Being and the beings in their ontological determination, messianicity is at once nothing but a variable yet determinate structure inherent in all messianisms *and* that in light of which all these messianisms are intrametaphysical and, in a sense, dogmatic or idolatrous (Kant would say sectarian or pagan) phenomena:

> In a certain aspect of itself, *différance* is certainly but the historical and epochal *unfolding* of Being or of the ontological difference. The *a* of *différance* marks the *movement* of this unfolding.
>
> And yet are not the thought of the *meaning* or *truth* of Being, the determination of *différance* as the ontico-ontological difference, difference thought within the horizon of the question of *Being,* still intrametaphysical effects of *différance?* The unfolding of *différance* is perhaps not solely the truth of Being, or of the epochality of Being.[26]

But in the final analysis, each of these structural analogies is only of limited importance. Neither the structural systematicity of the Saussurian model in its enabling function with respect to every *parole,* nor the quasi-transcendental "infrastructure"—to quote Rodolphe Gasché—that marks *différance* in its distinction and relation-without-relation to the ontico-ontological difference, nor, finally, the psychoanalytic structure of repression and the belatedness of the traumatic effect, can fully account for the relation (again without relation) that interests us here. In his most recent work, Derrida introduces or mobilizes other concepts and other figures, which pay tribute to an even older or, rather, more anachronistic, more

26. Derrida, *Margins of Philosophy,* 22 / 23.

heterodox, and more heretical tradition. This is nowhere clearer than in his rearticulation of such notions as the kenosis and the sacrifice. But the notions of the apocalypse, the mystical postulate, the shibboleth, and many others are no less relevant here.

Should one base one's thinking of the open future — of the to-come — on the events and the names of particular, historically unique or positive religions? Or should one, conversely, situate these events and names in a structure of revealability that is the very possibility of their manifestation or occurrence? Does this distinction constitute a genuine alternative or a dilemma? On more than one occasion,[27] Derrida has made very clear what a careful reading of his recent writings should have stressed all along, namely, that one cannot simply choose here. More precisely, that here it is irresponsible to choose. Or, conversely, that one cannot but choose both of these focal points or points of departure. In any experience and in any analysis, each of them is always already relied on, that is to say, affirmed. Messianicity and messianism thus stand in a relation of mutual implication and oscillation, of an elliptical movement in which the one pole calls forth the other, even though the one and the other are, in a sense, incommensurable. Strictly speaking, the former can no longer be considered as the condition, the possibility or the condition of possibility, of the latter. For within the logic of possibility — which is a "logic of presupposition" — one should add that they are at least as much each other's *un*-condition or *im*possibility. As a consequence, they subtract themselves from any logic of the possible and the metaphysical *possibilism* on which it rests.

If one keeps the word *messianic* and does not forget its reference to proper names, if one keeps it, without excluding the option that one will have to drop it one day, in a different historical and political constellation, then this citation is at once strategic and more than simply strategic.

The word *messianic* serves to remind us that the whole problematic of opening and closure goes all the way back to someone called the Messiah. More precisely, it is only because there has been a series of events naming the messianic or the Messiah, because there has been such a thing as religion, because there have been the so-called religions of the Book, that the thematization of a universal structure and the universalization of *Offenbarung* in terms of *Offenbarkeit* have been "possible," or, rather, nec-

27. The present exposition draws on a roundtable with Derrida at the Amsterdam School for Cultural Analysis, Theory and Interpretation (ASCA) in July 1994.

essary and pertinent at all. It would be impossible to speak of revealability without there having been references to purported revelations.

WE ARE DEALING HERE with a general observation that applies to other tropes or genres as well. "[I]t would be naive to think that one knows what is the essence, the provenance, or the history of autobiography outside events like Augustine's *Confessions*," Derrida writes, for example (SN 38 / 22).[28] This is not to say that every subsequent autobiography relates to St. Augustine's *Confessions* in the sense that it must be "interpreted in the same horizon" or have "the same structure." Moreover, Augustine's *Confessions* was already "an act of memory" in its own time and context (SN 40 / 26). Clearly, the relation between the one and the other is not that between the original or the paradigm, on the one hand, and the copy and the example, on the other; nor even that of the first and the later. For while Augustine's *Confessions* form the most authoritative and powerful document of the tradition of autobiography, of testimony and confession, they are themselves, in turn, already "an act of memory" (SN 40 / 26). But of what precisely, if anything?

And yet, conversely, the revelations of the Book could only have been thought or experienced against the background of an opening that was already preunderstood or postulated (not to say presupposed) by them. (At first sight, "Violence and Metaphysics" would seem to side with Heidegger against Levinas in this regard, but Derrida leaves no doubt that the question of Being might well depend at least as much on answering the question of the to-God as the other way around.)

The structure of revealability and of messianicity, Derrida would seem to suggest, is much larger than the cultural space in which (and as which) religions manifest themselves. Messianicity, thus defined, is no longer restricted to those who, in history, have in fact addressed themselves to the Messiah. It is the universal structure folded into every relation to the past, the present, the future, to life, and to death. As such, it neither keeps to itself nor in giving itself holds anything of itself in reserve. It holds nothing back. In this sense, precisely, Derrida's analysis of the structure of messianicity differs fundamentally from Heidegger's interpretation of the gift of Being. In Heidegger's view, the gift of Being is at once marked by a

28. On the autobiographical dimension of philosophy and the philosophical dimensions of autobiography, see the opening pages of Stanley Cavell's *A Pitch of Philosophy: Autobiographical Exercises* (Cambridge, Mass.: Harvard University Press, 1994).

certain reserve.[29] It retains a potential, as it were, that is not given in what it gives, in the presence or as this presence, but withholds and retreats within itself. In other words, for Heidegger, the gift remains premised on an irreducible refusal (*Verweigerung*).

The question of whether we should start from messianicity or, conversely, from messianism—as, Derrida suggests, Walter Benjamin was inclined to do—cannot be decided on reasonable grounds alone. Between these two moments or movements, it is not possible and, what is more, not responsible to choose *in advance* or *once and for all*. Here, Derrida adds, one should turn a certain hesitation (*not* a refusal) to choose into a matter of principle, at least provisionally. For, if one were to determine the specificity of our world today, one could not but point to the oscillation between these two orders, which, when left to themselves, resemble the worst of all possible worlds. Given this constellation, then, the words *messiah* and *messianic* are both necessary, but in speaking of messianicity, we must take care neither to reduce it to any single messianism nor to turn it into a mere (abstract, formal or general) intelligible structure over and above—before or beyond—concrete, historical messianisms.

Derrida only seems to rejoin those contemporary thinkers who attempt to uphold the distinction between phenomenology and theology in terms of differentiation between thinking revelation as a possibility and thinking it as historicity or, rather as historical in the sense of a singularly dated occurrence rather than, say, a historical or epochal event. Like Heidegger, Patočka, Levinas, Marion, and perhaps Ricoeur, Derrida accentuates, as *The Gift of Death* formulates it, a "non-dogmatic double of dogma, a philosophical, metaphysical in any case thinking double which 'repeats' without religion, the possibility of religion" (GD 49 / 53).

This gesture is marked by a "doubling" of the resources of religion that, Derrida goes on to suggest, is in the final analysis *neither theistic nor atheistic* and irretrievable by Heideggerian *Wiederholung*, but reminiscent of yet another phenomenological rupture with the metaphysical tradition, notably the one that Marion identifies as a "*relief* for theology."[30] Moreover, this possibility—or, rather, that which gives rise to this possibility—does not let itself be reduced to the source or to *one* source of *one* positive religion in particular or even to religion in general. As such, it is

29. See Jean-Louis Chrétien, "La Réserve de l'être," in *Martin Heidegger*, ed. Michel Haar (Paris: Éditions de l'Herne, 1983), 233–60.
30. Marion, "Metaphysics and Phenomenology."

abstracted from the very content, if not the form, of all cultural formations. Yet, it is no less true that the possibility for which it stands or that
it calls into being cannot immunize itself against its always possible —
indeed inevitable — *reinscription* into any such given, particular, positive
religion, into its theology, its dogma, its symbols, and its ritual practice.
In being caught in this *performative contradiction* it resembles the very
concept and structure of responsibility and the whole series of notions
that come with it and that interest us here (justice, decision, testimony,
the secret, the gift, the sacrifice the confession, the shibboleth).

All this then becomes a question of striking the right balance between historical revelation and a quasi-transcendental revealability, between messianism and messianicity. Whenever a thinker reduces the one
to the other, inferring one from the other, this balance ipso facto shifts in
a philosophically — and, for the present, politically — irresponsible fashion. Neither the future "in and of itself" nor the forms taken by acts and
archives over time — neither the critical spirit (or, rather, the spirit of critique) nor the dead letter — independently account for the repetition and
renewal that marks the inheritance of traditions. What is more, this relation would be unthinkable without reference to the rhythmic return and
the athetic or nonspeculative structure of the death wish or "destructive
instinct" that Freud introduces in *Jenseits des Lustprinzips* (*Beyond the
Pleasure Principle*) and *Das Unbehagen in der Kultur* (*Civilization and Its
Discontents*), which are the starting point for Derrida's "Spéculer — sur
'Freud'" and form the background to his references to Freud in *Aporias.*
In "Archive Fever," Derrida seems to reiterate his position on these mat-
ters when he comments on Yerushalmi's interpretation of Freud, Freud's
Moses, Freud's Judaism:

> If repetition is thus inscribed at the heart of the future to come, one must also
> import there, *in the same stroke*, the death drive, the violence of forgetting. . . .
> This is why Freud might not have accepted . . . the alternative between . . .
> "hope" and "hopelessness," the Jew and the non-Jew, the future and repeti-
> tion. The one is alas, or happily, the condition of the other. And the Other is
> the condition for the One.[31]

At issue, then, is the necessity and the task, not to choose one side or other
in these binary oppositions, but, rather, to *do justice* to both of them.
This does not mean that the two poles should be dialectically mediated or

---

31. Derrida, "Archive Fever," 51–52 / 126.

that some prudent compromise is possible between them, but they must not be forgotten. In Yerushalmi's book *Zakhor: Jewish History and Jewish Memory*, Derrida recalls, it is suggested that rather than *remembering*, the antonym of *forgetting* might be *justice*. But this justice is not so much distributive as it is *absolute* and characterized by a certain temporal immediacy and urgency here and now. The "modalities" of the future to-come "orchestrate" what Derrida calls "places of opening" or "doors." The reference is to Walter Benjamin's "Thesen über den Begriff der Geschichte" ("Theses on the Philosophy of History"), which in a topologico-temporal figure evoke the "narrow door" through which the Messiah may pass "at each second" (in Harry Zohn's translation: "For every second of time was the strait gate through which the Messiah might enter").

The ultimately de-transcendentalizing movement of inscription, uprooting, and reinscription of these theologemes should be clearly distinguished from all historicist, culturalist, or empiricist attempts to relativize or secondarize the abstract and formal, elusive and, in that sense, absolute status of the to-come. The emphasis on its inevitable performative contradiction or aporia should be understood as an *apophatic* no less than *emphatic* rearticulation of the well-known crisis of the phenomena as well as of the phenomenology that describes them. Not that there could be a phenomenology of apophatics, strictly speaking, but the movement in question comes down to a radicalization, if not eradication, of phenomenology (as a method and an ontology) in light or in view of the *apophasis*, in the direction of an apophatics that is not without a philosophical moment and momentum of its own.

In *Sauf le nom*, Derrida writes that what makes apophatic discourse "formalizable," "mechanizable and easily reproducible," and "falsifiable" but also invincible, an uncanny tautology, as it were, a logic of the same, or of the "almost the same," is the fact that "the statement of negative theology empties itself by definition, by vocation, of all intuitive plenitude" (SN 50/46). One way of reinscribing this procedure in a more familiar theological and philosophical idiom and context, Derrida goes on to suggest, is to translate the concept of kenosis found in Philippians 2:7, where St. Paul says that Christ "made himself nothing" (*New English Bible*) or "emptied himself" (ἑαυτὸν ἐκένωσεν), into the language of phenomenology. (Book 2 of Kant's *Religion Within the Boundaries of Mere Reason*, a work Derrida might be said to have rewritten, is in fact an indefatigable meditation on the figure of the kenosis.)

Apophatics multiplies *only the names*. But since every word or phrase that is repeated here is devoid or stripped of its semantic, metaphorical, and deictic value, we are also dealing here, in a sense, with everything but *distinctive* names. Of this "kenosis of discourse," Derrida says:

> If a phenomenological type of rule is followed for distinguishing between a full intention and an empty or symbolic intending [*visée*] forgetful of the originary perception supporting it, then the apophatic statements *are, must be* on the side of the empty and then of mechanical, indeed purely verbal, repetition of phrases without actual or full intentional meaning. Apophatic statements represent what Husserl identifies as the moment of *crisis* (forgetting of the full and originary intuition, empty functioning of symbolic language, objectivism, etc.). But in revealing the originary and final necessity of this crisis, in denouncing from the language of crisis the snares of intuitive consciousness and of phenomenology, they destabilize the very axiomatics of the phenomenological, that is also, the ontological and transcendental critique. Emptiness is essential and necessary to them. If they guard against this, it is through the moment of prayer or the hymn. But this protective moment remains structurally exterior to the purely apophatic instance, that is, to *negative theology* as such, if there is any, in the strict sense, which can at times be doubted. The value, the *evaluation* of the quality, of the intensity, or of the force of events of negative theology would then result from this *relation* that articulates *this* void [*vide*] on the plenitude [*sic!*] of a prayer or an attribution (theo-logical, theiological, or onto-logical) negated [*niée*], let's say denegated [*déniée*]. The criterion is the measure of a *relation,* and this relation is stretched between poles, one of which must be that of positivity de-negated. (SN 50–51 / 46–47)

Here, the "de-negated positivity" is *both* that of whatever *thesis* language comes up with or comes up against—in short, every predication based upon a full or fulfillable intuition—*and*, in the second place, of the purported "plenitude" of the prayer or the hymn that is said to give the *logoi* a spiritual, albeit not necessarily protective, quality. The two poles around which this ellipsis revolves would be that of the *said,* which in the pendular movement is being *unsaid,* and the *saying,* whose gesturing or positing or posturing in this alternation is also exposed to an *unsaying.*[32] Most important: *each is the abyss and the sublime of and for the other,* which is just

---

32. It is in precisely this sense that Levinasian terminology—speaking of the *dit* and the *dédit,* of the *dire* and the *dédire*—helps us to understand this relation, which structures and unsettles all the texts that we shall be addressing throughout this study and will become clearer as we proceed.

another way of saying that neither of them *is,* that is, stabilizes itself in any presence or present.

Prayer has a double function here. It prevents the stripping (*dépouillement*) of names, concepts, qualities, and predicates becoming merely mechanical and guards against the petrifaction of the apophatic in one or more privileged traditions.

Of course, one is tempted to ask at this point whether there is not perhaps a contradiction in stressing that prayer as pure address should be distinguished from predication — the hymn, that is, or the encomium — since only this demarcation guarantees that prayer is not already *this* or *that* (e.g., Christian) address, while at the same time casting doubts on the pertinence of a similar, indeed, parallel distinction (or is it separation?), namely, that between so-called revealability and revelation. And yet raising doubts concerning this distinction is exactly what Derrida does in the final paragraphs of "How to Avoid Speaking."

I would argue that the rearticulation of the relation between *Offenbarkeit* and *Offenbarung* in terms of messianicity and messianism and, more particularly, of kenosis and sacrifice, provides an answer to this problem. Thus, in *Specters of Marx, Sauf le nom,* "Archive Fever," and "Faith and Knowledge," Derrida addresses more centrally the fact that the formal and quasi-transcendental notion of revealability and the singular, historical phenomenon of so-called revelation stand in a relation of mutual implication as much as of exclusion. Somehow, once more, each conditions and destabilizes the other. Again, this conditioning and its opposite should not primarily be understood in terms of a making *possible* or *impossible.* A different modality than that of the possible and of possibilization is at work here:

> the absence of a common measure between the opening, openness [*apérité*], revelation, knowledge on the one hand and on the other a certain absolute secret, nonprovisional, heterogeneous to all manifestation. This secret is not a reserve of potential [*potentiel*] knowing, a potential [*en puissance*] manifestation. And the language of ab-negation or of renunciation is not negative: not only because it does not state in the mode of descriptive predication and of the indicative proposition simply affected with a negation ("this is not that"), but because it denounces as much as it renounces; and it denounces enjoining; it prescribes overflowing this insufficiency; it orders: *it is necessary* to do the impossible, *it is necessary* to go . . . there where one cannot go [alluding to Angelus Silesius's "Geh hin, wo du nicht kanst . . ."]. Passion of the place

again. . . . *il y a lieu de* (which means: "il faut," "it is necessary," "there is ground for") rendering oneself *there where* it is impossible to go. To go where it is possible to go would not be a displacement or a decision, it would be the irresponsible unfolding of a program. The sole possible decision passes through the madness of the undecidable and the impossible: to go where . . . it is impossible to go. (SN 59 / 62–63; trans. modified)

The apophatic path of the *über,* of the *überunmöglichste,* the most impossible or more than impossible, is attested to as *möglich,* as possible; this movement of elevation, transcendence, hyperbole, rhetorical exaggeration, and excess paradoxically coincides with a descent and humiliation, a coming down to earth, or incarnation of the concept, of ontology, of phenomenology, as well as of their deconstruction. This kenosis of discourse means that "the very functioning of these statements resides in a formalization. This formalization essentially does without, tends essentially to do without all content and every idiomatic signifier, every presentation or representation, images and even names of *God, for example,* in this tongue or in that culture" (SN 51 / 48; emphasis added). It is clear, however, that the tendency toward abstraction and generalizable structures — and thereby toward the philosophical concept of a revealability that can be analytically distinguished, if not simply separated, from any concrete account of revelation is already inherent in negative theology itself. Whatever is formally determinable in it reveals the structure of revealability. And, to the extent that this formalization can never be total and retains an element or remainder of the opaque, the singular, the idiomatic, and the idiosyncratic, however minimal, *the structure of revealability reveals the traces of positive revelations no more than it is revealed by them.*

This conclusion might well be seen as a derailment of the phenomenological project. But in this context, where a resonance between the aporias of the *via negativa* and those of phenomenology is at issue, it should not be forgotten that the risk of kenosis is not reserved to the *logoi,* neither true nor false, that are called prayers. At the beginning of *Being and Time,* Heidegger himself reminds us of the fact that an unavoidable threat looms especially where the phenomenological analysis approaches its origin. Typically, the peril — for Heidegger, the possibility of *Entartung,* Degeneration (and "in the field of ontology, any 'springing-from' is degeneration" [BT 383 / 334]) — does not exclusively or primarily lie in the "concrete phenomenological labor itself." Its chances increase to the extent that its concepts and statements are shared or communicated, become public and, in a sense, mediatized events. One is reminded here of Heidegger's derogatory remarks about the radio, the telephone, newspapers, and cinema, all of which are without further ado relegated to the realm of *das Man*, to the fallenness of the quotidian, to the ambiguities of irresoluteness and improper existence:

> Whenever a phenomenological concept and proposition [*Begriff und Satz*] is drawn from primordial sources, there is a possibility that it may degenerate if communicated in the form of an assertion. It gets understood in an empty way and is thus passed on, losing its indigenous character [*Bodenständigkeit*], and becoming a free-floating thesis. Even in the concrete work of phenomenology itself there lurks the possibility that what has been primordially "within our grasp" may become hardened so that we can no longer grasp it.[33]

An exception is made only for the *Bezeugung*, the testimony, of this testimony that can only be given in silence, in the *Verschwiegenheit*, or reticence, that marks Dasein, or existence properly speaking.

FINALLY, IT SHOULD BE NOTED that the rearticulation of the phenomenological project in terms of kenosis recalls Derrida's earliest discussions of the work of Husserl. The argument of *Specters of Marx*, Derrida writes, allows one to draw two consequences: "(1) the phenomenal form of the world is itself spectral; (2) the phenomenological *ego* . . . is a specter. The *phainesthai* itself (before its determination as phenomenon or phantasm, thus as phantom) is the very possibility of the specter, it brings death, it gives death (*donne la mort*), it works at mourning (*travaille du deuil*)."[34]

33. BT 60–61/36.
34. Derrida, *Specters of Marx*, 135/215. Here, Derrida extends the logic of the "it haunts," "*es spukt*," "*ça revient*," "*ça revenante*," and "*ça spectre*" well beyond the analysis of the Marxian critique of Max Stirner's *cogito* and into the domain of Cartesianism, Kantianism, and phenomenology. A note reminds the reader of Derrida's own earlier analysis, in *La Voix et le phénomène* (Paris: Presses universitaires de France, 1967), 98ff., trans. David Allison as *Speech and Phenomena* (Evanston, Ill.: Northwestern University Press, 1973), 88ff., in which the "strangely murmured implication" of death, "not only of an 'I am mortal' but of an 'I am dead,'" comes to unsettle—and, indeed, haunt—the very "declaration" of the assertion "I am" (see *Specters of Marx*, 189 n. 3/212 n. 1).
    It is in the same context that Derrida devotes a long note to the possible contours of a "phenomenology of the spectral" based on Husserlian premises. In such a phenomenology, he observes, "the narrow and strict concept of the phantom or the *phantasma* will never be reduced to the generality of the *phainesthai*" (ibid., 189 n. 6/215 n. 2). Instead, Derrida continues, it has a specificity—a positivity and concreteness, of sorts—that is neither regional nor ontic and therefore nonempirical. Needless to say, we touch here, again, upon the important motif of

This suggestion that the phenomenological "principle of principles" and the logic of the specter do not so much converge as resemble and condition each other in a manner that escapes the classical thought of mimesis, the modern logic of presupposition, and thus the legacy of transcendental philosophy, becomes clearer if we recall that Derrida has asked earlier: "[W]hat is a *phenomenology* if not a logic of the *phainesthai* and of the *phantasma*, therefore of the phantom?"[35] And just as there is no fundamental, or ultimately tenable, analyzable, perceivable distinction between the appearance of the things themselves and the appearance (or *revenants*) of phantoms, there is no way of distinguishing between spirit and specter, as Marx goes "to desperate lengths" to show, Derrida asserts.[36]

---

the relationship between transcendental historicity and idealization, albeit an idealization this time that obtains all the qualities (or, rather, modalities) of the spectral. It would almost seem as if the phenomenology of the spectral that Derrida sums up here takes up an intermediary position between the Husserlian analysis of historicity (retraced in Derrida's earliest writings) and Husserl's more isolated references to the "Absolute" and the "transcendent" that should be distinguished from the absoluteness of the transcendental ego, on the one hand, and the transcendence of the world, on the other (and that Derrida addresses in his more recent explorations of the relationship between the apophatic and the phenomenological reduction, crisis, delocalization, etc.). The spectral is not quite the singular exemplarity or eidetic singularity that illuminates historicity; nor is it the theological moment that phenomenology must bracket. Neither purely intelligible or transcendental nor merely empirical or conditioned, neither abstractly general and formal nor simply singular, the specter — or the spectral — would be whatever it is that leaves its trace in intentional experience without ever belonging to it as such. Original impression and constitution at once, it "is" that which makes experience possible, but is also, paradoxically, made possible by it in turn. Derrida implies as much when he writes:

> [T]he radical possibility of all spectrality should be sought in the direction that Husserl identifies . . . as an intentional but *non-real* [*non-réelle*] component of the phenomenological lived experience, namely the *noeme*. Unlike the three other terms of the two correlations (*noese-noeme, morphè-hulè*), this non-reality [*non-réellité*], this intentional but *non-real* inclusion of the noematic correlate is neither "in" the world nor "in" consciousness. But it is precisely the condition of any experience, any objectivity, any phenomenality, namely of any noetico-noematic correlation, whether originary or modified. It is no longer [*n'est plus*] regional. Without the non-real-inclusion of this intentional component (therefore inclusive *and* non-inclusive inclusion: the noeme is included without being a part), one could not speak of any manifestation, of any phenomenality in general (that being-for-a-consciousness, that appearing appearance which is neither consciousness nor the being that appears to it). Is not such an "irreality" [*irréellité*], *its independence both* in relation to the world *and* in relation to the *real* stuff of egological subjectivity, the very place of apparition, the essential, general, non-regional possibility of the specter? Is it not also what inscribes the possibility of the other and of mourning right onto the phenomenality of the phenomenon? (*Specters of Marx*, 189 n. 6 / 215–216 n. 2)

35. Derrida, *Specters of Marx*, 122 / 199. See also FK 6 / 15: "*phos, phainesthai, phantasma,* hence specter, etc."
36. Derrida, *Specters of Marx*, 122 / 199.

It would seem, then, that each pole of this relation, materialism and idealism, but also phenomenology and hauntology, is at once a repetition and the outcome of the other. Although, paradoxically, they are the alpha and omega of all thought, of all experience, and of all decision, neither is first; neither is last. Which is another way of saying that there will always have been at least two sources of faith and knowledge.

Why speak of two elements alone? Is that inevitable or owing to the limitations of philosophy, of what can be said within the scope of mere reason (whether in its metaphysical and, if possible, post- or transmetaphysical determination)? Are other disciplines, discourses, institutions, and practices limited in the same way? What about literature? Or religion?

## The Confessional Mode

Two tentative answers might at this point suggest themselves to the question with which we started out: How does the philosophical relate to the theological or the religious, to God, to Being, to the Being beyond, to the beyond of Being, to the "Being" beyond "Being," and so on? One, for lack of a better word and with many reservations, I am tempted to call crypto-pragmatic. The other, with more confidence, I am inclined to call testimonial, or even confessional. These answers, however, spell out moments that are to be analytically distinguished but that are nonetheless aporetically linked to each other. Were they not, they would turn respectively into the violence (ultimately, *la pire violence*) of mere pragmatism, in the form of opportunism, and into the terror of self-indulgent idiosyncrasy.[37] The one inscribes and uproots the other; the one articulates and displaces the other; the one engenders and supplements the other.

The first, pragmatic, answer consists in the reference, however indirect or provisional, to the overdetermined givens of a context, a history, a tradition, a culture. Whatever is determinable in the analysis of a given phenomenon, a corpus of texts, or tradition remains overdetermined or — in Derrida's more recent terminology — haunted by what is not yet determinable or, more likely, will forever be indeterminable. Here, any formalization reaches its limit and touches upon singular traits that only

---

37. See Derrida, *L'Autre cap*, 23–24: "[I]l faut aussi anticiper et garder le cap car, sous le motif, qui peut devenir slogan de l'anticipable ou de l'absolument nouveau, nous pouvons craindre de voir revenir le fantôme du pire. . . . Nous ne connaissons que trop le 'nouveau', en tout cas la veille rhétorique, la démagogie, la psychagogie du 'nouveau'-et parfois de l''ordre nouveau'. . . . Nous devons nous méfier *et* de la mémoire répétitive *et* du tout autre [We must be suspicious *both* of repetitive memory *and* of the totally other]."

a singular attestation renders, if not present, then at least indirectly or obliquely readable, audible, visible. Here, moreover, we are dealing in part with the necessity of what Derrida has introduced under the name *pragrammatology,* a provocative neologism that evokes the task and the study of the intersections between the quasi-transcendental structure of the trace and the empirical or the ontic (history, society, the self, the symbolic).

The second, testimonial, answer depends on the recognition—indeed the affirmation—of a singularity, of a singular inscription, or incision and circumcision (of the heart or the body). In the same vein, the very choice of an example, or, for that matter, the acknowledgment of a privileged example (of the theological, of negative theology, or of one particular heterodox rather than canonical author, for example, Angelus Silesius) remains marked by the "accident" or "contingency" of an "autobiographical chance [*aléa*]" (SN 85 / 113).

Yet, in spite of or, rather, thanks to this idiomatic trait, the testimonial is also capable of triggering the "passage through the transcendental" (to quote Geoffrey Bennington's "Derridabase")[38] that liberates it from the pitfall of mere empiricism, even from the empiricism that could be said to be absolute, from historicism, even from the historicism that is presented as new, in short, from any method or practice of archivization or documentation. Each of these two theoretical positions (empiricism and historicism) contextualizes and demarcates a position from which the theme and the topic of religion is presented or engaged. But both attempt to fix or determine its referent in vain. As Jean-Luc Marion says, they put God between quotation marks, affirming or negating the compatibility of the referent with some preestablished conceptual scheme. Whatever their avowed methodological atheism, agnosticism, or iconoclasm, they thereby commit idolatry. In proving or refuting the existence of God, they reinscribe themselves into the very ontotheology they set out to overcome or that they decry as meaningless, a mere *flatus vocis.* They measure the distance to an idol called "God" and are in turn measured by it.

By contrast, Derrida's more recent view seems to explain how one can—and, perhaps, should—be neither at home in the tradition called

---

38. Geoffrey Bennington, "Derridabase," in Geoffrey Bennington and Jacques Derrida, *Jacques Derrida* (Paris: Seuil, 1991), 7–292, 250, trans. Geoffrey Bennington as "Derridabase," in Geoffrey Bennington and Jacques Derrida, *Jacques Derrida* (Chicago: University of Chicago Press, 1991), 3–316, 271.

religious or theological nor simply alien to it. Everything depends on the chances and the necessities of the given situation, which is always made up of more than facts and fiction alone. Here, moreover, everything awaits the testimony of the self, of the other, of the self as other even to itself. This circumstance is exemplified by the homage Derrida seems to pay the confessional genre in *Glas, The Postcard,* "Before the Law," "Shibboleth," and "Circumfession." In these "examples," if examples they are, Derrida neither resorts to a mystification of the personal nor simply subscribes to the great Western tradition of journeys into selfhood. Autobiography's most graphic details reveal a completely different structure of self (*autos*), of life (*bios*), and of writing (*graphein*): one, moreover, that resembles the most salient features of the temporal structure of the poetic "date."

Interviewed by Derek Attridge, in *Acts of Literature,* Derrida explains why this "autobiographical trait" is never a merely subjective or individual, let alone psychological, feature, but, on the contrary, marks a place where the singular and the universal touch. More exactly still, the said "trait" provides the space where the singular and the universal simultaneously — paradoxically or, rather, aporetically — *annul* and *invoke* each other:

> In a minimal autobiographical trait can be gathered the greatest potentiality of historical, theoretical, linguistic, philosophical culture. . . . I try to understand its laws but also to mark in what regard the formalization of these laws can never be closed or completed. Precisely because the trait, date, or signature — in short, the irreplaceable and untranslatable singularity of the unique — is iterable as such, it both does and does not form part of the marked set. To resist this paradox in the name of so-called reason or of a logic of common sense is the very figure of a supposed enlightenment as the form of modern obscurantism.[39]

Instead, Derrida suggests, we are dealing here with the *secret* at the heart of any confession, of any religion, and of any other testimony. This secret recalls the confession, made in "How to Avoid Speaking," that the Greek, Christian, and the Heideggerian paradigms investigated throughout this text in fact "surround a resonant space ['a certain void, the place of an in-

---

39. Jacques Derrida, *Acts of Literature,* ed. Derek Attridge (London: Routledge, 1992), 43. See the central problem addressed in "To Speculate — on 'Freud,'" in Derrida, *Postcard,* 305 / 325: "[H]ow can an autobiographical writing, in the abyss of an unterminated self-analysis, give to a worldwide institution [here psychoanalysis] *its* birth?"

ternal desert'] of which nothing, almost nothing, will ever be said" (HAS 31/562–63).[40] What Derrida is silent about is the tradition of Jewish and Arab apophatics. Or so it seems. For not only is to intend to say or write "nothing," let alone "almost nothing," not the same as saying or writing nothing. In order to *avoid* all speaking about the Judaic and the Arabic as forms of belonging without belonging, a secret in the strict sense of the word—an apocryphal, esoteric, absolutely obscured or guarded truth— would have to be possible or be kept in the first place. *Quod non.* The reasons for this are clear enough and Derrida introduces them as follows:

> How to ascertain absolute dissimulation? Does one ever have at one's disposal either sufficient criteria or an apodictic certainty that allows one to say: the secret has been kept . . . , one has avoided speaking? Not to mention the secret that is wrested by physical or mental torture, uncontrolled manifestations that are direct or symbolic, somatic or figurative, may leave in reserve a possible betrayal or avowal. Not because everything manifests itself. Simply, the nonmanifestation is never assured. According to this hypothesis, it would be necessary to reconsider all the boundaries between consciousness and the unconscious, as between man and animal and an enormous system of oppositions. (HAS 18/550)

If the paradigms that Derrida discusses are not only questioned insofar as their metaphysical presuppositions are concerned (in their assumption of a hyperessentiality, in their privileging of a semantic or propositional interpretation of language) but also with respect to their promise to *remain silent* about what inspires them; if it is demonstrated that none of the examples given can avoid speaking, then the same could be said of Derrida's texts as well. Involuntarily, unintentionally, unwittingly, they betray and share "his secret." Our task, then, would not simply be to evade this subject (Derrida himself), but to address it as carefully (as reluctantly, disciplinedly, discretely) as possible. On that note, the essay "How to Avoid Speaking"—*in spite* or, rather, *because* of its attempted silence— might well be read as "the most 'autobiographical' speech"[41] Derrida has ever given.

40. See also Derrida, *Glas,* 45/37: "This is what I want to show by deporting you as swiftly as possible to the limits of a basin, a sea, where there arrive for an interminable war the Greek, the Jew, the Arab, the Hispano-Moor. Which I am also (following), by the trace" ("Que je suis aussi, à la trace").

41. HAS 66 n. 13/562 n. 1: "[H]ow not to speak of oneself? But also: how to do it without allowing oneself to be invented by the other? or without inventing the other?" *Specters of Marx* suggests as much when it speaks of "a self-confession that *confesses the other*" (21/46).

But the secret is telling in yet another sense: in order to be able to truly respect or address the Other, one ought to and must allow this Other at least the possibility, of taking another form and, therefore, of presenting itself as *other than other*, as the other of the Other, and therefore even as the Same. The stripping (*dépouillement*) of names and qualities, Derrida writes, must "remain at work" and therefore refuse to settle itself down in any work or oeuvre, in order for the loved or desired Other to remain other.

It is against this background, Derrida writes, that the *Gelassenheit* that plays such an important role in Angelus Silesius's peregrinations is practiced and "forced to undergo the practice" of a certain "indifference" with respect to the particular other.[42] It is here, moreover, that all genuine praise or veneration must run the risk of touching upon blasphemy, anthropomorphism, and idolatry, of yet another kenosis, so to speak, that may well turn out wrong, like a false prophecy or a prematurely announced messiah: "The other is God or no matter who [*qui*], some singularity [*une singularité quelconque*], from the moment that every other is totally other [*dès lors que tout autre est tout autre*]. For the most difficult, even the impossible [*sic*] resides there: there where the other takes his [its] name or can change it in order to become no matter what other [*n'importe quel autre*]."[43]

In his quasi-autobiographical "Circumfession," Derrida circumscribes himself, with a tone that is at once ironic and deadly serious, as "the last of the Jews that I still am" (*le dernier des Juifs que je suis encore*).[44] This statement—a phrase whose "modality," Derrida cautions, is "of course

42. "[T]he *Gelassenheit* exerts itself in us, it is *exerted* on this indifference by some other" ("[L]a *Gelassenheit* s'exerce en nous, elle *est exercée* à cette indifférence par l'autre quelconque"), Derrida writes (SN 74/92). This motif is not absent from Derrida's own writing either. In the *Envois* in *Postcard*, 149/162, for example, we find the following passage: "One must leave [*laisser*] things to be done (one *must* not even, *it leaves* [*ça laisse*], in any event), and the scene to be unfolded by itself; it's very ancient but it also has only just begun, this is what I try to resign myself to. And then it is the only proof of love, if there is any."

43. SN 74/92; trans. modified. This passage forms part of a longer section that has been omitted in the first English translation.

44. Jacques Derrida, "Circonfession: Cinquante-neuf périodes et périphrases écrites dans une sorte de marge intérieure, entre le livre de Geoffrey Bennington et un ouvrage en préparation (janvier 1989–avril 1990)." In Geoffrey Bennington and Jacques Derrida, *Jacques Derrida* (Paris: Éditions du Seuil, 1991), 7–291. Translated by Geoffrey Bennington under the title "Circumfession: Fifty-nine Periods and Periphrases Written in a Sort of Internal Margin Between Geoffrey Bennington's Book and Work in Preparation (January 1989–April 1990)," in id. and Jacques Derrida, *Jacques Derrida* (Chicago: University of Chicago Press, 1991), 3–315; 190/178.

everything"[45]—may well take by surprise and lead astray the reader, if only because it conveys several conflicting messages at once. In a recent interview, Derrida elucidates this enigmatic phrase in detail. It suggests not only that one is the latest or the last in a line of inheritance, after all, regardless of everything else, the last to come and to speak with authority—and this with perhaps more authority than was ever possible before—but also, conversely, that one is the last in the sense of *the least,* who can claim the status of a witness or martyr: as if the most advanced testimony (historically or chronologically, but also theoretically, technologically, and, perhaps, even ethically and politically speaking) is also, necessarily, the most risky, the most unfaithful, "the end" or "the death of Judaism," no less than its "singular chance of living-on,"[46] in any case, the one most likely to be misunderstood. Finally, one cannot fail to notice that the phrase echoes the passage in the New Testament in which St. Paul—in a sense, the last of the apostles—presents himself as "the least of the apostles, unfit to be called an apostle," because he has "persecuted the church of God": "But by the grace of God I am what I am, and his grace toward me was not in vain. On the contrary, I worked harder than any of them" (1 Corinthians 15:9–10).

What, then, does it entail to claim to testify to that "openness to the future" that Derrida, following Yerushalmi, takes to be the paradoxical essence of Judaism, of messianism, or, rather, messianicity? What, moreover, does it mean to consider oneself the last of the eschatologists—"I shall always have been eschatological, if one can say so, in the extreme, I am the last of the eschatologists [*le dernier des eschatologistes*],"[47] Derrida writes somewhat earlier in "Circumfession"—as the last of the last, but also as the least of the last, as the last of the least, as the last and the least, that is, of those who know, tell of, foretell, the last and the least, the "last things" (*ta eschata*), the eschatology that, as Adorno remarks in the final pages of his *Negative Dialectics,* does not accidentally constitute the last and least elaborated part of the confession of positive religions? What, finally, does it imply to understand and to present oneself *simultaneously* and *with the same gesture* as the latest and the least of the eschatologists? But also one who is at once *close to* and *at the furthest remove from* tradition?

45. Interview with Derrida, "Zeugnis, Gabe: Jacques Derrida," in *Jüdisches Denken in Frankreich,* ed. Elisabeth Weber (Frankfurt a./M.: Suhrkamp, 1994), 63–90, 66.
46. Ibid., 67.
47. Derrida, "Circumfession," 75/74.

if I am a sort of *marrane* of French Catholic culture, and I also have my Christian body, inherited from SA [St. Augustine] in a more twisted line . . . , I am one of those *marranes* who no longer say they are Jews even in the secret of their own hearts, not so as to be authenticated *marranes* on both sides of the public frontier, but because they doubt everything, never go to confession or give up enlightenment.[48]

What is at issue here is what Derrida in a similar context, in *Aporias,* formalizes as the "irreducibly double inclusion" of the singular in the general and of the smaller in the larger, and this to the extent to which "the including and the included regularly exchange places in this strange topography of edges."[49] But if this is the case, then Derrida's own confessional mode is reminiscent of the aporia that characterizes the fundamental ontological and existential analysis of death in its impossible demarcations from metaphysics, anthropology, biology, psychology, and theology. In other words, the relevance of Derrida's analysis in *Aporias* extends well beyond the analysis of death and my being toward death put forward by *Being and Time.*

While the richest or most necessary anthropo-thanatology cannot found itself in any other way than on presuppositions that do not belong to its knowledge or its competence, and while these presuppositions therefore constitute a style of questioning of which Heidegger, Freud, and Levinas are remarkable witnesses, conversely this fundamental questioning cannot protect itself from a hidden bio-anthropo-thanato-theological contamination. . . . [S]ince this contaminating contraband remains irreducible, it already insinuates itself through the idiom of the existential analysis. . . . What is analysis witness to? Well, precisely to that from which it demarcates itself, here mainly from the culture characterized by the so-called religions of the Book. Despite all the distance taken from anthropo-theology, indeed from Christian onto-theology, the analysis of death in *Being and Time* nonetheless repeats all the essential motifs of such onto-theology, a repetition that bores into its originarity right down to its ontological foundation, whether it concerns the fall, the *Verfallen,* into the inauthenticity of relaxation or distraction, or the *sollicitudo,* the *cura,* and the care (*Sorge*), or sin and originary guilt (*Schuldigsein*), or anxiety, and, regarding the texts, whether it concerns St. Augustine,

48. Ibid. 170–71 / 160.
49. A 80 / 139. In a different context, I address the problems raised by this "strange topography of edges" and the question of how it produces or resembles a utopography or, rather, utopology (see my "Theotopographies").

Meister Eckhart, Pascal, Kierkegaard, or a few others. Whatever the enigma of this repetition, as well as of the concept of repetition deployed by Heidegger . . . neither the language nor the process of this analysis of death is possible without the Christian experience, indeed, the Judeo-Christiano-Islamic experience of death to which it testifies. Without this event and the irreducible historicity to which it testifies.[50]

While every ontic exposition, for example, of death or God, must be conditioned by a virtually "universal delimitation" of the concept or the phenomenon in question, the reverse of this "logic of presupposition" holds true as well. Thus, "just as legitimately," Derrida writes, one might be "tempted" to interpret *Being and Time* as "a small, late document, among many others *within* the huge archive where the memory of death in Christian Europe is being accumulated" (A 80–81/140).

In sum, this would entail a certain "anachronism," a belonging to more than one age, that is to say, to no more of one age, and thereby a having of more than one past or future. Again, the figure, the historical presence, and the specter of the Marrano is cited as the very incorporation of this *poly-temporal existence:*

> Let us figuratively call Marrano anyone who remains faithful to a secret that he has not chosen, in the very place where he lives . . . , in the very place where he stays without saying no but without identifying himself as belonging to. In the unchallenged night where the radical absence of any historical witness keeps him or her, in the dominant culture that by definition has calendars, this secret keeps the Marrano even before the Marrano keeps it. Is it not possible to think that such a secret eludes history, age, and aging?
>
> Thanks to this anachronism, Marranos that we are, Marranos in any case, whether we want to be it or not, whether we know it or not, Marranos having an incalculable number of ages, hours, and years, of untimely histories, each both larger and smaller than the other, each still waiting for the other, we may be incessantly younger and older, in a last word, infinitely finite [or finished? *finis*].[51]

50. A 79–80/138–39. "The same could be said for Freud's and Levinas's thought, *mutatis mutandis*" (A 80/139). With respect to their work in relation to Heidegger's, we could speak of an "irreducibly double inclusion" (ibid.).

51. A 81/140–41. On the figure of the Marrano, see also "Archive Fever," 46/111, which reminds us that the "crypto-Judaic history" with which Derrida himself has "always secretly identified" also "resembles" that other secret genealogy to which "To Speculate — on 'Freud'" only obliquely alludes by revealing the formal structure of any inheritance, and to which the

Like Patočka, then, Derrida adopts or, rather, lets himself be adopted by a *doubly heretical* tradition marked by a certain secrecy: one that is heterodox with respect to Judaism as well as with respect to Christianity, one that challenges, without ever blurring, the distinction between the Judaic and the Christian. In short, one that peregrinates between the inner conviction and the outer appearance or vice versa, partaking of both while belonging to no one strictly speaking. It is as if one carried a certain tradition along with oneself, as that which can be neither excluded nor included, that is neither totally alien nor intimately familiar, neither distant nor nearby, or both.[52]

By the same token, Derrida's "Shibboleth" comments on Paul Celan's poetics, which situates the Jewish identity in that of the poet, "but also in every man circumcised by language or led to circumcise by a language." Indeed, Derrida continues, the so-called spiritualization or interiorization that is thus found to consist in "extending the meaning of the word beyond the sense of the cut into the flesh does not date from Saint Paul; it is not limited to the circumcision of the soul or the heart. . . . Before Saint Paul, the Bible writes of the circumcision or uncircumcision of the lips, which is to say, . . . , of the tongue (Ex. 6:12, 30), of the ears (Jer. 6:10), and of the heart (Lev. 26:41)."[53] The Judaic thus not only predates but also prefigures the Christian, as well as, for the matter, the poetic. But, in

---

discussion of Yerushalmi's *Freud's Moses* returns in startling detail: that of the origin and the future of psychoanalysis.

52. This is a formal analogy, I would suggest, between the structure of the "belonging without belonging" to a tradition and the way in which Derrida reads that singular passage in *Being and Time* according to which Dasein carries "the voice of the friend along with itself," or *bei sich*. See Derrida, *Politiques de l'amitié*, 344. As Derrida points out, the singular modality of the nonacoustic and nonpsychological, nonphysiological *hearing* to which Heidegger alludes here plays a pivotal role throughout, from this curious passage in *Being and Time* through the texts on Hölderlin (and the *Überhören* of the poet) all the way to the later text on the *Horchen*, the *Zusammengehören* and the *Gehörigkeit*. Following the premises of *Being and Time*, hearing (*Hören*) is an enabling condition for discourse (*Rede*) and, indeed, for all understanding (*Verstehen*): "Das Hören konstituiert sogar die primäre und eigentliche Öffentlichkeit des Daseins für sein eigenstes Seinkönnen" (cited in *Politiques de l'amitié*, 356). What is more important for our present purposes is the fact that, according to Derrida, the analysis of this singular modality (if that is what it is) cannot be reduced to that of a psychology, a sociology, an anthropology, a morality, or a politics. A radically different sociality (Derrida speaks of an originary *socius*) is at play here, one that resembles the very structure of mourning, and thus of haunting.

53. Jacques Derrida, *Schibboleth: Pour Paul Celan* (Paris: Galilée, 1986), 99, trans. Joshua Wilner as "Shibboleth: For Paul Celan," in *Word Traces: Readings of Paul Celan*, ed. Aris Fioretos (Baltimore: Johns Hopkins University Press, 1994), 3–72, 59.

a sense, the reverse is no less true. For the very future of the Judaic cannot be thought or lived without the reference to a double that in its manifest (Christian) features — indeed in its mondialatinization — mimics as much as its haunts, distorts, and threatens, or that in its radical poetization consists in a relentless profanation (as is nowhere clearer than in Celan's *Die Niemandsrose*).[54]

In "Circumfession," Derrida describes a similar testimonial confessional structure of a "belonging without belonging" in at least two ways. For although they are contradictory, each of these references to the theological generates or solicits the other, to the point of collapsing into that other. There are in this enigmatic text at least two addresses directed to the figure or the name of God, two appearances of God, two Gods, or so it appears.

The first is the invocation of the ontotheological notion of the omniscient and omnipresent God, resembling the God of St. Augustine's *Confessions*. It is introduced as if it belonged to the very structure of the confession itself and makes clear that not unlike the letter to the Philippians, where Paul takes God as his witness, Derrida himself in "Circonfession" testifies to God while needing God as a witness:

> [I]f avowal cannot consist in declaring, making known, informing, telling the truth, which one can always do, indeed, without confessing anything, without *making* truth, the other must not learn anything that he was not already in a position to know for avowal as such to begin, and this is why I am addressing myself here to God, the only one I take as a witness, without yet knowing what these sublime words mean, and this grammar, and *to*, and *witness*, and *God*, and *take*, take God, and not only do I pray, as I have never stopped doing all my life, and pray to him, but I take him here and take him as my witness.[55]

54. Ibid., 59, 64/99, 106. See my "Le Schibboleth de l'éthique: Derrida avec Celan," in *L'Éthique du don: Jacques Derrida et la pensée du don*, ed. Jean-Michel Rabaté and Michael Wetzel (Paris: Métailié-Transition, 1992), 212–38, trans. as "Das Schibboleth der Ethik: Derrida und Celan," in *Ethik der Gabe: Denken nach Jacques Derrida*, ed. Jean-Michel Rabaté and Michael Wetzel (Berlin: Akademie, 1993), 57–80.

55. Derrida, "Circumfession," 56–58/56–57. Cf. id., *L'Oreille de l'autre: Otobiographies, transferts, traductions. Textes et débats avec Jacques Derrida, sous la direction de Claude Lévesque et Christie V. McDonald* (Montréal: VLB, 1982), trans. Peggy Kamuf as *The Ear of the Other: Otobiography, Transference, Translation. Texts and Discussions with Jacques Derrida*, ed. Christie V. McDonald (New York: Schocken Books, 1985), 83: "In the case of Augustine, it is finally God who is presumed to sign." *Sauf le nom* makes this even clearer:

—When he [Augustine] asks (himself), when he asks in truth of God and already of his readers why he confesses to God when God knows everything, the response makes it

This motif of the absolute witness surfaces on at least two other occasions in Derrida's writings. "I would like everyone (no, not everyone, the best telescopic soul of the universe, call it God if you wish) to know, to testify, to attend. . . . it is for this, with sights set on this that I write when I can," he says in the *Envois* of *The Postcard*.[56] And in *The Gift of Death*, Derrida expands on Kierkegaard's elucidation in *Fear and Trembling* of the paradox of faith: "[A]nyone who loves God needs no tears, no admiration; he forgets the suffering in the love. Indeed, so completely has he forgotten it that there would not be the slightest trace of his suffering left if God did not remember it, for he sees in secret and recognizes distress and counts the tears and forgets nothing."[57]

The quoted passage alludes to the "your father who sees in secret" (ὁ πατήρ σου ὁ βλέπων ἐν τῷ κρυπτῷ; in Latin: *qui videt in abscondito*) of the Sermon on the Mount (Matt. 6:6), a phrase Derrida analyzes at some length in the final chapter of *The Gift of Death*. In Derrida's reading the phrase epitomizes the relation to the *tout autre* and "hence an absolute dissymmetry" (GD 91/97) of a gaze that faces me, sees me, or sees

appear that what is essential to the avowal or the testimony does not consist in an experience of knowledge. Its act is not reduced to informing, teaching, making known. Stranger to knowing, thus to every determination or to every predicative attribution, confession shares [*partage*] this destiny with the apophatic movement. . . . Confession does not consist in making known — and thereby it teaches that teaching as the transmission of positive knowledge is not essential. The avowal does not belong in essence to the order of cognitive determination; it is quasi-apophatic in this regard. . . . As an act of charity, love, and friendship in Christ, the avowal is destined to God and to creatures, to the Father and to the brothers in order to "stir up" love, to augment an affect. . . . Augustine speaks of "doing the truth" (*veritatem facere*), which does not come down to revealing, unveiling. . . . [Moreover, it is] as if the act of confession and of conversion having *already* taken place between God and him, being as it were written (it is an *act* in the sense of an archive or memory), it was necessary to add a *post-scriptum* — the *Confessions*, nothing less — addressed to brothers. . . . But the address itself to God already implies the possibility and the necessity of this *post-scriptum* that is originarily essential to it. Its irreducibility is interpreted finally, but we won't elaborate on that here, in accord with the Augustinean thought of revelation, memory, and time. (SN 38–40/22–25)

The elaboration of this relation between the confessional and the significance of tradition, mourning, and temporality takes place most clearly in the context of an analysis of the structure of the date in the poems and the poetics of Paul Celan. On the *veritatem facere*, see also Derrida, *Given Time*, 121/213. It is worthwhile noting that this interpretation resembles the one given in Derrida's *Limited Inc.: abc* . . . (Baltimore: Johns Hopkins University Press, 1977) of Descartes's "second" proof of the existence of God in his *Meditations*.

56. Derrida, *Postcard*, 46/53.

57. Søren Kierkegaard, *Fear and Trembling*, vol. 6 of *Kierkegaard's Writings*, ed. and trans. Howard V. Hong and Edna H. Hong (Princeton: Princeton University Press, 1983), 120. See GD 81/79.

through me without being seen by me in return. The relation to the other, to God—but every other is other and thus, in a sense, "God"—is not that of a "face-to-face exchange of looks between God and myself, between the other and myself" (ibid.) Yet while I can only learn from God by hearing from Him, from others, from innumerable others—"most often I have to be led to hear or believe him [*on me doit le donner à entendre*], I hear what he says, through the voice of another, another other, a messenger, an angel, a prophet, a messiah or postman, a bearer of tidings, an evangelist, an intermediary who speaks between God and myself" (ibid.)—God, the Absolute Referent and the Absolute Beginning of the exchange (of words and of hearsay, of gazes and of curiosity) must nonetheless be *there, given, giving*, a necessary postulate that is less a theoretical assumption unwarranted by proof than an affirmation that resembles the mystical.

God must witness the witness witness if the witness is to witness at all. But, then again, if God, the absolute witness, is the witness, then to witness is, in a sense, merely secondary or even superfluous, that is to say, not to witness or to witness in vain.[58]

The second type of address, the second and more singular, if not idiosyncratic, motif, which makes its appearance somewhat later in the text of "Circumfession," is introduced in a different, virtually iconoclastic tone. But then again, if the logic of inheritance sketched above is at all convincing, the second passage might, for all its heretical reminiscences, also be the more consequent and the more daring one: the last and least possible confession, the last and the least of the confessions. It recalls the infinite substitution of the infinite, more precisely, the endless series of nonsynonymous substitutions of the finite and the infinite, that is to say, of every single other (*tout autre*) *as* totally other (*tout autre*). Here it is:

> [T]he constancy of God in my life is called by other names, so that I quite rightly pass for an atheist, the omnipresence to me of what I call God in my absolved, absolutely private language being neither that of an eyewitness nor that of a voice doing anything other than talking to me without saying anything, nor a transcendent law or an immanent *schechina*, that feminine figure of a Yahweh who remains so strange and so familiar to me, but the secret I am excluded from. . . .[59]

58. See FK 27/40: "Without God, no absolute witness. No absolute witness to be taken as witness in testifying. But with God, a God that is present, the existence of a third . . . that is absolute, all attestation becomes superfluous, insignificant or secondary."

59. Derrida, "Circumfession," 155/146–47.

"God," then, is not only the unavoidable "theological trap" of which Derrida's *Dissemination* speaks, and of which Rodolphe Gasché reminds us. "God" is not only the "dream of an absolute erasure of the trace" in favor of a "positive infinity and full presence." [60] For not only does the trace as an "endless negativity" call for its own negation and thereby—whatever its resistance to dialectics—for its own opposite. Not only should one recall, as Gasché does, that "since a trace is only a trace if it is erasable—[that a] non-erasable trace would be a 'Son of God,' according to Derrida—[that] it harbors in a structural fashion the possibility and the site of its occultation and oblivion by the idea of God." [61] It is equally clear that "God" may well be the most proper name for this trace itself. As the trace, God calls forth His own erasure in the virtual infinity or presence that, in turn, remains for ever determined and suspended by the referral to other—to other others (or Others)—and that, for that reason, can never come into its own. God is truly the alpha and omega of everything and all. *Causa sui*, God is no less His own cause than His own effect. And yet there can be no doubt that the traditional, metaphysical or ontotheological, dogmatic doctrines of infinity are in their very repetition or doubling infinitely displaced here. More precisely, they are at once parodied and respected for what they are in truth: testimonies to yet another fact of reason, the differential and more than differential nature of the divine, of its essence, its existence, its attributes, and its so-called revelations. On this reading, it seems, Derrida, like Heidegger, justifies everything—everything remains the same after the passage through apophatics—and nothing! [62] But in (or with) this justification or affirmation, something may well have taken place without taking the place of tradition. This is "the generous repetition" in all the ambiguity and aporetics of the Levinasian and Derridean understanding of the future, the *avenir*, as the *à venir*, the to-come, and, perhaps, even as the *a-venir*, the not-coming, the coming

60. Gasché, *Inventions of Difference*, 161; see Derrida, *Dissemination*, 258 / 290.

61. Gasché, *Inventions of Difference*, 161; see Derrida, *Writing and Difference*, 230 / 339.

62. Here would be the major difference between the interpretation submitted here and the one proposed by Caputo in *Prayers and Tears of Jacques Derrida*, esp. 288, but also 284, who throughout gives the departure from the classical interpretation of "God" and Derrida's calling "God" by other names more prominence than the reaffirmation pure and simple. The reading that I advocate in this study, however, gives almost equal weight to the *adieu* and the *à dieu*; almost, since the apophatic element gains a certain privilege over the cataphatic moment in Derrida too. But then again, this apophatic moment never fully severs its ties with the most orthodox of all theological aspirations. Caputo does therefore not fully exploit the explosive consequences of the formula "[J]e suis le dernier . . ." that I use as my interpretative key.

of a "not" (*pas, sans,* etc.), as well as, more speculatively still, the coming of the letter *a,* the alpha or aleph, and everything it calls forth, the first and the last, and everything that is consonant with it, the best and the worst. In a sense, then, the two incommensurable notions of God (God as full presence or absence, and as the trace, the trace of the trace, or the trace par excellence) are juxtaposed, and this through parataxis. Yet one also implies, produces, effects or, rather, evokes and provokes the other. How can this be?

One answer might be found in the reference Derrida makes somewhere in the middle of *Specters of Marx* to a "Post-Scriptum" by Alexandre Kojève. Here, he notes, one finds the insight that it is precisely at the very limit of history and of man, where a certain concept of history and of man comes to its end, that the "historicity of history" or the "humanity of man" *may* signal itself. It is as if the dialectical sublation of the concreteness of history and man into Absolute Knowledge opens onto "an other history" and an "other man," onto history and man *"as other"* (i.e., not *comme telle* but *comme autre*). Derrida suggests that this is also the precondition for any future "re-politicization" and of "an other concept of the political." [63] Mutatis mutandis, the one concept of God—of God as the One—gives way to the concept (if it is one, just one) of the *à dieu* and another sense of the religious and the theological. Of course, all this happens in a space that allows different responses, for the best and for the worst. As is suggested by *Specters of Marx* and "Faith and Knowledge," the diverse political totalitarianisms that have marked this century and more recent religious fundamentalisms are reactions to the anxiety that surrounds this experience of the "ghost" or the phantomatic (face to face with *le fantôme en général*). [64] Another answer to the question lies in the extension of the figures of kenosis and sacrifice and their structural characteristics well beyond their historical appearance, their temporal and spatial delimitations as well as their mere phenomenality.

To sum up: any consequent thinking of the trace would have to affirm that the theological is, as Gasché puts it, "not an illusion that could be simply disposed of. . . . Without the possibility of its effacement in the name of God, the trace could not be more 'originary' than God." [65] This, Gasché suggests, is the implication of those well-known words from the opening part of *Of Grammatology:* "The 'theological' is a determi-

---

63. See Derrida, *Specters of Marx,* 74–75 / 125–26.
64. See ibid., 105 / 170.
65. Gasché, *Inventions of Difference,* 161.

nant moment in the total movement of the trace."[66] Which would be another way of saying that God is as much the "*exemplary* revelation" of the "quasi-transcendental structure" of the trace as its "most violent occultation."[67] But if "God" is one of the names—indeed the most exemplary name—of the trace, then the latter is no more originary than the former. Rather, the trace and God—or whatever absolute comes to substitute in His place—could be said to be co-originary, and this in a way that is neither logical nor ontological nor, for that matter, chronological, and that is, therefore, difficult, perhaps, impossible to understand. No aporia strictly speaking could be assumed or understood as such. Here as elsewhere, one must resort to figures, theological or not, such as that of the oscillating moment of elliptical poles, each of which constitutes an at least analytical, yet in itself divided, moment of the other. It is this figure of the ellipse, indicated here in an all too elliptical fashion, that I attempt to illuminate below.

One final reservation needs to be mentioned in this context: it is not certain that the erasure of the trace of the other always, let alone necessarily, produces the Other as God. *On the Name* cautions against this reading by broaching the topic of the Other's *impossibility,* which introduces itself inter alia as *chōra.*[68] There Derrida quotes Heidegger's *The Principle of Reason,* which quotes Leibniz as saying that some of Angelus Silesius's most daring "metaphors" are characterized by the fact that they "incline almost to godlessness" (*beinahe zur Gottlosigkeit hinneigend* [SN 36 / 16–17]). Derrida takes this observation as an occasion to dwell on the well-known paradox that when pushed to its limit, atheism reverses itself in theism and vice versa. One exception though remains, as is clear from the following dialogue:

> —If on the one hand apophasis inclines almost toward atheism, can't one say that, on the other hand or thereby, the extreme and most consequent forms of declared atheism will have always testified [*témoigné*] to the most intense desire of God? Isn't that from then on a program or a matrix? A typical and identifiable recurrence?
> —Yes and no. There is one apophasis that can in effect respond to, corre-

66. *Of Grammatology,* 47 / 69, quoted in Gasché, *Inventions of Difference,* 161.
67. Gasché, *Inventions of Difference,* 162. Gasché formulates this aporetics as follows: God can be seen as the "*self-presentation* of the structure of the trace," but of this self-presentation it must immediately be added that it "can only come into its own by forgetting the trace of the referral to the Other" (ibid.), that is to say, itself.
68. See Margel, *Tombeau du dieu artisan.*

spond to, correspond with the most insatiable *desire of God,* according to the history and the event of its manifestation or the secret of its nonmanifestation. The other apophasis, the other voice, can remain readily foreign to all desire, in any case to every anthropotheomorphic form of desire. (SN 36–37 / 18–19)

One question, therefore, is left unanswered: namely, what is it precisely, if anything, that *necessitates* no less than *obligates* the rearticulation of traditional theologemes of which we have been speaking? Must the continued citation of all of these theologemes be assumed in a reaffirmation of what one has not chosen and of what one would, perhaps, not choose here and now? Or can and must it also be testified to *strategically*—in the present historical and political constellation—in view, if not of their political relevance, then at least of their being able to renegotiate the limits and aporias of the very concepts in which history and the political are often framed?

# Chapter Six
## Apocalyptics and Enlightenment

DERRIDA SETS OUT the complex task of this chapter[1]—namely, rethinking the premises of the historically overdetermined phenomenon called Enlightenment, while still somehow, perhaps inevitably, continuing to subscribe to its very idea or practice—in what he himself has described as a "very, very ambivalent" essay,[2] entitled "On a Newly Arisen Apocalyptic Tone in Philosophy,"[3] originally presented in Cerisy-la-Salle in 1982 as the keynote address at the first major conference devoted to his work. This motif, in turn, may well be viewed as an oblique reference to Heidegger's preoccupations in the early lectures on St. Paul, lectures whose notes and annotations were, of course, not published at the time that Derrida wrote his essay, but whose topic was roughly known and whose topicality may not have escaped him. Indeed, one is tempted to read Derrida's *Aporias* as a preliminary exploration of the systematic parameters and a possible context of interpretation for this pièce de résistance of fundamental ontology and, indeed, of philosophy in general.

"On a Newly Arisen Apocalyptic Tone in Philosophy" reemphasizes the paradoxical nature of every attempt at deconstructing philosophemes such as those related to the problematic of Enlightenment "critique" in the work of Kant. Derrida reaffirms the peculiar movement of this displacement by maintaining that, in its interrogation of a classical figure of

1. A shorter version of this chapter appeared in *Enlightenments: The Debate Between Critical Theory and Recent French Thought,* ed. Harry Kunneman and Hent de Vries (Kampen, Neth.: Kok Pharos, 1994).

2. "Jacques Derrida in Discussion with Christopher Norris," in *Deconstruction: Omnibus Volume,* ed. Andreas Papadakis, Catherine Cooke, and Andrew Benjamin (New York: Rizzoli, 1989), 71–75.

3. Jacques Derrida, *D'un ton apocalyptique adopté naguère en philosophie* (Paris: Galilée, 1983), also in *Les Fins de l'homme: A partir du travail de Jacques Derrida,* ed. Ph. Lacoue-Labarthe and Jean-Luc Nancy (Paris: Galilée, 1981); trans. J. P. Leavy, Jr., as "On a Newly Arisen Apocalyptic Tone in Philosophy," in *Raising the Tone of Philosophy: Late Essays by Immanuel Kant, Transformative Critique by Jacques Derrida,* ed. P. Fenves (Baltimore: Johns Hopkins University Press, 1993), 117–71.

thought, deconstruction derives its force precisely from the very thing it seem to question. Deconstruction does not negate, or denegate, let alone sublate, what it puts under erasure. In the unending closure of meta-physics, its logic is neither that of a dialectical progression nor that of a Heideggerian "step back" (*Schritt zurück*).[4] Rather, Derrida suggests here, it receives its "light" and "vigilance" from an elliptical "remainder" or "remaining" (*restance*) of whatever it is that it seeks to deconstruct. The logocentric presuppositions of a given, historically and socially estab-lished form of Enlightenment can only be effectively and responsibly invoked, Derrida tells us, when this is done in the name of a new idea or, rather, reenactment of that very same institutional and more than merely institutional force of which modern Enlightenment is the succes-sor. But in this process, Enlightenment no longer coincides with "itself," nor can it be put to rest in a historical archive. It is marked by an intrinsic duplicity—a nonspeculative, spectral doubling—not describable by the age-old philosophical dichotomy of appearance and essence.[5] The task of thought—a task that is also a necessity—is to articulate the doubling of this "double bind" in view of a more subtle, more elliptical (and, perhaps, also more enlightened?) *Aufklärung* than the one Kant and his followers, as well as his opponents, deemed possible or justifiable.

At least since the publication of "On a Newly Arisen Apocalyptic Tone in Philosophy," then, there should no longer be room for any sincere doubt: Derrida may be said to be "in favour"[6] of *Aufklärung*, of its critical and more than critical potential or import, of its institutions and more than simply institutional effects. From now on, deconstruction can thus be understood in light of *Les Lumières* (and the *plurale tantum* is not with-out significance here), just as much as, conversely, Enlightenment, like the tradition of metaphysics of which it forms yet another moment, was ex-posed to a reading bringing to light the deconstructibility of its presuppo-sitions, argumentative procedures, and ethico-political imperatives.

In this chapter, I delineate some of the most compelling insights promised by this mutual illumination, both in the aforementioned essay

4. See Martin Heidegger, *Identität und Differenz* (Pfullingen: Neske, 1978), 39ff.
5. In the preface to *Du droit à la philosophie* (Paris: Galilée, 1990), 20–21, Derrida lays claim to a certain essentialism or originarism, on the one hand, and a nominalistic pragma-tism or conventionalism and contextualism, on the other, which presuppose each other. The "thought" that Derrida prepares here and elsewhere seeks to escape this opposition.
6. "Jacques Derrida in Discussion with Christopher Norris," in *Deconstruction*, ed. Papa-dakis, Cooke, and Benjamin, 75

on Kant and in some of Derrida's later juridico-political writings. I argue that the form this illumination takes in these texts reveals the singu-lar — elliptical — structure of an Enlightenment divided in (and against) "itself," and for that reason aporetic and given only in the plural. When-ever and wherever there is to be Enlightenment, Derrida tells us, it will always be (will always have been) in the form of *ellipses,* that is to say, in the irreducible and infinitely reaffirmed and reaffirmable form(s) of Enlightenments. In what follows, I describe the most significant features of this multiple appeal and the attention it provokes, first, by retracing some of the steps of Derrida's reading of Kant in "On a Newly Arisen Apocalyptic Tone in Philosophy," and, second, by focusing on his more general remarks on the so-called apocalyptic genre, of which Kant's essay turns out to be a telling example. The ellipsis of Enlightenment that Der-rida proposes must, it appears, be comprehended as a nonphenomeno-logical and nonreductionist "reduction" of *Aufklärung* to what is called a *"lucid vigil(ance),"*[7] and the urgency of this vigil haunts every ethico-political decision that deserves the name. I then circle back to the critique of pure practical reason, recalling some of Derrida's observations with re-spect to Kantian institutional politics and addressing the intriguing rela-tion of the (first) ellipsis of Enlightenment — *qua* vigil — to the dominant interpretations of reason as formal discourse and its institutionalization. This relation can, again, be described elliptically. This second ellipsis (or,

---

7. The phenomenological *terminus technicus* "reduction" should, of course, be used with as much precaution as possible. Like the notion of *epochē,* it implies a movement *"in the name and in sight of* meaning" (Derrida, *Writing and Difference,* 268 / 393), which is not identical with the vigilance that will concern us here. In the opening of *Speech and Phenomena,* Derrida in-sists that he is less concerned with the problem of whether or to what extent the metaphysical tradition has imposed limits upon the vigilance of the phenomenologist. What is at issue, he writes, is rather whether this vigilance is not in its very *"phenomenological* form" determined by the metaphysics of presence. While this problem exceeds the scope of this book, Derrida's statement allows one to spell out some of the striking similarities and dissimilarities between his notion of vigilance and the argument set forth in Levinas's "De la conscience à la veille: A partir de Husserl," first published in 1974 and reprinted in his *De dieu qui vient à l'idée,* 34–61. For Derrida, the notion of vigilance is not so much of Husserlian descent as reminiscent of the early Heidegger's (and, indirectly, St. Paul's) concept of wakefulness, as well as of Kant. "By its difficulty, its failure [*échec*], perhaps, one will measure the depth of vigilance in the Kantian 'limitation'," Derrida writes (*Edmund Husserl's "Origin of Geometry": An Introduction,* trans. John P. Leavy, Jr. [1978; reprint, Lincoln: University of Nebraska Press, 1989], 42 n. 32 / 25 n. 2; trans. modified). For an analysis of the parallels between Kant and Husserl in a more general sense, as well as with regard to the particular motif of the Copernican revolution in its relation to the phenomenological *epochē* and reduction, see Paul Ricoeur, "Kant et Husserl," in *A l'école de la phénoménologie* (Paris: Vrin, 1986), 227–50, 231.

rather, ellipse) is less a rhetorical than a geometric figure, even though it is impossible, for reasons that will be come clear, to draw a line of demarcation between these two.

Before demonstrating this in detail, however, I also examine how the reconsideration of the question of law—of the law of genre, of the law of laws, as much as of juridical law—in Derrida's reading of Kafka's short story "Vor dem Gesetz" ("Before the Law") can be juxtaposed with the narrativity of Kantian moral law. Here again the religious idiom plays a crucial role. This becomes especially clear in a passage where Derrida draws on yet another analysis of the mystical light, commenting indirectly on remarks made in *Glas,* this time with reference to Hegel's early theological writings, in *Der Geist des Christentums* (The Spirit of Christianity).

## Idolatry and Hyperphysics

"On a Newly Arisen Apocalyptic Tone in Philosophy" develops its thesis by way of a careful rereading of Kant's essay "Von einem neuerdings erhobenen vornehmen Ton in der Philosophie" ("On a Newly Arisen Superior Tone in Philosophy"), originally published in the *Berlinische Monatschrift* in 1796. In this, Kant defends a formally defined idea of rationality against what he considers to be the obscurantist claims of enthusiastic or exalted mystagogues. More precisely, he attacks "the most recent German wisdom [which] exposes its exhortation *to philosophize by feeling* [*durchs Gefühl zu philosophieren*] (not, as the one that is several years older [i.e., Kant's own], to *strengthen* and motivate [or empower] moral *feeling* by philosophy) [*durch Philosophie das sittliche Gefühl* in Bewegung und *Kraft zu versetzen*]" (NAS 66–67 / 390–91; trans. modified).[8] The so-called *Schwärmer* who indulged in this philosophizing through feeling had accused Kant of amputating a vital—*the* vital—part of reason. Kant, however, rebuts the charge and turns it against his accusers. If ever there was an amputation of reason, then surely it was on the part of these renewers of an obsolete Neoplatonic tradition, which appeals to something that can never become an object of experience and thus con-

8. Immanuel Kant, "Von einem neuerdings erhobenen vornehmen Ton in der Philosophie," in *Werke in zehn Bänden,* ed. W. Weischedel, (Darmstadt: Wissenschaftliche Buchgesellschaft, 1983), 5: 377–97, trans. Peter Fenves as "On a Newly Arisen Superior Tone in Philosophy," in *Raising the Tone of Philosophy: Late Essays by Immanuel Kant, Transformative Critique by Jacques Derrida,* ed. Peter Fenves (Baltimore: Johns Hopkins University Press, 1993), 51–72. On the different qualifications of *tone* throughout Kant's writing, see Willi Goetschel, *Constituting Critique: Kant's Writing as Critical Praxis* (Durham, N.C.: Duke University Press, 1994), 162–66.

tributes nothing to the progress of theoretical knowledge. For them, the true object of philosophy is thought to present itself in a divination or intimation (*Ahnung*) or vision (*Anschauung, Vision*) of the supernatural, which is given only to some. Kant, for his part, argues that these purported modes of experience entail a dangerous transition or a leap (*Übersprung*) from the generality of concepts to what lies beyond them, the so-called things as they are in themselves (*Dinge an sich*). In philosophy, he fears, this comes down to nothing less than a "*salto mortale*" (NAS 62/386). To operate with "concepts" in this transcendent realm at best offers a "surrogate" (*Surrogat*) of knowledge: a "mystic illumination" (*mystische Erleuchtung* [NAS 62/386]) that is not only the "death" of all genuine discursive thought but also a form of idolatry (or *Idololatrie*), in that it puts an end to all rational—that is to say, transcendental, rather than, say, transcendent, negative, or mystical—theology: "*Theophany* . . . makes an *idol* of Plato's Idea, and this idol can be honored only superstitiously [*abergläubisch*]; in contrast, *theology*, which proceeds from the concepts of our reason, sets up an *Ideal*, which compels us into worship [*Anbetung*], since it itself arises from the most sacred duties that are themselves independent of theology" (NAS 67 n/391 n; trans. modified).

To extrapolate the givens of our experience in an attempt to determine their highest aggregation (*Aggregat*) or sum total (*Inbegriff*) in order to attain to most real Being (*ens realissimum*) is, Kant claims, at best an empty gesture and at worst a sure sign of anthropomorphism. It means to ignore the fact that the highest Being can only be thought of as the necessarily abstract transcendental ground (*Grund*) or condition of possibility of everything real. Only a rational theology that "has been carefully detached from all empirical threads [*von allen empirischen Fäden sorgfältig abgelöset*]," Kant writes (NAS 64 n. 5/389 n), deserves, as it were, absolution and has an unconditional—absolute—character:

> The transcendental concept of God, as the *most real* being of all, cannot be avoided in philosophy, however abstract it may be. For it belongs to the binding and at the same time to the purification of all concrete concepts that are afterward to enter into applied theology and the doctrine of religion. . . . God is the being that contains the ground of everything in the world, *in addition [wozu] to which we human beings need [nötig haben] to assume an intellect* (e.g., for everything purposive in the world); it is the being in which the existence of every worldly being [*das Dasein aller Weltwesen*] has its origin, not from the necessity of its *nature* (*per emanationem*) but in accordance with a

relationship for which *we human beings* must assume *a free will* in order to make the possibility of the relationship comprehensible to us. Now, in this case, what the *nature* of the highest being (objectively) is can be entirely unfathomable to us and indeed can be posited entirely beyond the sphere of all possible theoretical knowledge we are able to attain, and yet (subjectively) this concept can nevertheless remain in place *in a practical respect* (with the respect to the way of life). (NAS 64–66 n. 5 / 389–90 n; trans. modified)

The transcendental concept of God, then, serves as quasi-ontological touchstone — and, as it were, formally indicative correction — for any concept that may find its way into biblical, historical, dogmatic, or practical theology. It purifies its interpretative possibilities and guards against the derailment of free-floating speculation, on the one hand, and against all-too-human predication, on the other.

By CONTRAST, it is obvious (*leuchtet von selbst ein*), Kant writes, that to follow the secret path proposed by the *Schwärmer* only leads to a derailment of thought, resulting in a "mistuning of heads into exaltation" (*Verstimmung der Köpfe zur Schwärmerei*) (NAS 62 / 386), which is at odds with the illumination of an ever-vigilant critique (*Beleuchtung einer immer wachsamen Kritik*). It is, Kant suggests, the abuse of the art of "a certain Plato" or rather "Afterplato" that has ignited the spreading fire of these other illuminati, who are neither awake nor asleep but, in a sense sleepwalking, unaware of the dangers they risk. But ultimately, Kant suspects, it is no one less than Plato himself who must be held responsible. Especially the esoteric, unacademic Plato of the apocryphal letters — Plato the writer of the questionable letters, Kant surmises, has "kindled the torch of exaltation" (*zur Schwärmerei die Fackel angesteckt*) (NAS 54 n. 1 / 380).[9] Kant starts by taking issue with the polemical explanatory remarks with which one year earlier, in 1795, the *Gefühlsphilosoph* Johann Georg Schlosser had presented a new annotated translation of Plato's letters. The book in question was published in Kant's own Königsberg and entitled *Platons Briefe über die syrakusanische Staatsrevolution, nebst einer historischen Einleitung und Anmerkungen* (Plato's Letters on the Revolution in the State of Syracuse, together with a Historical Introduction and Annotations).[10]

9. On Plato's letters, see Derrida, *Postcard*, 92 ff. /102 ff.
10. See Johan van der Zande, *Bürger und Beamter: Johann Georg Schlosser, 1739–1799*

However, much more is at stake in Kant's vehement and satirical riposte. His main target is not so much this translation or its translator as, more generally, the tendency of which, in his eyes, this publication is symptomatic. For Kant, this text illustrates once more the urgent need to defend the primacy of a restrictive, formal, and discursive interpretation of the tribunal of reason over and against its dogmatic inflation and devaluation in light of merely subjective feeling (*Gefühl*) and presentiment (*Vorempfindung, praevisio sensitiva* [NAS 61/386]). At issue, therefore, is nothing less than the privilege of conceptual labor over an *"aesthetic mode"* of presentation or representation (*eine ästhetische Vorstellungsart* [NAS 71/396]). The exalted "hyperphysics" (*Hyperphysik* [NAS 64 n. 5/ 389 n]) that accompanies the mystic illumination does not inquire into the formal principles and regulative ideas of practical reason but gives a confused theory of the supernatural—in particular concerning the existence and the essence of God, as well as of the human spirit—which is composed of threads from different categorical realms in a manner that is hardly subtle (*nicht gar so fein* [NAS 64 n. 5/389 n]). And instead of painstakingly justifying its propositions, this pseudo-philosophy has recourse to a more elevated, immediate insight based on the affirmation of the seemingly indisputable fact (*Faktum*) that philosophy has its tangible secrets (*fühlbaren Geheimnisse* [NAS 59/384]). It is thus in a *philosophia arcani* (NAS 56/382) that the enthusiasts find the source of inspiration for their poetic talents as well as for their social power. For, the "overlordly" superior tone that is denounced here is also institutionally overdetermined. It not only rests on epistemological presuppositions that have become untenable in light of the critique of pure (practical) reason, Kant argues, but destabilizes the state and favors the private (i.e., subjective and thereby particular) interests of mystagogues and their initiated adepts. In his advocacy of a blind faith—a *sacrificium intellectus* of sorts—the mystagogue, whatever his popularity or populism, is despotic. In his role of self-appointed guide, he is a "club member" (*Klubbist* [NAS 63/388]) who, whether he knows and intends it or not, places himself in opposition to the people, betraying a curious and paradoxical mixture of *ressentiment* and veiled power. Kant writes:

---

(Wiesbaden: Steiner, 1986) and the characterization of Schlosser as "antikritischer Philosoph" in Kant's *Verkündigung des nahen Abschlusses eines Traktats zum ewigen Frieden in der Philosophie* (Announcement of the Near Conclusion of a Treaty for Eternal Peace in Philosophy), originally published in the *Berlinische Monatschrift* in 1796 (*Werke,* 5: 405–16, 413–15).

Thus the egalitarians of the political constitution are not only those who, in accordance with Rousseau, want all citizens of a State to be equal to one another, because each is all [alles], but also egalitarians who want everyone to equate with one another, because they are all nothing [nichts] except One and who are [therefore] monarchists out of envy; conscious of their own inability to think on their own [selbst zu denken], sometimes they exalt Plato on the throne and sometimes Aristotle in order not to suffer a despised comparison with those who are currently alive [e.g., Kant himself]. (NAS 57–58 n. 2/383 n; trans. modified)

Now, what deserves our special interest in Derrida's reconsideration of this debate is not only that it directs our attention to one of Kant's more unfamiliar writings and provides us with an even more unfamiliar reading of its unresolved tensions. What is even more important is that Derrida focuses here on the uncanny circumstance that this short essay in many respects sets the stage for the by now all-too-familiar controversy about the purported end of metaphysics and its transformation into a supposedly postmetaphysical form of thinking. This transformation, it has been argued by Jürgen Habermas and others, continues an "uncompleted project" of modernity by protecting the rigorously "prosaic" character of its philosophical discourse, just as Kant did, against the temptations and permanent threat of rhetorical devices, bodily desires, and strategic—indeed, economic—interests.[11] The positions taken by Kant and his alleged antagonists would thus show how the recourse to certain, supposedly unshakable, premises and arguments mimics and settles a much older conflict. In retrospect, Derrida suggests, the present debate might well prove to be nothing but a repetition and parody: "[I]t could be demonstrated that today every slightly organized discourse is found or claims to be found on both sides, alternately or simultaneously. . . . Each of us is the mystagogue and the Aufklärer of another" (NAA 142/53).

Moreover, both the call for Enlightenment and its alleged mystification may well have coexisted, struggled for our recognition, or appealed to our vigilance from the very beginning of philosophy. And as far as we know, they have always done so in the name of some original or ultimate —unveiled—truth. Even the deconstructive unmasking of the nature or

---

11. "At bottom, all philosophy is indeed prosaic; and the suggestion that we should now start to philosophize poetically would be just as welcome as the suggestion that a businessman should in the future no longer write his account books in prose but rather in verse," Kant writes (NAS 72 n. 6 /397 n).

rather the conditions of possibility of this dialectic that marks philosophy from its assumed beginning to its purported end would still, in a sense, contribute to its prolongation. Indeed, throughout his reading, Derrida leaves no doubt that we cannot hope to find a solution to this conflict or overcome our dependency on the positions involved. There has always been and there will always be a desire to find, to uphold, or to restore reason in its very purity and self-sameness. It has always been the dream of philosophical "allocution" to express an unambiguous meaning or attain universal import by neutralizing all *tonal* differences or by making them *"inaudible"* (NAA 142 / 53).[12] The tone, Derrida summarizes, never passed for essentially philosophic. Conversely, there has always been a desire to let oneself be enticed by what — from a formal, rational viewpoint — is "impure" or "other." And, indeed, more often than not this seduction has manifested itself in what Kant considers to be an illegitimate use of figural (re)presentations in the very determination of the essence of the moral law.

12. Derrida had already noted the difficulty Hegel has in coming to terms with the resistance of the *Klingen* and the *Klang* to the philosophical concept in *Glas*. Derrida speaks here of an "affinity between *Klang* and writing": "without the conception of the concept, it [language] is a dead language, writing, and defunct speech, or resonance without signification (*Klang* and not *Sprache*). . . . Insofar as the *Klingen* of *Klang* resists, withstands conception, it plays for the Hegelian logos the role of mute or mad sound, a kind of mechanical automaton that triggers and operates within itself without meaning (to say) anything" (*Glas*, 9–10; see also 249–50, 254 / 16; see also 277–79).

It is no accident, then, that the polemical preface to Hegel's *Grundlinien der Philosophie des Rechts* (1833; ed. J. Hoffmeister, Hamburg: Meiner, 1962), 5, decries the "formless" back and forth of mere opinions characterized by a certain despicable "Ton." The tone is depreciated as much as the "perhaps" discussed above.

And let us not forget that Derrida's "On a Newly Arisen Apocalyptic Tone in Philosophy" is as much a discussion of Heidegger as of Kant. Even though Derrida never makes mention of the way in which Heidegger invokes Kant's "On a Newly Arisen Superior Tone in Philosophy" in *Grundprobleme der Phänomenologie* as a witness to the task of philosophy properly speaking, it is clear that the reading that interests us here targets a host of Heideggerian figures: the *Betonung* of which Heidegger speaks in *The Principle of Reason* (see also *Of Spirit*, 79 / 126), the *Verstimmung*, and the *Geschick*, to name a few examples. In the same vein, Heidegger writes in "Vom Wesen des Grundes" (On the Essence of Ground) that "it remains valid for all prepredicative manifestness that making manifest never primarily has the character of a mere presenting [*Vorstellens*] (intuiting), not even in 'aesthetic' contemplation" ("für alle vorprädikative Offenbarkeit gilt, dass das Offenbarmachen *primär* nie den Charakter eines blossen Vorstellens (Anschauens) hat, selbst nicht in der "ästhetischen" Betrachtung") (*Pathmarks*, ed. McNeill, 103 / 28). This is almost an oblique reference to the concluding paragraph of Kant's essay.

There seems at least one other example of the debate that "On a Newly Arisen Apocalyptic Tone in Philosophy" stages in all its formal and figural characteristics: I mean the one between Marx and Max Stirner, which Derrida analyzes at length in *Specters of Marx* (137, 191–92 n. 14 / 219, 230 n. 1).

Yet if Kant's critique is directed against an improper imitation or mimicry of superior tone in the philosophical discipline, rather than against genuine — social — superiority itself, this implies that a confusion between two different voices has at least been possible. In order for the tone to feign genuine superiority, Derrida claims, the simulacrum must have been sufficiently close to its purported original. The tone makes a difference that is therefore not simply that of thematic, stylistic, or even rhetorical distinction. Rather, Derrida surmises, it consists in an uncanny *doubling,* which leaves us almost no room to discern what, if anything, came first and what was merely an echo.

Everything in Kant's text is centered around this problem of a recurrent temptation, seduction, or "lure" (*Verleitung* [NAS 52 / 377]) away from a supposed original pretension to philosophical meaning(fulness). Everything revolves around the possibility of a radical misconception of the task of philosophy with respect to the questions of what can be known, what should be done, and what can be hoped for. In this, Derrida quickly points out, the text under consideration operates according to the protocols of academic and public debate expressed two years later, in 1798, in the *The Conflict of the Faculties.* Here Kant also castigates professional scholars who are not just theoretically but also morally and politically in the wrong in failing to respect the limits set to their academic freedom, which was accorded to them by the state as well as, more indirectly, by reason.

On the one hand, Kant describes the derailment of raising the tone as a contamination owing to mere misapprehension. On the other hand, however, one can just as easily find passages where Kant seems forced to admit that the derailment accompanies philosophy from its first origin and, in a sense, constitutes it from within. Derrida elaborates on a hint that Kant gives in order to explain why, from the outset of philosophical thought, there was a flight away from the labor of thinking into mystification and speculation. Ever since it had been possible to use the word *philosophy* without a secure reference to its first context and proper sense, this deviation had been possible, and "no mystagogic speculation would have been credible or efficient, nothing or no one would have clashed [*détonné*] in philosophy without this errancy of the name far from the thing, and if the relation of the name philosophy to its originary sense had been insured against every accident" (NAA 126 / 25; trans. modified). This originary accident thus haunts all philosophical discourse as a "continuous catastrophe" (NAA 134 / 38–39), tied as it is to the structure of language as such or, rather, as we know it. From the very first moment that we speak or write or listen, hermeneutic seduction is inevitable. The souring of the proper tone (or, more precisely, of philosophy's atonality) is given with the emergence and diffusion (and progress?) of discourse and thought as such.

It has been suggested that two "different things" pervade the structure of Derrida's reading.[13] One the one hand, "Of a Newly Arisen Apocalyptic Tone in Philosophy" appears to "side with Kant" and defend the lucid vigil of the faculty of reason against the obscurantist claims of an immediate, mystagogic illumination or vision. On the other hand, however, Derrida's text at times also seems to change, if not to raise, its tone to reiterate, mimic, or parody what Kant fears will lead to the certain death of philosophy as such (and not just the death of a certain philosophy). On this reading, Derrida's text maintains that if philosophy (or thought) is to survive its own apparent end or closure, Kant's critique is both indispensable and in need of opening up. To bring out the force and the weaknesses of Kant's critique thus demands that one engage in a highly convoluted exchange of gestures and speak in more than one tongue. Instead of relying on a single and ultimately monological voice of practical reason that dictates and orients a theoretical discourse that — in and for itself — is without tone, the Enlightenment of (and enlightenment by) this given, historically determined form of *Aufklärung* would therefore have to speak with many different voices at once. Moreover, it could be shown that this multiplicity or variety and change of tone also takes place within one and the same discursive utterance, within one and the same word, within one and the same syllable, in short, within one and the same mark.

But how could this occur? How can Derrida's reading claim to be simultaneously inside and outside the Kantian project? How can Derrida simply refuse to "take sides" with the parties involved and instead bring to light "the old solidarity of these antagonists or protagonists" (NAA 138 / 45)? Derrida writes that in "repeating" what Kant does, he is "going to come round to doing the contrary — or preferably something else" (NAA 125 / 23). How so?

It is, Derrida notes, Kant's proposal to resolve the conflict ("Aber, wozu nun aller dieser Streit . . . ?" [NAS 70 / 395]) between argument and intuition or divination and to pave the way toward a possible future consensus, coexistence, or even cooperation that indicates that we can hardly

13. "Jacques Derrida in Discussion with Christopher Norris," in *Deconstruction*, ed. Papadakis, Cooke, and Benjamin, 75. See also Christopher Norris, "On Derrida's 'Apocalyptic Tone': Textual Politics and the Principle of Reason," *Southern Review* 19, no. 1 (1986) 13–30.

speak here of a real "antinomy" (NAA 142 / 52), let alone a *différend*. For Kant concludes his essay by declaring the discrepancy—or lack of harmony—between philosophy's atonality and the increasing cacophony of voices ultimately null and void ("much noise about nothing [*ein Lärm um nichts*]," or even a noise produced *around* nothing). It is a controversy that because of the common aim of the parties involved is in demand of mere mutual explication in order to bring the dissension to an end. It is, in other words, a "disunity out of a misunderstanding in which no reconciliation [*Aussöhnung*] but only a reciprocal clarification is needed in order to conclude a treaty that makes future concord [*Eintracht fürs künftige*] even more heartfelt" (NAS 71 / 395).

Kant and his opponents, Derrida notes, have in common that they both exclude something as "*inadmissible*" (NAA 142 / 52). In foregrounding a striking sexual metaphorics that Kant takes up from Schlosser and simply turns against him, Derrida first of all points to the fact that both parties express a desire to uncover, denude, or unveil truth *without castrating the logos*—that is, without stripping reason of its "phallus." The debate between philosophy and its poetic seduction is thus readable as centered around an anxious attempt to prevent or circumvent the emasculation (*Entmannung* [NAS 64 / 389–90]) of reason.[14] On the one hand, there is the emasculation of which Schlosser accuses Kant: a castration that supposedly occurs whenever reason cuts from itself everything that exceeds the narrow bounds of formal reason. In this operation, reason loses its substance and quasi-divine nature through a "metaphysical sublimation" and runs the risk of becoming so thin or "delicate" (*feinnervig*) that it becomes impotent and unable to stand up against seduction of idolatry and

14. In the third essay of the *Zur Genealogie der Moral,* Nietzsche, too, invokes the threat of castration in his assault on the "contradictory" concept of "pure reason": "[T]he *more* affects we allow to speak about one thing, the *more* eyes, different eyes, we can use to observe one thing, the more complete will our 'concept' of this thing, our 'objectivity,' be. But to eliminate the will altogether, to suspend each and every affect, supposing we are capable of this— what would that mean but to *castrate* the intellect?" (*On the Genealogy of Morals,* trans. Walter Kaufmann and R. J. Hollingdale [New York: Vintage Books, 1989], 119). Aside from its interiorization of violence, the critique of pure (practical) reason consists, Nietzsche asserts, in the "shameful emasculation of feeling" (ibid., 124, cf. 142).

In Derrida, the figure of castration appears in many context; see for example, *Positions,* 112ff. / 84ff., where Derrida notes that the notion of castration is "indissociable" from that of dissemination; and *Glas,* 41–42 / 50–52, which discusses circumcision as a "symbolic castration," notes that circumcision and the "sacrifice of Isaac" are "analogous gestures," and goes on to observe that the figure of castration "has an essential relation here with the simulacrum and does not let itself be thought as a real 'event' in the current sense of the word."

blasphemy or "vice" (*Laster*) (NAS 65 / 389–90). On the other hand, there is the emasculation of reason of which Kant, in turn, suspects Schlosser. This castration supposedly takes place whenever reason permits itself to be enticed by subjective, intuitive, or sensualistic devices and becomes caught up and lamed (*gelähmt*) in the metaphor of a—feminine—veil and therein forgets its own formidable "strength" (*Stärke*) (NAS 65 / 390).

Kant criticizes in particular the *personification* that compares the moral law to a veiled goddess, to the figure of Isis, who—as the "murderess of Osiris, all of whose pieces she later recovers, except for the phallus" (NAA 143 / 55) [15]—reminds us by her very name of the castration complex that seems to haunt this text. Even though Kant does not establish an explicit link between the feared castration of reason and the sudden appearance of Isis, there is, Derrida suggests, a "tropical continuity" (NAA 136 / 43) between these two citations. And for all the difficulties related to its very concept, it is precisely as a trope or "simulacrum" (NAA 139 / 47), rather than as an anatomical incision, that what is called castration here affects a given symbolical order and indeed threatens its "phallus." [16]

We should, Kant urges, not personify the law, which is transcendent, not only in relation to things but, in a sense, also vis-à-vis persons, who only deserve our respect "insofar as they offer an *example* of the moral law," which, Kant holds, is "the only cause" of this respect. [17] Indeed, the

15. Derrida is mistaken: in the myth, Isis was the devoted wife, not the killer, of Osiris, who was murdered by their brother Set. The latter cut the body into fourteen pieces, but Isis searched for and found all of these, except for the phallus, "which had been greedily devoured by a Nile crab, the Oxyrhynchid, forever accursed for this crime" (*New Larousse Encyclopedia of Mythology* [London: Hamlyn, 1968], 18; and see also 19–20).

16. For discussion of "castration," its "concept" and "metaphor," see Derrida, *Dissemination*, 26, 41 n. 39, 32, 47 n. 24; *La Vérité en peinture* (Paris: Flammarion, 1978), trans. Geoff Bennington and Ian McLeod as *The Truth in Painting* (Chicago: University of Chicago Press, 1987), 119–21 / 136–38; *Éperons: Les Styles de Nietzsche* (Paris: Flammarion, 1976), trans. Barbara Harlow as *Spurs: Nietzsche's Styles*, French-English version (Chicago: University of Chicago Press, 1979), 59, 61 / 58, 60; and *Positions*, 84, 86–87 / 112, 118–19, 120–21.

17. See Jacques Derrida, "Préjugés—devant la loi," in *La faculté de juger*, ed. Jean-François Lyotard (Paris: Éditions de Minuit, 1985), 87–139, trans. as "Before the Law" by Avital Ronell and Christine Roulston, in Derrida, *Acts of Literature*, ed. Attridge, 183–220, 190 / 87–139, 53. The notion of respect is analyzed by Kant in his *Kritik der praktischen Vernunft*, trans. Mary Gregor as *Critique of Practical Reason* (Cambridge: Cambridge University Press, 1997), 1.1.3, which deals with the so-called "incentives" (*Triebfedern*) of pure practical reason. Derrida explains that his reading in "Before the Law" takes place against the background of Heidegger's discussion of *Achtung* in his *Kant und das Problem der Metaphysik* (Bonn: F. Cohen, 1929), trans. Richard Taft as *Kant and the Problem of Metaphysics* (5th ed., Bloomington: Indiana University Press, 1997), ch. 30, where "respect" is understood in relation to the so-called transcendental imagination. "*[R]espect* of the moral law belongs to neither the rational order of the law nor to

moral law is not based on the assumption of any pre-given unity of divine nature and human freedom that is said to announce itself in our deepest sentiments, as the most subtle representative of the *Genieschwärmerei* and *Popularphilosophie*, Friedrich Heinrich Jacobi, against whom Kant implicitly polemicizes in his pamphlet, had assumed.

Jacobi's *Briefe über die Lehre von Spinoza* (Letters on the Teaching of Spinoza), published in 1785, had embarrassed the Kantian party by initiating a debate in which the criticism of the *Aufklärung* threatened to be identified with a position from which it deemed itself removed at a safe distance, namely, Spinozism, atheism, and nihilism.

According to Jacobi, who dedicated his book *Allwill* to Schlosser in 1792, the inalienable awareness of freedom and moral consciousness, the synthetic character of our experience as well as the conviction that we are affected not just by phenomena or the mere appearances of things but by the *things as they are in themselves,* remains totally incomprehensible to philosophy if it uses *demonstration* and *mechanical reasoning* as its privileged methods of inquiry. Jacobi and the other philosophers of faith maintain that along these lines we shall never be able to infer or to affirm the existence of the *ens realissimum,* that is to say, of God, since the formal rational argument forbids the use of categories such as *cause* and *substance* outside the realm of the spatio-temporal—and, in Kant's view, merely phenomenal—world.[18] Kant's practical postulates, premised as they are on formally defined theoretical reasons, are therefore nothing but inconsequent and inconsequential declarations that have no *fundamentum in re,* which only a renewed primacy of faith and revelation could give them.

Nihilism is the final result of a thought that refrains from knowing the thing itself, that looks for the beautiful in beautiful forms, that reduces positive religion to mere awareness of duty, and that turns the will into the mere form of a general will, loses all substance, and ultimately wills nothing. In the formal determination of reason, all singular and context-specific—and, Jacobi suggests, lawless—givens are lost, and they precisely enable what it means to be human. In the philosophy of understand-

---

the order of psychological phenomena; the *interest* of reason and in general the whole schematism of transcendental reason is still what, raising the opposition, *suspends the leap,*" Derrida writes in *Glas* (216 / 242).

18. See H. Timm, "Die Bedeutung der Spinozabriefe Jacobis für die Entwicklung der idealistischen Religionsphilosophie," in *Friedrich Heinrich Jacobi, Philosoph und Literat der Goethezeit,* ed. K. Hammacher (Frankfurt a./M., 1971), 68 n. 81, and also Frederick C. Beiser, *The Fate of Reason: German Philosophy from Kant to Fichte* (Cambridge, Mass.: Harvard University Press, 1987), 44ff., 122ff.

ing that Kant and Fichte have pushed to its extreme, Jacobi says, there is no room for these irrational moments. They find their proper place in the heart, in sentiment, and in faith. Jacobi condemns the idealist concept of reason because it makes all reality depend on subjectivity. Kant's and Fichte's philosophies seek the conditions of justification in subjective reason alone and acknowledge nothing and nobody that falls outside this frame. Such a conception of a reason that is fundamentally only responsive to itself, Jacobi concludes, could well be called nihilistic. Kant's and Fichte's systems, in which there is no real—constitutive—place for a transcendent God, are a logical consequence of Spinozistic pantheism. In Fichte's subjective idealism, which liquidates the "thing in itself" (which Kant still respected), Spinoza's doctrine of a God who is immanent in the world and identical with reason is pushed and folded back into itself.

To be sure, Jacobi acknowledged in a letter to Fichte in 1799, one could launch a similar criticism at his own position, according to which the reality of God, men, and things is not given to us in knowledge but in the familiarity of an internally given image or faith. Here we would seem to be dealing with what in terms of conceptual mediation seems a mere chimera (Chimärismus). The alternative to the supposed atheism of the Enlightenment would be an irrational "obscurantism,"[19] whose fundamentum in re is no more warranted than the formal aprioris of mechanical reason. In other words, the said nihilistic trait would seem characteristic of all philosophizing. But if this is indeed the case, the question must be raised of which nihil is most conducive to life, morality, religion. Is it the nothingness of diffuse feelings or the emptiness of abstract concepts and formal reasoning?

INDEED, IN KANT'S EYES the critique of pure and pure practical reason excludes any possibility of an intellectual intuition of the ultimate telos, the highest good or summum bonum that it must nonetheless presuppose. Because of its elusive—some would say, absolute—nature, the secret of the moral law subtracts itself from the realm of what is potentially or actually visible or, for that matter, visible in its very invisibility (as would be, say, the idol or the icon). In words that anticipate the analysis proposed by "How to Avoid Speaking," Derrida here argues that the incomprehensibility of the law is in a paradoxical way

19. Otto Pöggeler, "Hegel und die Anfänge der Nihilismus-Diskussion," in Der Nihilismus als Phänomen der Geistesgeschichte in der wissenschaftlichen Diskussion unseres Jahrhunderts, ed. D. Arendt (Darmstadt: Wissenschaftliche Buchgesellschaft, 1974), 307–49.

more in tune with the essence of the voice that hears/understands itself but
neither touches nor sees itself, thus seeming to hide itself from every external intuition. But in its very transcendence the moral voice is nearer, and thus
more auto-affective, more autonomous. The moral law then is more auditory,
more audible than the mystagogic oracle still contaminated by feeling, illumination, or intuitive vision, contact and mystical tact. (NAA 133 / 37)

The voice of practical reason says "nothing describable" (NAA 132 / 35)
but only prescribes — only prescribes itself, that is, unconditionally, categorically. Yet, even though this may be exactly the reason why it thus
"gives rise to autonomy" (NAA 132 / 35-36), Kant also acknowledges that
it expresses itself in a manner that rests upon a certain heteronomy; it resounds from the height of a sublimity that has nothing to do with superiority, perhaps only with genuine superiority: "[E]very human being finds
in reason the Idea of duty and trembles as he listens to its adamant voice
when inclinations, which try to make him deaf and disobedient to this
voice, arise within him" (NAS 68 / 392). (But how, Derrida asks in passing,
can one determine the voice of the other than oneself — or, for that matter,
of oneself as other — in oneself? How, moreover, can a philosopher like
Kant, who throughout insists on limiting the knowable to what is general
and necessary, pretend to discern a singular tone? Put otherwise: how can
he differentiate between the voice of the oracle and that of reason? And is
their always possible confusion not precisely constitutive of the possibility
of the moral law in its very sublimity?) With formulations that, yet again,
broach a topic and announce a reading carried through elsewhere, Derrida here already conjures up the very horror that obligation toward the
moral law must apparently also entail for humankind: "Although it gives
rise to autonomy . . . it even thunders in him, for man *trembles* [*zittert*] to
hear this brazen voice that, from the height of its majesty, orders him to
*sacrifice* his drives, to resist seductions, to forgo his desires" (NAA 132-33 /
35-36).

Moral law speaks with authority — a sure sign of a divine power, force,
and, perhaps, violence (*Gewalt,* as Kant says, long before Benjamin) —
only since, as Derrida puts it, "the law it dictates is as little flexible, as
little subject to free interpretation as if it came from the completely other
in me" (NAA 132 / 36). In an enigmatic or rather aporetic way, human autonomy and reason, limited in their *Gewalt,* and heteronomy (or divine
*Gewalt*) are referred to each other or go hand in hand. These poles
strangely and uncannily meet in the heart of a necessary — and, as we shall

see, necessarily oblique or doubled—postulate that Derrida, following Montaigne and Pascal, calls "mystical," and that Kant, for his part, seeks before anything else to strip of its mystagogic or numinous potential:

> It is . . .in the categorical imperative of practical reason according to its matter—an imperative that says, "I will that your action harmonize with the final purpose of all things"—that the presupposition [*Voraussetzung*] of a legislating will is already at the same time thought, a will that contains all power [*Gewalt*] (of the divine) and that does not need to be imposed [*aufgedrungen*] in any special way. (NAS 62 n / 387 n; trans. modified)

This said, it comes as no surprise when, in the final paragraph of his essay, Kant reluctantly or almost indifferently associates the veiled Isis with his own understanding of the sublimity of the moral law. It is at this neurological point of the present yet absent moral law that the extremes, that is to say, critical philosophy and so-called obscurantism, touch upon each other, if only temporarily and, Kant seems to think, accidentally and strategically (or, as he puts it, didactically: for the difference between pedagogy and mystagogy seems all that matters here, and is, moreover, based on the putative point of departure or subjective attribution, not on any difference in the formal structure ascribed to the law):

> The veiled goddess before whom we of both parties bend our knees is the moral law in us, in its inviolable majesty [*das moralische Gesetz in uns, in seiner unverletzlichen Majestät*]. We do indeed perceive her voice and also understand very well her command [*Gebot*]. But when we are listening, we are in doubt whether it comes from man, from the perfected power of his own reason [*aus der Machtvollkommenheit seiner eigenen Vernunft*], or whether it comes from an other, whose essence is unknown to us and speaks to man through this, his own reason. At bottom we would perhaps do better to rise above and thus spare ourselves research into this matter; since such research is only speculative [*bloss spekulativ*] and since what obliges us (objectively) to act remains always the same, one may place one or the other principle down as a foundation. (NAS 71 / 395)

Therefore, in spite of the analogy, the identification of the moral law with a sensible, veiled, feminine figure—or, more precisely, her *body*—remains an aesthetic mode of (re)presentation even when it ascribes no other characteristics to this law than those (already or separately) discovered by discursive and prosaic demonstration. Nevertheless, this personification would be more appropriately invoked *after* the principles of morality have been uncovered. Only then could one feel justified in resorting to images from the senses, to using an "analogical representation" (*analogische Darstellung* (NAS 71/396), in order didactically to encourage — and socially, politically, and institutionally diffuse — rather than philosophically to ground moral principles and rules of conduct. By reversing this proper order, by deducing morality from sentiments or sensuous images, one is, Kant asserts, in danger of conflating the law with some mystic vision, which, again, comes down to the demise of all moral philosophy — this time in its scholarly delimitation within the institution of the university — and the rise of mere arbitrary opinion, demagogy and anarchy:

> To be able to have a presentiment of [*ahnen*] that goddess would therefore be an expression that means nothing more than to be led to concepts of duty by moral *feeling* before one could have *clarified* the principles on which this feeling depends; such an intimation of law, as soon as methodical [*schulgerechte*] treatment lets it pass into clear insight, is the authentic occupation of philosophy without which the expression of reason would be the voice of an *oracle* that is exposed to all sorts of interpretations.[20]

Kant claims that, unlike the sensible and singular voice of the oracle, the voice of (practical) reason, that is to say of moral law, does not (or

20. NAS 71–72/396; trans. modified. Kant could nonetheless also write: "Vielleicht ist nie etwas Erhabneres gesagt, oder ein Gedanke erhabener ausgedrückt worden, als in jener Aufschrift über dem Tempel der Isis (der Mutter Natur): 'Ich bin alles was da ist, was da war, und was da sein wird, und meinen Schleier hat kein Sterblicher aufgedeckt'" (*Kritik der Urteilskraft*, vol. 8 of *Werke in zehn Bänden*, ed. Wilhelm Weischedel [Darmstadt: Wissenschaftliche Buchgesellschaft, 1983], 417 n). These words are added to a passage that evokes the sublime (*erhabene*) feelings caused by the virtuous, intelligible character, feelings that are compared to the limitless prospect of a joyful future unattainable by any definite (*bestimmten*) concept. On the one hand, Kant leaves no doubt that this aesthetic idea is a representation of the imagination (*Einbildungskraft*), which simply supplements a given concept (*eine einem gegebenen Begriffe beigesellte Vorstellung*) and is bound up with a multitude of partial and freely deployed representations, said to surround the given concept with much that has to remain ineffable (*Unnennbares*), thus allowing the cognitive faculties to be experienced more vividly or quickened (*belebt*, ibid., 417) and binding the mere letter of language to its spirit. On the other hand, however, this logical and temporal order of conceptual thought and aesthetic imagination can apparently also be reversed. The said note explains approvingly that J. A. von Segner, in his *Naturlehre* used the temple of Isis as an emblematic figure in order to inspire his pupil ("um seinen Lehrling, den er in diesen Tempel zu führen bereit war, vorher mit dem heiligen Schauer zu erfüllen, der das Gemüt zu feierlicher Aufmerksamkeit stimmen soll" (ibid.). Derrida briefly refers to this passage in "Economimesis," in S.Agacinksi et al., *Mimesis: Des articulations* (Paris: Aubier-Flammarion, 1975), 57–93, 73.

should not) lend itself to any such misinterpretation or misappropriation. It is only when this voice is mimicked and parodied, when it is mistaken for (or mixed with) a voice that does not speak to all of us in the same unequivocal way, but, on the contrary, only through the veil of particular, sensible tropes, that it loses its proper tone and its true or genuine secret. The very universality of the law forbids it to speak a private language. And yet, if the secret (or *Geheimnis*) thus also has a certain intimacy or domesticity (as is suggested by the *heim* or *heimisch* that Derrida reads in the German *Geheimnis*), it is at the same time also transcendent, to the point of being uncanny (or *unheimlich*). Small wonder, then, that in the eyes of his immediate successors, Hegel among them, Kant's morality was seen as an excessively critical and formalist *Schwärmerei*.[21] For Kant, the sublimity of the moral law consists precisely in the fact that it speaks from a distant height. It becomes unclear *what* precisely, if anything, the law *is*.[22]

On closer scrutiny, Derrida contends, this remains true for the *Schwärmer* as well. For although Kant at one point accuses the mystagogues of being "strong men [*Kraftmänner*] who have recently proclaimed with great enthusiasm [*Begeisterung*] a wisdom that costs them no effort because they pretend to have seized this goddess at the tip of her garment and to have brought her into their power" (NAS 66 n / 391 n), he is also aware of the fact that they do not, cannot, and must not penetrate her veil either. The most they can hope for is to "approach so near to the goddess Wisdom that one can perceive the rustling [*Rauschen*] of her garment" (NAS 64 / 389; trans. modified), for the veil itself cannot be lifted. The *Schwärmer* only make it so thin that they can continue pretending to divine (*ahnen*) a presence behind it. And while it remains unclear how thin the veil is made, Kant suspects them of leaving it ultimately intact and in any case thick enough so as to allow them to take the apparent specter (*Gespenst*) behind it for whatever they please. What seems to attract them in the figure of Isis is thus more the veil itself than what lies behind it. It is the veil, then, that, Derrida concludes, "unleashes what Freud calls *Bemächtigungstrieb*" (NAA 140 / 48). This drive is evoked by a relative absence or, rather, presence-absence, that the veil, playing *around* the figured or imagined body—which is nothing determinable or, at least, nothing that we could bear to see—symbolizes, allegorizes, supplements in a suggestive metonymy, for as long as it last. For the desire cannot con-

21. See Jean-Luc Nancy, *L'Impératif catégorique* (Paris: Flammarion, 1983), 8.
22. See J. Hillis Miller, *Ethics of Reading: Kant, de Man, Eliot, Trollope, James, and Benjamin* (New York: Columbia University Press, 1987), 19, 20.

quer its object without destroying its—fatal—attraction, without liquidating what it strives for: the figure of Isis is constituted and constructed from within as that which eludes and excludes all vision, all touching, and every conceptual or poetical appropriation. "The mystagogues of modernity, according to Kant, do not simply tell us what they see, touch, or feel. They *have a presentiment of*, they anticipate, they approach, they smell out, they are men of imminence and the trace," Derrida concludes (NAA 136–37 / 43).

To the extent that the mystagogues respect the veil and do not grasp, let alone violate or incorporate, the body of the goddess whose existence is evoked behind (and by) the veil, they would thus seem to observe the very same logic of veiling that Derrida studies with so much fervor in *Spurs*. In this reading of some of Nietzsche's most enigmatic fragments, the "truth" of "woman" is also described in terms of a play that allows no material, corporeal, or ontological essences at all. In what measure, then, does Derrida's analysis here repeat the gesture that Kant condemns in the enthusiasts, who, we have just learned, are not only "men of imminence," but also "men of the trace"?

Surely it is also telling that in *Glas* (in a passage to which he returns in his reading of Kafka in "Before the Law"), Derrida makes much of the "violation" by Pompey of the Jewish temple mentioned in Hegel's early theological writings. Pompey "pulls off the veils" only to discover that the curtains of the tabernacle in fact hide nothing, or at least nothing that can be seen, touched, smelled, or heard. There is a difference here between the secret (*Geheimnis*) of the Jewish God that, it is recalled, "has nothing to show," that rests in a secret that remains secret, "into which a man could not be initiated," and the enthusiasm aroused by the Eleusinian gods.[23]

And lest we take this for a reading that reflects on Hegel, Kant (who in this respect is "Jewish"), and Freud, we should not forget that in what seems an autobiographical reference, Derrida recalls a scene from the synagogue in which the Torah is "brought forth from behind the curtains" in a "robe" and "bands," in which it is "wrapped" and that cover its "body."[24] The whole ceremony, described almost in passing, revolves around a similar "movement" of the veil, an unwrapping that ends with the sacred text being covered over again.

23. Derrida, *Glas*, 49–51 / 59–61. The better-known analysis of the *Fort-Da* that Derrida puts forward in "To Speculate—on 'Freud'" also revolves around a scene that hides itself behind—or in—curtains and veils (see Derrida, *Postcard*, 315–16 / 336–37).

24. Derrida, *Glas*, 213 and 240–41 / 238 and 268–69, respectively.

What is excluded by both Kant and the *Schwärmer* is the *body* behind the veil.[25] For Kant, the desire surrounding the feminine figure (whether that of her veil or her body) is always in danger of confusing the voice of reason, which is bestowed with a univocal meaning and thereby guarantees universality, with a sensible, all too audible or at least falsely sounding voice, which speaks in private and seduces like a siren's call. Speaking with two tongues, as it were, this call is in danger of conflating two distinctive feelings, each of which, Kant acknowledges, has a function of its own. Adopting for his part an almost medical or psychoanalytic register, if only to distance himself from it as much as possible,[26] Kant notes:

> The pleasure (or displeasure) [*Lust oder Unlust*] that must necessarily precede the law [*vor dem Gesetz*] in order for the act to take place is *pathological* [*pathologisch*]; the pleasure or displeasure, however, that the *law* has to precede in order for this act to take place is *moral*. The former has empirical

25. In the *Conflict of the Faculties (Der Streit der Fakultäten)*, trans. Mary J. Gregor (1979; reprint, Lincoln: University of Nebraska Press, 1992), Kant mentions the notion of the Incarnation as an example of a theoretical doctrine that, like those of the Trinity (*Dreieinigkeitslehre*), the Resurrection, and the Ascension (*Auferstehungs- und Himmelfahrtsgeschichte*), has to be interpreted in light or, more precisely, in the interest (*zum Vorteil*), of pure practical reason. How, then, should we understand the teaching that "one Person of the Godhead became man?" Kant writes: "[I]f we think of this God-man [*Gottmensch*], not as the idea of humanity in its full moral perfection, present in God from eternity and beloved by Him, but as the divinity 'dwelling incarnate' [*leibhaftig wohnende*] in a real man and working as a second nature in him, then we can draw nothing practical [*Praktisches*] from this mystery [*Geheimnisse*]: and to the extent that we cannot require ourselves to imitate a God, we cannot take him as an example" (67). This passage reiterates the analysis in *Religion Within the Boundaries of Mere Reason,* where Kant expands on this complex issue. The *Conflict of the Faculties* summarizes it by asking "why, if such a union [*Vereinigung*] is possible in one case, God has not let all men participate in it, so that everyone would necessarily be pleasing to him?" (ibid.). Kant attempts to demonstrate the fatal consequences of dogmatic interpretation of the Incarnation with the help of an *argumentatio ad absurdum*. The aporias hidden in the common representation became especially clear, he writes, in the *Schwärmerei* of Postellus (Guillaume Postel) in Venice in the sixteenth century, an extreme example of the "rational rage" (*mit Vernunft zu rasen*) that tends to arise when people "transform the perceptible rendering of a pure idea of reason into the representation of an object of the senses" (ibid., 67 n). Postellus drew the logical and, Kant implies, absurd consequence of this subreption. "For if we understand by that idea not humanity in the abstract [*das Abstractum der Menschheit*] but a real being, this person must be of one or the other sex" (ibid.). Postellus, then, was only consistent to search for a female divine daughter or "expiatress" (*Versöhnerin*) who would redeem the sins characteristic of that other sex. Ever ironical, Kant notes that he even believed himself to have found her "in the person of a pious Venetian maiden" (ibid.).

26. See *Glas*, 215–17 / 241–42, where Derrida sketches a "speculative *mise en scène,*" in which Kant seeks to exorcise the threat of *Schwärmerei*, not in the least by attempting to "subtract his discourse from the psychoanalytic instance."

principles (the matter of the elective will), the latter a pure principle a priori at its foundation (wherein it simply concerns the form of the determination of the will).[27]

Since the apriorical form of the law has to preside over every concrete — in Kant's word, material — determination of the will (*Willensbestimmung*), all desire should always be summoned *before the law* that precedes it. The righteous moral disposition (*Gesinnung*) only obeys the law insofar and as long as it neglects all motivational drives, whether they be inspired by an ideal of beatitude (*Glückseligkeit*) or by any other empirical interest. For these supplements to pure duty contaminate (*verunreinigen*) the categorical character of true obligation, even though they may very well form part of its ultimate horizon (the highest good), a horizon, to be sure, that is guaranteed and may be granted — indeed, given — from elsewhere, that is to say, by God alone.

Yet the very attempt to immunize reason against all seduction by preventing it from making a surreptitious slip from the noumenal into the phenomenal — "a leap from concepts to the unthinkable or the irrepresentable" (NAA 131/34) — also confronts thought with the danger of yet another eclipse or apocalypse. For, the defense of a neutrality of tone in philosophy, the pretense that philosophy could leave tonal differences behind, ultimately comes down to condemning it to a certain death. While Kant's purported "progressivism" thus overcomes a certain dogmatic, mystagogic metaphysics, it at the same time inaugurates another, more subtle, more formal and fundamental and transcendental eschatology.[28] On what grounds, if any (the question of the ground being precisely what is in question), does Derrida draw this conclusion?

27. NAS 59 n. 3/384–85 n; trans. modified. Many analogies could be drawn here between Kant's insistence on a certain order of reason — from the most simple, general, unequivocal, and necessary, to the complex, particular, equivocal, and contingent — and, say, the writings of Descartes and the logic of presupposition at work in Husserl and Heidegger. In *Du droit à la philosophie*, Derrida addresses the aporias involved in Descartes's *Discourse on Method* and *Metaphysical Meditations*, which follow a short cut to establishing the truth of *ego cogito* in its incorporeality and asexual essence or nature. Such a strategy, he notes, "produces ambiguous effects. It opens the access of women to a universal community and to philosophy (something one can consider as progress) but at the price of a neutralization of sexual difference" (*Du droit à la philosophie*, 321–22, trans. HdV). Mutatis mutandis, neither Husserl's attempt to reduce the reification of the *res cogitans* in the transcendental ego nor Heidegger's fundamental ontology or existential analytic of Dasein escape, let alone thematize, this difficulty.

28. For a critique of this conclusion, see J. Simon, "Vornehme und apokalyptische Töne in der Philosophie," *Zeitschrift für philosophische Forschung*, 1986: 489–519.

## Kant and Kafka

Before attempting to answer that question, let me briefly return to Derrida's suggestion, taken up elsewhere, in his reading of Kafka's short story "Vor dem Gesetz" ("Before the Law"), that the condition of possibility of any critique of *pure* practical reason is the impossible par excellence. Caught up in a double bind, the fundamental presupposition that the law be pure *must* but *cannot* be sustained. What does that mean?

In Derrida's "Before the Law," the reading of Kafka's "Before the Law" is related to a reconsideration of the major paradoxes of Kant's moral philosophy.[29] Kafka's text, Derrida notes, obliquely addresses the problem of the quasi-literary, indeed quasi-fictional, presentation and concealment of the law of pure practical reason, which in Kant's words—which would seem to anticipate Kafka's idiom here—is the guardian (*Aufbewahrerin*) and narrow gate (*enge Pforte*) of all moral conduct.

Indeed, it is not difficult to see how Kant's "On a Newly Arisen Superior Tone in Philosophy" would almost seem to anticipate or prefigure some of the most salient features of Kafka's parable. It is as if Schlosser, the *Glaubensphilosoph,* presents himself as holding the key (or one of the many keys) to the gate of the law (the castle, the tabernacle), but also as the one who closes it, playing the role of jealous guardian, whereas Kant, by contrast, adopts the position of the countryman who thinks that the law should be equally accessible to all.

At stake in Derrida's reading of Kant in light of Kafka—and vice versa—is first of all the suggestion that moral law must be thought of as parasitic on the contingent, phenomenal world of tropes and figures, that is to say, on all those a posteriori—impure and, as Heidegger would say, ontic—carriers of experience from which the Kantian notion of the law has to set itself apart in order to sustain its decidedly philosophical and nonempirical, intelligible, noumenal, and therefore universal character. The Kantian law, Derrida suggests, cannot proclaim its authority or articulate even the most formal of its prescriptions, in particular its categorical imperative, without a minimal narrative wording. Its very first example betrays it.

This aporia appears at numerous places throughout Kant's work, some of which are analyzed at length by Derrida in *Glas;* in the notes to "Les

29. Derrida, "Before the Law," 183–220 / 87–139. For a discussion, see Beardsworth, *Derrida and the Political,* 25ff.

Fins de l'homme" ("The Ends of Man"), in *Margins of Philosophy;* and in "Parergon," in *La Vérité en peinture* (*The Truth in Painting*). These inquiries into the intersection of practical philosophy and literature prepare the elaboration of a "narrative pragmatics" (a term Derrida uses in "Before the Law" with reference to Jean-François Lyotard and Jean-Loup Thébaud's *Au juste* [*Just Gaming*]). Kafka's short narrative, Derrida explains, succeeds in teasing out the intricacies of all discourse on morality, whether Kantian, Freudian, Heideggerian, or even Pauline, illuminating a "literariness" (rather than, say, "fictionality") at the very heart of practical reason, a literariness that is at work in the moral law's arousal of respect, and in the effects and accounts that this respect solicits and commands. This "singular text," Derrida notes, "names or relates in its way this conflict without encounter between law and singularity, this *paradox* or *enigma* of being-before-the-law; and *ainigma,* in Greek, is often a relation, a story, the obscure words of a fable."[30] Narrativity is evident in Kant's most intriguing expressions, Derrida points out, such as his references to a typology (*Typik* as opposed to the "schematism") of practical reason, to a symbolic presentation of the moral good, to the form of respect aimed at examples of the moral law, and, finally, to the "as if" (*als ob*) in the formulation of the categorical imperative ("Act as if the maxim of your act were by your will to turn into a universal law of nature").[31] It is for this reason, Derrida writes, that although the very "authority" and "rationality" of the law "seems alien to all fiction and imagination — even the transcendental imagination — it still seems a priori to shelter these parasites."[32] And to the extent that Kafka describes this paradox or aporia, it becomes almost impossible to decide whether Kafka's *récit* "proposes a powerful philosophic *ellipsis,*"[33] or whether (the critique of) pure practical reason is ultimately dependent upon nonphilosophical resources and retains an element of the fantastic, the fictional, or the fabulous:

> It seems that the law as such should never give rise to any story. To be invested with its categorical authority, the law must be without history, genesis, or any possible derivation. That would be the *law of the law.* Pure morality has no

30. Derrida, "Before the Law," 187/104; and, a little later in the text: "[T]he law is fantastic . . . its original site and occurrence are endowed with the qualities of a fable" (ibid., 199/117).
31. See ibid., 190/108.
32. Ibid.
33. Ibid., 191/109; emphasis added.

history: as Kant seems at first to remind us, no intrinsic history. And when one tells stories on this subject they can concern only circumstances, events external to the law and, at best, the modes of its revelation. Like the man of the country in Kafka's story, narrative accounts would try to approach the law and make it present, to enter in a relation with it, indeed, to enter and become *intrinsic* to it, but none of these things can be accomplished. The story of these maneuvers would be merely an account of that which escapes the story and which remains finally inaccessible to it. However, the inaccessible incites from its place of hiding. One cannot be with the law, or with the law of laws, whether at close range or at a distance, without asking where it has its place and whence it comes.[34]

Of course, "Before the Law" is hardly a systematic treatise in disguise, reconstructible at wish in a formal argument. Perhaps for this very reason, its narration (its *récit*) can be called literary. But the demarcation of philosophy and literature does not prevent the intermingling of the ethical and narrative regime from having far-reaching implications. For if it is characteristic of a specifically literary text that it give us neither the criteria nor the strict methodological guidelines that enable us to get hold of its central idea; if it is plausible, moreover, that we — as its addressees — *cannot avoid* deciding on its purported meaning, however "unjust" or arbitrary that might be, then an intriguing problem arises. Derrida characterizes it in the following terms: what if the so-called law of literature and of reading is analogous to the — often enigmatic and disturbing — way in which the moral law manifests itself: "what if the law [i.e., moral law], without being itself transfixed by literature, shared the conditions of its possibility with the literary object?"[35] What might *a quasi-literary constitution of all practical reason(ing)* teach us about the viability, the hermeneutics, the application, and the possible deconstruction of a spe-

---

34. Ibid., 191/109. Derrida continues: "What remains concealed and invisible in each law is . . . presumably the law itself, that which makes laws of the laws, the being-law of these laws. The question and the quest are ineluctable, rendering irresistible the journey toward the place and the origin of the law. The law yields by withholding itself, without importing its provenance and its site. This silence and discontinuity constitute the phenomenon of the law. To enter into relations with the law which says "you must' and "you must not" is to act as if it had no history or at any rate as if it no longer depended on its historical presentation. At the same time, it is to let oneself be enticed, provoked, and hailed by the history of this non-history. It is to let oneself be tempted by the impossible: a theory of the origin of law, and therefore of its non-origin, for example, of moral law" (ibid., 192/109–110).
35. Ibid.

cific—for instance, Kantian—ethics? And what, conversely, would the parallelism between the two laws imply for the ethics of deconstruction itself?

The *récit* and the law "appear together [i.e., before their common law, before the law of the law] and find themselves summoned one before the other," Derrida says.[36] Can we infer from this formulation that these two apparently extreme positions—the unconditionality and pure intelligibility of the law (for which, in Derrida's text, Kant stands) in opposition to its fictional or fabulous "presentation" or "manifestation" (for which Kafka stands here)—are in truth nothing but *oscillating poles* that incessantly refer to each other like the foci of one and the same ellipse, and this to such an extent that the first cannot be thought without the other, and vice versa? I shall return to this possibility at the end of this chapter. It recalls, of course, the earlier discussion of the "two sources" of religion (and morality, as Bergson had it), but, perhaps, also the double and co-orginary constitution of all phenomenological understanding (as well as all theological knowledge).

Derrida never simply conflates the spheres of law and morality with those of the fictional or the fabulous. Moral and legal principles, he stresses, are "not things found in nature, but . . . symbolic inventions, or conventions, institutions, that in their very normality as well as in their normativity, entail something of the fictional."[37] This does not mean that they are "the same as novels," but it does mean that they are "not 'natural entities' and that they depend upon the same structural power that allows novelesque fictions . . . to take place"; and this explains "why literature and the study of literature have much to teach us about right and law."[38]

One of the things Kafka's text could well teach us in this regard is that the question of law, ethics, and politics is from the outset one of place, space, topography, and topology, or, as Derrida puts it, of "topolitology" and "utopology." "Before the Law" indicates as much: "Did the man from the country wish to enter the law or merely the place where the law is safeguarded? We cannot tell, and perhaps there is no genuine choice, since the law figures itself as a kind of place, a *topos* and a taking place [avoir-

36. Ibid.

37. Derrida, *Limited Inc.*, 134 / 243–44.

38. Ibid. See in this context also Richard A. Posner, *Law and Literature: A Misunderstood Relation* (Cambridge, Mass.: Harvard University Press, 1988), especially ch. 4 (on Kafka and legal theory), and id., *Overcoming Law* (Cambridge, Mass.: Harvard University Press, 1995), 471–97.

*lieu*]." [39] The ethical intersects with the topological. "*Il y a lieu de,*" Derrida notes, also means "*il faut,* it is prescribed." [40]

Inquiry into the quasi-secret origin and enigmatic appeal of moral law and literature underscores the need for elaboration, not so much of pure practical (or formal pragmatic) philosophy, as of what Derrida calls "narrative pragmatics," and requires perhaps that we first confront some issues that are commonly relegated to poetics. [41] It would seem, in other words, that what can be said about the *récit* holds true for the poem. Or, more carefully, the poem, the structure of the poematic, as Derrida calls it, is the example par excellence of the literariness and quasi-fictionality of the law.

Finally, let us not forget that his reading of Kafka's "Before the Law" is also one of the contexts in which Derrida construes an intimate link between the aporia of the law and everything for which it stands — that is to say, the structure of experience and decision "as such" (and this precisely in the very "lack" of any such "as such") — and the religious tradition. The reference is once more to the New Testament and, more particularly, to St. Paul's interpretation of the law in the Epistle to the Romans, as well as to an unspecified tradition of rabbinical commentary, epitomized, remarkably, by the priest figure who in the famous cathedral scene toward the end of Kafka's *Der Prozess* (*The Trial*) takes on the guise of a rabbi (or is it the other way around?). Derrida writes:

> *Before the Law* perhaps gives rise to, in a kind of movement or trembling between the Old and New Testament, a text which is both archived and altered, such as the Epistle to the Romans 7. More time needs to be devoted to the relationship between these two texts. Paul reminds his brothers, "people who know the law," that "the law exercises its power over man as long as he lives." And the death of Christ would be the death of this old law by which we "know" sin: dead along with Christ, we are released, absolved from this law, we are dead to this law, to the great age of its "letter," in any case, and we serve it in a new "spirit." And Paul adds that when he was without law, he lived; and when, along with the law, the commandment came, he died. [42]

39. Derrida, "Before the Law," 200/118.

40. Ibid., 210/127.

41. This argument is one I make on the basis of an extensive discussion of the later work of Paul Ricoeur. See my "Attestation du temps et de l'autre," in *Paul Ricoeur*, ed. Greisch, and especially my *Instances* (forthcoming). For a recent exploration of the concept of narrative ethics, see also Adam Zachary Newton, *Narrative Ethics* (Cambridge, Mass.: Harvard University Press, 1995).

42. Derrida, "Before the Law," 203 n. 17; see also 217, 219/121 n. 7; cf. 135, 137.

Enigmatic and elliptical as these remarks remain, they make it clear that one's relationship to the law—moral and other—but also to God (*à Dieu*) is comparable to a certain death. This death, moreover, has a paradoxical structure. For while living under the old law, one is seen here as spiritually dead, and when dead to this law—and crucified with Christ—one truly lives, or, rather, lives again. Dying and living are portrayed here as singular—and, indeed, singularizing—instances (of mortification, conversion, and being born again) that underlie a repetition of which the *kairos* and the *parousia* (preceded by that other coming, that of the Antichrist and thereby the apocalypse) are not so much the terminus *a quo* or *ad quem* but rather the peculiar modality.

## The Revelation of John and the Ends of Philosophy

One of the most thought-provoking aspects of Derrida's reading of Kant's "On a Newly Arisen Superior Tone in Philosophy" is that it associates Kant's unmasking of the obscurantism of the *Schwärmer* with the quest for disclosure and uncovering that characterizes the apocalyptic tradition, in its religious and biblical overdetermination no less than in its supposedly secular translations.[43] Derrida claims that the denuding to which all critical, progressive discourses of modernity aspire—not unlike apocalyptics and the *via negativa* with which the latter has often made common cause—presupposes a vision of light and a spiritual enlightenment. Conversely, apocalyptic pathos often has shown a critical intent vis-à-vis the existing social and political order. Each of these two genres of discourse, apocalyptics and Enlightenment, as well as the historical formations they represent, inspire, or enable, throws light—of quasi-divine human reason and of divine illumination, respectively—on the other. Western tradition, Derrida contends, has been dominated by programs that proclaim the final end of the paradigms that precede them: the end of God and of morals, of history and class struggle, of the subject and of Oedipus, of art and of the university. As a result of these revolutions and reversals, each new Enlightenment, including the ones devoid of religious concepts, imageries, and overtones, can be read as yet another eschatology substituting for its predecessors. Even the proclamation of the "end

43. In *On the Genealogy of Morals,* Nietzsche calls Revelation, "the most wanton of all literary outbursts that vengefulness has on its conscience (one should not underestimate the profound consistency of the Christian instinct when it signed this book of hate with the name of the disciple of love, the same disciple to whom it attributed that amorous-enthusiastic Gospel [*jenes verliebt-schwärmerische Evangelium*]" (ibid., § 16, 53 / 286).

of the end," with which one might be tempted to identify Derrida's own position, partakes in this apocalyptic chorus (NAA 146 / 60).[44]

However, with typical precaution, similar to that orienting the discussion of negative theologies whose original structure, if it exists at all, can be respected by yet another negative theology — a *metapophasis*, as it were — Derrida asks here: who could ever claim to possess the "metalanguage" (NAA 146 / 60) that governs and organizes all eschatologies? Indeed, the supposition that there is "just *one* fundamental *scene, one* great paradigm" (NAA 150 / 67) that makes both these strategies possible still obeys what Derrida terms an onto-eschato-teleo-theological hermeneutics of sorts. This suggestion therefore can claim no other status than that of a self-defeating projection, a performative contradiction, or, in other words, a fiction and fable. This said, it comes as no surprise that Derrida begins his remarks by saying quite explicitly that he will not only write *on* but also *in* an apocalyptic tone. The first sentence of our text reads: "Je parlerai donc d'un ton apocalyptique en philosophie." As so often, Derrida's reading does not so much explore a theme, even though it does that as well, but is in the first place a practice of writing, reinscription, and unwriting.

On a "Newly Arisen Apocalyptic Tone in Philosophy" listens to the resounding of the *glas,* the death knell, of apocalyptics and eschatology and asks: what is it that remains of this genre, what of the critique, both of (pure) reason and of ideology in all its different Marxist, Nietzschean, and Freudian forms? Are not the distinctions between these devices in the final analysis, as Heidegger, perhaps, would have said, "measured as deviations in relation to the fundamental tonality of this *Stimmung* audible across so many thematic variations?" (NAA 145 / 49). Or is it the other way around, and should this ontological tonality be seen as fundamentally parasitic on a specific — eschatological, for example, Pauline — experience from whose ontic features it can never abstract? Derrida does not address this issue, so central, we have seen, to the concerns of *The Gift of Death* and *Aporias,* in this particular context. Instead, he raises the rhetorical question of whether the successive overcomings — according to a logic not of presupposition but of hyperbolic overdrive — do not reinforce the positions that they had sought to outwit. And they do so, if not thematically, then at least in the very formality of their structure: "Haven't all the *différends* taken the form of a going-one-better in eschatological eloquence, each

44. See also the essays in *Apocalypse Theory and the Ends of the World,* ed. Malcolm Bull (Oxford: Blackwell, 1995).

newcomer, more lucid than the other, more vigilant and more prodigal too . . .?" (NAA 145 / 59)

And if one can only refute one eschatology by appealing to another, more sophisticated one, would this not mean that eschatology has come over us even *before we have uttered a word,* raised a question, or leveled a suspicion? Seen in this light, every critique, destruction, and overcoming, as well as every deconstruction, in Derrida's sense of the word, would always already have responded to a call—a debt and promise or, for that matter, a threat, an inspirational fire, as well as an "all-burning fire" or "flame"—that in "itself" can never be questioned, but only affirmed, as a necessary fatality, an originary catastrophe, but also as a chance. If eschatology indeed "surprises us at the first word" (NAA 147 / 63), what is it that we can or should say and do?

Although Derrida does not discuss the question of whether *all* past paradigms are equally arbitrary and mortal or even lethal, he remarks in parentheses that one eschatology in particular—the one that claimed that morality should (or could) be overcome—was the "most serious" of all these "naïveté[s]" (NAA 145 / 59). This remarkable statement introduces (and, at least in part, motivates) Derrida's adoption of the Kantian idea of Enlightenment and its subsequent transformation into an elliptical notion of unconditional lucid vigilance or guardedness. The latter exceeds and precedes the false dilemma of formal reasoning and intellectual *illuminatio,* both of which, Derrida holds, mutilate and suffocate all responsible thought. In short, the wake—that which remains of *Aufklärung*—is the minimal concept of an emphatic idea of reason and the sum total of the answer to questions of the Kantian type: What can and must I do?[45] What may I hope for? What is man? Yet, this wake is not only a task, a duty, an obligation of sorts, but also a necessity, that which comes in a wake alone, whether it be of metaphysics, of theology, of the death with which philosophy is perpetually threatened or with which—perennially—it threatens itself. The wake is the form of reason, reduced itself to the unavoidable; its *anankē* just as much as it is its first and final *chance:*

> In the light of today we cannot not have become the heirs of these *Lumières.* We cannot and we must not—this is a law and a destiny—forgo the *Aufklärung,* in other words, what imposes itself as the enigmatic desire for vigilance, for the lucid vigil [*veille*], for elucidation, for critique and truth, but for a truth that at the same time keeps within itself enough apocalyptic desire . . .

45. Cf. Derrida, *Points . . . ,* 192 / 205.

to demystify, or if you prefer, to deconstruct the apocalyptic discourse itself
and with it everything that speculates on vision, the imminence of the end,
theophany, parousia, the last judgement. (NAA 148 / 64–65)

Unlike Kant and his opponents, Derrida does not identify this summoning with any specific — or exclusively — ethico-political or religious
obligation, let alone with some aesthetic playfulness or gravity. The differing and deferral that characterizes this elusive law and destiny, and that
leaves its trace in each word and each act — and that turns each of them
into a trace of itself as much as of others — is rooted neither in nature nor
in culture nor in any noumenal realm. And yet, paradoxically, it entails an
appeal that demands immediate response. In "On a Newly Arisen Apocalyptic Tone in Philosophy," this call is exemplified, as it were, with a citation of the "Viens!" ("Come!") that accompanies the opening of each of
the seven seals in the Revelation of John. This text, Derrida stresses, can be
read as the paradigm of the vigil that surrounds all known ends, as well as
those still to come. Indeed, without ever being able to turn its (last) page,
every wake, anticipating, preparing, or announcing an end, unwittingly
re-cites Revelation, or, Derrida clarifies, "at least the fundamental scene
that already programs the Johannine writing" (NAA 152 / 71), its fable, the
structure of its messianicity (as *Specters of Marx* puts it) or, more appropriately, its Christianicity, as the revealability of this particular revelation.

Derrida assumes that a careful rereading of Revelation — "beyond or
before a narratology" — could retrace the aleatory character of the "narrative voice" in this text (NAA 153 / 72).[46] For, according to the prologue to
Revelation, John is quoting the words of Jesus, which have been transmitted to him by a messenger or angel, and sends them to the seven communities, or, more precisely, to their angels. As a result, Derrida concludes,

46. Derrida's reading takes its lead from André Chouraqui's translation and presentation
in *Un Pacte neuf: Lettres, Contemplation de Yohanân* (Paris, 1977). See in particular the latter's
"Liminaire pour l'Apocalypse" (ibid., 157–60). It should be noted here that Derrida explicitly
refers to Revelation and the way in which it is read throughout *Glas* in the context of his discussion of Maurice Blanchot, in *Parages*, 170, 173, 175. Writing and teaching here themselves take
the form of an apocalypse, in all of its relevant meanings as revelation, eschatology, and catastrophe. Moreover, speaking of "passion" — or, rather, of an "arch-passivity" — Derrida reminds
us that it is Blanchot who, other than Levinas, insists on analyzing "a certain neutrality," that of
*le neutre*, that would be characteristic of the "narrative voice" (*voix narrative*), the voice "without a person" (*voix sans personne*) that should be distinguished from the "narrating voice"
(*voix narratrice*) "whose 'I' poses and identifies itself" (Jacques Derrida, "DEMEURE: Fiction
et témoignage," in *Passions de la littérature: Avec Jacques Derrida*, ed. Michel Lisse [Paris: Galilée, 1996], 21). See also my "'Lapsus absolu': Notes on Maurice Blanchot's *The Instant of My
Death.*" *Yale French Studies*, no. 93 (1998): 30–59.

we no longer know "who addresses what to whom" (NAA 156/77), because too many voices occupy the "line" (NAA 155/75); what is more, it is
no longer even certain (if ever it was) "that man is the exchange [*le central*] of these telephone lines or the terminal of this endless computer"
(NAA 156/77). Since, however, this uncertainty defines the apocalyptic or
angelic tonality and renders every determinate tone discordant, a crucial
question imposes itself:

> if the *envois* always refer to other *envois* without decidable destination, the
> destination remaining to come, then isn't this completely angelic structure,
> that of the Johannine apocalypse, isn't it also the structure of every scene of
> writing in general?: . . . wouldn't the apocalyptic be a *transcendental condition*
> of all discourse, of all experience even, of every mark or every trace? And the
> genre of writings called "apocalyptic" in the strict sense, then, would be only
> an example, an *exemplary* revelation of this transcendental structure. In that
> case, if the apocalypse reveals, it is first of all the revelation of the apocalypse.
> (NAA 156–57/77–78)

To the extent that it reveals nothing determinate, Revelation enlightens
the structure of language, of all experience, in short, of "the mark in general: that is, of the divisible *envoi* for which there is no self-presentation
nor assured destination" (NAA 157/78). In so doing, Revelation is the example par excellence of a general structure. The latter is brought to light
by the former and never rids itself of all of the traits that marked the
historical manifestation in its singular occurrence. It is made possible by
what it makes possible: this is what Heidegger thematizes under the heading of the formal indication, and what Derrida addresses when he speaks
of the paleonymic use of concepts and names, of the readability of whatever is crossed out or erased. Examples of this abound.

It is tempting to recognize in these and other passages a reiteration
and radical inversion of the project of transcendental, critical philosophy.
Instead of the identical spatio-temporal structures of perception and the
categories of understanding, Derrida seems to argue that it is, on the contrary, the unstable differing and deferral of the *différance* of all marks in
general that can be seen as the *quasi*-transcendental condition of possibility of all experience. A real appeal or event, then, is only possible on
the basis of the—properly speaking impossible—experience of the arbi-
trariness of the categories of all experience. Like Kant, Derrida makes it
plausible that the claims of formal reason *and* the presentiments of obscurantism ultimately obey one and the same law. To be sure, Derrida

leaves no doubt that there is no Archimedian point beyond the Kantian principle of reason. Moreover, the principle of (this) reason — in its Leibnizian formulation, "Nihil est sine ratione" — is not in itself simply reason.[47] But this does not imply that responsible thought should stop here. For, without having had an "idea" or, more likely, a presentiment of the abyss that surrounds occurrences and decisions, as well as all the risks involved, we would be unable to take a single new step; we would never be open or vulnerable to the gift and burden of future possibilities. Nothing would exist but a universe of causality, everything would come to a halt or — what comes down to same — be merely programmed. Paradoxically, only if the other gives the law — that is to say, if there is heteronomy — can there be autonomy, in Kant's sense of the word. Instead of focusing on the rational foundation and explication of what can be known or done or hoped for, one should therefore rethink a certain heteronomical unconditionality as the quasi-transcendental condition of all rational thought, conduct, judgment, and belief. Yet this unconditionality is far from unequivocal or univocal: it speaks with more than one voice at once, or so it must appear. It may be a threat as well as a promise, an apocalypse no less than a revelation. And this, Derrida points out, is no deplorable accident or a sure sign of philosophy's death, but, on the contrary, the very life — or, if one wishes, life-death — of the concept, of acts, and, again, of judgment (reflective and other):

> Generalized *Verstimmung* is the possibility for the other tone, or the tone of another, to come at no matter what moment to interrupt a familiar music . . . . *Verstimmung*, if that is henceforth what we call the derailment, the sudden change . . . of tone . . . , is the disorder or the delirium of the destination (*Bestimmung*), but also the possibility of all emission. The unity of tone, if there were any, would certainly be the assurance of destination, but also death, another apocalypse. (NAA 150 / 67–68)

Every attempt to demystify, criticize, or deconstruct the apocalyptic genre has to rely on this very same paradoxical or rather aporetic structure and let itself be inspired, diffused, and — inevitably — confused by a similar desire for more light. It has to share the same pathos: that is to say, that which Kant deemed pathological but that Derrida, following Levinas and an ultimately biblical topos, would eventually come to describe in terms of a passion. Every denunciation of false prophets still speaks in

---

47. Cf. Derrida, *Du droit à la philosophie*, 470, 471.

the prophetic mode that it, in this form or another, seeks to overcome or leave behind. There is nothing that could bring to an end this perennial process of demystification, that is to say, of negation and denegation, denial and sublimation, elevation and relief.

To be sure, these processes of unmasking are not simply wrong-headed and ought to be pushed "as far as possible" (NAA 159 / 81), a task that is interminable, since no inquiry will ever be able to "exhaust the overdeterminations and the indeterminations of the apocalyptic stratagems" (NAA 159 / 81). One should, indeed must, deploy or mobilize all the empirical and hermeneutic resources one can think of, whether socioeconomic, psychoanalytic, linguistic, rhetorical, or pragmatic. For, deconstruction, even when it "does not stop there," Derrida notes, can never succeed without this preliminary yet ultimately "secondary work" (NAA 149 / 66). This said, however, none of these modes of explanation and interpretation that the critiques of ideology provide can hope to reduce the "ethico-political motif or motivation" of their targets, as well as of themselves, to something "simple" or to what would seem to be a single "cause" (NAA 159 / 81).

The apocalyptic genre therefore cannot be judged in light of Kant's indictments alone. More often than not, it has misled those in control of the political and symbolical power. By multiplying the detours of signification, by destabilizing fixed meanings and hierarchies, Schwärmerei has been most successful in undermining the principle and the practice of censorship, whose hegemony relies in the first place on the establishment of certain identifiable codes of speech, and thus of thought as well as action. Apocalyptics might be seen as the very first — or last? — instance of a strategy that at given times and places, when all historical and political opportunities for resistance have either been played out or not yet emerged, can still upset an exclusivist discourse by challenging its dominant idiom. In Derrida's words: "Nothing is less conservative than the apocalyptic genre. And as it is an apocalyptic, apocryphal, masked, coded genre, it can use the detour to mislead another vigilance, that of censorship" (NAA 159 / 82–83). It was, Derrida points out, no accident that the apocalyptic genre flourished especially when the censorship in the Roman Empire was at its most intense. But the situation in which Kant found himself during the construction of a public sphere that has determined political modernity ever since was no exception to this general rule.

Now the most important reason for the irreducibility that gives the apocalyptic stance its capacity to resist is, Derrida surmises, not so much that its structural indetermination is yet another proof—albeit an example par excellence—of the finitude inherent in all empirical and hermeneutic inquiry, "but the (perhaps) more essential" (NAA 160 / 83) limit inscribed *in advance* in every attempt to demystify, whether the object of the critique is the apocalyptic discourse itself or not. It is the circumstance that any proclamation of ends has always already *responded* to a "Come" that calls it into being, without itself ever becoming part, let alone a describable property, of the revealment or event of this being. Derrida's whole analysis rests on the hypothesis that it is precisely that the acknowledgment (or, in his own words, the affirmation) of this internal margin— a pocket or "invagination" of a singular otherness or other in the very constitution of the most autonomous of thoughts, acts, or gestures—that marks the difference, indeed the *différend,* between the practice of deconstruction and the modern Kantian interpretation of Enlightenment critique.

No onto-eschato-teleo-theology, to use the contrived formulation with which Derrida captures the premise and the goal of metaphysics of presence and its successors and functional equivalents, is capable of determining, defining, or analyzing this coming, to-come, or advent of critique and the vigilance to which it testifies. Only a "spectrography of the tone" (NAA 165 / 92) could try to retrace the "writing" of this calling that does not let itself be represented as a theme, intentional object, figure or trope, symptom or speech act, each of which would categorize its injunction and inscription. In fact, any such semantic, phenomenological, rhetorical, psychoanalytic, or pragmatic analysis would be simply *off the mark.* As a "citation without past present" (NAA 165 / 92), the "Come!" of which and from which Derrida speaks here, gives itself only to be *read* (not seen or touched) in different narrations or *récits* (in Revelation, in the writings of Maurice Blanchot that Derrida analyzes in detail in *Parages*). But what does reading mean? This question should trouble us for, as Derrida is quick to point out, the "Come!" in question—the *Viens!* at the heart of any question—resounds as a "recitative and a song whose singularity remains at once absolute and absolutely divisible" (NAA 165 / 92). No existing or possible ontology or grammar, no narratology or, for that matter, phonology, could ever *decompose,* let alone *synthesize,* this tone or answer the question as to what it is in fact or in its very essence, in its function, in its intentional structure, in its socio-historical or political and aesthetic effects, and so on and so forth.

The reason for this is as simple as it seems irrefutable, based as it is on a formal structure whose analytical potential may seem limited—a *petitio principii* and a *circulus vitiosus*—to some, whereas it might strike others as a mere reprisal of the Kantian assumption of (or belief in) the so-called *Faktum der Vernunft*. For the very question "What is?" Derrida explains, "belongs to a space . . . opened [and traversed] by a 'come' come from the other" (NAA 166 / 93). As a consequence, the tone cannot but be affirmed and reaffirmed. The tone—the very word or concept or figure of the tone—here stands for that which cannot be denied, denegated, or, for that matter, avoided.

In this respect, as the unavoidable—*that without which not*—the "Come!" resembles the Heideggerian motif of the promise, or rather the *Zusage*. In other words, it involves what Derrida calls "acquiescing to language," or, more simply "the mark,"[48]—implied and forgotten by every questioning, be it that of the Kantian type of transcendental critique or, even by Heidegger's own account, of fundamental ontology. We would touch upon a singular affirmation which is also that of a radical *singularism*. For "the mark" in question (preceding even every possible question that one could raise about it) is neither an "I know not what"—more precisely, in its "Je ne sais quoi" sense it is fundamentally different from the Lockean "I know not what"—nor a "basic particular" of the kind from which Peter Strawson departs in the so-called descriptive metaphysics of his *Individuals*. The singular "mark" is hardly a "basic logical subject," even though, in its own way, it is a condition of the possibility of any reference, conceptualization, and, more broadly, experience. To miss the mark is, perhaps, what—at the most fundamental level—constitutes sin (in Greek ἁμαρτία, as in ἁμαρτάνω, "I miss the mark"). And lest we forget, the Greek word μάρτυς, eye- or ear-witness, lies at the origin of the classical, New Testament, and modern understanding of *martyr*. To sin, then, would thus precisely be to fail to bear witness.[49] Here, again, we would be at once close to and at an infinite remove from Heidegger's analysis, in *Sein und Zeit*, of originary guilt (*ursprünglichen Schuldigsein*), of testimony (*Bezeugung*), and so on (see BT 325–35 / 280–89).

The "Come!" can, moreover, hardly be identified with an imperative

---

48. Jacques Derrida, "'Il faut bien manger' ou le calcul du sujet," *Cahiers Confrontation* 20 (1989): 91–114, trans. as "'Eating Well,' or the Calculation of the Subject: An Interview with Jacques Derrida," in *Who Comes After the Subject?* ed. E. Cadava, P. Connor, and Jean-Luc Nancy (London: Routledge, 1991), 96–119.

49. I am indebted to Peter Dreyer for having reminded me of this important parallel.

or an order of sorts. But things are far from simple here, as Derrida explains in hindsight in one of the interviews published in *Points . . .* :

> When I said [that the "Come!" is] anterior to any desire, I meant less "anterior" to any order or any desire in itself — since it is at once an order and a desire, a demand, etc. — than "anterior" to all logical and grammatical *categories* of order, of desire as these have come to be determined in Western grammar or logic and which permit us to say: "come" is an imperative, thus "come" is an order. It is anterior to these categories that have been fixed since the origin of the Greco-Latin thought and grammar in which we think.[50]

Although it inhabits and traverses the concepts and categories of this world, and thus is not otherworldly, the "Come!" is not itself of this world. Neither immanent nor transcendent (or, in a sense, both immanent and transcendent), it is an order or imperative as though it were not one, in the mode of the ὡς μή.

Yet the "vigil" provoked or entailed by this originary affirmation — or "yes," as Derrida will say, time and again — is itself beyond any question, indeed, the very "beyond of the question" must be considered as "anything but precritical."[51] For the "beyond-question," the "gage" or "engage" of language, of the mark, always already offers itself as split, as at least double or doubled, as a "yes, yes." The affirmation in (the) question hardly takes a dogmatic, firm, or closed, thetic, apodictic or even deictic, form.

Moreover, to speak of *a* tone or of *tonality,* in empirical or general, conceptual terms, comes down to saying either too much or not merely enough. There could never be a "first," "last," "single," "universal," unequivocal, or uni-vocal call. Not only are the tone(s) divided in themselves, the difference between the "Come!'s" can, in turn, only be tonal. This difference is that of a breath, an accent, a timbre, or gesture that sup-

50. Derrida, *Points . . .*, 150/159.
51. Derrida, "Eating Well," 109. The most extensive discussion of the originary affirmation is the often discussed — longest — footnote in *Of Spirit* (129–36 n. 5/147–54 n. 1). Cf. in this context Heidegger's formulations in the "Afterword" to "What is Metaphysics?" which underscore the similarities and the differences. Derrida seems to start out from the miracle that there is, not Being or even beings, but "the mark," before any question about it can even arise. Between Heidegger's insistence, first, on the prominence of man, more in particular on his being the sounding board for the voiceless voice (*die lautlose Stimme*) of Being, and, second, on a certain pathos (characterized by some as the *Sehnsucht nach Härte und Schwere*), and Derrida's reluctance with respect to Heidegger's humanism, or the emphasis, for his part, on a certain laughter, the differences couldn't be greater. Derrida plays with the French here: *affirmation* "is" without *fermeté* and *fermeture,* but this *without* "is" without negativity or mere privation.

ports none of the classifications that we know from speech-act theory, not even that of the performative. For whereas the performative is an act whose success or failure depends on the fulfillment of certain contextual requirements, the tonal difference is nothing but "the gesture in speaking, that gesture that does not let itself be recovered by the analysis—linguistic, semantic or rhetorical—of speaking" (NAA 166/93–94). The very *location* of the tone, then, becomes uncertain or was undecidable from the start: it is and is not a trait (rather than, say, a property, quality, attribute, or modality) of discourse: "A tone decides; and who shall decide if it is, or is not, part of discourse?" [52]

We would almost seem to be dealing here with what Derrida calls a "pure differential vibration." But what does that mean, and how is this notion, if it can be thought of in any coherent way at all, to be reconciled with what one is still tempted to consider the structure and substance (the heart, the subject matter, the stuff) of factical life, both in its authentic and inauthentic modes, in other words, at its best and worst moments? Once more, a retrospective formulation in one of the interviews in *Points . . .* may help us further:

> In saying "pure differential vibration," one has the impression of seeing any identity, presence, fullness, or content disappear; from then on, one is dealing with only a vibrating or resonating system of relations. One would thus have only disappointment or lack. But I don't imagine that any bliss [ *jouissance*] . . . is thinkable that does not have the form of this pure difference; a bliss that would be that of a plenitude without vibration, without difference, seems to me to be both the myth of metaphysics—and death. If there is something that can be called living bliss or life, it can be given only in this form of painful bliss which is that of differential vibration. No self-identity can close on itself. . . . I cannot imagine a living bliss that is not plural, differential. This is marked in a minimal fashion by the fact that a timbre, a breath, a syllable is already a differential vibration; in a certain way, there is no atom.[53]

The "Come!" does not originate in a divine, masculine or female voice or direct itself to a subject, be it individual or collective, already constituted and identical to itself. Instead, the "Come!" seems the very

52. Derrida, *Signéponge/Signsponge,* 2; trans. modified. Pascal also notes that it is the tone—here the tone of voice influenced by imagination—that modulates discourse no less than a poem (see *Pensées,* ed. Léon Brunschvicg [1905; Paris: Garnier-Flammarion, 1976], 43: "Le ton de voix impose aux plus sages, et change un discours et un poème de force").

53. Derrida, *Points . . . ,* 137/146–47.

"disaster" or "catastrophe" of all of these sites and the passages between them. In terminology explored (and exploited) here, one could therefore rather call the "Come!" an apocalypse. An apocalypse, this time, without a cause, without a sender, messenger, message, or addressee. But also an apocalypse "without apocalypse" (NAA 167/95), that is to say, without the revelatory visions or final judgments that — at least historically, at the critical junctures of the Western monotheist religions, their victories, and demises — have characterized this particular genre.

The a-apocalyptic "Come!" therefore consists of *envois*, that is to say, dispatches or sendings, in the plural and plural in "themselves." And, in the light of this "immediate tonal duplicity in every apocalyptic voice" (NAA 157/78), the very regulative idea of a formal (however cautiously or hypothetically reconstructed) "unity of reason within the diversity of its voices"[54] must seem ruined in advance. While pragmatically valid, and thus far from obsolete, such an analysis would nonetheless find that some of its systematic philosophical claims cannot be warranted, but remain premised on, or, as Derrida would say, haunted by, that which it must also exclude or ignore.[55]

Furthermore, no thought of Being as event or *Ereignis*, no λέγειν of the ἀλήθεια, no *Geschick* of the *Schicken* could harbor hopes of gathering or re-collecting these sendings in one single hand. Instead — but the logic at work here is not simply one of opposition or negation, let alone denegation, nor, to be sure, of problematization and critique — the motif of the sending(s) that is put to work in "On a Newly Arisen Apocalyptic Tone in Philosophy," and earlier in the first part of *The Postcard*, is linked to a thinking of the mistaking of all destination (i.e., of *destinerrance* and *clandestination*) that goes far "beyond the Heideggerian protocols,"[56] even beyond the "erring of Being" (*Irre des Seins*), toward a more singularizing *and* universalizing thought and practice of chance (*la Chance*) as necessity (*la Necessité*).[57] Derrida writes:

54. See Jürgen Habermas, "Die Einheit der Vernunft in der Vielheit ihrer Stimme," in id., *Nachmetaphysisches Denken: Philosophische Aufsätze* (Frankfurt a./M.: Suhrkamp, 1988), 198; trans. W. M. Hohengarten as "The Unity of Reason in the Diversity of Its Voices," *Postmetaphysical Thinking: Philosophical Essays* (Cambridge, Mass.: MIT Press, 1992), 115-48.

55. For a more sustained exposition of this argument, see my *Theologie im pianissimo* (trans. forthcoming), ch. 1.

56. Derrida, *Points . . .*, 136/145-46. See chapter 4, n. 73.

57. On chance and *tuchē*, cf. Derrida, *Du droit à la philosophie*, 46. In the discussion included in the small volume *Altérités*, Derrida explains quite clearly that it is "la Nécessité" — here a "proper name" for *différance* — that, paradoxically, is "the chance of desire" (Jacques

there would be no more chance, save chance itself, for a thought of good and evil whose announcement would come to *gather* itself in order to be with itself in a revelatory speaking; (no) more chance, unless a chance, the unique, chance itself, for a collection of truth, a *legein* of *alētheia* that would no longer be a legendary unveiling; and (no) more chance even for such a gathering of gift, *envoi*, destiny (*Schicken, Geschick*), for the destination of a 'come' whose promise at least would be assured of its own proper event. (NAA 167 / 95–96)

This is therefore yet another investigation of the limits of Heidegger's project. Not that there could be chance or necessity or, say, "apocalypticity" as such, pure and simple. For the argument made in an earlier chapter with regard to messianicity and Christianicity holds true here as well. Likewise, the nonsynonymous substitutions of the structure of apocalypticity are numerous, and in principle innumerable. Indeed, too, each one is divided in and against itself and thus marked by an irrevocable multiplicity. In an interview, Derrida seems to acknowledge as much when he states:

> [I]t is at the moment when what [Heidegger] calls the "ontological differ-
> ence," or the "truth of being," seems to guarantee the most comprehensive
> reading of philosophy that . . . it is imperative to question this very compre-
> hensiveness, this presumption of unity, and to ask what the reading excludes
> or what it once again reduces to silence. . . . Does one have a right to speak of
> a — of *the* — Western metaphysics, of its language, of a single destiny or "send-
> ing forth of Being" [*Geschick des Seins*], etc.? Consequently, everything re-
> mains open, still to be thought. . . . Multiplicity, furthermore, needn't always
> invoke a labyrinth, some device of theatrics or typography. On the contrary,
> it might just make a simple sentence quaver, tremble, or, for that matter, a
> word, a tone. . . .[58]

Paradoxically, and by announcing itself beyond or, rather, before good and evil, albeit not in any logical, chronological, or genealogical sense, this "apocalypse" — in Blanchotian terms, an apocalypse-without-apocalypse — could be viewed as the apocalypse of all possible (past, present, and future) apocalypses. No longer simply mystagogic or anagogic, it would thus also appear as "an-archic" at its very origin and as "an-

---

Derrida and Pierre-Jean Labarriere, *Altérités* [Paris: Osiris, 1986], 93): "It is not simply the mortal limit of failure [*échec*], it is also the respiration of desire" (ibid.).

58. Interview in *Derrida and Différance*, ed. Robert Bernasconi and David Wood (Evanston, Ill.: Northwestern University Press, 1988), 77–81, 81.

agogic" in its ethical or sociopolitical effects. We are dealing here with yet another hyperbolic figure of the kind encountered above: with *plus d'un apocalypse,* that is to say, an apocalypse that is more than one, more just this one, and thus more than itself, but also no longer one, no longer this one, and thus, in a sense, less than itself. In other words, an apocalypse that appropriates and expropriates its own concept and figure, an apocalypse-that-is-more-and-therefore-less-apocalyptic-than-the-apocalypse-strictly-speaking. But which one, precisely, is the apocalypse strictly speaking? And which one comes first, which is the one that opens up the other? Is it the apocalypticity of the apocalypse (without apocalypse) that forms the condition of possibility of the apocalypses marking the religions of the Book? Or is it the other way around? Should we not accept, then, that the answer to this question must remain open, indeed aporetic, and part ways with the logic of presupposition and pos-sibilization? Can one, finally, resort to another—alternative if not merely opposite—model of relating the poles inherent in the very notion of apocalypse, just as we did before with regard to revealability and revela-tion, messianicity and messianism? May we simply assume that the quasi-transcendental instances in each of these relations—apocalypticity and messianicity, revealability and Christianicity—are principally or structur-ally the same; that is to say, not so much something identical, *das Gleiche,* in any formal or empirically determinable sense, but *das Selbe,* quasi-ontologically speaking (to employ Heidegger's famous distinction from *Identity and Difference*)? Yet, while Derrida clearly refrains from gather-ing these instances in one hand—let alone one word, for example, Being, whether as *Sein, Seyn,* or *Ereignis*—but insists, on the contrary, on a multiplicity of nonsynonymous substitutions, he also leaves no doubt that we should not mistake these latter for empirically determinable or histori-cally specific referents. What is more, this proliferation or dissemination must also keep its distance from the Hegelian or Weberian understanding of historical and socioeconomic differentiation, as well from that other expropriation that Heidegger in his later writings calls the *Enteignis,* al-though the lines are very difficult to draw here. For the latter, Derrida sug-gests in the context of a commentary on Hegel and, more indirectly, on Heidegger, goes hand in hand with its metaphysical counterpart: "Abso-lute appropriation is absolute expropriation. Onto-logic can always be reread or rewritten as the logic of loss or of spending without reverse."[59]

59. Derrida, *Glas,* 167/188.

Nonetheless, a question remains: why and how is it that Derrida's writings are increasingly marked by the attempt to retain certain names rather than others; names, moreover, that are overdetermined and highly charged by particular — and more often than not particularistic — traditions? What motivates, enables, and justifies this turn to religion? And in what relation, finally, does this turn stand to the earlier turns to the paradigms — examples par excellence — of writing, literature, the new technological media (beginning with postal and telephone systems), but also ethics, democracy, and others?

Let's leave this question for a moment and move on to some of the inevitable consequences of this uncertainty, indeterminacy, or even undecidability. For inasmuch as it subtracts itself from the historical or conceptual and figural characteristics of the apocalyptic genre as we know it from so-called positive religion, it necessarily runs the "risk," Derrida points out, of being reappropriated by "conductive violence" and an "authoritarian 'duction' [lead]" (NAA 166 / 94). This danger, Derrida admits, is "ineluctable"; the abuse or derailment "threatens the tone as its double" (NAA 166 / 94).[60] And this is precisely what explains its historical and ethico-political ambiguity. Kant's uneasiness with regard to the reappearance of the superior or apocalyptic tone — both in his own day and at the very origin of the philosophical project, before Plato even, when the term *philosophy* started to circulate and ipso facto lost its unequivocal meaning — is therefore fully understandable and, indeed, justified.

WHILE KANT SEEMS in his pamphlet on the whole intent on exorcising the "double" by neutralizing the tone, his position is in fact far from being unequivocal. This is already clear from the acknowledgment, albeit implicitly, that a tone — not unlike skepticism — accompanies and challenges philosophy from the start. But this ambiguity can be verified throughout Kant's work. One example may suffice here. In a different yet related context, Derrida reminds us that, in the *Critique of Practical Reason,* Kant himself acknowledges that experience never permits us to exclude the possibility that a secret motive (*geheimer Triebfeder* or *Antrieb*) may be at work, even though we genuinely believe ourselves to be obeying the voice of conscience and the categorical imperative it dictates. Now if this uncertainty is permanent, structural, or at least inherent in our finitude, then,

60. In "Signature, Event, Context," in *Limited Inc.,* 15, 17 / 141, 143, Derrida calls this risk a "*law.*"

Derrida infers, it takes on the form of an enigma, for good and ill. We are dealing here with a "secret," and one, moreover, that "no more offers us the prospect of some interpretation [déchiffrement], even infinite, than it allows us to hope for a rigorous decontamination between 'in conformity with duty' [pflichtmässig] and 'out of pure duty' [aus reiner Pflicht]." [61]

This "decontamination" is not impossible

> by virtue of some phenomenal or empirical limit, even if indelible, but precisely because this limit is not empirical: its impossibility is linked *structurally* to the possibility of the "out of pure duty." Abolish the possibility of the simulacrum and of external repetition, and you abolish the possibility both of the law and of duty themselves, that is, of their recurrence. Impurity is principally inherent in the purity of duty, i.e., its iterability. Flouting all possible oppositions: *there* would be the secret [là serait le secret]. The secret of passion, the passion of the secret. To this secret that nothing could confine, as Kant would wish, within the order of "pathological" sensibility, no sacrifice will ever disclose its precise meaning. Because there is none.[62]

The very ground, then, of responsibility—its chance no less than its fatality, its risk no less than its necessity or fatality—is *something secret.* For better and for worse, for the best and the worst. For the resonance between the words "Il y a là du secret"[63] and the formulation "Il y a là cendre," chosen by Derrida in another context, in *Dissemination* and *Feu la cendre* (*Cinders*), is hardly a coincidence. For the formulation that there is something secret—not any particular secret, let alone the secret as such—means here that no semantic content and no specific moral— even categorical—imperative is "separable ... from its performative tracing,"[64] and thereby from the perils epitomized by the figures of cinders, ruins, ashes, and specters. This disturbing fact—yet another fact of reason—that impurity is given with the very purity of duty manifests itself solely in a "feeling" from which we cannot simply "detach ourselves" and "whose linguistic or cultural conditioning is difficult to assess."[65]

---

61. Jacques Derrida, *Passions* (Paris: Galilée, 1993), 88 n. 11, trans. David Wood as "Passions: 'An Oblique Offering,'" in SN 142 n. 12.

62. Ibid. 142 n. 12 / 88–89 n. 11.

63. Ibid., 24 / 56.

64. Ibid. Derrida adds: "We shall not say from its performative *enunciation* or from its *propositional argumentation;* and we keep in reserve a number of questions about performativity in general" (ibid.)

65. Ibid., 132 n. 3 / 75 n. 3.

More troubling still, only a feeling makes us aware of the paradox that an act that does not go "beyond duty" or that was merely performed "out of duty" — in view of some "restitution" or "discharge of a debt" — will have to be considered as fundamentally "*a-moral.*" [66] For such an act falls short of affirming the very condition, or rather "in-condition," of its possibility, which is neither a condition nor a possibility *sensu stricto,* let alone a "possible" in Kant's or Heidegger's sense, but rather, Derrida writes, an "unlimited, incalculable or uncalculating giving, without any possible reappropriation, by which one must measure the ethicity or the morality of ethics." [67] Given this measure — a measure, that is, beyond or before any possible measure and thus incommensurable — a genuine duty, in a sense, "ought to prescribe nothing." [68] The obligation that falls upon the good will (to be distinguished from so-called good and thereby ipso facto false conscience) prescribes, on this view, nothing in particular, nothing in general, and nothing categorically; it prescribes that there be prescription, that the prescription be obeyed.[69] This distinction between a will that acts in conformity with the mere legality of duty (in Kant's words, the *virtus phaenomenon*) and one that stems from duty pure and simple (as Kant puts it, the *virtus noumenon:* "the same duty as an enduring *disposition* towards such as actions from duty because of their morality"),[70] is one of the elements of Derrida's subtle differentiation between *le droit* and *la justice.*

In order to remain faithful to itself, duty ought not to demand any acquittal of a debt. And to the extent that no duty and no normative rule is possible without the institution, circulation, and sublimation of debt, responsibility must consist in avoiding that one act merely *in conformity with, in virtue of,* or even *out of respect* for duty as such. Duty entails more than duty, *plus d'un devoir.* It demands at once the absolute appropriation and the absolute expropriation of duty, duty in itself, as well as the other of duty, that is to say, the duty before duty, beyond duty, and indeed *in*

66. Derrida "Passions," 133 n. 3, 75 n. 3.

67. Ibid.

68. Ibid.

69. For a similar, more extensive, analysis of this structure of "Kant's Imperative," see Werner Hamacher, *Premises: Essays on Philosophy and Literature from Kant to Celan,* trans. Peter Fenves (Cambridge, Mass.: Harvard University Press, 1996), 85 ff.

70. Immanuel Kant, *Die Religion innerhalb der Grenzen der blossen Vernunft,* vol. 7 of *Werke in zehn Bänden,* ed. Wilhelm Weischedel (Darmstadt: Wissenschaftliche Buchgesellschaft, 1983), 649–879, 661; trans. George di Giovanni as *Religion Within the Boundaries of Mere Reason* (Cambridge: Cambridge University Press, 1996), 65.

duty, for lack of duty, in a certain disregard even of duty, no less than out of duty or in conformity with duty. Mutatis mutandis, a similar structure is at work here as in the context of negative theology and apocalyptics. Here as well Derrida operates with a logic of the *hyper* and the *without*, of the X without X and the X over X, the X that is at once more and less than X, the X par excellence that is also at the furthest thinkable remove from X, in sum, of the superlative of X that is at the same time its innermost ruin.

A given ethics of discussion, Derrida notes, might not always sufficiently "respect" this silent feeling that accompanies the excessiveness of this demand remaining "foreign to speech [*la parole*]." [71] But it could never reduce it to something else or render it obsolete. For the secret continues to "impassion" us, even if it ontologically speaking does not exist as such, in the singular and identical with itself. And since this "passion," Derrida claims, precludes all "direct intuition" it must be "non-'pathological' " in Kant's sense of the word. It is, Derrida continues, not even a "psychophysical secret, the art hidden in the depths of the human soul, of which Kant speaks in connection with the transcendental schematism and of the imagination (*eine verborgene Kunst in den Tiefen der menschlichen Seele*)." [72] Neither conscious nor unconscious, neither profane nor sacred or mystical, private nor public, the secret must be characterized as neither phenomenal(izable) nor noumenal; nor is it even thinkable. [73] Unthinkable and aporetic, the secret could thus be said to escape the "play of veiling/unveiling, dissimulation/revelation." [74] It no longer determines itself in the service of some ultimate, promised truth, whether that of adequation or of *alētheia,* nor is it the latter's merely abstract negation. Its "nonphenomenality," Derrida concludes, is "without relation, even negative relation, to phenomenality." [75] It exceeds the metaphysical overdeterminations of even Kant's true *Geheimnis,* Freud's *Unheimliche,* and a certain apophatic mode of silence characteristic of negative theology.

Again, it is precisely the nonphenomenality of the secret that makes it at once immune to every critique that is leveled against it and vulnerable

71. Derrida, "Passions," 27 / 62.

72. Ibid., 24 / 57. In *Being and Time,* Heidegger writes: "In the end, those very phenomena which will be exhibited under the heading of 'Temporality' in our analysis, are precisely those *most covert* [*geheimsten*] judgments of the 'common reason' for which Kant says it is the 'business of philosophers' to provide an analytic" (BT 45 / 23).

73. Derrida, "Passions," 25–26, 58–61.

74. Ibid., 26 / 60.

75. Ibid.

to the worst of abuses. One can always turn it into a seductive power or use it to seduce. That, Derrida notes dryly, "happens [*se produit*] every day."[76] However, he continues, "this very simulacrum still bears witness to a possibility which exceeds it. It does not exceed it in the direction of some ideal community, rather toward a solitude without any measure common to that of an isolated subject . . . or with that of a *Jemeinigkeit* of *Dasein* whose solitude, Heidegger tells us, is still a modality of *Mitsein*."[77]

Precisely because it calls these modalities into being, without thereby letting them come into their own, the secret solitude, Derrida hastens to add, "never allows itself to be captured or covered over by the relation to the other, by being-with or by any form of 'social bond.'"[78] What counts, if anything, is this exceeding of the simulacrum by its possibility, although it is not testified to by any "definite witness" or "martyr."[79] Every moral utterance, every action, then, remains "problematic" or, rather, "of an order other than problematicity"; and this circumstance — which is the circumvention of every stance or stasis, whether that of the actor or the act — should not only be considered a tragedy (which indeed it is) but also "a stroke of luck": "Otherwise, why speak, why discuss?"[80]

## Speech Tact

What emerges from this is the need to revise the major premises of speech-act theory, as well as of the "ethics of discussion" commonly associated with it. The reasons for this should be clear by now. Derrida insists that without the permanent risk of derailment and perversion, no "call to action," indeed, no voice of conscience, could ever claim to be unconditional, let alone just. On the contrary, instead of announcing itself categorically and with absolute urgency, its manifestation would — like the Austinian performative — remain guaranteed and stabilized by past or present contexts of origination, as well as by future horizons of expectation. In so doing, however, it betrays its singular structure no less than its universal appeal. Indeed, Derrida maintains throughout his discussion of Austin and Searle, notably in "Signature, Event, Context," in *Margins of Philosophy,* and more extensively in *Limited Inc.,* especially in its afterword, "Toward an Ethic of Discussion,"

---

76. Ibid., 30 / 69.                          77. Ibid.
78. Ibid. 30 / 70.                           79. Ibid., 31 / 70; trans. modified.
80. Derrida, *Limited Inc.,* 120 / 218.

the very least that can be said of unconditionality (a word I use not by accident to recall the character of the categorical imperative in its Kantian form)
is that it is independent of every determinate context, even of the determination of a context in general. It announces itself as such only in the *opening*
of context. Not that it is simply present (existent) elsewhere, outside of all
context; rather, it intervenes in the determination of a context from its very
inception, and from an injunction, a law, a responsibility that transcends this
or that determination of a given context.[81]

The call, Derrida notes elsewhere, "comes from nowhere" and only thus
"institutes" a response and responsibility that lies "at the root of all ulterior responsibilities (moral, juridical, political) and of every categorical
imperative."[82] In order to be what it is, the call must remain at a distance from all of these determinations. Only the "irreducible opening" of
all contexts everywhere creates the space in which the call is (perhaps)
able to give itself, if it gives itself at all—or as such—which can always
be doubted. For, out of necessity—in order to generate any effect or inspire any respect—the call can only protect its singularity and otherness
by retaining an almost fictional, fabulous element and by remaining "a
sheer supposition,"[83] albeit one that is not theoretical and that therefore
does not take the form of a hypothetical presupposition, not even that of
a postulate, strictly speaking. *Almost* like literature, *the call must seem to
say just about anything;* rather than speaking to *all* in the same clear and
univocal way, and regardless of time and place, it must in principle speak
to one—in solitude—and do so in a virtually infinite range of possible
modes, and haunted by the specter of totally different (past, present, and
future) engagements.

Although he uses the term *unconditionality* in reference to the structure of the Kantian categorical imperative, Derrida is careful not to push
the analogy between moral law and the "injunction that prescribes deconstructing"[84] too far. Speaking of this "injunction," he hastens to add:

81. Ibid., 152 / 281.
82. Derrida, "Eating Well," 110. Referring to Paul de Man's reading of Rousseau in *Alle-
gories of Reading*, Derrida recalls that the "illocutionary mode" of making the law is that of
the "promise." The law is *proleptic, to-come.* See Derrida, *Mémoires: Pour Paul de Man* (Paris:
Galilée, 1988), trans. Cecile Lindsay, Jonathan Culler, Eduardo Cadava, and Peggy Kamuf as
*Memories: For Paul de Man* (New York: Columbia University Press, 1989), 127.
83. Derrida, "Eating Well," 110.
84. Derrida, *Limited Inc.*, 153 / 282.

Why have I always hesitated to characterize it in Kantian terms, for example, or more generally in ethical or political terms, when that would have been so easy and would have enabled me to avoid so much criticism . . . ? Because such characterizations seemed to me essentially associated with philosophemes that themselves call for deconstructive questions. Through these questions *another language and other thoughts* seek to make their way. This language and these thoughts, which are also new responsibilities, arouse in me a respect, which, whatever the cost, I neither can nor will compromise.[85]

That the tone of the appeal to vigilance denotes nothing, that it exceeds the formal structure of the Kantian categorical imperative, does not imply that the ellipsis of Enlightenment leaves us speechless or blind. And the absence of definition, rather than signaling a new obscurantism, "respectfully pays homage to a new, very new *Aufklärung*."[86] In what sense, then, does this elliptic transformation of Enlightenment into an unconditional vigilance that calls forth "other thoughts," "another language," and "new responsibilities" situate itself beyond the confines laid out by both the Kantian grounding of practical reason and its recent reconstruction in terms of a quasi-transcendental, formal pragmatics?

First of all, Derrida argues that the call can never stand alone or give itself as such, pure and simple. For even if no context is ever completely closed (or, in its turn, enclosed), this does not contradict the fact that "there are only contexts," or, more precisely, that "nothing *exists* outside context."[87] Yet, if the unconditional appeal consists in opening up *every* given ontic (empirical, historical, textual) context or ontological dimension, then it follows that its manifestation eludes every phenomenological description. It is in this that the appeal of which Derrida speaks distances itself from the so-called "saturated phenomenon" that Jean-Luc Marion sees as the privileged mode of appearing—without horizon, without visibility, and, in a sense, without appearing—of "God," of "distance," and of the "icon." Derrida's analysis here is at odds with the heterology, the theological "relief," and the "indifference" that Marion deems possible with regard to the tradition of metaphysics, its central concepts, and its institutionalized practices.

In addition to escaping all modifications of the phenomenological reduction, the unconditionality of the appeal escapes the transcenden-

85. Ibid., emphasis added.
86. Ibid., 141 / 261.
87. Ibid., 152 / 282.

Apocalyptics and Enlightenment 407

tal deductions that Kant entrusts to the faculty of pure practical reason. If anything, it is an enigmatic "otherwise than being," to quote Levinas, a call that is only there for those whose attentiveness — or vigil — allows them to hear it. Thus, as a further consequence of this ethics of response, the originary split of the call could be said to be *echoed* or *doubled* in the response or responsiveness that it had provoked in the first place, but without whose sounding board it would have remained nothing, without effect, anything but ethical, or pre-ethical. For the affirmation of this appeal entails an iteration — an unconditional "yes, yes" — that marks and doubles (or triples, quadruples, etc.) even the most singular "Hello!" or "Here I am!" ("Me voici!").

Now it is precisely this necessary repetition and alteration, Derrida claims, that eventually forces us "to articulate this unconditionality with the determinate (Kant would say, hypothetical) conditions of this or that context; and this is the moment of strategies, of rhetorics, of ethics, and politics."[88] Because of this repeated intervention in given contexts, deconstruction, along with the responsibility it implies or calls forth, "does not exist somewhere, pure, proper, self-identical, outside of its inscriptions in conflictual and differentiated contexts; it 'is' only what it does and what is done with it."[89] And, inasmuch as one cannot speak or write without thereby transforming a context, the very inception of any such speech and writing *necessarily implies politics*, "insofar as it involves determination, a certain non-'natural' relationship to others"[90] (whether human or not, whether in the past, the present, or the future, whether in our proximity or far away). For although the interrogation of the purported stability of pragmatic values and normative claims exceeds the realm of reference and truth, of science and ontology (and therefore exceeds Being *as such* or at least disrupts the *unity* of Being), it should also be acknowledged that this analysis never takes place in a vacuum, outside "pragmatically determined"[91] situations. For the singular truth that it unravels — in particular its insight into the structural instability or at best into the "relative," "provisional," and "finite" stability of all meaning — must also "submit" itself "in large measure" to the requirements of a given context.[92]

88. Ibid.                              89. Ibid.
90. Ibid., 136 / 251.                   91. Ibid., 150 / 278.
92. Ibid. That "no stability is absolute, eternal, intangible, natural" is, Derrida notes, "implied" in its very concept: stability is not "immutability" and therefore always "destabilizable" (ibid., 151 / 279). The pragmatic moment — the translation of untranslatable singularities — is therefore, in turn, imbedded in a frame, network, or, if one wishes, texture and play of differential relations that make it impossible to determine the *kairos* of its moment(um). In order to

For instance, deconstruction should—indeed must—take into account the generally accepted procedures as well as the restraints of academic debate, even though its arguments are in themselves "neither false, nor nontrue . . . , nor context-external or meta-contextual," but, rather, the exposition of a quasi-, simili-, ultra- (also in the sense of *hyper-* and the French *plus,* as more and no longer) transcendental "'truth'" that does not simply belong to the order of ontology, semantics, pragmatics, or even discussion and communication. And it is here that the often debated *double science* comes in to play: the fact that Derrida's writings are thus composed of two—not just seemingly but in fact—contradictory gestures. For this discourse persists in respecting or accepting the rules of the game of which it nonetheless "exposes the deconstructibility." And the reasons for this are clear. For, as Derrida reminds us, "without this tension . . . would anything ever be done? Would anything ever be changed?"[93]

"Pragrammatology" is the provisional name for the necessarily incomplete topography of the different gestures that will always already have marked the deconstructive intervention in those sites of tension that mark the ethical, the political, the economic, and much more. It is not

-----

avoid the misleading assumption that there could be a radical rupture with or escape from this law of *différance,* Derrida remarks that the logic of decision has never been that of *coupure,* or break, but at best that of "stricture" (Derrida, *Parages,* 214). It is at this critical juncture that the question of *tonality* again comes into play. For "*tonos,* tone," Derrida recalls, "first signified the tight ligament, the cord, the rope, when it is woven or braided, cable, strap—briefly, the privileged figure of everything that is subject to *strict-ure*" (NAA 127/69; emphasis added). Since, however, the occurence of stricture within—and *with*—the realm of differentiality is ipso facto and of necessity that of a specific, concrete, or singular tonality, or rather tone, this tone can never be pure, neutral, or inaudible, as Kant would have it. Nor can it be taken for a *signifiance* that is identiable in a simple (complex, absolute) ethical meaning *alone;* unless, of course, this signifyingness is taken in its very indeterminacy, in its being already and forever split, totally other each time, the *illéité* mimicked, doubled, and haunted by the *il y a.* That this is how one must read Levinas, if one is to avoid bad metaphysics and irresponsible moralism, I have argued elsewhere: see my "Adieu, à dieu, a-dieu," in *Ethics as First Philosophy,* ed. Peperzak, and my "Violence and Testimony," in *Violence, Identity, and Self-Determination,* ed. de Vries and Weber.

The concept of iterability that plays such an important role in Derrida's exposition draws on the Sanskrit pronoun *í-tara,* meaning *other,* but also finds a cognate in the Latin *iterum.* Sir Monier-Williams's *Sanskrit-English Dictionary* (Oxford: Clarendon Press, 1899; reprint, New Dehli: Munshiram Manoharlal Publishers, 1994) reminds us of a certain logic of the counterpoint on which the concept of iterability—i.e., of repetition plus (or *qua*) change—rests: "*itara, itara,* the one–the other, this–that (*itara* connected antithetically with a preceding word often signifies the contrary idea)." I am indebted to Professor Karunatillake for this reference.

93. Derrida, *Limited Inc.,* 152/281.

always certain whether (or to what extent) this programmatology implies a certain shift in Derrida's earlier preoccupations: a shift, that is,
away from the analysis of the general economy of *écriture* toward the particular question of the "intersection" between the logic of grammatology
(or iterability), on the one hand, and so-called pragmatically determined
situations, on the other. Of course, Derrida argues: "Grammatology has
always been a sort of pragmatics, but the discipline that bears this name
today involves too many presuppositions requiring deconstruction, very
much like speech-act theory, to be simply homogeneous with what is
announced in *Of Grammatology*. A programmatology (to come) would
articulate in a more fruitful and more rigorous manner these two discourses."[94]

A programmatology, then, remains "to come." It is the *à venir* of deconstruction. In more than one sense. For, as the deconstructive logic of
iterability demonstrates, any such project will not only always be incomplete *in fact*. In a more radical sense, it is also essentially or structurally
interminable, unfulfillable. The linkages or "ties" between marks and
words, concepts and things, that it seeks to determine in a given context—
as well as, for that matter, the "deontological" standard that regulates
their discussion—is never "*absolutely*"[95] secured by any "metacontext"
or "metadiscourse." Since no adequate, let alone exhausting, conceptual
or figural representation of such a programmatology can ever be given,[96]
and since its very description always intersects with an interpretative and
institutional act, one might wonder how to think in a nonrepresenta-
tional or aesthetic mode the effects of the said unconditionality in the
realm of ethics, politics, rhetorics, and strategy (terms that at this point
of Derrida's exposition all seem to be synonyms for the intervention of
the "call" or the "Come!" in the regional domains of the empirical, of institutions, disciplinary demarcations, etc.). This politics or economics[97]
needs to be rethought as an "impossible and necessary compromise . . . an
incessant daily negotiation—individual or not—sometimes microscopic,

94. Ibid., 159 n. 16 / 274 n. 1.
95. Ibid., 151 / 279.
96. As Lyotard notes in the context of another discussion, a performative cannot "*represent* what it accomplishes but . . . *presents it*" (Jean-François Lyotard, "Levinas' Logic," in *Face
to Face with Levinas*, ed. Richard A. Cohen [Albany: State University of New York Press, 1986],
117–58, 172). See also my "On Obligation: Levinas and Lyotard," *Graduate Faculty Philosophy
Journal* 20, no. 2; 21, no. 1 (1998), 83–112.
97. Derrida, *Parages*, 214.

sometimes punctuated by poker-like gamble; always deprived of insurance, whether it be in private life or within institutions."[98] If any model could help us visualize this interaction, while respecting its rhythm (i.e., without synchronizing it with various apocalyptic choruses), it would be the dance, or, more precisely, choreography. This pragrammatological model—which for all its internal multiplicity and complexity remains nonetheless just one *topos* or rather *u-topos* among many possible others —is anything but a tribute to mere pragmatism, practical wisdom, or, for that matter, *phronesis*. For, as Derrida emphasizes in a closely related context, it is always "in the name of a more imperative responsibility"[99] that one questions—or inverts—a traditionally defined responsibility vis-à-vis existing political and conceptual formations. All genuine responsibility must respond to a "restless excess" that disrupts all "good conscience"[100] and does not let itself be expressed in merely juridical terms. For no rule and no law could be said to be commensurate with this responsibility, which, Derrida reiterates, "regulates itself neither on the principle of reason nor on any sort of accountancy," each of which—*pace* Kant—produce what remains "at best" a hypothetical imperative: "[R]esponsibility is excessive or it is not a responsibility. A limited, measured, calculable, rationally distributed responsibility is already the becoming-right of responsibility; it is at times also, in the best hypothesis, the dream of every good conscience, in the worst hypothesis, of the small or grand inquisitors."[101]

This excess of the idea of responsibility and of justice that pervades all of the passages quoted above is no longer that of the Kantian regulative idea that supplements the finitude of the human condition and entrusts it with a task of infinite approximation. Instead, it is closely intertwined with the experience and experiment of the undecidable that destabilizes every decision, including "just" ones, from within, and not because of

98. Derrida, *Points . . .* , 95 / 100–101. A little later Derrida notes that this first of all implies that one begin by taking so-called *"real"*—sociopolitical and economical—preconditions seriously: "These conditions often require the preservation (within longer or shorter phases) of metaphysical presuppositions that one must . . . question at a later phase—or another place— because they belong to the dominant system that one is deconstructing on a *practical level.* This multiplicity of places, moments, forms and forces does not always mean giving way either to empiricism or to contradiction. How can one breathe without such punctuation and without the multiplicities of rhythm and steps? How can one dance . . . ?" (ibid., 97 / 102)

99. Derrida, *Du droit à la philosophie,* 35.

100. Ibid., 35–36.

101. Derrida, "Eating Well," 118; cf. 108.

some particular, empirical, sensual, contingency, but in general, of necessity, a priori. For a decision, Derrida explains,

> can only come into being in a space that exceeds the calculable program that
> would destroy all responsibility by transforming it into a programmable effect
> of determinate causes. There can be no moral or political responsibility without
> this trial and this passage by way of the undecidable. Even if a decision
> seems to take only a second and not to be preceded by any deliberation, it is
> structured by this *experience and experiment of the undecidable*.[102]

The crucial terms here—*trial, passage, experience, experiment*—should be understood against the backdrop of the numerous detours Derrida makes through the reading of Kafka (*The Trial* and "Before the Law"), Paul Celan's invocation of the "No passarán!" of the Spanish Civil War, and, somewhat more indirectly, Georges Bataille's notion of an *expérience intérieure* that does not allow one time to anticipate, project, mediate, or meditate. All of these references testify to a certain passage through and endurance of the impossible, that is to say, of aporia.[103]

Of course, Derrida points out, if we define the concept of experience as the designation of "something that traverses and travels toward a destination for which it finds the appropriate passage," then surely it must be impossible to have an *experience* of this impossible in this sense: for an aporia, Derrida goes on to explain, is a "non-road." And yet, justice—*justice* or *Gerechtigkeit,* as used, albeit in fundamentally different ways, by Pascal and Levinas, Benjamin and Heidegger[104]—if anything at all, means or implies or entails precisely this impossible experience of the impossible:

> A will, a desire, a demand for justice whose structure wouldn't be an experi-
> ence of aporia would have no chance to be what it is, namely a call for justice.
> Every time that something comes to pass . . . , every time that we placidly
> apply a good rule to a particular case, to a correctly subsumed example, ac-

102. Derrida, *Limited Inc.,* 116 / 210.

103. For the parallels with Georges Bataille, cf. the remarkable formulations in *L'Expérience intérieure* (1943): "Without night, no one would have to decide. . . . Decision is what is born before the worst and rises above. It is the essence of courage, of the heart, of being itself. And it is the reverse of project (it demands that one reject delay, that one decide on the spot, with everything at stake . . .)" (Bataille, *Inner Experience,* trans. L. A. Boldt [Albany: State University of New York Press, 1988], 26; *Oeuvres complètes* [Paris: Gallimard, 1954], 39). According to Derrida's "Force of Law," 967, the process of making a decision can be described as an "acting in the night of non-knowledge and non-rule."

104. Derrida, "Force of Law," 927, 955.

cording to a determinant judgment, we can be sure that law (*droit*) may find itself accounted for but certainly not justice.[105]

Justice, then, is "incalculable," even though it, paradoxically, aporetically, "requires that one calculates [*exige qu'on calcule*] with the incalculable."[106] For Derrida, there is no room here for the "condescending reticence"[107] with which Heidegger at times speaks of the *rechnen* and *planen* that for him epitomize the technological coinage of metaphysics. Justice prescribes — "it is just," Derrida writes — that there be law and right, both of which are never just per se, that is to say, in and for themselves, but can lay claim only to being "the element" of an always "improbable" yet "nec-

105. Ibid., 947. At several points throughout these analyses, Derrida acknowledges that one might feel "tempted" to invoke Levinas's equation of justice and the relation to the other — and thus, one might add, to the infinite Other — and compare it with the emphatic — undeconstructable — idea of justice as distinct from the order of (natural or positive) law and right. Derrida recalls the formulation from Levinas's *Totality and Infinity:* "[L]a relation avec autrui — c'est à dire la justice." This relation, like the idea of justice discussed here, is just as irreducible to the order of right, in the sense of a codified set of norms, rules, customs, and jurisprudences. Justice in Levinas's sense is not part of *droit;* it is a *droit* of the other that extends itself infinitely, i.e., well beyond (and before) any distribution of rights and duties. One would be well advised, therefore, to view it first of all in terms of a *droiture,* an equity, a rectitude, an uprighteousness or even sanctity with respect to nothing but the welcome that the face demands. Levinas speaks of a *droiture de l'accueil fait au visage,* a formulation that seems to inform Derrida's thoughts on hospitality, developed elsewhere.

Yet Derrida does not follow up on the analogy between the two notions of "justice" in the context that interests us here. Instead, he simply says that "since Levinas's difficult discourse would give rise to other difficult questions," one should not pretend to be able "to borrow conceptual moves without risking confusions" (ibid., 959). But then again, what, precisely, would such a confusion entail? Could or should one avoid it, especially where matters of ethics, politics, economics, and of rights are at issue?

At one point, Derrida reinterprets another motif from Levinas's *Totality and Infinity* that is of equal importance here: "La vérité suppose la justice." Even the most disengaged constative utterance, he argues, relies in the final analysis — "at least implicitly" — on the singular "performative structure" (ibid., 966) of addressing oneself to the other. Yet, while for Levinas this ethical relation is impossible and unthinkable outside the realm of *intersubjectivity* — of a communality that cannot be reified in psychologistic, sociologistic, or even linguistic terms — Derrida retains from this relation only this: the fact that the communication it entails no longer takes place in a homogeneous space governed by the laws of interest and symmetric exchange. For both Levinas and Derrida, this dissymmetry does not only pertain to the purported immemorial origin of communication, but also to its very paradoxical structure, address and destination (sending or destinerrance). It is a "communication of communication, a signaling of the gift of the sign instead of any transmission of meaning" (Levinas, *Autrement qu'être ou au-delà de l'essence,* 153). It would be difficult to think of this singular communication in terms of a quasi-transcendental infrastructure. For the relation in question is a destructuring par excellence, "la dé-structure même" (Levinas, *De Dieu qui vient l'idée,* 110 n. 9).

106. Derrida, "Force of Law," 947.

107. Derrida, "Eating Well," 108.

essary" calculation (or negotiation), which should, moreover, be sharply distinguished from the dialectical concept of mediation.[108] For in order to be just, the calculation should—indeed *ought* and *must*—pass through the abyssal experience of the incalculable, and this ad infinitum, regardless of its radical finitude and in spite of its desire to reach firm new ground.

This said, we can understand that *Specters of Marx* should appeal to what Derrida calls the "political virtue" of the *contretemps*, for the right moment and its counterpart might very well never be on time—or timely —as such, which may be precisely its strength and efficacy. He writes: "I believe in the political virtue of contretemps. And if a contretemps does not have the good luck, a more or less calculated luck, to come *just in time,* then the inopportuneness of a strategy (political or other) may still *bear witness,* precisely [*justement*], to justice, bear witness, at least, to the justice which is demanded and about which we were saying just a moment ago that it must be disadjusted, irreducible to exactness [*justesse*] and to law [*droit*]."[109]

Different examples of these insoluble paradoxes could be given, but in fact, Derrida writes, there is here in fact only "one potential aporetic that infinitely distributes itself."[110] In all of those cases, however, one would be obliged to experience or to suffer "moments in which the decision between just and unjust is never insured by a rule."[111] What would be the foundation, the ground, of this requirement or demand of justice to abandon itself, to give itself (away), and to pervert itself in this very performance? Derrida writes: "If I were content to apply a just rule, without a spirit of justice and without in some way inventing the rule and the example for each case, I might be protected by law (*droit*), my action corresponding to objective law, but I would not be just. I would act, Kant would say in *conformity* with duty, but not *through* duty or *out of respect* for the law."[112]

Similarly, a judge cannot pass a just judgment if he blindly follows the letter of the law and applies its principles and rules in a merely mechanical way. The decision must to a certain extent "suspend" (or even "destroy") and reinvent the law. For each case that presents itself to him will be other and therefore asks for an *epochē* followed by a decision "which no existing, coded rule can or ought to guarantee absolutely."[113] And yet,

108. Derrida, "Force of Law," 947.          109. Derrida, *Specters of Marx,* 88 / 145.
110. Derrida, "Force of Law," 959.          111. Ibid., 947.
112. Ibid., 949.                            113. Ibid., 961.

conversely, we would not call the judge just if he stopped short "before the undecidable" or abandoned "all rules, all principles."[114] In order not to be neutralized, a just decision would thus have to have it both ways — that is, go through the aporia and *perform the contradiction*. No just decision — but also no history, no communication, no discussion — could occur without this feat, without this tour de force.

An example might concretize this seemingly abstract point. When asked by the French newspaper *Libération* to comment on the politics of modern institutions in France, some two years after the election of François Mitterand, Derrida observed that the socialist idea has always been caught in a so-called performative contradiction, which it shares with all reformist and, whether they know it or not, with all successful revolutionary political and cultural movements. It must at once obey and escape the economical and technological imperatives of the market: it cannot avoid the double bind of having both to satisfy and displace the demand imposed by the competitive mechanism of modern (global) market production.[115]

In fact, it is only in the experience of this aporia — an irresolvable tension that, Derrida insists, is not "in itself an absolute evil, a sin, an accident or a weakness" — that socialism can reasonably hope to create juster institutions.[116] This negotiation, nothing else, is the minimal truth, indeed, the truism of the making of any difference, that is to say, of any ethico-political decision at all.

The (impossible) experience of the impossible or the undecidable is

114. Ibid. One is tempted to invoke Hegel here. In the *Grundlinien der Philosophie des Rechts,* par. 12, Hegel states that it is through a certain resolve that the will is actual at all: "nur als beschliessender Wille überhaupt ist er wirklicher Wille." This resolve, which determines the will in its singularization and individualization, is governed by a dialectical opposition in which one of the terms (actuality) inevitably dominates the other (potentiality or possiblity). This same teleological and organic scheme can be recognized in Hegel's intriguing remark distinguishing the *etwas beschliessen* from a more indeterminate *sich entschliessen* that is equally constitutive of the form, the formation and the determination of the will (ibid., 36).

115. In *Specters of Marx,* the "spirit of Marxism" to which Derrida pays tribute seems to have been emptied of virtually all of Marx's economic, political, and institutional positions and predictions. Derrida's position calls to mind rather Eduard Bernstein's reformist manifesto *Die Voraussetzungen des Sozialismus und die Aufgaben der Sozialdemokratie* (1899), ed. and trans. by Henry Tudor as *The Preconditions of Socialism* (Cambridge: Cambridge University Press, 1993). In *Limited Inc.,* Derrida notes, however, albeit in passing, that an "economy taking account of effects of iterability" has to call into question "the entire philosophy of the *oikos* — of the *propre*: the 'own,' 'ownership,' 'property' — as well as the laws that have governed it." Such an economy would be "very different from 'welfare economics'" (*Limited Inc.,* 76 / 144).

116. Derrida, *Du droit à la philosophie,* 504–5.

therefore not that of an either/or. It is not even the back and forth of two conflicting or incommensurate imperatives urging us, for example in a juridical setting, to respect at once the equality of identical cases before the law and the uniqueness of every singular act when faced with that law. Furthermore, the experience of the undecidable is infinitely more complex than the experience of a mere tension between two or more equally valid or justifiable decisions. Rather, it is the "ordeal" (*l'épreuve*) of an obligation to exceed or suspend the principles and rules of right, of law and jurisprudence, while continuing somehow to take them into account.[117] Without this anxious "freedom" of man's being at once inside and outside the law — and only this simultaneity explains the *iterability* of the law — to be just would come down to being a moment in an "unfolding process" or simply "applying a program."[118]

We can only be just, then, to the extent that we belong to two realms at once. And yet, this dual status or stance, for all the resemblances to Kant's moral philosophy, also explains why no decision is justifiable on formal rational grounds alone, whether they be those of introspection and inner deliberation or of intersubjective argumentation. For the said double bind precludes ever resolving the questions of *whether* and *how* a decision has taken place in any decisive way. As Kant already knew, we are never in a position in which we can be absolutely sure that what presents itself as a decision, let alone as a just decision, has not in fact followed a psychological ruse or obeyed a social code, or, as Derrida adds, already transformed itself into a merely exemplary case subsumable under a general rule. At no point, then, can a decision claim to be "presently" or "fully" just.[119] It

117. It is for that reason that neither the "thoughtlessness" nor the "madness" of the decision (nor that of the "founding violence" that institutes a law for society) can be reduced to the "existentialist" pathos or to the "decisionism" ascribed to Kierkegaard and Carl Schmitt respectively, although neither of these two authors is remote from Derrida's analysis. Nor are we dealing here with the so-called *Restdezisionismus* that Schnädelbach retraces in Karl-Otto Apel's transcendental pragmatics (see Herbert Schnädelbach, *Vernunft und Geschichte: Vorträge und Abhandlungen* [Frankfurt a./M.: Suhrkamp, 1987], 167). Derrida does not explain the irreducibility of the "decision" (or violence) that founds states, conventions, and rules in terms of their "historicity" or in terms of their supposed empirical conditions. Rather, he relates their "invention" to a singular performativity that exceeds the premises and the theoretical framework of speech-act theory and formal pragmatics. Instead, it relies on a certain "force," "enforcement," or "enforceability," which is differential, that is to say, intertwined with other anterior "performatives" and conventions and ultimately based on an "irruptive" — "mystical" — "violence." And of the latter, Derrida concludes, it must be granted that it "no longer responds to the demands of theoretical rationality" as such ("Force of Law," 966).

118. Derrida, "Force of Law," 963.

119. Ibid.

is this uncertainty that ensures that the undecidable continues to haunt every decision as a specter that cannot be exorcised. Even in retrospect, we can never be certain that a decision, in the emphatic sense of the word, in fact took place, let alone that it was absolutely just. No phenomenology or criteriology allows us to track down its past, let alone to predict its future occurrence.

If there can never be a moment when we can "say *in the present* that a decision *is* just . . . or that someone *is* a just man—even less, 'I *am* just,' "[120] Derrida stresses, this disrupts the entire axiomatics that governs the Kantian critique of pure practical reason and its formal-pragmatic transformation into so-called communicative ethics. For these tie responsibility to "a whole network of connected concepts,"[121] which presuppose the postulation of this very presence, not only of justice as a regulative idea and highest good, but also of free and intentional moral agents to themselves. This is not to suggest that these concepts will simply disappear: "What is limited by iterability is not intentionality in general, but its character of being conscious or present to itself (actualized, fulfilled, and adequate), the simplicity of features, its *undividedness*. . . . The iteration structuring it a priori* introduces into it a dehiscence and a cleft [*brisure*] which are essential."[122]

120. Ibid., 961, 963.
121. Ibid., 955.
122. Derrida, *Limited Inc.*, 105 / 194–95. The last sentence is a direct self-citation from "Signature Event Context" in *Limited Inc.* (emphasis added by Derrida). Of course, what holds true of intentionality, Derrida claims, "is also valid, correlatively, for the object (*qua* signified or referent) thus aimed at" (ibid., 58 / 113). Both the intention and the referent, then, that carry an utterance or statement are precluded from ever being "*active* and *actual*" (ibid.). And this calls into question the very notion of the "act" in speech-act theory based also as it is on the presupposed presence of the first person singular—of "myself saying I"—to itself. Earlier in the text, Derrida had already pointed out that it is far from certain that the "I" or the "saying I" more than anything else forms a guarantee for the "idealizing hypothesis" that one can say what one means, in other words, that the "intention of the speaker" is "closest to, if not absolutely present in what is said" (ibid., 62 / 121). Indeed, he continues, "the functioning of the *I* . . . is no less iterable or replaceable than any other word. And in any case, whatever singularity its functioning might possess is not of a kind to guarantee any adequation between saying and meaning." (ibid.). Of course, this is not to suggest that there is no singular instance that in its very "passion" and interpellation can be held responsible. What can be said about intentionality in general is valid par excellence, Derrida writes, for the singular situation indicated or evoked by the phrase "myself saying I," which need not be taken as either a stable identity-pole (an *idem*) or a simple restless effacement without remainder of the "I" (as some philosophies of mind or supposed liquidations of the subject have it), but rather summons an *ipse* (to adopt the language used by Ricoeur in his *Oneself as Another*) that is *other to itself no less than it is other to others*. What would be uncertain here is the question of the precise ontological or pragmatic

A deconstructed or deconstructive responsibility, then, responds to an "interpellation,"[123] which can no longer be said to originate in (or arrive at) an addresser or addressee that is determined *in advance* in philosophical or psychological terms as, say, a will, conscience, intelligible character, person, intentional subject, Dasein, citizen, and individual. For, in the final analysis, all these concepts rest on the presupposition of an "organic or atomic indivisibility,"[124] that is to say, on concepts that remain "*conditions* and therefore *limitations* of responsibility, sometimes limitations in the determination of the unconditional, of the categorical imperative, itself."[125] In its full consequence, even the very concept of possibility and possibilization as it informs a long philosophical tradition — from the Aristotelian *dunamis*, the Spinozistic *conatus essendi,* and the Kantian *ultra posse nemo obligatur* down to the Heideggerian primacy of the possible over actuality, to say nothing here of the possible as a logical modality, as a mere theoretical, virtual, or fictional possibility — should be seen, paradoxically, as yet another restriction of the singular instance or instantiation of which the fable of responsibility is made up and in which the "who" is called into question: "The singularity of the 'who'

---

status of the agency of responsiveness and responsibility. Indeed, for the latter to be possible at all, the former *must* be undecidable in its very singularity:

> [T]he functioning of the mark, a certain iterability, here a certain legibility that is operative beyond the disappearance or demise of the presumed author, the recognition of a certain semantic and syntactic code at work in this phrase ["myself saying I"] — none of all this either constitutes or requires a full understanding of the meaning*fulness* of this phrase, in the sense of the complete and original intentionality of its meaning (to say), any more than for the phrase "I forgot my umbrella," abandoned like an island among the unpublished writings of Nietzsche [see Derrida's *Spurs*]. A thousand possibilities will always remain open even if one understands something in this phrase that makes sense (as a citation? the beginning of a novel? a proverb? someone else's secretarial archives? an exercise in learning a language? the narration of a dream? an alibi? a cryptic code — conscious or not? the example of a linguist or a speech act theoretician letting his imagination wander for short distances, etc?) (Derrida, *Limited Inc.,* 62–63 / 121–22).

These uncertainties do not reduce the "I" or "myself saying I" — or even the somewhat irresponsible phrase "I am just" — to nothing, as if they entailed some (logical or merely abstract) negation of the "I" and the utterances in which it functions: for something, if not some thing (or *res,* e.g., a *res cogitans*), remains that can, indeed, be said to somehow make sense. Here and elsewhere, however, the point is, Derrida claims, that "the minimal making sense of something (its conformity to the code, grammaticality, etc.) is incommensurate with the adequate understanding of intended meaning" (ibid., 64 / 124).

123. Derrida, *Du droit à la philosophie,* 408.
124. See Derrida, "Eating Well," 100.
125. Derrida, *Du droit à la philosophie,* 88.

[*qui*] is not the individuality of a thing that would be identical to itself, it is not an atom. It is a singularity that dislocates or divides itself in gathering itself together to answer to the other, whose call somehow precedes its own identification with itself, for this call I can *only* answer, have already answered, even if I am answering 'no.' "[126]

This said, and although the other responsibility that Derrida speaks of is both "older" and "younger" than its philosophical counterparts, as well as their politico-juridical implementations, it is neither "higher" nor "deeper."[127] In its very diachrony and incommensurability, the other, old-new responsibility is not totally alien to its philosophical appropriations, but always already "inscribed" or "engaged"[128] in them. This engagement—*l'en-gage*, as Derrida says in *Of Spirit*, playing on the French *gage* and *langage*—should not be understood in terms of a logical implication or dialectical mediation. Nor does it let itself be captured by an essentialist and teleological organicism (as if it were inherent in language and waiting to unfold). Nor, finally, can this inscription be thought as a mere empirical or pragmatic contingency (as if it overcame language by accident). For the other responsibility is in a sense given with language—or, more precisely, with the occurrence of every mark—as such.

The deconstructive account of the possibility of responsibility or of justice is thus oddly circular or elliptical. On the one hand, there can be no justice "except to the degree that some event is possible which, as event, exceeds calculation, rules, programs, anticipations and so forth"; on the other hand, however, the inverse statement can also be made: justice is "the chance of the event."[129] In this second sense, which is certainly harder to comprehend, justice is itself that which allows or enables historical change (tradition and progress, knowledge and communication) to take place at all (as the quasi-transcendental condition of its possibility or, perhaps, otherwise still). All deconstruction finds its force in the motivation, movement, or impulse—the *élan*,[130] Derrida writes, echoing Bergson—that justice makes possible, and that, in turn, makes justice possible.

126. Derrida, "Eating Well," 100–101.
127. Derrida, *Du droit à la philosophie*, 409 and 89.
128. Ibid., 28, 89.
129. Derrida, "Force of Law," 971.
130. Ibid., 957.

## Vigilance and the Ellipses of Enlightenment

It should be clear by now, why, in his afterword to *Limited Inc.*, Derrida calls the technical discussion of the performative speech act "at bottom an ethical-political one,"[131] in other words, why this witty and sometimes overly polemical analysis of the intricacies of the performative must culminate in a plea for an "Ethic of Discussion." For the reading of J. L. Austin's *How to Do Things with Words,* in "Signature Event Context," in *Limited Inc.*, problematizes "the metaphysical premises" of what is said to be a "fundamentally moralistic"[132] theory of linguistic utterance. To be sure, Derrida leaves no doubt that this problematization extends far beyond the opposition of so-called Continental and Anglo-Saxon or analytic schools of thought, and that the said premises also "underlie the hermeneutics of Ricoeur and the archeology of Foucault."[133] The reception of

131. Derrida, *Limited Inc.*, 116 / 210.

132. Ibid., 39 / 80.

133. Ibid. That Derrida's argument is not with so-called analytical philosophy per se should have been obvious in his discussion of Austin from the very start. In *Limited Inc.*, Derrida says so explicitly when he declares himself "to be in many respects quite close to Austin, both interested in and indebted to his problematic." And he continues: "[W]hen I do raise questions or objections, it is always at points where I recognize in Austin's theory presuppositions which are the most tenacious and the most central presuppositions of the *continental* metaphysical tradition" (*Limited Inc.*, 38 / 78). Somewhat further in this text, and in a passage that gives an important clue to its title, Derrida compares his claim that "*no* intention can *ever* be fully conscious, or actually present to itself" with Austin's statement, in "Three Ways of Spilling Ink" (cf. the *Inc*) that "the only general rule is that the illumination [shed by intuition] is always *limited,* and that in several ways" (ibid., 73 / 139). Yet the charge that metaphysics "in its most traditional forms" casts its shadow over the "heritage" of so-called ordinary language philosophy and speech act-theory from Austin to Searle and beyond sets the tone of Derrida's riposte against Searle's severe criticism of "Signature Event Context." It finds its most concise formulation in the two "indications" summarized on pp. 93 / 173–74 of *Limited Inc.*, indications that presuppose and reinforce each other:

1. The hierarchical axiology, the ethical-ontological distinctions which do not merely set up value-oppositions clustered around an ideal and unfindable limit, but moreover *subordinate* these values to each other (normal/abnormal, standard/parasite, fulfilled/ void, serious/nonserious, literal/nonliteral, briefly: positive/negative, and ideal/nonideal); and in this . . . there is metaphysical pathos. . . . 2. The enterprise of returning "strategically," ideally, to an origin or to a "priority" held to be simple, intact, normal, pure, standard, self-identical, in order *then* to think in terms of derivation, complication, deterioration, accident, etc. All metaphysicians, from Plato to Rousseau, Descartes to Husserl, have proceeded in this way, conceiving good to be before evil, the positive before the negative, the pure before the impure, the simple before the complex, the essential before the accidental, the imitated before the imitation, etc. And this is not just *one* metaphysical ges-

speech-act theory that has played such a crucial role in the linguistic turn in critical theory after Adorno is just one more illustration of the wider significance of this same phenomenon.

One example might suffice there. When it is argued that we often cannot fulfill the counterfactual pragmatic presuppositions from which all communicative practice starts out and "in the sense of a transcendental necessity *must* begin," when it is added that in everyday life these presuppositions are *at once* implicitly affirmed and denied,[134] then neither the nature of this transcendental "must" or "necessity" nor that of this "performative contradiction" can be accounted for without a certain logic of iterability or without a certain pragrammatology. Another structural force seems to be at work here besides (or *in*) the well-known "force of the better argument." This other, more differential force—which, like that of the better argument and the *Verständigung* that it allows, is neither natural nor based on mere convention—explains why any (for example, normative) validity claim can be made in the first place and why it always can (and indeed must) derail. Derailment, perversion, and parody (or some other misunderstanding) is a structural and therefore necessary possibility, that is to say, "a *general possibility inscribed in* the structure of positivity, of normality, of the 'standard' . . . [which] must be taken into account when describing so-called ideal normality."[135]

---

ture among others, it is *the* metaphysical exigency, that which has been the most constant, most profound and most potent.

For an important alternative account of Austin, see Stanley Cavell, *Philosophical Passages: Wittgenstein, Emerson, Austin, Derrida* (Oxford: Blackwell, 1995), 42–90; and id., *Pitch of Philosophy*, ch. 2.

134. Jürgen Habermas, *Der philosophische Diskurs der Moderne* (Frankfurt a./M.: Suhrkamp, 1985), 378.

135. Derrida, *Limited Inc.*, 157 n / 246 n; cf. 102 / 189. This, nothing more and nothing less, is Derrida's claim: "Once it is *possible* for x to function under certain conditions (for instance, a mark in the absence or partial absence of intention), the possibility of a certain non-presence or of a certain non-actuality pertains to the structure of the functioning under consideration, and pertains to it *necessarily*" (ibid., 57 / 112). This proves neither Derrida's commitment to the investigation of the universal conditions of possibility of phenomena in general, as in the tradition of modern transcendental philosophy and its quasi- formal-transcendental transformations; nor his allegiance to some form of metaphysical possibilism. Rather, it testifies to a formally indicative approach to all signification that seeks to steer clear of all relativism (whether cultural, psychological, sociological) *without* losing anything of its hypothetical or provisional character. The use of notions such as "possible" and "necessary" is therefore strategic at most (even though they may be the only categories available for the moment).

It has been argued that, in more than one respect, Derrida's approach therefore does not much differ *in its results* from that of Donald Davidson. See, e.g., Sarah Richmond, "Derrida

Any attempt to exclude this necessary possibility from the analysis of speech acts and to concentrate instead, "in the best Kantian tradition," on the ideal or pure conditions of their intentional fulfillment and performative success, unwittingly translates into "a politics."[136] Reiterating Hegel's critique of the Kantian concept of *Moralität*, Derrida recalls that the formalism that continues to govern speech-act theory is not incompatible with a certain "intrinsic moralism" and "empiricism."[137] And, insofar as all communicative ethics bases its reconstruction of the just procedures of the practical *Diskurs* on these very same deconstructible premises and thereby presupposes a determinable or stable (that is, formalizable) relation between intentions, rules, and conventions, it also reproduces and prolongs less the *ideal* conditions of *all* ethics as those of a given, dominant, and dogmatic discourse on ethics. So-called transcendental, universal, formal pragmatics is for essential reasons neither universal nor formal nor transcendental.

Not that there would be a direct and simple correspondence between the methodological exclusion of "parasitical" occurrences and an excommunication of, say, the unconscious, the marginal, or the foreign.[138] But any such speech-act theory or communicative ethics is forgetful of "other conditions," which, Derrida maintains, "are no less essential to ethics in general, whether of *this given* ethics or of *another* ethics."[139] These other conditions, which a careful deconstructive reading can bring to light, might very well be "anethical with respect to any given ethics," but they are therefore not necessarily "anti-ethical" as such; on the contrary, without ever qualifying as "ethical" or "just" themselves, they may nonetheless "open or recall the opening of another ethics."[140] The task of deconstruction is to articulate the aforementioned "other conditions" and the opening they provoke in yet "another form of 'general theory,'

---

and Analytical Philosophy: Speech Acts and Their Force," *European Journal of Philosophy* 4, no. 1 (April 1996): 38–62; Samuel C. Wheeler III, "Truth-Conditions, Rhetoric, and Logical Form: Davidson and Deconstruction," in *Literary Theory After Davidson*, ed. Reed Way Dasenbrock (University Park: Pennsylvania State University Press, 1993), 144–59; and Richard Rorty, *Objectivity, Relativism, and Truth*, vol. 1 of *Philosophical Papers* (Cambridge: Cambridge University Press, 1991), 125.

136. Derrida, *Limited Inc.*, 97, 135/180, 250. See also Barbara Herrnstein Smith, *Belief and Resistance: Dynamics of Contemporary Intellectual Controversy* (Cambridge, Mass.: Harvard University Press, 1997), 89–124.

137. Derrida, *Limited Inc.*, 97/180.

138. Cf. ibid., 134, 135, 96, 97/243, 244, 250, 180, 181.

139. Ibid., 122/221.

140. Ibid.

or rather another discourse, another 'logic.'"[141] In a far more rigorous manner than professed by the proponents of speech-act theory, this other logic should account for its own intrinsic, systematic—and not merely factual or accidental—incompleteness.[142] It can do so by substituting for the ontological and semantic presuppositions surreptitiously introduced into the study of utterances and acts a more complex—paradoxical, indeed aporetic—consideration of a spectrological and, as *Specters of Marx* puts it, hauntological nature. At work here are what Derrida, following Montaigne, Pascal, Benjamin, and de Certeau, calls mystical postulates: at the origin and in the heart of laws, rules, conceptual idealizations, and even—some would say, especially—of the idea of universality itself. In their relation to the singular occurrence, to the self and the other (to the self as other), each of these general notions involves a transcendental illusion of sorts, one that borders—or touches—upon the fictional, the literary, and, more precisely, the fable.[143] We are not dealing here any longer with the procedures of some transcendental or phenomenological reduction or categorial intuition, or, for that matter, with the formal indication that Heidegger distinguishes from generalization and abstraction. Neither an essentialism in disguise nor a perspectivism, psychologism, or fictionalism is advocated or implied here. A different logic is proposed, one that reflects on the paradoxical, indeed aporetic, status of its concepts and modes of argumentation.

Derrida suggests as much when he concludes that the concept of iterability not only helps us understand "the necessity of thinking *at once* both the rule and the event, the concept and the singular," but also casts a surprising—indeed, troubling—light on the meaning and status of this concept itself. There is thus a certain

> reapplication (without transparent self-reflection and without pure self-identity) of the *principle* of iterability to a *concept* of iterability that is never pure. There is no idealization without (identificatory) iterability; but for the same reason, for reasons of altering (iterability), there is no idealization that

141. Ibid., 117 / 212.

142. See Albrecht Wellmer, *Ethik und Dialog: Elemente des moralischen Urteils bei Kant und in der Diskursethik* (Frankfurt a./M.: Suhrkamp, 1986), trans. David Midgley as "Ethics and Dialogue: Elements of Moral Judgement in Kant and Discourse Ethics," in *The Persistence of Modernity: Essays on Aesthetics, Ethics, and Postmodernism* (Cambridge, Mass.: MIT Press, 1991), 113–231.

143. Cf. Derrida, *Du droit à la philosophie*, 325–26, who refers in turn to Jean-Luc Nancy's chapter "*Mundus est fabula*," in Nancy, *Ego sum* (Paris: Flammarion, 1979).

keeps itself pure, safe from all contamination. The concept of iterability is this singular concept that renders possible the silhouette of ideality, and hence of the concept, and hence of all distinction, of all conceptual opposition. But it is also the concept that, *at the same time*, with the same stroke marks the limit of idealization and conceptualization.[144]

With an inversion of Kant's argumentation in favor of the actual generality and universality of scientific statements and moral imperatives in particular, and while remaining faithful to the direction of transcendental reasoning—that is, by moving back from a given (here the fact of misunderstanding) to the conditions of its possibility—Derrida claims that if things were not this complicated, "word would have gotten around," and consensus on most theoretical questions would not only be possible in principle (that is to say, under ideal conditions), but perhaps also the rule. Since, however, this is very far from the case, to ignore the aforementioned and admittedly "disconcerting" formulation of the nature of conceptual thought—and, indeed, of phenomena, experience, and language, "in general," or, rather, in a wider sense—comes down to betraying the only plausible and responsible "spirit of the type of 'enlightenment' granted our time": "Those who wish to simplify at all costs and who raise a hue and cry about obscurity because they do not recognize the unclarity of their good old *Aufklärung* are in my eyes dangerous dogmatists and tedious obscurantists. No less dangerous (for instance, in politics) are those who wish to purify at all costs."[145]

In some respects, one could argue that the aforementioned incompleteness is further guaranteed and deepened by the circumstance that a deconstructed or deconstructive responsibility (or justice) must be characterized by an irreducible "infinity" that, Derrida maintains, is "owed to the other" or, more precisely, to "the other's coming as the singularity that is always other."[146] Derrida leaves no doubt that this infinity is hardly that of a regulative idea, of a messianic horizon, or of any

144. Derrida, *Limited Inc.*, 119/216. Cf. 71/135: "the unique character of this structure of iterability . . . lies in the fact that, comprising identity *and* difference, repetition *and* alteration, etc., it renders the *project* of idealization possible without leading '*itself*' to any pure, simple, and idealizable conceptualization. No process . . . of idealization is possible without iterability, and yet iterability '*itself*' cannot be idealized." Surely, Derrida concludes, this circumstance and the aporetics of logic, or aporetic logic, that follows from it are irreconcilable with any theory of speech acts in the traditional, scientific or philosophical, sense of the term *theory*.

145. Ibid.

146. Derrida, "Force of Law," 965.

other "eschato-teleology," whether of the "neo-Hegelian," "neo-Marxist," or "post-Marxist" type.[147] The reason he gives here for this reluctance to think of responsibility and justice in terms of a horizon, and to identify their pursuit with the march toward an infinitely removed or a definite end, is neither that the Kantian and messianic perspectives are each in their own singular way *totalistic* nor that they both fail to explain how the intelligible and empirical realm can come together as it is claimed they should. The decisive argument here is, rather, that every horizon entails a "space" and a "period" of "waiting."[148] Yet while heaven (the ultimate good) can wait, the justice demanded by responsibility cannot. Its "excessive haste" leaves no room and no time for a messianic or regulative "horizon of expectation."[149] It has no place in a future in which the antagonistic elements of the present and past are deemed (and, in a sense, doomed) to be reconciled at a stroke or brought together step by step in an asymptotic process of convergence. Justice cannot wait for the judgment of history, to cite another Levinasian topos. The modality of its singular *avenir* is that of an *à venir*, an always yet—and still—"to-come"[150] that at any given moment is equally close, inasmuch as it remains distant and has no common measure or horizon with the present.

However, justice is betrayed if we, for want of an appropriate language, or in view of a confusedly understood "strategy of delay," were to resort to formulating a post-Cartesian "provisional morality" of a quasi-Stoic nature. Rather, Derrida writes, given the "surplus of responsibility that summons the deconstructive gesture or that the deconstructive gesture . . . calls forth [and both summonings are to be thought and practiced *at once*, as two sides of the *double affirmation*—HdV], a waiting period is neither possible nor legitimate."[151] For, the motivation for deconstruc-

147. Ibid., 967. Nor, indeed, does Derrida seem to share the premises of the "prophetic pragmatism" argued for by Cornel West in his *The American Evasion of Philosophy: A Genealogy of Pragmatism* (Madison: University of Wisconsin Press, 1989), 211ff., esp. 236; see also his *Keeping Faith: Philosophy and Race in America* (London: Routledge, 1993), 21–22 and notably 302 n. 6, where West makes an interesting distinction between a "dialectical deconstructionism" à la Adorno and Jameson and a "poststructuralist deconstructionism" à la Derrida and de Man, the "major difference" being that "the theoretical impasse the dialectician reaches is not viewed as an ontological, metaphysical or epistemological aporia, but rather as a historical limitation owing to a determinate contradiction as yet unlodged because of an impotent social praxis or an absence of an effective historical revolutionary agent."
148. Derrida, "Force of Law," 967.
149. Ibid., 969.
150. Ibid.
151. Derrida, *Points . . .* , 286 / 300. It would appear, then, that the process of endless trans-

tion derives its unconditional and imperative character—which, again, "is not necessarily or only Kantian"—from precisely the circumstance that it is "ceaselessly threatened"; and this, Derrida holds, is precisely "why it leaves no respite, no rest": "its exigency can always upset, at least the institutional rhythm of every pause."[152] We should not let ourselves be guided, then, by prudence and pragmatism alone, whether it takes the form of practical wisdom or hermeneutic application, social engineering or a technology of the self, solidarity and irony, not to mention realism or opportunism. All of these run the risk of not being responsive or responsible enough or seem to acquiesce to one or the other side of the historico-political private-public divide.[153] Justice, by contrast, demands, and indeed implies the impossible.

When we feel, Derrida remarks, in taking up the central motif of "On a Newly Arisen Apocalyptic Tone in Philosophy," that we are no longer fully absorbed in our society's conceptual horizons, when we sense that we are no longer "in the running," this hardly means that we can "stay at the starting-line" and remain "spectators." For the fact that we are no longer part of the game and no longer naïvely move within an infinite horizon, toward the end or in the direction—under the regulation—

---

lation and reinscription of finite meaning must come to a halt somewhere, sometime, if only for a split second and even though the place of this *stasis* or rather *stricture* is also already divided, at least "potentially." The standstill or knot in the indefinitely expanded tissue of cross-references—a fixation that is, perhaps, the *"note tenue"* of which Levinas speaks?—can therefore not so much be ascribed to things as they are in themselves but remains to be decided. And this always means: to be decided by the other. As in the taking of a picture, the *gaze of the other* seems to freeze a given situation. Here, as always, the question of meaning would be indissociable from the question "Who reads?" (cf. Derrida, *Dissemination*, 253 / 224), that is to say, who singles out, who signs or addresses, and "[W]ho speaks to whom and in what tune?"

152. Derrida, "Eating Well," 117.

153. See, for a discussion, *Deconstruction and Pragmatism*, ed. Mouffe. We should not conclude too hastily that Derrida's formulations betray an anti-Marxist, let alone a pre-Marxist, stance. Nor, again, does Derrida here simply rebuke the premises of a social critique informed by the legacy of psychoanalysis. *Limited Inc.*, Derrida stresses, "which aside from its use-value in the legal-commercial code that marks the common bond linking England and the United States (Oxford and Berkeley [cf. Austin and Searle—HdV]), also *mentions* in translation a seal related to the French code (s.a.r.l. [*société à responsabilité limitée*—HdV]); *condenses* allusions to the internal regulation through which the capitalist system seeks to limit concentration and decision-making power in order to protect itself against its own 'crises'; [and] *entails* everything said by psychoanalysis about incorporation, about the *limit* between incorporation and non-incorporation, incorporation and introjection in the work of mourning (and in work generally)" (*Limited Inc.*, 84–85 / 158, 159; see also 36, 57, 75, 112, 110–11 n. 11 / 158 n. 1). *Limited Inc.* therefore echoes the work of *Glas* and *Fors*, Derrida notes, and can in addition be said to announce that of *Specters of Marx.*

of an idea, might well be what keeps deconstruction moving. The suspense increases its intensity and "urgency"[154] and "hyperbolically raises the stakes of exacting justice."[155] Without it, the belief in certain protocols of a "new, very new *Aufklärung*," for example in the form of an "ethics of discussion," would be based on nothing but a "naïve confidence"[156] or an ultimately complacent "good conscience."

Justice, then, is "that which must not wait";[157] it is one of the essential characteristics of a "just decision" (and only a decision, Derrida stresses, is just or unjust) that it is "required immediately,"[158] here, at this very moment. Moreover, it is demanded without mediation, absolutely, categorically. For, even if all the information about the general situation and the unique features of a given case were available; even if we had *all* the time we needed to collect this knowledge, and even if our mastery of these facts were virtually unlimited, the decision itself would still remain an infinitely "finite moment," and, theoretically speaking, a "precipitation" that could not be fully justified: a genuine decision only signals itself in the "interruption of the juridico- or ethico- or politico-cognitive deliberation that precedes it, [and that, Derrida immediately adds] must precede it."[159] For, a decision "in its proper moment, if there is one, must be both regulated and without regulation."[160] Strictly speaking, decisions always are too early or too late and never take place *on* time (or *in* time).

Again, that the idea of justice thus proves to be an aporetic notion, that it is indeterminable and therefore "unpresentable," "cannot and should not serve as an alibi for staying out of juridico-political battles."[161] And the doubleness of this command is that of a *necessity* and an *ought*. For even if we wished, we could not hope to protect the purported purity of justice by refusing to translate it into terms that are not its own. Justice must and should be "done."[162] Moreover, it is precisely when it is "left to itself" that justice as a pure idea resembles or, at least, "is very close to the bad, even the worst."[163] Not only can it "always be appropriated by the most perverse calculation."[164] In itself, if we can say so, it is no longer distinguishable from its opposite. We must (and should), therefore, "negoti-

154. Derrida, "Force of Law," 967.

155. Ibid., 955.

156. Derrida, *Limited Inc,* 157 n / 246 n.

157. Derrida, "Force of Law," 967.

158. Ibid.

159. Ibid.

160. Ibid., 961.

161. Ibid., 971.

162. Ibid., 951.

163. Ibid., 971.

164. Ibid.

ate," for, paradoxically, only the *compromise* — the translation and thereby betrayal — of justice protects it from "the worst."

And yet, in an uncanny, disturbing way, *the possibility of "the worst" is also the condition of "the best,"* "the best" not being here the "lesser evil" that Jean-François Lyotard defines as the "political good" (namely, a constellation that does not interdict the "occurrence" of "possible phrases" and in that sense no longer despises "Being"),[165] but rather the incessant negotiation of an impossible yet necessary "relation" between justice, on the one hand, and the order of law and rights, on the other. This negotiation should be taken "as far as possible" and its task, which is also the task of a necessary "politicization" of all discourse on justice and responsibility, is "interminable" — that is, never "total."[166] And yet, even the slightest step forward — Derrida does not hesitate to speak here of "emancipation"[167] — affects the whole of the existing law and all political institutions, since it obliges us to reinterpret, reinvent, and recast their very structure. Such an emancipation is not only emancipated from traditional prophetic hopes and grand teleological (metaphysical, narrative) schemes, however, but at the same stroke reaffirms or reengages, as it

165. Jean-François Lyotard, *Le Différend* (Paris: Editions de Minuit, 1983), trans. G. Van Den Abbeele as *The Differend: Phrases in Dispute* (Minneapolis: University of Minnesota Press, 1988), 140. This would be the place to ask oneself whether there not is in the end a *différend* between Derrida's invocation of a lucid vigil and the "vigil" of which Lyotard speaks. Of course, one could begin by responding in recalling that the latter is a "feeling," "anxiety," and "joy," in short, an "expectant waiting" for *every* "occurrence" (ibid., nos. 134, 135, trans. p. 80). But then again, there is no doubt that the notion, if not of justice, then of ethical obligation — mediated here, once more, through the work of Levinas — orients Lyotard's analysis as whole too. See my "On Obligation: Levinas and Lytotard," *Graduate Faculty Philosophy Journal* 20, no. 2; 21, no. 1 (1998), 83–112. For a critical discussion of Derrida's and Lyotard's conceptions of rights, justice, and "metapolitics," see Seyla Benhabib, "Democracy and Difference: Reflections on the Metapolitics of Lyotard and Derrida," *Journal of Political Philosophy* 2, no. 1 (1994): 1–23.

166. Derrida, "Force of Law," 971. One might compare the inescapable and infinite "negotiation" with the "politics" that Lyotard calls "the possibility of the différend on the occasion of the slightest linkage," a "politics" that is not "the genre that contains all the genres . . . not *a genre*" (*Le Différend*, no. 192, trans. p. 139), but, rather, "the fact that language is not a language, but phrases, or that Being is not Being, but *There is*'s [*des Il y a*]" (ibid., no. 190, trans. p. 138); a "politics," finally, that is "immediately given with a phrase as a differend to be regulated concerning the matter of the means of linking onto it" (ibid., no. 198, trans. p. 141). Lyotard urges us not to confuse this "necessity" with an "obligation": "To link is not a duty, which 'we' can be relieved of or make good upon. 'We' cannot do otherwise." For a discussion of the concept of "the political" that is relevant to these contexts, see also Philippe Lacoue-Labarthe and Jean-Luc Nancy, *Le Retrait du politique* (Paris: Galilée, 1981), trans. as *Retreating the Political*, ed. Simon Sparks (London: Routledge, 1997).

167. Derrida, "Force of Law," 971.

were, the singular structure (*l'engage, le langage*) of messianicity, of the promise, of the "Believe me!" that is the very heart—indeed, the spirit and the specter, the vigil and the wake—of Enlightenment, as well as of its precursors and heirs (Marxism and psychoanalysis among them).[168]

It is impossible to conceptualize or fully formalize the double—or doubly oriented—gesture of a back and forth that Derrida, at one point, characterizes as being contrary to any "ethico-political motive."[169] In what sense could one read this movement as yet another ellipsis of Enlightenment, one that is, as it were, bifocal and, consequently in its very reduction and for all its supposed formalism, or rather kenosis, speaks with more than one voice at once? So far, I have been using the figure of ellipsis with reference to a rhetorical trope. Just as the word *ellipsis* can be read rhetorically as descriptive of the suppression or omission of at least one of the linguistic elements necessary for a complete syntactic or narrative construction or composition, the ellipsis of Enlightenment was introduced as the spectral remainder of a certain order and discourse of meaningfulness, which, in order to be able to speak at all, must risk losing all determinacy. However, one might be tempted to stretch the use of *ellipsis* a little further and stress that it also invokes another—nonrhetorical—figure that helps to circumscribe (or even visualize) the constitutive duality or polarity of tradition and renewal, universality and singularity, appropriation and distanciation, the same and the other, the "archaic" and the "new," "fidelity" and "infidelity," "responsibility" and "lightness [*légèreté*] of heart,"[170] that characterizes the double gesture discussed above. For the term *ellipsis* also evokes a figure (an ellipse) that falls short of completing a certain movement and resists filling up a certain middle but instead draws a line or traces a loop—an oval figure—that no longer encircles *one* fixed focus as the purported origin or center of this movement. This geometric ellipse is a structurally incomplete circle whose center has been omitted, evacuated, or split and doubled into two foci at a variable distance, which orient the place of every other point on

168. See Derrida, "Remarks on Deconstruction and Pragmatism," in Mouffe, *Deconstruction and Pragmatism,* 77–88, 82. All this, however, does not prevent Derrida from contrasting the motif of *l'engage* with "the remnant of *Aufklärung* which still slumbered in the privilege of the question" (*Of Spirit,* 131 n / 150 n) in Heidegger's later use of the *Zusage,* or the *acquiescence* and promise of language, especially in *Being and Time.*

169. Derrida, *Points . . . ,* 363 / 374. The French text has *mobile.*

170. Ibid., 150 / 160. See also ibid., 151 / 161, and see *Specters of Marx,* 87 / 144, where in the French original Derrida uses the words *s'entrelacer* and *s'entre-impliquer.*

the periphery.[171] Whereas the rhetorical ellipsis prevents the geometric—oval—elliptic figure from rounding itself off into a circle, the latter, in turn, forces upon the first a movement of repetition and change (in other words, imposes iterability) thus reinforcing its doubling (its double bind) and intensifying its uncanny and haunting character.

No "equilibrium" could contain this rhythm between the extremes of this pendular movement of oscillation, a movement Derrida also compares to the Hölderlinian *Wechseln der Töne,* and, more prosaically, to the televisual habit of "zapping."[172] The tension between these poles or postures should instead be made as great as possible or as intense as thought and experience allow. For each of them, when taken in itself, is madness, irresponsible, death, the worst.[173]

BOTH ELLIPSES OF ENLIGHTENMENT, then, imply and illuminate each other mutually and hint obliquely—elliptically—at a theoretico-ethico-political task or attentiveness that exceeds (or precedes) philosophical reason at every instant because it is the very condition of its possibility, as well as of its intrinsic incompletion. This explains why, for all its use of vivid imagery, this analysis is still a formalization, which in itself cannot immediately justify or translate into anything determinate, for example, institutional politics. For the rhythm not so much takes place *within* this formalization as *with it.* It is for this reason, Derrida admits, that the de-

171. The short text entitled "Ellipse" that concludes and recapitulates the trajectory of Derrida's *Writing and Difference* describes this iteration in the following words: "Repeated, the same line is no longer exactly the same, the ring no longer has exactly the same center, *the origin has played.* Something is missing for the circle to be perfect" (ibid., 296, 431). Any reading that, like "Ellipse" itself, succeeds in retracing this kind of repetition, this doubling of a singular, virtual point (or *point de vue*), would be elliptical. See also *Margins of philosophy,* 169ff./202ff., and *Psyché,* 192; and see Jean-Luc Nancy, "Sens elliptique," *Revue philosophique* 2 (1990), 325–47, 336; Werner Hamacher, "Hermeneutic Ellipses: Writing the Hermeneutic Circle in Schleiermacher," in *Premises,* 44–80; and Jean Greisch, "Le Cercle et l'ellipse: Le Statut de l'herméneutique de Platon à Schleiermacher," *Revue des Sciences philosophiques et théologiques* 73 (1989): 161–84, cf. 163, 183–84.

172. See Derrida, "On a Newly Adopted Apocalyptic Tone in Philosophy," *Postcard,* and "Circumfession," 176, 164–65: "I knew how to 'zap' even before television gave me that pleasure, as I have always zapped in writing, *Wechseln der Töne* which leaves the other rooted to the spot from one sentence to the next, in the middle of a sentence, dead or vigilant at last." One can easily comprehend the force of the figure of the modulation of tones if one contrasts it with Levinas's characterization of the "processus du présent" as a " 'note tenue' dans son *toujours,* dans son identité du même, dans la simultanéité de ses moments" (*De Dieu qui vient à l'idée,* 101).

173. Derrida, *Points . . . ,* 150–51, 160–61.

constructive analysis, for all its political relevance, can hope at best to spell out a "negative wisdom" — a formulation Derrida borrows from Kant[174] — or, what comes down to the same thing, to provide us with "protocols of vigilance"[175] in view (and in light) of a "new *Aufklärung.*"[176]

But doesn't the respect and responsiveness vis-à-vis the unconditional appeal that is said to institute the tribunal of reason entrap this thinking in a paralyzing dilemma of having to choose between discursive betrayal, on the one hand, and a silent, apophatic or mystical, respect, on the other? And even if the act of instituting reason could ever be concretized or materialized — if not in all purity, then at least through a certain limited, albeit transgressive, practice — what sociopolitical or cultural institution could hope to live up to this singular gesture and take responsibility for it?

No better answer to this question can be found than the one Derrida offers in his analysis of Kantian writings on the institution of the university, of the inevitable conflict of academic philosophy with biblical and dogmatic theology, of censorship, tolerance, and so on. For it is here that Derrida makes it clear what it means for deconstruction to revolve in all its central aspects around the institution. By explicating the double meaning of this word *institution,* as both founding act and founded edifice, Derrida shows here how it relates to philosophy — in the case of the university, even to the institution of philosophy — without therefore being itself strictly or even primarily philosophical. Based as it is on a so-called "mystical postulate," it resembles an absolute performative that enables both the best and the worst, and that lets itself be experienced — and experimented with — in *horror religiosus* alone.

174. Kant, *Conflict of the Faculties,* 168–69.
175. Derrida, *Du droit à la philosophie,* 496.
176. Ibid., 496.

# Epilogue

To a greater or lesser extent, all discourses concerning Western modernization—be they on social differentiation or on the phylo- and ontogenetic decentering of consciousness—rest on the assumption that it is possible to make a clear-cut distinction between myth and *logos,* or reason, between the divine and the human, the sacred and the profane, the Christian and the secular. It is far from clear whether the thinkers who celebrate postmodernity have in fact succeeded in subverting these last, and most persistent, of all binary oppositions. On the contrary, more often than not, the postmodern understands itself as the secular become sacred, the modern esoteric turned exoteric. In a sense, it is the apotheosis of the public sphere, that most cherished child of the emerging Enlightenment.

No doubt the range of issues pertaining to the "return of religion" that I have discussed in this book constitutes an important field of research for philosophers, historians, and cultural analysts alike. However, I have chosen to examine the role and the implications of religious tropes, not so much in their historical or present cultural setting, or in their empirical effects, as in relation to the unexpected and far-reaching systematic or conceptual twists and turns they imply, evoke, or provoke. I have also suggested that the religious—the word and the figure of "God," for example, and everything that comes to take its place—is a singular performative instance rather than, say, a general structure of performativity whose essential features could be fully explained in a theory of speech acts or, more broadly, a philosophy of language, culture, and meaning.[1] The performa-

---

1. To the extent that the performative instance is linked to the problem of naming—to the "initial baptism" and "rigid designation" of names, "God," for example—one might indeed side here once again with Saul Kripke, whose *Naming and Necessity,* while putting forward or rather reiterating certain "intuitions," and even "doctrines," refrains from formulating a *theory* in the strict sense of the word. See *Naming and Necessity,* 64, where Kripke surmises that the "only defect" of the so-called "cluster concept theory of names" is one that is "common to all philosophical theories. It's wrong." To this he hastens to add: "You may suspect me from proposing another theory in place; but I hope not, because I'm sure it's wrong too if it's a theory" (ibid.).

tive instance I have sought to *re*trace (and that I have thus also traced otherwise and inevitably distorted) is never merely secondary, accidental, or ornamental, and is therefore irreducible to the better-known classical and modern interpretations of tropology,[2] such as the aesthetic, the literary, the poetic, the symbolic, the metaphoric, the metonymic, and so on. Furthermore, this singular performative instance is at odds with all the known and possible varieties of semantic reference, or, for that matter, semantic innovation. And while this means that the religious, its hints, *Winke,* echoes, and citations cannot be captured or rephrased in terms of some propositional, ontological, or metaphorical truth, we must not conflate its undeniable prescriptivity with a simple imperativity or normativity. The reason for this seems clear enough and is in fact a central insight of so-called deconstruction. For while it is true that because it is "also ethico-political," deconstruction is not "essentially theoretical, thetic, or thematic," this statement, as Derrida hastens to add, also "calls for the strictest vigilance and quotation marks."[3] The question was raised, therefore, as to whether vigilance with respect to the ethical and the political can be simply ethical or political. Might its invocation be ethical and political in a radically new sense of these words? What, precisely, gives rise to the need to quote at all? And is it necessary to quote the notion of the ethical or of the political rather than something else? Why quote them, but only "under erasure," *sous rature?* Neither an empirical — psychological or biographical — nor an ontological, let alone aestheticizing, answer to these questions seems to do justice to the problems involved, and it is in the space left open by this very silence that the "turn to religion" has emerged.

In a sense, Derrida's analysis leaves both the orthodox and the heterodox interpretations of religious topoi and theologemes intact. But then again, an analysis that allows both the literal or spiritual and the frivolous or heretical readings of authoritative texts is itself strictly speaking neither orthodox nor heterodox, fundamentalist or liberal, denominational or secular, modern or postmodern. It situates itself before or beyond, and in any case at an infinite distance from the conflicts of interpretation arising

2. On the notion of tropology and its pertinence for historical and historiographical discourse, see F. R. Ankersmit, *History and Tropology: The Rise and Fall of Metaphor* (Berkeley and Los Angeles: University of California Press, 1994).

3. Jacques Derrida, "Some Statements and Truisms about Neologisms, Newisms, Postisms, Parasitisms, and Other Small Seismisms," trans. A. Tomiche, in *The States of Theory: History, Art and Critical Discourse,* ed. D. Carroll (New York: Columbia University Press, 1990), 63–95, 87.

out of each of these positions, no less than from their temporary irenic or ecumenic interruptions.

This is not to say that Derrida's analysis is intent on severing its ties with the philosophical, religious, and, indeed, ontotheological tradition it deconstructs. Although it adopts a stance of indelible indifference with respect to these demarcations, it does not constitute a counterposition. In Derrida's analyses, the same texts, topics, and tropes become readable otherwise. But this repetition or reiteration is hardly a *Wiederholung* in the Heideggerian or even Kierkegaardian sense. As I have argued here and elsewhere, the procedure or transformation at issue here is reminiscent of the textual practices of the mystics. But to be struck by such reminiscence is not to construe a genealogy, let alone a historical continuity. Nor can Derrida's dealings with the history of religions be described as so many in-stances of parody. Even the Kierkegaardian concept of irony perhaps falls short of grasping the implications and reverberations of the "turn" that interest us here. If anything, we are dealing with a peculiar *self-irony* of a tradition that, depending on the historical context, takes the form of a performative contradiction, whose critical force we should do well never to dismiss beforehand, albeit without thereby losing sight of its poten-tial — or even fundamental — conservatism and possible reactionaryism. The latter will always cast its shadow over the former.

This ambiguity of the semantic — and more than merely semantic but also but also formal, figurative, differential, and *ruinous* — potential of the heritage called religious need not surprise us if we bear in mind what Derrida says about the hegemony and deconstructibility of metaphysical concepts "in general" (that is to say, during most of the history of Western thought). Speaking of Platonic, Cartesian, and Kantian motifs, Derrida writes: "A text is never totally governed by 'metaphysical presupposi-tions.' . . . there is a domination, a dominant, of the metaphysical model, and then there are counterforces which threaten or undermine its au-thority. These forces of 'ruin' are not negative, they participate in the pro-ductive or instituting force of the very thing they seem to be tormenting."[4] My central claim, then, has been that mutatis mutandis the same holds true of religious practices and institutions in relation to their conceptual underpinnings (philosophemes and theologemes). It is as if deconstruc-tion is at work precisely in the self-irony of these motifs. As a consequence, deconstruction has, in a sense, nothing to add: it leaves everything as

4. Derrida, *Acts of Literature*, ed. Attridge, 53.

it is, albeit it in a different way than the one envisioned by Wittgenstein's *Philosophical Investigations,* and yet leaves nothing untouched. It assists in a process that *seems* at once tautological and heterological but that *is*—strictly or ontologically speaking—neither simply tautological nor heterological as such. It is in the very *negotiation,* both analytically and practically, between these two conceptual extremes (of tautology and heterology) that the contribution, indeed, the therapeutic effect (alluding to Wittgenstein just once more), of philosophy's turn to religion consists.

It has often been noted that Derrida's strategy from the mid 1960s up until the early 1970s was to argue that the traits that—in a metaphysical reading—"*distinguish* writing from speech belong equally to *both.*" This "generalization" of the concept of writing resulted both in a virtually unlimited widening of the "scope" of this term—which could now no longer be limited to (the practice of putting) words on paper—and in a certain qualification of our understanding of, for example, speech, which was now shown to have its own " 'graphematic' properties."[5]

Again, I have been claiming throughout that mutatis mutandis the same strategic move holds sway over Derrida's rearticulation or redeployment of the religious in its relation to the philosophical (the ethical, the political, the aesthetic, the theological). Here as well we are invited to rethink language and experience no less than the traditionally established disciplines and institutions, such as philosophy (but this example by no means stands on its own) in light of the paradoxical and aporetic notion of a *generalized religion.* Yet I would claim that the shift from generalized writing to generalized religion is by no means trivial or the mere transposition of an old discussion and a fixed "conceptual matrix" that, for example, in the first part of *Of Grammatology* was formulated in opposition to a certain dominant, say, structuralist, discourse to a different intellectual, cultural, and political climate (characterized by new technologies, globalization, and, indeed, the return of religion). This would be only one way to read Derrida, and, I believe, not the most productive one. For all the formal similarities that we may want to observe, the turn to religion studied here constitutes, in my opinion, also the most significant of all nonsynonymous substitutions to date. The strategic rearticulation and redeployment of religion maintains an even more outspoken or dramatic link than writing to the historical singularities in which even the most

5. Sarah Richmond, "Derrida and Analytical Philosophy: Speech Acts and Their Force," *European Journal of Philosophy* 4, no. 1 (April 1996): 40.

abstract—and formally indicative—analyses find their source, impetus, and corroboration. The invocation of religion, its concept no less than its historical manifestations, better enables one to highlight the most pressing questions of ethics and politics and give these concepts a renewed urgency, while avoiding the pitfalls of moralism, good conscience, or any other supposed correctness.

My central claim has therefore been that insistence on "Tout autre est tout autre" neither excludes an ethics or politics nor simply includes or implies one: however, its supposed *an-ethicity* does entail a certain formalization of the obligation and respect toward the other and toward others that resembles a famous line from Dostoyevky's *The Brothers Karamazov* often quoted by Levinas to illustrate the very idea of a nonsynonymous—and in Levinas's view: ethical—substitution:

> *All* of us are guilty of *everything* and responsible for *everyone* in the face of *everything* and I more than the others.

The term *adieu* conveys and economically summarizes this complicated and asymmetrical structure that any plausible or responsible turn to "religion" seems—so far—to take upon itself. In the very ambiguity of its meaning—once again, a turning "toward" (*à Dieu*) and "away from" (*adieu*) the absolutely other, a turning, moreover, that is never without risk, because never simply reciprocal or returned—it expresses the secret alliance and, perhaps, the co-originarity, of revelation and profanation, of the sacred and the secular, of the infinite and the infinitely finite, of prayer and blasphemy, of theology and idolatry, of violence and nonviolence, of the self and the other, and, indeed, of religion and philosophy.

# Bibliography

Adorno, Theodor W. *Negative Dialektik.* Frankfurt a./M.: Suhrkamp, 1966. Translated by E. B. Ashton under the title *Negative Dialectics* (New York: Seabury Press, 1973).

Adorno, Theodor W., and Max Horkheimer. *Dialektik der Aufklärung: Philosophische Fragmente.* Frankfurt a./M.: Fischer, 1979. Translated by John Cumming under the title *Dialectic of Enlightenment* (New York: Continuum Books, 1993).

Arendt, Hannah. *Lectures on Kant's Political Philosophy.* Edited by Ronald Beiner. Chicago: Chicago University Press, 1982.

Ariès, Philippe. *L'Homme devant la mort.* Paris: Éditions du Seuil, 1977. Translated by Helen Weaver under the title *The Hour of Our Death* (New York: Oxford University Press, 1991).

Asad, Talal. *Genealogies of Religion: Discipline and Reason in Christianity and Islam.* Baltimore: Johns Hopkins University Press, 1993.

Augustine, Saint. *Confessiones.* Translated by Henry Chadwick. New York: Oxford University Press, 1991.

——. *Confessions.* Translated by W. Watts. Cambridge, Mass.: Harvard University Press, 1996.

Austin, J. L. *How to Do Things With Words.* 1962. Cambridge, Mass.: Harvard University Press, 1975.

Bailly, Christoph. *Adieu: Essai sur la mort des dieux.* La Tour d'Aigues: Éditions de l'Aube, 1989.

Balthasar, Hans Urs von. "Kénose." In *Dictionnaire de spiritualité ascétique et mystique,* 8: 1705–12. Paris: Beauchesne, 1974.

Barash, Jeffrey Andrew. *Heidegger et son siècle: Temps de l'être, temps de l'histoire.* Paris: Presses universitaires de France, 1995.

Bataille, Georges. *L'Expérience intérieure.* Vol. 1 of *Somme athéologique.* Paris, 1945. Translated by Leslie Anne Boldt under the title *Inner Experience* (Albany: State University of New York Press, 1988).

——. *Somme athéologique.* 3 vols. Paris: Gallimard, 1945–54.

Beardsworth, Richard. *Derrida and the Political.* London: Routledge, 1996.

Beiser, Frederick C. *The Fate of Reason: German Philosophy from Kant to Fichte.* Cambridge, Mass.: Harvard University Press, 1987.

Benhabib, Seyla. "Democracy and Difference: Reflections on the Metapolitics of Lyotard and Derrida." *Journal of Political Philosophy* 2, no. 1 (1994): 1–23.

Benjamin, Walter. *Gesammelte Schriften.* Edited by Rolf Tiedemann and Hermann Schweppenhäuser with the assistance of Theodor W. Adorno und Gershom Scholem. Frankfurt a./M.: Suhrkamp, 1972–89.

———. "Theses on the Philosophy of History." In *Illuminations,* 253–64. Translated by Harry Zohn. Edited and with an introduction by Hannah Arendt. New York: Schocken Books, 1969.

Bennington, Geoffrey. "Deconstruction and the Philosophers (the Very Idea)." *Oxford Literary Review* 10 (1987): 73–130.

———. "Derridabase." In Geoffrey Bennington and Jacques Derrida, *Jacques Derrida,* 7–292. Paris: Éditions du Seuil, 1991. Translated by Geoffrey Bennington under the title "Derridabase," in id. and Jacques Derrida, *Jacques Derrida* (Chicago: University of Chicago Press, 1991), 3–316.

———. *Legislations: The Politics of Deconstruction.* London: Verso, 1994.

Benveniste, Émile. *Le Vocabulaire des institutions indo-européennes.* 2 vols. Paris: Éditions de Minuit, 1969. Translated by Elizabeth Palmer under the title *Indo-European Language and Society* (Coral Gables, Fla.: University of Miami Press, 1973.

Bergson, Henri. *Le Deux Sources de la morale et la religion.* Paris: Presses universitaires de France, 1932, 1951. Translated by R. Ashley Audra and Cloudesley Brereton, with the assistance of W. Horsfall Carter, under the title *The Two Sources of Morality and Religion* (Notre Dame, Ind.: University of Notre Dame Press, 1986).

———. *Essais sur les données immédiates de la conscience.* 1889. Translated by F. L. Pogson under the title *Time and Free Will: An Essay on the Immediate Data of Consciousness* (1910; New York: Humanities Press, 1971).

Birault, Henri. "Philosophie et théologie: Heidegger et Pascal." In *Heidegger,* ed. Michel Haar, 514–41. Cahier de l'Herne. Paris: Éditions de l'Herne, 1983.

Birus, Hendrik. " 'Ich bin, der ich bin': Über die Echo eines Namens." In *Juden in der deutschen Literatur: Ein deutsch-israelisches Symposium,* ed. Stéphane Moses and Albrecht Schöne, 25–53. Frankfurt a./M.: Suhrkamp, 1986.

Boer, Karin de. *Denken in het licht van de tijd: Heideggers tweestrijd met Hegel.* Assen, Neth.: Van Gorcum, 1997.

Boyarin, Daniel. *A Radical Jew: Paul and the Politics of Identity.* Berkeley and Los Angeles: University of California Press, 1994.

Brenner, Frederic, and Yosef Hayim Yerushalmi. *Marranes.* Paris: Éditions de la Différence, 1992.

Brkic, Pero. *Martin Heidegger und die Theologie: Ein Thema in dreifacher Fragestellung.* Mainz: Matthias Grünewald, 1994.

Bull, Malcolm, ed. *Apocalypse Theory and the Ends of the World.* Oxford: Blackwell, 1995.

Butler, Judith. *Bodies That Matter: On the Discursive Limits of "Sex."* London: Routledge, 1993.

Caputo, John D. *The Prayers and Tears of Jacques Derrida: Religion Without Religion.* Bloomington: Indiana University Press, 1997.

Carabine, Deirdre. *The Unknown God: Negative Theology in the Platonic Tradition, Plato to Eriugena.* Louvain: Peeters Press, W. B. Eerdmans, 1995.

Caruth, Cathy. *Unclaimed Experience: Trauma, Narrative, and History.* Baltimore: Johns Hopkins University Press, 1996.

Casanova, José. *Public Religions in the Modern World.* Chicago: Chicago University Press, 1994.

Castells, Manuel. *The Information Age: Economy, Society and Culture.* Vol. 1: *The Rise of the Network Society.* Oxford: Blackwell, 1996.

Cavell, Stanley. *A Pitch of Philosophy: Autobiographical Exercises.* Cambridge, Mass.: Harvard University Press, 1994.

———. *Philosophical Passages: Wittgenstein, Emerson, Austin, Derrida* (Oxford: Blackwell, 1995).

Certeau, Michel de. "La Fiction de l'histoire: L'Écriture de *Moïse et le monothéisme*." In id., *L'Écriture de l'histoire.* Paris: Éditions du Seuil, 1975. Translated by Tom Conley under the title "The Fiction of History: The Writing of *Moses and Monotheism,*" in *The Writing of History* (New York: Columbia University Press, 1988), 308–54.

———. *La Fable mystique: XVI^e–XVII^e siècle.* Paris: Gallimard, 1982. Translated by Michael B. Smith under the title *The Mystic Fable* (Chicago: University of Chicago Press, 1992).

Chouraqui, André. *Un Pacte neuf: Lettres; Contemplation de Yohanân.* La Bible traduite et présentée par André Chouraqui, 22. Paris: Desclée de Brouwer, 1977.

Chrétien, Jean-Louis. "La Réserve de l'être." In *Martin Heidegger,* ed. Michel Haar, 233–60. Cahier de l'Herne. Paris: Éditions de l'Herne, 1983.

———. *La Voix nue: Phénoménologie de la promesse.* Paris: Éditions de Minuit, 1990.

Cohn, Norman. *Cosmos, Chaos and the World to Come: The Ancient Roots of Apocalyptic Faith.* New Haven: Yale University Press, 1994.

———. *The Pursuit of the Millennium: Revolutionary Millenarians and Mystical Anarchists of the Middle Ages.* 1957. Reprint, London: Pimlico, 1970. Rev. and expanded ed., New York: Oxford University Press, 1970.

Courtine, Jean-François. *Heidegger et la phénoménologie.* Paris: Vrin, 1990.

———. "Les Traces et le passage du Dieu dans les *Beiträge zur Philosophie* de Martin Heidegger." *Archivio di filosofia* 1, no. 3 (1994): 519–38.

Coward, Harold, and Toby Foshay, eds. *Derrida and Negative Theology.* Albany: State University of New York Press, 1992.

Critchley, Simon. *The Ethics of Deconstruction: Levinas and Derrida.* Oxford: Blackwell, 1992.

Dastur, Françoise. "Entretien avec Jan Patočka." In *Jan Patočka: Philosophie, phénoménologie, politique,* ed. Etienne Tassin and Marc Richir. Grenoble: Éditions Jérome Millon, 1992.

———. *Heidegger et la question du temps.* Paris: Presses universitaires de France, 1990.

———. "Heidegger et la thèologie." *Revue philosophique de Louvain* 2, no. 3 (May–August 1994): 226–45.

———. *La Mort.* Paris: Hatier, 1994.

———. "Patočka et Heidegger: La Phénoménologie et la question de l'homme." *Cahiers de Philosophie,* nos. 11–12 (Winter 1990–91), special issue, *Jan Patočka: Le Soin de l'âme.*

Derrida, Jacques. *Adieu à Emmanuel Levinas.* Paris: Galilée, 1997.

———. *Apories.* Paris: Galilée, 1993. Translated by Thomas Dutoit under the title *Aporias* (Stanford: Stanford University Press, 1993).

———. *L'Autre Cap.* Paris: Éditions de Minuit, 1997. Translated by Pascale-Anne Brault and Michael B. Naas under the title *The Other Heading: Reflections on Today's Europe* (Bloomington: Indiana University Press, 1992).

———. "Avances." In Serge Margel, *Le Tombeau du dieu artisan: Sur Platon,* 11–43. Paris: Éditions de Minuit, 1995.

———. *La Carte postale: De Socrate à Freud et au-delà.* Paris: Flammarion, 1980. Translated by Alan Bass under the title *The Postcard: From Socrates to Freud and Beyond* (Chicago: Chicago University Press, 1987).

———. "Circonfession: Cinquante-neuf périodes et périphrases écrites dans une sorte de marge intérieure, entre le livre de Geoffrey Bennington et un ouvrage en préparation (janvier 1989–avril 1990)." In Geoffrey Bennington and Jacques Derrida, *Jacques Derrida,* 7–291. Paris: Éditions du Seuil, 1991. Translated by Geoffrey Bennington under the title "Circumfession: Fifty-nine Periods and Periphrases Written in a Sort of Internal Margin Between Geoffrey Bennington's Book and Work in Preparation (January 1989–April 1990)," in id. and

Jacques Derrida, *Jacques Derrida* (Chicago: University of Chicago Press, 1991), 3–315.

———. "Comment ne pas parler: Dénégations." In *Psyché: Inventions de l'autre*, 535–95. Paris: Galilée 1987. Translated by Ken Frieden under the title "How to Avoid Speaking: Denials," in *Languages of the Unsayable: The Play of Negativity in Literature and Literary Theory*, ed. Sanford Budick and Wolfgang Iser (New York: Columbia University Press, 1989).

———. *De la grammatologie.* Paris: Éditions de Minuit, 1967. Translated by Gayatri Chakravorty Spivak under the title *Of Grammatology* (Baltimore: Johns Hopkins University Press, 1976).

———. *De l'esprit: Heidegger et la question.* Paris: Galilée, 1987. Translated by Geoffrey Bennington and Rachel Bowlby under the title *Of Spirit: Heidegger and the Question* (Chicago: Chicago University Press, 1989).

———. "DEMEURE: Fiction et témoignage." In *Passions de la littérature: Avec Jacques Derrida*, ed. Michel Lisse, 13–73. Paris: Galilée, 1996.

———. "Des tours de Babel." In *Psyché: Inventions de l'autre*, 203–35. Paris: Galilée, 1987. Translated in *Difference in Translation*, ed. Joseph F. Graham, 165–248 (Ithaca, N.Y.: Cornell University Press, 1985).

———. "La Différance." In *Marges de la philosophie*, 3–29. Paris: Éditions de Minuit, 1972. Translated by Alan Bass under the title "Différance," in *Margins of Philosophy*, 3–27 (Chicago: University of Chicago Press, 1982).

———. *La Dissémination.* Paris: Éditions du Seuil, 1972. Translated by Barbara Johnson under the title *Dissemination* (Chicago: University of Chicago Press, 1981).

———. "Donner la mort." In *L'Éthique du don: Jacques Derrida et la pensée du don*, ed. Jean-Michel Rabaté and Michael Wetzel, 11–108. Paris: Métailié-Transition, 1992. Translated by David Wills under the title *The Gift of Death* (Stanford: Stanford University Press, 1995).

———. *Donner le temps: La Fausse Monnaie.* Paris: Galilée, 1991. Translated by Peggy Kamuf under the title *Given Time: I. Counterfeit Money* (Chicago: University of Chicago Press, 1992).

———. *Du droit à la philosophie.* Galilée: Paris, 1990.

———. *D'un ton apocalyptique adopté naguère en philosophie.* Paris: Galilée, 1983. Also in *Les Fins de l'homme: A partir du travail de Jacques Derrida*, ed. Ph. Lacoue-Labarthe and Jean-Luc Nancy (Paris: Galilée, 1981). Translated by J. P. Leavy, Jr., under the title "On a Newly Arisen Apocalyptic Tone in Philosophy," in *Raising the Tone of Philosophy: Late Essays by Immanuel Kant, Transformative Critique by Jacques Derrida*, ed. Peter Fenves, 117–71 (Baltimore: Johns Hopkins University Press, 1993).

————. "Economimesis." In S. Agacinksi et al., *Mimesis: Des articulations,* 57–93. Paris: Aubier-Flammarion, 1975.

————. *L'Écriture et la différence.* Paris: Éditions du Seuil, 1967. Translated by Alan Bass under the title *Writing and Difference* (London: Routledge, 1978).

————. *Edmund Husserl: L'Origine de la géométrie. Traduction et introduction.* Paris: Presses universitaires de France, 1962, 1974. Translated into English by John P. Leavy, Jr., under the title *Edmund Husserl's "Origin of Geometry": An Introduction* (Stony Brook, N.Y.: Nicolas Hays, 1978; reprint, Lincoln: University of Nebraska Press, 1989).

————. "En ce moment même dans cet ouvrage me voici." In *Psyché: Inventions de l'autre,* 159–202. Paris: Galilée, 1987. Translated by Ruben Berezdivin under the title "At This Very Moment in This Work Here I Am," in *Rereading Levinas,* ed. Robert Bernasconi and Simon Critchley, 11–48 (Bloomington: Indiana University Press, 1991).

————. *Eperons: Les Styles de Nietzsche.* Paris: Flammarion, 1976. Translated by Barbara Harlow under the title *Spurs: Nietzsche's Styles* (Chicago: University of Chicago Press, 1979).

————. *Feu la cendre.* Paris: Des Femmes, 1987. Translated by Ned Lukacher under the title *Cinders* (Lincoln: University of Nebraska Press, 1991).

————. "Foi et savoir: Les Deux Sources de la 'religion' aux limites de la simple raison." In *La Religion,* ed. Jacques Derrida and Gianni Vattimo, 9–86. Paris: Éditions du Seuil, 1996. Translated by Samuel Weber under the title "Faith and Knowledge: The Two Sources of 'Religion' Within the Limits of Mere Reason," in *Religion,* ed. Derrida and Vattimo, 1–78 (Stanford: Stanford University Press, 1998).

————. *Force de loi: Le "Fondement mystique de l'authorité."* Paris: Galilée, 1994. Translated by Mary Quaintance under the title "Force of Law: The 'Mystical Foundation of Authority.'" *Cardozo Law Review* 2, nos. 5–6 (July–August 1990): 920–1045.

————. "Forcener le subjectile." In Jacques Derrida and Paule Thévenin, *Antonin Artaud: Dessins et portraits,* 55–108. Paris: Gallimard, 1986. Translated by Mary Ann Caws under the title "To Unsense the Subjectile," in Jacques Derrida and Paule Thévenin, *The Secret Art of Antonin Artaud,* 61–157 (Cambridge, Mass.: MIT Press, 1998).

————. "Fors." In Nicolas Abraham and Maria Torok, *Cryptonymie: Le Verbier de l'homme aux loups.* Paris: Aubier Flammarion, 1976.

————. *Glas.* Paris: Galilée, 1974. Translated by John P. Leavey, Jr., and Richard Rand under the same title (Lincoln: University of Nebraska Press, 1986).

————. "'Il faut bien manger' ou le calcul du sujet." *Cahiers Confrontation* 20

(1989): 91–114. Translated under the title " 'Eating Well,' or the Calculation of the Subject: An Interview with Jacques Derrida," in *Who Comes After the Subject?* ed. E. Cadava, P. Connor, and Jean-Luc Nancy (London: Routledge, 1991), 96–119.

———. "Jacques Derrida in Discussion with Christopher Norris." In *Deconstruction: Omnibus Volume*, ed. Andreas Papadakis, Catherine Cooke, and Andrew Benjamin, 71–75. New York: Rizzoli, 1989.

———. *Limited Inc.: abc. . . .* Baltimore: Johns Hopkins University Press, 1977. Presentation and translation into French by Elisabeth Weber. Paris: Galilée, 1990.

———. "La Main de Heidegger (*Geschlecht* II)." In *Psyché: Inventions de l'autre*, 415–51. Paris: Galilée, 1987. Translated by John P. Leavy, Jr., under the title "*Geschlecht* II: Heidegger's Hand," in *Deconstruction and Philosophy: The Texts of Jacques Derrida*, ed. John Salis, 161–96 (Chicago: University of Chicago Press, 1987).

———. *Mal d'archive: Une Impression freudienne.* Paris: Galilée, 1995. Translated by Eric Prenowitz under the title "Archive Fever: A Freudian Impression," *Diacritics* 25, no. 2 (Summer 1995): 9–63.

———. *Marges de la philosophie.* Paris: Éditions de Minuit, 1972. Translated by Alan Bass under the title *Margins of Philosophy* (Chicago: University of Chicago Press, 1982).

———. *Mémoires d'aveugle: L'Auto-portrait et autres ruines.* Paris: Éditions de la Réunion des musées nationaux, 1990. Translated by Pascale-Anne Brault and Michael Naas under the title *Memories of the Blind: The Self-Portrait and Other Ruins* (Chicago: University of Chicago Press, 1993).

———. *Mémoires: Pour Paul de Man.* Paris: Galilée, 1988. Translated by Cecile Lindsay, Jonathan Culler, Eduardo Cadava, and Peggy Kamuf under the title *Memories: For Paul de Man* (New York: Columbia University Press, 1989).

———. "Mochlos: or, The Conflict of the Faculties." In *Logomachia*, ed. R. Rand, 1–34. Lincoln: University of Nebraska Press, 1992.

———. *Le Monolinguisme de l'autre.* Paris: Galilée, 1996. Translated by Patrick Mensah under the title *Monolingualism of the Other; or, The Prosthesis of Origin* (Stanford: Stanford University Press, 1998).

———. "L'Oreille de Heidegger." In *Politiques de l'amitié.* Paris: Galilée, 1994. Translated by John P. Leavy Jr. under the title "Heidegger's Ear. Philopolemology (*Geschlecht* IV)," in *Reading Heidegger: Commemorations*, ed. John Salis, 163–218 (Bloomington: Indiana University Press, 1993).

———. *L'Oreille de l'autre: Otobiographies, transferts, traductions. Textes et débats avec Jacques Derrida, sous la direction de Claude Lévesque et Christie V. McDon-*

*ald.* Montréal: VLB, 1982. Translated by Peggy Kamuf under the title *The Ear of the Other: Otobiography, Transference, Translation. Texts and Discussions with Jacques Derrida,* ed. Christie V. McDonald (New York: Schocken Books, 1985).

———. *Parages.* Paris: Galilée, 1986.

———. "Passions: 'An Oblique Offering.' " In *Derrida: A Critical Reader,* ed. David Wood, 5–35. Oxford, Eng., and Cambridge, Mass.: Blackwell, 1992.

———. *Points de suspension: Entretiens.* Paris: Galilée, 1992. Translated by Peggy Kamuf et al. under the title *Points . . . : Interviews, 1974–1994* (Stanford: Stanford University Press, 1995).

———. *Politiques de l'amitié.* Paris: Galilée, 1994. Translated by George Collus under the title *Politics of Friendship* (London: Verso, 1997).

———. *Positions.* Paris: Éditions de Minuit, 1972. Translated by Alan Bass. Chicago: Chicago University Press, 1981.

———. "Préjugés—devant la loi." In *La Faculté de juger,"* ed. Jean-François Lyotard, 87–139. Paris: Éditions de Minuit, 1985. Translated by Avital Ronell and Christine Roulston under the title "Before the Law," in *Acts of Literature,* ed. Derek Attridge, 183–220 (London: Routledge, 1992).

———. *Psyché: Inventions de l'autre.* Paris: Galilée, 1987.

———. *Sauf le nom (Post-Scriptum).* Paris: Galilée, 1993. Translated by John P. Leavey, Jr., in *On the Name,* ed. Thomas Dutoit (Stanford: Stanford University Press, 1995).

———. *Schibboleth: Pour Paul Celan.* Paris: Galilée, 1986. Translated by Joshua Wilner under the title "Shibboleth: For Paul Celan," in *Word Traces: Readings of Paul Celan,* ed. Aris Fioretos, 3–72 (Baltimore: Johns Hopkins University Press, 1994).

———. *Spectres de Marx.* Paris: Galilée, 1993. Translated by Peggy Kamuf under the title *Specters of Marx* (London: Routledge, 1994).

———. *Signéponge / Signsponge.* Translated by Richard Rand. New York: Columbia University Press, 1984.

———. *Ulysse gramophone: Deux mots pour Joyce.* Paris: Galilée, 1987.

———. *La Vérité en peinture.* Paris: Flammarion, 1978. Translated by Geoff Bennington and Ian McLeod under the title *The Truth in Painting* (Chicago: University of Chicago Press, 1987).

———. "Violence and Metaphysics." In *L'Écriture et la différence,* 117–228. Paris: Éditions du Seuil, 1967. Translated by Alan Bass in *Writing and Difference* 79–153 (London: Routledge, 1978).

———. *La Voix et le phénomène.* Paris: Presses universitaires de France, 1967. Translated by David B. Allison under the title *Speech and Phenomena, and*

*Other Essays on Husserl's Theory of Signs* (Evanston, Ill.: Northwestern University Press, 1973).

Derrida, Jacques, and Bernard Stiegler. *Échographies de la télévision: Entretiens filmés.* Paris: Galilée / Institut national de l'audiovisuel, 1996.

Derrida, Jacques, and Pierre-Jean Labarriere. *Altérités.* Paris: Osiris, 1986.

Dufrenne, Mikel. *La Notion d'apriori.* Paris: Presses universitaires de France, 1959. Translated by Edward S. Casey under the title *The Notion of the A Priori* (Evanston, Ill.: Northwestern University Press, 1966).

———. "Pour une philosophie non-théologique." In id., *Le Poétique*, 7–57. 1963. 2d ed. Paris: Presses universitaires de France, 1973.

Felman, Shoshana, and Dori Laub. *Testimony: Crises of Witnessing in Literature, Psychoanalysis and History.* London: Routledge, 1992.

Flew, Anthony. "Theology and Falsification." In *The Philosophy of Religion,* ed. Basil Mitchell, 13–15. Oxford: Oxford University Press, 1971.

Freud, Sigmund. *Jenseits des Lustprinzips.* Vienna: Internationaler Psychoanalytischer Verlag, 1920. Translated by James Strachey under the title *Beyond the Pleasure Principle* (New York: Liveright, 1970).

———. *Totem und Tabu: Einige Übereinstimmungen im Seelenleben der Wilden und der Neurotiker.* 2d ed. Leipzig: Internationaler Psychoanalytischer Verlag, 1920. Translated by James Strachey under the title *Totem and Taboo: Some Points of Agreements Between the Mental Lives of Savages and Neurotics* (New York: Norton, 1989).

Gasché, Rodolphe. "God, for Example." In *Phenomenology and the Numinous.* Pittsburgh: Simon Silverman Phenomenology Center, 1988.

———. *Inventions of Difference: On Jacques Derrida.* Cambridge, Mass.: Harvard University Press, 1994.

———. "Perhaps — A Modality? On the Way with Heidegger to Language." *Graduate Faculty Philosophy Journal* 16, no. 2 (1993): 467–84.

———. *The Tain of the Mirror: Derrida and the Philosophy of Reflection.* Cambridge, Mass.: Harvard University Press, 1986.

Goetschel, W. *Constituting Critique: Kant's Writing as Critical Praxis.* Durham, N.C.: Duke University Press, 1994.

Greisch, Jean. "Le Cercle et l'ellipse: Le Statut de l'herméneutique de Platon à Schleiermacher." *Revue des Sciences philosophiques et théologiques* 73 (1989): 161–84.

———. "L'Herméneutique dans la 'phénoménologie comme telle': Trois questions à propos de *Réduction et donation.*" *Revue de Métaphysique et de Morale* 96, no. 1 (1991): 43–63.

————. "Nomination et Révélation," *Archivo di filosofia* (1994): n. 1–3, 577–98.

————. *Ontologie et temporalite: Esquisse d'une interprètation intègrale de "Sein und Zeit."* Paris: Presses universitaires de France, 1995.

Haas, Alois M. *Mystik als Aussage: Erfahrungs-, Denk-, und Redeformen christlicher Mystik.* Frankfurt a./M.: Suhrkamp 1996.

Habermas, Jürgen. "Die Einheit der Vernunft in der Vielheit ihrer Stimme." In id., *Nachmetaphysisches Denken: Philosophische Aufsätze.* Frankfurt a./M.: Suhrkamp, 1988.

————. "Kants Idee des ewigen Friedens — aus dem historischen Abstand von 200 Jahren." In id., *Die Einbeziehung des Anderen: Studien zur politischen Theorie,* 192–236. Frankfurt a./M.: Suhrkamp, 1996.

————. *Der philosophische Diskurs der Moderne.* Frankfurt a./M.: Suhrkamp, 1985.

————. "The Unity of Reason in the Diversity of Its Voices." In id., *Postmetaphysical Thinking: Philosophical Essays,* trans. W. M. Hohengarten, 115–48. Cambridge, Mass.: MIT Press, 1992.

Halbertal, Moshe, and Avishai Margalit. *Idolatry.* Translated by Naomi Goldblum. Cambridge, Mass.: Harvard University Press, 1992.

Hamacher, Werner. *Premises: Essays on Philosophy and Literature from Kant to Celan.* Translated by Peter Fenves. Cambridge, Mass., 1996.

Hanssen, Beatrice. *Walter Benjamin's Other History: Of Stones, Animals, Human Beings, and Angels.* Berkeley and Los Angeles: University of California Press, 1998.

Hart, Kevin. *The Trespass of the Sign. Deconstruction, Theology and Philosophy.* Cambridge: Cambridge University Press, 1989.

Hegel, G. W. F. *Der Geist des Christentums und sein Schicksal.* Edited by Gerhard Ruhbach. Gütersloh: Gütersloher Verlagshaus G. Mohn, 1970.

————. *Glauben und Wissen: Oder die Reflexionsphilosophie der Sujektivität, in der Vollständigkeit ihrer Formen, als Kantische, Jacobische, und Fichtische Philosophie.* Edited by Hans Brockard and Hartmut Buchner. Hamburg: Meiner, 1986. Translated by Walter Cerf and H. S. Harris under the title *Faith and Knowledge* (Albany: State University of New York Press, 1977).

————. *Grundlinien der Philosophie des Rechts.* 1833. Edited by J. Hoffmeister. Hamburg: Meiner, 1962.

————. *Wissenschaft der Logik.* Vol. 1. Frankfurt a./M.: Suhrkamp, 1986. Translated by A. V. Miller under the title *Hegel's Science of Logic* (Atlantic Highlands, N.J.: Humanities Press International, 1969).

Heidegger, Martin. *Being and Time.* Translated by John Macquarrie and Edward Robinson. San Francisco: Harper, 1962. Oxford: Blackwell, 1993.

———. *Beiträge zur Philosophie: Vom Ereignis.* Edited by Friedrich-Wilhelm von Herrmann. Vol. 65 of *Gesamtausgabe.* Frankfurt a./M.: Klostermann, 1989.

———. "Brief über den Humanismus." In *Wegmarken,* 311–60. Frankfurt a./M.: Klostermann, 1978. Translated under the title "Letter on Humanism," in *Basic Writings: From "Being and Time" (1927) to "The Task of Thinking" (1964),* ed. David Farrell Krell, 213–65 (New York: Harper Collins, 1993); and by Frank A. Capuzzi, in *Pathmarks,* ed. William McNeill, 239–76 (Cambridge: Cambridge University Press, 1998).

———. *Die Grundprobleme der Phänomenologie.* Vol. 24 of *Gesamtausgabe.* Frankfurt a./M.: Klostermann, 1975.

———. *Identität und Differenz.* Pfullingen: Neske, 1978. Translated by Joan Stambaugh under the title *Identity and Difference* (New York: Harper & Row, 1969, 1974).

———. *Kant und das Problem der Metaphysik.* Bonn: F. Cohen, 1929. Translated by Richard Taft under the title *Kant and the Problem of Metaphysics* (5th ed., Bloomington: Indiana University Press, 1997).

———. *Phänomenologie des religiösen Lebens.* Vol. 60 of *Gesamtausgabe.* Frankfurt a./M.: Klostermann, 1995.

———. "Phänomenologie und Theologie." In *Wegmarken,* 45–78. Frankfurt a./M.: Klostermann, 1978. Translated by James G. Hart and John C. Maraldo under the title "Phenomenology and Theology," in *Pathmarks,* ed. William McNeill, 39–62 (Cambridge: Cambridge University Press, 1998).

———. *The Question Concerning Technology and Other Essays.* Translated by William Lovitt. New York: Harper & Row, 1977.

———. *Der Satz vom Grund.* Pfullingen: Neske, 1957. Translated by Reginald Lilli under the title *The Principle of Reason* (Bloomington: Indiana University Press, 1992).

———. *Unterwegs zur Sprache.* Pfullingen: Neske, 1990. Translated by Peter D. Hertz under the title *On the Way to Language* (New York: Harper, 1971).

———. *Vorträge und Aufsätze.* Pfullingen: Neske, 1954.

———. "Was ist Metaphysik?" In *Wegmarken,* 103–21. Frankfurt a./M.: Klostermann, 1978. Translated by David Farrell Krell under the title "What Is Metaphysics?" in *Pathmarks,* ed. William McNeill, 82–96 (Cambridge: Cambridge University Press, 1998).

———. *Wegmarken.* Frankfurt a./M.: Klostermann, 1978. Translated under the title *Pathmarks,* ed. William McNeill (Cambridge: Cambridge University Press, 1998),

———. *Zur Sache des Denkens.* Tübingen: Niemeyer. 1969.

Held, Klaus. "Husserls These von der Europäisierung der Menschheit." In *Phänomenologie im Widerstreit: Zum 50. Todestag Edmunds Husserls*, ed. Christoph Jamme and Otto Pöggler. Frankfurt a./M.: Suhrkamp, 1989.

Henry, Michel. *Phénoménologie matérielle*. Paris: Presses universitaires de France, 1990.

Husserl, Edmund. *Ideen zu einer reinen Phänomenologie und Phänomenologischen Philosophie*. Vol. 1 edited by Walter Biemel. *Husserliana*, vol. 3. The Hague: Martinus Nijhoff, 1950. Translated under the title *Ideas Pertaining to a Pure Phenomenology and to a Phenomenological Philosophy* (The Hague: Martinus Nijhoff, 1980–82).

———. *Die Krisis der europäischen Wissenschaften und die transzendentale Phänomenologie: Ein Einleitung in die phänomenologische Philosophie*. Edited by Walter Biemel. *Husserliana*, vol. 6. The Hague: Martinus Nijhoff, 1962. Translated by David Carr under the title *The Crisis of European Sciences and Transcendental Phenomenology: An Introduction to Phenomenological Philosophy* (Evanston, Ill.: Northwestern University Press, 1997).

———. *L'Origine de la géométrie*. Translated and introduced by Jacques Derrida. Paris: Presses universitaires de France, 1974.

Imdahl, Karl. *Das Lebens verstehen: Heideggers formal anzeigende Hemeneutik in den frühen Freiburger Vorlesungen*. Würzburg: Könighausen & Neumann, 1997.

Jabès, Edmond. *Le Livre des questions*. 3 vols. Paris: Gallimard, 1963–65. Translated by Rosmarie Waldrop under the title *The Book of Questions* (Middletown, Conn.: Wesleyan University Press, 1983).

Jacobi, Friedrich Heinrich. *The Main Philosophical Writings and the Novel "Allwill."* Translated from the German by George di Giovanni. Montréal: McGill-Queen's University Press, 1994.

———. *Über die Lehre des Spinozas in Briefen an den Herrn Moses Mendelssohn*. 1785. Breslau: G. Löwe, 1789.

Janicaud, Dominique. *Le Tournant théologique de la phénoménologie française*. Combas: Éditions de l'Éclat, 1991.

Jaspers, Karl. *Psychologie der Weltanschauungen*. Berlin: Springer, 1919. Reprint, 1960.

Jay, Martin. *Downcast Eyes: The Denigration of Vision in Twentieth-Century Thought*. Berkeley and Los Angeles: University of California Press, 1993.

Kaegi, Dominic. "Die Religion in den Grenzen der blossen Existenz: Heideggers religionsphilosophische Vorlesungen von 1920/21." *Internationale Zeitschrift für Philosophie* 1 (1996): 133–49.

Kant, Immanuel. *The Conflict of the Faculties (Der Streit der Fakultäten)*. Translated by Mary J. Gregor. 1979. Reprint, Lincoln: University of Nebraska Press, 1992.

—. *Grundlegung zur Metaphysik der Sitten.* 1785. Translated by H. J. Paton under the title *Groundwork of the Metaphysic of Morals* (1948; reprint, New York: Harper Torchbooks, 1964).

—. *Kritik der praktischen Vernunft.* Translated and edited by Mary Gregor under the title *Critique of Practical Reason,* with introduction by Andrews Reath (Cambridge: Cambridge University Press, 1997).

—. *Kritik der reinen Vernunft.* Vols. 3 and 4 of *Werke in zehn Bänden,* ed. Wilhelm Weischedel. Darmstadt: Wissenschaftliche Buchgesellschaft, 1983. Translated by Norman Kemp Smith under the title *Critique of Pure Reason* (New York: St. Martin's Press, 1965).

—. *Kritik der Urteilskraft.* Vol. 8 of *Werke in zehn Bänden,* ed. Wilhelm Weischedel. Darmstadt: Wissenschaftliche Buchgesellschaft, 1983.

—. *Prolegomena zu einer jeden Künftigen Metaphysik, die als Wissenschaft wird auftreten konnen.* Riga: J. F. Hartknoch, 1783. Translated by Gary Hatfield under the title *Prolegomena to Any Future Metaphysics That Will be Able to Come Forward as Science* (Cambridge: Cambridge University Press, 1997).

—. *Die Religion innerhalb der Grenzen der blossen Vernunft.* Vol. 7 of *Werke in zehn Bänden,* ed. Wilhelm Weischedel. Darmstadt: Wissenschaftliche Buchgesellschaft, 1983. Translated by George di Giovanni under the title *Religion Within the Boundaries of Mere Reason,* in the Cambridge Edition of the Works of Immanuel Kant, ed. Paul Guyer and Allen W. Wood (Cambridge: Cambridge University Press, 1996), and by Theodore M. Greene and Hoyt H. Hudson under the title *Religion Within the Limits of Reason Alone* (New York: Harper Torchbooks, 1960).

—. *Schriften zur Ethiek und Religionsphilosophie.* Vol. 7 of *Werke in zehn Bänden,* ed. Wilhelm Weischedel. Darmstadt: Wissenschaftliche Buchgesellschaft, 1983.

—. *Schriften zur Anthropologie, Geschichtsphilosophie, Politik und Pädagogik.* Vol. 9 of *Werke in zehn Bänden,* ed. Wilhelm Weischedel. Darmstadt: Wissenschaftliche Buchgesellschaft, 1983.

—. *Verkündigung des nahen Abschlusses eines Traktats zum ewigen Frieden in der Philosophie.* Originally published in the *Berlinische Monatschrift* in 1796. In *Werke in zehn Bänden,* ed. Wilhelm Weischedel, 5: 405–16, 413–15. Darmstadt: Wissenschaftliche Buchgesellschaft, 1983.

—. "Von einem neuerdings erhobenen vornehmen Ton in der Philosophie." 1796. In *Werke in zehn Bänden,* ed. Wilhelm Weischedel, 5: 377–97. Darmstadt:

Wissenschaftliche Buchgesellschaft, 1983. Translated by Peter Fenves under the
   title "On a Newly Arisen Superior Tone in Philosophy," in *Raising the Tone of
   Philosophy: Late Essays by Immanuel Kant, Transformative Critique by Jacques
   Derrida,* ed. Peter Fenves, 51–72 (Baltimore: Johns Hopkins University Press,
   1993).
———. *Zum ewigen Frieden: Ein philosophischer Entwurf.* Konigsberg: F. Nicolo-
   vius, 1795. Vol. 16 of *Kant im Original.* Erlangen: Fischer, 1984. Translated by
   M. Campbell Smith under the title *Perpetual Peace: A Philosophical Essay* (New
   York: Garland, 1972).
Kelly, J. N. D. *Early Christian Creeds.* Longman: New York, 1972.
Kierkegaard, Søren. *The Concept of Dread.* Translated by W. Lowrie. London,
   1944.
———. *Fear and Trembling.* Vol. 6 of *Kierkegaard's Writings,* ed. and trans. How-
   ard V. Hong and Edna H. Hong. Princeton: Princeton University Press, 1983.
———. *The Sickness unto Death.* Translated by W. Lowrie. Princeton, 1941.
Kisiel, Theodore. *The Genesis of Heidegger's "Being and Time."* Berkeley and Los
   Angeles: University of California Press, 1993.
Kittel, Gerhard et al., eds. *Theologisches Wörterbuch zum Neuen Testament.* Stutt-
   gart: W. Kohlhammer, 1973. Translated and abridged in one volume by Geof-
   frey W. Bromiley (Grand Rapids, Mich., and Exeter, Eng.: William B. Eerdmans
   and Paternoster Press, 1985).
Kockelmans, J. J., ed. *A Companion to Martin Heidegger's "Being and Time."* Wash-
   ington, D.C.: Center for Advanced Research in Phenomenology and University
   Press of America, 1986.
Kripke, Saul A. *Naming and Necessity.* Cambridge, Mass.: Harvard University
   Press, 1972, 1980.
Lacan, Jacques. *L'Éthique de la psychanalyse, 1959–1960.* Translated by Dennis
   Porter under the title *The Ethics of Psychoanalysis, 1959–1960* (New York: Nor-
   ton, 1992).
Lacoue-Labarthe, Philippe, and Nancy, Jean-Luc. *Le Retrait du politique.* Paris:
   Galilée, 1981. Translated by Simon Sparks as *Retreating the Political* (London:
   Routledge, 1997).
Lehmann, Karl. "Christliche Geschichtserfahrung und ontologische Frage beim
   jungen Heidegger." In *Heidegger: Perspektiven zur Deutung seines Werkes,* ed.
   Otto Pöggeler, 140–66. Königstein: Athenäum, 1984.
Levinas, Emmanuel. *Autrement qu'être ou au-delà de l'essence.* The Hague: Marti-
   nus Nijhoff, 1974. Translated by Alphonso Lingis under the title *Otherwise than
   Being, or Beyond Essence* (The Hague: Martinus Nijhoff, 1981).
———. *De Dieu qui vient à l'idée.* Vrin: Paris, 1982.

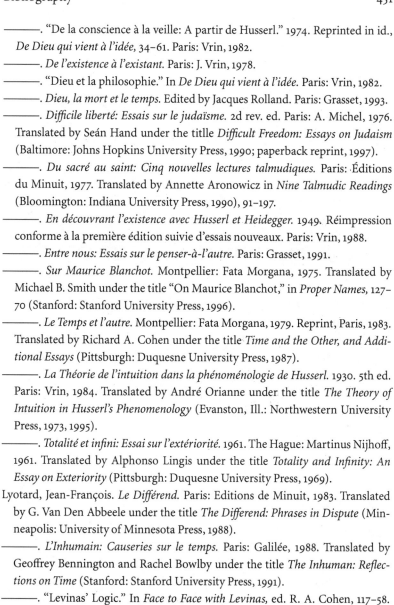

———. "De la conscience à la veille: A partir de Husserl." 1974. Reprinted in id., *De Dieu qui vient à l'idée,* 34–61. Paris: Vrin, 1982.

———. *De l'existence à l'existant.* Paris: J. Vrin, 1978.

———. "Dieu et la philosophie." In *De Dieu qui vient à l'idée.* Paris: Vrin, 1982.

———. *Dieu, la mort et le temps.* Edited by Jacques Rolland. Paris: Grasset, 1993.

———. *Difficile liberté: Essais sur le judaïsme.* 2d rev. ed. Paris: A. Michel, 1976. Translated by Seán Hand under the titlle *Difficult Freedom: Essays on Judaism* (Baltimore: Johns Hopkins University Press, 1990; paperback reprint, 1997).

———. *Du sacré au saint: Cinq nouvelles lectures talmudiques.* Paris: Éditions du Minuit, 1977. Translated by Annette Aronowicz in *Nine Talmudic Readings* (Bloomington: Indiana University Press, 1990), 91–197.

———. *En découvrant l'existence avec Husserl et Heidegger.* 1949. Réimpression conforme à la première édition suivie d'essais nouveaux. Paris: Vrin, 1988.

———. *Entre nous: Essais sur le penser-à-l'autre.* Paris: Grasset, 1991.

———. *Sur Maurice Blanchot.* Montpellier: Fata Morgana, 1975. Translated by Michael B. Smith under the title "On Maurice Blanchot," in *Proper Names,* 127–70 (Stanford: Stanford University Press, 1996).

———. *Le Temps et l'autre.* Montpellier: Fata Morgana, 1979. Reprint, Paris, 1983. Translated by Richard A. Cohen under the title *Time and the Other, and Additional Essays* (Pittsburgh: Duquesne University Press, 1987).

———. *La Théorie de l'intuition dans la phénoménologie de Husserl.* 1930. 5th ed. Paris: Vrin, 1984. Translated by André Orianne under the title *The Theory of Intuition in Husserl's Phenomenology* (Evanston, Ill.: Northwestern University Press, 1973, 1995).

———. *Totalité et infini: Essai sur l'extériorité.* 1961. The Hague: Martinus Nijhoff, 1961. Translated by Alphonso Lingis under the title *Totality and Infinity: An Essay on Exteriority* (Pittsburgh: Duquesne University Press, 1969).

Lyotard, Jean-François. *Le Différend.* Paris: Editions de Minuit, 1983. Translated by G. Van Den Abbeele under the title *The Differend: Phrases in Dispute* (Minneapolis: University of Minnesota Press, 1988).

———. *L'Inhumain: Causeries sur le temps.* Paris: Galilée, 1988. Translated by Geoffrey Bennington and Rachel Bowlby under the title *The Inhuman: Reflections on Time* (Stanford: Stanford University Press, 1991).

———. "Levinas' Logic." In *Face to Face with Levinas,* ed. R. A. Cohen, 117–58. Albany: State University of New York Press, 1986.

Lyotard, Jean-François, and Jean-Loup Thébaud. *Au juste: Conversations.* Paris: C. Bourgois, 1979. Translated by Wlad Godzich and Brian Massumi under the title *Just Gaming* (Minneapolis: University of Minnesota Press, 1985).

Man, Paul de. *Blindness and Insight*. Minneapolis: University of Minnesota Press, 1989.

———. *The Rhetoric of Romanticism* (New York: Columbia University Press, 1984).

Margel, Serge. *Le Tombeau du dieu artisan: Sur Platon*. Paris: Éditions du Minuit, 1995.

Marion, Jean-Luc. *La Croisée du visible*. Paris: Éditions de la Différence, 1991.

———. *Dieu sans l'être: Hors texte*. 1982. Reprint, Paris: Quadrige, 1991. Translated by Thomas A. Carlson under the title *God Without Being: Hors-Texte* (Chicago: University of Chicago Press, 1991).

———. "De la 'mort de Dieu' aux noms divins: L'Itinéraire théologique de la métaphysique." In *L'Être et Dieu*, ed. D. Bourg et al., 103–30. Paris: Éditions du Cerf, 1986.

———. "The End of the End of Metaphysics." *Epoché*, 1996: 1–22.

———. *Étant donné: Essai d'une phénoménologie de la donation*. Paris: Presses universitaires de France, 1997.

———. *L'Idole et la distance: Cinq études*. Paris: Grasset, 1977.

———. "Metaphysics and Phenomenology: A Relief for Theology." Translated by Thomas A. Carlson. *Critical Inquiry* 20, no. 4 (Summer 1994): 572–91.

———. *Réduction et donation: Recherches sur Husserl, Heidegger et la phénoménologie*. Paris: Presses universitaires de France, 1989. Translated by Thomas A. Carlson under the title *Reduction and Givenness: Investigations of Husserl, Heidegger, and Phenomenology* (Evanston, Ill.: Northwestern University Press, 1998).

———. "Réponses à quelques questions." *Revue de Métaphysique et de Morale* 96, no. 1 (1991): 65–76.

———. *Sur la théologie blanche de Descartes: Analogie, création des vérités éternelles et fondement*. Paris: Presses universitaires de France, 1989; Quadrige, 1991.

———. *Sur le prisme métaphysique de Descartes*. Paris: Presses universitaires de France, 1986.

———. *Sur l'ontologie grise de Descartes: Savoir aristotélicien et science cartésienne dans les Regulae*. Paris: Vrin, 1975, 1981.

Marrati-Guénoun, Paola. *La Genèse et la trace: Derrida lecteur de Husserl et Heidegger*. Dordrecht and Boston: Kluwer Academic Publishers, 1998.

Mauss, Marcel. *Essai sur le don*. Translated by W. D. Halls under the title *The Gift: The Form and Reason for Exchange in Archaic Societies*, with foreword by Mary Douglas (New York: Norton, 1990).

McCormack, Bruce L. *Karl Barth's Critically Realistic Dialectical Theology: Its Genesis and Development, 1909–1936*, Oxford: Clarendon Press, 1997.

Merleau-Ponty, Maurice. *L'Oeil et l'esprit*. With a preface by Claude Lefort. Paris: Gallimard, 1964, 1973. Translated by Michael B. Smith under the title "Eye and Mind," in *The Merleau-Ponty Aesthetics Reader: Philosophy and Painting*, ed. Galen A. Johnson, 121–49 (Evanston, Ill.: Northwestern University Press, 1993).

———. *Phénoménologie de la perception*. 1945. Reprint, Paris: Gallimard, 1976.

Milbank, John. *Theology and Social Theory: Beyond Secular Reason*. Oxford: Blackwell, 1990.

Miller, J. Hillis. *The Ethics of Reading*. New York: Columbia University Press, 1987.

Mitchell, W. J. T. *Iconology: Image, Text, Ideology*. Chicago: University of Chicago Press, 1986.

———. *Picture Theory: Essays on Verbal and Visual Representation*. Chicago: University of Chicago Press, 1994.

Mondzain, Marie-José. *Image, icône, économie: Les Sources byzantines de l'imaginaire contemporain*. Paris: Editions du Seuil, 1996.

Mouffe, Chantal, ed. *Deconstruction and Pragmatism*. London: Routledge, 1996.

Nancy, Jean-Luc. *La Communauté désoeuvrée*. Translated by Peter Connor, Lisa Garbus, Michael Holland, and Simona Sawhney under the title *The Inoperative Community*, ed. Peter Connor (Minneapolis: University of Minnesota Press, 1991).

———. *L'Expérience de la liberté*. Paris: Galilée, 1988. Translated by Bridget Mc-Donald under the title *The Experience of Freedom* (Stanford: Stanford University Press, 1993).

———. *Des Lieux divins*. Mauvezin: Trans-Europ-Repress, 1987. Translated by Michael Holland under the title "Of Divine Places," in Jean Luc Nancy, *The Inoperative Community*, ed. Peter Connor (Minneapolis: University of Minnesota Press, 1991), 110–50.

———. *Ego sum*. Paris: Flammarion, 1979.

———. *L'Impératif catégorique*. Paris: Flammarion, 1983.

———. "Sens elliptique." *Revue philosophique* 2 (1990): 325–47.

Natorp, Paul. *Religion innerhalb der Grenzen der Humanität: Ein Kapital zur Grundlegung der Sozialpädagogik*. Tübingen: J. C. B. Mohr, 1908.

Neurath, Otto. "Soziologie in Physikalismus." *Erkenntnis* 2 (1931): 393–431.

Newton, Adam Zachary. *Narrative Ethics*. Cambridge, Mass.: Harvard University Press, 1995.

Nietzsche, F. W. *Unzeitgemässe Betrachtungen*. In *Sämtliche Werke*, Kritische Studien Ausgabe, ed. Giorgo Colli and Mazzino Montinari, 1: 157–510. Berlin: Walter de Gruyter. Translated by Richard T. Gray under the title *Unfashionable Observations* (Stanford: Stanford University Press, 1995).

———. *Zur Genealogie der Moral*. 1887. In *Sämtliche Werke*, 5, 246–412. Translated by Walter Kaufmann and R. J. Hollingdale under the title *On the Geneal-ogy of Morals* (New York: Random House, Vintage Books, 1989).

Norris, Christopher, "On Derrida's 'Apocalyptic Tone': Textual Politics and the Principle of Reason." *Southern Review* 19, no. 1 (1986): 13–30.

Ollig, Hans-Ludwig, ed. *Materialien zur Neokantianismus-Diskussion.* Darmstadt: Wissenschaftliche Buchgesellschaft, 1981.

Otto, Rudolf. *Das Heilige: Über das Irrationale in der Idee des Göttlichen und sein Verhältnis zum Rationalen.* 1917. Munich: C. H. Beck, 1997. Translated by John W. Harvey as *The Idea of Holy: An Inquiry into the Non-Rational Factor in the Idea of the Divine and Its Relation to the Rational* (New York: Oxford University Press, 1958).

Overbeck, Franz. *Christentum und Kultur: Gedanken und Anmerkungen zur modernen Theologie.* Edited by Albrecht Bernoulli. 1919. Reprint, Darmstadt: Wissenschaftliche Buchgesellschaft, 1973.

———. *Über die Christlichkeit unserer heutigen Theologie.* 1873. Reprint, Darmstadt: Wissenschaftliche Buchgesellschaft, 1981.

Pascal, Blaise. *Pensées.* Edited by Léon Brunschvicg. 1905. Paris: Garnier-Flammarion, 1976.

———. *Pensées.* Translated by A. J. Krailsheimer. New York: Penguin Books, 1966.

Patočka, Jan. *Essais hérétiques sur la philosophie de l'histoire.* Lagrasse: Verdier, 1981. Translated by Erazim Kohák under the title *Heretical Essays in the Philosophy of History,* ed. James Dodd (Chicago: Open Court, 1996).

———. "Questions et réponses: Sur *Réponses et questions* de Heidegger." In id., *Liberté et sacrifice: Écrits politiques.* Grenoble: Éditions Jérôme Millon, 1990.

Pöggeler, Otto. *Der Denkweg Martin Heideggers.* 1963. Reprint, Pfullingen: Neske, 1983.

———. "Hegel und die Anfänge der Nihilismus-Diskussion." In *Der Nihilismus als Phänomen der Geistesgeschichte in der wissenschaftlichen Diskussion unseres Jahrhunderts,* ed. D. Arendt, 307–49. Darmstadt: Wissenschaftliche Buchgesellschaft, 1974.

Ponge, Francis, *Proêmes.* Paris: Gallimard, 1948.

———. *Tome premier.* Paris: Gallimard, 1965.

Posner, Richard A. *Law and Literature: A Misunderstood Relation.* Cambridge, Mass.: Harvard University Press, 1988.

———. *Overcoming Law.* Cambridge, Mass.: Harvard University Press, 1995.

Pseudo-Dionysius. *The Complete Works.* Translated by Colm Luibheid in collaboration with Paul Rorem. New York: Paulist Press, 1987. For the Greek text, see the version edited by B. Corderius in *Patrologia Graeca,* ed. J. P. Migne, vol. 3 (Paris, 1857).

Putman, Hilary. "Wittgenstein on Religious Belief." In id., *Renewing Philosophy.* Cambridge, Mass.: Harvard University Press, 1992.

Richmond, Sarah. "Derrida and Analytical Philosophy: Speech Acts and Their Force," *European Journal of Philosophy* 4, no. 1 (April 1996): 38–62.

Ricoeur, Paul. *Le Conflit des interprétations: Essais d'herméneutique.* Paris: Éditions du Seuil, 1969. Translated under the title *The Conflict of Interpretations: Essays in Hermeneutics,* ed. Don Ihde (Evanston, Ill.: Northwestern University Press, 1974).

———. "Kant et Husserl." In id., *A l'école de la phénoménologie,* 227–50. Paris: Vrin, 1986.

———. *Soi-même comme un autre.* Paris: Éditions du Seuil, 1990. Translated by Kathleen Blamey under the title *Oneself as Another* (Chicago: University of Chicago Press, 1992).

———. *Temps et récit.* 3 vols. Paris: Éditions du Seuil, 1983–85. Translated by Kathleen McLaughlin and David Pellauer under the title *Time and Narrative* (Chicago: University of Chicago Press, 1984–88).

Rockmore, Tom. *Heidegger and French Philosophy: Humanism, Antihumanism, and Being.* London: Routledge, 1995.

Rogozinski, Jacob. "It Makes Us Wrong: Kant and Radical Evil." In *Radical Evil,* ed. Joan Copjec, 30–45. London: Verso, 1996.

Rorty, Richard. *Contingency, Irony, and Solidarity.* Cambridge: Cambridge University Press, 1989.

———. *Philosophical Papers.* Vol. 1: *Objectivity, Relativism, and Truth.* Vol. 2: *Essays on Heidegger and Others.* Cambridge: Cambridge University Press, 1991.

———. *Philosophical Papers.* Vol. 3: *Truth and Progress.* Cambridge: Cambridge University Press, 1998.

Ryle, Gilbert. *The Concept of Mind.* 1949. Chicago: University of Chicago Press, 1984.

Safranski, Rüdiger. *Ein Meister aus Deutschland: Heidegger und seine Zeit.* Munich: Carl Hanser, 1994.

Sartre, Jean-Paul. *L'Existentialisme est un humanisme.* Paris: Éditions Nagel, 1946. Reprint, 1970. Translated by Philip Mairet under the title *Existentialism and Humanism* (1948; reprint, Brooklyn, N.Y.: Haskell House, 1977).

Scheffler, Johann. *Des Angelus Silesius Cherubinischer Wandersmann.* Jena: E. Diedrichs, 1905. Critical edition by Louise Gnädinger. Stuttgart: Reclam, 1984. Translated by Maria Shrady under the title *The Cherubinic Wanderer* (New York: Paulist Press, 1986).

Scheler, Max. "Die Idole der Selbsterkenntnis." In *Gesammelte Werke,* vol. 3: *Vom Umsturz der Werte,* 215–92. Bern: Francke, 1955. Translated with an introduction by David R. Lachterman under the title "The Idols of Self-Knowledge," in *Selected Philosophical Essays*, 3–97 (Evanston, Ill.: Northwestern University Press, 1973).

Schnädelbach, Herbert. *Vernunft und Geschichte: Vorträge und Abhandlungen*. Frankfurt a./M.: Suhrkamp, 1987.

Searle, John R. *Speech Acts: An Essay in the Philosophy of Language*. Cambridge: Cambridge University Press, 1969, 1977.

Sheehan, Thomas. *The First Coming: How the Kingdom of God Became Christianity*. New York: Random House, Vintage Books, 1986, 1988.

———. "Heidegger's 'Introduction to the Phenomenology of Religion,' 1920–21." In *A Companion to Martin Heidegger's "Being and Time,"* ed. J. J. Kockelmans, 40–62. Washington, D.C., 1986],

Shields, Philip R. *Logic and Sin in the Writings of Ludwig Wittgenstein*. Chicago: University of Chicago Press, 1993.

Simon, J. "Vornehme und apokalyptische Töne in der Philosophie." *Zeitschrift für philosophische Forschung*, 1986: 489–519.

Smith, Barbara Herrnstein. *Belief and Resistance: Dynamics of Contemporary Intellectual Controversy*. Cambridge, Mass.: Harvard University Press, 1997.

Smith, Jonathan Z. "A Matter of Class: Taxonomies of Religion." *Harvard Theological Review* 89, no. 4 (1996): 387–403.

Strawson, P. F. *Individuals: An Essay in Descriptive Metaphysics*. London: Methuen, 1959. Translated into German under the title *Einzelding und logisches Subjekt (Individuals)* (Stuttgart: P. Reclam, 1972).

Taubes, Jakob. *Die politische Theologie des Paulus*. Edited by Aleida Assmann and Jan Assmann. Munich: Wilhelm Fink, 1993.

———. *Vom Kult zur Kultur: Bausteine zu einer Kritik der historischen Vernunft*. Edited by Aleida Assmann, Jan Assmann, Wolf-Daniel Hartwich, and Winfried Menninghaus. Gesammelte Aufsätze zur Religions- und Geistesgeschichte. Munich: Wilhelm Fink, 1996.

Taylor, Charles. *Sources of the Self: The Making of the Modern Identity*. Cambridge, Mass.: Harvard University Press, 1989.

Taylor, Mark C. *Erring: A Postmodern A/theology*. Chicago: University of Chicago Press, 1984.

———. "Failing Reflection." In id., *Tears*, 87–103. Albany: State University of New York Press, 1990.

Theunissen, Michael. *Negative Theologie der Zeit*. Frankfurt a./M.: Suhrkamp, 1991.

Thomä, Dieter. *Die Zeit des Selbst und die Zeit danach: Zur Kritik der Textgeschichte Martin Heideggers, 1910–1976*. Frankfurt a./M.: Suhrkamp, 1990.

Towler, Robert. *Homo Religiosus: Sociological Problems in the Study of Religion.* London: Constable, 1974.

Tugendhat, Ernst, and Ursula Wolff. *Logisch-semantische Propädeutik.* Stuttgart: Reclam, 1983.

Vaihinger, Hans. *Die Philosophie des Als Ob: System der theoretischen, praktischen und religiösen Fiktionen der Menschheit auf Grund eines idealistischen Positivismus.* Leipzig: Felix Meiner, 1920.

Veer, Peter van der. *Religious Nationalism: Hindus and Muslims in India.* Berkeley and Los Angeles: University of California Press, 1994.

Vorländer, Karl. "Einleitung." In Immanuel Kant, *Die Religion innerhalb der Grenzen der blossen Vernunft,* ed. Karl Vorländer. Leipzig: Meiner, 1937.

Vries, Hent de. "Adieu, à dieu, a-dieu." In *Ethics as First Philosophy: The Significance of Emmanuel Levinas for Philosophy, Literature and Religion,* ed. Adriaan T. Peperzak, 211–20. London: Routledge, 1995.

———. "Antibabel: The 'Mystical Postulate' in Benjamin, de Certeau and Derrida." *Modern Language Notes* 107 (1992): 441–47.

———. "Attestation du temps et de l'autre: De *Temps et récit à Soi-même comme un autre.*" In *Paul Ricoeur: L'Herméneutique à l'école de la phénoménologie,* ed. Jean Greisch, 21–42. Paris: Beauchesne, 1995.

———. " 'Lapsus absolu': Notes on Maurice Blanchot's *The Instant of My Death.*" *Yale French Studies,* no. 93 (1998): 30–59.

———. "On Obligation: Lyotard and Levinas." *Graduate Faculty Philosophy Journal* 20, no. 2; 21, no. 1 (1998), 83–112.

———. *Theologie im pianissimo: Zur Aktualität der Denkfiguren Adornos und Levinas.* Kampen, Neth.: J. H. Kok, 1989. Forthcoming in English translation from the Johns Hopkins University Press.

———. "Le Schibboleth de l'éthique: Derrida avec Celan." In *L'Éthique du don: Jacques Derrida et la pensée du don,* ed. Jean-Michel Rabaté and Michael Wetzel, 212–38. Paris: Métailié-Transition, 1992. Translated into German under the title "Das Schibboleth der Ethik: Derrida und Celan," in *Ethik der Gabe: Denken nach Jacques Derrida,* ed. Jean-Michel Rabaté and Michael Wetzel, 57–80 (Berlin: Akademie, 1993).

———. "Theotopographies: Nancy, Hölderlin, Heidegger." *Modern Language Notes* 109 (1994): 445–77.

———. "*Winke.*" In *The Solid Letter,* ed. Aris Fioretos. Stanford University Press, forthcoming.

Vries, Hent de, and Harry Kunneman, eds. *Enlightenments: Encounters Between Critical Theory and Contemporary French Thought.* Kampen, Neth.: Kok Pharos, 1993.

Vries, Hent de, and Samuel Weber, eds. *Violence, Identity, and Self-Determination.* Stanford: Stanford University Press, 1997.

Wahl, Jean. *Traité de métaphysique: Cours professés en Sorbonne.* Paris: Payot, 1953, 1957.

Weber, Elizabeth, ed. *Jüdisches Denken in Frankreich.* Frankfurt a./M.: Suhrkamp, 1994.

Weber, Samuel. *The Legend of Freud.* Minneapolis: University of Minnesota Press, 1987.

————. *Mass Mediauras: Form, Technics, Media.* Stanford: Stanford University Press, 1996.

Wellmer, Albrecht. "Ethics and Dialogue: Elements of Moral Judgement in Kant and Discourse Ethics." In *The Persistence of Modernity: Essays on Aesthetics, Ethics, and Postmodernism,* trans. David Midgley, 113–231. Cambridge, Mass.: MIT Press, 1991.

West, Cornel. *The American Evasion of Philosophy: A Genealogy of Pragmatism.* Madison: University of Wisconsin Press, 1989.

————. *Keeping Faith: Philosophy and Race in America.* London: Routledge, 1993.

Wheeler, Samuel C., III. "Truth Conditions, Rhetoric, and Logical Form: Davidson and Deconstruction." In *Literary Theory after Davidson,* ed. Reed Way Dasenbroch, 144–59. University Park: Pennsylvania University Press, 1993.

Williams, Raymond. *Keywords: A Vocabulary of Culture and Society.* 1976. Rev. ed. New York: Oxford University Press, 1983.

Wittgenstein, Ludwig. *Lectures and Conversations on Aesthetics, Psychology, and Religious Belief.* Compiled from notes taken by Yorick Smythies, Rush Rhees, and James Taylor. Edited by Cyril Barrett. Berkeley and Los Angeles: University of California Press, 1966. Reprint, 1972.

————. *Philosophical Investigations.* 1953. Edited and translated by G. E. M. Anscombe and R. Rhees. Oxford: Blackwell, 1963. 2d bilingual ed., 1997.

————. *Tractatus logico-philosophicus.* With an introduction by Bertrand Russell. London: K. Paul, Trench, Trubner; New York, Harcourt Brace, 1922.

————. *Vermischte Bemerkungen.* Bilingual edition. Translated by Peter Winch under the title *Culture and Value.* Edited by G. H. von Wright. Chicago: University of Chicago Press, 1984.

Wolf, Ursula, ed. *Eigennamen: Dokumentation einer Kontroverse.* Frankfurt a./M.: Suhrkamp, 1985.

Yerushalmi, Yosef Hayim. *Freud's Moses: Judaism Terminable and Interminable.* New Haven: Yale University Press, 1991.

————. *Zakhor: Jewish History and Jewish Memory.* Seattle: University of Washington Press, 1982. Reprint, 1996. Translated into French under the title *Zakhor: Histoire juive et memoire juive* (Paris: La Decouverte, 1984).

Zande, Johan van der. *Bürger und Beamter: Johann Georg Schlosser, 1739–1799.* Wiesbaden: Steiner, 1986.

Zarader, Marlène. *La Dette impensèe: Heidegger et l'héritage hébraïque.* Paris: Éditions du Seuil, 1990.

———. *Heidegger et les paroles de l'origine.* Paris: Vrin, 1986.

Ziff, Paul. *Philosophical Turnings.* Ithaca, N.Y.: Cornell University Press; London: Oxford University Press, 1966.

Zišek, Slavoj. *The Sublime Object of Ideology.* London: Verso, 1989.

# Index

Library of Congress Cataloging-in-Publication Data

Vries, Hent de.
    Philosophy and the turn to religion / Hent de Vries.
        p.    cm.
    Includes bibliographical references and index.
    ISBN 0-8018-5994-8 (alk. paper). — ISBN 0-8018-5995-6
(pbk. : alk. paper)
    1. Philosophy and religion — History.    I. Title.
B56.V75    1999
291.1′75 — dc21          99-10359  CIP